AUSTRALIAN TRADE POLICY
1942-1966

AUSTRALIAN TRADE POLICY
1942-1966

A Documentary History

by

J. G. CRAWFORD

assisted by

Nancy Anderson and Margery G. N. Morris

Co-Editors

CANBERRA
Australian National University Press

University of Toronto Press
TORONTO

First published 1968

Australia and New Zealand: Australian
National University Press, Canberra;
North America: University of Toronto Press,
Toronto; *United Kingdom, Europe:* Longmans,
Green and Co., London

Printed and manufactured in Australia by
Halstead Press Pty Ltd, Sydney

Designed by A. R. Stokes

Library of Congress Catalog Card No. 68-12555

PREFACE

The purpose of this book is to outline the development of Australian trade policy from 1942 to 1966 as it appears from published documents of the period. These were mainly *Parliamentary Debates* (Hansard) and *Parliamentary Papers*, ministerial statements, and some other official papers and statements published or made during the period.

The study was not confined to official papers: an attempt has been made to locate the more important published comments on official policies at the time of their announcement or development. There has been no attempt to match official pronouncement or action with an equal unofficial reaction in press or Parliament, favourable or otherwise. In any case this would not have been possible, for the harvest of non-official comment and analysis has not been a rich one. This in itself points to a lack of sustained public debate on issues of trade policy, although a definite improvement has occurred in recent years. This improvement probably reflects the development of economic journalism, of more highly organised and articulate business groups like the Associated Chambers of Manufactures of Australia and the Associated Chambers of Commerce of Australia, and a welcome re-entry into the arena of debate of public affairs of academic economists. The bibliographical references in the later sections of the book reflect this. Whatever the true explanation of the relative paucity of non-official papers, it is this paucity which goes some way to explain the heavy weighting of ministerial statements in this book. Nevertheless it is not the complete explanation, as the central interest of the book is the development of official trade policies—clearly the responsibility of government and only to be found in statements by government spokesmen.[1] For this reason the principal documents, relating as they do to key decisions of Government in the period, are mainly official papers, regardless of the abundance or otherwise of published non-official comment and discussion.

However, there is a difference between ministerial and other official pap-

---

[1] Even so, the relegation of academic comment to bibliographical references somewhat exaggerates the weighting. The purpose of the book is to provide documentation of official policy, so when we found that space had to be conserved we naturally gave preference to exposition of policy, being careful, however, to draw attention to serious academic and semi-official papers known to us. It cannot be said that the excluded papers would make a balanced volume of readings in trade policy for, unfortunately, as we have occasion to notice from time to time, academic interest in some aspects of trade policy has been virtually nil.

ers: too few of the latter are readily available. Only as recently as 28 April 1966, in the House of Representatives, F. Crean said,

> Again I would point out the great difficulty in Australia in finding readily available documentation in respect of those bodies (i.e. GATT and UNCTAD). Australia sends representatives to annual and committee meetings of GATT. Australia is also a participant in UNCTAD and we are also members of the Economic Commission for Asia and the Far East—ECAFE. Nevertheless, little information is available to members of this House on how those important bodies operate.

Much could be done in trade policy matters by departments directly concerned along the lines of the Treasury White Papers now appearing from time to time on economic policy (and incidentally trade) matters. More can be done, too, to make available papers about which no reticence is required. It is particularly disappointing to read in published volumes statements by Australian delegates to the General Agreement on Tariffs and Trade (GATT) which are prone to be treated in Canberra as restricted papers long after they have been declassified and publicly released by GATT officials in Geneva.[2] Such papers should be automatically available to interested people in Australia as they are, for example, in Washington.

To assist in the difficult task of making the selection of documents manageable, the issues of trade policy have been confined to those arising within the framework of principles, law, administrative regulation and practices within which the country's export and import trade has been conducted. The main factors studied, therefore, have been those influencing Australia's current account—i.e. trade in goods and services—with principal emphasis on the annual trade in goods. The reader will find little here about the 'invisibles' of the trade accounts—insurance, freights, tourism, dividends—and as little also about capital inflow and the problems of overseas investment. In some of the comment these factors do receive incidental mention, more particularly in comments on the balance of payments situation in Sections 15 and 16.

This limited definition of trade policy serves one other very important purpose. As is argued in the final review section, trade is a reflection of production capacity and market opportunities for export and of the needs of home and domestic production for imports of raw material, components, and capital equipment, as well as of consumer demands for finished imported goods. Trade policy is therefore necessarily related, in important measure, to general economic policies including those directly bearing on the domestic structure and competitive efficiency of agriculture and industry and on the incomes and tastes of consumers. A study of trade policy all too easily, therefore, leads to an examination of domestic agricultural policies (e.g. income and price stabilisation schemes) and of the structure of secondary and tertiary indus-

---

[2] This is particularly true of papers quoted in Curzon (68).

tries. This temptation has been resisted. Nevertheless, where agricultural and other decisions of economic policy impinge directly on trade policies, documents have been selected accordingly. In illustration, the documents announcing a 'new deal' for agriculture in 1952 (Section 13) are important as reflecting a conviction that export earnings were lagging or would be likely to lag dangerously in relation to our growing needs for foreign exchange.

The approach to trade policy adopted in this book has emphasised its economic aspects. With the notable exceptions of the British preferential tariff system and the sterling area system in which the 'political ties that bind' were formerly more important than they are now (Sections 4 and 10) and the negotiation of the Japanese Trade Treaty (Section 10), in which political objectives were important, there has been little in trade policy which could be described as an extension of political aims, domestic or international. We do control trade in some strategic items but otherwise we encourage rather than discourage trade with Communist countries in notable contrast to the practice of the United States. Recently we have made some special tariff arrangements on behalf of less developed countries (Section 6). These could be regarded as politically inspired, although the thesis is widely accepted that in the long run expanded trade opportunities for these countries will also be in Australia's economic interest. Australia's aid policies have political objectives but curiously, again in contrast to most advanced countries, these policies have been mostly in terms of grants with very little emphasis on tied loans or other forms of continuing trade links between Australia as donor and the recipient countries. All told, as will be apparent in the documents, trade policy for Australia is very much a matter of its economic policies.

Trade policy is by its nature international in operation. It reflects and supports domestic circumstances and economic objectives, but it is conducted and negotiated internationally, bilaterally with trading partners, and multilaterally in special world and regional organisations established for the purpose. Accordingly, most of the documents necessarily reflect this fact. The key decisions affecting trade policy mentioned below reflect not only the debate in Parliament and in Cabinet at home but also the debate and negotiation in United Nations bodies generally and in special organisations such as GATT (which is not part of the formal United Nations machinery). They also reflect the communiqués announcing the results of Commonwealth economic conferences and bilateral negotiations with other nations, which frequently result in formal trade treaties such as those with the United Kingdom and Japan.

The story that emerges from the documents is one of great change in the international framework in which Australian trade policy has been formed and conducted but also in the complexity of the detailed content of trade policy as developed by successive Australian governments. Presenting the documents in chronological order would be one, but not the most effective, way of presenting the story. Instead, they have been arranged to reflect the chronological order of events, modified by subject matter divisions. The arrangement is best understood by expressing the historical evolution of policy in terms of a series of *key decisions*—decisions which have proved critical in that they have had, and many continue to have, an important influence on the character of Australian trade policy. These and other documents are numbered and keyed to the section in which they are placed for ease of reference and cross-reference.

We have listed fourteen primary decisions, although many others of importance are also revealed in the documents. These do much to explain the contrast between the pre-war milieu in which the Ottawa Agreement dominated Australia's external economic relations and the post-war developments which represent a marked retreat from that system. This change is also commented on in the final review section which concludes the book. For ease of understanding of the arrangement of the documents and of the general theme of the book the fourteen key decisions essential to the understanding of present-day policy are listed chronologically below. Of these, twelve were made by Australian governments alone or in agreement with other national governments while in two (Nos. 11 and 12), of great importance to it, Australia was not itself a principal.

1. *Article VII of Mutual Aid Agreement, September 1942:*

In accepting the agreement Australia agreed to take action directed to the expansion of international trade, the elimination of discriminatory treatment in international commerce such as that represented in American minds by the Ottawa Agreement of 1932, and to the reduction of tariffs and other trade barriers (Section 1).[3]

2. *White Paper on Full Employment, May 1945:*

This paper made full employment in Australia and abroad the keystone of Australia's domestic *and* external economic policies. It confirmed various specific domestic policies—tariff protection, import controls rather than deflation to counter adverse export returns, stabilisation of returns for primary producers, and willingness of the government to work with other nations for expansion of trade and to mitigate fluctuations in export prices (Section 2).

---

[3] Subsequent decisions to join the International Monetary Fund (IMF), the International Bank for Reconstruction and Development (IBRD), the GATT, and the Food and Agriculture Organization (FAO), may be regarded as directly flowing from the declaration in Article VII. It is in this sense that Article VII may be regarded as committing Australia to a multilateral trade policy. The decision to support FAO is not listed as a critical decision. It was expected that it might provide the machinery for post-war international commodity agreements; in the event all agreements—tin, sugar, wheat, coffee—were negotiated under United Nations auspices.

Preface

3. *Australia accepts membership of International Monetary Fund, August 1947:*

This provided 'rules' for dealing with changes in exchange rates and assured support to meet balance of payments difficulties. This decision was of no great significance in the fifties but has since become a major part of Australia's overseas reserve policy, IMF support representing the so-called 'second line' of reserves. Membership of the IBRD was accepted at the same time and regarded as a related decision. In the event it has proved to be an important decision of practical significance (Sections 3 and 15).

4. *Australia accepts provisional application of General Agreement on Tariffs and Trade, November 1947:*

In accepting GATT Australia confirmed some negotiated tariff concessions, but more importantly accepted rules for governing international trade including the operation of the non-discriminatory most-favoured-nation rule, the no-new-preference rule, and an undertaking to avoid quantitative import restrictions for protective purposes (Sections 3 and 5). A decision, thought to be of more far-reaching importance, related to the International Trade Organization (ITO) which, however, failed to come into being. GATT subsequently developed in ways originally not intended, and in part met the needs represented by ITO.[4]

5. *General import restrictions imposed, March 1952 (restrictions lifted February 1960):*

These widened the controls already operating in respect of goods from dollar areas and from Japan to embrace sterling area goods as well (Sections 4 and 15).

6. *Agricultural production to be increased: five-year targets adopted, April 1952:*

This program followed failure of the rural economy to expand adequately for developmental and balance of payments needs (Section 13).

7. *Australia agrees to the 'Collective Approach' to sterling convertibility and world trade at Commonwealth Economic Conference, London, December 1952:*

This was designed to strengthen the sterling area (including Australia) and to enable it to gain the benefits of 'freer trade and payments' (Section 4).

[4] The decision to establish an ITO was taken by the Havana Conference in March 1948. Ratification by Australia was made dependent upon ratification by the United States which, however, was not forthcoming. Even so, it deserves special mention, for it did indicate an approach to commodity problems then satisfactory to the Australian government (Sections 3 and 7).

8. *Australia decides to seek a review of* GATT, *August 1953, which took place in 1954-5:*

This was designed to redress the 'imbalance' in the rules of trade resulting from the failure to ratify ITO and from neglect of the concerns of countries dependent upon trade in primary products. This decision has been included because it did result in an important clarification of Australian policies and substantial amendments to GATT. The move, however, was not designed to effect an alternative to the multilateral principle inherent in the GATT (Section 5).

9. *Australia seeks revision of the Ottawa Agreement: a new trade agreement signed with the United Kingdom, November 1956:*

Substantial changes were effected in contractual preferences extended to the United Kingdom by Australia; room for tariff negotiations with other countries was gained; and assurances received on wheat sales (Section 9).

10. *Trade Agreement with Japan signed, July 1957:*

This treaty arose out of political and economic considerations: it was designed to preserve and enlarge Australian export markets while safeguarding Australian industry from disruption (Section 10).

11. *European Economic Community established by Treaty of Rome, March 1957:*

This treaty established 'The Common Market' and, regardless of the later British decision to apply for admission, immediately raised serious issues of policy for Australia (Section 8).

12. *Britain makes application to join the European Economic Community, July 1961:*

This was officially regarded as a decision almost certain to be adverse to Australia's economic and political interests, for it was bound to require large changes in the mutual preferential tariff relations of the United Kingdom and Australia (Section 8). Although that application came to nought, the issue may well arise again in the current (1966) United Kingdom approaches to the common market. The decision remains in the list because it did give a considerable impetus to efforts to diversify export markets and confirmed the wisdom of maintaining the trade treaty with Japan.

13. *Australia agrees to join in the 'Kennedy Round' of* GATT *negotiations, May 1963:*

The agreement to negotiate was largely conditional on the possibility of obtaining reductions in the non-tariff barriers to trade (Section 5). The decision is listed here because of its highly critical bearing on agricultural protectionism in general *and* on the future of world wheat trade in particular. The outcome is still (December 1966) problematical but vital, whether favourable to Australia's interests or otherwise.

14. *United Nations Conference on Trade and Development, May 1964, results in a permanent organisation—Trade and Development Board:*

This conference and the outcome have focused the attention and power of the 'less developed countries' on major areas of trade policy which are of concern to them and which could be of vital interest to Australia, both as an exporter of primary products and as an affluent nation possibly thought to be unduly restricting the market for raw materials and low cost 'simple' manufactures from the underdeveloped countries. The decision by Australia in May 1965 to offer some preferential advantages to exports from underdeveloped countries, although taken within GATT, reflects a positive reaction to the pressures now evident both in GATT and in the Trade and Development Board (Section 6).

Notable among particular omissions are the international and Commonwealth commodity agreements and understandings—to some extent referred to in the comment on FAO above (n. 3). They were important achievements omitted from the list as being secondary to the general decision to join international economic organisations (including the Economic and Social Council of the United Nations (ECOSOC)) for this purpose.[5] The subject, however, receives special treatment in Section 7. No less striking is the omission of reference to sales of wheat to China. These sales do present political problems for some, but are not inconsistent with Australia's official policy, noted above and clearly declared in both United Nations and GATT, of willingness to trade with Communist countries. Again, relations with the United States have been of major importance although they do not impinge on any particular decision (other than Article 7).

Tariff policy looms large in the economic affairs of Australia. No particular decision stands out, although the White Paper on Full Employment confirmed the continued use of the Tariff Board as the principal authority in this field. The subject nevertheless called for a special section (Section 14).

Probably the most important feature of post-war policy of which no clear hint is given in these decisions is the development of an 'export drive' (not always sustained at high pressure). The drive for exports received special impetus at times of great difficulty in the balance of payments situation. However, it has come also to be regarded as a continuing necessity of general economic policy as governments and the community alike have become more

---

[5] The reader will find early reference to Figure 4 in Section 18 of value in seeking a perspective on the framework of international bodies most relevant to Australian trade policies.

aware of the vital relationship between economic growth in Australia and its ability to expand its trade both as importer and exporter. Its significance has grown not merely because of frustration in some major markets for agricultural products but also because the exports of manufactured goods seem particularly responsive to marketing incentives in one form or another (see especially Sections 16 and 17).

Each section of documents is introduced by a comment which has in each case a limited objective. They are not essays on the subject matter of the documents or on the key decisions represented in the section. They do—sometimes drawing on the author's special knowledge of the circumstances—seek to clarify and explain where some help seems advisable. They do go further than this in two directions. On the one hand they invite attention to the principal questions leading to or posed by the decisions, leaving the official argument to speak for itself, but seeking at the same time to encourage students—economists and historians—to take up some of these questions for detailed study. On the other hand, I have not felt it necessary always to conceal my own views which, in any case, are sometimes revealed in the bibliographical references. There is admittedly danger in commenting at all, for in many of the decisions I have been personally involved and my judgment may be warped. All I can say is that I believe the comment may be helpful and that I have tried to be objective.

The arrangement within each section containing documents is simple. The general comment comes first in the belief that this best assists the reading of the documents. In many sections special documents have been prepared (and acknowledged to the authors) to assist understanding of the documents or of the background. These follow the comments as Annexes but are in fact a special kind of document and may be regarded as part of the documentary material which forms the final and major part in each section. Section 17 is a statistical appendix, including some explanatory material, designed to provide a statistical picture of the course and pattern of Australian trade since the war. Section 18 is a review commentary on the period and the documents as a whole. Finally, the master set of documents has been deposited with the Menzies Library at the Australian National University. It includes many which had to be excluded from this volume for lack of space, and the full version of many statements appearing here only in part. It is hoped this action will assist those who wish to take their reading and research further.

J. G. CRAWFORD

Canberra
March 1967

ACKNOWLEDGMENTS

This book grew out of an official project initiated by me when Secretary of the Department of Commerce and Agriculture, and it was carried on after the Department of Trade was established in January 1956. The project was simply to have the official records associated with major decisions of government so ordered as to ease the task of archivists, historians, and officials daily needing access to what had happened in possibly similar situations before. By the time I left the Service in 1960 the project was certainly not complete, but the state of the records, especially those bearing on ministerial submissions to Cabinet, had been considerably improved. This comment does not imply that officials were slipshod in their approach to their daily work; rather, it recognises that the day-to-day functional records are not automatically the best way of ordering the papers for after-the-event examination.

It was natural to think of providing a documentary record of public statements to match the official decisions for which the detailed papers considered by Cabinet or forming the material of intergovernmental negotiations could not yet be made available publicly. This thought led to this book.

That the book has appeared at all is due to the loyal and sustained enthusiasm of my two colleagues. Miss Margery Morris not only supervised the work in its stages as an official project in the Department of Trade; she advanced the book greatly in 1960-1 by tirelessly hunting for and selecting from the vast number of documents now produced or otherwise listed in this book. With the co-operation of my successor as Secretary of the Department of Trade, Sir Alan Westerman, Miss Morris spent a year as Public Service Fellow at the Australian National University. During this year the book took shape and our initial thinking about the 'key' decisions of the post-war period and the related documents was well tested in a seminar paper given by her in July 1961 to a number of interested people at the University.

After Miss Morris returned to the department to other duties her interest nevertheless continued. We have both been fortunate in having Mrs Nancy Anderson join my staff as Research Assistant late in 1961. Only recently from the Public Service, Mrs Anderson quickly understood what was in hand and, with Miss Morris's occasional help, managed to carry our researches further. It is almost entirely due to her efforts that we have been able to keep pace with new documents made available after 1961.

The commentary on the documents and the final general review at the

Acknowledgments

end of the book are entirely my responsibility. On my colleagues has fallen the main burden of the editorial work on the documents; I have shared in it, but only in slight degree. A number of documents have been prepared solely for the book, several by Mrs Anderson and one by Dr S. F. Harris. Miss Elaine Realf assisted in the preparation of the statistical tables in Section 17.

Many people have helped us. These include my former secretary, Miss G. Joyce, who, both in Commerce and Agriculture and in Trade, supervised my personal records. These have in fact formed the essential nucleus of both the official project and this book. Officials in the Commonwealth departments have co-operated at all times both during my term as Secretary and—most pleasing to me—since. Ministerial statements naturally figure largely in the book. Co-operation has been readily extended, not from motives of the incidental publicity represented by the book, but rather from interest in our work. On a few occasions access to documents (some written by me) was sought to establish the sequence of certain events. Acting strictly in accordance with the rules, the officers concerned in the Prime Minister's Department unfortunately felt unable to help. This has not affected the documentation in the book, for no classified material is used. As is inevitable and perhaps one of its values, the commentary on the documents reflects the special knowledge gained by me as a senior Commonwealth official in the period 1942 to 1960. Nevertheless, I believe I have faithfully met the requirements of the Official Secrets Act, although at times temptation was strong.

To many others our thanks are due and gladly given. Not least among these are Mrs Eileen Murphy, Mrs Dorothy Binnie, and Mrs Eunice Cochrane who have bravely, efficiently and with good humour, stuck to the long and often wearying task of typing documents and the accompanying text.

Several people, both academics and officials, have been kind enough to read the book, or pieces of it in draft form. Two former colleagues in the Department of Trade, Messrs L. Corkery and G. J. Hall, read the whole manuscript in its near-final stages and offered useful criticisms. Other former colleagues also offered to read the manuscript but, to my loss, the peripatetic habits of senior officials of the department finally made this impracticable. Dr W. M. Corden and Dr R. T. Shand, colleagues at the Australian National University, also read sections of the manuscript and made some helpful suggestions. Nevertheless, having acknowledged the great help received, the responsibility for the defects of views expressed or argued in the commentary remains with me and with myself and my fellow editors in respect of the selection and editing of the documents. It is our hope that the book's usefulness and interest will in some measure offset its shortcomings.

J.G.C.

ABBREVIATIONS

ACMA	Associated Chambers of Manufactures of Australia
BPT	British Preferential Tariff
CAP	Common Agricultural Policy (of the EEC)
CET	Common External Tariff
C.P.D.	*Commonwealth Parliamentary Debates*
C.P.P.	*Commonwealth Parliamentary Paper*
CSIRO	Commonwealth Scientific and Industrial Research Organization
ECAFE	Economic Commission for Asia and the Far East (United Nations)
ECOSOC	Economic and Social Council (United Nations)
EDC	Export Development Council
EEC	European Economic Community
EFTA	European Free Trade Association
EPIC	Export Payments Insurance Corporation
FAO	Food and Agriculture Organization (United Nations)
GATT	General Agreement on Tariffs and Trade
Haberler Report	GATT, *Trends in International Trade . . .*
IBRD	International Bank for Reconstruction and Development
IMF	International Monetary Fund
ITO	International Trade Organization
LDCs	Less Developed Countries
MFN	Most Favoured Nation
MIAC	Manufacturing Industries Advisory Council
OECD	Organization for Economic Co-operation and Development
OEEC	Organization for European Economic Co-operation
P.D.	*Parliamentary Debates* (United Kingdom)
The SIX	Members of the European Economic Community
The SEVEN	Members of the European Free Trade Association
UNCTAD	United Nations Conference on Trade and Development
UN	United Nations
Vernon Report	Australia, *Report of the Committee of Economic Enquiry*

CONTENTS

Contents

DIAGRAMS

xviii

LIST OF DOCUMENTS

Section 4: 'The Collective Approach': Sterling Convertibility

Section 5: The General Agreement on Tariffs and Trade

List of Documents

List of Documents

Section 8: The Common Market and the European Free Trade Association

Section 9: Ottawa Reviewed

Section 10: Japan

List of Documents

Section 14: Tariff Policies and Procedures

Section 15: Balance of Payments: General Import Controls, March 1952 to February 1960

List of Documents

*Section 16: Balance of Payments: Export Promotion and the Case for a
Sustained Export Drive*

*Section 17: Statistical Appendix: Some Characteristics of Australian Trade:
Growth and Pattern, 1948-9 to 1965-6*

A

WAR-TIME AND
POST-WAR DECISIONS

1

ARTICLE VII
OF THE MUTUAL AID AGREEMENT

In 1942 Australia was preoccupied with the war in the South-west Pacific and dependent upon the United States for ultimate success in the war against Japan (Doc. 1:10). In the larger area of war in all theatres the resources of the United Kingdom and the United States were totally employed in turning defeat and setback into organisation, material strength, and military offensives for victory. It is against this background that Article VII of the Mutual Aid Agreement,[1] a quite remarkable statement of economic post-war aims, must be understood.[2] The several mutual aid agreements between the United States and British Commonwealth governments were primarily agreements on mutual lend-lease arrangements drawn up in the interests of the joint war effort of each government with the United States (1:2). Article VII, although linked with the terms of settlement in return for United States aid, was very much wider in its commitment to the sort of general international economic relations to be followed in the post-war period.

The Atlantic Charter (the Joint Declaration of August 1941 mentioned in the Article) presaged an agreement of the type of Article VII (1:1). For Australia the requirements of the Article represented a strong challenge to, if not quite the 'flat contradiction' of, 'Australia's historic policy of protection and preference', suggested by the authors (including some government officials) of the 'Canberra' memorandum for the Institute of Pacific Relations (1:3). The challenge is in the reference to 'agreed action' by signatories to the Article,

> directed to the expansion, by appropriate international and domestic measures, of production, employment, and the exchange and consumption of goods, which are the material foundations of the liberty and welfare of all peoples; to the elimination of all forms of discriminatory treatment in international commerce; and to the reduction of tariffs and other trade barriers (1:2).

Australian trade policy of the thirties had been marked by firm adherence to the Ottawa Agreement and especially its preferential principles. Some in-

[1] Throughout the remainder of the comment in this and later sections the term 'Article VII' refers to the Mutual Aid Agreement. Any similarly numbered article in some other agreement, if referred to, will be explicitly identified.

[2] A useful account of Article VII is to be found in Gardner (78), pp. 54-68. See also Crisp (65), pp. 199-201.

dependent trade treaties there had been to moderate some of the resentment against this preferential system; and some reductions of preference had been accorded to make a United Kingdom-United States trade treaty possible (11:2). There had been a very unhappy attempt at 'trade diversion' in 1936 and 1937 which had not profited Australia economically and which had done nothing to help Australian political relations with Japan and the United States.[3] By 1939 some of the acrimony had been removed from United States-Australian relations but a trade treaty seemed a long way off still. Economic relations with Japan had improved and there appeared to be prospects of a comprehensive trade treaty. During the war bulk-purchase agreements had continued more firmly the export dependence on the United Kingdom and had raised questions about the possibility of intergovernmental trading after the war (7:1). Australian trade policies were due for review but, in fact, the content and direction of the review were forced on the war-time government by the necessity to accept Article VII.

The necessity to accept Article VII as a means of ensuring 'material aid for the prosecution of the war'[4] on lend-lease terms can be readily under-stood. However, the Article can also be interpreted as an economic rallying point for the Allies, whether already overrun or still fighting—a guarantee against the resurgence of the economic nationalism of the thirties. There is no doubt that to the Americans the Ottawa Agreements contributed heavily to discriminatory economic nationalism, against which the Article was directed (1:11). It was also true that to many in Washington the United States economy seemed ripe for, and in need of, freer world trade conditions.

It was no secret, therefore, that the United States would look to the elimination of preferences (3:5), and not unnaturally some officials and many in Congress interpreted the Article as a promise to forgo the preferential system as a *quid pro quo* for the lend-lease system thought likely to be a net drain on United States economic strength, despite its mutual aid character. In the event, this was an overstatement of the position—for it became clear at least by 1945 that no preferences would be abandoned or tariff barriers lowered except as part of agreed (and presumably mutually balancing) negotiations. Nevertheless, substantial, if not complete, loss of the preferences had been expected, and there was uncertainty about which world system would actually prevail and fear lest this system might prejudice Australia's economic development. Despite its worries and uncertainty the Australian government was in no position to refuse to approve the Article—as the Prime Minister, J. B. Chifley, showing a marked sympathy for the United Kingdom position, was later (1948) to confirm (1:10). In the outcome, its fears were found to be

[3] For accounts of Australia's trade diversion policy see Copland and Janes (42), pp. 259-346; Australia, Tenth Report of the Rural Reconstruction Commission 1946 (12), pp. 51-2; Nicholson (132), pp. 8-10, 83, 110-15, 120-2.

[4] As printed in the Mutual Aid Agreement cited in 1:2n.

exaggerated. Yet the public documents of the early years, by avoiding the topic, most certainly understated the reality. The work of the Canberra group previously mentioned (1:3) was one of the few public warnings before the end of the war.[5] It was not until the early post-war years that the uncertainty that had prevailed became fully evident. Chifley's 1948 statement (1:10) is therefore best understood as a reflection of the earlier interpretation of the changes to be expected to flow from Article VII.

Moreover, the Americans did exert considerable pressure, especially during the period of loan negotiations between the United Kingdom and the United States in 1945. That it resulted finally in no more than the General Agreement on Tariffs and Trade 'no new preference' rule (see Section 3 below) and some modest reductions in preferential margins, negotiated in 1947, no doubt disappointed the Americans. A complete explanation requires more information than is available in Australian public documents, but some leads can now be suggested.

First, it was probably not possible before the war ended to develop to the full the American pressures implied in the Article, let alone make any very helpful public statements on such a difficult subject (1:11, final para.). For the good reasons that the shape of events to come could not be stated clearly enough to inform the public and that any comment might only make subsequent negotiations more difficult, there was no considered public statement by ministers on the nature and significance of the United States pressure to eliminate preferences. (Mention is made implicitly in 1:7 to 1:10, and 3:5.) However, the absence of an authoritative statement for the government did not altogether eliminate public realisation that something was in the wind. The very terms of the Atlantic Charter and Article VII answered some speculation. Moreover, the views contained in 1:3 were significant if only because of their authorship, despite the limited circulation of this document. (See also R. G. Menzies's call for 'Empire trade planning' in 1:6.)

[5] Among the relatively few early public documents of importance the following must be included: Firth (77), pp. 1-15, written after the U.K.-U.S. Agreement but before the acceptance of Article VII by Australia; Australian Institute of International Affairs (16), which reflects academic and official thought and does not appear to have had much impact beyond the circle of the Institute (see extract in 1:3); Brigden (27); Copland (40), a valuable document, but nevertheless notable for the almost complete absence of analysis of the preference question. It is good background to Sections 2 and 3 and reflects the greatly expanded American interest in world trade problems and the high hopes attached to this by Australia's intellectuals; Australia, Tenth Report of the Rural Reconstruction Commission (12), which attempts to examine the implications for Australian export prospects. It was published in August 1946 before the important 1947 international negotiations, which resulted in GATT, but it aroused little public discussion. In addition, speculation by Members of Parliament about the possible effects on Australia of Article VII is worth glancing at—see remarks by R. G. Menzies (1:6); J. P. Abbott on 25 March 1943; J. W. Leckie on 30 September 1943; G. J. Bowden on 12 October 1943; J. P. Breen on 13 October 1943; Archie Cameron on 31 March 1944; and J. McEwen on 18 July 1944.

B

While much was achieved in study and more or less informal and non-public negotiation by the war's end (3:2), these discussions served to moderate any thought, held strongly by some in Washington, that some single act on the part of Commonwealth members committed to Article VII would end the preferential system. The more modest outcome of the high hopes of some Americans and perhaps some Englishmen (1:11) (and of the fears of many in the Commonwealth) was undoubtedly in part assured by the famous Churchill speech of 21 April 1944, in which he denied the abandonment of the preferential system (1:4, 1:5). Chifley might later call the speech ambiguous (3:6) but at least it made more likely the possibility that any change in the preferential system would be by negotiation, not by unilateral cession as a *quid pro quo* for war-time aid. This did not become clear finally until December 1945 (3:2).

Until December 1945 there was—to the extent that the public worried about it at all—an expectation, not allayed by the Churchill speech, of more considerable and more rapid change than in fact occurred. Indeed, the informal examinations in which Australian officials participated from 1942 on covered the possibility of agreed ceilings to tariffs and formula cuts which would result in heavy reductions in and even elimination of margins of preference. Moreover, even in December 1945 when it was finally and publicly agreed that no single step, let alone unilateral action, eliminating preferences was possible, the Americans still adhered to elimination as their objective. On this point, moreover, they have remained consistent in the two decades since, except in respect of customs unions and free trade areas as provided for in Article XXIV of GATT (Sections 5 and 8). The continued hostility of the United States was made evident in 1962 in public and private exchanges between Canberra and Washington occasioned by Australian reactions to the British application to enter the Common Market (Sections 8 and 11).

While the British successfully resisted the attempt to link immediate and substantial action on the preferential issue directly with the negotiation of the Anglo-American loan in 1945, they did agree to a more precise formulation of the principles for negotiations on tariffs and preferences (1:8). This agreement was published in December 1945 as 'Proposals . . . for Consideration by an International Conference on Trade and Employment' (3:1, 3:2). In these proposals, the two countries agreed to an 'initial step in the process of eliminating tariff preferences' (3:1).

The principle of negotiation within the framework of commercial policy was thus established, but the expectation of considerable change remained strong. (In Section 3 more light will be thrown on developments after 1945.) However, once the principle of mutual negotiations in terms of balancing concessions was accepted, it was perhaps inevitable that forces against quick and substantial change would reassert themselves. These forces included Commonwealth interests freed from the worst pressures of war and now

6

more calmly looking for alternative forms of trade security if preferences were to go. The same circumstances also enabled American protectionist interests to organise their strength. They proved not at all anxious to contemplate heavy reductions in the United States tariff as the price for dismantling the Commonwealth preferential system.

It is clear enough, from the public documents (1:3) as well as from Chifley's more oblique reference (3:3), that there was in Australia some, even though not well informed, expectation of considerable change in the preferential system. At least one responsible observer expected compliance with United States demands.[6] In fact, while the precise future of the preferential system remained uncertain, Australian officials, encouraged by Chifley, developed quite strongly a viewpoint which promised to make expected adjustments in tariff and preferences easier to handle. This was the theme of full employment, not unique to Australia but made very much the distinguishing mark of Australia's initiative in international economic affairs during and after the war. It became in Australian official thinking a highly important solvent for some of the difficulties otherwise inherent in Article VII (2:1). Full employment was seen as ensuring growth in trade opportunities for Australia and that growth would make otherwise unpalatable adjustments easier. The doctrine itself is developed in the documents in Section 2.

This comment on Article VII has deliberately given pride of place to the preferential issue. It was the central political issue in Article VII for the good reason that the threat to preferences was rightly seen as a threat to the major foundation of Australia's pre-war external economic policy. Article VII incorporated that threat; but it also incorporated more positive possibilities for expansion in trade and employment and for securing stability in world commodity trade. Chifley and his ministers, especially H. V. Evatt and J. A. Beasley, seized upon these possibilities (see, for example, 2:1 and 3:3). The 'full employment' theme continues its importance throughout the period and will be developed in later sections.

A great deal of the foundation for other Australian policies well articulated in the two post-war decades was strongly laid down in the three or four years immediately following Article VII and can fairly be said to be consistent with that Article.

In retrospect, some twenty years later, the gains to our trade resulting from the practical achievement of full employment in the leading industrial countries of the world[7] and, no less important, the relatively high rates of

---

[6] Bailey (17), p. 26.

[7] The comment made by Menzies in 1948 (3:5) that to this end no document was needed to persuade governments to promote full employment had a measure of truth in it. Yet it discounts too heavily the importance of the international discussions among officials and ministers, whose determination vigorously to promote full employment was clearly strengthened by the stimulus so given to public interest and support for full employment measures.

7

economic growth that have prevailed in most of them since the mid-fifties, must be ranked as far outweighing any loss of preferences that might be held to the account of Article VII. In the event Australia's economic interests have dictated the continued retreat from Ottawa which began with Article VII and was finally assured by acceptance of GATT (Sections 3 and 5). Ironically, the two forms of preferential system approved by GATT—customs unions and free trade areas—have produced a far more direct threat to our export interests than our inability to take further advantage from the Ottawa system (Section 7).

The most significant outcome of Article VII was the commitment in theory —and in important measure in practice—to a system of multilateral trading relations. This was to receive expression in the rules of GATT, which attempted not merely to prevent a return to unrestrained economic nationalism but also to bind nations in a system of tariff rules which gave promise of substantial lessening of barriers (Section 5).

The fuller significance of these other aspects of Article VII for Australia will emerge in later sections of these documents. Article VII certainly launched Australia on a course of policy governing her trade relations with other countries not foreseen in 1938 and not clearly understood in 1942. All major developments in Australian post-war trade policy, at least up to the late 1950s, can be traced back to the commitment in Article VII.[8] Initial uncertainty and some fear of impairment of Australia's basic relations, especially with the United Kingdom, are apparent in the documents. Some imprecise references to Australia's future with Asia may be found, and a strong current of expectation of greater economic dependence on the United States is apparent.[9] It was not until well into the fifties that the content, advantages, and limitations of the trade policies evolved in world councils (in which Australia shared) and accepted by Australia were to be clearly discerned. All that was certain in 1942 was that change was afoot. What finally emerged was less damaging to previous economic relations with Britain than had been feared but also a good deal less fruitful in the more positive aspects of world co-operation than Australian ministers and officials perhaps had hoped. At this time, as already noted, public debate was limited, largely because of pre-occupation with the war and ministerial inability to give firm public guidance. However, on one positive matter—full employment policy—public debate was begun in 1943 and vigorously promulgated as government policy in a notable White Paper. This is the core of the documents in Section 2.

[8] This statement needs modifying to the extent that Australia's propensity for fairly high tariffs for some industries is not altogether consistent with the spirit of Article VII, although it is quite within the framework of tariff-making machinery allowed by GATT.

[9] This expectation was based on the even then obvious and great significance of the full employment policies in the United States, whose subsequent rather restrictive import policies, as affecting Australia, were not then foreseen.

1:1 ATLANTIC CHARTER

Extracts from 'Declaration of Principles, known as the Charter, issued by the Prime Minister of the United Kingdom and the President of the United States of America, 14 August, 1941'.[1]

PREAMBLE TO ATLANTIC CHARTER

The President of the United States of America and the Prime Minister, Mr Churchill, representing His Majesty's Government in the United Kingdom, being met together, deem it right to make known certain common principles on which they base their hopes for a better future for the world. . . .

Fourth, they will endeavour, with due respect for their existing obligations, to further the enjoyment by all States, great or small, victor or vanquished, of access on equal terms, to the trade and to the raw materials of the world which are needed for their economic prosperity.

Fifth, they desire to bring about the fullest collaboration between all nations in the economic field with the object of securing, for all, improved labour standards. economic advancement and social security; . . .

Source: *League of Nations Treaty Series,*
vol. 204, p. 384.

[1] The Declaration of Principles was signed by President Roosevelt and Prime Minister Churchill on 12 August 1941. However, 14 August, the date of the announcement. is the date officially given to it.

1:2 MUTUAL AID AGAINST AGGRESSION

Agreement between the Government of the United Kingdom and the Government of the United States of America on the Principles applying to Mutual Aid in the Prosecution of the War against Aggression. Signed at Washington, 23 February 1942.[1]

ARTICLE 7

In the final determination of the benefits to be provided to the United States of America by the Government of the United Kingdom in return for aid furnished under the Act of Congress of the 11th March [Lend-Lease], the terms and conditions thereof shall be such as not to burden commerce between the two countries, but to promote mutually advantageous economic relations between them and the betterment of worldwide economic relations. To that end, they shall include provision for agreed action by the United States of America and the United Kingdom, open to participation by all other countries of like mind, directed to the expansion, by appropriate international and domestic measures, of production, employment, and the exchange and consumption of goods, which are the material foundations of the liberty and welfare of all peoples; to the elimination of all forms of discriminatory treatment in international commerce, and to the reduction of tariffs and other trade barriers; and, in general to the attainment of

[1] An agreement in similar terms between Australia and the United States was announced by the Prime Minister (J. Curtin) on 3 September 1942. see *C.P.P.* no. 95 of 1940-3.

all the economic objectives set forth in the Joint Declaration made on the 14th August, 1941, by the President of the United States of America and the Prime Minister of the United Kingdom.

At an early convenient date conversations shall be begun between the two Governments with a view to determining, in the light of governing economic conditions, the best means of attaining the above-stated objectives by their own agreed action and of seeking the agreed action of other like-minded Governments.

Source: *League of Nations Treaty Series*, vol. 204, p. 389.

1:3 AUSTRALIA'S COMMERCIAL POLICY AND ARTICLE VII

Extracts from paper submitted by members of the Canberra Branch, Australian Institute of International Affairs, to the Eighth Conference of the Institute of Pacific Relations at Mont Tremblant, Quebec, in December 1942.[1]

Under Article VII of the Mutual Aid Agreement between the United Kingdom and the United States of America . . . the 'agreed action . . . open to participation by all other countries of like mind' is to be directed, in addition to 'the attainment of all economic objectives' set out in the Atlantic Charter, to: (a) 'the expansion, by appropriate international and domestic measures, of production and employ-ment, and the exchange and consumption of goods, which are the material foundation of the liberty and welfare of all peoples . . .'; and to (b) 'the elimination of all forms of discriminatory treatment in international commerce, and to the reduction of tariffs and other trade barriers. . . .'

Fulfilment of (a) should imply the solution of the 'balance of payments problem', which has plagued Australia (in common with many other countries) ever since the depression. On the other hand, (b) appears to require extensive changes in some of the cardinal features of Australia's commercial policy.

. . . the requirements of objective (b) stand in flat contradiction to Australia's historic policy of protection and preference. . . .

Source: Australian Institute of International Affairs, *Australia and the Pacific* (Princeton University Press, 1944), pp. 195-6. Reprinted by permission.

[1] See also Bailey (17).

1:4 SAFEGUARDS FOR IMPERIAL PREFERENCE

Extract from a speech by the Prime Minister of the United King-dom (W. S. Churchill) in the House of Commons, 21 April 1944.

What I am concerned to do is to show to the House, and also to Members of my own Party, how strictly I have, during my stewardship, safeguarded the structure of Imperial Preference, which has arisen out of the controversies and achieve-ments of the last 40 years, against any danger of being swept away in the tumult of this war. At my first meeting with the President of the United States at Argenta in Newfoundland, at the time of the so-called Atlantic Charter and before the United States had entered the war . . . I asked for the insertion of the following words which can be read in that document:

'With due respect for their existing obligations.' Those are the limiting words, and they were inserted for the express purpose of retaining in the House of Commons, and the Dominion Parliaments, the fullest possible rights and liberties over the question of Imperial Preference. Again, in February, 1942, when the United States was our closest ally, I did not agree to Article 7 of the Mutual Aid Agreements, without having previously obtained from the President a definite assurance that we were no more committed to the abolition of Imperial Preference than the American Government were committed to the abolition of their high protective tariffs. The discussions as to how a greater volume of trade and a more harmonious flow of trade can be created in the immediate post-war years in agreement, leaves us, in every respect, so far as action is concerned, perfectly free.

Source: P.D. (H. of C.), vol. 399,
pp. 579-80.

1:5 IMPERIAL PREFERENCE HARMFUL IN ITS OTTAWA MANIFESTATION

The two-day debate on Commonwealth relations in the House of Commons last week elicited from the Prime Minister one of his most felicitous and states-manlike speeches and from the House generally an impressive witness to the strength of the invisible bonds that knit the British nations together. The debate was opened by a speech by Mr. Shinwell, which was perhaps less remarkable for its substance than for the fact that he delivered it—but was still remarkable enough in the fervour of its imperial attachment to stir some protest in his own party. There can be no doubt of the desire of the people of the United Kingdom, as voiced by their representatives, to lose no opportunity of increasing the cohesion of the Commonwealth—not as a policy directed against any other nation, or against any universal association of the nations, but as the one sure fundamental in an unsure world. The imminence of the Premiers' Conference, and the divergent views that have been expressed by the Prime Ministers of Canada and Australia, prevented any very far-reaching discussion in the debate of the political side of Commonwealth relations. The effect was to give the subject of imperial preference an importance greater than it really deserves. The Prime Minister not only underlined the reservation he had inserted in the Atlantic Charter to protect the system of imperial preference, but also revealed that before accepting the Lend-Lease Agreement, with its famous Article Seven, he had secured from President Roosevelt a declaration that the United Kingdom was no more committed to its abolition than 'the American Government was committed to the abolition of their high protective tariff'. It was clear from the debate that the Parliamentary resistance to the one act of abolition would be fully as strong as the Congressional resistance to the other. This forthright statement has aroused some irritation in the United States. But it should also serve to clear the air. As a matter of fact, and not of desirability, there is no chance that the British Parliament would consent to the abolition of the system of imperial preference save

11

possibly as part of a very large reconstruction of international trade involving concessions by other countries far larger than any that are yet in prospect. There is no reason to suppose that the feeling in the Dominions is any less strong. These are facts that cannot be ignored. But when it comes to the question whether they are welcome or unwelcome facts, it is permissible to regret that so much of the symbolism of something as desirable as Commonwealth unity has come to be concentrated in a system of preferential duties which is of questionable virtue in any form and of downright harm in its Ottawa manifestation.

Source: *The Economist*, 29 April 1944,
vol. 146, p. 564.

1:6 REVIVAL OF EMPIRE TRADE NEEDED

Speech by the Leader of the Opposition (R. G. Menzies) in the House of Representatives on 13 September 1944.

I believe that it is high time that British countries got together to do a bit of Empire trade planning. . . In the past we had the Ottawa Conference, and later there were trade conferences in Great Britain. Unfortunately, it has become the fashion now to discount the Ottawa Conference, and to discount Empire preference. Influenced by some rather vague expression in the Atlantic Charter, or by some phrase in the lend-lease agreement, people are saying, 'Of course, we have finished with preference. After this war all countries must trade on the same footing.' I would not be so sure myself that the days of British Empire preference have gone . . . the first contribution, in point of time, that we can make to the revival of world trade is to do what we can to bring about a revival of Empire trade . . . We should not, on the assumption that a new world order is beginning, wipe out the advantages which Empire countries give one to another, but should assist one another in every way possible.

Source: C.P.D., vol. 179, pp. 724-5.

1:7 ELIMINATION OF EMPIRE PREFERENCES: GOVERNMENT'S ATTITUDE

Questions asked in the House of Representatives on 30 October 1945 and 6 March 1946.

Mr. McEwen: . . . Will the right honorable gentleman give an assurance that the government will resist the elimination of Empire preferential tariffs in representations to the British Government, if such a proposal . . . emanates from the U.S.A.?

The Prime Minister (J. B. Chifley): I have no official intimation that the representative of the U.S.A. will insist upon the abolition of Empire preference. I should like to be able to make a more complete statement to the House, but the position is still fluid . . . All I can say is that everything possible will be done. I have my own ideas regarding the best course of action, but they do not necessarily represent the view of the Government.

Mr. White: Why has the Prime Minister never made an announcement that he believes that reciprocal Empire trade should go on?

Mr. Calwell: He has never said that it will not be continued.

Mr. White: But why does he not announce that it will be?

Source: *C.P.D.*, vol. 185, p. 6342, and
vol. 186, p. 35.

1:8 UNITED KINGDOM PREPARED TO CONTRACT EMPIRE PREFERENCES

Speech by the Prime Minister of the United Kingdom (C. V. Attlee) in the House of Commons on 6 December 1945.

There is one particular matter arising out of the terms of Article VII of the Mutual Aid Agreement which is of especial interest and importance to the British Commonwealth and Empire—that is the question of tariff preferences. I would therefore refer shortly to that aspect of the American document which deals with both tariffs and tariff preferences.

The statement sets forth the procedure to be followed by common consent in considering, in the context of a general lowering of tariffs and other trade barriers, what contribution can be made from our side by way of reduction or elimination of preferences.

The statement makes it clear that, in pursuit of the objectives of Article VII of the Mutual Aid Agreement, we for our part are ready to agree that the existing system of preferences within the British Commonwealth and the Empire will be contracted, provided there is adequate compensation in the form of improvement in trading conditions between Commonwealth and Empire countries and the rest of the world.

The statement further provides that in entering negotiations for the reduction of tariffs the parties concerned will not refuse to discuss the modification of particular preferences on the ground that these are the subject of prior commitments; on the contrary, all margins of preference will be regarded as open to negotiation, and it will of course be for the party negotiating the modification of any margin of preference which it is bound by an existing commitment to give a third party, to obtain the consent of the third party concerned.

Further points to be noted are:

(i) The statement makes it clear there is no commitment on any country in advance of negotiations to reduce or eliminate any particular margin of preference. The position is that each country remains free to judge in the light of the offers made by all the others, the extent of the contribution it can make toward the realisation of the agreed objective.

(ii) It is recognised that reduction or elimination of preferences can only be considered in relation to, and in return for reductions of tariffs and other barriers to world trade in general which would make for mutually advantageous arrangements for the expansion of trade. There is thus no question of any unilateral surrender of preferences. There must be adequate compensation for all parties affected.

The statement does not in advance of the detailed negotiations lay down how far the process of reduction and elimination of preferences will be carried at this immediate stage. It must be realised that some preferences are of particular importance to the economy of certain parts of the world just as some tariffs are important in others. The elimination of all preferences would be such a step as would require a most substantial and widespread reduction of tariffs and other trade barriers by a large number of countries. Thus it is recognised that the degree to which the final objectives can be reached at the initial stage can only appear at the negotiations themselves and as the result of a mutually advantageous settlement. . . .

Source: *P.D. (H. of C.)*, vol. 416, pp. 2667-70.

1:9 UNITED STATES PRESSURE ON AUSTRALIA TO REDUCE PREFERENCES

Press statement by the Minister for Post-War Reconstruction (J. J. Dedman) on 7 October 1947.

The Australian delegation at Geneva had resisted all pressure by the United States to reduce tariffs and preferences which would result in sacrifices by Australian industries, the Minister for Post-War Reconstruction (Mr. Dedman) said today.

Mr. Dedman said that throughout the negotiations the United States had been pressing for reductions in preferences. . . .

1:10 BACKGROUND TO BRITISH AND AUSTRALIAN ACCEPTANCE OF ARTICLE VII

Speech by the Prime Minister (J. B. Chifley) in the House of Representatives on 26 February 1948.

I do not believe that Mr. Churchill was ever anxious to have Article VII, relating to tariff revision, included in the Mutual Aid Agreement . . . He knew that the United States had always looked with strong disfavour on Imperial preferences, and he knew also that Canada had never been keen on contractual Imperial preference obligations. I think I may thus interpret the utterances of the Prime Minister of Canada, who has been the leader of that country for a long time, without committing a political libel. I do not say that he did not believe in some sort of preference, but it is evident that he has never been enthusiastic about being bound by contractual obligations.

President Roosevelt had great political problems in his own country at that time. For a long time the policy of a great majority of the people of the United

States had been to 'keep out of Europe'—not to engage in any conflict on that continent, either militarily or otherwise. Therefore, President Roosevelt had to offer to his people something in return for what was one of the most generous gestures in history—the provisions of Lend-Lease under the Mutual Aid Agreement. On the other side of the bargain, we had a great leader in Mr. Churchill, who realized the desperate straits of his country. He knew that the United Kingdom had been selling its foreign securities to obtain credits, and that this reserve was becoming rapidly depleted. Indeed, the United Kingdom had to make its purchases abroad on a cash-and-carry basis. Mr. Churchill knew that if this situation were continued there could be only one end—that Britain could not carry on the war . . . It was very doubtful at that time whether 60 per cent. of the American people were in favour of participation in a European conflict. Confronted with these tremendous problems, Mr. Churchill and Mr. Roosevelt agreed to insert in the Lend-Lease Agreement the conditions contained in Article VII which provided that consideration was to be given after the war to a general reduction of tariff barriers. No doubt Mr. Churchill agreed to that provision reluctantly. At that time Australia was in a most desperate position, and it had no alternative but to join in the undertaking given to the United States by the United Kingdom. At that time the United Kingdom could not help us because physically it was incapable of doing so, and it was only because of the volume of aid supplied by the United States in the form of personnel, aircraft, equipment and services that Australia was not invaded. . . .

In the circumstances prevailing at the time the action taken by the Australian Government was completely justified. Of course, if the matter had been left to us, we should not have initiated a conference to discuss the reduction of world tariff barriers, but, as I said previously, we were under a contractual obligation to do so. Moreover, other factors entered into the matter. The United Kingdom desperately needed a reduction of world trade barriers if its economy were to survive in the aftermath of war. The Australian Government realized fully the position of Britain, and because of that, and because of our contractual obligation —or, should I say, moral obligation—we agreed to the provisions of Article VII of the Lend-Lease Agreement. . . .

Australia participated in the International Conference on Trade and Employment for three main reasons. In the first place, we were morally obliged to do so because of Article VII of the Lend-Lease Agreement, and in any event, we wanted the benefit of the favourable provisions of that article. Secondly, the British Government was convinced that an agreement, such as was eventually reached at the conference, was absolutely essential to its economic existence, and finally we had our own privileges to preserve.

I pay tribute to the members of the delegation which represented Australia at that conference . . . I am convinced that our representatives accomplished something really worthwhile, something at least comparable with the achievement of the British delegation. It was no easy task to assist the United States Government to convince its people that it was justified in doing things for other countries. Australia has suffered no real loss as a result of the agreements or the tariff schedules that will be discussed later. It has played its part in world affairs and has contributed to the assistance of Great Britain. . . .

In this world one cannot take all and give nothing. Australia has not given very much materially, although we have contributed a great deal through the industry and ability of our representatives at international conferences.

Source: C.P.D., vol. 196, pp. 253-6,

1:11 ARTICLE VII AND COMMONWEALTH PREFERENCES

There emerged at length (February 1942) the 'Master Agreement . . . on the Principles Applying to Mutual Aid in the Prosecution of the War Against Aggression.' This Agreement, which became the model of many others signed between the United States and its Allies, most signally merited the adjective 'unsordid'; so too did the financial terms of the settlement made in its spirit after victory had been achieved. Nevertheless, one of its articles—and that the one on which liberal economists, both British and American, set most store—became the cause, both then and later, of much controversy and misgiving in Britain and the British Commonwealth. This was the famous Article VII, which, after providing that the final determination of the benefits due to the United States on account of lend-lease aid would not be of such a nature as to impede world trade, went on to pledge both Governments to work for the 'elimination' of discriminatory practices and the 'reduction' of tariffs.

The discriminatory practices which the American negotiators had most prominently in mind were the trade preferences of the British Commonwealth. To many people in the United States these preferences seemed economically, if not morally, wrong; but many people throughout the Commonwealth regarded them as a family arrangement that was neither unvirtuous nor damaging to the world's prosperity: indeed, the very reverse. Among professional economists in Britain opinion was divided; some thought that speedy progress could be made after victory towards a world of impartial trade policies, but others believed that the attempt to move quickly in this direction would damage world trade and would in particular gravely endanger Britain's efforts to rebuild her shattered balance of payments.

This more remote aspect of the history of lend-lease could not in the present chapter be passed by, for it was prominent in the despatches, memoranda and minutes of 1941 and the early months of 1942. But for the historian of British war economy it must remain a minor theme, recognised but not pursued. After all, the British in 1941 were not devoting much of their time to blue-printing the world's commercial future or safeguarding their own. They were absorbed in the immediate struggle. Lend-lease made it possible for them to put more power into the struggle. That was its chief significance.

Source: Hancock and Gowing, *British War Economy*. History of the Second World War, United Kingdom Civil Series (H.M.S.O.), pp. 246-7. Reprinted by permission.

2

WHITE PAPER OF 1945:
'FULL EMPLOYMENT IN AUSTRALIA'

The central document in this section is the White Paper on 'Full Employment in Australia', of May 1945 (2:2). It reflects the work of Chifley as Treasurer and, earlier, Minister for Post-War Reconstruction, and of his successor in this portfolio, J. J. Dedman. In adopting the White Paper the Curtin government made 'full employment' their central policy. This was indeed a key decision. It coloured and governed many approaches to economic and social policy, not least trade policy: it was a domestic policy to be strengthened by its sale to other countries (2:2, para. 46).

Memories of the depression were still vivid (2:2, para. 23), and the effects of fuller employment on war-time production achievements had not been unremarked. No less important, it seemed possible to achieve full employment by following appropriate investment and expenditure policies (2:2, para. 23). Full employment readily became a key domestic policy. What was more novel was the development of the link between policies of full employment in advanced countries and buoyant trade and prosperity in countries like Australia (2:2, para. 19). The interdependence of nations became a strong theme for the war-time Labor government and full employment as an objective of international policy was seen as a way of handling the difficulties anticipated or feared when Article VII was accepted.

While the White Paper represented the most comprehensive statement of the government's economic aims for post-war reconstruction, much of its content had been foreshadowed in earlier statements, especially those covering the international activities of Evatt and Beasley (2:1). These reveal the Australian government's attempt to develop the positive aspects of Article VII. It may therefore appear curious that the White Paper does not mention Article VII, although para. 46(b) refers to it obliquely. Nevertheless this is understandable, for the Anglo-American discussions on the preference issue were still proceeding, with the outcome almost unpredictable. The White Paper was published in May: it was not until December that the Anglo-American agreement on proposed procedures for negotiating tariffs and preferences was announced (3:2).

The Chifley government immediately disclosed its knowledge of the discussions leading to the proposals and its willingness 'without prior commitment' to make concessions on preferences in terms of the proposed procedures (3:3). However, it could and did make clear, both before and after December 1945, its view that an international understanding on full employment was, or ought to be, a condition precedent to negotiations on commercial policy.

It is the primacy of full employment that is asserted in these early international efforts and in the White Paper itself. There is no attempt to deny the importance of other matters such as tariff negotiations, international monetary policy, commodity agreements—see, for example, paragraph 46 of the White Paper. Nevertheless, with a persistence and a conviction that earned prominence (and also respect) for Australian efforts internationally, our delegates stressed the relationship between the level of incomes and employment, on the one hand, and the volume of world trade, on the other. They argued that employment policy was basic to all else in the economic field. As Brigden observed in a review article on *Australia and the Pacific*:

> Australian policy takes the doctrine of 'full employment' right into the international field and tries to make it the criterion for all future economic action.[1]

Other aspects of trade policy were to gain in importance as the post-war period developed. Nevertheless the Federal elections of December 1961, held at a time of recession, appeared to demonstrate the hold full employment, at least as a domestic policy, has continued to have on the Australian people.

Among the more interesting and sometimes prescient elements in the White Paper are the comments on the effect of full employment in Australia on the balance of payments. In particular, in paragraphs 49 and 85 and elsewhere, full employment is recognised as increasing the demand for imports of equipment and raw materials (also see 3:19). The 'spill-over' effect of full employment on demand for imports is, however, less clearly spelt out than the danger of inadequate export returns, especially in periods of downward fluctuations. In general terms it is seen that full employment may call for curbs on imports to levels manageable in relation to available earnings and reserves of foreign exchange. Deflation leading to unemployment is firmly ruled out as a method of dealing with a situation of falling export returns (2:2, para. 90). Neither the government nor its advisers could have foreseen the reality, in the decades ahead, of all the issues posed in its White Paper.

Naturally enough, domestic tariff policy received attention (2:2, para. 72). A moderate policy of tariff protection was propounded, its moderation in part due to the increased awareness of the fact that Australia could not live in economic isolation. The role of the Tariff Board was clearly reaffirmed. In the event, to an unexpected degree, the Board's role was to be

[1] Brigden (27), p. 327.

minimised first by reductions on imports from dollar areas, second by the shortage of imported goods in the early years of reconstruction in Britain and Europe, and third by the general imposition of import restrictions following the sudden rush of imports in 1951-2. Import restrictions and tariff policy are discussed more fully in Sections 14 and 15. The important point here is to note the clear prediction of policies relating to balance of payments later put into effect by a different government.

Other documents in this section show due recognition of domestic and international agricultural problems. There is some recognition of concern for the welfare of underdeveloped (poor) countries and a recognition that their welfare, too, is linked with Australia's and, of course, with full employment in the advanced industrial countries. There is a clear recognition in govment and some non-official documents of the importance of restoring the fortunes of agriculture badly affected by war-time droughts and post-war shortages of materials (2:3). The proposal for an export trading corporation (2:2, para. 86) came to little, although in 1956 the Export Payments Insurance Corporation, established by a Liberal government, gave partial expression to the idea Chifley expressed in 1945 (16:1).

In retrospect it seems natural that the theme of full employment should have dominated Australian government thinking both at ministerial and official levels. Its relevance to domestic post-war aims was apparent to all. Hardly less apparent were the motives for so strongly arguing the relevance of full employment as a *world* policy to Australia's external economic problems, especially those concerned with trade. The fear that the United States and the United Kingdom could all too easily slump into depression and pass its effects on to the Australian economy was strongly entrenched in both official and non-official economic thinking. There was less clear articulation before December 1945 of the possibility that full employment might resolve the international difficulties expected in respect of tariffs and preferences.[2]

[2] There was a good deal of comment in the newspapers immediately after the publication of the White Paper. It emphasised full employment and some of its problems but paid little attention to related trade problems, despite the emphasis placed by ministers and officials on the significance of full employment for trade expansion (2:1). Not till the fifties, thanks to the surge of interest in the experience of full employment and in the problems of growth (in both advanced and underdeveloped areas), was much written on the direct connection between trade and growth, and under full employment conditions. A considerable review occurs in the *Report of the Committee of Economic Enquiry* (better known as the Vernon Report (11)) presented by the Commonwealth in May 1965.
Australian professional economists wrote little on the White Paper itself. Those who did include Merry and Bruns (128) and Wilson (167).
Perhaps the most useful recent official reminder of the importance to Australian trade of continuing full employment and economic growth in the industrial countries of the world is contained in the February 1966 Supplement to the *Treasury Information Bulletin* (5), which devotes three pages (34-6) to this topic.

The merit of the White Paper and other statements on full employment is their recognition that expanding economies could afford more liberal attitudes on trade and commercial policies—although it would be claiming too much to assert that the possibility of continuous economic expansion or 'growth' under conditions of full employment was as clearly seen as the merits of full employment. Thinking was still very much in terms of a simpler proposition: the depression of 1930 must not be allowed to happen again.

Exercising the privilege of hindsight, one can fairly observe that full employment was overstated as a solvent for some of the difficult issues of trade policy. Even Dedman's explicit recognition of these other problems (3:14) does not effectively remove the impression that full employment held pride of place in government thinking about trade policy. In the mid-fifties Australian delegations were sometimes—especially in Commonwealth conferences —hoisted with their own petard of 1945: 'full employment' was frequently offered to Australia by the United Kingdom as the best policy for handling instability in commodity trade and even for mitigating agricultural protectionism. By the mid-fifties, however, Australian governments had cause, without discounting the prime importance of high levels of income and employment everywhere, to stress the need for more direct action on excessive agricultural protectionism and the rather-too-wide fluctuations in world prices for primary products. Australia can still experience economic chills when recessions occur in Britain, Europe, North America, and now Japan: but general buoyancy does not dispose of the problems of non-tariff barriers to trade and the year-by-year uncertainty in price levels.

2:1 AUSTRALIA PROPOSES EMPLOYMENT AGREEMENT

Speech by the Minister for Supply and Shipping (J. A. Beasley) on 24 April 1944.[1]

What I have now to say outlines the conclusions which have been reached, and the further steps which the Australian Government considers should first be taken to implement Article V of the Atlantic Charter, and Article VII of the Mutual Aid Agreement. . . .

It is, therefore, with satisfaction that the Australian Government notes that, by

[1] The Minister was speaking at the fourth sitting of the International Labour Organization Conference at Philadelphia, United States of America, on Items I and II of the agenda, the former referring to future policy, program and status of the International Labour Organization and the latter containing recommendations to the United Nations for present and post-war social policy.

This is the fullest exposition on this topic selected from statements made by Beasley and also by the Prime Minister (J. B. Chifley), the Minister for External Affairs (H. V. Evatt) and the Minister for Post-War Reconstruction (J. J. Dedman).

signing the Atlantic Charter and the Mutual Aid Agreement, the United Nations have pledged themselves to pursue policies designed to raise living standards everywhere in the world. It needs to be emphasized that the raising of living standards is primarily a matter of domestic policy. The instruments for increasing investment, consumption and employment, and for distributing purchasing power among the community lie in the hands of the institutions and governments of each nation. But it must be emphasized also that the raising of living standards is not wholly a domestic matter, particularly for those countries which are under-developed or are highly dependent on foreign trade or the financial policies of other countries. For them domestic policies to maintain high levels of employment and to increase standards of living are restricted by the necessity of balancing external payments. In other words, the success of the domestic policies of many small countries depends, not only upon their own domestic planning, but also upon world demand for their exports. . . .

The most important single factor determining the demand for goods entering world trade is world level of income and consumption, and particularly, the level of income and consumption in the larger and industrially developed countries. High levels of income and consumption throughout the community are dependent, in their turn, on high and stable levels of employment. . . .

. . . we are led to the conclusion that the critical factor controlling the raising of standards of living and the level of trade throughout the world will be the kind of domestic policies which are followed by the larger economies such as those of the United States of America and Britain. This being the case, higher levels of employment throughout the world, and in particular higher levels of employment in the more developed countries, should be the first goal to be sought in international economic collaboration. . . .

Australia attaches great importance to increased consumption as a post-war objective; but the immediate means of achieving this objective is to start at the base by increasing employment.

Monetary planning to maintain stable exchange rates and increase the availability of foreign credits, as is contemplated in Britain and United States plans now under discussion, is another goal . . . Under any scheme, a country maintaining high levels of employment, requiring as a result increased imports will find its credits restricted if other countries do not also maintain high levels of employment and increase their imports.

Another goal of international economic collaboration is the removal of trade restrictions. In the absence of full employment, the removal of restrictions cannot guarantee increased world trade. In fact, removal of restrictions might easily set in motion a trend towards decreased world demand by causing increased local unemployment. In any case, in practice, all countries have found that barriers to trade cannot be removed while unemployment exists. The dominating problem of every nation before the war was the continuous under-employment of its population. The main factor preventing international economic collaboration was the fear that international collaboration involving agreements to reduce trade barriers would cause and not cure the urgent local problem of employment. This defensive attitude towards international obligations was, and still is, justified by uncertainty about domestic policies in the major areas of world consumption.

Similar uncertainty regarding their operation surrounds buffer-stock plans, international commodity agreements, and other devices which are other goals of international economic collaboration. Uncertainty and doubt about the effectiveness of such proposals will only be removed by a conviction that governments will pursue domestic policies of expansion, and recognize this as the first and most important contribution to international economic collaboration.

It can be seen that employment and consumption policies, which have traditionally been regarded as of domestic concern only, exercise far more influence on the affairs of other nations than do exchange rate, tariff, and export subsidy policies which have conventionally been classified as of international concern. The Australian Government considers, therefore, that national policies of employment should come within the scope of matters subject to international discussion and agreement. An agreement between Governments to maintain high levels of employment would not imply any interference with sovereign rights by an international institution, except the sovereign 'right' to cause unemployment in other countries by allowing unemployment and low living standards to persist within the national boundaries. Every country would be free to use the means which seem most appropriate in the circumstances to maintain its own employment level and prevent unemployment. It hardly seems conceivable that democratic Governments would hesitate to undertake to maintain high levels of employment. They cannot afford to hesitate, having regard to the experiences of the great depression, and the undoubted claims every demobilized serviceman and producer of war goods will have upon his government to see that a proper place will be found for him in the economic life of his country when this war is over. . . .

All the United Nations have already undertaken, by implication, the obligation to maintain employment. They have endorsed the Four Freedoms, and in particular the Freedom From Want. They have endorsed the Atlantic Charter, and in particular the objective of 'security for all, improved labour standards, economic advancement, and social security'. They have endorsed Article VII of the Mutual Aid Agreement, and in particular the undertaking 'to promote mutually advantageous economic relations' by 'appropriate international and domestic measures, of production, employment, and the exchange and consumption of goods'. The only objection that could be raised to a formal agreement is that some countries might take advantage of it as an excuse to restrict trade. . . .

The Australian Government delegation, therefore, will wish later to put forward the recommendation to the Governments of the United Nations, that a United Nations agreement on employment be sought . . . I attach to this statement a draft agreement in order that this recommendation may be put forward in a practical way. The main features of the draft agreement are that each government agrees—

To declare its responsibility to its own people and to the peoples of other countries to maintain high levels of employment.

To improve its statistics of employment and unemployment.

To furnish other countries regularly with these statistics and an account of the domestic employment position.

To consult with others through an appropriate international agency, when employment levels are low and threaten the security of employment of others. . . .

Full employment is the central pivot of the Australian Government's domestic policy. . . .

It can be seen that an employment agreement has an important bearing upon other aspects of international economic collaboration. We consider, and I believe I have shown, that without an employment agreement, other international economic proposals will be no more than a dangerously deceptive veneer simply covering the fundamental problems of international society. . . .

I do not imply that the Australian Government is not in favour of these other international agreements. In fact it is an anxiety to see that they are successful in carrying out their primary aims of increasing living standards and providing peace that prompts us to emphasize full employment as the fundamental basis. . . .

Source: Digest of Decisions and Announcements, no. 82, pp. 7-14.

2:2 FULL EMPLOYMENT IN AUSTRALIA

Extracts from the text of the White Paper of 30 May 1945.

PART I.—INTRODUCTION

Full employment is a fundamental aim of the Commonwealth Government. The Government believes that the people of Australia will demand and are entitled to expect full employment, and that for this purpose it will be able to count on the co-operation of servicemen's associations, trade unions, employers' associations and other groups. Because the Referendum was not carried, the co-operation of State Governments and local authorities will be particularly necessary.

2. Despite the need for more houses, food, equipment and every other type of produce, before the war not all those available for work were able to find employment or to feel a sense of security in their future. On the average during the twenty years between 1919 and 1939 more than one-tenth of the men and women desiring work were unemployed. In the worst period of the depression well over 25 per cent. were left in unproductive idleness. By contrast, during the war no financial or other obstacles have been allowed to prevent the need for extra production being satisfied to the limit of our resources. It is true that war-time full employment has been accompanied by efforts and sacrifices and a curtailment of individual liberties which only the supreme emergency of war could justify; but it has shown up the wastes of unemployment in pre-war years, and it has taught us valuable lessons which we can apply to the problems of peace-time, when full employment must be achieved in ways consistent with a free society. . . .

6. There will be no place in this full employment policy for schemes designed to make work for work's sake. Moreover, full advantage must be taken of modern methods of production and training in all branches of industry, and the economic system must be flexible enough to meet changing needs. In these conditions, full employment has advantages to offer to every section of the community. To the worker, it means steady employment, the opportunity to change his employment if he wishes and a secure prospect unmarred by the fear of idleness and the dole. To the business or professional man, the manufacturer, the shopkeeper, it means an expanding scope for his enterprise, free from the fear of periodic slumps in spending. To the primary producer, it means an expanding home market and—taking a world-wide view—better and more stable export markets. To the people as a whole, it means a better opportunity to obtain all the goods and services which their labour, working with necessary knowledge and equipment, is capable of producing. . . .

23

8. The Government has proposed in current international discussions that an employment agreement should be concluded whereby each country would undertake to do all in its power to maintain employment within its own territories. The Government is also taking part in discussions relating to other forms of international collaboration designed to expand world trade and to mitigate fluctuations in prices of raw materials and foodstuffs. A domestic policy of full employment in Australia will prove of benefit to other countries. . . .

PART II.—EMPLOYMENT AND EXPENDITURE

12. The amount of employment available at any time depends on the volume of production being undertaken. This in turn depends on the demand for goods and services—that is, on expenditure by individuals, firms, public authorities and oversea buyers. Full employment can be maintained only as long as total expenditure provides a market for all the goods and services turned out by Australian men and women, working with available equipment and materials, and fully employed after allowing for the need for leisure. . . .

Variability of Expenditure

18. Spending from overseas on Australian goods and services has in the past been extremely variable. All other countries have suffered substantial fluctuations in their levels of employment and total income and their spending on our exports has varied accordingly.

Scope for Stabilization of Expenditure

19. One of the chief threats to full employment is, therefore, the instability of private capital expenditure and of expenditure from overseas. Unfortunately, neither type of expenditure is capable of being completely stabilized. The prospect of a high and stable level of demand will encourage businessmen to maintain a steady flow of capital expenditure, but many other factors on which their judgments depend are necessarily variable. We must also be prepared for continued fluctuations in spending from overseas. This will be less serious to the extent that oversea governments succeed in raising and stabilizing their people's employment and incomes. Domestic measures to promote stability of primary producers' incomes will also tend to stabilize spending and employment in Australia.

23. The essential condition of full employment is that public expenditure should be high enough to stimulate private spending to the point where the two together will provide a demand for the total production of which the economy is capable when it is fully employed. The effectiveness of public expenditure in stimulating employment generally is vividly brought home by our experience at the beginning of this war. There were then more than a quarter of a million unemployed. The Commonwealth Government directly absorbed some of these people into the armed forces, into clothing and munition factories, and into building new factories, aerodromes, and similar establishments for war purposes. The balance of the unemployed was quickly absorbed by private enterprise to produce goods and services to meet the demands of these newly-employed workers, and to meet the demands of the government for war goods. During the war, the high level of government expenditure required to achieve our war effort has not only resulted in full employment, but has caused a continual strain on available resources, and has involved a contraction and diversion of private enterprise because of the scarcity of resources.

24

PART III.—MAINTENANCE OF FULL EMPLOYMENT

Net Expenditure from Overseas

46. In the past, the chief fluctuations in total spending and employment in Australia have arisen from changes in the value of Australian exports, in response to the varying prosperity of world markets. In order to meet this threat to the maintenance of full employment in Australia, the Government's policy will be based upon the following principles:—

(a) to seek agreement now with other nations—particularly the major industrial countries of the world—by which countries undertake to do all in their power to maintain employment within their own territories, and thereby expand demand for internationally-traded goods;

(b) to participate in developing other forms of international collaboration designed to expand world trade and to mitigate fluctuations in prices of raw materials and foodstuffs;

(c) to prepare now for the post-war development and diversification of Australian export markets for both primary and secondary products;

(d) to develop measures to stabilize the income, and hence the expenditure, of Australian export producers, so as to offset the effect of short-term fluctuations in the demand for Australian exports;

(e) to stabilize total expenditure and employment in Australia in the face of any expected reduction in spending from overseas on Australian goods and services, by bringing about a compensating expansion in public capital expenditure and by other appropriate means; this will require a continual review of export prospects, in order that these measures may be taken in good time. . . .

47. In seeking to offset fluctuations in receipts from overseas, it will obviously be desirable to stabilize farm incomes as far as possible, in order to give primary producers the same sense of security as we are seeking for the rest of the community. In the past, measures have been adopted to maintain essential activity by rural producers, even though at times their financial position has been jeopardized by a serious slump in prices, or by an adverse season. These measures, however, did not eliminate the serious fluctuations in the expenditure of export producers which have been the cause of wide variations in total expenditure in Australia. To meet this problem and to eliminate this element of instability, the Government proposes to seek the co-operation of the States through the Australian Agricultural Council in maintaining greater stability of income to rural producers.

48. Australian spending on imports is not a significant factor in maintaining full employment in Australia since it affects employment in other countries. The chief problem here from the Australian point of view is whether our receipts from abroad will provide sufficient oversea funds to pay for all the imports which, in conditions of full employment, Australians will wish to buy.

49. This problem of the balance of payments is dealt with in Parts IV and V of this paper. It is important, however, to point out here that if, at any time, we are obliged, because our export income is insufficient, to impose quantitative import restrictions in order to keep our spending on imports within the limit of our available oversea funds, there will be a tendency for local resources to find employment in industries which can attract spending previously devoted to imports. To the extent that this happens, employment will be maintained with a

smaller expansion of public and private capital expenditure. However, Australia will have urgent need of certain imported materials and will impose quantitative import restrictions only if they become necessary to keep our oversea purchases within the limits of our oversea income. . . .

PART IV.—SPECIAL PROBLEMS OF A FULL EMPLOYMENT ECONOMY

Efficiency

72. While the tariff and other methods of protection are legitimate devices for building up industries appropriate to our economy, the grant of protection by the Government to producers is a privilege which carries with it the responsibility for maintaining the highest possible level of efficiency. Protection must not be protection of excessive costs, inefficient methods and obsolete equipment, nor should it encourage the practice of relying on rings, cartels, tariffs and a guaranteed home market, rather than on efficient production. Protection in the past has been granted upon the advice of the Tariff Board, and the Government proposes to continue to rely upon this body. The Tariff Board has ample powers to investigate and report upon the efficiency of protected industries. It is the Government's intention that the Board shall carry out these investigations and make regular reports. . . .

Balance of Oversea Payments

85. A policy of full employment, brought about through the maintenance of high levels of expenditure, will necessarily involve an increased demand for imports. Australia has always been a heavy importer of materials and, with an expanding national income, will continue to be so in the future. But the amount we can spend on imports is limited by the amount of export proceeds, together with reserves of oversea funds, which are available for this purpose.

86. The Government is taking measures designed to expand and stabilize post-war markets for Australia's exportable products, which will help to achieve greater stability in our export incomes. An Export Advisory Committee, consisting of representatives of the Government and of those interested in exports, has already been established to provide a means of contact and collaboration. The Government has under consideration the establishment through the Commonwealth Bank of export credit guarantee facilities which would reduce the financial risks of the export trade, and also the establishment of a joint Government and Commercial Export Trading Corporation which would actively promote Australia's export trade in primary and manufactured goods. The scope and quality of our trade representation overseas is being examined to bring it up to the standards required. The Government is also seeking opportunities to negotiate trade treaties with countries where there are possibilities of expanded commercial relations after the war.

87. The full success of these measures, however, depends upon the general state of employment and economic activity throughout the world, which largely determines the demand for internationally traded goods. The Government is therefore seeking an international agreement among important trading countries to maintain high levels of employment within their own territories.

88. Australia must be prepared for some fluctuations in the balance of payments. Difficulties may arise from a decline in the world demand for Australian exports, either because of a failure on the part of important trading countries to maintain employment and spending, or because of a shift in world demand to

products different from the ones we have been exporting. There are also climatic and other temporary factors which will continue to have an important effect on exports.

89. Minor fluctuations in export income will, as in the past, be met by running down oversea reserves in poor export years, and building them up in good years. The Government's banking legislation provides the Commonwealth Bank with adequate powers to mobilize our foreign exchange reserves and will ensure that the best use is made of them.

90. If there is a prolonged and severe fall in export incomes, it will not be possible to meet the deficit in the balance of payments merely by drawing from oversea reserves, and we shall then have to reduce expenditure on imports. In the past, necessary reductions in imports have usually been allowed to come about by permitting a fall in export incomes to result in reduced spending by export producers, thus bringing about unemployment and a general fall in incomes to the extent necessary to reduce imports to the level at which they could be paid for from export income. This deflationary method is inconsistent with a full employment policy, and serves the interests neither of the people of Australia nor of the people of the countries with which Australia trades. The Government will not countenance this method in future.

91. Other means of reducing imports will thus be required. If the deficit in the balance of payments is primarily due to a permanent decline in oversea demand for Australian products, and if it is not possible to restore export income by shifts of productive resources to meet changes in world demands, an alteration in the exchange rate may be the appropriate method of correction. If, however, the fall in export income is one which, although prolonged and severe, is not permanent, the more appropriate method may be quantitative restriction of imports.

92. The kind of action taken to control imports would depend on the Government's assessment at the time of the causes and probable duration of the deficit in the balance of payments. The Government considers there are good grounds for expecting a reasonably steady expansion of export income in the future. If, however, there should be a serious deficit in the balance of payments, import spending will inevitably have to be reduced. It would be in the interests neither of the world nor of ourselves to make the reduction by means of unemployment in Australia. Australia will make its maximum contribution to the flow of world trade by maintaining full employment at home, and by allowing the consequent high level of expenditure to become effective in demand for imports up to the limit of our available funds.

PART V.—CHANGE-OVER FROM WAR TO PEACE

Controls in the Transition

104. Although it is at present impossible to foresee in detail how difficult will be the problem of the balance of payments in the transition period, there is good reason to take precautions in advance against possible difficulties in finding the means of payment for the imports we shall require. Not only will it be necessary to meet urgent needs for some imported materials and equipment for our industries, together with the accumulated arrears of consumption goods, but it is also possible that the prices of the goods we import will have risen to a greater extent than the prices of the goods on the export of which we rely for obtaining oversea exchange. Time may be needed, moreover, before our export industries get back

into full production. For all these reasons, therefore, it will be necessary to retain the machinery for controlling imports, in order to keep our international accounts in balance and to make the best use of our available foreign exchange. In particular, it may be necessary to give priority to imports of essential materials and equipment needed for industry, building and construction.

Source: *C.P.P.*, no. 11 of 1945-6.

2:3 A RURAL POLICY FOR POST-WAR AUSTRALIA

Current Commonwealth policy in relation to Australia's primary industries. Extracts from a statement authorised by the Prime Minister (J. B. Chifley), 1946.

II. OBJECTIVES OF AGRICULTURAL POLICY

5. The Government feels that certain general objectives may already be clearly stated:

(i) To raise and make more secure the levels of living enjoyed by those engaged in and dependent upon the primary industries.

(ii) To secure a volume of production adequate to meet domestic food requirements, to provide the raw materials for our developing secondary industries, and to enable an expanding volume of exports to pay for necessary imports.

(iii) To encourage efficient production at prices which are fair to the consumer and which provide an adequate return to the producer.

(iv) To develop and use our primary resources of water, soil, pastures and forests in a way which conserves them and avoids damaging exploitation.

These general objectives may be translated into more specific terms, namely:

(i) To promote a successful general economic and employment policy—domestic and international—to ensure adequate markets for rural industries.

(ii) To provide greater stability and security of farm incomes.

(iii) To promote more efficient farm practices and so reduce the cost per unit of output.

(iv) To conserve and develop water, soil and other natural resources.

(v) To improve the conditions of country life.

III. GENERAL ECONOMIC AND EMPLOYMENT POLICY

6. The Government regards high levels of employment both in Australia and overseas as a necessary prerequisite of continued agricultural prosperity. It has taken this view consistently in its domestic policy and in international discussions. . . .

IV. STABILITY AND SECURITY OF FARM INCOMES

International Commodity Agreements

18. Where a large proportion of our production is exported, the stability of prices and returns to primary producers is largely dependent in the long run on

export or world prices. With this in mind the Government has sought to conclude international agreements with other countries in order to secure stability in world prices of primary products, and to introduce other measures to safeguard the producer from violent and sudden changes in his returns. At the forthcoming United Nations Conference on Food and Agriculture and on Trade and Employment, proposals for the improvement of the conditions of world trade will be considered in detail.

VIII. AGRICULTURE AND GENERAL WELFARE

67. Prosperity like peace cannot be secured in sections. Agricultural prosperity depends in the long run upon general welfare. Allowing prices to rise to a level that burdens the consuming public is certain to restrict demand and react upon the interest of producers. On the other hand, where the general level of employment and prosperity are high the demand for agricultural products expands.

68. No country stands to gain more than Australia from an expansionist world policy. The agricultural prosperity of Australia depends upon the widening of world trade. Our soil and climate enable us to produce a relatively few but important products for which world markets are needed. If these are denied us our special advantages are lost and our development retarded. It is for these reasons that Australia is vitally interested in an expansionist rather than an isolationist world policy. If security and prosperity can be widely spread the demand for food and fibre will expand and Australia's future will be secure, provided agriculture is efficient and costs not inflated. The Commonwealth Government is convinced that this attitude towards world policy is essential to our welfare and will devote itself to securing these aims.

Source: Reproduction of roneoed
document at Central Drawing Office,
Maribyrnong.

3

AUSTRALIA CHOOSES
INTERNATIONAL ECONOMIC COLLABORATION

The element of decision—the acceptance of membership of several international organisations—in the documents in this section is the natural outcome of the commitment to Article VII of the Mutual Aid Agreement (Section 1) and of the Australian declarations of policy in the 1945 White Paper on Full Employment (Section 2). Australia decided, not without considerable debate in Parliament and within the government party, the Australian Labor Party (A.L.P.), to accept the obligations and privileges of the proposed ITO as set out in the Havana Charter 1948 (3:14), the GATT (3:11), the IMF (3:18, 3:19), the IBRD (3:19), and the FAO (3:22).[1] In accepting the Charter of the United Nations in 1945[2] it had accepted the Economic and Social Council with its wide range of economic and social objectives.[3]

Between them the obligations amounted to a comprehensive undertaking to conduct the country's foreign economic policies under agreed rules amounting, for trade policy *per se*, to a code of fair trade. These obligations were designed to give effect to the objectives stated in Article VII and altogether represented a quite remarkable move forward in international cooperation compared with the situation prevailing between the two world wars.

ITO and GATT

However, the intended principal instrument—the Charter for an International Trade Organization—was finally not ratified by its prime mover, the United States. That chaos in trade relations did not reign after President Truman admitted defeat on the ITO issue in December 1950[4] was largely due

[1] In October 1943 Australia decided to accept the proposals to establish a permanent FAO, which came into existence on 16 October 1945; in November 1946 she decided to join the IMF and IBRD and formally became a member on 5 August 1947. Then in October 1947 Australia decided to accept the draft agreement on Tariffs and Trade; and in December 1948 the International Trade Organization Act came into operation, approving Australia's decision to accept GATT and providing for her conditional acceptance of the ITO.

[2] This was not without its specific importance for trade policy. The United Nations has sponsored conferences resulting in specific commodity agreements, especially wheat, sugar, and tin.

[3] See 'Charter of the United Nations', *C.P.P.*, no. 24 of 1945.

[4] See Nicholson (132), p. 163; Gardner (78), p. 379. Gardner's book is a good general reference book for the ground covered in Section 3.

to the somewhat surprising but increasingly evident strength of GATT, which had been provisionally adopted in November 1947. Something of the relationship of the GATT and the stillborn Havana Charter will be made clear in this comment and in the annexes prepared by Nancy Anderson. Before becoming even slightly involved in this rather tangled story, it will be well —if the documents are to make sense—to draw attention again to the Australian government's declared policy objectives.

The commitment in Article VII in 1942 was to find measures

> directed to the expansion . . . of production, employment, and the exchange and consumption of goods, . . . to the elimination of all forms of discriminatory treatment in international commerce, and to the reduction of tariffs and other trade barriers (1:2).

At times Chifley was clearly apologetic for being dragged along by this primary undertaking, itself the direct product of war-time circumstances, more particularly those in which the United Kingdom found itself (cf. early paras. of 3:6). His harassment under Menzies's forceful and well-prepared criticisms (3:5) was understandable. Nevertheless, more clearly than the published documents show, the Australian delegations, throughout the many conferences in London, Washington, New York, Geneva, and Havana, worked hard and constructively to obtain full expression of, and opportunity for, Australian policy objectives. Later, too, Menzies, when Prime Minister, upheld the decision to accept the obligations of GATT, although his views on the ITO Charter were never put to any official test.

In the first two comments in Sections 1 and 2 we have already seen something of these policy objectives. However, they emerge rather more clearly in the documents in this section, reflecting, naturally enough, the years of argument and negotiation which followed 1942 (3:11, 3:14). Dedman is perhaps the most explicit in 3:14—his Second Reading speech in presenting the International Trade Organization Bill on 30 September 1948. As Dedman stated it, the interests of the country required:

(a) maintenance of full employment, especially in the major industrial countries;

(b) greater stability in prices for primary products;

(c) freedom for Australia to protect its industries, to protect its balance of payments, and to stabilise its primary industry;

(d) no elimination or reduction of tariff preferences except in return for compensating concessions;

(e) limitations on undue restrictions of imports of Australian agricultural produce into countries protecting their domestic agriculture; and

(f) the development of underdeveloped areas in the interests of trade expansion.

This is among the clearest and most comprehensive statements of trade policy to be found in the post-war period. With varying degrees of emphasis the objectives Dedman stated have remained those of successive Australian ministries. They do not make easy bedfellows in the practical areas of international agreements or in the administration of domestic policies (e.g. through the Tariff Board), as there will be occasion to note. Nevertheless, the international agreements, represented in the documents in this section, did manage to find and even stress the consistencies in these objectives, by recognising the use of the tariff for protective purposes. At no time was this right given away by the Australian government (or any other government). True, the emphasis was on lowering all barriers to trade, including tariffs. However, the 'rules' established sought not merely to limit the growth of protection but also to define the circumstances in which freedom to vary the tariff or to use non-tariff devices for such objectives as protecting the external balance of payments was permissible.

Before turning to the ITO and the fate that befell it, one other comment on Dedman's statement (3:14) is allowable. Up to this point it was reasonably fair to argue (as we have in Sections 1 and 2) that the Australian government saw full employment as the major solvent for the problems of international trade in Australia's primary products. Dedman showed a clear recognition that other factors were relevant: the advantages of full employment do not include adequate stability in price levels or prevent the excessive agricultural protectionism which was to reach its full expression in the Treaty of Rome of 1957.

The post-Article VII discussions finally resulted in agreement between the United Kingdom and the United States on principles which would govern international negotiations (3:2). The Americans put forward proposals to establish an international trade organisation, clearly designed to give effect to the declaration of Article VII whilst recognising the principles of negotiation agreed with the British (3:1, 3:2). It is not the purpose of these notes to trace in detail the successive steps from which emerged concurrently the Havana Charter, or ITO—the subject of Dedman's speech (3:14)—and the GATT. There is ample scope for a close student of the history of international economic affairs to undertake this task, although it could not readily be done from the public documents alone. Some help is offered in a short statement of chronological steps given in A3:1 to these notes.

For our purposes it is important to note that negotiations for an international trade organisation were concurrent with, but clearly separable from, those which led to GATT. The Preparatory Committee for the United Nations Conference on Trade and Employment which led in 1948 to the Havana Charter for an International Trade Organization also, *inter alia* as it were, prepared the draft text for a General Agreement on Tariffs and Trade. Those articles of the Charter thought most appropriate were used to govern the actual tariff negotiations in 1947. They also became collectively the instrument governing the subsequent operations of the Agreement. Some of the articles of GATT were therefore common to GATT and ITO; but the failure to bring ITO into being did not impair the binding force of those articles in GATT.

All this is rather difficult to follow in the documents, but for the lay reader it is perhaps unnecessary. For the articles in GATT, and those in ITO but not in GATT, a quick perusal of A3:3 will convey a useful impression of the apparent setback Australia suffered when the United States Congress rejected ITO.

Fortunately or not, then, the GATT survived as an effective instrument of international co-operation in the field of commercial policy (principally tariffs), whereas the more comprehensive and ambitious ITO failed to secure ratification where ratification most mattered—in the Congress at Washington.

A full précis of the Havana Charter is given in A3:2. It shows that Dedman's declared policy objectives did receive expression in the Charter. A careful reading will show, too, that the final text was a decided improvement on the early drafts from Australia's point of view. For example, in his powerful and trenchant review (3:5) of the report of the First Session of the Preparatory Committee, Menzies challenged the proposal to allow the proposed organisation to determine in its wisdom whether Australia's stabilisation schemes were in breach of the charter. The final version made it mandatory on the organisation to approve them provided the unique features of these schemes were clearly evident (e.g. the fact that export prices could and did rise above fixed domestic prices, so offsetting the circumstance in which export prices often fell below the home price).[5]

Perhaps the greatest irony in Menzies's speech (3:5) rests in the fact that the 'two things' in the draft charter which he most strongly criticised—the threat to preferences and the most-favoured-nation clause—were the provisions which, by being transferred to GATT, survived the demise of the ITO Charter to govern our international economic relations until the time of this writing (1966).[6] As Prime Minister he learned to live with the new 'trade rules', albeit not always willingly.

While it would be an interesting exercise it is beyond our scope to comment in detail on the charter. Documents 3:4 to 3:6, 3:14, and 3:15 give something of the political considerations. However, the subject matter of the

---

[5] The point remained critical to the final (and sympathetic) interpretation of Article XVI of GATT (Subsidies) secured at the Review Session of GATT in 1954-5 (see Section 5).

[6] However, had one particular article of the Charter (XVII) been transferred to GATT, the dismantling of preferences might have proceeded faster than it has. This article required a member to enter into negotiations for the reduction of tariffs and preferences at the *request* of another member (A3:2).

several chapters of the charter is given in A3:2 to these comments.[7] This indicates those principal elements of the charter which survived by being incorporated in GATT (3:10, 3:11). It will be readily seen that it was principally the commercial policy provisions of the charter, appropriate to an agreement on tariffs, which survived in GATT.

The rejection of ITO—a fact not clear until after Chifley's ministry was defeated in December 1949—meant that much of Australia's hard effort in negotiation had apparently come to nought. This was especially true of its representations concerning policies of full employment, its efforts to promote commodity agreements, and its emphasis on the need to develop underdeveloped areas. Yet it could be argued that the loss was more apparent than real.

A final judgment on this point must await later sections, but a few preliminary observations are in order. There was no great debate in Australia on the failure to establish ITO. This was not merely because Menzies had subsequently come into power, holding the views expressed in 3:5. Certainly, Chifley's indication (3:18) that if ITO failed to come into being, membership of the World Bank and the IMF would be reviewed, was not taken up by his successor. Under Menzies, indeed, Australia became an early and regular borrower from the Bank. And his views, as we have noted, did not lead him to withdraw our membership of GATT—the repository of much that he criticised in ITO—strong as may have been his inclination to do so. Nor did the steady opposition of the Associated Chambers of Manufactures of Australia (ACMA) (3:16) weaken this resolve, although its views played a part in the decision in 1953 to seek a review of the GATT articles. Probably it became clear that advanced countries had accepted—without the stimulus of formal international agreement—the importance of full employment for domestic policy reasons.[8] Again, post-war prosperity and especially the Korean War boom took away much of the apparent war-time sense of urgency to do something about the instability of trade in primary produce. The Americans were particularly concerned to set a limit to the boom in wool prices (Section 11). Finally, the fact that ITO was stillborn meant the loss of potentially useful obligations towards economically underdeveloped areas. Yet in the event the many United Nations programs, the massive United States and other multilateral and bilateral aid programs of today far exceed anything in the minds of the drafters of the ITO Charter.

One of the more unfortunate results of the collapse of ITO was that responsibility for promoting international commodity arrangements became uncer-

---

[7] In view of the later political importance of attempts in GATT and UNCTAD designed to assist underdeveloped countries, the considerable stress given by Dedman to this matter (3:4) is worth noting. See also 3:14.

[8] Thus, the commitment had already been taken by the Congress of the United States when it passed the Employment Act of 1946.

tain.[9] We have not tried here or in Section 8 to document this rather vexing (and at times pathetic) story of international administrative confusion. Suffice it to say the United Nations itself acted as convener of the conferences which gave rise to the International Agreements on Wheat, Sugar, and Tin (and later Coffee). The Trade and Development Board, which resulted from the 1964 United Nations Conference on Trade and Development (Section 6), has now assumed the United Nations mantle. However, GATT has also now developed, after failure of efforts at the Review Session to develop a special agreement on commodity arrangements,[10] a practical working interest in commodities—at least those relevant to the Kennedy Round (Section 5). It had been expected that the FAO would be a major international power in this respect. This did not happen for reasons noted later.[11]

Altogether, the death of ITO produced no great lamentation—although it became more fondly recalled by some in the debate on desirable changes in GATT in 1954-5 (Section 5). The immediate achievement, albeit residual in character, was GATT itself, which incorporated certain important rules of fair trade and a schedule of the tariff concessions negotiated in 1947. It is not possible here, if anywhere at all, to assess the significance of the actual tariff concessions.[12] Suffice it to say that Australia did offer some concessions in her Most-Favoured-Nation (MFN) tariff rates and accept some (very slight) cuts in her preferences in the United Kingdom, Canada, and New Zealand, affecting mainly canned and dried fruits. There is ample scope here for investigation by an economic historian: it would not be surprising if his inquiries established that despite the persuasive implication to the contrary in Menzies's statement (3:7) and in the *Age* leader (3:13), Australia gave rather less by way of concessions that 'hurt' Australian industry in some degree than was given to Australia. Nevertheless, the bargain was accepted by her partners as mutually fair, fully justifying Australian complaints a few years later when it became evident that some European and United States tariff concessions in respect of Australian exports were practically worthless because of overriding non-tariff measures for protecting the home industries concerned (Section 5).

Australia accepted the GATT articles, at first provisionally (3:10 to 3:12) but, as time wore on, substantively. These meant that no new preferences

[9] The Australian government's support for an improvement in international commodity arrangements is clearly set forth in a press statement by the Minister for Post-War Reconstruction (J. J. Dedman) on 13 December 1947.

[10] An account of these efforts, which does rather less than justice to the Australian position, but is valuable nevertheless, is given in Curzon (68), especially pp. 170 *et seq.*

[11] Moreover, the final paragraph of 3:21 leaves in some doubt whether FAO itself or an organisation like ITO would be the appropriate organisation.

[12] See Nicholson (132), p. 15. His book gives a very full treatment of the tariff negotiations under GATT. Another useful source is *Australia in Facts and Figures*, No. 19, December 1947, pp. 15-16.

could be extended where none existed before and existing preferences could not be widened beyond their October 1946 *absolute* level[13] and that all reductions in MFN rates would reduce preferential margins unless British Preferential Tariff rates were simultaneously reduced.[14] Moreover, all reductions in MFN rates had automatically to be extended to all countries accepted as members of GATT.[15]

This last point is worth a little more emphasis, if only to round off the stress given to the preference issue in Section 1. Article VII had foreshadowed—or so it must have seemed to most of the Allied governments—the end of the imperial preference system. Article I of GATT was the outcome of five years of discussion and negotiation. It represented far less than the Americans had hoped, for the preferential structure remained substantially intact. Indeed, the actual concessions made in the tariff negotiations of 1947 were neither numerous nor very damaging. For these same reasons, Commonwealth countries, especially the United Kingdom, Canada, Australia, and New Zealand, had apparent cause for relief: the new rules of trade promised trade expansion without requiring the prior loss of well tested and valuable preferences.

Nevertheless, in adhering to GATT the Americans had succeeded better, in the early meetings of GATT, than they appeared to realise. In the first place, the no-new-preference rule set an effective limit—subsequently strongly enforced by the GATT members (Contracting Parties)—to any further development of preferential British Commonwealth trade ties (see further comment in Sections 5 and 9).

The second reason for suggesting a greater American success than was conceded at the time rested in Article XXIV of GATT, which provided for customs unions and free trade areas. Partly because the United States favoured economic integration of Europe as a vital element in political unity, but also because it saw economic merit in large free trade areas like the

[13] The placing of a ceiling on existing preferences and the forbidding of new preferences became known as the no-new-preference rule. The reference to the October 1946 *absolute* level can be simply illustrated. If at that time the MFN rate were 45 per cent and the British Preferential Tariff (BPT) rate were 30 per cent, the *absolute* preferential margin or difference was 15 per cent. It could not be expressed, for example, as one-third of the MFN rate and raised to 20 per cent if this rate were subsequently raised to 60 per cent. Should the latter happen, the BPT rate, to comply with the no-new-preference rule, would have to be raised to 45 per cent. As is shown in Section 5, however, the GATT no-new-preference rule bore most harshly on preferences expressed in specific rates such as 5s per cwt. Rising prices in the post-war period have eroded the *ad valorem* equivalent of such specific margins.

[14] It is probable that a preference once reduced by negotiations could later be restored to its base level, although strong protests might well be expected.

[15] Under Article XXXV Australia was able to deny recognition of Japan as a member for purposes of extending Australian MFN tariff concessions (Sections 5 and 10), a provision which greatly lessened some of the dangers of the MFN treatment expounded by Menzies in 1947 (3:5).

United States itself, America supported this article, despite the fact that it provided for a preferential area! The United States was not as inconsistent as some Australian spokesmen suggested: British Commonwealth preferences resulted mostly from raising duties against *outsiders* with clear damage to them; while customs unions and free trade areas can proceed only by removing barriers on 'substantially all trade' in the area (i.e. among the *insiders*) and are expected not to worsen thereby the market access of the non-members to the customs or free trade area considered as a whole.

One particular irony about Article XXIV of GATT is not so much the American approval of a preferential system as the ultimate challenge it was to present the British Commonwealth when Britain decided in 1961 to seek entry into the European Common Market (Section 8).[16] The British decision in 1961 to seek entry required a British willingness to forgo the preferential system in the British tariff and implied their resignation to the loss of preferences in Commonwealth markets. It would be legally possible under Clause 9 of Article XXIV for Britain to negotiate the retention of at least some of its existing preferences: but in practice it would seem to be impossible on any significant scale, except for preferences extended to former colonies which might be treated like the existing Associated Territories under the Treaty of Rome. In a very real sense the combination of the no-new-preference rule of GATT and the practical operation of the Treaty of Rome would spell the end of the Ottawa preference system, should Britain be admitted to membership of the European Economic Community.

There is little in the documents in this section about the importance of development in the underdeveloped areas of the world. As we have seen, Dedman's speech (3:14) gives emphasis to the subject which was, in fact, one to which Australian delegations gave a good deal of active consideration at the conference tables of the time. The subject received explicit recognition in the ITO Charter, but a good deal less in GATT.

Today it is apparent that while the importance of economic growth in these areas was recognised it took a minor place alongside full employment in advanced countries and the rules of trade appropriate to them.[17] True, special exceptions were provided for the underdeveloped countries (see Article XVIII). They could use tariffs and non-tariff devices with more freedom than other members—but always with the proviso that the organisation (ITO) or contracting parties (GATT) approved. This became an issue of greater and greater importance in the sixties (Sections 6 and 18).

[16] By 1963 some of the American keenness for the Common Market had been blunted. It is doubtful whether the Americans adequately assessed the degree of agricultural protectionism inherent in the Rome Treaty. The fuller realisation came when progress in the Kennedy Round was badly checked by the unwillingness of the EEC to negotiate freely in respect of barriers to trade in agricultural commodities.

[17] This was inevitable in a period in which the 'new' nations of the fifties and sixties were not yet represented as independent principals in the relevant negotiations.

37

There are two documents—3:7 and 3:8—which call for some explanation if they are to be properly understood. The tariff negotiations in Geneva in 1947 were not without difficulty. For Australia the principal target was a 50 per cent reduction in the United States wool tariff on greasy wool imports of 34 cents a pound, clean content, equivalent.[18] During the course of the negotiations, in which the United States was willing to give a 25 per cent reduction, Congress passed an Act which could substantially have *increased* import charges on wool. This was the 'internationally provocative' proposal referred to by Chifley (3:8).

The concern of the Australian government—clearly supported by Menzies's initiative in the House (3:7)—is understandable. A complex negotiation of tariff concessions in the Australian tariff and some politically difficult concessions in our preferences in the United Kingdom and Canada (at the expense of the canned and dried fruit industries) was at stake. The concession on wool sought from the United States was the key to the whole arrangement, for reasons worth recalling.

The prevailing wool duty of 34 cents per pound clean content was equivalent to about 58 per cent of the average Australian auction price in 1946-7.[19] Then, as now, wool was the principal Australian export; then, as now, the United States, alone of the important markets for wool, imposed a high duty on imports; then, as now, the argument was that the interests of both United States producers and Australian growers would be served by stimulating consumption by lowering the duty and hence prices of final woollen products. In 1966 the incidence of the tariff at 25·5 cents per pound clean content is considerably less[20]—but the argument for a further tariff cut still retains validity in the context of keener competition with synthetic fibres.

More than the crucial wool concession was at stake: for Australia, and for other countries, too, the effective leadership of the United States was in question. President Truman clearly recognised this in vetoing the Congressional Bill, declaring (3:9) that

> it would be a blow to our leadership in world affairs. It would be interpreted around the world as a first step on that same road to economic isolationism down which we and other countries travelled after the First World War with such disastrous consequences.

[18] Australian greasy wool on average yields about 55-60 per cent clean (scoured) content. Greasy wool costing 60 cents a lb, yielding 55 per cent clean wool, would be worth 109 cents per lb clean.

[19] Greasy average price 24·5d, clean 'yield' per lb greasy about 55 per cent, giving a clean content price of 44d per lb. The then rate of exchange was $3·2 = £A1, from which the 34 cents duty can be expressed as 58 per cent of the clean content equivalent of the Australian auction price. At the lower prices of pre-war and war-time years the incidence was naturally even higher.

[20] At current rates of exchange ($2·24 = $A2) and 1962-3 prices (about 100 cents per lb clean content), the incidence of 25·5 cents is about 27 per cent of the Australian auction floor price.

As Chifley stressed (3:8), much of Australia's hesitation about the new forms of international economic co-operation had only been resolved by belief in the reality and importance of United States participation in measures for expanding trade. This occasion was to prove but one of many in subsequent years in which Australia was inclined to regard Washington as better able to offer precept in world commercial policies than practice in the (for Australia) vital area of trade in agriculture and mineral produce (Section 11).

There has been no attempt here to offer a commentary in detail on the many articles of ITO or GATT. The purpose has been to emphasise the general nature of Australia's commitment to international economic co-operation, to note the failure of ITO to come into being, to observe that this caused less immediate disturbance than might have been expected, to stress the survival of GATT, and to note the special problem of uncertain and changing leadership on the part of the United States. The rejection of ITO pointed to an imbalance between Australia's hopes on the one hand and her commitments on the other. This became apparent by 1953 and is the subject of some of the documents in Section 5.

IMF, IBRD, and FAO

Although the ITO and GATT were seen as the major commitments to international economic co-operation in trade policy, they were not the only ones. In concluding this comment some brief reference to the other institutions— the International Bank for Reconstruction and Development, the International Monetary Fund, and the World Food and Agriculture Organization —is called for (3:17 to 3:22). Our interest cannot be in the details of these organisations nor even the serious schism in the A.L.P. provoked by the IMF (Bretton Woods) Agreement:[21] it is limited to their direct significance for trade policy.

Of the three organisations named, FAO has turned out to be least directly relevant to Australian trade policy. In supporting this organisation the Australian government clearly hoped that its influence on trade would be important in two ways. First, it could lend weight to the promotion of intergovernmental commodity agreements designed to stabilise trade in agricultural products. The organisation has never developed strong executive initiatives in the first field, being overshadowed early on by the expectation that ITO would accept full responsibility in terms of Chapter VI of the Charter.[22]

[21] So far, the best account is in Crisp (65), ch. XIV. Good primary accounts of opposed Australian Labor Party views are Dedman (71) and Ward (161).

[22] FAO came into being in 1945; the draft of ITO was not completed until 1948. FAO has, however, been of major importance in the realm of ideas and data on commodities and in evolving principles designed to limit commercially damaging use of food surpluses.

The second influence has proved important in the policies of many countries, but its value as a stimulus to trade has for several reasons been less than expected. When, in 1935, S. M. Bruce (now Lord Bruce) and F. L. McDougal argued that improved nutritional standards would help world trade, they assumed that as incomes rose throughout the world the demand for meat, fruit, dairy produce (all these being classed as nutritionally 'protective' foodstuffs), and sugar would rise relative to that for grains. The general argument is valid enough, and FAO has in its frequent reviews of the world food situation sustained attention on the importance of nutritional standards to the world's populations. But, in terms of trade prospects for Australia, the campaign has had limited application: this is in part because a high degree of agricultural protectionism in Europe and North America has limited the scope for imports of temperate foodstuffs, although the world markets for meat are growing, despite barriers, as incomes rise in North America, Europe, and Japan. Again, most of the underdeveloped areas have had to concentrate—with considerable help from FAO—on raising home production of basic grains to meet the needs of rapidly increasing populations. Also, and more importantly, for most of these countries export earnings have been too inadequate to allow significant imports of the relatively expensive 'protective' foods.

Where FAO has been more directly helpful to Australia's interests is in persuading governments to operate plans for the disposal of United States food surpluses in ways designed to minimise damage to commercial marketing. It can be said in passing, however, that this problem will not be satisfactorily settled until surplus disposals—whether originating in burdensome stocks (i.e. temporarily unmarketable in ordinary commerce) or from production especially encouraged for the purpose—become an integral part of world agreements on cereals and other 'surplus' foods. This is one aspect of commodity talks under the Kennedy Round in GATT (Section 5).

By way of contrast the two financial institutions (IMF and IBRD) have had more influence than might have been expected immediately after the war. Opinion among the political parties in Australia ranged from deeply-felt hostility based on fear for the national interest to doubts whether any value would result at all. The two political leaders (Chifley and Menzies) saw value in Australian membership, but naturally enough could not foresee the precise nature of the return it would yield.

This return can be seen from the schedule of International Bank loans (A15:2) and the Annual Reports of the Australian Treasurer under the International Monetary Fund Acts. Australia has in recent years drawn on the IMF and has, beginning in 1950, borrowed extensively from the Bank. Of the latter it can be said unequivocally that these borrowings at all times usefully supplemented Australia's capital resources needed for development.

40

Even more significant, at least in the case of the borrowings before 1959, the Bank loans lessened the adverse impact of the severe dollar shortages. Recovery in agricultural output, and hence in badly lagging export sales, in the period 1945-51, was particularly aided by the added supplies of American equipment made possible by the loans (Section 13).

Views on the IMF continue to be somewhat controversial but neither serious enough to justify the fears of its opponents in 1947 nor sufficient to outweigh the firm role it now plays in ensuring a 'second line' of reserves in our balance of payments. This matter is further dealt with in Section 15.

While the documents in this section do not make for easy understanding of a complex period of decision-making by the Federal government, they are important to the story of Australia's trade in the years since. A system of world trading rules has emerged in GATT which has provided the chief framework for Australia's international commercial diplomacy. In Section 5 the documents tell more of its strengths and weaknesses in terms of Australia's interests; and in Section 18 there is comment on its likely staying power in the years ahead. In the technical language of its delegates, GATT has provided the framework for a system of multilateral trade, freer and more expansive than the contrasting system of bilateralism, economic nationalism, and the rather disruptive (even if understandable) preferential system established in the Ottawa agreements.

We have not attempted to document the other decisions in such detail. But of these the IMF may be regarded as the financial counterpart of GATT in a conjoint system of freer or multilateral trade and payments; for the IMF has been designed (and with a large degree of success) to provide rules to govern alterations in rates of exchange between currencies and the means to assist members through temporary difficulties in their external balance of payments. The International Bank has fitted into this system by supplementing the Fund's emphasis on the short-term, with assistance for longer-term economic development. These important roles of the three institutions, together with the technical assistance programs, were to prove key elements in the major economic decisions of the British Commonwealth of Nations. In December 1952 the Commonwealth prime ministers firmly agreed upon a course of action which can be called 'The Collective Approach towards Freer Trade and Payments'. This is the subject of the next section.

41

A3:1 STEPS LEADING TO HAVANA CHARTER AND GENERAL AGREEMENT ON TARIFFS AND TRADE

PREPARED BY NANCY ANDERSON

1. *December 1945:*

   United States and United Kingdom agreed on principles of commercial policy and suggested an International Trade Organization (see 3:2).

2. *1946:*

   United States issued revisions of its draft charter for ITO.[1]

3. *October-November 1946:*

   First Session of Preparatory Committee of the United Nations Conference on Trade and Employment met in London to discuss United States' draft charter. The results were:
   (a) substantial modifications, including the addition of a new section on economic development;
   (b) a recommendation that tariff negotiations be brought under the sponsorship of the United Nations.

4. *March 1947:*

   Drafting Committee recommended drafting changes to the charter and also prepared a text for a General Agreement on Tariffs and Trade. This text established the principles which were to govern the tariff negotiations and the subsequent operation of the agreement.

5. *April 1947:*

   Tariff negotiations at Geneva began concurrently with resumption of discussions on the draft charter by the Second and Final Session of the Preparatory Committee. Tariff negotiations were kept distinct from charter discussions so that they could be brought into effect without waiting for the implementation of ITO under the charter.

6. *18 November 1947:*

   The results of the April negotiations were incorporated in a draft GATT which Australia applied provisionally from 18 November 1947 (see 3:11).

7. *21 November 1947 to 3 March 1948:*

   Havana Conference considered the draft charter for ITO as it emerged from the Geneva Session in April 1947. This consideration resulted in the Havana Charter (see A3:2).

8. *24 March 1948:*

   Final Act of the United Nations Conference on Trade and Employment was signed by fifty-four countries, including Australia.

9. *March 1948 and August-September 1948:*

   Amendments made to GATT to bring rule-making and structural sides into line with changes at Havana to text of ITO.

[1] Published, among other places, as an Appendix to *Report of First Session of the Preparatory Committee of the United Nations Conference on Trade and Employment.*

10. *17 December 1948:*

Australian International Trade Organization Act came into effect under which acceptance of GATT and the Havana Charter were made conditional on acceptance by United Kingdom and United States (see 3:14).

11. *28 March 1949:*

President of United States submitted Havana Charter to Congress, but no action was taken.

12. *7 November 1950:*

United States elections.

13. *11 December 1950:*

President Truman of United States issued statement that proposal to authorise United States participation in ITO would not be reintroduced into Congress, which would, however, be asked to approve legislation making United States participation in GATT more effective.

A3:2 HAVANA CHARTER FOR AN INTERNATIONAL TRADE ORGANIZATION: SUMMARY OF ARTICLES

PREPARED BY NANCY ANDERSON

CHAPTER I—PURPOSE AND OBJECTIVES

Article 1

In order to realise the aims of social and economic progress envisaged in Article 55 of the United Nations Charter, the Parties to the Havana Charter pledge themselves to promote national and international action to increase the production, consumption and exchange of goods; to foster the economic development of underdeveloped countries; and to promote the reduction of tariffs and other barriers to trade and the elimination of discriminatory treatment in international commerce. They establish the International Trade Organization through which to achieve their objectives.

CHAPTER II—EMPLOYMENT AND ECONOMIC ACTIVITY

Articles 2-7

The avoidance of unemployment or underemployment is necessary for the achievement of the aims set out in Chapter I. Internal measures by individual countries to avoid unemployment should be supplemented by concerted action under the sponsorship of the Economic and Social Organization of the United Nations in collaboration with the appropriate intergovernmental organisations.

The Organization shall have regard to the need of Members to safeguard their economies against inflationary or deflationary pressure from abroad.

CHAPTER III—ECONOMIC DEVELOPMENT AND RECONSTRUCTION

Articles 8-15

The industrial and general economic development, particularly of underdeveloped countries, and the reconstruction of those countries devastated by war will expand international trade and raise levels of real income.

Provision is made for assistance to underdeveloped countries, and to those devastated by war, by means of studies and advice on development, and the provision of capital, materials and technical and managerial skill. It is recognised that protective measures to promote particular industries or branches of agriculture in such countries may be justified, and they may, under stated conditions, be released from restrictions placed on certain types of protection such as quota restrictions on imports, and the establishing of new tariff preferences. In the latter case the territories of the parties to the agreement must be contiguous, or all parties must belong to the same economic region.

CHAPTER IV—COMMERCIAL POLICY

Section A.—Tariffs, Preferences and Internal Taxation and Regulation

Articles 16-19 General Most-Favoured-Nation Treatment

Unconditional most-favoured-nation treatment is to be accorded by Members to all other Members in respect of customs duties and charges of any kind on international commercial transactions. Exceptions to this provision include *existing* British Commonwealth preferential arrangements. No margin of preference shall be increased. If a Member fails to become a contracting party to GATT within two years of the entry into force of the Charter, most-favoured-nation treatment is no longer required in respect of this Member.

Each Member, on the request of any other Member or Members, is to negotiate for the substantial reduction of the general level of tariffs and other charges on imports or exports and for the elimination of preferences on a reciprocal and mutually advantageous basis.

Negotiations are to be conducted on a selective product-by-product basis, and Members shall be free not to grant concessions on particular products.[1]

The binding against increase of low duties or of duty-free treatment shall in principle be recognised as a concession equivalent in value to the substantial reduction of high duties or the elimination of tariff preferences.

Section B.—Quantitative Restrictions and Related Exchange Matters

Articles 20-24

General elimination of quantitative restrictions on both imports and exports is required. Some exceptions are allowed, including:

(a) export restrictions to prevent critical shortages of foodstuffs;
(b) restrictions necessary for the application of international trade standards;
(c) restrictions to prevent domestic shortages, and to regulate domestic production;
(d) restrictions to safeguard the balance of payments.

The Organization is to pursue a co-ordinated policy with the International Monetary Fund with regard to exchange questions, quantitative restrictions and other measures.

[Articles XI to XV of GATT incorporate the provisions of Articles 20-24 of the Charter. See A5:1 for a fuller summary of these measures.]

---

[1] This principle is in sharp contrast to those favoured by the U.S. Trade Expansion Act, 1962, in which the U.S. authorised 'linear' negotiations, i.e. tariff cuts, 'across the board' in contrast to careful pre-selection of individual items for negotiation.

SECTION C.—Subsidies

Articles 25-28

Members must furnish information regarding subsidy schemes to the Organization and discuss with any Member considering itself seriously prejudiced by such subsidies or with the Organization the possibility of their limitation.

Export subsidies resulting in lower export prices than the comparable domestic price are generally prohibited two years from the date the Charter comes into force, but special treatment is provided for primary commodities. Thus stabilisation schemes for such commodities which result at times in a lower export price are considered not to involve an export subsidy if the system is also designed to result in an export price higher than the comparable domestic price; and if it is designed so as not to stimulate exports unduly or otherwise seriously prejudice the interests of other Members. Members granting primary commodity subsidies are to co-operate in efforts to negotiate international agreements in respect of such commodities. Export subsidies must not result in a Member acquiring more than an equitable share of world trade in the commodities concerned.

SECTION D.—State Trading and Related Matters

Articles 29-32

State enterprises, in their import and export transactions, are to act consistently with the general principles of non-discriminatory treatment prescribed in the Charter. They are to make purchases or sales solely in accordance with commercial considerations. These provisions do not apply to imports of products for consumption solely in governmental use.

A Member maintaining a monopoly of the importation or exportation of any product, if so requested by another Member substantially interested in trade with the Member in the product concerned, must negotiate to reduce the amount of protection the monopoly affords to a domestic user or producer, or to assure exports in adequate quantities at reasonable prices, or to relax the limitation on exports.

Liquidation of non-commercial stocks of primary products is to be carried out in a manner that will avoid serious disturbance to world markets.

SECTION E.—General Commercial Provisions

Articles 33-39

Goods, vessels and other means of transport are to be accorded freedom of transit through the territory of each Member country. Most-favoured-nation treatment is to be accorded in the case of all transit charges, regulations and formalities.

Anti-dumping and countervailing duties to offset the injurious effects of dumping on an established industry, or the retarding of the establishment of a domestic industry are permitted under certain defined conditions.

General principles to be followed in valuation of goods for customs purposes are set out.

Fees and charges in connection with imports and exports should be limited to the approximate cost of the services involved and should not represent an indirect protection to domestic products or a taxation for fiscal purposes.

In the case of laws and regulations relating to marks of origin, most-favoured-nation treatment is to be accorded to each Member, who will work towards the elimination of unnecessary marking requirements.

Laws, regulations, judicial decisions and administrative rulings of general application to imports and exports are to be published promptly.

Members are to furnish statistics covering their external trade to the Organization.

[Articles V to X of GATT incorporate the substance of Articles 33-38 of the Charter. See A5:1.]

SECTION F.—Special Provisions

Articles 40-45

Article 40 Emergency Action on Imports of Particular Products

Provision is made for the suspension of obligations incurred by a Member under Chapter IV, including tariff concessions, if, as a result of unforeseen developments, they lead to the import of any product under such conditions as to cause or threaten serious injury to domestic producers of a like or directly competitive product.

[Article XIX of GATT incorporates the substance of Article 40 of the Charter—see A5 : 1.]

Article 41 Consultation

Adequate opportunity for consultation is to be afforded on all matters affecting the operation of Chapter IV.

Article 42 Territorial Application of Chapter IV

The provisions of Chapter IV apply to the metropolitan customs territories of the Members and to any other customs territory in respect of which this Chapter has been accepted in accordance with the provisions of Article 104.

Article 43 Frontier Traffic

Chapter IV shall not prevent advantages accorded to adjacent countries to facilitate frontier traffic.

Article 44 Customs Union and Free Trade Areas

[The provisions of Article XXIV of GATT are the same as those in Article 44 of the Charter. They are rather lengthy and can be studied in A5:1.]

Article 45 General Exceptions to Chapter IV

[These exceptions are similar to those for GATT as listed in Article XX of the Agreement. See A5:1 for summary.]

CHAPTER V—RESTRICTIVE BUSINESS PRACTICES

Articles 46-54

Appropriate measures shall be taken by Members to prevent, on the part of private or commercial enterprises, business practices affecting international trade which restrain competition, limit access to markets, or foster monopolistic control, wherever such practices have harmful effects on the expansion of production or trade and interfere with the achievement of any of the objectives of Article I.

CHAPTER VI—INTER-GOVERNMENTAL COMMODITY AGREEMENTS

SECTION A.—Introductory Considerations

Articles 55-57

International trade in some primary commodities may be affected by special difficulties such as the tendency towards persistent disequilibrium between production and consumption, the accumulation of burdensome stocks and pronounced fluctuations in prices. Such difficulties may necessitate special treatment of international trade in such commodities through inter-governmental agreement. Such agreements are appropriate for the achievement of the following objectives:

(a) to prevent or alleviate the serious economic difficulties which may arise when adjustments between production and consumption cannot be effected by normal market prices alone as rapidly as the circumstances require;

(b) to provide a framework for the consideration and development of measures which have as their purpose economic adjustments designed to promote the expansion of consumption or a shift of resources and manpower out of over-expanded industries into new and productive occupations;

(c) to prevent or moderate fluctuations in the price of a primary commodity on the basis of prices fair to the consumer and providing a reasonable return to producers;

(d) to maintain, develop and conserve natural resources;

(e) to provide for the expansion of production of a primary commodity, with advantage to consumers and producers, including in appropriate cases, the distribution of basic foods at special prices;

(f) to assure the equitable distribution of a primary commodity in short supply.

SECTION B.—Inter-governmental Commodity Agreements in General

Articles 58-61

Substantial consumer participation is required, as well as that of producer countries.

The following types of agreement are specified:

(a) commodity control agreements—i.e. those involving the regulation of production or the quantitative control of exports or imports of a primary commodity and which have the effect of reducing, or preventing an increase in the production of, or trade in that commodity; or the regulation of prices; and

(b) other inter-governmental commodity agreements.

Commodity control agreements may be entered into only when a finding has been made through a commodity conference or through the Organization by consultation and general agreement among Members substantially interested in the commodity, that:

(a) a burdensome surplus of a primary commodity has developed or is expected to develop which could not be corrected by normal market forces in time to prevent serious hardship to producers;

(b) widespread unemployment or underemployment has developed or is expected to develop which could not be corrected by normal market forces in time to prevent widespread and undue hardship to producers.

Under such agreements importing and exporting countries shall have equal voting power.

Participating countries shall adopt programmes of internal economic adjustment adequate to ensure as much progress as practicable within the duration of the agreement towards solution of the particular commodity problem.

Any inter-governmental organisation deemed to be competent by the Organization, such as the Food and Agriculture Organization, shall be entitled to take part in international commodity consultations and activities.

Exceptions are provided for in the case of certain inter-governmental agreements.

CHAPTER VII—THE INTERNATIONAL TRADE ORGANIZATION

Articles 71-91

The internal structure, functions and rules of the Organization are laid down. The Conference is the main body, consisting of all Members of the Organization. It may delegate some of its functions to an Executive Board and may set up a number of commissions to carry out particular functions. The Organization shall be brought into relationship with the United Nations as one of its specialised agencies as soon as practicable.

Special functions set out for the Council include:

  (i) collection, analysis and publication of information relating to international trade;
  (ii) promotion of bilateral and multilateral agreements designed to expand the volume and improve the bases of international trade;
  (iii) studies of the potentialities of underdeveloped countries;
  (iv) promotion of establishments for technical training necessary for development;
  (v) in collaboration with the Economic and Social Council of the United Nations and other appropriate inter-governmental organisations, studies of the relationship between world prices of primary commodities and manufactured products; and, where appropriate, to recommend international agreements on measures designed to reduce unwarranted discrepancies in those prices.

CHAPTER VIII—SETTLEMENT OF DIFFERENCES

Articles 92-97

Provisions are made for consultation and arbitration when any Member considers that any benefit accruing to it under the provisions of the Charter is being nullified.

CHAPTER IX—GENERAL PROVISIONS

Articles 98-106

No Member shall enter into any new arrangements with a non-Member which preclude the latter from according to other Member countries any benefit provided for by such arrangement. A Member must not accord to the trade of any non-Member treatment more favourable than that accorded to another Member, if such treatment would injure the economic interests of a Member country.

Provisions are made for general exceptions (mainly of a security nature) and amendments to, withdrawal from and termination of the Charter, and for its entry into force and registration. The date of the Charter is to be 24 March 1948, and it is to be known as the Havana Charter.

Source: Based on *Final Act and Related Documents of the United Nations Conference on Trade and Employment held at Havana, Cuba, from November 21, 1947, to March 24, 1948.*

A3:3 HAVANA CHARTER: PRINCIPAL ELEMENTS INCORPORATED IN GATT

SUMMARY PREPARED BY NANCY ANDERSON

Chapter I: Purpose and Objectives (Article 1)

See A3:2. A condensed version became preamble of GATT.

Chapter II: Employment and Economic Activity (Articles 2-7)

No article transferred to GATT.

Chapter III: Economic Development and Reconstruction (Articles 8-15)

Only Article 13 transferred, as Article XVIII of GATT—a contentious but so far not very effective clause—designed principally to make the requirements of the other articles on tariff and quantitative import controls rather less restrictive for underdeveloped countries.

Chapter IV: Commercial Policy (Articles 16-45)

All but Articles 26-8 (some aspects of export subsidies and stimulation of exports of primary products) transferred as principal articles of GATT. These covered especially the treatment of preferences (Article I of GATT), most-favoured-nation clause (Article I), export subsidies (XVI), circumstances permitting quantitative import restrictions (XI, XII, and XIII), Customs Union and Free Trade Areas (XXIV),[1] Emergency Action (XIX). These illustrations do not cover all the articles of GATT including the key tariff schedules (II) and the rules covering impairment of concessions (XXIII) and providing for renegotiation (XXVIII).

Chapter V: Restrictive Business Practices (Articles 46-54)

No article transferred to GATT.

Chapter VI: Inter-Governmental Commodity Agreements (Articles 55-70)

No article transferred to GATT.

Chapter VII: The International Trade Organization (Articles 71-91)

No article transferred to GATT.

A3:4 MAIN INTERNATIONAL ORGANISATIONS CONCERNED WITH COMMODITY ARRANGEMENTS

PREPARED BY NANCY ANDERSON

UNITED NATIONS ORGANISATIONS

1. *Economic and Social Council of the United Nations (ECOSOC)*

The council is responsible for promoting conditions of economic progress and is empowered to make or initiate studies and reports on international economic matters and to make recommendations thereon to United Nations agencies and to the specialised agencies concerned. The existing international agreements on wheat, sugar, tin and coffee were made under its aegis.

[1] Article under which consistency with GATT is claimed for Treaty of Rome setting up the European Economic Community.

To help it discharge its functions the council appoints commissions to deal with particular aspects of its work. For commodity arrangements it established the two bodies referred to in 2 and 3 below.

2. *Interim Co-ordinating Committee for International Commodity Arrangements (ICCICA)*

The committee was established by ECOSOC in March 1947 to facilitate intergovernmental consultation or action on commodity problems. Its chairman was nominated by the contracting parties to GATT, and one of its members was chosen by FAO.

ICCICA convened intergovernmental study groups, made recommendations on convening commodity conferences, and co-ordinated activities of individual commodity study groups and councils.

For some years it prepared an annual *Review of International Commodity Problems* which dealt with their relation to economic conditions. However, in 1954 responsibility for this passed to the Commission on International Commodity Trade. Following the setting up of UNCTAD, ICCICA formally ceased to exist, although some of its functions survived in the new Advisory Committee to that body (see 5 below).

3. *Commission on International Commodity Trade (CICT)*

The commission was established by ECOSOC in 1954 to examine measures designed to avoid excessive fluctuations in prices of and the volume of trade in primary commodities, and to keep under review their situation in world markets.

In 1958 it was given the following terms of reference: to study and analyse developments and trends in international trade and their effect on both the international and domestic economic positions of countries participating in international commodity trade, especially on the economic development of the less developed countries.

The commission prepared an annual *Commodity Survey* and a periodical memorandum entitled *Recent Commodity Developments*, but with the emergence of UNCTAD it ceased to exist (see 5 below).

4. *Food and Agriculture Organization (FAO)*

The Organization was set up in 1945 as a specialised agency. One of its functions is to promote national and international action towards the improvement of all aspects of the production, marketing, processing and distribution of agricultural commodities. It maintains relations with intergovernmental organisations which have a particular interest in commodity problems.

Its Committee on Commodity Problems keeps under review problems of an international character, and prepares a factual, interpretative, annual survey of the world commodity situation, the *F.A.O. Annual Commodity Review*. It also publishes a series of Commodity Bulletins and Commodity Reports.

5. *United Nations Conference on Trade and Development (UNCTAD)*

UNCTAD was set up on 30 December 1964 as an organ of the General Assembly. Its main functions are to seek solutions to world trade problems, and more particularly to the urgent trade and development problems of the developing countries; to review and facilitate the co-ordination of activities of other institutions within the United Nations System in the field of international trade and related problems of economic development; and to co-operate with the General Assembly and ECOSOC concerning the performance of their charter responsibilities for co-ordination.

The Trade and Development Board is the permanent organ of the Conference and it has established a Committee on Commodities to carry out functions previously performed by CICT and ICCICA. The latter still exists in the more limited form of an Advisory Committee to the Board and to the Committee on Commodities.

GENERAL AGREEMENT ON TARIFFS AND TRADE (GATT)

6. Although (as seen in Section 3) Chapter VI of the Havana Charter dealing with intergovernmental commodity agreements was not incorporated in GATT, the latter has been actively interested in commodity arrangements in the course of carrying out its general objectives of expanding international trade and reducing obstacles to it. In fact, any commodity arrangements between contracting parties involving, for example, import or export quotas, would involve GATT approval.

Also, the vital importance of commodity trade for many of the contracting parties has resulted in annual discussions of trends and developments and the annual publication *International Trade* contains information on these.

Specific examples of actual commodity arrangements concluded by GATT were the short-term arrangements regarding international trade in cotton textiles in July 1961 and long-term arrangements for the same commodities in February 1962.

More recently, in November 1964, the contracting parties drew up a new Part IV of the Agreement in which, *inter alia*, it is provided that they shall, through international arrangements, seek to provide improved access to world markets for primary products of interest to less developed contracting parties and to stabilise their prices.

3:1 EXPANSION OF WORLD TRADE AND EMPLOYMENT

Proposals by the Department of State, U.S.A., developed by a technical staff within the Government of the United States in preparation of an International Conference on Trade and Employment and presented for consideration by the Peoples of the World.

CHAPTER III

GENERAL COMMERCIAL POLICY

Section B. Tariffs and Preferences

1. *Import tariffs and preferences.* In the light of the principles set forth in Article VII of the mutual aid agreements, members should enter into arrangements for the substantial reduction of tariffs and for the elimination of tariff preferences, action for the elimination of tariff preferences being taken in conjunction with adequate measures for the substantial reduction of barriers to world trade, as part of the mutually advantageous arrangements contemplated in this document.

As an initial step in the process of eliminating tariff preferences it should be agreed that:

   a. Existing international commitments will not be permitted to stand in the way of action agreed upon with respect to tariff preferences.

b. All negotiated reductions in most-favoured-nation tariffs will operate automatically to reduce or eliminate margins of preference.

c. Margins of preference on any product will in no case be increased and no new preferences will be introduced.

2. *Export tariffs and preferences.* Export duties should be open to negotiation in the same way as import duties. Members should undertake not to impose export duties which differentiate by reference to the destinations to which the goods are exported.

3. *Emergency action.* Commitments with regard to tariffs should permit countries to take temporary action to prevent sudden and widespread injury to the producers concerned. Undertakings for reducing tariffs should therefore contain an escape clause to cover such contingencies. . . .

Section C. Proposals Concerning an International Trade Organisation

The purposes of the Organisation should be:—

1. To promote international co-operation by establishing machinery for consultation and collaboration among member governments regarding the solution of problems in the field of international commercial policies and relations.

2. To enable members to avoid recourse to measures destructive of world commerce by providing, on a reciprocal and mutually advantageous basis, expanding opportunities for their trade and economic development.

3. To facilitate access by all members, on equal terms, to the trade and to the raw materials of the world which are needed for their economic prosperity.

4. In general, to promote national and international action for the expansion of the production, exchange and consumption of goods, for the reduction of tariffs and other trade barriers, and for the elimination of all forms of discriminatory treatment in international commerce; thus contributing to an expanding world economy, to the establishment and maintenance in all countries of high levels of employment and real income, and to the creation of economic conditions conducive to the maintenance of world peace.

Source: Department of State Publication,
no. 2411, November 1945.

3:2 ANGLO-AMERICAN ECONOMIC AND FINANCIAL AGREEMENT

Speech by the Prime Minister of the United Kingdom (C. V. Attlee) in the House of Commons on 6 December 1945.

The economic and financial discussions between officials of the United States and United Kingdom Governments, meeting in Washington, have now been completed. These discussions have been concerned with the major problems affecting the basic economic and financial relations between the two countries, in the light of the provisions of Article VII of the Mutual Aid Agreement between their Governments, signed on 23rd February, 1942. They have covered the questions of financial assistance from the United States to the United Kingdom, and the demobilisation of war-time trade and monetary restrictions, the settlement of Lend-Lease, the disposal of surplus war property in the United Kingdom owned by the United States, and finally, long-range commercial policies in the broad sense embracing the fields of trade barriers and discrimination, the policies in respect of commodities in world surplus, cartels and international trade organisation, and international aspects of domestic measures to maintain employment. . . .

Next I should like to read to the House the Joint Statement regarding the understanding reached on Commercial Policy. The Secretary of State of the United States has made public today a document setting forth certain 'Proposals for consideration by an International Conference on Trade and Employment.' These proposals have the endorsement of the Executive branch of the Government of the United States and have been submitted to other Governments as a basis for discussion preliminary to the holding of such a conference. Equally, the Government of the United Kingdom is in full agreement on all important points in these proposals, and accepts them as a basis for international discussion, and it will, in common with the United States Government, use its best endeavours to bring such discussions to a successful conclusion in the light of the views expressed by other countries. . . .

To this end, they have undertaken to begin preliminary negotiations at an early date between themselves and with other countries, for the purpose of developing concrete arrangements to carry out these proposals, including definitive measures for the relaxation of trade barriers of all kinds. These negotiations will relate to tariffs and preferences, quantitative restrictions, subsidies, State trading, cartels and other types of trade barriers treated in the document published by the United States and referred to above. The negotiations will proceed in accordance with principles laid down in that document. . . .

During this preparatory period extending over two years our experts held a series of informal and most valuable consultations with experts from the Dominions and India who made a number of very helpful contributions on the various topics discussed. . . .

While we have kept closely in touch with them during the conversations, it is quite understood that each of the (Dominion) Governments concerned will be able to approach the international discussions with full freedom of action in relation to the various matters dealt with in the proposals. . . .

It is to be noted that the preamble to the document stresses the vital need for high and stable levels of employment in all countries, and the necessity for all countries to adopt domestic measures for the preservation of a high level of economic activity. . . .

Source: *P.D. (H. of C.)*, vol. 416, pp. 2662-70.

3:3 AUSTRALIA READY TO JOIN IN DISCUSSIONS ON INTERNATIONAL TRADE

Statement by the Prime Minister (J. B. Chifley) on 7 December 1945.

As publication of the United States commercial policy proposals for consideration by an international conference on trade and employment might cause misunderstanding it is necessary to give some explanation and to define the position of the Australian Government.

The proposals published have been drawn up by representatives of the United States Government after consultation with representatives of the British Government. The British Government has kept us informed of the progress of its negotiations but the Australian Government has not in any way participated in the Anglo-American discussions out of which the proposals arose and is not associated with their publication. In these circumstances, the Australian Government is not in any way committed to the proposals.

It is the view of the United States Government that a conference of the United Nations should be held during 1946 to consider the proposals and to take action to realize them. In addition, a preliminary conference will probably be held at which the more important trading countries (including Australia) will be asked to negotiate reciprocal bi-lateral trade arrangements among themselves so that concrete arrangements for relaxation of tariffs and trade barriers can be submitted for consideration by the United Nations Conference. Australia will accept the invitations, when they are received, to attend these conferences. The Australian Government has been in the forefront in proposing that countries adopt policies designed to bring about full employment and it welcomes detailed consideration of this subject by the United Nations.

The Australian Government is also ready to join in discussions on international trade, and to engage in bi-lateral negotiations with a desire to reach a satisfactory settlement on the basis of making concessions in return for equivalent reciprocal concessions by other countries, particularly the United States, which would enable trade to be expanded and employment and living standards to be improved.

The Australian Government considers it essential, however, to approach such discussions free of any prior commitment ...

In particular, the Commonwealth Government will enter the proposed negotiations and take part in the discussions without any prior commitment or implied obligation to make any specific concessions in respect of tariffs or Empire preferences. Any proposals in these fields will be dealt with on their merits and any concessions agreed to must be counter-balanced by fully equivalent concessions which will enlarge the market opportunities for Australia's exports, both primary and secondary.

Source: Digest of Decisions and Announcements, no. 109, pp. 6-7.

3:4 INTERNATIONAL TRADE ORGANIZATION AND AUSTRALIA'S FUTURE DEVELOPMENT

Statement by the Minister for Post-War Reconstruction (J. J. Dedman) in the House of Representatives on 27 February 1947, when tabling the 'Report of the First Session of the Preparatory Committee for the United Nations Conference on Trade and Development.'

The Preparatory Committee consists of the representatives of eighteen nations appointed by the Economic and Social Council. The purpose of the London discussions was to provide for an informal exchange of views on international action which could be taken to promote the maintenance of full employment; the production, exchange, and consumption of goods; the reduction of trade barriers;

and whether these purposes could be promoted by the establishment of an international trade organization. It is intended that, associated with these general discussions which will be continued in April, 1947, at Geneva, direct negotiations for the conclusion of a multilateral trade agreement providing for 'mutually advantageous' exchanges of tariff concessions should be conducted between participating countries. At some date following the Geneva meeting it is proposed that there shall be a conference of all United Nations to consider the final report of the Preparatory Committee.

. . . the Government is entering into these negotiations with an open mind. It will stand by its traditional policy of fostering the progressive industrial development of Australia, but it will be prepared to consider modifications of tariffs where these can be conceded without endangering this general objective, and where they are part of an exchange of concessions generally advantageous to Australia. A final decision will not be made until the Government is in a position to review the outcome of the negotiations as a whole.

Important though the tariff negotiations will be, the establishment of an international trade organization and the adoption of a charter embodying agreed principles for the conduct of international trade may well be of even greater importance to the future development of Australia. It is important that there should be no misunderstanding about the nature of Australia's participation in the work of the Preparatory Committee. It was made clear by the Australian delegation that they were not in any sense committing the Government to acceptance of the charter or to participation in the organization. At the same time, it was clear that the establishment of the organization and the general world-wide adoption of a charter governing international trade would be of great importance to Australia as a major trading nation. . . .

I review briefly the major points on which the Australian delegation sought to have the proposals which had been placed before the Preparatory Committee amended to accord with the Government's policy. In doing this, I make it clear that the Government is not committed to accepting the charter in its present form. A final decision will not be made by the Government until the whole of the proposals are before it and Ministers are in a position to judge whether it is in Australia's interests to accept them.

A major success for Australia was the acceptance of the principle that the charter of the International Trade Organization must be written around the positive aims of full employment and economic development throughout the world, rather than around the negative idea of merely reducing trade barriers, to which the draft charter submitted to the Preparatory Committee by the United States gave most of the emphasis. Within the British Commonwealth there is now a gratifying measure of agreement on the employment approach to trade expansion problems, for no country under the necessity of exporting large quantities of staple commodities can shut its eyes to the need for continuing full employment in the consuming countries if there is to be effective international demand for its output. The American delegation to the London Conference showed a positive interest in the employment policy aspects of problems confronting the International Trade Organization. The draft charter now includes a positive obligation for all countries to maintain full employment with high levels of effective demand. This is as much a condition of the charter as is the obligation to negotiate for an exchange of tariff concessions. Failure to fulfil this obligation, and failure by a country to maintain a high level of demand for imports from others, would mean a breach of one of the conditions of the charter, and under the terms of the charter could be followed by a review of the obligations of members affected by that failure. It means to Australia that we can examine any proposed modification of trade barriers against the background of satisfactory international markets for our exports. In other words, if demand does fall off because of the failure of other countries to maintain high levels of employment and economic activity, it would be open to us to have reviewed any tariff concessions or other obligations which we had accepted.

Australia received a sympathetic and encouraging response to its insistence that any trade charter must contain provisions which will actively assist industrial development in new or under-developed countries. A country in a process of rapid industrialization cannot give up its choice between protective tariffs, quantitative restrictions on imports, and payment of production subsidies as means of fostering its industrial growth. While they are in their present stages of growth such countries can, at most, agree to discuss questions of 'how much' and 'in what circumstances', and to develop criteria for answering these questions in practice. Australia found it necessary to press for concrete recognition of our right to use such protective measures and clear provision for their use in appropriate circumstances.

Representations by Australia and other countries with a similar viewpoint resulted in a decision that the draft charter of the International Trade Organization should include a special chapter on economic development containing the following features:—

Specific undertakings by all members to promote industrial and general economic development and to facilitate access by less-developed countries to the facilities necessary for their development. Recognition that special governmental assistance in the form of tariffs and subsidies and other protective measures may be necessary and legitimate means of promoting the establishment and reconstruction of particular industries; and

Provision for the International Trade Organization itself to furnish technical assistance to members towards their plans and programmes of economic development, and to sponsor or grant in appropriate cases release from international obligations (such as to be contained in reciprocal trade agreements negotiated under the charter) which might prove in conflict with the objective of economic development.

In the event of a country such as Australia being confronted with a difficult balance of payments position, she would wish to adopt measures to safeguard her position and to prevent such a flow of imports as would endanger her international reserves. Provision has been made in the draft charter for a country to impose import restrictions in the event of balance of payments difficulties threatening, and at the instance of Australia provision has been made for subsequent agreement with the International Trade Organization regarding specific criteria which would enable the imposition of restrictions without challenge by any other member. The draft charter also provides that, generally, there shall not be discriminatory administration of quantitative restrictions. This means that, in the event of any other country imposing quantitative restrictions, Australia's exports will not be discriminated against, and that we will secure a fair share of the reduced level of imports which that other member can afford.

The Preparatory Committee recognized the special difficulties facing primary producers, and the necessity to provide special arrangements for overcoming these difficulties. The charter enables the continuance of subsidies provided that these do not operate to increase the exports of a product or reduce the imports of such product into the member's country. It is expected that the charter will protect the continuance of Australian stabilization plans such as those that have operated for butter and sugar. In addition, Australia succeeded in having a special provision made for international commodity arrangements in order to stabilize the prices of primary products which may from time to time be in surplus supply. These international commodity arrangements will provide for consultation between the producers and consumers, and will provide for stabilization of the incomes of farmers.

One of the proposals in the charter is that members will, at the request of each other, engage in negotiations for the reduction of tariffs and preferences. Reductions agreed between any of the members will be extended to all other members of the organization. As a first step towards the realization of this objective of the charter, the members of the Preparatory Committee, concurrently with the further drafting of the charter, will meet at Geneva to discuss mutually advantageous reductions of tariffs. These discussions will consider also requests for the modification of existing margins of preference within the British Commonwealth. The negotiations will be on a product-by-product basis, and the parties will be free to reserve from negotiation particular items of importance to their domestic policies.

In considering the effect of these negotiations on particular industries likely to be affected two points should be borne in mind: firstly, that the charter leaves the participating governments free to assist industries by other means, and provides specifically for the modification of a concession if it proves to injure seriously an industry affected. Finally, the Government will review the whole outcome of the negotiations before reaching a decision as to whether, on balance, they are to Australia's advantage.

The establishment of an International Trade Organization with a suitable charter, and the freeing of the barriers to world trade holds the promise for a great expansion in international trade from which Australia has everything to gain. If we can avoid a reversion to the restrictions of the 1930's, we shall have made an advance which will increase the welfare and standards of the people of Australia, and at the same time provide for the changing conditions of our economy, and the progressive development of this country. If an International Trade Organization can be established on an effective and satisfactory basis, we may well have achieved one of the most positive instruments for promoting world prosperity, and world peace.

Source: Digest of Decisions and Announcements, no. 124, pp. 5-9.

3:5 INTERNATIONAL TRADE ORGANIZATION AND THE BRITISH PREFERENTIAL SYSTEM

Speech by the Leader of the Opposition (R. G. Menzies) in the House of Representatives on 26 March 1947.

I begin by describing the debate, if we engage in it fully, as the most important debate that will take place in this House this year. . . .

In the eyes of the Government the only problem is—'Have we something here on paper, and does it go far enough?' I reiterate a view which I and other honorable members have frequently expressed, namely, that we are much more likely to get somewhere by taking one step at a time—for example, by hammering out the trade relations of the British Empire countries and then the relations between those countries and the United States of America, to take two magnificent and important steps—than by endeavouring to achieve some sort of universal result in one hit. It is unhappily true about these things that the more ambitious the scheme the less likely it is to succeed. The second statement by the Minister which I quote is this—

> A major success for Australia in the discussions was the acceptance of the principle that the charter of the international trade organization must be written around the positive aims of full employment and economic development throughout the world. . . The draft charter now includes a positive obligation for all countries to maintain full employment with high levels of effective demand.

Those are good words, but I ask two questions which I invite all honorable members to consider seriously. First, is it soberly thought that any nation not otherwise disposed to seek full employment and to take measures for its own economic development, will be induced to do so because of the existence of a document of this kind? It is against all human nature to suppose so. If a country has a government so obtuse as not to want to get rid of unemployment, so unaware of its own destiny as not to want to develop its community economically, then all the charters in the world, all the sheets of paper, all the long words and all the short words written by other nations will not compel it to do those things. Secondly, is it really thought that anything can be described as a 'positive obligation'—I quote the Minister's words—which in its very nature is plainly unenforceable? The third statement that the Minister made was this—

> A country in a process of rapid industrialization cannot give up its choice between protective tariffs, quantitative restrictions on imports, and payment of production subsidies as a means of fostering its industrial growth.

I pause there to say that I subscribe to that view. I shall return to this point later. The Minister added—

> Australia found it necessary to press for concrete recognition of its right to use such protective measures and clear provisions for their use in appropriate circumstances.

Setting aside the fact that anybody who looks for a clear provision for anything in this document will be hard pressed to find it, I say that that statement, and others which followed in the Minister's speech, seem to indicate that the existing state of affairs, broadly speaking, is to continue. An accurate description of the existing state of affairs is that we have preserved a 'choice between protective tariffs, quantitative restrictions on imports, and payment of production subsidies'. If all that is to be done by the proposed charter is to continue that system, then the charter will achieve nothing. However, unfortunately for that simple view, reference to the draft charter will show that, in all probability—and I use that expression because nobody will ever know to a certainty—the intention is, not to preserve our choice of quotas and subsidies, but to eliminate them. If honorable members when they have a spare fortnight in which to peruse this draft, will examine Article 25, they will find that it provides, under the heading of 'General Elimination of Quantitative Restrictions'—

> Except as otherwise provided in this Charter—

Those words are always occurring in this document—

> Except as otherwise provided in this Charter, no prohibition or restriction, other than duties, taxes or other charges, whether made effective through quotas, import licences or other measures, shall be imposed or maintained by any member on the importation of any product of any other member or on the exportation or sale for export of any product destined for any other member.

There, in relatively clear English is a clean sweep of quotas, import licences, and other measures of the kind which were referred to in the Minister's statement. There are certain exceptions. Some of them do not matter, and others are garnished with provisos which make them difficult to understand. But at the least, export or import quotas can still be imposed under inter-governmental commodity agreements, such as the proposed wheat agreement; and then, in Article 26, there is the provision that members may need to use import restrictions as a means of safeguarding their external financial position, and as a step towards the restoration of equilibrium on a sound and lasting basis, particularly in view of an increased demand for the imports that are needed to carry out their domestic employment, reconstruction development or social policy. If Article 26 is to be given its full effect, then it may very well be said that it has the effect of cancelling out Article 25. I should not be surprised if it did. But as it is not a normal method of interpretation to say that a second article contradicts that which immediately precedes it, and one must attempt to reconcile them, all that I can say is that the nett result of it all is one of two results—either those provisions will, in the long run, make it impossible to resort to quantitative restrictions and to restrictions upon imports by means of licences and the like, or the result of the articles will be to leave the position exactly as it is to-day, and if so, the usefulness of entering into this cumbersome piece of international machinery is not very clear to me.

The fourth sentence in the Minister's speech to which I refer is this—

The Charter enables the continuance of subsidies—

The honorable gentleman was talking particularly about primary products—

provided that these do not operate to increase the exports of a product or reduce the imports of such product into the member's country. . . .[1]

There are two (other) things in this proposal that I want to concentrate my own attention upon, two things which stand out as vital in the proposed charter, in the proposed scheme for a world trade organization. They are, first, the elimination of preferences; and secondly, general, unconditional, most-favoured-nation treatment among all members of the International Trade and Employment Organization. I should say, in order to avoid confusion—because this is a difficult subject, I admit—that the organization is at present only something which exists just over the rim of the horizon. Its constitution is unknown. The method by which it will be governed is unknown. Our representation on it is unknown. So that, at the moment, it is rather a mystical conception. But there is nothing mystical about that section of this charter which indicates the end of preferences, and the institution of universal, unconditional, most-favoured-nation treatment among all the members of the organization. I want to take them in that order, and say something, first, about the elimination of preferences. Good-

---

[1] Menzies's comments on this subject have been omitted for reasons of space only. They are pertinent to any examination of Australia's 'two-price' schemes for primary products. Menzies attacked the proposed right of ITO, in possible defence of Australia's views, to determine whether such schemes represent non-allowable subsidies.

ness knows, what I have to say will not even pretend to be exhaustive. All that one can do is to indicate some prominent aspects of the matter. . . .[2]

. . . Article 24 of the draft charter . . . states—

> Each member . . . shall upon the request of any other member or members enter into reciprocal and mutually advantageous negotiations with such other member or members directed to the substantial reduction of tariffs and other charges on imports and exports and to the elimination of import tariff preferences.

It is as well to have the exact words before us, because an attempt has been made to create ambiguity. Article 24 ties up with page 9 of the report, on which it is stated as a principle—

> that existing preferences, which are of long standing and which have important effects on the economics of the countries concerned, should be excepted from the Most Favoured Nation clause pending their elimination by negotiations pursuant to the provisions of Article 24.

In the long run, therefore—and it might not be so long a run—the charter aims at the destruction of the British preferential system. I say this without any equivocation about a great and friendly power, that the pressure to this end has unquestionably come from the United States of America, which propounded the charter in its original form, and which has felt for a long time that there is something anomalous and objectionable in the British preferential system. There are two anomalies in that attitude. The first is that the United States of America itself represents a complete customs union between the individual States, with absolute freedom of interstate trade. There, you have a great community with a far greater white population than the British Empire has or ever had, and the system in operation there represents a triumph of the principle of preference in internal trade—preference having been carried to the point of free trade. Why this should be unexceptionable in the case of the United States of America—as I agree it is— but objectionable discrimination in the case of the British Empire, it is impossible for me to understand.

The second point is that if Empire preference goes then, in an economic sense, the British Empire will be 'balkanized' . . . if this new principle is to be assented to, the major economic units of the western world will be arranged like this: the United States of America will have complete internal preference. The British Empire will be converted into a series of separate units without preference. Europe will continue as a set of separate units without preference. Then, on the other side of the map, there will be the Soviet Union occupying a position like the United States of America, with complete internal preference. That will represent a loss of economic balance which I cannot believe to be good.

I do not want to overload the record of proceedings with figures, but there can be no doubt about the effects of the Ottawa Agreement, and the mutual establishment of preference which reached its flower in the Ottawa Agreement. Not only did Britain substantially increase its trade with the Dominions and the Dominions with Great Britain, but all of them substantially increased their trade with foreign countries; because, of course, their new internal level of prosperity reflected itself, as will always be the case, in more trade with the rest of the world. . . .

I turn from that to the other fundamental principle of these agreements, the

[2] The next section of the speech is omitted here. It was a review of Churchill's statement on imperial preference (see 1:4).

provision dealing with the most-favoured-nation clause. As honorable members know most-favoured-nation clauses have been found in international trade treaties for between 200 and 300 years. They began, in fact, with the Anglo-Danish Treaties of 1660 and 1670. From that time onwards clauses by which a contracting nation undertakes to give to another nation with which it makes a bargain, terms and conditions no less favourable than those it gives to other nations, so that, in a short phrase, it gives to its contracting party most-favoured-nation treatment in relation to everything, have been an essential feature of British commercial policy. Since those treaties were made at the end of the seventeenth century, this principle has been applied by Great Britain not only to goods and ships but also to the determination of the conditions under which British subjects may enter other countries. Any one who looks over the history of this important matter will soon realize that adherence to most-favoured-nation clauses was part and parcel of the larger policy of universal free trade. Consider the England of the nineteenth century when most of these developments occurred. The most-favoured-nation principle was looked upon as a means of reducing customs barriers. Indeed, in the circumstances of those days, it was. Great Britain as a free-trade country had only to negotiate with certain other countries which had imposed tariffs for many years and which gave it most-favoured-nation treatment, and it was thereby in a position to get the benefit of all tariff reductions that might be made by various contracting countries. Any Englishman in the nineteenth century would have looked upon the most-favoured-nation clause as a means of reducing customs barriers and would have unhesitatingly agreed that when universal free trade had been reached the whole purpose and utility of the most-favoured-nation clause would have disappeared. Here is where we come to a difficulty. There were at least two schools of thought about the most-favoured-nation clause, the English and American schools. The United Kingdom practically always used an unconditional most-favoured-nation clause of the kind we now find in this draft charter; but the United States of America nearly always used a conditional clause, that is, one in which the grant of most-favoured-nation treatment to any other nation was not automatic, but was made conditional upon the receipt of certain compensating concessions. In other words, the Americans said, 'We do not give you most-favoured-nation treatment just because you happen to be a party to an agreement with us. If you want such protection you must make your own bargain with us'. The British most-favoured-nation treatment was extended automatically to all nations with whom it traded, but the American most-favoured-nation treatment was extended, not automatically, but only after a series of special negotiations in which the receiving country had to provide something in exchange. Those were two fundamentally different conceptions of most-favoured-nation treatment. Where the clause was conditional there was still room for useful tariff negotiations, and individual foreign powers could not merely sit back and automatically obtain the benefit of what other nations had succeeded in obtaining by means of negotiation. In the draft charter the proposed most-favoured-nation clause is unconditional. Article 14, which expressed quite plainly what other nations are to receive, provides—

> Any advantage, favour, privilege or immunity granted by any member to any product originating in or destined for any other country shall be accorded immediately and unconditionally to the like product originating in or destined for all other members.

I invite honorable members to take a realistic view of the results of that provision. No doubt it will be said that it is directed towards assisting negotiations for tariff reductions. Quite plainly, it will not achieve that purpose; on the contrary, it will probably impede it because a negotiating nation may be very reluctant to reduce its tariff in favour of another country when it knows that the benefits of that reduction must immediately and unconditionally be extended to all other member countries, some of which may be free trade, some highly protectionist, some highly industrialized, and all with varying costs of production. Under this provision, should this country make tariff concessions to any other member of the International Trade Organization the clause automatically extends those concessions to all other members of the organization. One has no great difficulty in understanding that a country, by making use of this unconditional clause, may secure for itself the lowest rates prevailing in low tariff areas and, at the same time, itself impose a very high tariff upon imports, and maintain high tariffs by saying, 'We make no bargain at all; we do not need to do so; we keep our own tariffs; we enter into no negotiations; as a member of this organization we are at the receiving end of all tariff reductions made by all other countries belonging to it'. I am at a loss to understand why this nineteenth century expedient should now be revived so categorically, unless it be specifically designed, as it may be, to protect the position of highly developed industrial countries and to prevent the development of industrialization in other and younger countries. Take the case of Australia, which is a country with a small population, with developing resources. Suppose we had, side by side during the last 30 years, no Empire preference and the unconditional most-favoured-nation clause as now suggested in this draft charter. What industrial development would we have had? What markets would we have developed overseas, particularly in Great Britain, for our primary products? Honorable members themselves must answer those questions, because if the obvious answers are to be given to them, then it seems abundantly clear that when we are asked to adopt this charter in its present form we are being asked to destroy the whole foundations upon which the progress of our primary and secondary industries has been built. Whilst I put it in this fashion, I do not want to be misunderstood; I am not saying that the Government at the present time is advocating the charter, or seeking to force it upon the House. It is giving to honorable members an opportunity to exercise the privilege of debating it while there is yet effective time to do so. Honorable members will recall that the most-favoured-nation clause, although it has had a lot of lip-service paid to it, has in reality been increasingly evaded in modern times; and this is another condemnation of it. It has been evaded, particularly in the last 40 years, by import quotas, exchange restrictions, specialization of tariff rates and sometimes by subtle classifications in the schedule, and sometimes by State trading. Honorable members might be amused to recall what must be the most classic example of evasion of the most-favoured-nation provision by subtle classification. It was contained in item No. 103 of Germany's convention tariff of 1902. That item, in order to give preference to Switzerland without violating most-favoured-nation obligations to Russia and Holland, gave a special rate to—

> . . . large dappled mountain cattle or brown cattle reared at a spot at least 300 metres above sea level—
>
> That cut out Holland with a vengeance—
>
> and which have at least one month's grazing each year at a spot at least 800 metres above sea level.

If anybody complained, the reply would be, 'Oh, dear me, we are prepared to give exactly the same treatment to you, my dear fellow'. They would say to

Holland, 'Certainly, if you bring along your dappled, or brown, cattle that have lived at the necessary height above sea level we are prepared to take them'. We look at it, and it seems absurd; but it only happens to be the most absurd example out of thousands of examples which the Minister knows have occurred over that period. We must try to accommodate our desire to make some special bargain with a country with our obligation in respect of most-favoured-nation treatment. So, an expedient is looked for. Are those various devices to evade most-favoured-nation treatment really excluded by the new charter? If they are excluded, then the effects will be simple even though from our point of view they may be destructive. Let me illustrate them. If all those devices are gone under this charter, so that we come right back to the most-favoured-nation clause and the abolition of Empire preference, what happens? Australia will be ultimately compelled to give the same rates of duty on cotton textiles to India and Japan as it does to Great Britain. How does that line up with our desire to preserve our substantial market in Great Britain for our own commodities? Great Britain in its turn will be required to give the same rate of duty and the same treatment, without quotas and licences, to sugar from Java and Cuba as it gives to sugar from Australia. How does that line up with our conception of the future of the sugar industry of Australia? All those things will happen if the two great principles of this charter become effective and these methods of evasion are effectively prohibited. The alternative is that they are not effectively prohibited; and what will be the effect if these devices to evade the most-favoured-nation clause continue in operation? Quite plainly, in those circumstances, the existence of the International Trade Organization will make no real difference in the practice of the last 40 years, and the whole document might just as well be torn up. It will be useless and unnecessary, and, therefore, dangerous. . . .

Source: *C.P.D.*, vol. 191, pp. 1197-204.

3:6 INCREASED AUSTRALIAN OUTPUT AND UNITED KINGDOM PURCHASES

Speech by the Prime Minister (J. B. Chifley) in the House of Representatives on 26 March 1947.

In this debate, the Government is not attempting to commit the Parliament in any way to the adoption of any particular policy. I also make it clear that the representatives of Australia who will attend the conference will not have the authority to commit this Parliament, this Government, or this country to the adoption of any particular class of tariffs. Despite their undoubted eloquence, the Leader of the Opposition and the Leader of the Australian Country Party had considerable difficulty in revealing the realities of this position. . . . The Leader of the Opposition found it most difficult to make these proposals comprehensible . . . He said that the document was complex and difficult to understand. I, too, consider that, of all the proposed international agreements, the one now under discussion is amongst the most difficult to understand and to make decisions upon.

I shall deal with the realities of the position. We face in the world today a great economic re-orientation. Apparently there can be no escape from this impending change because of the economic circumstances of various countries, particularly the United Kingdom. I make perfectly clear at the outset that, had the initiative been with the Commonwealth Government, it probably would not have attempted to take part in any such organization as is proposed in the draft charter or, indeed, to join in discussions. . . .

I believe that both the Leader of the Opposition and the Leader of the Australian Country Party will freely admit that there has been a vast change in the economic condition of the world and in the relative economic positions of nations since 1932. There has never been any suggestion from this Government, as far as I know, for the implementation of proposals regarding employment and trade such as are contained in the draft charter. I qualify that by saying that any Commonwealth government which did not look beyond the British market for the expansion of Australia's overseas trade might be adopting an unwise policy. I envisage possible developments in relation to the capacity of the British people to buy our products, which I hope will never occur. In view of the terrific economic struggle in which Great Britain is now engaged, the population of that nation in 20 or 25 years may be much less than it is today, and, even allowing for a higher standard of living than the pre-war standard, the British people may not be able to buy Australia's increased output of goods. This is a problematical subject, but possibly it would be extremely unwise for Australia to rely upon the United Kingdom to purchase its ever-increasing output of primary and secondary products. . . .

However, in relation to international trade and employment, it is essential that we should look far ahead. Although this Government, or any other government, might be satisfied to allow circumstances to remain as they are, we canno* afford to take the risk that in future we shall be able to dispose of our increased exportable surpluses of primary and secondary goods under existing arrangements. The United Kingdom to-day is in a very difficult economic situation. . . .

This Government certainly would be glad to continue under the old system. . . .

If the people of the United Kingdom, rightly or wrongly were to say, 'Much as we desire to continue what has been a very happy arrangement for both of us, namely Empire preferences, because of economic circumstances, the welfare and even the survival of our country depend upon our being able to enter other markets and to have other avenues of trade. Believing that to be our greatest need, we shall have to modify Empire preferences, or no longer be a party to them', . . . What would Australia and New Zealand be able to do? Would they stick their heads in the sand and say, 'We are not going to abandon Empire preferences?' . . . If . . . the United Kingdom, Canada and other dominions decided, with great reluctance and considerable sorrow, that in the best interests of all, Empire preferences must go . . . it would be the height of foolishness if we were to sulk in Australia and not even attempt to improve the position or to lessen the blow to our own industries . . . I have had from the outset some doubt as to whether it is practicable to make such a world arrangement . . . but I am confident that out of all the discussions something may emerge. . . .

The Government considers that whatever the final decision may be, if it will enable us to expand our trade and give the maximum employment to our people it will be to Australia's advantage. I agree with the Leader of the Opposition that the nations of the world should not be bound merely by charters to strive for full employment in their respective countries. I trust that some realization of their own economic interest and the welfare of their people, particularly the workers, will inspire the Government of every country to do its utmost to achieve this without the necessity for charters. Of course, the mere writing of words in a statute book cannot by itself achieve that; but it does point the way, and it is a clear signal of the way we are going. I think that justifies the Government in the attempt it is making to achieve this. . . .

My private opinion is that, in its own interests, the British Government believes that world trade talks would help it in lowering tariff barriers, and would at the same time assist other countries in a freer exchange of goods, with consequent increase of employment. . . .

The whole matter resolves itself into the simple question: 'Should we take part in the discussions and should we try to mitigate the effect of any arrangements made which may be detrimental to this country?' Do honorable members suggest that we should simply absent ourselves from the conference and when the final arrangements have been made say: 'We will have nothing to do with them; it is perfectly true that we might have done better had we taken part in the discussion, but on principle we refuse to take part'.

I do not intend to say a great deal more. This matter was placed on the business paper to give to honorable members an opportunity to express their views on what is a very difficult, and, indeed, extraordinarily complex subject, and to hear the views of honorable members. I repeat that the only issue is: Should Australia take part in this conference? It will be an attempt to see if any arrangement can be made to solve this problem. The Leader of the Opposition quoted Mr Churchill's statement as follows:—

That we were no more committed to the abolition of Imperial Preference than the American Government were committed to the abolition of their high protective tariffs.

Mr Churchill, at the height of his eloquence, could never have uttered a more ambiguous statement than that. He must have known very well that if any one wanted America's high tariffs to be reduced something would have to be given in return. As it stands, the statement does not mean anything. . . .

If the United States of America tariff on wool were reduced from 34 cents to 17 cents per lb., it would confer one of the greatest boons possible on the wool industry in Australia. If there could be a corresponding reduction of the tariff on butter it would result in a tremendous expansion of the butter industry in New Zealand, and much the same applies to lamb. Of course, if some tariff sacrifices were made in regard to canned and dried fruits in order to obtain tariff reduction on wool, butter and lamb, it would be difficult to persuade the producers of canned and dried fruits that the resulting economic benefit would be worth more to Australia than the survival of their industry. Human nature being what it is, I can imagine the producers of fruit not taking kindly to such an argument. They would have strong words to say of any proposal which, although it might benefit Australia generally, would drive them off their orchards. Those are the problems with which we are confronted. Everybody is trying to get the best he can for himself without giving anything away. It is a problem which faces the United Kingdom, and even the United States of America itself. The latter country will not be able to sell its goods to other countries if it refuses them an opportunity to sell their goods in the United States of America. . . .

Source: *C.P.D.*, vol. 191, pp. 1209-15.

3:7 GATT GENEVA NEGOTIATIONS: UNITED STATES PROPOSED DUTY ON WOOL HALTS NEGOTIATIONS

Speech by the Leader of the Opposition (R. G. Menzies) in the House of Representatives on 29 May 1947.

The object of this [adjournment] motion is to give the House a brief opportunity . . . to express its views—which I do not imagine will be determined by the party complexion of any honorable member—on one or two very important aspects of the Geneva trade negotiations . . . the whole basis of the Geneva negotiations is an endeavour to stimulate world trade to the advantage of all the nations of the world, and not for the advantage of one to the disadvantage of another. The present negotiations, so far as they concern Australia, clearly contemplate certain matters. . . .

In the first place, these negotiations contemplate the making of concessions in the Australian tariff. Any concession that is made in that tariff, quite obviously, is a matter of immense importance to Australian secondary industry. Again, the negotiations contemplate the modification of Empire preferences to Australia— that is to say, the preferences which at present we enjoy in other British countries —and any modification of those preferences is naturally a matter of immense importance to Australian primary industries, and in particular to such industries as sugar, dried fruits, and canned fruits, which are well in what might be described as the fighting line in these discussions. The negotiations contemplate the modification of Empire preference to the United Kingdom, by countries like Australia —modifications of the preferential position which the United Kingdom now occupies in relation to our own tariff. In exchange for all those modifications, or for one or more of them, it is contemplated that there will be reductions of the United States of America tariff on British goods so as to enable a substantial entry of United Kingdom products into the United States of America market, and the modification of the United States of America tariff to provide for increased entry into the United States of America of Australian products, such as wool, dairy products, and meat. . . .

The United States of America has taken a prominent part in negotiations and proposals to free world trade a little, and to stimulate it. Ever since the beginning of the secretaryship of Mr Cordell Hull, who was prominently associated with the matter, the United States of America has been the leading sponsor of tariff revision. I cannot say that it has been a leading practitioner of tariff revision, because it has not, but it has been the leading sponsor, and tariff revision it is said, is designed to increase international trade. . . .

Well, despite all that, and despite the position occupied by the United States of America, the Geneva talks have halted on the central and crucial matter of the United States of America duty on wool. . . Wool, of course, is Australia's greatest single industry. Year by year, it constitutes more than 40 per cent in value of all our exports. I heard it described admirably within the last few hours as our principal international currency, which is, indeed, a graphic and substantially accurate way to describe it. The present duty on scoured wool entering the United States of America is 34 cents per lb. My memory goes back to negotiations before the war in which attempts were made to obtain trade treaties with the United States of America, and at that time the duty on wool entering the United States of America was the stumbling block, as the right honorable member for Cowper [Sir Earle Page] will well remember. That duty of 34 cents per lb. was, before the war, quite frequently greater than the price obtained by Australian growers for their wool. Therefore, in certain circumstances, it would amount to an absolute prohibition against the entry into the United States of America of certain kinds of wool. Now, in 1947, the wool duty is again up for discussion. The United States of America, as a sponsor of tariff revision for the purpose of increasing international trade, comes into the conference and, so far as Australia is concerned, the United States of America duty on wool is in the very centre of negotiations, this duty which has been a notorious stumbling block to success on previous occasions. . . .

As a young country in point of development, we cannot accept any doctrine which requires us to 'stay put'. We want to see in this country, and in others, high levels of employment and purchasing power. We want to see higher levels of employment and higher purchasing power in other countries because, amongst other things, these mean for us growing markets, growing production, and growing population. But we are in no mood to drop the bone for the shadow or to impose difficult re-adjustments upon the primary industries of Australia or upon sections of our economy unless, on balance, the result of the trade negotiations is to enable us and Great Britain, and our sister dominions, to move forward with expanding enterprise. . . .

Source: *C.P.D.*, vol. 192, pp. 3112-14.

3:8 GATT GENEVA NEGOTIATIONS: UNITED STATES PROPOSED WOOL LEGISLATION CRITICISED

Speech by the Prime Minister (J. B. Chifley) in the House of Representatives on 29 May 1947.

The Australian Government merely agreed to be represented at Geneva on condition that we were uncommitted. We were prepared to participate in the discussions believing that they might resolve some of the difficulties that confronted the nations of the world. These discussions on world trade present grave difficulties to a country such as Australia. We are closely associated, not only in bonds of kinship, but also economically, with the United Kingdom. The representatives of the United Kingdom Government attended the conference in pursuance of the promise made to the United States Government, believing that the economic circumstances of Great Britain might be bettered by such an arrangement as was proposed in the American formula. As the economic welfare of Australia is so closely wrapped up with that of the United Kingdom, we believed that Australia should be represented at these discussions in order to ascertain whether some of the proposals put forward would be of benefit not only to the United Kingdom but also to ourselves. We believed that whatever concessions Australia might have to make in imperial preferences it would receive other concessions to offset them and that the final agreement would be mutually advantageous to both countries. On that basic principle we went to the conference. The Leader of the Opposition (Mr Menzies) has, of course, covered some of the ground. . . . Although we are anxious to do that [assist the United Kingdom reach trade agreements with the United States and other countries], we are not prepared to give away something without receiving anything in return. In view of the importance of wool in our economic life, I think, although not every one will agree with me, that a substantial reduction of the American duty of 34 cents on our wool would bring to this country an aggregate national advantage far and above any benefit that we get out of Empire preference. . . .

We are prepared to go a long way to help Great Britain in that respect; but it would not be fair to the people of Australia to place before the Commonwealth Parliament for ratification proposals that meant that we should give everything away and not get anything in return. I am not saying that some proposals made by the United States of America about individual commodities would not be of advantage to the producers of those commodities. They would be; but still wool is the overriding consideration. I must confess my complete astonishment that the country that originated and preached the proposals under consideration at Geneva in all the councils of the world should have, at the time attempts were being made to negotiate an agreement, precipitated a proposal that to my mind is internationally provocative [i.e. U.S. Congress's Bill to increase wool duties: see 3:9]. It was made by politicians. They are of our own fraternity, so to speak. I am not complaining about the State Department. Without pretending to know all about it, I think the State Department was probably as astonished as we were at the proposals that have come from the Senate and House of Representatives of the Congress of the United States of America, because its representatives have been the preachers of the doctrine of international trade. The legislation proposed in America is a complete repudiation and contradiction of that doctrine, which, in a broad, general way dates as far back as statements made by President Roosevelt. . . .

Source: *C.P.D.*, vol. 192, pp. 3114-16.

3:9 UNITED STATES PRESIDENT VETOES WOOL BILL

Advice from the President of the United States (H. S. Truman) to the Senate, 26 June 1947.

To the Senate of the United States:

I return herewith, without my approval, S.814, entitled 'The Wool Act of 1947'.

This bill contains features which would have an adverse effect on our international relations and which are not necessary for the support of our domestic wool growers.

As originally passed by the Senate, the bill directed the Commodity Credit Corporation to continue until the end of 1948 to support prices to domestic producers of wool at not less than 1946 levels. It further authorized the Commodity Credit Corporation to sell wool held by it at market prices. I have no objection to these provisions.

As passed by the House, the bill carried an amendment intended to increase the tariff on wool through the imposition of import fees. This was done to provide a means of increasing the domestic price for wool to approximately the support price, thus shifting the cost of the support from the Treasury to the consumers of wool products. The prices of these products are already high.

The conferees of the two Houses agreed upon a measure closely following the House bill, but empowering me to impose import quotas as well as import fees.

The enactment of a law providing for additional barriers to the importation of wool at the very moment when this Government is taking the leading part in a United Nations Conference at Geneva called for the purpose of reducing trade barriers and of drafting a charter for an International Trade Organization, in an effort to restore the world to economic peace, would be a tragic mistake. It would be a blow to our leadership in world affairs. It would be interpreted around the world as a first step on that same road to economic isolationism down which we and other countries travelled after the First World War with such disastrous consequences.

I cannot approve such an action.

The woolgrowers of this country are entitled to receive support. There is still ample time for this Congress to pass wool legislation consistent with our international responsibilities and the interests of our economy as a whole. I urge that the Congress do so promptly.

A bill based on the general principles and policy of the original Senate bill would be acceptable to me, although I would prefer a more permanent wool program, as suggested in my memorandum which was made public on March 12, 1946.

For these reasons I am returning S.814 without my approval.

HARRY S. TRUMAN

The White House,
June 26, 1947

Source: *Congressional Record*, vol. 39,
pt. 6 (Senate), p. 7687.

3:10 AUSTRALIA ACCEPTS DRAFT GATT

Speech by the Minister for Post-War Reconstruction (J. J. Dedman) in the House of Representatives on 29 October 1947.

The Australian Government believes that the proposed agreement will prove advantageous to Australia. Accordingly, it has decided to accept and apply, provisionally, the draft general agreement on tariffs and trade. . . .

Later, after conclusion of the Havana conference and within six months of the tabling of the draft agreement, the Government will decide whether Parliament is to be asked to confirm the agreement and, if it so decides, will seek Parliament's approval for this course. . . .

I can assure the House that the Government is convinced that the draft agreement will create new export opportunities of great value to Australia. Throughout the negotiations the Government has maintained the closest collaboration with other members of the British Commonwealth. The agreement takes full account of the legitimate interests of both primary and secondary industries in this country; and, in relation to imperial preferences, the agreement conforms to the policy enunciated by the Government from time to time in this House. . . .

Source: *C.P.D.*, vol. 194, p. 1435,

D

3:11 GATT: OUTLINE OF DRAFT AGREEMENT

Statement by the Minister for Post-War Reconstruction (J. J. Dedman) in the House of Representatives on 11 November 1947.

The tariff negotiations have been quite distinct from the charter discussions, and the aim has been to bring the results into effect without necessarily waiting for the establishment of the International Trade Organization. The results have been incorporated in a Draft General Agreement on Tariffs and Trade for the consideration of governments, which will be published on 18th November, 1947, and which the Government has decided to apply provisionally from that date. . . .

The agreement is in three parts.

Part I contains—

(a) the schedules of tariff reductions which have been negotiated by all the countries concerned;

(b) an undertaking to extend most-favoured-nation treatment to other parties except for existing preferences which are formally recognized as valid to the extent that they have not been altered in the current negotiations.

Part II contains undertakings regarding commercial policy. These are necessary primarily to prevent tariff concessions granted being offset by other protective measures and follow closely chapter IV of the draft charter. In practice they involve no significant change in Australian commercial policy. In particular they preserve—

(i) the right to impose new duties for protective purposes except where we specifically have accepted, or may accept, as binding in tariff negotiations [*sic*];

(ii) the right to impose import restrictions to protect our balance of payments;

(iii) the right to preserve stabilization schemes for primary products at present operating in Australia, and the right to establish such schemes for other products in similar circumstances;

(iv) the right to take emergency action if any industry is endangered by any tariff or preference reduction negotiated.

Part III contains mainly machinery provisions. . . .

The negotiations have been conducted against an economic background dominated by the slow recovery of war-devastated countries, and by the world-wide shortage of dollars. . . The results of the negotiations as a whole must, therefore, be judged primarily by their effect on the trade relationship between the United States and the rest of the world. While it is easy to exaggerate the effect of tariff reduction, it is clear that a serious endeavour has been made to open the United States' market to imports. The effect of this should be apparent as soon as production in countries other than the United States reaches levels capable of taking advantage of the changes.

On the other hand, the agreement permits the maintenance of quantitative restrictions for balance of payments reasons and until dollars are available also permits discrimination against United States' goods. So long as the present international payments difficulties being experienced by practically all countries except the United States persist, the United States cannot expect to benefit fully from concessions granted to it. The agreement as a whole, therefore, should be a significant contribution to a restoration of a more reasonable balance between dollar and non-dollar payments. . . .

I summarize briefly the direct and indirect benefits which may be expected to accrue as a result of the proposals arising from the Geneva negotiations if they are confirmed by the respective governments concerned. The tariff concessions affecting Australian exports take the form of actual reductions in existing rates of duty or, where duty-free entry or low duties already operate, the binding of such duty-free entry or low rates. In many items such binding is of material value because of the insurance it gives against increases in tariff rates which now stand at low levels. Tariff concessions have been offered to Australia on almost all the principal products which Australia exports or can expect to export, to the individual countries concerned. Generally, the offers have been made directly to Australia, but in some cases the benefits will arise indirectly from offers made to a third country which is a more important supplier of the particular product. The concessions should be of real importance in relation to the future development of primary production in Australia. Further, they include items of importance to Australian secondary industry.

Trade opportunities may also be expected to arise in respect of a number of products of export interest to Australia on which tariff concessions have been offered to other countries. Indirect benefits will also affect a wide range of manufactured products in which there is opportunity for expansion of Australian production and exports. The reductions of duties obtained in the course of the present negotiations are important, not only in themselves, but also by reason of the fact that they ensure a relatively advantageous starting point for future negotiations. This is specially important in the case of the United States, where a 50 per cent. reduction in duties is the maximum cut permissible in any one agreement under the United States Reciprocal Trade Agreements Act. It is only by such negotiations that high duties can be progressively reduced to reasonably low levels.

To secure the above-mentioned benefits, Australia has been obliged to offer some concessions. These have taken the form of concurrence in the reduction of certain preferences at present enjoyed in Empire countries and of concessions in the Australian tariff. Both were unavoidable. We cannot expect to obtain the advantage of such negotiations without making some concessions ourselves. In assessing the outcome, it is essential to have regard to the likely effect on the Australian economy. We have not concurred in any proposed reductions in preferential margins except where such concessions are considered to be within the capacity of the Australian industries affected and where satisfactory compensation concessions have been offered in return. The other concessions which Australia was required to make in return for the benefits offered were in the protective tariff. Most of the concessions proposed are individually small but they cover a very wide field. The Government has every confidence in the ability of Australian industry to withstand the concessions. Price levels in Australia have risen much less than in most overseas countries. This has resulted in Australian industries enjoying greater competitive advantages and an ability to compete within the shelter of a lower tariff wall than that provided by the present Customs Tariff. . . .

It is to the outcome of our negotiations with the United States that the Government attaches paramount importance. This market, whatever its vicissitudes, is by far the world's greatest. It matches an industrial output which is at least equal to that of the rest of the entire world. Even since the outbreak of

World War II, the population of the United States has increased by almost double the total population of Australia. At the same time rising living standards and soaring incomes have greatly increased average purchasing power per head. It is a country where agricultural costs, despite increasing efficiency, steadily outpace those of other countries. At the prices at which we could afford to supply, the American public would buy a very much larger quantity of foodstuffs. But in recent years exorbitant tariffs have barred the way to meeting this demand.

A significant section of Australian industry is geared to dollar imports, without which, as we are finding now, our industrial capacity is handicapped. Further development in the future will require much greater supplies of dollars for the purchase of equipment and essential supplies. Not only Australia, but also the whole sterling area is starved for dollars. The only way to increase the supply permanently is to increase exports to the United States. Any increase in our earnings would benefit not only us but also nearly all our best customers. It would help to redress the world balance against the dollar. The cardinal point of our policy throughout the negotiations has been to break down this great barrier to the further expansion of Australia's greatest primary industries. Throughout the inter-war period market factors, not technical, inhibited their growth. Wool, beef, butter and lamb were all held back by the closure of the American market not only to our produce but also to that of our competitors. When one looks beyond the immediate dislocation and exceptional circumstances of today, to the market prospects of coming years, two factors stand out—shrinking markets in western Europe, including Britain, and a growing one in the United States. The population of western Europe is likely to start declining within a few years accompanied probably by stationary if not falling income *per capita*. To make matters worse, Britain, our main market for foodstuffs, is embarking on policies of increasing self-sufficiency. This will in turn increase its production costs and weaken its competitive power still further, thus lessening its international purchasing power upon which we have depended so heavily in the past. Dislocation in Asia, too, is likely to reduce the flow and increase the price of many of the foodstuffs and raw materials needed to sustain the industry and purchasing power of Western Europe.

Very different trends are manifest in America. So convinced has the Government been of the necessity to break down the barriers to all exports to the United States, not only of foodstuffs, that for a while, as became well known, we risked a breakdown of the whole of the Geneva negotiations in the period immediately preceding the veto by President Truman of the United States Congress bill to increase wool duties. In short, if the draft agreement is accepted by the governments concerned, it should make a significant contribution to a solution of the problems created by the world-wide shortage of dollars. It should materially assist Britain in its economic difficulties and thus help to maintain its international purchasing power, and above all it holds out the prospect of greatly increasing our earnings of foreign exchange by extending the range of our export opportunities, especially in the United States, thus paving the way for the further expansion and development of Australian primary and secondary industries.

Although our negotiations with the United States of America over-shadow the rest, the latter are in the aggregate of considerable significance. We conducted negotiations with seventeen different countries, including Britain, in relationship to which we are in a very special position. The outcome of these negotiations will become apparent when the general agreement on tariffs and trade is published on 18th November. If and when the general agreement is accepted by the requisite number of parties, an Interim Tariff Committee will be established on which each accepting country will be represented on a basis of equality. In due course, it is hoped that other countries will negotiate sufficient tariff reductions to satisfy existing members and thus qualify for membership of the Interim Tariff Committee. The treatment to be accorded to non-members is still unresolved, but it is likely to be as favourable as that extended to members at least until they have had sufficient time to negotiate appropriate reductions and have failed to do so. Eventually, if the International Trade Organization is set up and the most important trading countries become members of both the International Trade Organization and the Interim Tariff Committee, the latter will be dissolved and its functions and membership transferred to a tariff committee within the International Trade Organization. Thereafter the Tariff Committee will be the competent body for the conduct of all International Trade Organization activities in regard to tariffs.

Source: *C.P.D.*, vol. 194, pp. 1880-8.

3:12 GATT: AUSTRALIA SIGNS PROTOCOL OF PROVISIONAL APPLICATION

Statement by the Minister for Commerce (R. T. Pollard) in the House of Representatives on 18 November 1947.

In accordance with the arrangements entered into at Geneva, the provisional application of the General Agreement on Tariffs and Trade was made dependent on the signature by the following eight key countries of the Protocol of Provisional Application, namely, Australia, Belgium, in respect of its metropolitan territory, Canada, France in respect of its metropolitan territory, Luxemburg, the Netherlands in respect of its metropolitan territory, Britain in respect of its metropolitan territory, and the United States. All eight countries have now signed the protocol and the texts of the final act, the general agreement on tariffs and trade, and of the protocol of the provisional application were released for publication at 9.30 a.m. today Australian eastern standard time.

The protocol was signed on behalf of the Australian Government by the Minister for External Affairs (Dr. Evatt) and the following statement was issued on behalf of the Government:

The Australian Government undertake to apply provisionally, provided all other countries do likewise, the tariff reductions negotiated with the other countries whose representatives have been engaged at Geneva during the greater part of 1947. This action will be consequent upon my signing, on behalf of the Australian Government, the protocol of provisional application of the general agreement on tariffs and trade.

The Australian Government will apply the new rates provisionally from 18th November. At a later date the Government will decide whether to recommend to Parliament that the provisional agreement be confirmed.

The breadth of the negotiations conducted by a committee established by the Economic and Social Council of the United Nations is without precedent. More than 120 separate negotiations ranging over a vast number of products were compiled by representatives who met to attempt mutually advantageous arrangements to free the channels of world trade. Australia negotiated with a full conviction of the benefits to be gained, not only to herself, but by the whole world from a satisfactory settlement and a selective reduction of present trade barriers.

The negotiations have to be considered in the light of concurrent efforts to get agreements, in the form of a charter from an International Trade Organization, to commitments upon countries to maintain employment and the demand for goods, which are the basis of trade, and to adhere to agreed rules of good trade conduct.

These commitments are intended to supplement those which the members of the United Nations have already accepted in the United Nations charter—namely, to promote jointly and severally, higher standards of living, full employment and conditions of economic and social progress and development.

The project embarked on by the Economic and Social Council, through its preparatory committee and the world conference which is to assemble shortly in Havana, is one of the most constructive endeavours of the United Nations. The progress already made in tariff negotiations and the decision by a substantial number of the governments to bring tariff reductions into provisional effect lay a sound basis for successful achievement of a significant improvement in world trading conditions and for a solution of the present economic crisis.

I lay on the table the following papers:—

United Nations Conference on Trade and Employment—General Agreement on Tariffs and Trade—

Ministerial Statement, 18th November, 1947.

Explanatory Statement by the Acting Minister for Post-War Reconstruction, 18th November, 1947, together with accompanying documents.

Text of Agreement, together with—

Protocol of Provisional Application.

Final Act.

Schedules of Tariff Concessions (Volumes I and II).

This is the text of the general agreement on tariffs and trade, which includes general articles, tariff schedules covering all the countries concerned, and annexed protocols. The changes involved in the Australian tariff are contained in the resolutions and explanatory memorandum which I lay on the table. Statements have also been assembled which, in conjunction with the tariff resolutions and explanatory memorandum, contain the latest information bearing upon the effect of the general agreement on trade and tariffs on Australia's interests if the agreement is eventually adopted by the governments concerned.

Source: *C.P.D.*, vol. 194, pp. 2172-4.

3:13 GATT: AUSTRALIA'S ROLE IN NEW TRADE PLANS[1]

While some time must necessarily elapse before the full effects of the new rates will be known in certain of our Commonwealth industries, the tariff

[1] Leading Article in the *Age* of 19 November 1947. This article stands out at a time marked by an almost complete absence of the more analytical articles we have now become accustomed to in newspaper editorials or the *Australian Financial Review*. See also a broadly similar leader in the *Sydney Morning Herald* of 20 November 1947.

schedules based on the international trade agreements reached at Geneva constitute for this country the most important and decisive developments in Commonwealth fiscal policy since the Ottawa Agreement. . . .

The fact that it has been found possible to effect these agreements among so many different countries, each with its own special problems of trade, illustrates a genuine desire among most Governments of the world to quicken the flow of normal commerce, and in general stimulate post-war collaboration among the nations. From a Commonwealth as well as an Empire standpoint, the results could have been much worse! Fears that Imperial preference might be scrapped or mangled out of all recognition have not been realised. The system which the Commonwealth and other parts of the Empire have such a vital interest in maintaining has substantially survived, and obviously has been recognised and accepted by the United States as an integral part of the Geneva agreements to which so many countries of both hemispheres have been signatories. Australia is deeply committed in this general agreement because she has signified her willingness to accept the reduction or elimination of Imperial preference on not less than 21 per cent of her Empire trade. That is a very considerable sacrifice, but substantial concessions obtained in return may effectually redress the balance.

One notable concession is that which opens the hitherto sealed United States market to Australian fine wools. The concession of 25 per cent reduction of import duty in this case is one that will greatly encourage the Australian wool industry. It should be able as the result of a vigorous marketing drive substantially to increase the sale of our wool to the United States, thereby making a material contribution to the balancing of the dollar account. Reductions of duty have also been obtained from the United States in respect of Australian beef, mutton, lamb and butter.

In return for these concessions from the important American market, the largest in the world, Australia necessarily has had to give a substantial quid pro quo. She has indicated her readiness to accept reductions or elimination of preferential duties on a fairly wide range of exports. Notable among these is the fruit industry. Australia has surrendered important concessions in respect of fresh, dried and canned fruits . . . The extent to which the Australian fruit export industry will be adversely affected by these concessions has yet to be ascertained. At first sight there appear to be grave dangers for some branches of the industry, which has passed through many critical periods. It survived mainly by virtue of the existing rates of preference in the British market, and a careful analysis of future trends should be made before ratification of an agreement which may hazard the future of a developing Australian industry.

The general agreement, so far as it affects Australia, must be accepted in a spirit of reasonable compromise. It has been created under the stress of abnormal conditions and the pressure of world trends and events. Its permanent acceptance by the Commonwealth and its value to the national economy must depend upon the extent to which this country finds it possible to meet the conditions of an international agreement and at the same time build up under the shelter of her protective walls all those secondary industries which are essential to Australian needs. . . .

That is the background against which the results flowing from the present Agreement must be weighed and watched. With reservations necessitated by self-interest in regard to the development of her own manufacturing and export industries, Australia will nevertheless accept the agreement as the first really effective evidence of international co-operation since the end of the war.

3:14 INTERNATIONAL TRADE ORGANIZATION BILL

Speech by the Minister for Post-War Reconstruction (J. J. Dedman) in the House of Representatives on 30 September 1948 during second reading.

This bill is concerned with Australian acceptance of two distinct but related documents, the charter for an International Trade Organization and the General Agreement on Tariffs and Trade.[1] The charter was laid on the table of the House on the 16th June, 1948, and a copy has been circulated to all honorable members. The International Trade Organization will, if it is established, encourage, and to some extent, supervise and regulate international action aimed at increasing the volume of world trade as a contribution to the full employment and rising standards of living of member nations, and will assist in the creation of conditions of stability and well-being necessary for peaceful and friendly relations among nations. It will be essentially a rule-making and supervising body. . . .

ITO

Australia has been closely connected with the negotiations since the proposal for an International Trade Organization was adopted by a resolution of the Economic and Social Council in February, 1946. The council set up a Preparatory Committee of nineteen countries, in which Australia participated actively and subsequently convened the world conference which drafted the Havana charter. . . .

The charter will enter into force on the sixtieth day following the day on which a majority of the governments which signed the final act at Havana have deposited instruments of acceptance with the Secretary-General of the United Nations. If, however, by the 24th March, 1949, it has not so entered into force, it will enter into force on the sixtieth day following the day on which twenty of the governments that participated in the conference at Havana have deposited their instruments of acceptance. It is likely that most of the countries which participated in the conference will defer the deposit of instruments of acceptance until the Congress of the United States has considered the charter, which is not likely to occur before January, 1949. [The charter was not accepted by the United States and did not come into being.]

GATT

The General Agreement on Tariffs and Trade, the second document with which this bill is concerned, is closely linked with the charter of the International Trade Organization. It contains the tariff rates negotiated at Geneva in 1947 on the basis of mutual concessions between the participating countries. Honorable members will recall that the agreement was laid before the Parliament earlier this year and debated by this House in February and March. That debate was followed by legislation ratifying changes in the rates of duty to bring them into accord with the agreement. The agreement is at present being operated provisionally by 22 countries which were concerned with its construction. While operation is

[1] The Bill covers both ITO and GATT. Subheadings have been inserted in the text to help the reader keep the important distinction between GATT and the Charter for the ITO.

provisional, any member country may withdraw on 60 days' notice and need not take the full legislative steps regarding trade policy which are required by full adherence. Full adherence pledges member countries not to withdraw before 1951. It is, I think, unlikely that any country will make full acceptance of the General Agreement on Tariffs and Trade, as distinct from applying it provisionally until a decision has been made on the entry into force of the charter. I might point out to honorable members that once a sufficient number of countries are applying the agreement definitively, they are empowered to declare that a country which is only applying it provisionally is no longer a contracting party to the agreement.

Some amendments were made to the terms of the general agreement at sessions of the contracting parties at Havana in March of this year, and again at Geneva in August and September. The main purpose of these amendments, which were effected by a series of protocols, was to bring the general agreement, on its rule making and structural sides, into line with amendments made at Havana to the text of the International Trade Organization charter. Two of those protocols are concerned entirely with rectifications of the tariff schedules contained in the general agreement, but these only pick up slips and misprints between the schedules as negotiated and as originally printed. . . .

ITO

Now I desire to say something about the charter of the International Trade Organization. It is designed—(a) to establish an acceptable commercial code of rules and mutual obligations which the member governments undertake to observe in their relations with one another; (b) to set up an International Trade Organization which is intended to act as a means of consultation, collaboration and joint action for member governments in the field of international commercial policy, and to provide a medium of settlement of trade dispute among its members.

I have supplied honorable members with a detailed statement describing the provisions of the charter and the manner in which they will operate and will therefore confine my remarks to an outline of the broad implications confronting Australia in accepting or rejecting them.

Throughout its participation in the negotiations the Australian delegation sought to secure a charter adapted to the interests of this country. It particularly sought to establish—

(a) the importance of maintaining employment and effective demand, particularly in the major industrial countries of the world that will continue to represent the biggest markets for our exports;

(b) the need for greater stability of prices for primary products in order to stabilize the incomes of primary producers and to reduce the undesirable economic fluctuations resulting from extreme variations in prices for these goods;

(c) freedom for Australia to deal with economic problems of particular concern to it, for example—(i) industrial development by tariff protection; (ii) protection of the balance of payments; and (iii) stabilization plans for primary industries;

(d) the principle that British Commonwealth countries should not be required to reduce, or eliminate, preferences except in return for compensating concessions and that these preferences are a recognized exception to the general most-favoured-nation principle;

77

(e) limitations on the use of restrictions on imports of agricultural products by countries which in the past maintained domestic agriculture at uneconomic levels by means of import quotas and other impediments to imports and by so doing reduced their demand for Australian exports; and

(f) the necessity to promote actively the development of under-developed areas and by raising living standards in these territories to increase the demand for imported goods.

I believe that the charter can be examined in the light of the foregoing objectives and will be found to meet them. It has been the policy of the Australian Government that no commitments in relation to commercial policy, particularly those which required a reduction in restrictions on imports, could successfully be maintained unless the conditions under which Australia could continue to export to the full capacity of its industries are maintained. Primarily this requires conditions of full employment and high levels of effective demand in the major industrial countries of the world. In recognition of this the charter contains a chapter devoted to employment and economic activity and in Article 3 each country accepts an obligation to take action designed to maintain full employment and a large and steadily growing demand. In the event of a failure of others to maintain employment and demand, the provisions of the charter enable a country, such as Australia, whose exports would be affected, to seek from the organization a review of its obligations on commercial policy, or even to obtain release from continuing obligations to maintain low levels of tariffs or from other responsibilities under the charter. In any case there is provision within the charter for a country to take emergency action with respect to tariff concessions granted if conditions threaten domestic industry.

One of the principal duties of the organization will be the promotion of agreements between governments relating to the international marketing of primary commodities. The purpose of these agreements will be to ensure that producers can plan their production ahead with a knowledge of a guaranteed return for their exportable surpluses. Such agreements are not for the purpose of reducing the return to producers but for overcoming the wide fluctuations in the actual returns to growers and, consequently, to give them a greater stability of income. Commodities for which such special international agreements are completed will then be exempt from the other provisions of the charter which might conflict with any undertakings in those agreements.

The development of Australian industry has for many years been encouraged by tariff protection granted by Parliament after inquiry by the Tariff Board. The charter imposes no restriction on the raising of tariffs and the only obligation is in respect of duties that are bound against increase for a period of time under the general agreement. It was the policy of the Government in the course of the Geneva negotiations to refrain from negotiating items whose future industrial development it was felt might require the raising of the tariff sooner than the expiration of the three-year period for which the general agreement will initially be in force. Moreover, the charter recognizes the right of a country to seek to withdraw from the general agreement its commitment under any tariff items before the end of a three-year period in order to raise the duty for the purpose of assisting industrial development. Whilst this procedure requires the consent of substantially all the affected parties it is a clear and important recognition of the right to seek to re-negotiate a duty in special circumstances.

Past experience has shown that countries must, at times, take immediate action to protect their international monetary reserves. Balance of payments difficulties are, at the present time, a matter of concern to most of the countries in the world and the use of quantitative restrictions to control a decline in their foreign exchange reserves is an essential part of the policy of those governments. The charter recognizes completely the need of countries to use quantitative restrictions to safeguard their balance of payments and a special exception for this purpose is contained in Article 21. This article, and the provisions of Article 23, relating to the discriminatory use of quantitative restrictions, are highly technical and complex. However, they cover our need to apply and maintain quantitative restrictions, if there should be a decline, or a threatened decline, in our international reserves.

For many years domestic marketing schemes, such as those covering butter and wheat, have operated in Australia for the purpose of stabilizing returns to primary producers. These schemes, with which honorable members are fully familiar, have resulted at times in higher prices being paid by Australian consumers than by overseas purchasers, while at other times the reverse has been the case. Recognition of this type of marketing scheme has been obtained for the purposes of the charter and the provisions of the charter restricting export subsidies do not apply to these Australian stabilization arrangements.

Article 16 of the charter, which contains a statement of the most-favoured-nation principle, specifically excludes from that generalization preferences exchanged between members of the British Commonwealth prior to various dates laid down. There is no obligation for these margins of preference to be reduced except by agreement of all the parties concerned. Any such action would be taken only in return for tariff concessions made by other countries as part of a bargaining process having mutually advantageous results, as was the case with the Geneva tariff negotiations. It is to be noted that no new preference may be created and that this extends in principle to all the members of the organization. However, as honorable members are aware, no other British country has extended a new preference of importance to Australia for many years, and the Government of the United Kingdom is, irrespective of the charter, formally committed against such an extension of preference. It is also known that the Government of Canada is opposed to an extension of, or the creation of, new preferences. On the other hand, this prohibition on the exchange of preferences applies generally to all other members of the organization, and it has been apparent in the course of the negotiations leading to the formulation of the charter that a number of those countries which are in the same economic region or have complementary economies would, but for this obligation, have sought to create new preferences to a far greater extent than the charter now permits. New preferences may be permitted only in the interests of economic development or reconstruction or under a customs union arrangement, and in all cases with the approval of the organization. Detailed criteria must be complied with before consent will be forthcoming. Past experience has shown the extent to which overseas markets for Australian exports of agricultural products have been closed by the imposition of quantitative restrictions. These restrictions have been imposed by older industrial countries, which have sought by this means to protect high cost agricultural production. The charter provides for a general prohibition on the use of import quotas in this manner except in temporary circumstances or under conditions in which the domestic production of the article is also restricted. Rising living standards in the under-developed countries of the world would increase the demand for imported goods, particularly foodstuffs. More than a recognition of this need for development is required, and the charter places on the organization the responsibility for actively encouraging the development of these areas by advising members and providing them with assistance in their planning. Positive action of this type should ensure an expanding volume of international trade from which Australia, as an important supplier of food, would benefit considerably.

I think honorable members will agree that these points amply show that the charter includes provisions which meet the main requirements of Australian interests. In making a decision whether it would be advantageous to become a member of the organization, we should, I think, consider a little further the following four aspects of the question:—

(a) the contribution that the organization can make to the solution of world economic problems and to the maintenance of healthy economic conditions;

(b) the effect of the charter on Australian export markets for primary products and manufactured goods, by its application to the economic policies of other countries;

(c) the effect which the charter may have on the economic policies of Australia; and

(d) the attitude of other countries.

On these points I shall make some observations for the consideration of honorable members. The charter requires, as a condition for freer commercial policies, an undertaking by all countries to pursue policies designed to maintain high and stable levels of employment and effective demand. The present world conditions of shortages of goods and scarcity of hard currencies mask the ultimate need to ensure that there are maintained in our overseas markets steady levels of employment and consequent increasing demand for our primary exports. If these obligations are successfully carried out, these market conditions for all internationally traded goods will be assured. If there is a failure to carry out these undertakings by the major marketing countries, then Australia and the other countries adversely affected will have strong justification under the terms of the charter for taking emergency action to protect their own economies against the impact of adverse economic conditions overseas, and also a sound basis for urging in the organization international action to correct the decline of demand.

Members of the organization undertake, in Article 4, that, if their balance of payments shows a persistent excess of exports over imports and is thus creating balance of payments difficulties for other countries, they will play their full part in restoring equilibrium. This, for instance, would require such a country as the United States actively to pursue policies designed to correct a disequilibrium between dollar and non-dollar currencies. The absence of successful action provides a basis for complaint by affected countries and for the urging of international action through the organization. On the other hand, for countries whose balance of payments is unfavourable, provisions have been inserted to ensure that measures to prevent a continuing decline in monetary reserves may be taken.

Although some of the principles set out in the charter are subject to exceptions which may be applied to meet the specific needs, for example, of under-developed countries, countries in balance of payments difficulties, and countries dependent on primary exports, the general effect of the charter will be to secure recognition of the need to follow non-restrictive trade policies to the fullest practicable degree. Some of the main industrial countries may require to make use of some of the exceptions until the war damage to their economies has been overcome, but others, notably the United States, will be in a position to apply the charter terms from the beginning practically without recourse to the exceptions provided in the charter. This alone will undoubtedly be to the benefit of the rest of the world because of the expanding market which the United States provides for exports from other countries, especially in view of the restraint imposed by the charter upon the adoption of restrictive practices which may have the effect of providing unreasonable protection for domestic industries and so limiting competition with those industries.

Honorable members are well aware that international trade disputes in the past have frequently had widespread and detrimental effects resulting from action taken by individual countries without regard to the effects upon others. The establishment of the International Trade Organization will provide a forum in which there can be prior consultation tending to limit the scope of trade disputes and lead to their earlier settlement. For this reason Chapter VIII of the charter provides for extensive consultation and arbitration. It will also be possible for members to refer to the organization, for advice and study, developments inimical to international trade as they become apparent. The adoption of a generally accepted code in international trade, which provides adequately for the realization of legitimate national and commercial objectives, will also tend to eliminate the detrimental effects resulting from the grosser forms of national self-sufficiency.

Australian exports will benefit directly from the maintenance of good demand conditions in the world and particularly from the adoption of non-restrictive trade policies by highly developed countries such as the United States of America. Future tariff negotiations of the kind concluded in Geneva can lead to further benefits for our industries. The development of new export markets for Australian goods will increase the benefits to be obtained from direct negotiations with those countries and indirectly from the negotiations which may be undertaken by other countries. The limitation on the use of quantitative restrictions by importing countries, from which Australian exports of primary products have suffered in the past, will also strengthen our export position. Moreover, our existing schemes for the stabilization of primary export industries are fully protected.

On the other hand, the charter leaves the main structure of existing imperial preferences substantially preserved . . . the Australian delegation has secured recognition in the charter for the basic elements of policy followed by Australia in connexion with international trade. This relates particularly to the protection for Australian manufacturing industries, stabilization plans for primary industries and restrictions necessary for the protection of the balance of payments. It can be said that the charter requires no change in Australian policies and few changes, and those only minor, in the present Australian commercial legislation or practices, and that it will not prevent our dealing adequately with any economic problem likely to arise in the future as a result of our adherence to the charter.

Of the 56 governments represented at Havana, all except Argentina and Poland signed the final act of the conference authenticating the text of the Havana charter. The United Kingdom delegation stated that its Government, in deciding to sign the final act, had also decided to submit the charter to the Parliament with the Government's support. It seems likely that the charter will not be submitted to the Congress of the United States of America until 1949.

This bill makes Australian acceptance of the International Trade Organization membership conditional on United States and United Kingdom acceptance . . .

81

The usefulness and success of the organization will depend upon the willingness of such major trading nations to accept membership. As joint sponsors, the United Kingdom and the United States are indispensable to the organization's effectiveness. . . On the other hand, it would be almost certainly disadvantageous for us to decline membership if British and American acceptance is forthcoming, because the organization and its members would, in fact, constitute a large and powerful trading group whose members would exchange most-favoured-nation treatment from which we would be excluded.

There is no need for me to enter here into details of the International Trade Organization . . . the powers and duties of the organization given to it by the charter will be carried out by the conference of the members. The conference will also determine the policies of the organization. It may, by a simple majority decision, assign to the executive board any power or duty of the organization. The executive board is to consist of eighteen members selected regularly by the conference. In the event of our accepting membership, Australia would appear to have an excellent chance of election to this executive board. There should be ample room, therefore, for Australia to take an active part in the formulation of the policy of the International Trade Organization when it is established, both in the conference and the executive board. Outside the organization we could have little or no voice at all in formulation of world trade policies.

GATT

I turn now from the International Trade Organization charter to the distinct but related General Agreement on Tariffs and Trade. In pursuance of the principle of reductions in tariffs, the members of the Preparatory Committee present in Geneva negotiated last year the General Agreement on Tariffs and Trade. The agreement is in practice intimately linked with the charter. Any tariff concessions which may be agreed upon as a result of any future negotiations completed under the charter, will be fitted into the framework of the general agreement on terms to be agreed upon by the parties concerned. By the operation of the general most-favoured-nation treatment provided for in the charter, Australia stands to gain from such negotiations, even though it may not participate in every one of them. When the charter comes into force, the general clauses of the agreement will be suspended, or rather merged into the corresponding sections of the charter. The agreement will then consist of the tariff concessions and the unconditional most-favoured-nation clause, together with Part III, which contains certain machinery provisions directly related to the operation of those concessions.

If the charter is accepted by the Australian Government, there will be no purpose in failing to accept the General Agreement on Tariffs and Trade, which has been provisionally applied by Australia since the 1st January, 1948. The period of the agreement is initially for three years, but may run on thereafter, subject to withdrawal by individual contracting parties on six months' notice or to the re-negotiation or withdrawal of individual tariff concessions. The Government is now seeking authority for the definitive, as distinct from provisional, application of the general agreement at such time as the governments of the United Kingdom and the United States of America shall have taken action to apply the agreement definitively to their respective countries. . . .

ITO

In preparation for the first conference of the organization, an Interim Commission has been established and an executive committee of eighteen members has been elected. Australia was one of the countries elected, and is participating

82

actively in the work of the Interim Commission, thus preserving a link that was established when the project was commenced. A session of the executive committee of the Interim Commission has been concluded at Geneva during this month. Thus it is hoped to assist in the determination of the early policy of the organization in a manner that will ensure its development on sound lines and in the interests of Australian development in international trade.

The charter should provide conditions in which an expanding volume of international trade will be secured, and Australia, as a large and growing export country, has a very material interest in such a development. The charter does not require important changes in our present practices. If our hopes for expanding world trade are not realized, then the conditions which restrict our exports will provide an acceptable reason for a review of our own commitments in respect of the charter, and we shall therefore be no worse off for having attempted to co-operate with other countries in the achievement of this objective. The price of isolationism will be at the least a failure to derive benefits from tariff concessions exchanged between the major trading countries of the world that are members of the organization. But there are wider reasons, equally compelling, for giving the International Trade Organization every opportunity to prove itself. As I suggested earlier, success by this body could go very far indeed in creating conditions of stability, co-operation and trust among the nations on which alone we and all nations may live together in freedom and good neighbourliness. For these reasons, the Government has decided that, on balance, it will be in Australia's interest to accept membership in the organization and to accept the general agreement, and therefore it commends the bill to the House.

Source: *C.P.D.*, vol. 198, pp. 1052-9.

3:15 INTERNATIONAL TRADE ORGANIZATION CHARTER AND AMERICAN ECONOMIC IMPERIALISM

Speech by T. W. White (Opposition Member) in the House of Representatives on 18 November 1948, during second reading debate on International Trade Organization Bill.

The purpose of the bill before us is to approve of the acceptance by Australia of the General Agreement on Tariffs and Trade and of the Havana Charter for an international trade organization. It is one of the most important measures that have been brought before the Parliament, as it will vitally affect the economic future of this country and will have far-reaching repercussions on trade and employment. It is contended by the Opposition, and by many competent authorities, as I shall show, that both are endangered by it . . . I believe that we should not take this course, because, by doing so we should be committed to accepting damaging changes under the most-favoured-nation clause of the charter. . . .

Under the charter, we have given away our economic sovereignty. The fixing of our tariffs is to be left to a number of foreign nations, instead of being under our own control. . . .

Its ultimate interpretation is sure to lead to endless contention and delay, and the operation of its main provisions can only lead to further economic dominance by the United States of America, and the disintegration of the Empire into separate economic fragments. Our own Constitution, which has been a fruitful source of litigation that has kept the High Court busy, is a simple document compared with this draft. . . .

The [Ottawa] Agreement is to be discarded; not immediately, of course, as the Minister will remind me when he replies to the debate but it will go when the provisions of the charter begin to apply. Clause 16 of the charter drives a wedge between Britain and the Dominions, in that they are to be regarded as separate entities for tariff purposes, neither Britain nor the Dominions being able to grant a concession to one another without granting it to all countries alike.

Article 17 of the charter obliges members to negotiate for a tariff reduction, and the elimination of preferences, when required. Hitherto, tariff revision was the prerogative of the Government, which was advised by the Tariff Board, and those governments which accepted the advice of the board acted well. The international body which is to be set up under the charter is not an advisory body. It will have executive powers. The change is vital as far as the Empire is concerned, because it must lead to ultimate extinction of Empire preference and early Empire commercial disunity. As comparatively weak trading units in a free-trade world, Empire countries will be defenceless against America's economic imperialism. . . .

Source: *C.P.D.*, vol. 200, pp. 3207-15.

3:16 ASSOCIATED CHAMBERS OF MANUFACTURES OPPOSE RATIFICATION OF GATT

Proceedings in the House of Representatives on 24 November 1948.

E. J. HARRISON: I have received the following telegram from the Director of the Associated Chambers of Manufactures:

Following resolution of Annual Conference Associated Chambers of Manufactures of Australia is hereby transmitted:

'That this annual meeting of the Associated Chambers of Manufactures of Australia deprecates the action of the Government of the Commonwealth of Australia in proposing to ratify the general agreement of tariffs and trade and expresses its considered opinion that such action is a complete abrogation by Australia of its sovereign rights to manage its own affairs and is based on a vain hope that a commercial and trade Utopia can be manufactured from international action of the kind contemplated and further expresses its unyielding opposition to the Government's proposed action.'

Will the Prime Minister, even at this late stage, withdraw the International Trade Organization Bill, which is now before the House, so that he may consider the points raised in the telegram from the Associated Chambers of Manufactures?

J. B. CHIFLEY: I do not know of any matter which has received greater consideration by the Government than the International Trade Organization. It has been the subject of discussion at dozens of meetings of Cabinet Sub-Committees. I respect the views of the Associated Chambers of Manufactures on this subject, but I do not intend to withdraw the International Trade Organization Bill.

Source: *C.P.D.*, vol. 200, p. 3400.

3:17 UNITED NATIONS MONETARY AND FINANCIAL CONFERENCE

Documents relating to the conference held at Bretton Woods, U.S.A., 1-22 July 1944.

SUMMARY OF PROCEEDINGS OF THE CONFERENCE AS PREPARED
BY THE SECRETARIAT OF THE CONFERENCE

I. *The International Monetary Fund*

Since foreign trade affects the standard of life of every people, all countries have a vital interest in the system of exchange of national currencies and the regulations and conditions which govern its working. Because these monetary transactions are international exchanges, the nations must agree on the basic rules which govern the exchanges if the system is to work smoothly. When they do not agree, and when single nations and small groups of nations attempt by special and different regulations of the foreign exchanges to gain trade advantages, the result is instability, a reduced volume of foreign trade, and damage to national economies. This course of action is likely to lead to economic warfare and to endanger the world's peace.

The Conference has therefore agreed that broad international action is necessary to maintain an international monetary system which will promote foreign trade. The nations should consult and agree on international monetary changes which affect each other. They should out-law practices which are agreed to be harmful to world prosperity, and they should assist each other to overcome short-term exchange difficulties.

The Conference has agreed that the nations here represented should establish for these purposes a permanent international body, the International Monetary Fund, with powers and resources adequate to perform the tasks assigned to it. Agreement has been reached concerning these powers and resources and the additional obligations which the member countries should undertake. Draft Articles of Agreement on these points have been prepared.

II. *The International Bank for Reconstruction and Development*

It is in the interest of all nations that post-war reconstruction should be rapid. Likewise, the development of the resources of particular regions is in the general economic interest. Programmes of reconstruction and development will speed economic progress everywhere, will aid political stability and foster peace.

The Conference has agreed that expanded international investment is essential to provide a portion of the capital necessary for reconstruction and development.

The Conference has further agreed that the nations should co-operate to increase the volume of foreign investment for these purposes, made through normal business channels. It is especially important that the nations should co-operate to share the risks of such foreign investment, since the benefits are general.

The Conference has agreed that the nations should establish a permanent international body to perform these functions, to be called the International Bank for Reconstruction and Development. It has been agreed that the Bank should assist in providing capital through normal channels at reasonable rates of interest and for long periods for projects which will raise the productivity of the borrowing country. There is agreement that the Bank should guarantee loans made by others and that through their subscriptions of capital all countries should share with the borrowing country in guaranteeing such loans. The Conference has agreed on the powers and resources which the Bank must have and on the obligations which the member countries must assume, and has prepared draft Articles of Agreement accordingly.

The Conference has recommended that in carrying out the policies of the institutions here proposed special consideration should be given to the needs of countries which have suffered from enemy occupation and hostilities.

The proposals formulated at the Conference for the establishment of the Fund and the Bank are now submitted, in accordance with the terms of the invitation, for consideration of the Governments and people of the countries represented. . . .

Purposes of Fund

The Monetary Fund is intended—

(1) to promote international monetary co-operation;

(2) to facilitate the expansion and balanced growth of international trade by—
    (a) providing member countries with working balances of international funds;
    (b) maintaining orderly exchange arrangements among members; and
    (c) preventing members from imposing restrictions on payments, other than of capital, without the approval of the Fund;

(3) to influence countries to correct maladjustments in their balance of payments and to fulfil their obligations under the Fund. . . .

Source: *C.P.P.*, F.5402, 1944.

3:18 AUSTRALIA TO JOIN INTERNATIONAL MONETARY FUND AND INTERNATIONAL BANK FOR RECONSTRUCTION AND DEVELOPMENT

Statement by the Prime Minister (J. B. Chifley) on 19 November 1946.

Cabinet decided today to make the following recommendation to the Federal Parliamentary Labor Party:—

That Australia will join the International Monetary Fund and the International Bank for Reconstruction and Development, but at the same time, makes clear to Britain, the United States and other interested countries, that the Australian Government regards the fund and the bank and the International Trade Organization as being closely linked, and that the Government will review the question of continuing Australian membership of the fund and the bank when the outcome of the International Trade Organization discussions are known.

Source: *Digest of Decisions and Announcements*, no. 121, p. 19.

3:19 INTERNATIONAL MONETARY AGREEMENTS BILL 1947

Second Reading speech by the Prime Minister and Treasurer (J. B. Chifley) in the House of Representatives on 13 March 1947.

The purpose of the Bill is to seek approval by the Parliament of Australia becoming a member of the International Monetary Fund and of the International Bank for Reconstruction and Development.[1]

Australia has consistently maintained the view that the successful working of international economic organizations, and the expansion of international investment and trade, depend to a very great degree on the achievement and preservation of full employment in the major industrial countries. After a long series of formal and informal discussions at London, Washington, Hot Springs, the Philadelphia Conference of the International Labour Organization and at the Bretton Woods Conference, we finally succeeded, at San Francisco in June, 1945, in amending the purposes of the United Nations to include the promotion of 'high standards of living, full employment and conditions of economic and social progress and development'. Since then, with the strong support of the United Kingdom Government, we have gained the acceptance of the Preparatory Committee on Trade and Employment to the inclusion of an International Employment Agreement in the proposed Trade Charter.

But employment and trade undertakings can be defeated by exchange manipulations, and it is the special object of the International Monetary Fund to avoid the recurrence of these evils. Competitive exchange depreciation, discriminatory exchange controls and the blocking of currencies were destructive weapons in the economic warfare, which raged throughout the thirties and contributed to the outbreak of armed conflict in 1939. Their effect was to deprive international trade of a stable basis, and by greatly diminishing its volume, to impoverish people in all countries, especially in those which, like Australia, depend largely upon external trade. By providing a permanent institution to promote international monetary co-operation, it is hoped to avoid these evils, to facilitate the expansion and balanced growth of international trade and to contribute thereby to the promotion and maintenance of high levels of employment and real income.

The International Monetary Fund represents an attempt to avoid the errors of the past. It has already been commenced with 44 member governments. The chief nations which have not yet joined are Australia, New Zealand and Russia. The articles of the fund are the result of two years' intensive study by representatives of over 40 countries. Australia was represented at the several conferences and successfully pressed important amendments. Inevitably, they represent, at certain points, a compromise; and experience may well prove that some changes are required. The fund is an inter-governmental organization and is wholly controlled by governments. On the board of governors, which determines policy, each member government has one representative, and voting power is allocated according to quotas. At present, the Chancellor of the Exchequer in the United Kingdom, Sir Hugh Dalton, is chairman of the board of governors of both the

---

[1] The purposes, membership, quotas, articles of agreement etc. of the Fund and the Bank are set out in *The Schedules to the International Monetary Agreements Act 1947* published in Commonwealth Acts 1901-1950, vol. III, pp. 2311 ff. Australia formally accepted membership of both organisations on 5 August 1947.

fund and the bank. Day to day management rests with executive directors, of whom there are at present twelve.

Broadly, the fund comprises on the one hand an international pool of gold and currency reserves to meet emergencies, and, on the other hand, a code of rules to regulate exchange relationships between members. Each member joining the fund is assigned a quota which measures two things: First, its obligation to contribute to the pool of gold and local currencies; and, secondly, its right to draw foreign exchange from the fund. Australia's quota is £A.62,500,000 of which £A.2,000,000 to £A.3,000,000 would be paid in gold, and about £A.60,000,000 would be subscribed either in its own currency, or by transferring to the fund non-negotiable non-interest bearing securities. Australia's subscription could only be used for expenditure in Australia by other countries and could only be so used if we had a favourable balance of payments.

Our drawing rights would total about £A.65,000,000. This would constitute an addition of that amount to our international exchange reserves, and would be available if our overseas funds should run down, for instance, as the result of drought. It would also assist overseas loan obligations in time of difficulty. Australia would be entitled to draw foreign currencies from the fund at a rate not greater than 25 per cent. of the quota in a twelve-months period. Under certain conditions, and with the consent of the fund we could draw on the pool beyond these limits.

Certain obligations are undertaken by member countries under the fund agreement in relation to exchange controls and the par value of their currencies. In general, members may not impose restrictions upon payments or transfers for current international transactions with other members. This, however, does not apply to capital movements, and it is subject to what is known as the 'transition period clause' which, broadly, allows members to retain necessary exchange restrictions for five years after the fund begins operations.

When a country joins the fund, it must agree with the fund its initial par value, i.e., its exchange rate. In all cases to date members have agreed their existing exchange rates, and, in our case, the Government would propose to retain the present exchange rate of £A.125 to £100 sterling. Thereafter, exchange rates may be altered only to correct a fundamental disequilibrium. A member can, however, make one alteration of ten per cent. upwards, or downwards, without the consent of the fund. All other changes must be approved by the fund, but the fund is compelled to approve any change necessary to correct a fundamental disequilibrium.

Finally, there is the important provision that a member may withdraw at any time without penalty. A more detailed exposition of the articles of agreement of the fund is available to honorable members in the review made by the leader of the Australian delegation to the Bretton Woods Conference which is contained in Parliamentary Paper No. 13b of 1944.

The undertakings which a member gives regarding exchange stability and the convertibility of its currency in respect of current transactions are clearly important commitments. There are, however, adequate safeguards to ensure that reasonable exchange stability shall not become excessive exchange rigidity, and that movements in exchange rates required for employment reasons shall be achieved. I have already explained that the fund is compelled to concur in movements in exchange rates required to correct a fundamental disequilibrium. It is further provided that the fund may not object to a proposed change because of the domestic, social or political policies of the member proposing the change.

Like ourselves, the United Kingdom Government is pursuing a full employment policy, and, as a further and final safeguard, the United Kingdom Government sought and obtained from the fund a ruling that 'steps necessary to protect a member country from chronic or persistent unemployment arising from pressure upon its balance of payments are among the measures necessary to correct a fundamental disequilibrium'. As the Chancellor of the Exchequer has stated, this 'removes any doubts which may be lingering in men's minds regarding the interpretation of the phrase "fundamental disequilibrium" in relation to employment'.

Further, in return for the exchange undertakings given, a member is assured of assistance from the fund in time of need and is freed from the fear of its external trade being disrupted by fluctuations in the exchange rates of other countries and by the restrictive currency practices which caused so much trouble in the past. External trade is in itself an important determinant of levels of employment, especially for countries like Australia. Our major primary industries and all their related trades and services depend upon the sale of proceeds of our exports, while much other economic activity depends upon the flow of imports. It is a point too often overlooked that a great part of Australia's secondary industry relies upon imported materials, equipment and some processed goods, and this need will grow as secondary industry expands.

The par value of the currencies of members is to be expressed in terms of gold as a common denominator or in terms of the United States dollar, and this has been described as equivalent to the gold standard. But that is not so. The central feature of the gold standard was rigid exchange rates, with currencies so linked to gold that countries were compelled to expand or contract the volume of credit within their territories as gold flowed in or out of their reserves. In contrast the monetary fund envisages controlled flexibility of exchange rates and also, by providing additional currency reserves for members, seeks to avoid the need for contractions of credit where members are subject temporarily to an adverse balance of payments.

The purpose of the International Bank for Reconstruction and Development is to provide a source of capital funds for the reconstruction of countries devastated by war and for the development of industrially backward countries. The bank has a share of capital to which member countries subscribe according to quotas, our quota being £A.62,500,000, the same as for the monetary fund.

Source: *C.P.D.*, vol. 190, pp. 590-3.

3:20 OPPOSITION SUPPORTS INTERNATIONAL MONETARY AGREEMENTS BILL

Speech by the Leader of the Opposition (R. G. Menzies) in the House of Representatives on 20 March 1947, during second reading debate.

I do not propose to speak for more than a few minutes on this measure, partly because it would not seem to be, in any event, useful to engage in a long and detailed examination of the provisions of the agreement . . . However, it is, perhaps, desirable to state one or two broad principles. This is not a party matter. It is a matter of international significance, and there may be many different views about it in many minds. My own mind runs substantially along the same channel as did that of the Prime Minister when he was delivering his second-reading speech. The experience of the world between the two wars showed very clearly and, indeed, very bitterly, that violent fluctuations of exchange rates can be extraordinarily damaging to world trade, and that close controls over exchange, such as those practised by Germany between the two wars, can themselves do immeasurable harm to international trade. If there is one thing about which we all ought to agree it is that one of the tasks of the world particularly during the next few years, is to restore the volume of international business, and to maintain its continuity and steadiness, because this will render policies of full employment in each country more practicable than would be otherwise possible. Our experience between the two wars demonstrated the desirability of some genuine international experiment in the stabilization of exchanges, and in the maintenance of some constancy and reason in the control of currencies used in international trade.

The experience gained during the recent war has taught us another thing—that there are at least some nations which have been brought almost to the verge of ruin, and which have problems of difficult reconstruction that they can hardly undertake to solve out of their own resources. If those nations are to be assisted, we must endeavour to set up an international bank of some kind which, backed by the nations of the world, can provide assistance for those nations faced with this tremendous problem of reconstruction.

Those few observations contained in themselves the primary justification for the creation of an international monetary fund, and for the creation of an international bank. It is quite true that, so much having been stated—so much having been agreed upon even—an immense argument arises over details. I am not at all convinced that argument about those details can be particularly useful at present. Forty nations have gone into this proposal. Australia is among the few which are still suspending judgment. We may criticize individual proposals in the agreement, but we will not change those proposals. We may engage in an academic argument about articles V. or X., or about clause 17, but it will not get us anywhere. Broadly speaking, we must be either in favour of this experiment, or we must reject an experiment of this kind altogether. I am not prepared to reject an experiment of this kind. I think, on the contrary, that it must be made, and we all hope that it will succeed. . . .[1]

Source: *C.P.D.*, vol. 190, pp. 934-6.

[1] In the remainder of his speech, Menzies dealt with criticisms that the Bretton Woods Agreement would result in some loss of national sovereignty; that it would involve a return to the gold standard; and that control over Australia's domestic policies would be handed over to an international body.

3:21 UNITED NATIONS CONFERENCE ON FOOD AND AGRICULTURE 18 MAY-3 JUNE 1943

Resolution II. *Interim and Permanent Commissions for Carrying Out the Recommendations of the United Nations Conference on Food and Agriculture.*[1]

[1] On 16 October 1945 the Constitution of the Food and Agriculture Organization was accepted by thirty-seven nations, including Australia. The functions as set out in the Constitution closely followed the suggestions contained in this document.

... The United Nations Conference on Food and Agriculture

Recommends:

1. That the governments and authorities here represented recognize and embody in a formal declaration or agreement the obligation to their respective peoples and to one another, henceforth to collaborate in raising levels of nutrition and standards of living of their peoples, and to report to one another on the progress achieved;

2. That the governments and authorities here represented establish a permanent organization in the field of food and agriculture; and

Resolves:

1. That in order that every practicable step may be taken to attain these and the other appropriate objectives set forth in the declaration and specific recommendations of the Conference, an Interim Commission for carrying out the recommendations of the United Nations Conference on Food and Agriculture be established. ...

6. That in considering the functions and duties to be assigned to the permanent organization the Interim Commission take into account:

(a) the promotion of scientific, technological, social and economic research;

(b) the collection and dissemination of information and provision for the exchange of services;

(c) the submission to member governments and authorities of recommendations for action with regard to the following:

(i) nutrition;

(ii) standards of consumption of food and other agricultural products;

(iii) agricultural production, distribution, and conservation;

(iv) statistics and economic studies in the field of agriculture and food, including the study of the relation of agriculture to world economy;

(v) education and extension work in the field of food and agriculture;

(vi) agricultural credit;

(vii) problems of agricultural population and farm labor; ...

RESOLUTION XXIV. *Achievement of an Economy of Abundance*

WHEREAS:

1. The first cause of hunger and malnutrition is poverty;

2. The promotion of the full employment of human and material resources, based on sound social and economic policies, is the first condition of a general and progressive increase in production and purchasing power;

3. The sound expansion of industry in undeveloped and other areas, with equality of access to materials and markets, serves also to expand production and purchasing power and is therefore indispensable to any comprehensive program for the advancement of agriculture;

4. Tariffs and other barriers to international trade, and abnormal fluctuations in exchange rates, restrict the production, distribution, and consumption of foodstuffs and other commodities;

5. Progress by individual nations toward a higher standard of living contributes to the solution of broader economic problems, but freedom from want cannot be achieved without effective collaboration among nations;

91

The United Nations Conference on Food and Agriculture

Recommends:

1. That the governments and authorities here represented, by virtue of their determination to achieve freedom from want for all people in all lands, affirm the principle of mutual responsibility and coordinated action:

(a) To promote the full and most advantageous employment of their own and all other people and a general advance in standards of living, thereby providing for an increase in both production and purchasing power; ...

(e) To maintain an equilibrium in balances of payments, and to achieve the orderly management of currencies and exchange;

(f) To improve the methods and reduce the cost of distribution in international trade;

(g) As an integral part of this program, to reduce barriers of every kind to international trade and to eliminate all forms of discriminatory restrictions thereon, including inequitable policies in international transportation, as effectively and as rapidly as possible; ...

RESOLUTION XXV. *International Commodity Arrangements*

WHEREAS:

1. Excessive short-term movements in the prices of food and agricultural commodities are an obstacle to the orderly conduct of their production and distribution;

2. Extreme fluctuations of the prices of food and agricultural products aggravate general deflationary and inflationary tendencies, which are injurious to producers and consumers alike;

3. The mitigation of these influences would promote the objectives of an expansionist policy;

4. Changes in the scale and character of production to meet more effectively the world's need for food and agricultural products may in certain instances require a period of transition and international cooperation to aid producers in making necessary readjustments in their productive organization;

5. International commodity arrangements may play a useful part in the advancement of these ends but further study is necessary to establish the precise forms which these arrangements should take and whether and to what extent regulation of production may be needed;

The United Nations Conference on Food and Agriculture

Recommends:

1. That international commodity arrangements should be designed so as to promote the expansion of an orderly world economy;

2. That, to this end, a body of broad principles should, through further international discussion, be agreed upon regarding the formulation, the provisions, and the administration of such international commodity arrangements as may be deemed feasible and desirable and should include assurance that:

(a) such arrangements will include effective representation of consumers as well as producers;

(b) increasing opportunities will be afforded for supplying consumption needs from the most efficient sources of production at prices fair to both consumers and producers and with due regard to such transitional adjustments in production as may be required to prevent serious economic and social dislocations;

(c) adequate reserves will be maintained to meet all consumption needs;

(d) provision will be made, when applicable, for the orderly disposal of surpluses;

3. That an international organization should be created at an early date to study the feasibility and desirability of such arrangements with reference to individual commodities and, in appropriate cases, to initiate or review such arrangements to be entered into between governments, and to guide and co-ordinate the operations of such arrangements in accordance with agreed principles, maintaining close relations with such programs as may be undertaken in other fields of international economic activity to the end that the objective of raising consumption levels of all peoples may be most effectively served.

*Source: Final Act and Section Reports of
the United Nations Conference on Food
and Agriculture, 18 May-3 June 1943,*
United States Government Printing Office,
Washington, 1943.

3:22 AUSTRALIAN IMPLEMENTATION OF FOOD AND AGRICULTURE PROPOSALS

Speech by the Minister for External Affairs (H. V. Evatt) in the House of Representatives on 14 October 1943.

I shall refer, first, to the United Nations' Conference on Food and Agriculture, which was held in the United States of America in May and June last....

The Conference was ... of importance as it was the first occasion on which common action on a specific post-war economic problem was taken by the United Nations. It was of particular importance to Australia, first, because it represented a continuation of the work done by Australian representatives in the pre-war period in seeking the development of agriculture along lines which would at once promote sound nutrition and prosperous and stable agriculture; and, secondly, because it was the first step to implement the policy which this Government has advocated of common national and international action to improve the living standards of the people of the world....

The Government examined the recommendations put forward by the conference and was satisfied that if they were adopted generally an improvement should be effected throughout the world in the levels of nutrition, the efficiency of agriculture, and the standards of living of rural producers. The Government, therefore, welcomed the report of the conference, and proposes to implement its recommendations insofar as they are applicable to Australia.

A detailed report on the Food Conference by Dr Coombs, who was the leader of the Australian delegation, is attached to this statement, together with the official text of the Final Act of the conference.

Source: C.P.D., vol. 176, pp. 576-7.

B

MULTILATERAL POLICIES
IN OPERATION

4

'THE COLLECTIVE APPROACH ':
STERLING CONVERTIBILITY

The war ended in 1945 with immense problems of reconstruction facing Britain and Europe. The rather sudden ending of Lend-Lease arrangements in August 1945 greatly aggravated the dollar shortage. This shortage in turn exacerbated the difficulties of reconstruction, for until European industries could be restored to full capacity their dependence upon United States supplies, with civilian goods replacing war materials, necessarily continued. During the first five years of post-war reconstruction, an Anglo-American loan was negotiated and all too quickly exhausted (4:1, 4:2). While this loan failed to achieve and sustain the restoration of sterling viability (i.e. convertibility), the Marshall Plan did give Europe the aid needed to get industry started again.[1] By the time of the Korean War (1950) European industry was well on the road back, although it was not until 1951-2 that its recovery was so complete that Australia suffered its first post-war balance of payments crisis associated with a surge of imports in fulfilment of a large backlog of orders (Section 15).

The restoration of sterling convertibility and with it the key role of Britain as 'Banker for nations' was a major post-war objective, as Chifley's speech of 4 December 1947 reveals (4:2).[2] The return to convertibility in July 1947

[1] On the setting up of the Marshall Plan see Chambers, Harris and Bayley (38), pp. 834-6, 921-3. Briefly, the plan was called after the United States Secretary of State, General Marshall, who in June 1947 proposed that the nations of Europe put forward a plan for rehabilitation of their economies to be financed by the United States. Sixteen nations subsequently formulated a four-year recovery plan and on 20 December 1947 President Truman sought Congress approval for this plan and authorisation of the expenditure of United States funds of 17 billion dollars over the period. The Foreign Aid Bill which gave effect to the proposals was passed in April 1948. It provided that each country receiving aid from the United States would enter into an agreement with the latter to 'stimulate the production of specified raw materials, as may be mutually agreed upon, and to facilitate the procurement of such raw materials by the United States for stockpiling purposes from the excess above the reasonable domestic usage and commercial export requirements of the source country'. The very success of the Plan did much to gain support for subsequent aid programs for underdeveloped areas. By the same token, the lack of similarly spectacular results from these programs has given rise to disappointment—a disappointment not really justified when the difference between Europe and non-developed areas in experience, labour skills, and social capital is remembered.

[2] Once again Chifley's sympathetic understanding of Britain's difficulties comes through as clearly as his analysis of the implications for Australia. The same mixture of realism and genuine worry about Britain's position was evident in another speech made
(Continued on next page)

(a condition of the American loan) was shortlived, being suspended on 20 August of the same year. Although a devaluation of sterling took place in 1949, it was not accompanied by convertibility. Not until late in the fifties was sterling again convertible in practical terms, this time as the expression of a concerted Commonwealth policy of 'freer trade and payments'. This key decision is in the communiqué issued following the November-December 1952 Commonwealth Economic Conference, held at prime ministerial level (4:8). It will be noted, however, that this conference decided rather more than a currency question. Moreover, the decision to do something positive about the dollar shortage had its origins in Commonwealth meetings in 1947, 1949, 1950, and January 1952 (4:2, 4:3, and 4:7). This comment is confined to a reminder of Australia's participation in the policy of the sterling area in respect of the dollar and to an indication of the wider issues covered in the November-December 1952 conference.

Throughout the period of acute dollar shortages Australia accepted the restrictions on access to North American (and other dollar currency) supplies.[3] Chifley's speeches make his readiness to do this quite plain. In view of the Labor Party's general hostility to overseas borrowing, he was far more reluctant than his successor as Treasurer, A. W. Fadden (later Sir Arthur), to borrow even from the World Bank, membership of which had cost him some difficulties within his party.[4] Some idea of the sterling area shortages of gold and dollars is shown in the movement in reserves (including the loan proceeds) in 1945 to 1950. The position for Australia in the fifties is shown in the extract from J. O. N. Perkins's Book (A4:1).

Australia could not manage its dollar requirements independently of the pooling arrangement with Britain. Its direct earnings of dollars and other fully convertible currencies was not enough, except in 1950-1. It is, however, important to note Perkins's warning that Australia's contribution to dollar and gold reserves could not be measured without reference to her surpluses derived from trade with Europe which, in part at least, were offset against the direct deficit on trade with dollar areas (A4:1). Australia accepted the idea of restrictions worked out with London and applied without formal mechanisms and legal rules as between the members of the sterling area. Indeed, Australia always resisted any attempt to define the understanding in any precise or formal agreement.

---

earlier in the same year (3:6). Much of 4:2 has been omitted but what remains well illustrates the meticulous care he took in the matter of Britain's economic difficulties and Australia's responsibility in contributing to a solution. It will be noted that there was no discussion of any alternative to membership of the sterling area.

[3] For an account of the effect of the early post-war dollar shortage on Australia see Prest (141).

[4] Had Chifley been returned to office in December 1949 it is probable that he would have had to overcome this reluctance (4:4, last para.).

It is notable that there was no serious examination of the possibility of withdrawal from the sterling area. This was not merely because Australia believed in the British Commonwealth, for one important member (Canada) was associated with the dollar area. It was rather that Australia's working relations in trade and financial matters were and still are tied very closely to Britain. Moreover, Chifley almost certainly would have regarded the step as unhelpful to Britain even if he had thought it practical which, almost certainly, it would not have been. Even under the different circumstances of 1966, when the step is less fanciful, there would still be strong feelings, politically expressed, if such a move could be construed as likely to embarass Britain. The move may come, *de facto*, when the role of the IMF as major backstop to the world currency reserve systems is finally and adequately established. The continued major difficulties of sterling and the lesser ones of the dollar as world trading currencies may bring this about sooner rather than later. There is not likely to be any hasty independent move by Australia to transfer its allegiance from the sterling area.

In practical terms the Sterling Area Arrangement was a simple one. The United Kingdom agreed to sell to Australia for sterling any dollars needed to meet deficits in Australia's dollar transactions. For its part Australia agreed to conserve dollars by applying import, travel, and other restrictions broadly comparable with those applied by the United Kingdom. Rather less successfully on the whole, members of the sterling area also agreed to promote dollar exports and to supply each other with dollar saving (i.e. substitute) goods.

Australia took these obligations seriously and it was not until 1958, at the Montreal Conference (4:12) that a quite rapid dismantling of Australian discriminatory measures against the dollar began. The process was completed along with the virtual ending of general import controls in February 1960. During the interim, especially in the early fifties, the impact of dollar shortages was significantly offset by borrowing, especially from the World Bank (4:6, A15:2), and by the beginnings of private capital inflow from the United States, which supported some permitted imports of capital goods.

An incidental feature of dollar controls was the protection thereby afforded to important new industries—not the least of which was the motor industry. General Motors-Holden's, Ford, Chrysler, and International Harvester all responded to government encouragement and became established as makers of 'Australian' vehicles in the early post-war period under arrangements made possible by dollar import licensing and controls.[5]

Although there were not wanting people who saw no particular virtue in striving for sterling convertibility (and with it the abolition of discrimination

[5] For an account of the Australian government's encouragement of the Australian motor industry see Maxcy (121), pp. 504-5.

against dollar imports),[6] it can be said that American (and Canadian) pressure and the more positive policy aims of the United Kingdom, supported (sometimes prodded) by Australia, made it inevitable that the aim of policy would be to free trade and other transactions from restrictions under which sterling area members operated, if not suffered. The positive approach was embodied in informal agreements reached at Commonwealth conferences and finally, but informally, dubbed 'The Collective Approach to Freer Trade and Payments'.

As the documents show, the need for a positive policy was recognised in 1949, again in 1950 (after it was clear that British devaluation in late 1949 alone was not enough), and in January 1952. It was left to the November-December 1952 conference to give the policy detailed content, to be confirmed in Sydney in January 1954 and again in Montreal in 1958. The last conference was almost the end of the road back: *de facto* convertibility was in sight then and within the next two years practically arrived in the form it now is.[7]

Convertibility came as world trade expanded, and sterling, despite crises en route, managed to meet the calls on it. Some policy makers saw sterling convertibility as an end in itself,[8] but in fact it came in the only satisfactory way possible, when the movement of goods and payments was of such volume and pattern that the dollar ceased to be too 'hard' in relation to sterling and European currency generally.[9]

The Australian approach to this problem was somewhat inconsistent. Both in Chifley's time in office and in the early years of Menzies's administration, Australian officials were vigorous in promoting moves towards convertibility. There were some interests against it, notably those industries enjoying the artificial protection afforded by first the restrictions on dollar imports and then the more general restrictions imposed in March 1952. Yet on this matter the government's policy was clear: such restrictions were to go as soon as possible (Section 15).

It was clearly seen at Commonwealth conferences that the only way to get rid of restrictions—or, more significantly, to ensure viability in the balance of payments—was to expand trade. This was no less clearly seen, for reasons noted below, to be unlikely in any system which required the sterling area to live entirely within itself. True, it made good sense, while exchange difficulties continued, for Commonwealth countries to supply sterling area coun-

[6] See, for example, Balogh (19), various essays in vol. 2.

[7] The United Kingdom accepted the obligations of Article VIII of the IMF as from 15 February 1961, thereby announcing that sterling is convertible *de jure*. Australia took this formal step as from 1 July 1965. However, while sterling has now remained convertible for several years, it is not yet free from the recurrent stresses, even of increasing severity, associated with British balance of payments problems.

[8] See Balogh (19), especially his acid comment in vol. 2, p. 205.

[9] On the problems of this period generally see MacDougall (115).

tries, especially the United Kingdom, with goods which could compete with goods from dollar and non-sterling areas. But beyond this there was the need to expand total production for sale to world markets, especially those in Europe and North America. To this end the two keynotes were development and cost-reducing, especially anti-inflationary, measures (4:8, 4:9). All this pointed away from a closed 'Ottawa-type' system to the more open system first contemplated in Article VII (Sections 1 and 3).

Perhaps the communiqué of 11 December 1952 (4:8) fails to bring out adequately the critical nature of the decision taken to move away from discriminatory trade policies in favour of systems of multilateral trading. The meaning of the term 'multilateral' is better conveyed by the phrase 'freer trade and payments'. We noted this phrase in the last section and its association with the dual role of GATT and the IMF. 'Freer' does not mean free trade but a shift away from the restrictions and 'excessive' barriers to trade imposed by governments towards the system inherent in the rules of GATT. Under these rules trading and investment decisions are made in the market place, given a 'normal' system of non-discriminatory tariffs where protection for domestic industry is required, and given a ready convertibility of national currencies.

What the communiqué principally fails to communicate is that the 1952 conference really turned its back on the hopes of some (including those held by the Australian Prime Minister) that the Ottawa road would be further explored, turning the Commonwealth into a more tightly integrated economic unit. The debate was not difficult nor was it prolonged, but it was decisive (4:8, para. 16), simply because the case against was overwhelming.

This case had several elements. First, whatever the benefits Ottawa may have given, it had aroused antagonism. That antagonism was still reflected in American policy (as we have seen in discussing Article VII). American support was still vital to the Commonwealth;[10] an approach towards sterling convertibility was the only acceptable policy. To the United States any suggestion of going back on Article VII (and its expression in the GATT) was anathema despite its own recourse to a waiver from some of the GATT obligations (Section 5). Secondly, autarky was impossible for the Commonwealth. More than self-sufficient in many items of production and trade, its members were dependent upon non-Commonwealth countries for markets for important exports (Australia—wool, wheat, minerals), as well as for some key imports and for capital for development. Accordingly any system which hampered the growth of trade with non-Commonwealth countries was almost bound to be rejected, especially by Canada which was not a member

[10] Whether expressed through direct financial support of the sterling area reserves, as was then contemplated by the Commonwealth, or as transferred by backing IMF action in support of sterling as and when necessary (4:12, para. 12). Latterly (1966) European direct support has also been vital in preventing sterling devaluation.

E

of the sterling area and was necessarily opposed to any attempt to make the sterling area self-sufficient.[11]

Even Australia's interest in preferences in the British market and hopes for revitalising them (Section 9) could not blind it to these facts. Thirdly, GATT had established itself as an effective organisation of value to Commonwealth members who, for the most part, did not wish to flout its firm strictures against enlargement of preferential margins.[12]

Throughout the whole exercise, Australia sought the rehabilitation of its preferences in the United Kingdom (Section 9); but on the broad policy issue —the quest for sterling convertibility—it threw its weight behind the case for freer trade and payments. At times it sensed an irrational pursuit by London of 'convertibility' for its own sake, but for the most part accepted the 'approach' as being in its own trading interests. It also pursued its commodity policies and gained some recognition for them (4:8, para. 15) but, as will be seen in Section 7, progress in this area was to prove difficult and limited.

The facts attest the rightness of the decision to seek expansion beyond those markets open within a Commonwealth system. Reference to Sections 7 and 9-11, and to the statistical tables and notes in Section 17, will show that no great expansion of trade with the United Kingdom was possible and that, while there were difficulties elsewhere too, relatively greater expansion with non-Commonwealth markets was possible: so much so that marked changes in the pattern and direction of our trade have occurred since 1952, although without the emergence of Japan as a rapidly growing economy the story would doubtless have been less dramatic.

There were several meetings of Commonwealth prime ministers and of finance and trade ministers after 1952. None reversed the course set in December 1952. Although Montreal (September 1958) was convened as a conference to consider self-help within the Commonwealth,[13] it was more notable for its announcements of real progress towards 'freer trade and payments' and for reaffirmation of the wisdom of this course. Nor is any significant result yet apparent of Harold Wilson's frequent declarations of concern to provide intra-Commonwealth trade. Moreover, it is to be doubted whether Commonwealth trade interests would be allowed by Britain's Prime Minister to stand any more seriously in the way of British entry into the EEC than was true of his predecessor's attempt to gain entry (Section 8).

[11] This did not prevent a later Commonwealth government in Canberra seeking to encourage intra-Commonwealth trade in ways not calculated to reverse the growth of trade outside the Commonwealth.

[12] The embarrassment for most Commonwealth members inherent in the preferential systems provided for in Article XXIV (Customs Unions) was not yet apparent.

[13] It was at the time of the preparatory conference at Mont Tremblant a year earlier that there occurred the somewhat dramatic offer by the United Kingdom of free-trade relationship with Canada. Observers could be amused but the Canadians weren't (4:11).

A4:1 AUSTRALIA'S RELATIONSHIP WITH STERLING

An important aspect of the economic relationship between Britain and Australia is Australia's membership of the sterling area. During World War II and its aftermath this carried special obligations arising out of the co-ordination of the policies of the sterling countries over exchange control and import restrictions against goods from dollar countries. . . .

Since Australia holds almost all her international reserves in the form of sterling balances in London, the net balance of all her transactions—current plus capital—is reflected in changes in her sterling balances ('London funds', as they are usually called in Australia). As Australia's needs for non-sterling currencies are met by purchasing them from London by payment out of Australia's sterling balances, the United Kingdom's gold and dollar reserves are affected directly by Australia's net balance of transactions with non-sterling countries.

TABLE 24

AUSTRALIA'S REGIONAL BALANCE OF PAYMENTS

(£A million)

| | Net (direct) drawing on the dollar pool (−) or contribution thereto (+) | Current Account Balance with Non-dollar Countries | | | Non-sterling balance |
		Non-sterling Western Europe	Other non-sterling countries	Sterling countries	
	(1)	(2)	(3)	(4)	(5 = 1+2+3)
1950–1	+ 43	+148	+ 28	− 145	+219
1951–2	− 59	− 40	− 66	− 391	−165
1952–3	− 5	+125	+ 50	+ 76	−170
1953–4	− 43	+105	+ 45	− 109	+107
1954–5	− 54	+ 50	− 1	− 208	− 5
1955–6	− 40	+ 46	+ 17	− 194	+ 23
1956–7	− 23	+137	+ 99	− 51	+213
1957–8	− 70	+ 73	+ 51	− 170	+ 54
1958–9	− 69	+ 19	+ 45	− 142	− 5
	−320	+663	+268	−1,336	+611

As Table 24 indicates, the pattern of Australia's regional balance of payments with non-sterling countries during the 1950's has been that a large deficit (on current plus capital account) with dollar countries has been outweighed by a still larger surplus with non-dollar, non-sterling countries. Australia was a net drawer upon the sterling area's dollar pool, but that deficit was only about half as great as her surplus with Continental Western Europe, and only about a third as large as her surplus with all non-dollar, non-sterling countries. A surplus earned by a sterling country with Western Europe normally earned or saved gold for the sterling area (though not normally to the full value of the surplus earned) through the operation of the European Payments Union (which operated from mid-1950 until December 1958). Australia was therefore a net contributor to the area's

103

gold and dollar reserves, even on the very conservative assumption that surpluses earned by a sterling country with Western Europe brought gold to the sterling area to the extent of half the value of that surplus. In fact, gold was paid to or by the sterling area to the extent of 75 per cent of any surplus or deficit with the rest of the E.P.U. area in the later years, and to the extent of varying percentages in earlier ones.

Against Australia's large surplus with all non-sterling countries must be set her even larger current deficit with the sterling area. The remaining deficit was covered by the substantial inflow of capital from Britain (and minor amounts from other sterling countries) and by the use of the country's international reserves (which fell by over £A100m. during the 1950's).

But such regional analyses as these should not be used as an indication of whether a sterling country has been in some sense a 'good' or a 'bad' member of the area. They are cited here merely because some observers have tended to look at Australia's substantial dollar deficit and fail to take due account also of her substantial surplus with other areas, many of which paid gold or convertible currencies in settlement of their net balances with the sterling area.

Source: J. O. N. Perkins, *Australia and Britain: Economic Relationships in the 1950s* (Melbourne University Press), pp. 138-40. Reprinted by permission.

4:1 ANGLO-AMERICAN ECONOMIC AND FINANCIAL AGREEMENT

Statement by the Prime Minister of the United Kingdom (C. V. Attlee) in the House of Commons on 6 December 1945.

Agreement has been reached, subject to the approval of the legislatures of both countries, for the extension by the United States to the United Kingdom of a line of credits of 3,750,000,000 dollars on the terms stated in the Financial Agreement signed this day, for the following purposes: to facilitate purchases by the United Kingdom of goods and services in the United States; to assist the United Kingdom to meet transitional post-war deficits in its current balance of payments; to help the United Kingdom to maintain adequate reserves of gold and dollars, and to assist the United Kingdom to assume the obligations of multilateral trade. This credit would make it possible for the United Kingdom to relax import and exchange controls, including exchange arrangements affecting the sterling area, and generally to move forward with the United States and other countries towards the common objective of expanded multilateral trade. . . .

Source: *P.D. (H. of C.)*, vol. 416, pp. 2663-4.

4:2 AUSTRALIA ACTS TO CONSERVE DOLLARS AND HELP UNITED KINGDOM

Statement by the Prime Minister (J. B. Chifley) in the House of Representatives on 4 December 1947.

1. At present there is a practically world-wide shortage of United States dollars. Amongst the regions affected are the United Kingdom and Australia, New Zealand, India and the other countries of the sterling area, most of Europe, Canada and the South and Central American countries. For most of the world, Canadian dollars are also scarce whilst Canada itself is faced with an acute shortage of United States dollars.

2. Although other factors have contributed to this situation, the most important cause is the disparity between levels of production in the United States of America on the one hand and in Europe and Asia (including Indonesia) on the other hand. Restoration of the war-devastated countries has in general been slow, with the result that they have been able neither to produce the normal proportion of their own needs nor to re-establish their export trade. Hence there has been a concentration of demand upon the United States of America and Canada, where production has risen more rapidly than elsewhere. The position has been greatly aggravated by the increase which has occurred in United States prices, particularly during the past year.

3. On recent figures the rate of exports from the United States of America has exceeded the rate of imports by about 10 billion dollars per annum. Whereas during the early post-war period contributions such as those made under U.N.R.R.A. and the large dollar loans made by the United States of America and Canada eased the position for a number of countries, the greater part of such aid had by the middle of 1947 been exhausted and dollar deficits are now for the most part being met by drawings upon gold and dollar reserves. In most cases such reserves are dwindling rapidly and cannot sustain for long the present rate of drawings upon them. In efforts to reduce the dollar gap in their balances of payments, most countries have by now imposed severe restrictions upon United States goods.

4. There can be no satisfactory solution to the present dollar problem until European production and trade are brought into balance with Western Hemisphere production. To a large extent this will require a reconstruction of the European economy, and the Marshall Plan is based upon such a concept. . . .

The United Kingdom Dollar Position

6. The United Kingdom emerged from the war with her productive structure seriously impaired and her external income from exports and overseas investments greatly reduced. She needed a certain level of imports, largely from the United States of America, to maintain a reasonable living standard and to supply raw materials and replace capital equipment. With her overseas investments largely liquidated and her shipping depleted, exports were the only substantial means of payment remaining, but even these had fallen by the end of the war to 40 per cent. of the pre-war volume. It was estimated that the volume of exports would have to rise to 75 per cent. above pre-war before the United Kingdom's overseas pay-

ments would balance again. It was against this background that the United States loan of 3,750,000,000 dollars was negotiated to assist the United Kingdom in its transitional period.

7. The United States loan became available on 15th July, 1946. It was estimated that the loan would last for two to three years.

8. However, it was used up in just over twelve months, largely because of—

(a) the rapid increase in American price levels;

(b) the slow recovery of production in Europe and Asia;

(c) the severe 1946-47 winter in the United Kingdom, which dislocated British production; and

(d) the demands of other countries for conversion of sterling into dollars after 15th July, 1947, when sterling became formally convertible into dollars under the Loan Agreement. (Convertibility was suspended on 20th August, 1947).

United Kingdom and Sterling Area Reserves and Deficits

14. . . . On 7th August, 1947, the then Chancellor of the Exchequer (the Right Honourable H. Dalton) informed the House of Commons that the United Kingdom gold and dollar reserves amounted to about 2,400,000,000 dollars (Column 1679 of No. 159 of Volume 441 of Official Report). As there is a limit below which the United Kingdom Government could not permit these reserves to fall, it became necessary after exhaustion of the American loan to devise means of reducing the dollar deficit drastically enough to safeguard these reserves, which are the reserves not only of the United Kingdom but also of the whole sterling area.

15. The United Kingdom took the lead in imposing very heavy restrictions on dollar imports, instituting a renewed export drive and curtailing the use of dollars on travel, films, military expenditure, and so on. The effect of these restrictions was to reduce the United Kingdom's dollar import programme for 1948 by 400,000,000 dollars. . . .

19. It is clear that unless the rate of drain from reserves can be reduced by further cuts in dollar expenditure there will be no alternative for sterling area countries but to live within their current dollar earnings.

20. Even if the long-term proposals contained in the 'Marshall Plan' are approved and the United Kingdom benefits to some extent directly, any significant improvement in the United Kingdom position can only come from the restoration of the European countries.

21. These benefits can, however, be expected to mature only gradually. . . .

The Australian Position

22. The grave economic difficulties with which the United Kingdom is con-fronted, largely as a result of her sacrifices during the war, must be a matter of much concern to all other members of the British Commonwealth. Among the greatest of these difficulties is the dollar shortage. The Australian Government desires to do everything in its power to assist the United Kingdom in overcoming her dollar difficulties. For this reason the Government announced on 4th September, 1947, that it had been decided to sell, for the time being, current gold production to the United Kingdom as a special measure of assistance. Prior to this Australia's current production had been added to our gold reserves.

23. It must be realized that the normal pattern of Australia's overseas trade is such that we are usually net drawers on the sterling area dollar pool in respect of both United States of America and Canadian dollars.

24. During the war years, when a large number of American troops were stationed in Australia, our dollar accruals substantially exceeded our dollar outgoings. The net surplus of dollars was sold to the United Kingdom for sterling and was used by the United Kingdom in the prosecution of the war against the common enemy.

25. With the removal of the American troops from the Australian theatre and the cessation of hostilities (and with it, the termination of lend-lease) our international receipts and payments resumed their traditional pattern and it again became necessary to purchase dollars for sterling from the United Kingdom to cover our net dollar deficit. . . .

27. The conservation of both United States and Canadian dollars is, therefore, an inescapable necessity for Australia.

Dollar Exports and Imports

28. We can, of course, help by increasing our exports to the dollar area.

29. Wool is our greatest dollar earner but the scale of American wool purchases is governed by factors largely outside our control. . . .

33. Since the outbreak of war in 1939 imports from the dollar area have in general been limited to essential goods not available in adequate quantities from sterling sources of supply. However, in present circumstances, there are a great many items which are obtainable only from the dollar area and the great development which has taken place in Australian industry has increased the demand for imported machinery and raw materials.

34. During the period immediately following the cessation of hostilities, when reconversion of American production to a peace-time basis was incomplete, the level of dollar imports was limited by lack of availability. During the current year, however, American production has caught up with the backlag of domestic demand in many fields and many items have come into free supply for the export trade. This, coupled with the steep rise in dollar prices, has led to a very rapid growth in the value of dollar goods imported into Australia.

35. Our imports from the United States of America and Canada in 1946-47 were valued at £A63,000,000 on the recorded basis of f.o.b. plus 10 per cent. In the first four months of 1947-48 imports from the United States of America and Canada were about £A41,000,000—an annual rate of £A123,000,000.

Australia's Dollar Deficit

36. Accurate estimates of Australia's balance of payments with individual countries are difficult to obtain particularly because of the high proportion of our overseas trade which is financed through London. However, on 30th September, honorable Members were informed that on the basis of such information as is available it was estimated that in 1946-47 Australia's dollar deficit amounted to about 100,000,000 dollars.

The September Dollar Cuts

37. Following the suspension of convertibility of sterling into dollars and the exhaustion of the American loan, the Commonwealth Government took stock of

the position and decided on certain measures to reduce the size of Australia's deficit for the current financial year and thus reduce the demands we would have to make on the United Kingdom to provide us with dollars from their ultimate reserve of gold and dollars.

London Dollar Talks

38. Following the September decisions, Australian officials were sent to London at the request of the United Kingdom Government to participate in discussions between various sterling area countries on the general dollar situation and the steps required to meet it.

39. These talks revealed that the rate of drain on the United Kingdom gold and dollar reserves was even more serious than had been realized and the United Kingdom authorities requested that Australia should undertake to live within its current dollar income and to make no net claim on the United Kingdom for dollars.

40. The Commonwealth Government felt unable to give a rigid undertaking of this kind. Since our dollar earnings are apt to vary widely from year to year, there could be no certainty as to what such a commitment would entail. But it was evident that should our dollar income decline heavily we might find ourselves unable to fulfil such an undertaking without causing excessive dislocation to Australian industry.

41. The Government did, however, undertake to cooperate with the United Kingdom Government in reducing dollar expenditure to the fullest practicable extent.

Review of Outstanding Dollar Import Licences

42. When the September review was made no clear picture was available of the extent to which we were already committed to expenditure of dollars by import licences already granted. Statistics were available on the total value of licences issued, but it was not known to what extent the goods covered by these licences had already been imported or what proportion was still to come forward.

43. Accordingly, early in October all outstanding dollar import licences (except for certain commodities covered by special arrangements), were recalled for review. The purpose of the review was to establish more precisely the extent of our dollar commitments for imports during the current financial year and also to enable consideration to be given to the possibilities of further economies in dollar expenditure. . . .

48. The total value of dollar import licences recalled for review was £A52,000,000. Action is being taken to confirm these licences in all cases where (a) goods were in transit, (b) irrevocable letters of credit had been established and (c) the goods covered were included in the list of highly essential items announced on 30th October, 1947.

49. The Government had hoped that it would be possible to avoid cancellation of any licences but, in the light of the Inter-departmental Committee's report, it was felt that there was no alternative but to cancel all outstanding licences not falling within the above categories.

50. It is estimated that the effect of these decisions will be to confirm licences to a value of £A35,000,000 and to cancel licences to a value of £A17,000,000.

51. The major items involving dollar expenditure, such as newsprint, motor vehicle chassis, tobacco, petrol and film remittances, are being dealt with separately and were not covered in the general review of import licences. Further economies in these major items will, however, be inescapable and specific proposals will be submitted to Cabinet for decision at its next meeting. . . .

53. Despite the action already taken and the further action proposed, our inescapable commitments are so great that the possibilities of effecting reductions in dollar expenditure during the current year are limited. Even when all possible action has been taken it seems probable that imports from the United States of America and Canada during 1947-48 will be about £A90,000,000.

54. However, a marked tapering off in dollar imports may be expected during the second half of the financial year and imports during the calendar year 1948 from the dollar area will be reduced to a level bearing a much closer relationship to our current dollar earnings.

New Dollar Import Licences 1947-48

55. The Government appreciates that to meet cases of special urgency some new licences will have to be granted for the importation of goods from the dollar area during the current financial year. However, a ceiling figure has been placed on the value of such licences and the Inter-departmental Committee has been given the responsibility of recommending the allocation of licences within the ceiling figure.

Dollar Imports 1948-49

56. The Government is now considering the basis on which dollar import licences are to be issued for goods to be imported during the financial year 1948-49. It is proposed to establish quotas for the various classes of goods within a budget ceiling, and the Minister for Trade and Customs will announce as soon as possible the procedure to be followed in granting import licences.

CONCLUSION

57. The Government regrets the inconvenience and hardship which the cancellation of import licences and other dollar conservation measures have caused in the field of industry and commerce. It feels confident, however, that the Australian people as a whole will support the action taken, since failure on our part to reduce our dollar expenditure would inevitably increase the much greater hardships which are at present being endured by the people of the United Kingdom.

58. The United Kingdom is at present making sales from its reserves of gold and is borrowing from the International Monetary Fund to pay for imports of food and other essential goods and to meet the dollar deficit of other members of the sterling area. We in Australia must do what we can to help by reducing our net demands on the United Kingdom for dollars to the absolute minimum.

Source: *C.P.P.*, no. 54 of 1946-7.

4:3 COMMONWEALTH MINISTERS AIM AT MULTILATERAL TRADING SYSTEM FOR STERLING AND DOLLARS

Press Communiqué issued after the final session of the meeting of the Commonwealth Finance Ministers in London on 18 July 1949.

1. The final session of the meeting of Commonwealth Finance Ministers was held in London today.

2. The purpose of the meeting was to enable Ministers of the Commonwealth countries to exchange views on the urgent economic problems at present confronting their countries, with particular reference to the fall in the level of the gold and dollar reserves of the sterling area during recent months. . . .

6. Ministers reviewed the economic position of the Sterling Area both immediate and long term. They reaffirmed their conviction that the strength and stability of sterling are essential to the wellbeing, not only of each member of the sterling area, but also of the world as a whole.

7. Immediate steps necessary to check the continuing heavy drain on the central reserves of the sterling area were discussed and the Ministers concerned agreed to recommend to their Governments action comparable in its results to that already decided upon by the United Kingdom.

8. Emergency measures to stem the current drain on the sterling area's reserves are perforce negative and unconstructive. It was recognized that while the immediate action must be to protect the reserves of the sterling area, the problems of the past few months were an aggravation of long-standing difficulties. The meeting, therefore, was pleased to note that discussions had taken place between the United Kingdom, Canadian and United States Ministers and agreed with them that the aim must be the achievement of a pattern of world trade in which the dollar and non-dollar countries can operate together within one single multilateral system. The meeting noted with satisfaction that further discussions were being arranged to take place in Washington early in September to consider the action required to carry out this aim.

9. Ministers agreed that the achievement of this aim depended on the establishment of conditions which would make a single multilateral system of world trade and payments practicable. These conditions did not exist at present. It was agreed that the Governments represented would give consideration, in collaboration with other Governments concerned, to measures designed to establish these conditions, and that in endeavouring to solve the short-term problem, care should be taken to concentrate upon measures which would fit into the permanent pattern of world trade.

10. It was agreed that a lasting solution of the sterling area's difficulties could not be found without a very substantial expansion of the area's earnings of dollars, and the most effective use and development of the resources of each component part. Practical and positive measures designed to this end were discussed and accepted for recommendation to Governments. Ministers recognized the special position of those countries which are at present in a lesser or greater degree underdeveloped but which, with assistance, might not only improve the standard of living of their people, but also make a greater contribution to the resources available to the world.

11. These measures, to be effective, clearly call for close and continuous consultation between Governments, and the Ministers made recommendations for the necessary action to meet this need.

4:4 AUSTRALIA REDUCES DOLLAR EXPENDITURE AND CONSIDERS DOLLAR LOAN

Budget Speech by the Prime Minister and Treasurer (J. B. Chifley) in the House of Representatives on 7 September 1949.[1]

The Government has decided to adopt the recommendations of the London Conference and, as already announced, has reduced allocations of licences in the September quarter for imports of goods from the dollar area. The aim is to reduce dollar expenditure on imports to 75 per cent of the 1948 level as quickly as possible. This means that there will have to be a substantial reduction in dollar expenditure by government departments as well as cuts in practically all the major categories of commercial dollar imports. Dollar imports were already severely restricted in 1948. The reductions in the September quarter were the largest which could be applied immediately without causing severe disruption in Australian industries.

But the full 25 per cent saving in dollar import expenditure will not be possible of achievement in 1949-50 because of the commitment represented by outstanding licences. Australia must play its full part in avoiding a further drain on the limited gold and dollar reserves of the United Kingdom and the Government is examining the possibilities of borrowing as a means to provide additional dollars. The Government recognizes that this course may present difficulties. Generally, it has been averse to increasing the long-term dollar commitments of Australia. There are various possible sources of dollar borrowing, and the matter will be decided in the light of all the circumstances.

Source: *C.P.D.*, vol. 204, pp. 21-3.

[1] The earlier part of this speech included a review of the July Conference held in London.

4:5 DEVALUATION OF STERLING AND AUSTRALIAN CURRENCY

Statement by the Prime Minister and Treasurer (J. B. Chifley) in the House of Representatives on 20 September 1949.

As honorable members are aware, the United Kingdom Chancellor of the Exchequer, Sir Stafford Cripps, announced in a broadcast made in London on Sunday night, that is at 6.15 on Monday morning Canberra time, that the United Kingdom Government had decided to devalue the £1 sterling in terms of the United States dollar. The new rate fixed by the United Kingdom Government is 2.80 dollars to the £1 sterling. I was informed by Mr. Attlee at the week-end of the United Kingdom Government's decision. It was then necessary to reach an immediate decision concerning the rate of exchange to be fixed for the Australian £1 in the light of the new sterling-dollar rate.

Australia clearly could not maintain the former rates of exchange with both the £1 sterling and the dollar. The choices open were to maintain the existing relationship with the dollar and to appreciate against sterling, to maintain the existing relationship with sterling and to depreciate against the dollar, or to adopt a middle course involving some appreciation against sterling together with some depreciation against the dollar. After careful consideration of all the circumstances, it was decided to maintain the existing relationship between the £1 Australian and the £1 sterling, that is, the rate of £125 Australian to £100 sterling. This, of course, involved the consequential decision that the £1 Australian should be devalued in terms of the United States dollar by the same proportion as the £1 sterling, producing a new rate of 2.24 dollars to the £1 Australian. The International Monetary Fund was consulted and expressed agreement. . . .

The decision of the Government means that there will be no change in the exchange basis of our trading relationships with the United Kingdom, our most important export market. The proceeds in Australian currency received by exporters to the United Kingdom will not be reduced as a result of the exchange movements which have taken place. Neither will these movements reduce the price in Australia of goods imported from the United Kingdom. The Government had in mind the difficulties which would have been created for both export industries and industries producing for the local market if the existing exchange relationship with sterling had been altered. To have retained the former par value with the dollar would have meant that the Australian £1 would have been appreciated against sterling, and possibly against the currencies of a number of other countries in which we have important markets. This would have been to the disadvantage of exporters, and it would also have created the possibility that Australian industries would be undersold in their home market. If a mid-way course had been taken, the same possibilities would have been present, even though to a lesser degree. At the same time the Government recognized that to devalue our currency against the dollar to the same extent as sterling would tend in some respect to increase local costs.

At the new rate of 2.24 dollars to the Australian £1 currency costs of all imported goods which have to be paid for in United States dollars will be increased. . . .

Source: *C.P.D.*, vol. 204, pp. 339-40.

4:6 AUSTRALIA BORROWS $100,000,000 FROM INTERNATIONAL BANK FOR RECONSTRUCTION AND DEVELOPMENT

Second Reading speech by the Treasurer (A. Fadden) on the Loan (International Bank for Reconstruction and Development) Bill in the House of Representatives on 1 December 1950.

. . . The purpose of this bill is to authorize the borrowing of a sum of up to 100,000,000 dollars from the International Bank for Reconstruction and Development, in accordance with the loan agreement concluded with the bank on the 22nd August, last. . . .

'The Collective Approach': Sterling Convertibility

The Government decided to raise a dollar loan to remove one of the greatest obstacles standing in the path of industrial expansion and of the general development of Australia. That obstacle was the shortage of certain types of capital equipment and plant, which are indispensable to the furtherance of development in this country, and can be obtained only in the United States and Canada. Because of the shortage of dollars in Australia and all other countries of the sterling area, we were not getting these items in sufficient quantities. The Government therefore explored the possibilities of borrowing dollars to alleviate the position and when it found that a loan on reasonable terms was available, it had no hesitation in recommending its acceptance to the Loan Council.

For the programme of immigration and development upon which Australia has embarked vast and increasing supplies of capital equipment will be necessary. . . . However, because of the world-wide shortage of dollars which has prevailed since the war, our access to North American supplies has remained severely restricted. As honorable members know, Australia does not normally earn enough dollars to cover its dollar expenditure, and in most years we have to draw on the sterling area dollar pool for the balance. As a counterpart to this arrangement, we have followed a common policy with the other members of the sterling area in economizing on dollar expenditure. . . .

The Government determined from the outset that any dollars raised by way of loan should be expended only on items of an indispensable kind that could not be obtained elsewhere than in North America. A careful study was made of our likely requirement for developmental plant and equipment during the next few years, and of the possible availability of such plant and equipment from the United Kingdom and other non-dollar sources. This list of requirements was, at the Prime Minister's request, examined by the United Kingdom authorities in London. They confirmed that, given the rate of development desired by the Australian Government, it would in general be impracticable for Australia to obtain the listed goods from United Kingdom production or from any other easy currency sources. It was recognized that, if we were to get the goods in time to meet our needs, there was no alternative to buying them from dollar sources. . . .

After three weeks of intensive but cordial negotiations between Australian officials and officials of the Bank, a loan agreement was signed in Washington by the Australian Ambassador and the President of the Bank on the 22nd August. . . .

I shall now describe briefly the imports that are to be financed under the loan. The broad categories are—

Tractors and other agricultural equipment
Industrial crawler tractors and earth moving equipment
Locomotives and rail-cars, including component parts therefor, and ancillary railway equipment
Plant for development of productive capacity in the following industries—
Textile
Paper making and paper working, including printing
Steel
Engineering
Building materials
Glass making and working, including ceramics
Chemical and pharmaceutical
Food processing
Boot and shoe

The fifth category covers plant for the development of productive capacity in major manufacturing industries in Australia. The severe restrictions imposed on the importation of plant and equipment from North America in recent years have retarded technological development in many branches of Australian secondary industry. The availability of loan funds will not, of course, mean that Australian industrialists will be given licences to import whatever they may want in the way of new plant and machinery from dollar sources. They will still be required to produce evidence that the plant and machinery are needed for developmental purposes and cannot be obtained from non-dollar sources. . . .

Source: *C.P.D.*, vol. 211, pp. 3518-26.

4:7 COMMONWEALTH FINANCE MINISTERS AIM AT CONVERTIBILITY OF STERLING

Extracts from Statement issued on 21 January 1952, following Conference of Commonwealth Finance Ministers in London from 15 to 21 January 1952.

We recognise that the sterling area is faced with a very serious crisis which, if it is not effectively dealt with, will have far-reaching consequences. The crisis has arisen because the sterling area as a whole is spending more than it is earning, with the result that its gold and dollar reserves have been falling at a rapid rate. . . .

3. . . . measures taken to stop the drain upon reserves must form part of a long-term policy designed to restore and maintain the full strength of sterling. . . .

5. The urgency of the immediate situation, and the present level of the gold reserves, require that the sterling area as a whole should be in balance with the rest of the world at latest in respect of the second half of 1952. It is imperative that this should include at least a balance with the dollar area within the same period. . . .

8. The methods by which members will contribute to these ends are within the discretion of each country concerned and will vary according to their individual circumstances. The first, and most important, step is to ensure that the internal economy is sound and that all possible measures are taken to combat inflation. This is not only essential for an improvement in the balance of payments but it will also help to keep down the cost of living. Another important requirement is to increase exports and earning power. In some cases long-term borrowing from outside the sterling area may be practicable. Finally, so far as other methods do not fully achieve the desired results, it will be necessary, as a temporary measure, to reduce imports. . . .

18. . . . it is our definite objective to make sterling convertible and to keep it so. We intend to work towards that goal by progressive steps aimed at creating the conditions under which convertibility can be reached and maintained. . . .

4:8 COMMONWEALTH ECONOMIC CONFERENCE AND CONVERTIBILITY OF STERLING

Final Communiqué of Commonwealth Economic Conference issued in London on 11 December 1952.

1. The Commonwealth Economic Conference, which ended today, was convened with the aim of concerting measures for increasing the economic strength of the Commonwealth countries, including the Colonial territories, and creating conditions in which their peoples can play their part in securing prosperity and contentment for themselves and for the world.

2. In recent years the sterling area has been faced with recurrent economic crises which have forced its members to take emergency measures of trade and exchange restriction. These measures were necessary but they have inevitably tended to frustrate the long-term economic expansion on which our hopes and opportunities for the future are founded. This was recognised at the January meeting of Commonwealth Finance Ministers. The measures taken in accordance with the conclusions of that meeting have, however, enabled the present Conference to decide that a more positive policy can now be adopted, both by the Commonwealth countries themselves and in concert with other friendly countries, to promote the expansion of world production and trade.

3. The Conference agreed that Commonwealth countries would work together to achieve certain broad common objectives. They have no intention of seeking the creation of a discriminatory economic bloc: rather, their object is, by strengthening themselves, to benefit the world economy generally.

Accordingly the following principles were agreed upon as governing the approach to the whole range of subjects under discussion:—

   (a) Internal economic policies designed to curb inflation and rises in the cost of living should be steadily followed.
   (b) Sound economic development should be encouraged with the object of increasing productive strength and competitive power, providing employment and raising the standards of life.
   (c) A multilateral trade and payments system should be extended over the widest possible area.

4. The application of these principles will require individual action by Commonwealth Governments, co-operation among them and international action with other trading nations and existing international organisations.

INTERNAL MEASURES

5. All Commonwealth Governments have agreed to persevere in their efforts to curb inflation. Inflationary conditions frustrate the progress of sound development, both by increasing its cost and by destroying the savings necessary to finance it. Moreover, they damage the external balance by stimulating excessive imports and by diverting to internal use goods which would otherwise be available for export.

6. An adequate and stable external balance must be a first objective for all Governments. . . .

7. The Conference considered the extensive restrictions which some countries of the sterling Commonwealth have needed to impose upon imports from the United Kingdom and other Commonwealth sources. There was agreement that

restrictions imposed because of balance of payments problems should be relaxed as the external financial position of countries improved. . . .

8. The economic and social objectives of the Commonwealth countries, individually and in association, depend upon their ability to produce and supply under competitive conditions an expanding flow of exports. There was therefore general agreement in the Conference on the vital need to expand the earning power of all sterling countries.

9. *Development Policy.* Throughout the Commonwealth there is wide scope for expanding the production of the essential supplies which the whole world needs—food and agricultural products, minerals and engineering products—and improving the means for transporting them. This development of the basic essentials has on occasion been impeded by other development of a less sound and permanent kind, which has overtaxed the countries' resources and has failed to contribute to the building of economic strength. The Conference agreed that in sterling area countries development should be concentrated on projects which directly or indirectly contribute to the improvement of the area's balance of payments with the rest of the world. Such projects should strengthen the economy of the countries concerned and increase their competitive power in world markets and so, by improving their balance of payments, bring increasing prosperity to their peoples. In some countries of the area, however, development plans have been or are being made to provide for some basic improvement in the standards of living, which is a necessary foundation for further economic development. Some social investment is also urgently needed in the more developed countries, certain of which have rapidly increasing populations. The Conference recognised the need in such cases for these types of investment.

10. To enable development to go forward a sufficient flow of savings must be provided in the countries undertaking the development and also in other countries which are ready to invest their savings there. The amount of savings which will be available from external sources will at best be small in relation to the size of the development programmes of countries of the sterling Commonwealth, and it is therefore essential that these countries should themselves adopt policies which increase the flow of savings—although this is inevitably a slow process for countries with low incomes and little margin above the basic needs for existence. . . .

11. The United Kingdom is the traditional source of external capital for Commonwealth investment and has special responsibilities in the Colonial territories. The United Kingdom Government are determined that the flow of capital from London for sound development throughout the Commonwealth shall be maintained and increased. This will only be possible if the United Kingdom can sustain the necessary level of internal savings and can achieve a surplus on overseas account additional to that required to meet its heavy existing commitments.

12. The United Kingdom Government have, however, undertaken to make a special effort to provide additional capital for Commonwealth development by facilitating the financing of schemes in other Commonwealth countries which will contribute to the improvement of the sterling area's balance of payments. . . .

15. *Commodity Policy.* The Conference recognised that there was no one universal remedy for the problem of instability of prices for primary commodities. Each commodity must be considered on its merits, in the light of the conditions prevailing at the time; and the circumstances must determine what form of

arrangements would be appropriate. The Conference agreed that violent fluctuations and an uneconomic level of prices for primary commodities were against the interests of consumers as well as producers.

All Commonwealth Governments are therefore ready to co-operate in considering, commodity by commodity, international schemes designed to ensure stability of demand and prices at an economic level. They also recognise the need for an agreed procedure for calling together the Governments concerned to consider emergency action in the event of rapidly developing conditions of surplus or shortage of commodities entering into international trade.

16. *Imperial Preference.* There was general recognition at the Conference of the value of existing preferences.

On the initiative of the United Kingdom a discussion took place on a proposal that all Commonwealth countries should join in seeking release from the 'no new preference' rule in the General Agreement on Tariffs and Trade (G.A.T.T.) and this United Kingdom proposal was supported by the representatives of some countries. The representatives of other countries felt that such an approach would not advance the agreed objective of restoring multilateral world trade and the Conference was therefore unable to support it.

All Commonwealth Governments agreed, however, to co-operate with the United Kingdom Government in an approach to the other contracting parties to the G.A.T.T. to meet particular difficulties arising on the United Kingdom tariff. The object would be to enable the United Kingdom, consistently with the basic provisions of the G.A.T.T., to continue the duty-free entry for Commonwealth goods notwithstanding any increases that might from time to time become necessary in duties designed to protect domestic industry and agriculture in the United Kingdom. The Commonwealth Governments also agreed to consider sympathetically certain special tariff problems affecting the Colonies.

INTERNATIONAL ACTION

17. Resolute action in accordance with the conclusions recorded above will in itself do much to strengthen the economies of the sterling Commonwealth countries. But this is not enough. Action in a wider sphere is also necessary. The Conference therefore agreed to seek the co-operation of other countries in a plan to create the conditions for expanding world production and trade. The aim is to secure international agreement on the adoption of policies, by creditor and debtor countries, which will restore balance in the world economy on the lines of 'Trade not Aid' and will, by progressive stages and within reasonable time, create an effective multilateral trade and payments system covering the widest possible area.

18. *Trade.* The plan envisages positive international action for the progressive removal, as circumstances permit, of import restrictions imposed for the purpose of bringing a country's external accounts into balance. Action will be required by both creditor and debtor countries. The rate of progress in removing discrimination will depend upon the advance towards equilibrium between the United States and the rest of the world.

19. The sterling Commonwealth countries will not all be able to remove restrictions at the same time. In particular, the representatives of some countries have emphasised that they must continue to use their exchange resources in the manner which enables them to carry out their planned development programmes most effectively, and that they are likely to continue to need import restrictions for this purpose.

20. *Finance.* The Conference agreed that it is important, not only for the United Kingdom and the sterling area but also for the world, that sterling should resume its full role as a medium of world trade and exchange. An integral part of any effective multilateral system is the restoration of the convertibility of sterling, but it can only be reached by progressive stages. The achievement of convertibility will depend fundamentally upon three conditions:—

(a) the continuing success of the action by sterling Commonwealth countries themselves, as outlined above;

(b) the prospect that trading nations will adopt trade policies which are conducive to the expansion of world trade;

(c) the availability of adequate financial support, through the International Monetary Fund or otherwise.

21. *Procedure.* It is proposed to seek acceptance of this plan by the Governments of the United States and of European countries, whose co-operation is essential, and to work as far as possible through existing international institutions dealing with finance and trade.

22. The timing of the successive stages of this plan cannot be decided at present. This can only be judged as the necessary conditions are satisfactorily fulfilled.

23. *Conclusion.* The Conference is happy to be able to present this account of the confident understanding which exists between members of the Commonwealth and the wide measure of agreement which they have been able to achieve over the whole range of economic policy. The aims of their co-operation are entirely consistent with their close ties with the United States and the members of the Organisation for European Economic Co-operation. The Commonwealth countries look outward to similar co-operation with other countries, not inward to a closed association. It is their common purpose, by their own efforts and together with others, to increase world trade for the mutual benefit of all peoples.

4:9 AUSTRALIA AND THE LONDON ECONOMIC CONFERENCE

Press statement by the Prime Minister (R. G. Menzies) on 28 December 1952.

The London Conference was not a 'crisis' conference. It was convened for four purposes, each of them related to long-term policy and designed to ensure steady progress towards the development of resources, the promotion of production and trade, and the ultimate achievement of convertibility of currencies. The reaching of this goal will, by the widening of markets and the stimulation of a flow of international investment, give vital aid to further development, production and trade.

In other words, we were seeking positive policies, moving away from artificial restrictions and towards greater freedom in the movement of goods and money.

The four purposes were:

(a) A frank and full interchange of ideas, policies, and experience, enabling each of the eight governments represented to review their own internal

118

policies and to learn what the other governments were themselves doing in the financial and economic field.

(b) The formulation of a set of principles the effectuation of which would assist in the gradual elimination of restrictions by the promotion of development and trade.

(c) The discovery of ways and means of increasing public and private investment calculated to assist adequate trade and payments balances.

(d) The preparation of specific plans for achieving convertibility, limited at first, but ultimately complete, so as to break down the exchange barriers which now cause a serious interference in trade between the dollar and sterling areas. . . .

The long-range principles evolved by the Conference were unanimously agreed upon. Briefly, they were:—

A resolute continuation of anti-inflationary policies, including control of credit, with of course such flexibility of application as new circumstances may require.

Policies of investment designed to secure a sound balance of payments position by encouraging the movement of capital into industries producing additional exports or reducing the demand for dollar imports in particular.

Policies of development giving high priority to works calculated to increase production, strengthen competitive power in overseas markets, maintain employment, and so provide a real foundation for increased living standards.

These principles are not a mere form of words. They are completely opposed to the foolish notion that needed capital can be secured by an inflationary use of central bank credit. The Conference states plainly that:—

Inflationary conditions frustrate the progress of sound development, both by increasing its cost and by destroying the savings necessary to finance it. Moreover, they damage the external balance by stimulating excessive imports and by diverting to internal use goods which would otherwise be available for export. . . .

4:10 COLLECTIVE COMMONWEALTH APPROACH TOWARDS STERLING CONVERTIBILITY

Communiqué of the Commonwealth Finance Ministers' Conference issued in Sydney on 15 January 1954.

We have met as the financial representatives of the United Kingdom, including its Colonial Territories, Canada, Australia, South Africa, New Zealand, India, Pakistan, Ceylon and the new Federation of Rhodesia and Nyasaland. . . .

1. The object of our present meeting was to consolidate the economic progress made by the Sterling Area and the Commonwealth during the last twelve months, to seek means to accelerate that progress and to ensure that they make their full contribution to world prosperity.

2. During the last year the Sterling Area countries of the Commonwealth have made great strides towards the objectives which they set for themselves in January, 1952, and confirmed and amplified in December, 1952. The Commonwealth countries rejected then, and we reject now, the view that any solution of

our problems can be found in the creation of a closed system of discriminatory arrangements, which could lead only to chronic restrictions and recurring crises. We therefore re-affirm our agreed objectives, which are to strengthen the position of each country and of sterling as a currency, and to establish with other countries a wider and freer system of trade and finance in which convertibility of sterling is an essential part. Thus we shall serve the best interests of all, not only in our own countries but in the world as a whole.

The Outlook for World Trade

3. We have considered the outlook for world trade. The Commonwealth is responsible for about one-third of that trade. We are conscious of the vital importance which the actions and policies of our countries could have when, as must be the case from time to time, there is some uncertainty about the future.

4. Our first resolve is to ensure that our own actions and policies will be such as to inspire confidence. We stand prepared to take appropriate steps, both individually and in concert with each other, to sustain production and trade and the sound development of resources, and to ensure that temporary economic fluctuations are not permitted to interfere with our progress towards our long-term objectives. We are also ready to co-operate with other countries and international institutions to this end. . . .

Progress in the Short-Term

10. The Conference then discussed current policies, namely:—
   (a) the maintenance of a strong balance of payments position and the strengthening of the central gold and dollar reserves;
   (b) sound internal policies and the need to restrain inflation;
   (c) economic development of resources.

11. Considerable progress has been made in the application of these policies during the past twelve months, a period when, despite weakness in certain commodity prices, economic conditions have been generally favourable. In the result the overall deficit in the sterling area balance of payments in 1951-52 was turned into a surplus in 1952-53, the position of sterling in the world has been strengthened and the central reserves have steadily increased. But we realize that much still remains to be done.

Short-Term Balance of Payments

12. The policies adopted since the meeting of Commonwealth Finance Ministers in January, 1952, have been at the base of the remarkable change in the balance of payments of the Sterling Area. In the year ending 30th June, 1953, the Sterling Area had a surplus of over £400 million in transactions with the outside world, compared with a deficit of nearly £1,000 million in the year ending 30th June, 1952. This marked improvement in the fortunes of the Sterling Area, to which all members have contributed, brought with it an increase of about £250 million in the central reserves of gold and dollars. These reserves have continued to increase, although rather more slowly, in the second half of 1953, and at the end of the year stood at £900 million. Throughout the period sterling has gained strength.

13. The Conference reviewed the prospects for the coming year. We agreed that the Sterling Area as a whole would seek to maintain a substantial surplus in its payments with the rest of the world. Earlier the main emphasis was placed on

dollar earnings. Although the dollar situation has improved, we should not relax our efforts to achieve a dollar surplus; but it is just as important to-day, that we should earn a substantial surplus in other non-sterling currencies. We recognize that success in these aims will depend in part on the level of world trade, but we emphasize that the primary task of all Sterling Area countries in the forthcoming year is to increase their earnings by intensive efforts over the whole field of exports.

14. In this task we must show ingenuity, increased efficiency and competitive strength. We cannot afford to disregard any market, and we must develop our exports wherever we can. While we must continue to expand our traditional major exports, we must also expand our exports of the immense variety of other products which in the aggregate form so large a proportion of the total earnings of the Sterling Area.

15. The Communiqué of the Commonwealth Economic Conference in December, 1952, referred to the extensive restrictions which some countries of the sterling Commonwealth had needed to impose upon imports from the United Kingdom and other Commonwealth sources. There was agreement at that time that these restrictions should be relaxed as the external financial position of these countries improved. We note with satisfaction the progress in this matter which has since been made by several Sterling Area countries and the prospects of further progress made possible by continuing improvement in their balance of payments.

Internal Policies

16. We have reviewed the internal policies of our countries and have observed that considerable improvement has been made during the past year. But more remains to be done and the importance of this part of our task cannot be over-emphasized. On the application of sound economic policies depends the purchasing power of money, the cost of living and the ability to sell exports in increasingly competitive world markets. Shortcomings in the internal policies of any one member affect the external fortunes of the whole sterling area by creating excessive demand for imports, diverting resources from export industries and throwing the balance of payments out of equilibrium. Our Governments will continue to follow the policies which have served satisfactorily in the past year. Where necessary they will be adjusted so as to encourage increased production for export and to stimulate savings, upon which the development of the Commonwealth substantially depends. . . .

The Collective Approach to Freer Trade and Payments[1]

25. We reaffirm our support for the proposals shortly referred to as the Collective Approach, which emerged from the Commonwealth Economic Conference of December, 1952. These proposals, which are set out in full in paragraphs 17 to 22 of the communiqué of that Conference, are designed in general to bring about the widest possible system of multilateral trade and payments, the reduction and progressive elimination of import restrictions, and the convertibility of sterling and other important currencies. They are based on collective action, by debtor and creditor countries, to bring about a balance in the world economy on the basis of 'Trade not Aid'.

[1] The 'Collective Approach' became the generally adopted description of the policies initiated in December 1952 and reaffirmed in January 1954.

26. The growing confidence in sterling and the increasing strength and flexibility of the economies of the Sterling Area countries have enabled them to make progress in the move towards expanding trade and freeing currencies. But decisive action must be related to the fulfilment of the conditions indicated in the communiqué of the Commonwealth Economic Conference. These conditions are—

(a) The continuing success of internal policies of sterling Commonwealth countries;

(b) The prospect that trading nations will adopt trade policies which are conducive to the expansion of world trade;

(c) The availability of adequate financial support, through the International Monetary Fund or otherwise.

27. We have noted with great satisfaction the passage in President Eisenhower's recent message to Congress in which he referred to the creation of a healthier and freer system of trade and payments in which others could earn their own living and the United States economy could continue to flourish. All Commonwealth countries await with interest the detailed recommendations which the President will make to Congress after the Joint Commission on the Foreign Economic Policy of the United States has made its report. While stressing the importance of the policies, external and internal, which our own countries should pursue, we believe that the forthcoming declaration of United States policies will have a profound significance for the free world.

28. We reaffirm the intention of our governments to work as far as possible through existing international organizations dealing with trade and finance.

29. The functions which the G.A.T.T. and the I.M.F. perform will become even more important when moves to freer trade and currencies are concerted; their rules, procedures and organization need close examination and review in some respects if they are to play a full and effective part. We note the forthcoming review of the G.A.T.T. and agree that there should be prior consultation among Commonwealth countries about this in the light of the circumstances then existing.

30. The Sterling Area has a close interest in the European Payments Union through the membership of the United Kingdom in that Union and the use of sterling in it. We will follow with interest the studies now proceeding in the O.E.E.C. on convertibility and how a transition can be best effected from the E.P.U. to a wider system of trade and payments. . . .

Source: Current Notes on International Affairs, vol. 25, pp. 27-34.

4:11 CANADA'S COOL RECEPTION TO BRITAIN'S NEW FREE TRADE SCHEME

OTTAWA, September 30th. First reaction in official Canadian quarters has been cool to Britain's offer to eliminate tariffs on Canadian goods if Canada reciprocates.

Some authorities believe that Anglo-Canadian free trade would wreck big sections of Canadian industry because Canadian production costs are higher than Britain's in many cases.

They say that if such keenly competitive products as textiles were freed of duty, British manufacturers might swamp the Canadian market and smash Canadian production.

The Canadian Press news agency says one Canadian argument is that under her proposed link with the European industrial free trade area Britain will be producing for a vastly expanded European market. This might further reduce her manufacturing costs and give her an even greater chance to undercut Canadian goods.

The British Chancellor of the Exchequer, Mr Peter Thorneycroft, disclosed the British plan at a Press conference on Saturday night. He called it possibly the most adventurous way of implementing the Canadian Prime Minister, Mr John Diefenbaker's suggestion that Canada should switch 15 per cent of her imports from the United States to Britain.

The Canadian Finance Minister, Mr Donald Fleming, said the proposal presented formidable difficulties. . . .

A Reuter Correspondent says that the British offer has had a 'bombshell' effect on the 11-nation meeting of Commonwealth Finance Ministers at Mont Tremblant, Quebec.

OTTAWA, October 6th. Britain did not press Canada for an expression of opinion on the Anglo-Canadian free trade area proposal at the Ottawa trade talks which ended on Friday.

A joint statement issued at the end of the bilateral conference said that it had been agreed that an expansion in Anglo-Canadian trade is a primary policy of both Governments.

The statement said British Ministers had emphasised that Britain's free trade area proposal was a long-term one and not designed to come into full effect over a period of 12 to 15 years.

The Ministers for both countries therefore concentrated on the immediate problem of expanding the beneficial two-way flow of trade between Canada and Britain.

Source: *Sydney Morning Herald*,
1 October 1957, p. 3, and
7 October 1957, p. 3.

4:12 COMMONWEALTH MINISTERS REAFFIRM SUPPORT FOR MULTILATERAL TRADE AND PAYMENTS SYSTEM, WITH RETENTION OF COMMONWEALTH PREFERENCE

Report of the Commonwealth Trade and Economic Conference, Montreal, September, 1958.

7. It is our firm belief that Commonwealth countries should continue to work in no exclusive spirit towards a multilateral trade and payments system over the widest possible area. We are also convinced that there are many things which can appropriately be done to increase trade between one Commonwealth country and another. Commonwealth participation in the preferential system has proved to be of mutual benefit and we have no intention of discarding or weakening it. Some of the trade agreements between Commonwealth countries now require review, and work has begun on renegotiating them. It is our intention to work towards an expansion of Commonwealth trade by all practicable means, and we have explored a number of these. . . .

10. It remains our objective that sterling should be made fully convertible as soon as the necessary conditions have been achieved and that trade discrimination should continue to be progressively removed in view of the advantages to be gained by so doing. We were glad to note the progress that has been made and we received with particular satisfaction the announcements made by the United Kingdom of further steps in that direction. . . .[1]

12. We were greatly encouraged by the announcement made last month by President Eisenhower that the United States would propose that a substantial enlargement of the resources of the International Monetary Fund should be considered. We endorse that initiative and will give it full support in principle at the meetings that are shortly to be held in New Delhi. We will support the parallel initiative that is also to be taken by the United States for the consideration of a substantial increase in the resources of the International Bank for Reconstruction and Development. . . .

23. Progress has, however, been continued in the reduction of discrimination against the dollar area, and during the Conference some important new measures of liberalization of dollar imports were announced.

24. The Australian Government have just taken a further step to reduce discrimination, a step which will open a further 10 per cent of Australia's total imports to the competition of dollar sources of supply. Over half of Australia's imports are now dealt with on a non-discriminatory basis.

25. The United Kingdom Government which had by 1957 freed over 60 per cent of all dollar imports from restriction, took a number of important steps earlier this year, including the freeing of imports of chemicals. They announced to the Conference a number of further immediate measures and outlined their future programme. The changes that have just been made comprise the freeing of canned salmon, newsprint and most classes of machinery. In addition, the Colonial Governments have been invited to relax their restrictions on a wide range of dollar imports. With these changes almost all materials, basic foodstuffs and 'tools of trade' are free of restriction. It is the United Kingdom intention to proceed with the removal of controls of imports from dollar sources. All being well, the United Kingdom hopes to make a start next year with as wide a range of consumer goods and foodstuffs as possible. . . .

31. The United Kingdom Government confirmed its intention of maintaining as an important element in the preferential system the free and unrestricted entry of nearly all goods imported from the Commonwealth. . . .

35. The Conference agreed that subject to the provisions of international agreements, Commonwealth countries should endeavour as soon as possible to remove discrimination in trade in the form of quantitative restrictions between the Commonwealth sources of supply unless this is necessary for balance of payments reasons.

Source: *Report of the Commonwealth*
Trade and Economic Conference,
Montreal, September 1958. Common-
wealth of Australia, Paper No. 7819/58,
Government Printer, Canberra.

[1] See *Sydney Morning Herald*, 19 September 1958 (p. 1), for announcement by the President of the Board of Trade on 18 September in Montreal concerning the removal of controls on dollar imports of industrial, agricultural, and office machinery.

4:13 NEGATIVE PROGRESS REPORT FROM MONTREAL

It is very paradoxical at first glance that the United Kingdom should make a family conference of the British Commonwealth nations at Montreal the occasion for an announcement that it will ease the restrictions on dollar imports, giving the United States more competitive scope against members of the family. There seem to be a number of reasons why the Australian delegation, led by Mr. McEwen, took the announcement calmly. First, as Mr. McEwen said, Australia has always stood for a freer convertibility of sterling into dollars; but he might have added that some Australians had held the pretty simple view that convertibility would mean we could exchange our sterling freely into dollars without bearing the consequences of British importers being able to do likewise.

The second point is that the relaxations on dollar imports will probably benefit Canada, a member of the family, relatively rather more than the U.S.A. This may apply particularly to Canadian machinery products, but there will be other primary export lines in which Canada's gain could to some extent be Australia's loss. Mr. McEwen's third inhibition against complaining, or ground for some consolation, is that Australia itself has already been enjoying the liberty to import, without discrimination, some of the dollar lines that Britain now proposes to admit.

It is certainly embarrassing at any time to object to proposals for the liberalising of international trade, but this moderate windfall for the United States at a moment when its own trade policies have been making things especially difficult for others would only seem appropriate if it is intended to influence or shame the Americans into better behaviour. If it manages, for instance, to kill the proposals for higher U.S. tariffs against lead and zinc, Australia will be relieved. If it breaks down some of the American tariffs against U.K. manufactures, Britain will have been properly compensated.

The sad fact remains, however, that Australia's most serious objections to American economic policies at present—that the U.S. domestic position is depressing commodity prices, while its huge stockpiles and methods of disposal amounting to dumping are doing the same—are not on matters opposed to the natural interests of the United Kingdom, but quite the contrary. Mr. McEwen himself recognises that a further easing of Britain's dollar restrictions will affect a widening sector of our exports, beginning with canned, dried, and fresh fruits.

The proceedings at the trade talks at Montreal have so far been the very opposite of helpful to Australia's serious trading predicament. The talks have not yet, incidentally, produced a materialising of Mr. Diefenbaker's original bold ideas for inter-Commonwealth trade which largely inspired them. That such talks are of limited effectiveness when confined to Commonwealth countries has been underlined by the outside noises to be heard in Montreal of Russian inroads upon the tin market and American plans to depress lead and zinc even further.

Source: Leading article in the *Sydney Morning Herald*, 23 September 1958.

4:14 AUSTRALIA WELCOMES UNITED KINGDOM'S MOVE TOWARDS CONVERTIBILITY

Statement by the Treasurer (H. E. Holt) in December 1958.

United Kingdom: Commenting on December 27 on the United Kingdom Government's announcement of further measures being taken towards full convertibility of sterling, the Federal Treasurer, Mr. H. E. Holt, said that the decision indicated that, in the judgment of the United Kingdom Government, the position of sterling was not only strong, but likely to remain so. . . It had been recognised at Montreal that the final decision of timing of further moves toward convertibility must rest with the United Kingdom Government, which would take into account the interests of the Commonwealth as a whole in any such decision.

It did not seem that, apart from certain technical changes in exchange control regulations, there would have to be any immediate modification as a result of the new measures in the policies being followed in Australia in relation to overseas payments or to import licensing, Mr. Holt said. The Australian Government had already taken substantial steps towards reducing import licensing discrimination against dollar imports and towards liberalising other dollar payments, for example, by increasing the dollar travel allowance. It was the Government's policy to carry out, as circumstances permitted, an orderly programme of eliminating what remained of dollar discrimination. Those moves represented an advanced step towards achieving full convertibility of sterling, which the Australian Government had always strongly supported.

Source: Australia in Facts and Figures,
no. 60, p. 37.

5

THE GENERAL AGREEMENT
ON TARIFFS AND TRADE

Seven key decisions relate to the subject of this section. The first is the decision to accept the Articles and the results of the 1947 tariff negotiations carried out under them. This decision was reviewed in Section 3; but here we have provided more documents which explain the Articles themselves. The second is the decision in 1953 to seek a major review of the GATT (5:1). The third is the agreement to attempt a major and in important ways a novel round of tariff negotiations—the so-called 'Kennedy Round' (5:11, 5:12). The fourth decision, the adoption of a new Part IV, containing three Articles on trade problems of underdeveloped or 'developing' countries, is documented in Section 6 which is devoted to these problems. The fifth and sixth decisions—the formation of the European Common Market (the SIX, or EEC) and, separately, the European Free Trade Area (the SEVEN, or EFTA) under Article XXIV of GATT—are reviewed in Section 8, together with the seventh decision—the British application in 1961 to join the Common Market. The bearing of the last three decisions on the future of GATT receives some consideration also in the final Review, Section 18. In this section, then, the documents relate to the nature of the GATT contract, to the substantial review of it which took place in 1954 and 1955, and to the Kennedy Round.

We have seen, in Section 3, how GATT came to be accepted as a provisional instrument to cover tariff negotiations of 1947 (3:11, 3:12)[1] and, unexpectedly, as a residual and clearly more permanent arrangement, to fill the gap in international economic machinery which resulted from the failure to bring the ITO into being. Under the General Agreement as negotiated in 1947 the contracting parties agreed to contribute to the general aims of full employment and growing volume of real income and expansion of the production

---

[1] These tariff negotiations commenced in April 1947 and the resulting concessions were incorporated in the Schedules to Article II of GATT. They were signed by Australia on 30 October 1947 and came into force on 1 January 1948. Article II also incorporates the results of further tariff negotiations: in 1949, Annecy (France); 1950-1, Torquay (England); 1956 and 1960-1, Geneva. These negotiations were all conducted under agreed rules based on provisions of Article XVII of the abortive ITO Charter. The negotiations in the Kennedy Round are conducted under fresh rules specially drawn up to meet the new approach to tariff negotiations. See text below. On the early 1947, 1949 and 1951 negotiations see Nicholson (132).

and exchange of goods. To implement these aims they agreed to grant one another MFN treatment in respect of exports and imports; to enter into negotiations for reduction of tariffs; and to eliminate preferences. However, certain *existing* preferences, including British Commonwealth preferences, were to be retained, and customs unions or free trade areas were permitted.

A code of rules governing trade was also agreed to, covering such matters as international aspects of internal taxation and regulation, anti-dumping and countervailing duties, restrictions on imports and exports for balance of payments and protective reasons, and subsidies. As we have seen in Section 3 these were regarded as 'interim' rules only to cover the tariff negotiations in 1947 and to be superseded by the more comprehensive Havana Charter establishing the International Trade Organization. They have, however, provided the one international code binding an increasing number of members.[2]

Review of GATT

Document A5:1 is a summary of the Articles of GATT. The summary takes into account changes made as the result of the so-called Review Session (Ninth Session) of 1954-5.[3] This Review constitutes the first of the two principal subjects of this section. Australia had participated fully in the original tariff negotiations and had granted concessions and made gains, especially the cut in the U.S. wool tariff (Section 3). It was not any dissatisfaction with these tariff bargains that caused Australia to seek a review of the GATT (5:1); it was a sense that GATT was 'imbalanced' in relation to Australia's interests.

Feeling was strong: the question, 'Should Australia remain in GATT?' was not mere rhetoric used for bargaining purposes.[4] Australia's determination

[2] The original membership numbered twenty-three; at November 1966 it stood at seventy.

[3] Another, but less complete, Article by Article 'summary' is to be found in the Vernon Report (11), vol. I, ch. 12, where, however, the précis is mixed with some comments as to the significance of the Articles from the Australian viewpoint. It does, in this way, serve to clarify the technical language of many of the Articles. For a more detailed and primary study of the Articles, their meaning and origin, see

(a) *Provisional Consolidated Text of The General Agreement on Tariffs and Trade and Texts of Related Documents* (96);
(b) *Basic Instruments and Selected Documents. Volume III: Text of the General Agreement 1958* (80);
(c) 'Review of the General Agreement on Tariffs and Trade held at Geneva, 8th November, 1954 to 7th March, 1955' (13) (usually referred to as the White Paper). Extracts are given in 5:4.

The main text of this White Paper is a useful annotated comparison of pre-review text and amended text of the GATT Articles.

[4] This feeling had two strands. One was the highly vocal and often inaccurate criticism of GATT by the Associated Chambers of Manufactures of Australia (3:16). Their main worry was the alleged slowness to act on Tariff Board recommendations for increases in the tariffs where these increases required 'unbinding' of bound rates under

to consider the question in certain eventualities was taken seriously—and properly so—in both London and Washington. Nevertheless, the fact that the question was asked, and referred to seriously, reflected frustration rather than certainty that any satisfactory alternative was readily available. Certainly it cannot be said confidently that Australia would have withdrawn from GATT had the Review Session been a 'failure' from the viewpoint of Australian interests. As Document 5:1 makes clear, the strong presumption was against withdrawal. Nevertheless, the judgment made there was not conclusively shared by all ministers and officials of the government (5:3). In my mind the question was a valid one to raise, though I considered then (as I do today: see Review Section) that with all its continued shortcomings Australia's interests were best served by remaining in GATT.

The documents, especially 5:2, are unusually complete on the official reasons for Australia's disquiet about GATT. Perhaps the simplest way to sum up Australia's criticism is in terms of the lack of genuine reciprocation in the practical operation of the articles of GATT.[5] This sense of imbalance arose from the realisation that some tariff concessions gained from European countries and the United States in 1947 were being nullified by the operation of non-tariff devices, protective in effect and often in intention. It was felt that if the rules governing non-tariff restrictions on imports or subsidies on exports were properly applied, Australia's trade would suffer much less from these restrictions. Actual tariff concessions mutually agreed could only be in stable balance if all the rules were operated uniformly well by members. It seemed apparent that the rules most affecting Australia's export interests (such as those disallowing quantitative restrictions except under special circumstances) were the ones most likely to be observed in the breach.

A particular case of non-reciprocation relates to the practical impairment by some of Australia's partners of the MFN principle, which is the heart of a multilateral trading system. Under it (A5:1, Article I) any tariff concessions extended by one contracting party (i.e. a member of GATT) to another is automatically extended to all other members. In a compact in which mutual concessions and gains resulting directly and indirectly from negotiations are balanced as the result of the bargaining, it can be said that the MFN relationship is in balance. This is true even under the conditions of automatic exten-

---

Article XXVIII. The other strand stemmed more from official circles (especially the Department of Commerce and Agriculture), where frustration at failure to get the Contracting Parties to remove non-tariff barriers to agricultural trade was felt keenly. Their argument was that just given, namely, that Australia did not enjoy true reciprocation of benefits under the agreement.

[5] For an excellent discussion of the implications of the MFN clause, see Curzon (68), ch. III. Curzon's book is the best serious study of GATT and contains an excellent bibliographical list of GATT documents, including many of Australian origin (delegates' speeches) not easily available and not publicly known in Australia.

sion. Australia's case against GATT was that where tariff concessions affecting trade in primary products are negotiated, as they had been with the United States and some European countries later to become members of the Common Market, non-tariff barriers[6] appear to vitiate the concession. Mutual tariff concessions may be in balance on paper, but not in practice if one or more of the several parties undoes its tariff concessions by direct, non-tariff restrictions. Australia operated its tariff in accordance with MFN principles and unimpaired by non-tariff measures, but different and more restrictive policies, in practice if not in theory, seemed to apply to its export trade in primary products.

In short, Australia's trading partners have applied the MFN principles in their tariff, but have too often impaired both direct and indirect concessions by breach of other rules (such as Article XI—General Elimination of Quantitative Restrictions—and Article XVI—Subsidies) designed to safeguard the mutual balance of tariff concessions negotiated under the Agreement. Australia's further difficulty (and complaint) has been that even a willingness on her part to negotiate non-permissible but *de facto* non-tariff barriers of trade has met with poor response.[7]

That there were other difficulties for trade in primary products was becoming evident, too (Section 6); but these served only to add to frustrations under GATT. The problem of tariff-making procedures is fully outlined in 5:2 and was satisfactorily resolved.[8] The preference issue was elevated (5:1, 5:4) to a level of importance rather beyond any practical possibilities. It was known from Commonwealth talks (see for example 5:4 and 4:8) that not even the major Commonwealth countries were with us. The British affirmative vote was formal and reflected no measure of active assistance in the GATT

[6] Such as import quotas and embargoes restricting freedom of access which, under GATT, should (except when balance of payments difficulties apply) be restrained only by regular tariff barriers (Articles XI and XII). As one observer commented: 'There were to be no exceptions to this rule—not even for infant industries, for agriculture, or for industries considered essential to national security' (Gardner (78), ch. III, quoted by Curzon (68), p. 30).

[7] Probably the best response in these matters has come from Japan within the framework of the trade treaty with that country (Section 10).

[8] To the extent that Australia gained special facilities under Article XXVIII of GATT it may be said to have achieved some offset to the rigidity of the non-tariff restrictions imposed by others on her trade. This follows from the fact that Australia can move more quickly than most to unbind tariff concessions made by it. The tariff unbinding procedure is a highly technical matter, and those interested will be helped by the White Paper above cited, especially the notes on Articles XIX and XXVIII. See also Vernon Report (11), vol. I, ch. 12, para. 55 and footnote. It is a matter of some importance that Australia ranks second only to the United States in frequency of use of Article XIX. During periods of *firm* binding the procedures under Article XXVIII for unbinding are more restrictive than they are at certain regular intervals of time (for explanation see Vernon Report). For Australia, however, the degree of restriction is considerably less than for most members—a concession to its special 'mid-way' position.

negotiations, though it did have an important bearing on the subsequent review of the Ottawa Agreement (Section 9).

There certainly appears to be something illogical about a refusal to allow preference margins to be re-negotiated when 'bound' tariff rates are negotiable. Yet the limitation on preferences was the main outcome of the American hopes on this question under Article VII of the Mutual Aid Agreement and it was useless to expect flexibility in that quarter. Nor did the Prime Minister's reference to the preferences under Article XXIV, customs unions (5:1), now heavily in evidence in the EEC and EFTA (Section 8), elicit response.[9]

If the preference issue was a dead loss for Australian negotiators there were many gains, and it is fair to regard GATT as McEwen did, as a less unbalanced instrument after the Review than before.[10] It could not be said that full balance was restored, and the issue of agricultural protectionism was to continue to be the principal difficulty for Australia, along with slow progress in the matter of commodity agreements.[11] An especial disappointment was the insistence by the United States at the Review Session itself on a waiver (Article XXV) for its import quotas and for embargoes on certain agricultural products. The German situation, too, was fully ventilated and, while yielding some tangible benefit, served as a clear warning of difficulties to be faced in the years to come. It became more than ever apparent that it was not going to be practicable to treat trade in agricultural products in the same unequivocal way as trade in most industrial products.[12] In short, the prospects for an effective reciprocation of MFN treatment in the Australian tariff were not greatly advanced.

In the subsequent period Australia certainly benefited from the speedier procedures made available to it under Article XXVIII for tariff action other-

[9] The truth is that preferences under Ottawa had been accorded mostly by *raising* duties against third countries; under customs unions they are accorded to members, not by raising tariffs against third countries but by lowering and finally eliminating them for members only. This is a real difference.

[10] In view of the availability of a White Paper and the long review by McEwen in the course of the negotiations (5:3), as well as his opening speech at the Conference (5:2), his post-conference reviews have not been included. However, two very similar speeches give the political flavour of satisfaction with results in relation to those sought in his speech to the Conference. These are in an address in the House of Representatives on 2 June 1955 (*C.P.D.*, vol. 6, pp. 1411 ff.), and *The Recent Review of* GATT (118).

[11] Considerable energy was devoted to drawing up a special agreement on commodity arrangements, but for various reasons, including objections on Australia's part, this came to naught. See Section 3 for a brief comment on the confusion which has attended international administration of commodity matters. See also Nicholson (132), pp. 161-2.

[12] The word 'most' is necessary because it also became apparent at the Review Session that trouble was brewing over cotton textiles and other cheap manufactures from the underdeveloped countries.

wise limited by agreements under GATT.[13] It also gained distinctly from the improved Article XVI under which it was later able to secure limits to 'unfair' competition in flour markets by Germany and France (5:8, 5:9), and from the improved consultation procedures agreed to by the United States in respect of 'surplus disposals'. It also defeated attempts to make action under Article XII (import restrictions for balance of payments reasons) dependent upon GATT approval and gained recognition of Australia's 'middle' position: a country dependent upon primary exports but also on industrialisation and neither an advanced industrial country nor an underdeveloped one requiring the most liberal treatment provided in Articles XVIII and XXVIII *bis*. This 'middle-zone' position has become one of increasing difficulty, but its recognition in GATT has certainly helped in tariff matters.[14]

Despite the disappointments, especially over agricultural protectionism, enough redress was achieved to render unnecessary any post-Review examination of the wisdom of Australia's continued membership of GATT.[15] If the United States had forsaken GATT—a real prospect had the waiver been refused—there is little doubt that GATT would have floundered or have continued with the United States remaining in only by ignoring the voting result against it. For either situation Australia could not afford to be held responsible, as it might have been, for it led the attack on the United States policies and received vigorous support for its views on non-tariff barriers to trade.[16] Subsequent events—especially the emergence of the Common Agricultural Policy now in operation under the Rome Treaty (Sections 6 and 7)—have perhaps given renewed cause for re-opening the question of membership, but further comment on this is reserved until the final section.

One matter affecting Australia's interest on which progress in GATT has been very slow is the development of 'rules' to cover trade with state-trading (mostly Communist) countries.[17] Some progress is being made, with Australia keen to develop such rules. In this, however, the United Kingdom and some other industrialised countries are not enthusiastic. They

---

[13] It is well to remind readers that GATT imposes no limits on tariff making except where duties have been bound under negotiated agreements and, of course, except in respect of proposals to widen margins of preference. As seen, Article XXVIII preserves procedures for unbinding bound duties. Australia's special position under this Article (5:4) is particularly noteworthy recognition of its middle-zone position and of the nature of its tariff-making machinery.

[14] This concept receives further mention in the Review Section 18. For full explanation and analysis of the concept, see Vernon Report (11), vol. I, ch. 12, paras. 22-3, and especially Arndt (2).

[15] McEwen's conversion to GATT was somewhat overstated by the *Sydney Morning Herald* (5:5).

[16] This view, in my judgment, remains valid even though the expected organisation for trade co-operation—a *quid pro quo* for not opposing the waiver in the final vote—failed to materialise, again owing to difficulties with Congress.

[17] See Curzon (68), ch. X.

132

prefer firm bilateral commitments to any 'global' (i.e. comprehensive) quotas that might make access to Communist markets competitive in the GATT sense of multilateral trade. The issue has not been important enough to be reflected in public documents: it is doubtful whether Australia's trade interests have been greatly harmed.[18]

Another subject which receives little or no mention in the public documents is 'nullification and impairment'. Article XXIII provides for allowable retaliatory action by a complainant who fails to secure 'satisfactory adjustment' for a demonstrated damage. Thus Australia could proceed against the United States because of damage done by her import restrictions on agricultural products. (The *waiver* enjoyed by the United States does not absolve her from this risk.) However, as the Vernon Committee noted, the difficulty about the Article is to find action (e.g. against United States exports) likely to hurt the offender without hurting the complainant.[19] Australia has not invoked the Article although it has seriously considered doing so.

Something of the same problem exists when action is taken to unbind 'bound' duty rates, for the country whose interests are adversely affected is rarely satisfied with the alternative concession offered. This is the main reason why frequent Australian use of unbinding procedures available under Article XXVIII is not popular with the other contracting parties. Excessive use of freedom here is calculated to reduce respect for our complaints on other matters. This will be more and more the case with the less developed countries if we unbind tariff concessions of significance to their trade.

The Kennedy Round

The evolution of GATT did not stop with the amendments to its Articles accepted at the Review Session. There have been continuing efforts, especially in the detailed committee work of GATT (5:7), to provide for expansion of world trade and to deal with the growing and seemingly intractable problem of agricultural protectionism.[20] In the course of these efforts major problems have emerged. Some of them—those related to the less developed countries—have been so great politically that they have led to a new world trade organisation. This is the Trade and Development Board, dealt with in Section 6, which also reviews the persistent efforts of GATT itself to deal with the trading problems of the less developed countries.

It is interesting to note that the Haberler Committee appointed in 1957 to review, *inter alia*, agricultural protectionism as it affected exporters of primary products, was the result of an Australian initiative in GATT (5:6). Its

[18] The recent MFN treaty with Russia is referred to in Section 12.

[19] Vernon Report (11), vol. I, ch. 12, para. 52.

[20] As noted earlier, some tangible progress was achieved in respect of Australia's flour trade (5:8, 5:9).

133

F

Report served the Australian objective well,[21] for it undoubtedly brought out the obstructions to world trade in temperate zone agricultural products represented by agricultural protectionism, and so removed something of the defensive flavour of repeated Australian statements on the subject. The Report also admirably opened up discussion of the trading problems of the less developed countries and has contributed significantly to the greatly increased attention given in GATT to the problems of these countries. Only meagre progress has been made in stabilising and expanding trade opportunities both in temperate foodstuffs (Australia's interests) and in tropical produce (of more vital concern to the less developed countries), not to mention the difficult problem of quantitative restrictions imposed on exports of manufactures from underdeveloped countries and Japan (5:7). These problems receive comment in Sections 6 and 7.

One outcome of the program for expanding world trade was the 'Dillon Round' of tariff negotiations in 1960-2.[22] These were of no moment to Australia since the tariff on United States wool imports was not negotiable. Concurrent with these formal negotiations were efforts to devise a more spectacular means of tariff negotiation. The United States Trade Expansion Act of October 1962, sponsored by President Kennedy, gave the President powers to negotiate very large 'across the board' tariff reductions—at least of the order of 50 per cent of rates as they stood in October 1962.[23] This gave the United States administration room for spectacular initiative aimed especially at the Common Market. This initiative would have been the more spectacular had Britain joined the Common Market, for duties could have been eliminated altogether on articles in which 80 per cent of world trade was accounted for jointly by the United States and the EEC—a circumstance only likely to arise if the United Kingdom were a member of the EEC. The outcome was the decision of 21 May 1963 (5:11) providing for the linear 'across the board' approach to tariff cutting and for negotiations to begin in May 1964. These are the negotiations known as the Kennedy Round, Australia's interest in which forms the second principal subject in the documents of this section.

Document 5:12 indicates why this resolution placed Australia in a dilemma. Of great value to Australia were paragraphs 3 and 7 of the resolution under which the negotiations could include non-tariff barriers to trade and would attempt to 'provide for acceptable conditions of access to world mark-

[21] *Trends in International Trade* (the Haberler Report) (81) is a report by a panel of experts established in terms of a decision of the Twelfth Session of GATT. Professor Gottfried Haberler of Harvard acted as Chairman of the group, the other members being Campos, Meade, and Tinbergen. The Report remains highly relevant to the current problems besetting trade in primary products.

[22] See Curzon (68), pp. 99-100.

[23] The Common Market had offered to negotiate 'across the board' at an earlier date (up to 20 per cent), but at that time (1960) the United States lacked sufficient power.

ets for agricultural products'. Australian delegations had fought strongly for both these points for several years—against United States indifference and even opposition in the early stages. It was only when the Common Agricultural Policy of the EEC (Section 8) began to obstruct United States exports that Washington adopted a more positive approach. This approach was also influenced by the solid reporting of Committee II of GATT which dealt continuously with the problems of agricultural protectionism (5:7).

These were gains. On the other hand, Australia could not easily contemplate any 'across the board' cut in tariffs, especially a large one. Solid reasons are given in 5:12, including the improbability that any linear cut in tariffs on manufactures by the advanced industrial nations would significantly benefit Australia's export trade. Even if these reasons did not exist, it would be difficult to apply linear cuts to both MFN and BPT rates in the Australian tariff, should this be necessary to preserve obligatory preferential margins on imports of British goods.[24] Nevertheless, British participation in the Kennedy Round will necessarily lead to a review of preference margins extended to Britain, quite independently of MFN tariff cuts Australia may be prepared to make to the United States, European countries, and Japan, for Britain will almost certainly wish to offer countries like Denmark and the United States cuts in tariff rates applicable to their agricultural exports, thereby reducing preferences enjoyed by Australia. The greater part of Australia's difficulty, however, is that a linear cut in MFN rates would adversely affect several industries unable to survive without a substantial tariff. Yet Australia cannot expect to make gains in the shape of improved access for wool in the United States and for foodstuffs in Europe and be a beneficiary (although minor) of all the 'across the board' cuts in tariffs on manufactures by Europe and North America, without some reciprocation.[25] To this end—since Australia is fully committed to participation—the special but naturally confidential reports of the Tariff Board on the scope that exists for MFN tariff reduction will be of great importance.[26] This is provided—and always provided—any-

[24] Difficulties would not arise if cuts in the MFN rates could be made without impairing our contractual preferential obligations (mostly 10 per cent margin—see Section 9).

[25] Under the MFN rule of Article I of GATT Australia must be an automatic beneficiary of tariff reductions made by other contracting parties. Whether she can take practical advantage is another question. It needs to be noted that Australia may cut some MFN rates without hurting its industry. All such cuts can do is encourage import competition at Britain's expense in respect of such goods as are imported under the tariff items in question. Any tariff reduction that 'bites' must either impair the hold of the local producers on the Australian market or force them to share 'growth' in the total market or, preferably, so raise their efficiency through import competition that they can hold their own despite the apparently damaging tariff cut. Many items of the Australian tariff seem open to attack on the ground that they are too high to encourage this last kind of import competition (Section 14).

[26] There have been two general references to the Tariff Board, one in 1959 and the other in 1963 (5:13, 9:17).

135

thing of interest does happen by way of agreement on market opportunities for Australia's exports.

In this last connection it is to be noted that at the time of writing (December 1966), the Kennedy Round is reaching its final stages. It has not yet made significant progress, mainly owing to the internal difficulties of the Common Market, which have particularly hampered formal negotiations on agriculture (5:14). The deadline for the completion of the round is 30 June 1967. Nevertheless the GATT Trade Negotiations Committee is operating.[27] Of the three commodity groups mentioned in 5:12 the Cereals Group has been the most active (with full EEC support) and shows some promise of producing a result significant for Australia (Section 7).

The emergence of GATT as an active forum for commodity agreements, although clearly connected with the Kennedy Round, raises problems of its relations institutionally with FAO and the Trade and Development Board of UNCTAD. (See also Section 3 and Review Section.) It is beyond the scope of this book to document this institutional problem in detail.[28] At this point, however, it is important to stress again that if agreements within GATT are negotiated in terms offering a ceiling to agricultural protectionism, some assurances about minimum prices and some improvement in market access, Australia will have to reciprocate in some way.[29] This may be in terms of ceilings to export prices, production controls or restrictions under certain conditions, or in tariff concessions thought to match the improved market access.

In making this comment on the difficulties of Australia's participation in the Kennedy Round we have not referred specifically to her status as a middle-zone country. It is probably not a good term for use outside GATT, for reasons noted elsewhere (Review Section 18). Nevertheless, the acceptance of Australia's inability to negotiate 'across the board' is the most notable instance of its real significance for purposes of commercial diplomacy. Moreover, willingness to accept the Australian position is a reminder that access to the Australian market is of importance to the other contracting parties, especially the advanced industrial members. Since these countries have not, in the past, made any very helpful moves, even to negotiate, let alone improve access for Australia's agricultural products, the Kennedy Round will determine whether increased access to the Australian market renders it worth

[27] On the organisation of the Kennedy Round and the draft time schedule see Curzon (68), pp. 103-5, *The Activities of* GATT (79), and the Vernon Report (11), vol. 1, para. 12.57.

[28] See A3:4 for a brief account of some international institutions dealing with commodity problems.

[29] It is true that Australia may attempt to claim as an offset to any necessary reciprocation the degree of impairment of earlier 1947 tariff concessions by European countries already paid for, but not enjoyed, by Australia because of non-tariff barriers which have undone the benefit of the 1947 tariff concessions.

while for the advanced countries to pay the price demanded by Australia—reduction in agricultural protectionism or, in practical terms, assured and predictable access for her products. The outlook at this stage for any spectacular or even significant result is not hopeful. Nor is it yet hopeless.

A5:1 GENERAL AGREEMENT ON TARIFFS AND TRADE: SUMMARY OF ARTICLES

PREPARED BY NANCY ANDERSON

This summary is based on the original text of the General Agreement on Tariffs and Trade drawn up at Geneva in 1947 and incorporating certain subsequent protocols modelled on clauses in the 1947 Geneva draft of the Charter for an International Trade Organisation.

Important amendments made as a result of the review of the Agreement carried out between November, 1954 and March, 1955 are shown in brackets at the end of the relevant article.

ARTICLE I—*General Most-Favoured-Nation Treatment*

The article provides for the mutual accord by the parties thereto of unconditional most-favoured-nation treatment with respect to customs duties or charges on the import or export of goods, or on the international transfer of payments for imports or exports. Such treatment is also to be extended to formalities associated with imports or exports, and internal taxation and regulation of goods.

The article expressly permits the retention of preferences existing at certain specified dates (1947 or earlier) between certain groups of territories, including the British Preferential Area. No new preferences can be granted or margins of preference increased beyond the absolute level existing at the base date, which in the case of Australia is 15 October 1946.

ARTICLE II—*Schedules of Concessions*

The article provides that contracting parties shall accord to each other treatment no less favourable than that provided for in their Schedules of Concessions annexed to the Agreement.

The article also permits the imposition on imported goods of internal charges equivalent to those imposed on domestic goods, and allows the imposition of anti-dumping or countervailing duties consistent with Article VI.

Where a product subject to a concession is subject to a State monopoly the operation of the monopoly should not afford protection on the average in excess of the protection provided for in the schedule.

ARTICLE III—*National Treatment of Internal Taxation and Regulations*

The article provides for the exemption of imported products from internal taxes and charges of any kind in excess of those applied to like products of national origin. No new taxes on imported products may be instituted to afford protection to national products not similarly taxed, if there is no substantial production of such national products.

137

National treatment is to be accorded imported products in respect of all requirements affecting internal sale, purchase, transportation, etc. Differential transportation charges may be imposed based exclusively on economic operation of the means of transport, and not on the nationality of the product.

The article also contains provisions prohibiting regulations for the mixture, processing, etc., of domestic products where there is no substantial production of such products. Regulations already in force on a base date are excluded from operation of these provisions. The article does not apply to products purchased for governmental purposes and shall not prevent the payment of subsidies exclusively to domestic producers, and subsidies effected through governmental purchases of domestic products.

ARTICLE IV—*Special Provisions Relating to Cinematograph Films*

Regulations regarding cinematograph films are to take the form of screen quotas. Requirements to which such quotas shall conform are laid down.

ARTICLE V—*Freedom of Transit*

The article defines goods, vessels, etc. deemed to be in transit, and provides for freedom of transit. The article requires that most-favoured-nation treatment shall be accorded to such goods, vessels, etc. No unnecessary delays or restrictions are to be imposed.

ARTICLE VI—*Anti-Dumping and Countervailing Duties*

Dumping of products by one country in another country is to be condemned if it causes or threatens material injury to an established industry of a contracting party or materially retards the establishment of a domestic industry.

Certain limitations are placed on the imposition of anti-dumping and countervailing duties. No anti-dumping duty is to be levied on any product in excess of an amount equal to the defined margin of dumping under which the product is being imported. No countervailing duty is to be levied on any product in excess of an amount equal to the estimated bounty or subsidy determined to have been granted on the manufacture, production or export of such product in the country of origin or exportation.

[The Contracting Parties are to authorise the levying of countervailing duties to protect the industries of a third country against subsidisation of exports by another country where material injury is caused or threatened by such subsidisation.

In exceptional circumstances, where delay might cause damage difficult to repair, countervailing duties to prevent injury to an established domestic industry may be imposed without the prior approval of the Contracting Parties.]

ARTICLE VII—*Valuation for Customs Purposes*

The article sets out general principles to be followed in valuation of goods for customs purposes.

ARTICLE VIII—*Formalities Connected with Importation and Exportation*

Fees and charges in connection with customs formalities are to be limited to the approximate cost of the services for which they are levied. The article provides that no substantial penalties shall be imposed for minor breaches of customs regulations.

138

ARTICLE IX—*Marks of Origin*

The article provides for most-favoured-nation treatment of goods in relation to marking requirements. Such requirements are to be reasonable, and the article lays down general principles to be followed. The use of trade names, etc., with a view to misrepresentation of the true origin of the goods is not to be permitted.

ARTICLE X—*Publication and Administration of Trade Regulations*

The article provides for the prompt publication by parties to the Agreement of laws, regulations, judicial decisions and administrative rulings affecting classification of goods, rates of duty, etc., and requirements, restrictions, or prohibitions on imports or exports or on transfer of payments. The article covers all requirements affecting the import or export of goods, and provides that there shall be no enforcement of such laws, regulations, etc. before publication.

ARTICLE XI—*General Elimination of Quantitative Restrictions*

No prohibitions or restrictions other than duties, taxes or other charges shall be instituted or maintained by any contracting party on the importation of any product of the territory of any other party or on the exportation or sale for export of any product destined for the territory of any other party. These provisions do not apply to the following:

(a) export prohibitions or restrictions temporarily applied to prevent or relieve critical shortages of foodstuffs or other products essential to the exporting contracting party;

(b) import and export prohibitions or restrictions necessary to the application of standards or regulations for the classification, grading or marketing of commodities in international trade;

(c) import restrictions on any agricultural or fisheries product, imported in any form, necessary to the enforcement of governmental measures which operate:

(i) to restrict the quantities of the like domestic product permitted to be marketed or produced, or, if there is no substantial domestic production of the like product, of a domestic product for which the imported product can be directly substituted; or

(ii) to remove a temporary surplus of the like domestic product, or, if there is no substantial domestic production of the like product, of a domestic product for which the imported product can be directly substituted, by making the surplus available to certain groups of domestic consumers free of charge or at prices below the current market level; or

(iii) to restrict the quantities permitted to be produced of any animal product the production of which is directly dependent, wholly or mainly, on the imported commodity, if the domestic production of that commodity is relatively negligible.

Any restrictions applied under (i) above must not reduce the total of imports relative to the total of domestic production as compared with the proportion which might reasonably be expected to rule between the two in the absence of restrictions.

[A *decision* was recorded providing for waiving of obligations of Article XI to the extent necessary to allow the temporary maintenance of import restrictions which have afforded incidental protection to industries. The only actual amendment was to delete a paragraph which included in the definition of 'restrictions' those made effective through state-trading operations.]

Article XII—*Restrictions to Safeguard the Balance of Payments*

This article permits any party to restrict the quantity or value of merchandise permitted to be imported, in order to safeguard its external position and balance of payments. Import restrictions may be imposed only for the purpose of forestalling the imminent threat of, or stopping, a serious decline in its monetary reserves, or for achieving a reasonable rate of increase in its reserves.

Restrictions applied shall be progressively relaxed as conditions improve.

Difficulties of post-war adjustment and the need to use import restrictions for the restoration of equilibrium in balance of payments on a sound and lasting basis are recognised, and also the necessity of using restrictive measures in furtherance of the development of industrial and other economic resources in pursuance of domestic policies directed towards full and productive employment. Restrictions are not to be unreasonably employed with this object, and unnecessary damage to the interests of any other contracting party is to be avoided.

Provision is made for consultation between the party imposing import restrictions and the Contracting Parties and for complaints by one party against the restrictions applied by another. The Contracting Parties may recommend the withdrawal or modification of restrictions in the light of their investigations of a complaint that the restrictions are applied in a manner inconsistent with the provisions of this Article, or Article XIII (subject to the provisions of Article XIV). If the restrictions are not modified or withdrawn the Contracting Parties may release any contracting party from specified obligations under this Agreement towards the contracting party applying the restrictions.

In the case of persistent and widespread application of import restrictions under this article indicating a general disequilibrium which is restricting international trade, the Contracting Parties are to discuss whether other measures might be taken to remove the underlying causes of the disequilibrium.

[Contracting parties applying restrictions shall try to avoid causing serious prejudice to exports of a commodity on which the economy of a contracting party is largely dependent.

Contracting parties shall review all restrictions still applied under the article. One year after the review a system of annual consultations with contracting parties still applying restrictions (except underdeveloped countries) shall enter into force.

The Contracting Parties, when conducting consultations under this article, are to have due regard to special external factors which may influence the balance of payments position of the country concerned.]

Article XIII—*Non-Discriminatory Administration of Quantitative Restrictions*

No prohibition or restriction shall apply on the importation of any produce of any other party unless like products from all third countries are similarly prohibited or restricted. Shares of the product permitted to be imported are to be maintained in the proportions which would obtain in the absence of any restrictions. Quotas of permitted imports shall be fixed, where possible, but if this is not practicable restrictions may be applied by means of import licences or permits without a quota.

Information may be requested concerning the administration of import restrictions by other parties having an interest in the trade in the product concerned, and public notice of the total quantity or value of the product permitted to be imported during a specified period shall be given. Public notice of shares in a quota shall be given.

The principles of the article extend to export restrictions and to internal regulations under Article III.

ARTICLE XIV—*Exceptions to the Rule of Non-Discrimination*

Contracting parties who apply restrictions under Article XII or under Section B of Article XVIII, in the application of such restrictions are entitled to deviate from the rule of non-discriminatory administration of import restrictions in a manner having equivalent effect to restrictions on payments and transfers for current international transactions which the contracting party may apply under Articles VIII or XIV of the International Monetary Fund (Under Article VIII the discrimination would apply when a currency is declared 'scarce'. Under Article XIV the rule is more flexible but it can be said that any discrimination should be for currency reasons.) The GATT consultations under Article XII include consideration of discriminatory aspects.[1]

ARTICLE XV—*Exchange Arrangements*

Parties shall seek co-operation with the International Monetary Fund so that the parties to the Fund may pursue a co-ordinated policy with regard to exchange questions within the jurisdiction of the Fund and questions of quantitative restrictions and other trade measures within the jurisdiction of the parties. A party which is not a member of the Fund shall become a member within a time to be determined, or failing that, shall enter into a special exchange agreement with the parties to the Agreement. Provision is made that nothing in the Agreement shall preclude the use of exchange controls or exchange restrictions in accordance with the Articles of Agreement of the International Monetary Fund.

ARTICLE XVI—*Subsidies*

Any contracting party which grants or maintains any subsidy, including any form of income or price support which operates to increase exports of any product from or imports of any product into its territory must notify the Contracting Parties of its extent and nature, of its estimated effect and of the circumstances which make it necessary. Consultation is provided for if the subsidy causes serious prejudice to the interests of a contracting party.

[The Contracting Parties recognise that export subsidies may have effects prejudicial to trade and the achievement of the objectives of the Agreement and should seek to avoid their use on the export of primary products.

Where direct or indirect export subsidies are given on primary products they are to be applied so as to result in the subsidising country securing no more than an equitable share in the world export trade in the product concerned.

Provision is made for the elimination of existing subsidies and the prevention of new subsidies on manufactured goods which result in their sale abroad at prices lower than domestic prices.][2]

---

[1] This summary of Article XIV is taken direct from *The General Agreement on Tariffs and Trade*, prepared by the Department of Trade and Industry, Canberra, June 1965. (Roneoed.)

[2] The provisions concerning manufactured goods are only legally in force for some contracting parties which have signed a Declaration agreeing to apply them. The countries which have signed include the leading industrialised countries. Australia has not signed. The Declaration also lists a number of export incentives deemed to be subsidies.

ARTICLE XVII—*Non-Discriminatory Treatment on the Part of State-Trading Enterprises*

State-trading enterprises shall, in their purchases or sales of imports or exports, act in a manner consistent with the general principles of non-discriminatory treatment prescribed for governmental measures affecting imports or exports by private traders. Any such purchases or sales are to be made solely in accordance with commercial considerations.

The article does not apply to imports of products for consumption solely in governmental use.

[Notification is to be made to Contracting Parties of products the subject of state trading. On request, the mark up on unbound items must be supplied and information about how the state trading operations conform to the provisions of the Agreement.]

ARTICLE XVIII—*Government Assistance to Economic Development and Reconstruction*

It is recognised that special governmental assistance may be required to promote the establishment, development or reconstruction of particular industries or branches of agriculture, and that in appropriate circumstances protective measures are justified.

Authority may be given to a contracting party to impose non-discriminatory protective measures in the interests of its economic development or reconstruction. Contracting parties which consider that their trade is substantially affected by proposed measures by any party shall notify other contracting parties, who shall examine the measures. Adjustments may be decided upon after negotiations.

Any non-discriminatory measures in force on 1 September 1947, imposed for the establishment, development or reconstruction of particular industries, etc. may be maintained. Notification of products affected is to be made.

[The Article was completely re-cast. Its provisions no longer apply to industrialised countries for reconstruction purposes; they apply only (except in the case of Section D) to countries with a low standard of living and in the early stages of development. It is agreed that such countries should enjoy additional facilities to enable them (a) to maintain sufficient flexibility in their tariff structure to be able to grant the tariff protection required for the establishment of a particular industry and (b) to apply quantitative restrictions for balance of payments purposes in a manner which takes full account of the continued high level of demand for imports likely to be generated by their programs of economic development. Under Section C such contracting parties who need governmental assistance to promote the establishment of a particular industry to raise the general living standard of their people may deviate from obligations of the Agreement other than tariff bindings. The Contracting Parties may also grant a release from tariff bindings without the concurrence of materially interested contracting parties if satisfied that the interests of other contracting parties are adequately safeguarded. The rights contained in Section C are also extended to the special case of an industry which has in its initial period been incidentally protected by restrictions for balance of payments reasons and on the lifting of these is in need of continued protection. A contracting party affected by a measure introduced under this section has the right to take the necessary measures to redress the balance of benefits. Under Section D the benefits of Section C are extended to contracting parties whose economies are in the process of development but which are not classed as low standard of living countries and in the early stages of development. Australia is included in this category.]

ARTICLE XIX—*Emergency Action on Imports of Particular Products*

Provision is made for the suspension of obligations incurred by a party under the Agreement, including tariff concessions and preference reductions if, as a result of unforeseen circumstances, such concessions lead to the import of any product into the territory of a contracting party under such conditions as to cause or threaten serious injury to domestic producers of like or directly competitive products.

If practicable, advance notice in writing shall be given to parties interested with a view to consultation being arranged. In critical circumstances action may be taken provisionally without prior consultation, on condition that consultation shall be effected immediately after taking such action.

ARTICLE XX—*General Exceptions*

This article covers exceptions to the provisions of the General Agreement which are to be applied in a non-discriminatory way and must not constitute a disguised restriction on international trade.

The exceptions cover measures relating to protection of public morals, human, animal or plant life or health; importation or exportation of gold or silver; customs enforcement; the enforcement of monopolies operated under paragraph 4 of Article II and Article XVII; protection of patents, etc., and the prevention of deceptive practices; products of prison labour; national treasures; conservation of natural resources; measures undertaken in pursuance of obligations under approved inter-governmental commodity agreements conforming to the principles approved by the Economic and Social Council of the United Nations in its Resolution of 28 March 1947; and those involving restrictions on exports of domestic materials necessary to assure essential quantities of these to a domestic processing industry when the domestic price of such materials is held below world price as part of a governmental stabilization plan. Other exceptions relate to measures essential to the acquisition or distribution of products in general or local short supply* and the control of prices or liquidation of temporary surplus stocks following the war.* Any measures of the type mentioned in the preceding sentence which are inconsistent with the other provisions of the Agreement are to be removed as soon as the conditions giving rise to them have ceased.

[The type of commodity agreement covered by the article is widened to include any agreement which conforms to criteria submitted to the Contracting Parties and not disapproved by them or which is itself so submitted and not so disapproved.

The exceptions covered from * to * above are deleted.]

ARTICLE XXI—*Security Exceptions*

The Agreement shall not require any contracting party to furnish information contrary to its essential security interests, or to prevent action necessary for the protection of such interests relating to fissionable materials, traffic in arms, ammunition and implements of war, etc. or action taken in time of war or other emergency in international relations.

No contracting party is prevented from taking any action in pursuance of its obligations under the United Nations Charter for the maintenance of international peace and security.

ARTICLE XXII—*Consultation*

Opportunities are provided for consultation on any matter affecting the operation of the Agreement.

ARTICLE XXIII—*Nullification or Impairment*

If any contracting party considers that any benefit accruing to it under the agreement is being nullified or impaired because of (a) the failure of another contracting party to carry out its obligations, (b) the application by another contracting party of any measure, whether or not it conflicts with the provisions of the Agreement, or (c) the existence of any other situation, the party should complain to the contracting party or parties concerned. If no satisfactory agreement is reached the Contracting Parties may be asked to investigate and make recommendations or give rulings. They may authorise a contracting party to suspend the application to any other contracting party or parties of appropriate obligations and concessions. The contracting party against whom such action is taken may withdraw from the Agreement.

ARTICLE XXIV—*Territorial Application—Frontier Traffic—Customs Unions and Free Trade Areas*

Closer integration between the economies of contracting parties is permitted in the form of customs unions and free trade areas provided that these do not result in higher or more restrictive duties and other regulations being imposed on trade with contracting parties who are not members of the union or area. Notification of plans for such integration must be made to the Contracting Parties. If they consider that such plans will not result in a customs union or free trade area within a reasonable time they shall recommend modifications which the parties concerned must carry out before putting an agreement into force.

A customs union is defined as the substitution of a single customs territory for two or more customs territories, with the elimination of duties and other restrictive regulations of commerce on substantially all the trade between the constituent territories; and the application of the same duties and regulations by each member to the trade of those outside the union. A free trade area is defined as a group of customs territories in which duties and other restrictive regulations of commerce are eliminated on substantially all the trade between constituent territories.

The preferences in Article I are not affected by the formation of such unions or areas but may be eliminated or adjusted by negotiations with the contracting parties affected.

(The full text of clauses 8-10 of Article XXIV is given in A8:2).

ARTICLE XXV—*Joint Action by the Contracting Parties*

The article provides for representatives of the Contracting Parties to meet from time to time to give effect to the provisions of the Agreement involving joint action and to facilitate the operation of the Agreement. In exceptional circumstances the Contracting Parties may waive an obligation imposed upon a contracting party provided this is approved by a two-thirds majority of the votes cast and that such majority comprises more than half of the Contracting Parties.

If any contracting party has failed without sufficient justification to carry out negotiations concerning tariff reductions, the Contracting Parties may authorise the complaining party to withhold tariff concessions from the other. If the concessions are withheld, the other party may withdraw from the Agreement,

The General Agreement on Tariffs and Trade

ARTICLE XXVI—*Acceptance, Entry into Force and Registration*

The Agreement shall enter into force when it has been accepted by the Governments of the territories which account for 85 per cent of the total external trade of the territories of the signatories to the Final Act.

[The date of this Agreement shall be 30 October 1947.]

ARTICLE XXVII—*Withholding or Withdrawal of Concessions*

Any contracting party is free to withhold or withdraw any concession initially negotiated with a government which has not become, or has ceased to be, a contracting party. A contracting party taking such action shall, upon request, consult with the contracting parties which have a substantial interest in the product concerned.

ARTICLE XXVIII—*Modification of Schedules*

On or after 1 July 1955[3] any contracting party may, by negotiation and agreement with any other contracting party with which such treatment was initially negotiated, and subject to consultation with such other contracting parties with a substantial interest in such treatment, modify or cease to apply the treatment which it has agreed to accord under Article II to any product described in the appropriate schedule annexed to this Agreement.

If agreement cannot be reached modification or withdrawal may be made, but other contracting parties mentioned may withdraw substantially equivalent concessions initially negotiated with the contracting party taking such action.

[The revised article provides for the firm validity of the schedules of tariff concessions by three-year periods, but with greater flexibility for the right to renegotiate and in the procedures for negotiation, both during the periods of firm validity and at the end of each period. Paragraph 4 contains new provisions for renegotiations under authority obtained from the Contracting Parties in special circumstances and providing in certain circumstances for modification or withdrawal even if the negotiations are not successful. An interpretative note to paragraph 4 places an obligation on the Contracting Parties to authorise negotiations for those contracting parties which depend in large measure on a relatively small number of primary commodities and which rely on the tariff as an important aid for furthering diversification of their economies or as an important source of revenue.

ARTICLE XXVIII *bis.—Tariff Negotiations*

Under this new article the Contracting Parties, from time to time, may sponsor negotiations directed to the reduction of tariffs, as these are of great importance to the expansion of international trade. Negotiations may be carried out on a selective product-by-product basis or by the application of multilateral procedures, and may be directed towards the reduction of duties, the binding of duties at their existing levels or undertakings that individual duties or the average duties on specified categories of products shall not exceed specified levels. The binding against increase of low duties or of duty-free treatment shall, in principle, be recognised as a concession equivalent in value to the reduction of high duties.

The conduct of the negotiations is to take into account the needs of individual contracting parties and individual industries; the needs of less developed countries for a more flexible use of tariff protection to assist their economic development and the special needs of these countries to maintain tariffs for revenue purposes;

[3] The date was originally fixed as 1 January 1951.

and all other relevant circumstances, including the fiscal, developmental, strategic and other needs of the contracting parties concerned.]

ARTICLE XXIX—*The Relation of this Agreement to the Havana Charter*

The Contracting Parties undertake to observe to the fullest extent of their executive authority the general principles of Chapters I to VI inclusive and of Chapter IX of the Havana Charter pending their acceptance of it. Part II of the Agreement is to be suspended on the day on which the Havana Charter enters into force.

If the Havana Charter has not entered into force by 30 September 1949, the Contracting Parties are to meet before 31 December 1949, to agree whether the Agreement is to be amended, supplemented or maintained.[4]

ARTICLE XXX—*Amendments*

In general, amendments to the provisions of Part I of this Agreement or to the provisions of Articles XXIX and XXX will become effective when accepted by all the contracting parties. Other amendments will become effective, in respect of those contracting parties which accept them, upon acceptance by two-thirds of the Contracting Parties.

The Contracting Parties may decide that any amendment made effective under this article is such that any contracting party which has not accepted it within a specified period is free to withdraw from the Agreement, or to remain within it with the consent of the Contracting Parties.

ARTICLE XXXI—*Withdrawal*

The article provides for the withdrawal from the Agreement of any contracting party, or for its separate withdrawal on behalf of any of the separate customs territories for which it has international responsibility.

ARTICLE XXXII—*Contracting Parties*

These are defined as those governments which are applying the provisions of this Agreement under Articles XXVI or XXXIII or pursuant to the Protocol of Provisional Application. When the Agreement enters definitively into force contracting parties which have accepted it under Article XXVI may decide that any contracting party which has not so accepted it shall cease to be a contracting party.

ARTICLE XXXIII—*Accession*

Provision is made for the accession to the Agreement of governments not party to it.

ARTICLE XXXIV—*Annexes*

The annexes to the Agreement become an integral part of it.

ARTICLE XXXV

This Agreement or Article II of the Agreement shall not apply as between any contracting party and any other contracting party if:
- (a) the two parties have not entered into tariff negotiations with each other, and
- (b) either of the contracting parties, at the time either becomes a contracting party, does not consent to such application.

[4] At their Fourth Session the Contracting Parties decided that the meeting referred to should be held at such time as they might subsequently decide.

5:1 AUSTRALIA TO SEEK REVIEW OF GATT

Press statement by the Prime Minister (R. G. Menzies) on 27 August 1953.

The Commonwealth Government will press at the next session of the members of the General Agreement on Tariffs and Trade for a comprehensive review of the General Agreement itself. The session begins in Geneva on 17th September. There will be a prior meeting of the delegates of the Commonwealth countries in London a few days before the Geneva session begins.

The Government has been far from satisfied with the operation to date of the Agreement and has reached this latest decision after a general examination of the advantages and disadvantages of continued Australian participation in it.

Australia entered into the Agreement in 1947, when the Chifley Government was in power. At that time it was contemplated that an International Trade Organisation would be established and the G.A.T.T. was applied provisionally, largely as a stop-gap until the I.T.O. Charter should come into force. The main results, in a tariff sense, from G.A.T.T. have been the operation of the tariff concessions negotiated between the member countries, the extension of the most favoured nation principle between them and the freezing of all preference margins at the 1947 levels.

Although a Charter for an International Trade Organisation was drawn up in 1948, no country has ratified it. The United States rejected it. Consequently, the I.T.O. idea has lapsed. Meanwhile, the G.A.T.T.—which was intended only as a part of the wider I.T.O. and was in any case a makeshift—has carried on from year to year for almost six years.

During that period there have been many changes in the world trading situation. In many products what has been for many years a sellers' market has now become or is in the process of becoming a buyers' market. Some of the Government trading which has marked the post war years has disappeared. Some of the rights and obligations under G.A.T.T. have had rather less effect up till now than they might otherwise have had because markets generally have been favourable to sellers. With the changing conditions, however, some at least of the provisions of G.A.T.T. will be found more onerous. Moreover, new problems may require new provisions. In any case, an Agreement which affects so much of the world's trade must have a degree of flexibility and there is room to doubt whether as at present drafted the General Agreement meets this requirement.

The Australian Government, therefore, considers that a general review of the G.A.T.T. is overdue and the Australian Delegation has been instructed to seek a review to be held at an appropriate date some time during 1954. The Government feels that only in the course of a general review, leading to such revision of the Agreement as is necessary, can the present circumstances of world trade, and Australia's particular circumstances be satisfactorily met.

For example, we do not agree with the view which seems to be implicit in the G.A.T.T. that Empire preferences, no matter what the circumstances, conflict with what is known as multilateral trade. On the contrary, we consider that a strongly trading British Commonwealth will strengthen total world trade. The last time the world had what for practical purposes is multilateral trade was in the pre-war era—at a time when we had a full system of Empire preference.

It is interesting to note that while the G.A.T.T. sets itself against any extension of preferences, it accepts the principle that Customs Unions may be consistent with the objectives of the G.A.T.T. Yet a Customs Union, by allowing complete freedom of trade between its parties, in effect establishes a more complete system of preferences than anyone ever contemplated for Empire Preferences.

In reaching the decision that the G.A.T.T. is due for a review the Australian Government is not unmindful of the view, which has been at times vigorously expressed, that Australia should withdraw its provisional membership. But we have concluded that we would not profit by withdrawing in isolation from other Commonwealth countries and major trading nations.

If Australia alone ceased to be a party to the Agreement, those countries which still remained members of G.A.T.T. would not be free to negotiate with us new arrangements which gave us as a non-member any greater benefits than are available to countries still in G.A.T.T. Thus, if Australia withdrew alone, we would not, for example, be able to negotiate new preference for our exports any more readily than if we stayed in the Agreement. So far as international negotiations for Australia's benefit are concerned, we cannot do better if we alone are outside G.A.T.T. than if we are inside it. In fact, it does seem possible that we might do worse.

5:2 REVIEW OF GATT: AUSTRALIA'S CASE

Speech by the Minister for Commerce and Agriculture (J. Mc-Ewen) at the Plenary Session of the Ninth Session of the Contracting Parties of the General Agreement on Tariffs and Trade on 9 November 1954.

The high objectives set out in the preamble to the General Agreement on Tariffs and Trade were designed to provide a solid foundation upon which could be built an international trade organization capable of making a decisive contribution towards the solution of world trade problems.

Australia at the Eighth Session of the Contracting Parties pressed strongly for a comprehensive review of the GATT in accordance with the provision of Article XXIX.

Australia pressed for this Review because it saw the need for changes in the GATT. The desirability of 'order' in international trade in the interests of increased multilateral trade and payments is obvious. The need is for a manageable and equitable code of fair trade. Australia seeks now those changes which in its opinion could equip the GATT as a means to such desirable objectives.

In the light of our experience in the past seven years and of our assessment of our needs in the foreseeable future Australia's judgment on GATT is based on five points:

(1) It is incomplete as an instrument governing 'good trading' relations between nations.

(2) GATT embodies a range of rules providing some stability and predictability in tariff relations which are important in trade in manufactured goods. It does not provide anything like a comparable degree of stability and predictability for trade in foodstuffs and raw materials. Some countries have exploited the freedom which ineffective GATT articles permit. They have protected their own high-cost primary production by subsidies of a type

148

and magnitude certainly distorting the pattern of export trade which would exist if the tests of economic production were more seriously applied.

(3) Because of its incompleteness, GATT is in fact partial in content and operation—too much shaped by the interests of advanced industrial nations as exporters of finished goods and importers of food and raw materials.

(4) Being incomplete and partial, it is too rigid, and apparently in danger of becoming more so. Absolutely rigid instruments will break down, as it is found the dynamic needs of developing nations are not helped, but hampered by them.

(5) Quite apart from the need to review certain of the GATT articles themselves, the total benefits we have received under GATT have not been commensurate with the total price paid by Australia. Moreover, the very rigidity of GATT has made it impracticable to restore to their original balance certain highly important bilateral agreements to which Australia was a party long before GATT, and which have given historic shape to the pattern of Australian trade.

When the fifty and more nations met in the early post-war years and hammered out an agreement covering the whole gamut of trade problems, Australia did not visualise the possibility that one portion only of the total agreement—the code we now know as GATT—would become the sole code of trade rules. It is not to be wondered at that GATT, having originated in this manner, is, in the view of Australia, an incomplete document. Being incomplete, its benefits and obligations fall unevenly upon the Contracting Parties. It is therefore inequitable.

The Contracting Parties to GATT may be divided roughly into two categories. The first includes nations more or less fully developed whose trade largely consists of exports of industrial and consumer goods and imports of raw materials and foodstuffs. The second and complementary category is of nations, either undeveloped or in the stage of rapid development, whose trade largely consists of imports of manufactured goods and exports of raw materials and foodstuffs. The former—the developed nations—look to trade rules for shelter from import restrictions and high tariffs imposed by less developed countries for protective and other reasons. The latter—the undeveloped or rapidly developing countries— face dangers not of tariffs and import restrictions so much as of impairment of their markets by violent price fluctuations and by subsidies imposed by developed countries. Primary producers cannot adjust their production to meet these factors as can secondary producers.

An examination of GATT shows quite clearly that it is a fairly effective document so far as it operates to reduce or freeze tariffs and outlaw quantitative restrictions except for balance-of-payments reasons. It is therefore a substantially satisfactory document from the point of view of the needs of developed countries.

On the other hand it is equally clear that the omission from GATT of major sections of the Havana Charter has resulted in its being a completely unsatisfactory document for regulating subsidies and commodity policy. It fails thereby to foster and assist the economic progress of less developed countries some of which are in a stage of very rapid development.

Thus GATT provides valuable safeguards to developed countries and leaves other countries relatively unsheltered from the kind of dangers which are peculiar to their economies.

It is natural that Australia, along with all other countries, should approach GATT from basic national economic and security interests. These interests for Australia are those of an expanding economy with substantial unused material resources awaiting development. The rapid growth of population in the post-war period is likely to continue, with commensurate growth in requirements of consumer and capital goods, both home produced and imported.

Due to its geographic position, Australia has particular security considerations which are made more complex in a period of rapid economic growth. These present some special problems in capital investment and trade.

The various considerations to which I have referred determine Australia's approach to the GATT. We must safeguard the position of our important export industries which are largely but not entirely primary. On their welfare depends our ability to develop our resources in accord with our economic and security objectives.

We must and do look to a growing volume of export trade to finance a necessary and clearly expanding volume of capital and consumer goods from overseas. We must have regard also to the growing industrialization of Australia.

The development of our primary and manufacturing industries has enabled us to make a contribution to neighbouring countries which are anxious to raise their living standards by developing their own resources. Our special circumstances are such, however, that for our progress in development we require considerable flexibility in policies of capital investment and trade.

The flexibility we need is not sufficiently available to us in GATT. This, together with the important omissions I have outlined produces, for us, dissatisfaction with the GATT as it stands. Accordingly, I shall now indicate in fairly specific terms the major matters of importance to Australia in the Review Session.

Tariff Bindings

The binding of tariff schedules by Australia has presented my Government with very serious problems. It will be recalled that the firm rebinding for a period of eighteen months following the Eighth Session was undertaken only because of the assurance that a complete review of GATT would be carried out in the near future.

In considering a further rebinding, my Government would want to be satisfied that, when necessary, action could be taken to protect Australian domestic industries, particularly those in early stages of development. Study of Australia's tariff-making policy will show that the procedure of periodic renegotiation of concessions followed by firm binding of the concessions for fixed periods is wholly unsuited to Australia's requirements.

Successive Australian Governments have made it clear that they do not favour the use of quantitative restrictions for protective purposes, and they have not resorted to this means to protect Australian industries. Australian manufacturers have accepted the fact that they can expect protection against imported goods only by means of the Customs tariff.

To remove questions of tariff protection from the field of domestic pressure groups and party politics an independent tariff tribunal (known as the Tariff Board) was set up in Australia thirty-two years ago. Gradually this Tribunal built up a reputation for thorough investigation and independent recommendations.

Decisions in relation to the establishment of new industries or the extension of existing industries are left to private enterprise; the Australian Government does

150

not give any guarantee in relation to tariff protection in advance of these decisions. As a general rule, the Tariff Tribunal will not recommend protection until the production of the goods concerned has been undertaken on a commercial basis in Australia and until it can be demonstrated that there are sound opportunities for the success of the industry if reasonable tariff protection is afforded it.

Under existing procedures of GATT, the only feasible way of operating would be to withdraw all tariff concessions which may present a problem every time a firm rebinding of the schedules is being undertaken. For instance, we would need to withdraw tariff concessions in every case where the question of a protective duty for a commodity was before the Tariff Tribunal, or was likely to be referred to it in the foreseeable future. Such a procedure would result in unnecessary withdrawal of a considerable number of concessions. It is worth mentioning that, as a result of the implementation of recommendations of the Tariff Tribunal, the rates of duty now operating in the Australian Customs Tariff in respect of some products are below those bound under GATT.

From the time when the binding of rates of duty under GATT first took place in 1947, alarm arose among various interests in Australia who see in this commitment a grave danger of the destruction of the Tariff Tribunal system and a return to arbitrary decisions in relation to tariff levels, including lobbying tactics of pressure groups. These interests cannot reconcile the binding of the rates of duty over a large part of the Australian tariff, with a system under which the question of the level of duty required to encourage a worthwhile industry is determined on the basis of recommendations of an independent tariff tribunal. My Government, from the time it took office, has shared these misgivings.

Recently, my Government has made a thorough examination of the position. As Australia does not wish to change its present method of encouraging the development of industry by a careful and prudent use of the Customs Tariff an attempt has been made to pinpoint the particular difficulties which the GATT commitments present.

This examination has revealed that there is a need for adequate provision in GATT on the following point. Should circumstances arise in which delay in increasing a bound rate is likely to damage an Australian industry to an extent difficult to repair, my Government should be in a position to take action immediately, provided the negotiation of compensatory concessions is undertaken without delay.

As the GATT stands at present, emergency action to protect domestic industries in critical circumstances is permitted only where established industries are adversely affected by increased imports. Thus there is provision for a type of situation which gives most concern to countries in an advanced state of economic development. On the other hand, there is no provision for emergency action where a contracting party finds that a developing industry will face critical circumstances unless it is placed in a competitive position in the domestic market. Australia, as a rapidly developing country, must have sufficient freedom in this regard.

Preferences

I refer now to what is known as the No New Preference Rule—in other words that part of Article I of GATT which lays it down that margins of preference may not be increased.

In the discussion on GATT and the Havana Charter, this No New Preference Rule was accepted by Australia because it formed part of the package—including both benefits and restrictions—which the ITO Charter gave reasonable promise of providing. But, as I have said, the benefits which countries like Australia expected have not sufficiently materialized. It is impossible, therefore, for Australia to regard the No New Preference Rule as a satisfactory part of continuing obligations under GATT. It must be looked at on its merits.

On its merits, what the Australian Government finds is this—that this rule, which permits of no new preferences and therefore binds all preference margins against increase, imposes an unreasonable restriction on countries which had contracted preferential arrangements before entering GATT. Over the last decade, we have experienced the marked deterioration of the value of specific margins of preference—almost to vanishing point in some instances—and yet GATT denies us an opportunity to negotiate on these.

All tariff rates are subject, not to the complete binding which applies to preferences, but merely to a selective binding, agreed as the outcome of periodic negotiations. Not only that, but unbound tariff rates may be increased. That is of course subject to certain procedures which have already been used by several Contracting Parties. No parallel facilities for variation through negotiation and compensation are available in respect of margins of preference.

GATT does provide for and approve one form of new preferences—a Customs Union. The intended result of a Customs Union must be to benefit its members as against non-members. We concede that a Customs Union may be valuable to the circumstances of some groups and countries, notably in Europe. Yet no other method of new preference has any approval from GATT. GATT does not even include the important, although limited, provision of the ITO Charter, enabling Contracting Parties to enter into preferential agreements for developmental purposes.

Recent experience in Europe (the OEEC Liberalization Programme) has shown that in certain circumstances, new preferential arrangements within a geographical area have had beneficial results. It may well be that an extension of the principle of preferences may be relied on in connexion with European coal and steel arrangements. These do not appear to be compatible with the No New Preference rule.

We must draw attention to the inconsistency which presumes our support for a Customs Union or OEEC preferential arrangements while refusing us any right to adjust the terms of our own system.

GATT does not recognize the valuable and healthy influence which preferences have had in the past on the economic development of the countries concerned, with large consequential benefit to world trade. Furthermore, it rejects in summary fashion the possibility that preferences may play such a role in the future.

For these reasons the Australian Government, early in this Review Session, draws attention of the Contracting Parties to this defect in GATT. It expresses in particular the view that it is completely unrealistic to attempt to bind all preference margins against increase for the entire life of GATT. It points out that no effective compensation has ever been received for what amounts to a unilateral binding of its preferences.

Subsidies

(a) *Export Subsidies*

I turn now to the question of export subsidies. Australia regards the question of export subsidies—particularly on foodstuffs and raw materials—as one of the most serious and urgent issues with which the Contracting Parties will have to deal at this Review Session. The GATT and the ITO Charter both have application to surplus disposals through provisions on subsidies, which include any form of price support.

The failure of the ITO Charter (specifically Articles 25-28) has left only Article XVI of the GATT to which exporters can look for protection from the ill effects upon their trade of export subsidy policies of other countries. A glance at this Article even without the experience of the last few years shows quite clearly how ineffective GATT as at present constituted is likely to be.

The Charter Articles were intended to outlaw those subsidies which have the effect of giving a country an undue share of total exports in the commodity concerned, and thus seriously prejudicing the interests of another contracting party. They were designed to oblige a country granting a subsidy on a primary commodity to co-operate in attempts to negotiate an international commodity agreement and to provide that a subsidy should not give the country applying it more than an equitable share of international trade.

The present GATT provisions in this field are weak. They are confined to a requirement for consultation about those subsidies which tend to increase exports and about the right of an importing country to apply countervailing duties where imports of subsidized goods threaten a local industry.

The value of countervailing duties is limited by the absence of any obligation on contracting parties generally, to preserve the interests in their markets of member countries competing with subsidized exports from other countries.

A GATT provision which merely requires the Contracting Parties to 'discuss' is a totally inadequate safeguard for countries dependent largely upon the export of foodstuffs and primary products. In our view, it is essential as a first step that the Charter provisions, mainly those in Articles 26-28, be incorporated in GATT in appropriate form.

As an additional safeguard, the problem of dealing with subsidies in GATT should also be tackled from the importer's end. An obligation on exporting countries to refrain from using harmful export subsidies or from disposing of surpluses in a manner prejudicial to other exporters is not an adequate safeguard. In fact, under certain conditions it may not be a safeguard at all.

Emphasis has been given to the necessity for assuring fair import trade policies on the part of creditor countries under conditions of convertibility. This is very necessary but those policies must be matched by fair export policies by such countries.

Australia as an exporter of wheat, dairy products, canned goods and the like needs no great prescience to realize what might result from bargain sales to her traditional markets. The predicament is not confined to foodstuffs. Many other countries are also likely to be in the same situation in respect of other commodities.

Contracting parties who may be immediate beneficiaries of bargain-counter sales must realize that short-term advantages must be followed by downward adjustments to their own export trade. These adjustments would not only cancel out the temporary benefits of cheap food, and cheap raw materials, but would set in train a series of economic reactions which would leave them immeasurably worse off than if they had never received their 'bargains'. In short, the economies of many countries must be seriously impaired if world-trade patterns are to be distorted by uneconomic export subsidies with which they cannot possibly compete. Such subsidy policies are frequently necessitated by high domestic price-support programmes.

Under these circumstances, Australia will propose that GATT should not only impose an obligation on *exporting* countries to refrain from using export subsidies or disposing of surpluses in a manner prejudicial to other exporters, but should also place an obligation on *importing* countries to impose measures to protect the interest of third countries against subsidized goods disrupting their markets.

Finally, in the situation which exists at present—where large surpluses already exist or threaten to accumulate—GATT should set out safeguards governing the entry of surpluses into world trade and develop effective criteria for ensuring that subsidized goods do not obtain more than equitable shares of world trade.

(b) *Domestic Subsidies*

Australia would not argue that domestic subsidies of agricultural and other commodities are necessarily harmful to world trade.

It is clear, however, that they may operate in such a manner as to stimulate domestic production to the extent that trade opportunities of other contracting parties are impaired—or surpluses accumulated to an extent which affects confidence in world trade and prices.

They should, therefore, be subject to some kind of control equivalent in result, if not identical in form, to that operating in regard to tariffs and quantitative restrictions, and be subject to something more than formal reporting to the Contracting Parties.

There is no equity in a situation where certain countries are limited in their protection of secondary industry by either tariffs or quota restrictions, while other countries—principally the importers of foodstuffs and raw materials—are free to resort to the no less effective protective device of subsidies.

Commodity Arrangements

Australia considers that the vacancy in the commercial policy field created by the exclusion from GATT of the provisions of Chapter VI of the ITO Charter is an appropriate subject for the present Review Session of GATT. Certainly, the absence from GATT of positive provisions for effectively working-out arrangements designed to prevent in a measure the disequilibrium between production and consumption, the accumulation of burdensome stocks, and pronounced fluctuations in prices of primary products was not contemplated by Australia back in 1947.

While Chapter VI of the ITO Charter might be a starting point for drafting, Australia, in the light of the experience of international commodity agreements in the post-war period, considers that a number of additions or amendments may be necessary.

For example, I refer to two aspects of commodity policy where the ITO Charter falls short of what Australia would regard as desirable.

Commodity control agreements can only be concluded in harmony with Chapter VI of the ITO Charter in conditions of burdensome surpluses. This prerequisite condition of burdensome surpluses applies to agreements regulating prices as well as those controlling production and marketing. It is suggested that it would be desirable to reconsider this aspect.

The view is strongly held by Australia that, if the real purpose of commodity agreements is to prevent persistent disequilibrium between production and consumption and avoid pronounced fluctuations in price, then such commodity agreements must be effected in some cases in conditions where no accumulation of burdensome stocks actually exists. The justification for an agreement in such a case would lie in the previous history of supply, demand and price, in respect of the commodity concerned.

154

Both the ITO Charter and GATT have recognized that special difficulties exist for countries which are mainly exporters of primary commodities. Both concede that inter-governmental commodity agreements may be warranted, but the principles of Chapter VI make their achievement more difficult than necessary. Firstly, the procedural requirements are so cumbersome as to inhibit a quick settling down to the negotiation of terms of an agreement. Secondly, the principles governing participation are too universal; it should be open to smaller groups of countries (importing and exporting) to initiate agreements, upon terms which would not offend fair trading practices.

Further, it should not be impossible to envisage agreements among producer countries provided these comply with criteria laid down by GATT.

We are conscious of some confusion in existing and proposed international machinery for dealing with commodity problems. We recognize the valuable work already being done by FAO and we understand the anxieties which led to the recent ECOSOC decision to establish a Permanent Advisory Commission on International Commodity Trade. Again, there is the Interim Coordinating Committee for International Commodity Arrangements. To suggest that GATT has a role may seem, at first blush, to add to the confusion. We firmly believe, however, that the 1947 debates were on right lines and that GATT should have a provision which would make possible the development of effective principles and procedures for consultation and action on commodity problems. We will ask that the Review Session attend to this question—including, if necessary, the problem of overlapping among international bodies—concurrently with the other important matters before it.

Quantitative Import Restrictions for Balance-of-Payments Reasons

Certain contracting parties have said they consider that, in framing long-term trade rules to be applied in a convertible world, conditions more stringent than those in the existing GATT should be laid down to regulate the application of quantitative import restrictions on balance-of-payments grounds.

It has been suggested that such a tightening-up of the existing provisions might take the form that countries imposing such restrictions should be required not merely to consult with the Contracting Parties about them but to seek without delay the approval of the Contracting Parties for them and, if such approval were not forthcoming, to withdraw them. It has also been advocated that no restrictions imposed for balance-of-payments reasons should be allowed to be retained for longer than a fixed period.

My Government could not accept any greater limitations than those imposed by the existing GATT Articles on its freedom to apply quantitative import restrictions, deemed necessary in order to protect the national solvency. Nor could my Government agree that the duration of the application of such import restrictions should be determined by mere reference to the calendar, irrespective of the economic circumstances at the time.

These are objections of principle which my Government would regard as fundamental.

It is obvious that some countries are much more vulnerable to fluctuations in their balance of payments than others.

Australia is dependent for her export income mainly on wool, wheat and other primary products.

Seasonal considerations affect the *volume* of these exports and their *value* is subject to even more violent changes because of movements in world prices, particularly of wool.

To illustrate the scale of the swings that can take place in the Australian balance of payments, I might mention that in 1950/51 the surplus on current account was £A104 million. In the following year 1951/52, this was transformed into a deficit of no less than £A583 million, i.e., a swing in one year of £A687 million, equivalent approximately to the total export earnings of what might be termed a reasonable export year.

So far as Australia is concerned there is in any case a tendency for pressure to be exerted on the balance of payments by the very pace with which, for the highest political and strategic reasons, we have been pushing ahead with our economic development and encouraging a large intake of new migrants. The experience of early 1952 has established in our minds the strong conviction that when a Government is confronted with a balance-of-payments crisis, it must in the last resort be able to exercise its own judgment on the need to place quantitative restrictions on the flow of imports and on the extent of such restriction required to protect its solvency.

At the same time, Australia recognizes the need for some safeguards against the abuse of quantitative import restrictions. The existing GATT Articles were carefully drawn up with the dual objective of meeting the needs of countries in genuine balance-of-payments difficulties and, at the same time, of bringing pressure to bear on countries making improper use of the balance-of-payments escape clause. We do not consider that any case for amendment of these particular clauses of the GATT has been established.

There is also a suggestion that the GATT Articles should be revised in order to provide 'improved coordination' between the IMF and the GATT Contracting Parties in the matter of restrictions imposed to protect the balance of payments.

If 'improved coordination' means giving to the Fund greater powers in respect of trade questions than are now provided in GATT, my Government would not be able to entertain the proposal. The existing GATT Articles already adequately provide for close cooperation and consultation between the Contracting Parties and the Fund. We entirely support the view that the Contracting Parties should look to the Fund for information about the ascertainable facts of the financial position of countries invoking the balance-of-payments escape clause. However, we see no need to go beyond this.

In a balance-of-payments emergency, broad judgments have to be made not merely about the past but also about the probable trend of future events, the adequacy of available reserves and the all-important question of what has been called 'the confidence factor'. The Government of the country confronted with the problem must make the judgment in the first place and, if other countries consider that the action taken is unjustifiable or unduly damaging to their trade interests, the right of challenge and adequate consultation provisions are written into the existing GATT Articles. If we are to have an international trade organization, it cannot be a subordinate body.

Conclusion

I have now reviewed major issues of concern to Australia. There will be other particular points including an amendment to Article XX to ensure our right by quantitative restrictions on exports to conserve natural resources. These questions will be raised in appropriate Committees.

We have approached this Review Session confident that we have good cause to seek important amendments in, and additions to, the terms of GATT. While far from satisfied that GATT in its present form meets Australia's national interests, our criticisms have not been advanced in any carping spirit. They flow directly from real policy needs and experience. Moreover, the criticisms are not meant to destroy. Australia would prefer a revised GATT which will enable it to recognize and operate a manageable set of fair trading rules. We need to be able to negotiate trading relations which, while recognizing and complying with agreements made, will enable a tariff structure and trade arrangements more in keeping with the changing economic situation.

We therefore commend to the consideration of the Contracting Parties the changes we are putting forward in the belief that they will result in a more complete instrument, and a more acceptable and manageable set of international trade rules which will foster and protect an increase in multilateral trade.

We realize we are not alone in seeking changes impelled by our national interests. Moreover, there may well be controversial debate before the interests and needs of all are reconciled in a new GATT.

The final position of the Australian Government in GATT will be determined by the scope and content of any new document. Meanwhile, the Australian delegation will play a constructive role in the work of the Conference in the common effort to produce an Agreement which all governments, my own included, will regard as a realistic and acceptable instrument.

Source: Press Release GATT/184,
15 November 1954.

5:3 REVIEW OF GATT: ISSUES FOR AUSTRALIA

*Press statement by the Minister for Commerce and Agriculture
(J. McEwen) on 5 January 1955.*[1]

The G.A.T.T. Conference is, of course, not yet concluded and while discussions with the United Kingdom Government and Departments have resulted in important understandings the workout of some of the understandings is still proceeding between senior officials. . . .

International Competition

To keep the issues which have been argued in proper perspective, it is essential that all interested parties should always remember that world trade is, day by day, becoming both in total and for individual industries much less affected by what trade rules exist than by ability to compete in cost and quality in international markets. . . .

Other Issues

We have campaigned to convert the G.A.T.T. document to a more balanced and acceptable form from the Australian viewpoint by proposing to protect international trade in commodities from distortion through the operation of subsidies.

Our case has been that our primary commodity export trade must be given as much stability and predictability through rules governing subsidies as the rules regarding the binding of national trade in manufactured goods. Rules should also

[1] This statement has been greatly cut. The passages retained should be read in conjunction with 5:2.

be adequate to prevent distortion of normal trade by international gifts of surpluses to or their large scale disposal on special terms. . . .

I feel bound to express disappointment that there has not so far been more effective help in achieving solutions to Australia's problems on the part of some of the great nations who have undoubtedly understood our difficulties.

At Geneva there is great weight in favour of strong tariff and import quota rules which protect the position of the old established manufacturing exporting countries. There is an evident willingness to go a long way to accommodate the problems of the underdeveloped countries. Australia is in neither of these groups. This is the core of our problem, and quite frankly I do not feel that we, dependent upon export trade in primary products to finance needed development here, have had as yet sufficient of the assistance from our great friends which we might have expected.

Great Issues for Australia

. . . it is important that Australians interested in these great issues should understand what strength and what weaknesses there are in Australia's general bargaining position. If the rules of G.A.T.T. are unacceptable we do not necessarily solve our problem by withdrawing from G.A.T.T. if all the nations with which we trade remain members of that Organization and are still bound by those rules. So withdrawal is no simple remedy. Recovery of our unqualified freedom in protective tariff making by withdrawal implies freedom for every other country to take retaliatory action (in G.A.T.T. language withdrawal of concessions.) We must weigh carefully the total public interest. On the other hand, however, there are two situations which while they have not yet hurt us vitally could develop so intolerably as to demand a strong gesture by Australia. The first is that if the United Kingdom is unwilling to bind herself against buying subsidised products to the extent of damaging our trade, and in fact continues to do so (as in the case of Argentine wheat last year), then in my opinion we would have to consider reviewing our very generous import policies *vis à vis* British goods in order to force that issue.

The second issue relates to the United States. If they continue to declaim the need for fair trade rules as in G.A.T.T. they must do more on the issues of unfair export subsidies and on large scale disposal of their huge surpluses than their recent promises. On the surpluses their new undertaking amounts to a willingness to tell other interested parties who may be adversely affected, of their intended disposals, and, if practicable, give those interested parties an opportunity to voice their opinions in the rather uncertain hope that our vital interests may, thereby, be safeguarded. On top of this limited gesture the United States still wishes to curb agricultural imports into America despite tariff concessions which have been negotiated. I say with full consideration that it would be a reasonable response to this negative attitude to fair world trade rules for primary products for Australia to consider withdrawal from G.A.T.T. on the grounds that her great world trade interests were inadequately protected by G.A.T.T. For it must be understood by the great powers that commodity trade is at least as much our life blood as trade in manufactured foods is theirs. We should not take issue lightly with our great friends, neither should we, nor will we, be passive in defending our own great trade. . . .

5:4 RESULTS OF THE GATT REVIEW

Extracts from 'Review of the General Agreement on Tariffs and Trade'.[1]

10. As a result of the review amendments to the text of the General Agreement have been proposed for acceptance by Governments.[2] A comparison of the existing Articles of the Agreement with the new Articles proposed as a result of the review together with the brief explanatory notes on the intention of the amendments is given in Section 2 of this paper. The proposed changes in the Agreement of major importance to Australia are described in the following paragraphs.

Tariff Bindings

11. Article XXVIII is the Article which governs the continuance of the tariff concessions given and received by Australia in the course of the various tariff negotiations conducted under the General Agreement in 1947 and subsequently. This Article has been revised in certain important respects.

The redrafted Article provides specific procedures for the withdrawal of a binding on a tariff item. Four important points in connexion with the redrafted Article are:—

(a) during the three months immediately before 1st July, 1955, Australia is free to modify or withdraw—in accordance with the procedures set out in paragraphs 1 to 3 of the Article—individual concessions in the Australian tariff accorded to other countries. Shortly before the end of 1957, and at three-yearly periods thereafter, a similar arrangement will operate. Before the beginning of any three-year period Australia may if desired reserve the right in respect of the whole Australian Schedule to modify or withdraw concessions under this procedure during the ensuing three-year period.

(b) at other times, i.e. after 1st July, 1955, and in the course of subsequent three-yearly periods, selected individual items may be modified or withdrawn in accordance with the procedure set out in paragraph 4 of the Article.

(c) in the case of modification or withdrawal of individual items under (b), the new procedures could not delay action to increase a 'bound' rate of duty—so far as the General Agreement is concerned—more than 120 days from the time at which the first steps were taken under the General Agreement. Moreover Australia has gained special rights under these procedures which are noted in the next paragraph.

(d) any modifications or withdrawals of concessions made by Australia at any time (i.e. whether under (a) or (b) above) require the offer of compensatory

[1] These extracts are from a White Paper embodying the complete results of the Review Session presented to Parliament on 2 June 1955. A full perusal of the text is essential for any serious student, who will be equally as interested in the less formal and more politically directed remarks by the Prime Minister made in the House of Representatives when tabling the White Paper (see *C.P.D. (H. of R.)*, vol. 6, pp. 1407-14).

[2] It should be noted that Australia's ratification was not announced until 2 March 1956.

concessions, and in the event of lack of agreement on the question of compensation, substantially equivalent concessions may be withdrawn by the countries concerned. Also the right of Australia to withdraw a specific concession under procedures referred to in (b) above could be revoked in any case where Australia unreasonably failed to offer adequate compensation.

The new procedures are particularly favourable to Australia. The special position of countries heavily dependent upon a few primary commodities for their export income, and relying on the tariff as an important aid for diversifying their economies is recognized by a provision that for such countries authority to enter into negotiations for the adjustment of 'bound' rates on selected items will be virtually automatic.

The new procedures were adopted largely as a result of the insistence of the Australian Delegation that some provision should be made for Australia's circumstances.

Disposal of Surpluses

12. Prolonged negotiations resulted in the adoption of a resolution which should provide some safeguards against the ill-effects for Australian exports of the disposal of agricultural surpluses. The resolution records the expressed intention of countries holding any such surpluses to liquidate them so as to avoid undue disturbances on the world market. The resolution also calls for consultation with governments likely to be affected (Appendix B, Item 4). A similar resolution was adopted in respect of stockpiles accumulated for strategic purposes (Appendix B, Item 5).

Preferences

13. Insufficient support was forthcoming to secure the flexibility sought by Australia in the no-new-preference rule. This rule in the 1947 Agreement was regarded as vital by almost all countries outside the British Commonwealth and in fact few Commonwealth countries supported the Australian proposal for a relaxation in the rule. The Contracting Parties, however, officially recognized the right of countries exchanging preferences to consult together on an arrangement which included new or increased preferences and subsequently to bring such a proposed arrangement before the Contracting Parties for a waiver of the rule.

State Trading

14. New provisions (Article XVII) were achieved which require specified additional information about these practices to be supplied. Australia will thus be able to assess more precisely the extent to which these practices affect Australian exports, and will be in a better position to decide how to develop trade in products subject to these practices.

Export Subsidies

15. Increased protection has been obtained against disruption of trade by export subsidies. The new Article (Article XVI) recognizes that export subsidies may have harmful effects. Australia was not able to secure a complete banning of these subsidies but it is now stipulated that export subsidies on primary products should not be applied to capture for the exporting country more than an equitable share of the world market having regard to past trade and any special factors.

Another change in Australia's interest is that where injury or threat of injury can be shown countries importing for example Australian goods may now impose countervailing duties on subsidized products from third countries.

Quantitative Import Restrictions

16. There was strong pressure by some countries to insert new limitations upon the right of members to make their own decisions as to whether or for how long import restrictions should be imposed for balance of payments reasons. Notwithstanding this pressure, Australia retains its essential freedom to impose such restrictions to safeguard the level of overseas funds. This is a matter to which the Government attaches particular significance. The changes made in the Articles concerned (Articles XII to XV) are confined to improvements in the procedures for consultation with the contracting parties when restrictions are imposed. These changes may benefit Australian export trade in respect of import restrictions imposed in countries importing Australian products.

Transitional Import Restrictions

17. Under a Decision taken during the Review the Contracting Parties will exercise a strict scrutiny and a close control over any import restrictions maintained during a limited transitional period to avoid serious injury to a particular industry (Appendix B, Item 7). Another decision provides in a similar fashion for a strict scrutiny of measures taken by the United States to protect its system of agricultural price supports (Appendix B, Item 3).

Other Matters

18. The Delegation took an active part in discussions on other changes in the Agreement. These included the re-drafting of Article XVIII to meet the special position of under-developed countries and the decision concerning the special problems of dependent overseas territories of the United Kingdom (Appendix B, Item 6).

19. The Contracting Parties were also required to consider certain procedural matters in relation to the Agreement. One of these is the proposal to establish an Organization for Trade Co-operation to supersede the body known as the Contracting Parties which has so far administered the General Agreement. This proposal and its link with the General Agreement are described in Section 3 and the text of the proposed agreement for an Organization is given in Appendix A. Appendix B incorporates the text of certain important resolutions and decisions. Two of these are worth special mention. One concerns the definitive application of the Agreement (Appendix B, Item 1). The other relates to the continued application of the tariff schedules of the Agreement (Appendix B, Item 2).

Definitive Application

20. So far the General Agreement has been applied provisionally as distinct from definitively. Provisional application has meant that countries apply Part II of the Agreement—that is the general trading rules—'to the fullest extent not inconsistent with existing legislation'. In addition resignation is permitted on 60 days notice as compared with 6 months in the case of definitive application. It was recognized at the Review Conference that definitive application would contribute more effectively to progress towards attainment of the objectives of the Agreement.

161

21. It was also agreed that for some members immediate amendment of all inconsistent legislation would cause difficulties. Accordingly a resolution was adopted at the Review Session which will enable countries to accept the definitive application of the Agreement under Article XXVI subject to a reservation regarding existing legislation similar to that provided for in provisional application. The formula does not set any fixed time limit for the duration of the reservation but the general intent of the declaration and the detailed procedures is towards securing complete conformity between the legislation of all member countries and their obligations under the Agreement. The text of the reservation and conditions attaching to its acceptance is reproduced in Item 1 of Appendix **B**.

The Continued Application of the Schedules

22. The present period of assured life of the tariff schedules ends on 30th June, 1955. Most member countries indicated at the Review that they favoured a further extension of the assured life. Because the revised Agreement, Article XXVIII of which provides for automatic extensions, cannot become effective for some time, a Declaration was drafted which will prolong, until 31st December, 1957, the life of the schedules of those contracting parties which sign the Declaration. The Declaration will also bring into effect the provisions of paragraph 4 of the new Article XXVIII (see paragraph 11 above), for those countries, in advance of the formal amendment of the Agreement. This Declaration is reproduced in Item 2 of Appendix **B**.

Source: *C.P.P.*, no. 91 of 1954-5, pp. 6-8.

5:5 GATT SHOULD BE RENEWED

The Minister for Commerce has until recently been a severe critic of the General Agreement on Tariffs and Trade. Now he is converted to a warm supporter by the 'dramatic' differences resulting from the revision of the agreement. Australian objections to the agreement in its old form, and to some of the proposals brought to the Geneva meeting, have been almost wholly met. There should be no further hesitation over renewing the agreement. Australia, however, must also be prepared to observe it in spirit, without taking undue advantage of the greater latitude it allows. . . .

The gain in flexibility is welcome. But Australia still needs to view widespread increases in protective duties with great caution. Development is proceeding just as fast as labour, materials and capital supplies will allow, and we need to draw heavily on overseas sources for these things. In return, Australia must sell to other countries. 'The quality of the product and the price at which we can produce and sell it will be the determining factors', as Mr McEwen has said. Tariffs which raised internal costs and impaired the ability of Australia's customers to buy from her could be a two-edged weapon.

Source: Editorial in *Sydney Morning
Herald*, 4 June 1955.

5:6 GATT AND LESS DEVELOPED COUNTRIES' EXPORT NEEDS

Press statement by the Minister for Trade (J. McEwen) on 20 October 1958.

The Australian case for commodity price stabilisation he had put at the Montreal Commonwealth Conference had been launched into the wider international arena much more quickly than our highest expectations allowed us to hope for, the Minister for Trade (Mr. McEwen) said today.

He said to have the case launched with the immediate and positively vigorous endorsement of the United Kingdom and the United States Governments inspired confidence that the basic problems of world trade in primary products would be attacked with determination.

These and other great industrial nations might have been expected to be among the last to support the principles advanced by the Australian Government. Instead they had unstintingly backed them.

Mr. McEwen was commenting on reports that member countries of the General Agreement on Tariffs and Trade, (G.A.T.T.) in their opening review of the world trade situation in Geneva during the week-end, emphasised the necessity for international action to overcome the special problems of trade in the great bulk commodities.

These included violent fluctuations in prices, lack of predictability, widespread practice of a high degree of agricultural protection in industrial countries and the great importance of improving the trading position of the less developed countries.

Mr. McEwen said it was a striking vindication of the principles he had put forward so vigorously for the Australian Government that over 40 G.A.T.T. countries had agreed that a solution of international commodity problems was fundamental to the expansion of world trade.

Mr. McEwen said a prominent place had been given in the discussion to the report on trends in international trade prepared by a panel of independent economists, appointed on Australian initiative, by the G.A.T.T. at its 1957 meeting.

This report, called the Haberler Report after the Chairman of the Panel of Expert Economists, had clearly identified the special problems associated with trade in primary commodities.

Australia had been arguing for some time that action should be taken to improve conditions of international commodity trade and had taken the initiative in proposing the appointment by G.A.T.T. of the panel of expert economists. Their report substantially endorsed the Australian Government's views.

Mr. McEwen said that at the recent Commonwealth Conference at Montreal he had put Australia's case in the clearest terms and had pointed out that the political stability of the less developed countries, including those close to Australia in South-East Asia, depended on their economic well-being. . . .

Mr. McEwen said it was most gratifying to see that the G.A.T.T. countries had now accepted the view that a more rapid rate of expansion in the export trade of the less developed countries was essential to their economic development. This was of profound importance to many of Australia's neighbours in South-East Asia, as well as to Australia herself.

The G.A.T.T. countries had agreed that the more industrialised countries should avoid trade measures which harm the trade of less developed countries. They had coupled this agreement with a readiness to examine, on a commodity-by-commodity basis, means of reducing fluctuations in commodity prices. This meant that they had given international endorsement to the objectives of Australian policy for which acceptance by Commonwealth countries had been received at Montreal.

This international endorsement was particularly encouraging in that it came so closely after the Montreal Trade and Economic Conference. It was clear that the Australian and Commonwealth attitude was acceptable on a wide world front and would be the basis for concerted world efforts to deal with these difficulties over the next few years.

5:7 GATT, 15TH SESSION: AUSTRALIA OPPOSES DISCRIMINATION

Statement by Australian Delegate (Sir John Crawford) at Ministerial Meeting on 28 October 1959.

Trends in Trade

. . . The imbalance in the relative rates of growth of trade of industrialized and non-industrialized areas was given prominence in the Haberler Report. The G.A.T.T. publication 'International Trade 1957/58', issued recently, points out that this trend has generally continued since the Haberler Report was completed. The trend is sharply accentuated in periods of economic recession in the highly developed countries as was illustrated by sharp falls in the prices of many primary commodities in 1957/58. The response of these prices to improved economic conditions has been uneven. It is highly significant that the prices and demands which have recovered least are products which are excessively protected in the industrialized countries. In this fact there is indeed one important obstacle to expansion of world trade.

This situation is not solely attributable to 'natural economic causes' like excessive supplies [and] changes in consumer tastes; it is due in significant measure, as the Haberler Report noted, to measures of protection adopted by many countries which are contrary to the basic philosophy of G.A.T.T. There is an imbalance in trading conditions between the highly industrialized countries on the one hand and those heavily dependent on exports of primary products and minerals on the other. A great deal of the onus for rectifying the imbalance does rest with industrialized countries who will need to modify the more exaggerated policies of protection, particularly those of a non tariff kind. . . .

Indeed, the Australian Government believes that ultimately success in G.A.T.T. will not be measured by further reductions in tariffs but rather by its ability to modify the powerful non-tariff barriers to world trade and, no less important, by its ability to eliminate discriminations in trade. Non-tariff barriers to trade and discriminations together go far to destroy any real meaning in most favoured nation tariff treatment as extended originally in the 1947 tariff negotiations to the agricultural exporters of the world.

Discrimination

It has for some time been the Australian Government's view that the time was approaching when, due to the improved balance of payments position of a number of countries and the measures taken on external convertibility, a comprehensive attack could be made on the elimination of discrimination in import restrictions. . . .

The decision of the I.M.F. on discrimination marks a significant step forward for world trade. It is certainly significant for dollar countries. But it is much more. The I.M.F. decision means just what it says: discrimination by countries trading in convertible currencies can no longer be justified on balance of payments grounds.

In the light of this decision then, I repeat the view of the Australian Government that the time is ripe for a further comprehensive attack on all forms of discrimination. . . .

Programme for Expanding Trade: The Work of the Three Committees

. . . For my Government the Review Session accomplished modest but quite significant improvements which have already yielded measurable results in our trading relations with some members.

Another step forward was the report of the Haberler Committee and the three committees since established to provide the basis for moving forward in our trading relations and, more especially, to promote an expansion of trade. These committees are crucial to G.A.T.T. As I have said, we cannot expect dramatically quick results; but solid results we must look for if the imbalance outlined in the Haberler Report is to be rectified. . . .

Committee I

As I stated at the 14th Session in relation to Committee I, the value of a further round of tariff negotiations to Australia is dependent upon a recognition that non-tariff obstacles to trade are amongst the major impediments to our exports. We consider that countries maintaining these non-tariff devices should be prepared to consider requests for reduction in these forms of protection. We have indicated our willingness to negotiate reductions in some instances.

. . . Obviously it is quite meaningless to negotiate and pay for a tariff concession on a primary product only to find that other forms of protection will effectively prevent any increase in the exports of the particular commodity. Indeed, all too many of the tariff concessions negotiated by Australia in 1947 have been vitiated by non-tariff devices: this is an experience we have no wish to repeat.

The Australian Government has been quite discouraged by the reception which our proposals have received from Committee I. It is thought that countries have been far too cautious in their approach to the negotiability of non-tariff barriers. We see in this caution possibly an inability, I hope not a reluctance, to realise the importance of this issue for countries like Australia. . . .

The Haberler Report drew particular attention to the growth of agricultural protectionism and its adverse effect upon world trade. It is not only in directly limiting the markets for low cost non-subsidised producers that unreasonable protectionism hurts. The hurt extends to third markets as export subsidies are used to dispose of the 'spill over' of excessive production generated by high price supports.

The Australian Government looks to Committee II for progress under this head. The agreed procedures under which the very frank consultations are being held will provide the basis for coming to close grips with the real issues involved.

We see merit in these procedures despite their undoubted slowness. We can not expect rapid developments or changes over night. . . .

G

Two particular aspects of this problem which cause the Australian Government serious concern are the widespread use of bilateral agreements on agricultural products and the use of quantitative restrictions to protect agriculture. I have already commented that balance of payments consultations have contributed to our education. Australia had expected that as countries emerged from balance of payments difficulties they would, in accordance with the terms of the G.A.T.T. and agreed procedures, remove their import restrictions. In important cases, however, restrictions on agricultural products are being retained and the retention of these restrictions is, as I have already made clear, aggravated by the existence of discriminatory action arising out of bilateral agreements.

We would like to think that out of Committee II will emerge good faith efforts to improve access to markets and to lessen the type of import discrimination associated, almost as a corollary, with excessive agricultural protectionism.

Committee III

The work of Committee III is mainly concerned with those countries which are in urgent, almost desperate need for economic development. Their ability to export is a major factor in this. Almost all have the problems facing agricultural exporters and many, as the report showed, are faced with exclusion of their manufactures. Most, too, have low tariffs and cannot readily negotiate market entry in the ordinary way associated with G.A.T.T.

The need is too great to be ignored by G.A.T.T. and governments must consider the plea already advanced by Committee III. Yet the Chairman of the Contracting Parties was undoubtedly right in suggesting more specific lines of enquiry and consultation on behalf of this Committee.

Certainly it is the view of the Australian Government that there is probably no escape from detailed case work. We need to list clearly the practices which are hampering the export efforts of the less developed countries. We need then patiently to probe and discuss—'confront' if you will—in the hope of securing practical modifications to trade barriers of greatest concern to the less developed members of G.A.T.T. The plea for patience here is even less palatable than in other areas of G.A.T.T.'s work—for the need is so great. Yet we see no alternative and stand ready to support detailed exercises designed to advance the work of Committee III in quite concrete terms. . . .

Economic Integration

No general policy statement in G.A.T.T. on behalf of a member government can ignore the movement towards economic integration in Europe. The Australian Government, along with others, has repeatedly welcomed the prospects of effective economic integration as a major step towards political, social and economic stability in Western Europe. We have, nevertheless, felt it right to draw attention to some trade problems emerging, especially on the agricultural side, where the 'open door' policy is not yet obvious to us. These questions are very much before G.A.T.T. and our concerns are so well known that they perhaps call for no repetition. Yet events prior to this Session had not lessened those concerns of which I mention only three.

In the first place we have expressed fear that market opportunities would be lessened, not enlarged, to the extent that agricultural policies possibly became more, not less, protective under the Rome Treaty and under whatever finally governs the economic relations of the SEVEN. . . .

Secondly, the Australian Government is not happy that there should be two blocs: it will be better for world trade to see one Free Trade Area in some form or another consistent with Article XXIV of G.A.T.T. . . .

And this is my third point, Mr. Chairman. If G.A.T.T. is not able to reconcile regionalism in Europe with its broad concept of non-discriminatory multilateral trading, then G.A.T.T. as a system of fair trade rules may become of secondary instead of primary importance in leading and shaping the trading policies of the world.

For all three reasons the debate on European economic integration is of high importance, requiring all the accumulated and well tested wisdom of G.A.T.T. in the years immediately ahead of us.

Source: Department of Trade,
*Important Australian Policy Speeches
Relating to GATT, 1954-65*, pp. 38-43.
Roneoed document.

5:8 AUSTRALIA AND GERMAN FLOUR EXPORTS

Agreed minute of discussions between representatives of the Government of the Commonwealth of Australia and the Government of the Federal Republic of Germany on the exportation of flour from the Federal Republic of Germany to certain traditional Australian markets for flour.

Representatives of the Government of the Commonwealth of Australia and Representatives of the Government of the Federal Republic of Germany met in Canberra between the 7th and 14th October, 1959, to consider the difficulties arising from the system under which increasing quantities of German flour were being exported to traditional Australian flour markets.

The two Delegations reviewed trade developments in these markets over recent years and, as a result of the consultations, agreed that measures would be adopted which should lead to a solution to the problem at an early date.

In the course of these discussions it was agreed:

(1) The Government of the Federal Republic of Germany will reduce from 100 : 182 to 100 : 170 the conversion ratio used in allocating wheat to millers for the manufacture of the type of flour which is being exported to Australia's traditional markets. The German Delegation considered that such modification of the conversion ratio would reduce the problems which Australia had been experiencing from the competition of German flour in those markets.

(2) The Government of the Federal Republic of Germany will not grant any governmental assistance which would assist German flour exports or offset the effect of the reduced conversion ratio.

(3) The Government of the Federal Republic of Germany will, on a continuing basis, provide the Australian Commercial Counsellor in Bonn with monthly information on licences issued and, as soon as available, on the quantities of flour exported to the countries and places listed in the Annex to this Minute, and on request, with other information relevant to the provisions of this Minute.

(4) Each Government will at the request of the other enter into consultation on any matter relating to the operation of the provisions of this Minute. In the event of any difficulty arising in the operation of the provisions of this Minute either Government may request consultation for the purpose of resolving the particular difficulty and if after a period of one month from the date of such request for consultation the particular difficulty is not resolved, the Government requesting consultation will then be free upon not less than fourteen days' notice to terminate the provisions of this Minute.

The two delegations agreed that:

(a) the provisions of this Minute shall be regarded as coming into force on 1st January, 1960, with effect until 31st December, 1961;

(b) before 31st December, 1961, the two Governments will consult regarding the extension of the provisions of this Minute beyond that date.

Signed in Canberra on the fourteenth day of October, 1959, in duplicate, in the English and German languages, both texts being equally authentic.

G. P. PHILLIPS,
Leader of the Australian
Delegation.

WERNER VON BARGEN,
Leader of the German
Delegation.

ANNEX

Aden	Mauritius	Saudi Arabia
Brunei	Netherlands New Guinea	Singapore
Burma	North Borneo	Sudan
Ceylon	Nyasaland	Thailand
Goa	Pacific-Islands	United Kingdom
Hong Kong	Persian Gulf Ports	Zanzibar
Indonesia	Philippines	
Malaya	Sarawak	

Source: Commonwealth of Australia, *Paper No. 10612/59*, Government Printer, Canberra.

5:9 FLOUR AGREEMENT WITH FRANCE

Press statement by the Minister for Trade (J. McEwen) on 3 May 1960.

The Acting Prime Minister and Minister for Trade (Mr. J. McEwen) announced today that an understanding on flour exports had been reached in Paris recently between representatives of the Australian and French Governments. The understanding, he said, was designed to protect Australian flour exports from damage from subsidised French flour exports.

Several years ago exports of French flour to traditional Australian markets like Ceylon and Indonesia reached such proportions that the important Australian export trade to South-East Asia had been disrupted. French flour was able to undersell Australian because of substantial subsidies paid to the French millers and exporters.

The position became so serious that the Australian Government initiated discussions in the G.A.T.T. The G.A.T.T. Contracting Parties recommended that the French and Australian authorities should consult before France resumed exports to South-East Asian markets so that further serious damage to Australia's trade might be avoided. . . .

As a result of the discussions, Mr. McEwen added, the French Government had assured us that our flour export trade to traditional markets in South-East Asia would not materially be affected by French competition during the current French export season.

The French Government has also undertaken to avoid damaging Australia's flour export trade during the coming French export season, which commences on the 1st August, by keeping total exports of French flour to markets in South-East Asia within a reasonable figure and by avoiding undue concentration of their exports in any single market.

Both Governments have agreed to exchange information on exports of flour to all markets of interest on a regular monthly basis and to be prepared to consult if any difficulties arise.

Mr. McEwen concluded by saying that the understanding with France was the latest in a succession of actions by the Government over the last two years to protect Australian flour exports from unfair competition. The results of earlier actions were the protection gained in the Trade Agreement with the Federation of Malaya; the undertaking by Ceylon to buy specified quantities of Australian flour in 1959 and 1960; and the agreement by Germany last year to avoid further damage to Australia's flour trade.

5:10 GATT: AUSTRALIA SEEKS REDUCTIONS IN AGRICULTURAL PROTECTION, IMPROVEMENT IN PRICE LEVELS AND SOME COMMODITY AGREEMENTS

Statement by the Deputy Prime Minister and Minister for Trade (J. McEwen) at the Meeting of Ministers on 18 May 1963.

ITEM II: *Arrangements for the Reduction or Elimination of Tariffs and Other Barriers to Trade, and Related Matters*

ITEM III: *Measures for Access to Markets for Agricultural and Other Primary Products*

Mr Chairman, addressing myself from the Australian aspect to this issue of agriculture, our needs as exporters of temperate agricultural products are simply stated. Australia needs reasonable and predictable access to world markets, needs remunerative and more stable prices, for the products of which we are efficient producers. These simple objectives which I state have been pursued by Australia for many years in the GATT. We have had the experience of many disappointments and frustrations. Our terms of trade have continued to run against us and frankly we have been beginning to despair of the ability of GATT to cope with problems on agriculture. We have even been beginning to feel that we must look elsewhere. Now there is a new attempt at a break-through. We welcome the initiative of the United States; we welcome the initiative of the Kennedy Round as bold and comprehensive. It is also probably the last chance of the GATT to redeem all their failures to reduce the lack of balance between the various types of countries parties to GATT. As you said yourself, Mr. Chairman, whatever the outcome of this meeting the world will not be the same after it. I assume you mean it will be better from the trading point of view if we succeed. It will be worse if we fail. So we can only endorse and commend the United States proposals for massive and equal reductions in tariffs and other barriers to trade. We welcome the negotiations to be tied together as proposed by the United States, to achieve reductions to barriers of trade on all classes of products. Successful negotiations on agriculture are quite essential to an overall satisfactory conclusion. . . .

I note that the Working Party on Procedures for the Negotiations agrees that agriculture presents special problems. Problems of arrangements of methods, of scope, etc., are really not capable of a 'formula approach' or of broad commitment. Indeed much as we would welcome a simple commitment to reduce agricultural protection by 50 per cent, or a significant fixed amount, frankly we do not expect it and will not imperil the substantive success of the Kennedy Round by taking any unrealistic stand.

The GATT itself has recognized that there is a number of countries who depend for their export earnings on a relatively small number of primary products. The industrialized countries must accept that these countries cannot formulate reciprocal offers before the form and scope of benefits which they may receive become sufficiently apparent.

There are three areas in agricultural fields where we expect progress. First, reductions in levels of assistance given to domestic production. Here we expect commitments that will give us known terms of access. We do not want vague promises as were given us in 1947, but firm commitments to cover tariff and non-tariff devices. Whatever the means of protection used the results must be bound in the GATT schedules. Second, on the subject of international prices. There has been a complete failure of GATT to come to grips with this problem. Stripped to essentials the situation is that because of subsidies and variable levies and quantitative restrictions it is not unusual—indeed it is the rule—between industrial countries to be able to purchase their bulk agricultural commodities at depressed prices, frequently below the cost of production by efficient producers—certainly in every instance much below the prices which their own producers receive. We do not want extravagant or unreasonable prices but remunerative prices for efficient producers.

Present prices on a number of items are artificially low. Take, for example, wheat. Less than 15 per cent of the total world production of wheat enters into commercial international trade but this 15 per cent is, for my country, the export income on which we must plan our development and growth and it is being sold at prices far below the levels of price support in most of the consuming countries.

Any benefits to us from price improvements would be followed immediately by even larger benefits to industrialized countries from whom our imports come, who earn from us the invisible income—our freight—who profit from us in their dealings in the field of banking and public borrowings. There is known history to show that benefits to the primary exporting countries are more than offset, through their purchases, by benefits to the industrial exporters.

On the third aspect we believe that there is a need for comprehensive commodity agreements for bulk commodities. Action in this area could complement what is done in the first and the second areas that I have referred to—that is, domestic protection and price. Such agreements would cover all the appropriate

170

aspects of international trade as dictated by the needs of different commodities with reciprocal obligations for exporters and importers.

We accept that benefits to agricultural exporters cannot be brought by one single decision. Benefits of worthwhile value must include, in the first place, reductions in agricultural protection. In the second place improvements in international price level and the predictability of our trade. And in the third place, and we believe in a few cases only, comprehensive commodity agreements.

The meetings of the GATT groups on cereals and meat must resume at an early and firm date to really get to grips with the problems and to *negotiate*—certainly not to resume a study, but to get to grips, produce solutions and decisions.

Because the problems of agriculture are so separate and so complex, so important both to the industrial countries and the agricultural exporters alike, we believe that these problems are best tackled separately within the total negotiations—separate from the difficult enough problems of industrial tariff reductions—separate again from the urgent problems of the less-developed countries. Any attempt to sort out in one single negotiating group all these problems of the three areas would, I think, be doomed to failure and frustrations.

Accordingly, I suggest the establishment of a special temperate primary products negotiating group to be charged with the full task of determining the methods of handling agricultural problems and applying these methods finally in the negotiations. The existing GATT commodity groups for cereals and meat would henceforth, then, operate as negotiating bodies within the framework of the new agricultural group. It would be the responsibility, as I see it, of this temperate primary products negotiating group to have a final package in its sphere ready by the time the results of negotiations in the other two fields—of the less-developed and the industrial exporters have been finalized. The temperate primary products negotiating group would, as I see it, report progress made, and report difficulties arising not entirely within the province of its charter to an overall trade negotiations management committee, but I strongly put it, Mr. Chairman, that these three groups dealing with these quite identifiably separate problems would need to operate as autonomous groups and certainly not as sub-committees of some overall group. . . .

Source: GATT Press Release 793,
18 May 1963.

5:11 GATT: TRADE NEGOTIATIONS TO COMMENCE ON 4 MAY 1964

Extracts from 'Conclusions and Resolutions Adopted at Meeting of Ministers, 21 May 1963'.

Resolution Adopted on 21 May 1963 on Items II and III of the Agenda

The Ministers agreed:

A. PRINCIPLES

1. That a significant liberalization of world trade is desirable, and that, for this purpose, comprehensive trade negotiations, to be conducted on a most-favoured-nation basis and on the principle of reciprocity, shall begin at Geneva on 4 May 1964, with the widest possible participation.

2. That the trade negotiations shall cover all classes of products, industrial and non-industrial, including agricultural and primary products.

3. That the trade negotiations shall deal not only with tariffs but also with non-tariff barriers.

4. That, in view of the limited results obtained in recent years from item-by-item negotiations, the tariff negotiations, subject to the provisions of paragraph B 3, shall be based upon a plan of substantial linear tariff reductions with a bare minimum of exceptions which shall be subject to confrontation and justification. The linear reductions shall be equal. In those cases where there are significant disparities in tariff levels, the tariff reductions will be based upon special rules of general and automatic application.

5. That in the trade negotiations it shall be open to each country to request additional trade concessions or to modify its own offers where this is necessary to obtain a balance of advantages between it and the other participating countries. It shall be a matter of joint endeavour by all participating countries to negotiate for a sufficient basis of reciprocity to maintain the fullest measure of trade concessions.

6. That during the trade negotiations a problem of reciprocity could arise in the case of countries the general incidence of whose tariffs is unquestionably lower than that of other participating countries.

7. That, in view of the importance of agriculture in world trade, the trade negotiations shall provide for acceptable conditions of access to world markets for agricultural products.

8. That in the trade negotiations every effort shall be made to reduce barriers to exports of the less-developed countries, but that the developed countries cannot expect to receive reciprocity from the less-developed countries.

Source: GATT Press Release 794,
29 May 1963.

5:12 AUSTRALIA AND THE KENNEDY ROUND OF GATT TRADE NEGOTIATIONS

Press statement by the Minister for Trade (J. McEwen) on 31 May 1963.

I went overseas to attend a meeting of Ministers of the G.A.T.T. and to have talks with the Governments in Wellington, Washington, Ottawa and London.

Last year Britain faced the inevitability of the preference system being drastically revised when she sought entry to the Common Market.

Now the British willingness to reduce her tariffs in the new Kennedy Round of G.A.T.T. trade negotiations—and hence reduce preferences—confronts Australia with the virtual certainty of a substantial change in our reciprocal preferences with Britain.

This fact forms the background of my recent mission overseas. It poses an issue of great importance for the Government on the best course to be taken in planning to protect Australia's overseas trading and access to export markets.

In Washington I made it clear to the American administration that Australia supported the broad objectives of the United States in proposing that the Kennedy Round should embrace negotiations on the barriers to trade in agricultural products, and the trade problems of the less developed countries as well as on industrial tariffs. I left the Americans in no doubt that their proposal for a 50% across-the-board cut in tariffs was unacceptable and inappropriate for a country like Australia. The arguments I advanced were:—

(1) Because of our small domestic market, our industries do not enjoy the lower costs which go with large-scale production, whereas the giant industries of the great industrial exporting countries do have this benefit.

(2) The great bulk (90%) of our exports were agricultural and primary products. No industrialised country had agreed to reduce its protection on these products by the equivalent of a 50% linear cut. Therefore we would not know at the outset of the negotiations the benefits available to us.

(3) The advantages which could come to our small volume of industrial exports would bear no comparison with the disadvantages which would be imposed on our protected industries, if a general uniform, across-the-board tariff reduction were applied.

For these reasons, I made it abundantly clear that Australia could not accept the linear cut principle as the basis for negotiations. On the other hand, Australia was not seeking a 'free ride' and was prepared to pay for any benefits received in the negotiations. Britain's acceptance of the 50% linear cut proposal would mean that the negotiations could result in a serious decline in our preferences in the British market—a decline which for us must be offset in gains elsewhere, mainly in the field of primary exports. To the extent that present reciprocal preferences were not maintained in either the British or Australian markets then third countries, particularly the industrialised countries, would gain benefits which would be as valuable to them as those we would expect to get in their markets for our agricultural trade.

As the result of my discussions in Washington, I secured a full understanding of our position by the Americans.

At the outset of my bilateral discussions with British Ministers, I re-emphasised the over-riding importance which the Australian Government and farm industries attached to the assured and preferred market access provided in the United Kingdom/Australia Trade Agreement. I made it plain that the 'known' benefits of the United Kingdom/Australia Trade Agreement were for us better than the 'unknown' outcome of the Kennedy Round. This was especially the case because of our understanding of the basic difficulties the industrialised countries would have in offering in the Kennedy Round anything like the same reductions in agricultural protection as in industrial protection.

Because of the British Government's predisposition in favour of the Kennedy Round tariff and agricultural proposals, and because the British Government might still wish to join the Common Market, it was obviously necessary for me to have a very frank discussion with British Ministers on the implications of these policies for a renewed United Kingdom/Australia Trade Agreement to cover a further 5 year period. . . .

As the result of these talks I was left in no doubt that Britain saw it as vital to her interest to participate actively in the Kennedy Round of trade negotiations, on the basis of offering an across-the-board reduction in her tariffs for compensating benefits, particularly in the tariffs of the Common Market and the U.S.A. Although this policy decision by the British Government would, if implemented, obviously have an important impact on the preferences we now enjoy in the British market, it was apparent that they had taken this into consideration and that their decision was firm.

In the light of this British policy, it was obvious that there was no point in fixing a date for the re-negotiation of our Trade Agreement at that stage. We decided to review our mutual trading relationships at a later period when both Governments would be able to determine more clearly the extent of Britain's commitments in the Kennedy Round. . . .

The G.A.T.T. Meeting of Ministers was convened to discuss President Kennedy's proposals for trade and tariff negotiations, and was devoted to the consideration of proposals for the expansion of trade in three major areas.

(1) Measures for the expansion of the trade of less developed countries.

(2) Arrangements for the reduction or elimination of tariffs and other barriers to trade in industrial products.

(3) Measures to improve access to markets for agricultural and other primary products.

When at Washington I stressed from the outset the importance of the Americans adhering to their previously announced intention to require that liberalisation of agricultural trade should be a condition precedent to their offer of tariff reductions. The Americans assured me that they would do this. At Geneva the Americans adhered strongly to this line.

I obtained general acceptance in Geneva that linear tariff cuts would not be appropriate for countries such as Australia. Firstly, because it could not be expected that the countries engaging in agricultural protectionism would reduce their protection by 50% across-the-board. Secondly, as previously explained, the home industries of countries like Australia, geared to a small market and not having the cost advantages of the big industrialised countries, should not be sacrificed. . . .

The resolution as finally agreed is of great significance to Australia in that it makes explicit provision for dealing with the obstacles, tariff and non-tariff, which have stood in the way of commercial exporters of primary products. I have been arguing for years that while G.A.T.T. has brought worthwhile results to the major exporters of industrial products through the reduction of industrial tariffs, it has failed to deal with subsidies, quotas, and the other non-tariff devices facing agricultural exporters. The decisions of this conference mean that the industrial countries have now accepted that this paradox must be corrected. The barriers to the exports of primary products are at long last to be put in the negotiating ring alongside industrial tariffs, and the G.A.T.T. Trade Negotiations Committee has been instructed to find ways of obtaining a balance between industrial and equivalent agricultural concessions.

I hope that this will turn out to be a significant break-through for exporters of agricultural and other primary products. Indications as to what can be expected from these agreements on principles will become apparent from meetings to be held shortly of the G.A.T.T. negotiating groups on Cereals and Meat. A similar group on Dairy Products is also to be set up. Since the last abortive meeting of the Cereals group which was frustrated by Britain's attitude towards the crucial issue of low prices, Britain has announced changes in her agricultural policy. The forthcoming meeting of the Cereals group will provide an opportunity to see what effects this new policy will have on a successful outcome of the work of the group....

The final negotiating stage is to start on 4th May, 1964, when the final negotiations leading to decisions on tariffs and agricultural issues will be set in train. Without doubt this will be the toughest stage of all.

5:13 INQUIRY ON TARIFFS

The Tariff Board began on September 23 [1963] to enquire into a reference to it by the Minister for Trade linked with Australia's participation in forthcoming international tariff negotiations commonly referred to as the Kennedy Round. The Board has been asked to decide whether the most-favoured-nation rates of duty on 135 items should be reduced. The rates apply in all countries in the General Agreement on Tariffs and Trade to which special rates under other preferential tariffs do not apply. The tariffs suggested on the 135 items would make the rates equal to those under the preferential system between the United Kingdom and Australia. The Board's recommendations are sought by March 15, 1964.

Source: Australia in Facts and Figures,
no. 79, 1963.

5:14 KENNEDY ROUND NEGOTIATIONS

Paper given by J. McEwen to the Australian Institute of International Affairs in Brisbane, 5 July 1965.

Although the Kennedy Round was launched some two years ago it is only recently that the negotiations have begun to gather momentum. There have been various reasons for the delays, but the great unresolved problem is in agriculture.

Great difficulty is being experienced in finding a satisfactory basis for negotiations. The agreed approach has been to take the major commodities for separate examination and negotiation. G.A.T.T. Groups have been established for Cereals, Dairy Products and Meat.

A commencement has been made on negotiations on all these products. Since there has been more international experience on wheat it was agreed that the Cereals Group should press on with its study first. It is hoped that the outcome of the Cereals Group would prove a pattern for application, with appropriate modifications, to the other products. The Cereals Group has recently been engaged in quite intensive studies. Indeed the Group has reconvened in Geneva today.

Australia has tabled detailed and explicit proposals to the Cereals Group. We want assurances of remunerative prices for efficient producers. We also seek to put a limit on the highly protectionist policies of the industrial countries and limit and eventually eliminate dumping and excessive export subsidies.

We know that wheat has been produced in surplus to the commercial market in post-war years. These surpluses were relieved by their disposal to the needy countries. Part of our proposal to the Cereals Group is that this should now be converted from a separate and ad hoc approach to an agreed international approach.

We concede that the country which produces wheat surplus to its commercial opportunities ought to be prepared to sell some of that wheat at less than the commercial price to the needy. We further argue that the provision of wheat to the needy ought not to be the responsibility only of those countries which produce wheat in export quantities.

Our approach is that the more affluent countries, whether wheat importers or exporters, should make a financial contribution to an international Fund which would be used to buy wheat at less than the going commercial price and provide it on concessional terms to the needy.

Let me summarise the main features of what we are trying to do: the Cereals Group is an illustration of an attempt to achieve international order by the concentration of certain principles on one product at a time. These principles are profit for efficient producers; the avoidance of price exploitation in times of shortage; a code for the handling of quantities surplus to commercial demand and the taking into account, where appropriate, of the problems of the needy countries.

There would need to be different formulae applicable to the various bulk primary products.

If such principles could govern international trade in the bulk commodities, then not only would Australia's economic position be improved, but one of the factors in world-wide economic fluctuations would have been removed for the betterment of all.

As I have said earlier there are also G.A.T.T. Commodity Groups negotiating on Meat and Dairy Products. Sugar may be similarly treated or it may be sufficiently covered in a new International Agreement. . . .

Source: *Australia's Overseas Economic
Relationships* (Sixteenth Roy Milne
Memorial Lecture), pp. 18-19.
Reprinted by permission.

6

NEW PROBLEMS EMERGING: TRADE POLICIES FOR THE LESS DEVELOPED COUNTRIES

There are really two sets of documents here, one associated with one special aspect of the work of GATT in recent years and the other with the United Nations Conference on Trade and Development. The two sets are placed together because of the common subject represented: the problem of improving the conditions of trade for the so-called 'less developed countries'.[1] We have, on the one hand, in GATT, an attempt in the new Part IV (Articles XXXVI-XXXVIII) to mould and bend the old trade rules to fit the trade and development needs of the less developed countries (A6:1). We have, on the other hand, in UNCTAD, a wider and more political approach to the same problems (6:8). The latter approach is much more than a mere protest at the comparative failure of GATT to achieve much for the LDCs although there is an important element of this in it. That the LDCs have not been able, in GATT, to express themselves so politically as they have in United Nations organisations is in large measure due to the fact that GATT is a detailed mutual commercial policy contract among the members. The contract calls for oversight and review in a detailed fashion not conducive to frequent political debates. Nevertheless, their political weight has become increasingly manifest in the 'modernisation' of GATT, as the documents in this section attest.

Both these developments are important to Australia. Australia finds itself in a somewhat uncomfortable position in both GATT and the new Trade and Development Board, the executive arm of the United Nations Conference.[2] It has, in some respects, the same objectives in export trade policy (especially for primary products) as the LDCs. It also shares the objective of economic development but, at the same time, it shares the affluence of the advanced countries and much of their reticence about lessening the tariff barriers to exports of simple manufactures from the LDCs. The difficulties and limitations of this middle-zone position are referred to in the Review Section (18)[3];

[1] For convenience we will describe these 'underdeveloped nations' as 'LDCs'. They are, in general terms, the poorer countries of the world whose incomes are low and whose level of industrial development is relatively backward compared with the more affluent countries of North America, Europe, Australia, New Zealand, and Japan.

[2] For the distinction between the *Conference* and the *Board* see 6:8.

[3] For an interesting analysis of Australia's 'middle zone' position see Arndt (2); also Vernon Report (11), vol. I, ch. 12, paras. 22-3.

but many of its characteristics are described (and defended) in the documents contained in this section (see especially 6:4).

We observed in the concluding paragraphs of the comment in Section 5 that, following the Haberler Committee Report, GATT became much more active—through its Trade Expansion Program—in matters affecting the LDCs. Committee III was given the mandate

> to consider and report to the Contracting Parties on ... measures for the expansion of trade, with particular reference to the importance of the maintenance and expansion of export earnings of the less developed countries to the development and diversification of their economies.[4]

The detail of the work of Committee III is beyond the scope of this book and these comments.[5] However, to it belongs much of the credit for some small results on particular commodities so far achieved and, more significantly for the future, for the political pressure represented in the three main documents—the Declaration of November 1961 (6:1), the Program of Action (6:2) adopted by ministerial delegates at GATT in May 1963, and the new Protocol or Part IV (Articles XXXVI-XXXVIII) of the GATT (A6:1).[6] It is worth noting that the Program of Action (sponsored initially in 1962 by twenty-one LDC members of Committee III) is an attempt to translate the earlier Declaration into achievable practical steps.

Taken together, all three steps can be fairly said to indicate that Australia, despite the difficulties of its position (6:4), has taken a constructively sympathetic view. Its actual import policies are far from being as obstructive as those of some other advanced countries, and its difficulties are genuine.[7] This is what renders 6:4 of such interest and importance.

On the one hand, the Australian offer of preferences doubly challenges the older GATT members, and particularly the United States, where it hurts—both in principle and pocket. Preferences are anathema to many members. This is not necessarily assuaged by the fact that Australia seeks no reciprocation for the preferences—since if they prove effective the cost will be borne by the developed countries replaced by the LDCs as suppliers to the Australian market. To any charge that this is unfair, the Australian government can fairly retort that both in GATT and UNCTAD there has been strong

[4] One indication of the general respect held for Australian understanding of the problems of the LDCs is the fact that this Committee almost continuously operated under the chairmanship of an Australian. Its work was taken over by the Trade and Development Committee in 1965.

[5] On all the matters discussed in this section there is a good deal of official material available from GATT and from the United Nations. See in particular GATT (81)-(87); United Nations Organization (158)-(159) UNCTAD; and Curzon (68).

[6] As at 27 June 1966 a sufficient majority of contracting parties had accepted Part IV to enable it to operate. France alone among the EEC countries has not signed (December 1966), and this will weaken its effectiveness and the likelihood of EEC action.

[7] For an account of Australia's treatment of imports from developing countries see Vernon Report (11), vol. I, ch. 12, para. 39.

support for one-sided preferential treatment.[8] It can argue more cogently, as McEwen does in 6:4, that a reduction in the MFN rate available to all will not help the LDCs *vis-à-vis* the advanced countries, whose competitive position would remain unimpaired. Preferential quotas will at least give the LDCs some help in this respect, although in some cases the preferential margin won't be wide enough.

There is, however, another side to the offer of preferences, one that rather limits the apparently generous quality of Australia's action. The commodities chosen are not those in which Australian production is affected and, indeed, 6:4 makes the Australian reservation on this point clear. In simple effect an opportunity has been provided to the LDCs at the expense of other suppliers. For this we need not apologise but nor should we be upset if the special and limited nature of our action is the subject of comment.[9] While the case against across-the-board reductions in the Australian tariff is overwhelming and is accepted in GATT,[10] we can nevertheless expect pressure in due course to share in arrangements designed to help the trade of the LDCs in some of the products we also produce ourselves. We will be expected to share in whatever further steps are taken to lessen restrictions on exports of textiles and other simple manufactures from the LDCs.[11]

Although the formal reservation in applying paragraphs 1, 2 and 3 of Article XXXVII could be considered inept and unnecessary, it is at least an honest statement of Australia's position. A general acceptance of Part IV of GATT with a reservation that complete compliance would not be practicable because of Australia's special position as outlined by Hasluck (6:5) could have served the purpose as well if Australia intends to do what it feels it can in terms of the Article. The reservation leaves Australia legally free from formal constraint and allows it to be unco-operative if it feels it must: it will nevertheless not relieve it from criticism (6:3) or pressure to act in terms of the Article. The Japanese case is perhaps a good precedent justifying the reservation. The fact that we formally reserved our position under Article XXXV did not prevent us—in response to Japanese pressure and to serve our interests—according Japan much better MFN treatment under our first trade treaty than some members of GATT who had unblushingly accepted GATT obligations *vis-à-vis* Japan. Subsequently we withdrew that reservation, and when later progress is reported under the new GATT articles we may feel

[8] Perhaps 'pressure' or 'demand' would be the better word, since most 'support' comes from the LDCs themselves. Nevertheless, there are supporters in the ranks of the developed countries, and the Common Market virtually gives it to its Associated Territories.

[9] One of the strong supporters of Australia's action—Shri Manubhai Shah, Minister for Commerce in India—has, for example, felt constrained to draw attention to its limitations.

[10] See comments on Kennedy Round in Section 5.

[11] See some comment on the new Chapter in GATT, written before the announcement (6:5) of Australia's position in Vernon Report (11), vol. I, ch. 12, paras. 85-92.

able to withdraw this more general one. Meanwhile paragraph (b) of Hasluck's communication (6:5) indicates Australia's commitment to do what it may find possible. The judgment remains in the hands of the Australian government. The preference offer outlined by McEwen (6:4) which came into force on 12 April 1966 following a GATT waiver given on 28 March 1966, is a definite step, but a first step only, in the spirit of the Articles.

While the forum has been GATT, the Australian action on the preference issue may be seen as an action of political importance in the framework of UNCTAD. As this book is being prepared it is too early in the development of the new body to discern from the documents very much that is definitive for Australia's position. Certain points, however, appear to emerge.

The first is that Australia's position as neither fully advanced nor underdeveloped economically was not well, or even formally, accepted in UNCTAD. In the forum of this Conference (6:6 to 6:8), the political division of the world 'into two—and only two—economic categories' was sharply drawn (6:4). While Australia's special position continues to enjoy respect, it is not thereby freed from the pressures exerted by the '77' (LDCs) on all affluent (= developed) nations.

The second follows from the first. While commodity problems have a very large place in the functions of the new Trade and Development Board established in terms of the Final Act of the Conference (6:8), it is inevitable that emphasis will be in the areas of most interest to the LDCs—tropical products and minerals rather than cereals, meat, and dairy produce.[12] Australia may well find it necessary to push its interest in commodities in both GATT (cereals, meat, and dairy produce groups) and the new United Nations Board (sugar, minerals, and all tropical products of interest to itself and Papua-New Guinea). It will therefore necessarily have a vital interest in the institutional relations of the two bodies in respect of commodity policy. Even within GATT the growing influence of the LDCs will reduce the relative importance of temperate zone produce in the debates. For this reason the tying of wheat, meat, and dairy produce to the Kennedy Round is an important way of trying to assure adequate attention to them.

The third comment is perhaps less obvious in the documents and should be put in the form of a question. The documents show a parallel development of efforts—in GATT and in the wider United Nations framework—to meet the legitimate economic aspirations of the LDCs. The calling of UNCTAD undoubtedly reflected in part political frustration with lack of progress. The question is whether the Conference can free itself sufficiently from the political atmosphere and debating practices of the United Nations Assembly to get down to the realities of securing action on the many trade issues in its charter. In this respect GATT has decided advantages: its delegations are used

---

[12] It is not suggested that no LDCs have any interest in these. Argentina is a notable case in point.

180

to negotiating contracts and practical understandings within the framework of principles endorsed by its member governments at the political level. The techniques of consultations (really a form of non-political confrontation) have produced results—the more readily because the Articles, although emerging from original declarations of principle, are mostly specific and can be interpreted and applied readily to particular cases. The new Articles XXXVII and XXXVIII read rather more concretely than anything as yet emerging from UNCTAD. Nevertheless, GATT is still handicapped by the fact that it was drafted for, and remains still in the main a charter for, 'normal' trade as conceived by the advanced countries in 1947 and in 1954.[13] It is possible that the new body—with the LDCs as its central interest—will, nevertheless, take the most valuable leaf out of GATT's book and attempt to draft actual compacts or agreements. When it does this it will be in business. Like GATT it may find progress slower than desired but more real than that coming from repeated declarations limited to statements of principle and objectives.

Whatever the methods used by the Trade and Development Board to achieve results, it remains clear that Australia will be treated as an affluent country: not too much notice will be taken of its mid-way position if this is proffered as a reason for not accepting suggestions for liberalising trade opportunities needed by the LDCs.

A6:1 GATT: SUMMARY OF PART IV

PREPARED BY NANCY ANDERSON

ARTICLE XXXVI—PRINCIPLES AND OBJECTIVES

The Contracting Parties recall that the basic objectives of this Agreement include the raising of standards of living and the progressive development of the economies of all contracting parties, and consider that the attainment of these objectives is particularly urgent for less-developed contracting parties. They agree on the need for rapid and sustained expansion of the export earnings of these parties; for positive efforts to ensure them a share in the growth in international trade commensurate with their economic development needs; for provision of more favourable and acceptable conditions of access to world markets for their exports of a limited range of primary products; for measures to stabilize and improve conditions of world markets in these products; for increased access to markets under favourable conditions for processed and manufactured products of particular export interest to them; for collaboration between the Contracting Parties and the international lending agencies to alleviate their burdens; and for appropriate collaboration between the Contracting Parties and other intergovernmental bodies and the organs and agencies of the United Nations concerned with trade and development.

The developed contracting parties do not expect reciprocity for commitments to reduce or remove barriers to the trade of the less-developed contracting parties.

---

[13] See reference to this in GATT (87), statement by Balensi.

Article XXXVII—Commitments

To the fullest extent possible developed contracting parties shall accord high priority to the reduction and elimination of barriers to products currently or potentially of particular interest to less-developed contracting parties; refrain from introducing or increasing import barriers on these products; refrain from imposing new fiscal measures, and in any adjustment of fiscal policy accord high priority to the reduction and elimination of measures hampering the growth of consumption of primary products wholly or mainly produced in the territories of less-developed contracting parties.

If effect is not being given to these provisions the matter shall be reported to the Contracting Parties which shall consult with all interested contracting parties to reach satisfactory solutions.

The developed contracting parties shall make every effort, where a government determines the resale price of products produced in the territories of less-developed contracting parties, to maintain trade margins at equitable levels; consider the adoption of other measures to provide greater scope for the development of imports from less-developed contracting parties; and have special regard to the trade needs of less-developed contracting parties when considering the application of other measures permitted under this Agreement.

Less-developed contracting parties agree to take appropriate action in implementation of the provisions of Part IV for the benefit of the trade of other less-developed contracting parties, in so far as such action is consistent with their individual development, financial and trade needs.

Article XXXVIII—Joint Action

The Contracting Parties shall collaborate jointly within the framework of this Agreement and elsewhere, to further the objectives set forth in Article XXXVI. In particular they shall take action to provide improved conditions of access to world markets for primary products of particular interest to less-developed contracting parties and to devise measures to stabilize and improve conditions of world markets in these products, including stable, equitable and remunerative prices; seek appropriate collaboration in matters of trade and development policy with the United Nations and its organs and agencies, including any institutions that may be created on the basis of recommendations by the United Nations Conference on Trade and Development; collaborate in analysing development plans and policies of less-developed contracting parties and in examining trade and aid relationships in order to devise measures to promote the development of export potential and facilitate access to export markets for products thus developed; keep under continuous review the development of world trade with special reference to the rate of growth of the trade of less-developed contracting parties and make appropriate recommendations; collaborate in seeking methods to expand trade for economic development purposes, through international harmonization and adjustment of national policies and regulations, through technical and commercial standards affecting production, transportation and marketing, and through export promotion by the establishment of facilities for the increased flow of trade information and the development of market research; and establish institutional arrangements to give effect to the provisions and further objectives of Part IV.

Source: Based on the text of Part IV of GATT as printed in *The Developing Countries and the GATT: The New Chapter on Trade and Development*, Geneva, February 1965.

6:1 GATT DECLARATION ON PROMOTION OF TRADE OF LESS DEVELOPED COUNTRIES, 30 NOVEMBER 1961

1.   The Contracting Parties recognize that there is need for rapid and sustained expansion in the export earnings of the less-developed countries if their development is to proceed at a satisfactory pace. They recognize the magnitude of the task before the governments of those countries in increasing per capita incomes and raising the standard of living of their peoples. To achieve these ends, increasing amounts of foreign exchange will be required for financing the imports needed to sustain and develop the economy. Although international aid is now and will continue to be essential in covering these needs, aid can be no substitute for trade. In the final analysis, economic development will have to be paid for from the earnings of the countries concerned.

2.   The export trade of the less-developed countries is not growing at a pace commensurate with the growth of their foreign exchange needs or with the growth of world trade generally. The Contracting Parties accordingly recognize the need for a conscious and purposeful effort on the part of all governments to promote an expansion in the export earnings of less-developed countries through the adoption of concrete measures to this end. The success of the efforts of developing countries will depend to a great extent upon their ability to find the necessary markets. Accordingly, contracting parties should reduce to a minimum restrictions inhibiting access to markets for the export products of the less-developed countries. The governments of the major industrialized areas, on whose markets the less-developed countries must necessarily largely depend, recognize a particular responsibility in this respect.

3.   The Contracting Parties agree that, if the needs of the less-developed countries for enlarged and diversified export trade are to be met, these countries must develop trade in other than traditional products. They note that some developing countries already have the investment and technological resources for the processing of raw materials and are able to produce efficiently some manufactured goods. They recognize that it is desirable that these countries and others possessing the necessary materials and skills be provided with increased opportunities to sell in world markets the industrial goods which they can economically produce, and urge that governments give special attention to ways of enlarging these opportunities.

4.   The Contracting Parties recognize that governments can contribute to the general objectives outlined above by observing the following principles and taking into account the following facts regarding tariff and non-tariff measures affecting access to markets.

(a)   *Quantitative restrictions.* Governments should give immediate and special attention to the speedy removal of those quantitative import restrictions which affect the export trade of less-developed countries. Where it is necessary for a government to maintain such restrictions under appropriate provisions of the GATT, it should apply them in a non-discriminatory manner causing the minimum hindrance to international trade, pursue policies designed to remove the underlying conditions requiring the use of such restrictions and, pending their elimination, give careful and sympathetic consideration to progressive increases in quotas. Contracting parties which are in process of moving out of balance-of-payments difficulties should take particular care that liberalization benefits are extended

183

in the fullest measure to the trade of less-developed countries, having regard to the urgent need for helping these countries attain rapid, self-sustaining growth.

(b) *Tariffs.* Governments should give special attention to tariff reductions which would be of direct and primary benefit to less-developed countries. In this connexion, they should consider the elimination of tariffs on primary products important in the trade of less-developed countries. They should also consider reducing those tariffs which differentiate dispro-portionately between processed products and raw materials, bearing in mind that one of the most effective ways in which less-developed countries can expand their employment opportunities and increase their export earnings is through processing the primary products they produce for export.

(c) *Revenue duties.* Fiscal charges, whether imposed as tariff duties or internal taxes, may inhibit efforts directed towards increasing consumption of particular products important in the trade of less-developed countries and, even where applied equally to imports and to competing domestic products, can be a serious obstacle to the expansion of trade. The Con-tracting Parties appreciate that adjustments in a fiscal system may be a complex matter, with important financial, economic and other conse-quences which have to be taken into account. Bearing in mind, however, the urgent development needs of less-developed countries and the current financial and economic situation in the industrialized countries mainly concerned, they agree that the removal or considerable reduction of revenue duties and fiscal charges in industrialized countries would be a useful contribution to the foreign exchange earning capacity of less-developed exporting countries.

(d) *State trading.* Access to markets for products of the type studied by Committee III should not be unnecessarily impeded through the operations of State import monopolies or purchasing agencies. For many products exported by less-developed countries, the prices charged on resale by some State monopolies, whether in countries with centrally-planned economies or in others, involve an implicit heavy taxation of imports. Countries operating State import monopolies or purchasing agencies, should en-deavour to improve access to their markets for products of less-developed countries by decisions to import larger quantities of the products con-cerned and, if necessary, by reductions in the difference between import and sales prices.

(e) *Preferences.* Some less-developed countries benefit neither from the preferential tariff systems which were in operation when the GATT came into being nor from the preferential treatment being established in the new customs unions or free trade areas. The Contracting Parties appreciate the concern of these less-developed countries whose export trade in certain products may be placed at a competitive disadvantage by the preferred treatment given to certain less-developed suppliers. They note, however, that the benefits afforded participating less-developed countries may include not only tariff preferences but other forms of assurances in the marketing of the products concerned. While it was important that these various advantages should not operate to the detriment of other less-developed countries, it was also necessary that action to deal with this

184

problem should be on a basis that meets the marketing needs of supplying countries now enjoying preferred access to markets.

(f) *Subsidies.* The subsidization of either the production or export of primary products may restrict the market opportunities of less-developed countries. Where this is so, the governments concerned should seek to limit the use of the subsidies in question with a view to avoiding injury to the export earnings of less-developed countries.

(g) *Disposal of commodity surpluses.* Governments disposing of commodity surpluses should bear in mind that the products concerned are generally important in the export trade of one or more less-developed countries, and that this is an added reason for careful observance of the principles and guidelines regarding such disposals accepted in the GATT resolutions of 4 March 1955 on the Disposal of Commodity Surpluses and on the Liquidation of Strategic Stocks and in the FAO's Principles of Surplus Disposal.

5. In negotiations for reductions in barriers to the exports of less-developed countries, contracting parties should adopt a sympathetic attitude on the question of reciprocity, keeping in mind the needs of these countries for a more flexible use of tariff protection. In making arrangements to bring about a general reduction of tariffs, account should also be taken of the special needs of less-developed countries.

6. An important contribution to the expansion of export earnings can also be made by intensified efforts to improve the production and marketing methods of the less-developed countries. The efforts of the less-developed countries along these lines would be greatly assisted if the industrial countries would give greater attention to this matter in the framework of their technical and financial assistance programmes.

7. Efforts to expand the export earnings of the less-developed countries and efforts to lessen the instability of such earnings which results from fluctuations in primary commodity markets should proceed concurrently. Progress towards reducing market instability, or towards offsetting its effects on foreign exchange receipts, is essential if the maximum benefits of the trade expansion effort are to be realized; at the same time, progress towards a diversified export trade will reduce the vulnerability of primary exporting countries to market fluctuations.

8. Finally, it is recognized that there are important possibilities for encouraging sound economic development in the less-developed countries through increased trade among themselves and that these countries should keep this in mind in formulating their tariff, commercial and economic policy measures. Lest the development of this important trade potential be prevented or unduly delayed, they should strive to attain and preserve liberal access to one another's markets in the same manner as they now seek to secure improved access to the markets of the economically advanced countries.

Source: GATT, *Proceedings of the Meeting of Ministers (27-30 November 1961),* Geneva, February 1962.

6:2 GATT PROGRAM OF ACTION, MAY 1963

The Ministers during their meeting from 16 to 21 May 1963, discussed the question of measures for the expansion of trade of developing countries as a means of furthering their economic development. The Ministers had before them the reports of Committee III and of the Special Group on Trade in Tropical Products, and considered the following *Programme of Action* which had previously been examined in Committee III:[1]

(i) *Standstill provision*

No new tariff or non-tariff barriers should be erected by industrialized countries against the export trade of any less-developed country in the products identified as of particular interest to the less-developed countries. In this connexion the less-developed countries would particularly mention barriers of a discriminatory nature.

(ii) *Elimination of quantitative restrictions*

Quantitative restrictions on imports from less-developed countries which are inconsistent with the provisions of the GATT shall be eliminated within a period of one year. Where, on consultation between the industrialized and the less-developed countries concerned, it is established that there are special problems which prevent action being taken within this period, the restriction on such items would be progressively reduced and eliminated by 31 December 1965.

(iii) *Duty-free entry for tropical products*

Duty-free entry into the industrialized countries shall be granted to tropical products by 31 December 1963.

(iv) *Elimination of tariffs on primary products*

Industrialized countries shall agree to the elimination of customs tariffs on the primary products important in the trade of less-developed countries.

(v) *Reduction and elimination of tariff barriers to exports of semi-processed and processed products from less-developed countries*

Industrialized countries should also prepare urgently a schedule for the reduction and elimination of tariff barriers to exports of semi-processed and processed products from less-developed countries, providing for a reduction of at least 50 per cent of the present duties over the next three years.

(vi) *Progressive reduction of internal fiscal charges and revenue duties*

Industrialized countries shall progressively reduce internal charges and revenue duties on products wholly or mainly produced in less-developed countries with a view to their elimination by 31 December 1965.

(vii) *Reporting procedures*

Industrialized countries maintaining the above-mentioned barriers shall report to the GATT secretariat in July of each year on the steps taken by them during the preceding year to implement these decisions and on the measures which they

[1] The Action Program was sponsored in 1962 by the following GATT countries: Argentina, Brazil, Burma, Cambodia, Ceylon, Chile, Cuba, Ghana, Haiti, India, Indonesia, Israel, Federation of Malaya, Federation of Nigeria, Pakistan, Peru, Tanganyika, Tunisia, United Arab Republic, Uruguay, and Yugoslavia.

propose to take over the next twelve months to provide larger access for the products of less-developed countries.

(viii) *Other measures*

Contracting parties should also give urgent consideration to the adoption of other appropriate measures which would facilitate the efforts of less-developed countries to diversify their economies, strengthen their export capacity, and increase their earnings from overseas sales.

2. The Ministers of all industrialized countries, with the exception of the Ministers of the member States of the European Economic Community, agreed to the above Programme of Action[2] subject to the understandings set out in paragraphs 3 and 4. The Ministers of the member States of the European Economic Community endorsed, in principle, the general objectives of the Programme of Action and declared themselves ready to contribute, for their part, to the fullest extent possible, towards the development of the developing countries. With respect to the most appropriate methods of achieving the objectives mentioned above, the position of the Ministers of the member States of the European Economic Community is contained in paragraph 6.

3. It was agreed by the Ministers of the industrialized countries, other than those of the EEC, that, in the first instance, the above Programme of Action relates to the products identified by Committee III, it being understood that the Programme of Action might subsequently be extended to an enlarged list of products to be agreed upon. It was also recognized that acceptance of the Programme was without prejudice to the rights and obligations of contracting parties under the provisions of the General Agreement, under arrangements negotiated within the framework of the GATT or covered by international commodity arrangements. Further, it should be understood that where action under the Programme would affect the interests of third countries, as under preferential arrangements, countries granting such preferences would need to take into account the interests of the trade partners concerned. As regards tariffs on primary products, these Ministers indicated that their governments would work towards the elimination or, where this was not possible, at least towards the substantial reduction of tariffs on these products. In respect of tariffs on semi-processed and processed products of substantial interest to the developing countries, these Ministers indicated that their governments would work towards a substantial reduction of the tariffs on these products. Action in connexion with the reduction of tariffs on primary, semi-processed and processed products from less-developed countries would be taken within the framework of the GATT trade negotiations, and, while not precluding action in advance of the trade negotiations, these Ministers proposed to ensure, as far as possible, that these products would be included in their offer lists in the negotiations and not be excepted therefrom in accordance with the principles agreed on for the negotiations.

4. Ministers of industrialized countries, other than those of the EEC, stated that they would conform to the standstill provision except where special compelling circumstances rendered departure from it unavoidable, in which case adequate

[2] The additional conclusions of Ministers on the points of the Action Program relating to the removal of barriers to trade in tropical products (point (iii) and also point (vi)) are set out in paragraphs 10 to 23, while the conclusions on point (viii), relating to other action for assisting the less-developed countries, are taken up in paragraphs 24 to 31.

opportunity for consultation would be afforded to the developing countries mainly interested in the products concerned. Such consultation would occur prior to the introduction of measures constituting a departure from the standstill unless this were impossible or impracticable. The Austrian and Japanese Ministers indicated that, while it was their intention to remove quantitative restrictions maintained inconsistently with the GATT as soon as possible, they regretted that they might not be able to meet the target date of 31 December 1965 in respect of a few products. With respect to tariff reductions, the United States Minister pointed out that United States legislation required such reductions to be staged over a period of five years. . . .

5. The Ministers of a small number of countries, mainly dependent for their export earnings on a narrow range of primary products, welcomed the Action Programme and undertook to give effect to it to the best of their ability. However, since they, like many less-developed countries, were in the process of diversifying their economies through industrial development, they would have difficulty in accepting inflexible tariff commitments for certain products.

6. . . . The Ministers of the European Economic Community and the States associated with the EEC stated that, while they recognized that some of the points contained in the Programme could be regarded as objectives to which, to the fullest extent possible, concrete policies should be adapted, the first seven points of the Programme referred only to measures for the elimination of barriers to trade, whereas, in their view, more positive measures were required to achieve the marked and rapid increase in the export earnings of the developing countries as a whole, which was the fundamental objective. Accordingly, these Ministers urged:

(a) that international action should, in particular, be directed to a deliberate effort to organize international trade in products of interest to the less-developed countries. . . .

(b) that an effort should . . . be made to ensure increasing exports at remunerative, equitable and stable prices for the less-developed countries producing primary products. . . . As regards processed and semi-processed products, a study should be made to determine the selective measures, specially conceived to meet the needs of developing countries, which could assure these countries the necessary markets for the products in question. In this connexion various relaxations of present rules regarding non-discrimination might be considered (in particular the suggestions made at the ministerial meeting by Mr Brasseur, Minister for Foreign Trade and Technical Assistance of Belgium). A rapid study of them by a special group should enable decisions to be taken without delay. . . .

7. In the opinion of certain Ministers, the same special group could, as a matter of urgency, analyse the possibility and conditions for establishing within the framework of GATT a centre for trade information and market research with a view to the expansion of exports of the less-developed countries. . . .

9. The Ministers of the less-developed countries sponsoring and supporting the Programme of Action, expressed disappointment with the understandings and positions as set out by some industrialized countries and found them to be unhelpful . . . They trusted that industrialized countries would be able to make substantial tariff concessions on primary, semi-processed and processed products, exported by less-developed countries in advance of the forthcoming trade negotiations. . . .

Trade Policies for the Less Developed Countries

TRADE IN TROPICAL PRODUCTS—FREE ACCESS TO MARKETS OF INDUSTRIALIZED COUNTRIES FOR TROPICAL PRODUCTS

General conclusions

10. The Ministers other than those of the EEC and the States associated with the Community:

(a) endorsed the general objective of free access to markets for tropical products, in view of the great importance of these products to the foreign exchange earnings and economic development of many less-developed countries;

(b) agreed that the instability of prices and inadequacy of earnings are the principal problems affecting producers of tropical products;

(c) agreed that governments should not erect any new tariff or non-tariff barriers against trade in tropical products. If, in practice, a government for compelling reasons felt that it had to take any measures which would have such effects, it should afford adequate opportunity for prior consultations with the exporting countries mainly interested in the products affected;

(d) regretted the difficulties which had delayed the implementation of the relevant part of the Ministerial Declaration of November 1961 relating to the removal of revenue duties and internal charges and urged governments to take the necessary steps to secure such implementation as soon as practicable, but in any event not later than 31 December 1965;

(e) decided that, where prior action had not already been taken on barriers to trade and restraints on consumption of tropical products, these should be dealt with in the context of the forthcoming GATT trade negotiations.

11. The Ministers of the EEC and the States associated with the Community were unable to support the above general conclusions. They emphasized their belief that the general and primary objective was to organize markets and to increase the export earnings of the less-developed countries. With that end in view they referred to their Declaration concerning the Programme of Action as set forth in paragraph 6. . . .[3]

ADDITIONAL ACTION TO FURTHER THE TRADE AND DEVELOPMENT OF LESS-DEVELOPED COUNTRIES

24. The Ministers agreed that contracting parties should give urgent consideration to the adoption of other appropriate measures which would facilitate the efforts of less-developed countries to diversify their economies, strengthen their export capacity and increase their earnings from overseas sales. In this connexion it was suggested that one of the measures which should be studied promptly would be the accordance of preferential treatment to the semi-manufactured and manufactured goods exported by the less-developed countries. It was agreed that a working group should be established to study the following proposals and report to the Contracting Parties at their twenty-first session:

(a) the granting of preferences on selected products by industrialized countries to less-developed countries as a whole; and

[3] Paragraphs 12-23 are omitted from these extracts. They cover conditional agreement to the tropical products program by the Minister for Austria and conclusions on individual tropical products, viz. cocoa, coffee, bananas, tropical oilseeds and oils, tea, and tropical timber.

(b) the granting of preferences on selected products by less-developed countries to all other less-developed countries.

25. The Ministers agreed that industrialized countries, in drawing up and implementing their policies which affect the pattern of production and trade, should take full account of the need to facilitate the efforts of less-developed countries to strengthen their export capacity and to diversify their economies.

26. The Ministers agreed that the fundamental need of the less-developed countries in the field of trade was to achieve an increase in their export earnings. In those cases where under present conditions their export trade was heavily dependent on a limited number of primary products, efforts on the part of the less-developed countries to increase their earnings by a higher volume of exports were often frustrated by declining prices and violent price fluctuations. Effective joint action was required to arrest the deterioration of the terms of trade of the less-developed countries and to mitigate and eliminate excessive fluctuations in their exports and export earnings. Some Ministers felt that this action might, for instance, take the form of commodity agreements, price stabilization schemes, compensatory financing and market organizations.

27. The Ministers agreed that the work of Committee III should be extended, in collaboration with other interested agencies, particularly the lending agencies, through the adoption of concerted, systematic and prompt studies of trade and aid relationships in individual less-developed countries aimed at obtaining a clear analysis of export potential, market prospects and any further action that may be required to overcome any difficulties that the studies reveal. In this connexion many Ministers considered that the problem of financing the gap between the export proceeds and import requirements of the developing countries needed to be given careful consideration. Ministers of less-developed countries considered that in order to extend the activities of the GATT to embrace the financing aspect, and as a practical measure to achieve this end, a working group should be formed to study the ways and means for enabling the less-developed countries to obtain from the industrialized contracting parties loans on soft terms, and thus enable the GATT to realize its objectives of fostering trade between the contracting parties.

28. The Ministers recognized the need for an adequate legal and institutional framework to enable the Contracting Parties to discharge their responsibilities in connexion with the work of expanding the trade of less-developed countries.

29. The Ministers of the less-developed countries and of the EEC recognized that there was urgent need for an amplification of the objectives and for revision of the principles and rules of the General Agreement to enable the Contracting Parties to discharge these responsibilities, with a view to safeguarding the interests of these countries in their international trade and development programmes. This action should not prejudice, but contribute to, broader negotiations in which contracting parties might participate, such as the United Nations Conference on Trade and Development.

30. While many Ministers did not agree with the views expressed in paragraph 29 above, all Ministers agreed that a committee of the Contracting Parties should be established with instructions to examine all aspects of the problems outlined in paragraphs 28 and 29, taking full account of the views expressed by the Ministers, and to report with appropriate recommendations to the twenty-first session of the Contracting Parties.

31. The Ministers agreed that the Council of Representatives should take the action necessary to set up the working group and the committee referred to in paragraphs 24 and 30 above.

Source: GATT Press Release 794 of 29 May 1963.

6:3 AUSTRALIA'S MIDWAY POSITION AND PART IV OF GATT

Australia's failure to sign the GATT amendments designed to help the exports of less-developed countries is easy to justify in parish pump terms, but difficult to sustain in world forums where the maintenance of a healthy internal economy is not the only criterion.

The reasons given for Australia's refusal to sign the amendments which was readily agreed to by almost half the 64 members of GATT, has done our overseas image little service, particularly in those developing countries which have had cause to think us generous in the past.

They are basically a reiteration of the midway position argument which was formulated at last year's United Nations' Conference on Trade and Development.

There, the Minister for Trade and Industry, Mr McEwen, argued strongly that Australia was in a special position between the developed and undeveloped countries because of her dependence on overseas investment, and succeeded in having this position officially recognised as a reason for our failure to accept the general proposition that developed countries should aim to spend 1 per cent of their national income in aid to the less-developed countries.

Ever since the UNCTAD conference inserted the phrase 'having regard to the special position of certain countries which are net importers of capital' as an addendum to the generally accepted 1 per cent principle, Government spokesmen have assumed that the midway position has been officially recognised in international forums.

Australia's failure to have this formula written into the GATT amendment shows quite clearly that our argument is far from being accepted.

The Deputy Secretary of the Trade and Industry Department Mr A. T. Carmody, argued Australia's case as ably as possible under the circumstances.[1]

He signified the Government's complete agreement with the principle that developed countries should reduce the barriers on exports from less-developed countries and pointed out that the bulk of our imports from less-developed countries already enter free of duty, or at low rates.

He mentioned the recent abolition of duties on tea and cocoa and the virtually free entry of coffee as examples of our desire to aid the development of Papua and New Guinea and other less-developed countries such as India and Ceylon. . . .

Mr Carmody's statement was a clear indication of Australia's fear of any international action which would disturb the carefully erected tariff system.

It was also an honest statement because it expressed the determination of the Government to state its position firmly and frankly, despite the inevitable consequences of criticism by those countries which freely signed the protocol.

[1] This reference is to a statement of the middle-zone position made at Geneva on 8 February 1965 by Mr Carmody. However, this position was stated more comprehensively in 6:4 and the February statement has therefore been omitted.

191

This attitude might be contrasted with that of Britain, which announced its intention of signing 'in due course', inferring that the U.K. could wait until its export position improved sufficiently to allow it to abolish the 15 per cent surcharge.

The weakness of Australia's position lies in her attempt to put herself in a special position at the UNCTAD conference and to have that position recognised each time the question of aiding the less-developed countries is raised.

The fact that her attempt to write the same formula into the GATT amendment was rejected by what Mr Carmody termed 'a few industrialised countries' shows the degree of resentment which this argument has aroused.

There is still plenty of work to be done before the GATT amendment can be made to work.

A two-thirds majority of the 64 members is required by the end of the year to make it a legal part of the agreement, and the question of items which would be considered under its provisions has still to be considered.

Australia still has the opportunity to reverse or qualify her attitude before the agreement comes into force.

This would involve official recognition of the established fact that by any measurable standards Australia is a 'have' nation, and must help the 'have nots' even if this recognition involves some sacrifice.

Source: Leading article in *The Australian Financial Review*, 10 February 1965.

6:4 AUSTRALIA DECIDES TO ACCEPT PART IV OF GATT AND TO INTRODUCE PREFERENTIAL IMPORT DUTIES FOR LESS DEVELOPED COUNTRIES

Statement by the Minister for Trade and Industry (J. McEwen) in the House of Representatives on 19 May 1965.

The Government has taken two important decisions. It has decided to introduce preferential rates of import duties for a range of products of particular export interest to the less-developed countries. This will enable Australia to make a positive contribution towards overcoming the trade problems of these countries. It has decided also to accept new provisions of the G.A.T.T. designed to aid the trade of less-developed countries, subject to a reservation which will fully preserve our right to continue our own policies of using the tariff to assist Australian development. . . .

. . . I want to direct the attention of the House to recent attempts in the G.A.T.T. to tackle the . . . problems of the trade and development needs of the less-developed countries of the world.

As originally drafted in 1947, the G.A.T.T. had very few provisions directed towards these problems. It seems to have been based on the premise that rules having equal application for all members would give all countries equal opportunities to secure the benefits of international trade. This is manifestly absurd. Countries are not equal; and equal opportunities for unequals do not result in equal benefits.

Some consideration was given to this point when the Agreement was revised in 1954/55. The revision resulted in some limited relaxation of the general rules for the less-developed countries. It also resulted in explicit recognition that countries such as Australia, whilst obviously not in the position of less-developed countries, nevertheless needed greater flexibility than the major industrialised countries in regard to the use of tariffs. However, there was no significant change in the basic philosophy underlying the G.A.T.T.

The less-developed countries were, of course, far from satisfied with this half-hearted attempt to do something about their very real trade problems. As more and more of them achieved independence with their own voice in international affairs, they have in recent years been able to compel the G.A.T.T. and other international organs to give more attention to their needs.

One result was last year's United Nations Conference on Trade and Development. Another has been the negotiation of a series of new articles for insertion in the General Agreement. These new articles have been incorporated in a Protocol of amendment which has now been opened for acceptance by G.A.T.T. members.

In the negotiations leading up to the new articles, the less-developed countries rightly stressed the need for arrangements that would help them to stand on their own feet—their need for access on reasonable terms to external markets, particularly the volume markets of the major industrial nations. Improved access to these markets is essential if these less-developed countries are to have any prospect of financing the volume of imports which their development demands.

The less-developed countries laid particular stress on three specific objectives:

reduction and removal of tariffs and quantitative restrictions imposed on their exports;

reduction and removal of high internal taxes maintained particularly by European countries on consumption of such products as tea, coffee, and cocoa, which are of particular interest to the less-developed countries;

preferential entry for their exports of manufactured products.

The first two of these objectives were directed mainly towards improvement in the conditions under which the less-developed countries sell the products of their existing industries on world markets. The third was designed to enable them to export the products of new manufacturing industries, the establishment of which is essential to their overall development and improvement in their standards of living.

Australia gave full support to the general objectives of the less-developed countries. Sharing, as we do, their problems of severely limited access to export markets for primary products and being ourselves comparatively new exporters of manufactures, we are only too well aware of the kind of obstacles which must be overcome before the countries concerned can achieve adequate and pre-dictable returns from their exports to world markets. We live with the same problems as plague the efforts of the less-developed countries to maintain and expand returns from traditional and limited export lines. . . .

We therefore supported their general objectives and indicated our willingness to do as much as lies within our capacity to help them. However, we felt bound to maintain in respect of these new Articles of the G.A.T.T. what is recognised in the present Agreement—that there are significant differences between the economy of Australia and the economies of the mature industrial countries. We made it clear that whilst we wanted to play our part in contributing to an expansion of the trade of the less-developed countries, we could not be committed to obligations identical with those to be accepted by countries which already had highly-developed industrial structures. Our own development needs and policies, and our responsibilities for the development of Papua and New Guinea, set limits on our ability to help the less-developed countries in the particular ways they were seeking and which might well be the most appropriate ways for the mature industrial countries to contribute.

We therefore pressed to have included in the new articles, provisions which would carry forward the G.A.T.T. recognition that there are quite significant differences between the Australian economy and the economies of the industrial powers. We sought a provision which, whilst clearly not exonerating us from action to help the trade of the less-developed countries, would enable us to do so without negating our policies on the use of the tariff to protect our own economic development, or our policies for the development of Papua and New Guinea.

Our proposal was generally acceptable to the less-developed countries themselves. However it was rejected by a few of the more powerful industrial countries.

At the same time the major industrialised countries were themselves very cautious about accepting the commitments sought from them by the less-developed countries. They insisted that the new provisions relating to tariffs and quantitative restrictions be so written as to accommodate their own particular difficulties with the demands of the less-developed countries. They adopted the same stand in regard to fiscal charges. And some of the more important of them completely rejected the idea of preferences for the manufactured exports of the less-developed countries—which we have all along been prepared to accept. In the result, the new articles make no change in the rigid G.A.T.T. embargo on new preferences.

Since the volume markets of the major industrial countries were the prime target—indeed the main hope—of the less-developed countries, the latter were obliged to settle for the best that they could obtain from those countries. The result is a series of rules tailored to the circumstances of the highly industrialised countries, and in no way recognising that Australia's situation is not, in fact, identical with that of the highly industrialised countries. As I have said, the absence of such recognition was not due to opposition from the less-developed countries.

Let us look at the new articles which have emerged from these negotiations. The key article—and the one that presents Australia with real difficulty—is Article XXXVII.

Article XXXVII lays down two sets of rules. The first set applies to what are described as the developed countries and the second set, which reasonably enough is fairly nominal, applies to the less-developed countries. In other words, the article is based on the premise that the countries of the world fall into two—and only two—economic categories. This proposition is, of course, completely contrary to real life.

Under the new Article XXXVII, the so-called developed countries are to accept certain new commitments. The main ones are:—

> to accord high priority to the reduction and elimination of tariff and non-tariff barriers to products of actual or potential export interest to less-developed countries;
>
> to refrain from increasing tariff and non-tariff barriers against such products;
>
> to take similar action in regard to fiscal charges on raw or processed primary products produced in the less-developed countries.

These three commitments are backed up by a further provision obligating a country to enter into consultations—really confrontations—in the G.A.T.T. whenever it is unable to give full effect to them. As noted earlier, there is no provision for relaxing the G.A.T.T. ban on new tariff preferences.

We can accept the commitment on fiscal charges. But, in the absence of any provision for new preferences, the effect of the provisions on tariffs would be to severely curtail our right to increase, or even to maintain, tariffs on any products that might be designated—now or in the future—as being of actual or potential export interest to the less-developed countries. Because the range of products of export interest to the less-developed countries has not been established—and indeed is not likely ever to be established in the sense of being made subject to any limits—this would involve contracting out of our right to use the tariff over large and quite undefined areas of Australian production. It would involve giving a blank cheque, in a situation in which we have no real knowledge of the extent to which such action might impinge upon our own development policies.

It might be argued that Australia would suffer no real detriment if we were to remove duties from imports from less-developed countries, on the ground that Australian industries are not worthy of protection if they cannot compete with the industries of these countries. This ignores two things. It ignores, first, the fact that there are a number of products in which some less-developed countries are highly competitive, not only with Australian industry but also with the much older and much larger industries of other countries.

But more importantly, it ignores the continuing G.A.T.T. embargo on new preferences—an embargo which, as I have already noted, certain highly industrialised countries have so far declined to amend. If we were to remove or reduce duties on imports from less-developed countries, the provisions of G.A.T.T. would require us to remove or reduce also the duties on the same goods when imported from the industrialised countries. It would be those countries, rather than the less-developed countries, which would receive the major benefit from duty reductions on this basis.

Quite obviously, duty reductions on this basis would expose Australian industries to the most damaging competition from the highly developed countries. Australian industrialisation has not yet reached the stage where our industries can compete on a free-trade basis with the long established, high volume industrial complexes of the major industrial powers. If it had, we would not have protective duties.

To remove our protective duties in this situation would mean sacrificing much of what we have already achieved in the way of industrial development, and our hopes of further industrial development, with little or no benefit to the less-developed countries.

This is the crux of our difficulties with the new G.A.T.T. provisions. To accept those provisions unreservedly would place in jeopardy our future development, and much of the development we have already achieved. It would also limit our ability to use the Tariff for the benefit of Papua and New Guinea.

The Government is not prepared to do this. It has therefore decided to make its acceptance of the new articles subject to a formal reservation. The effect of the reservation is to limit Australia's obligations under the new articles to action that is consistent with our development needs and responsibilities.

This does not mean that the Government is not prepared to contribute towards the solution of the urgent trade problems of the less-developed countries. On the contrary, the Government is willing and anxious to help these countries to the limits of Australia's capacity. This is made clear in the reservation.

Concurrently with its examination of the new G.A.T.T. provisions, the Government has indeed studied what can be done, consistent with our own needs and policies, to afford real and practical help to the less-developed countries in their efforts to expand their export earnings. We have never been convinced that tariff reductions applicable to the industrialised countries as well as the less-developed countries, as provided for in the new G.A.T.T. articles, will in fact do very much at all to improve the trade of the less-developed countries. The relative competitive position of the less-developed countries will not be improved by this means. It would appear inevitable that the major part of the increase in trade flowing from across-the-board tariff cuts would accrue to those countries which already have vast industrial capacity.

The Government has therefore consistently backed the less-developed countries in their efforts to get for themselves preferential tariff reductions on their exports.

The first serious discussion of such preferences at Ministerial level was at a meeting of Commonwealth Trade Ministers in London in May 1963. At that meeting I argued that the G.A.T.T. rules needed to be changed to allow tariff preferences for selected imports from less-developed countries. I advocated this at a G.A.T.T. Ministerial meeting a few weeks later, and again at the United Nations Conference on Trade and Development in 1964.

There are, of course, many practical difficulties in introducing new preferential trading arrangements for a group of countries large in number and difficult to define. After very careful examination of the whole question, the Government is satisfied that arrangements for preferences that will assist the less-developed countries can be devised.

Protection of domestic industry would not be impaired. The essential interests of existing exporters to the Australian market would not be jeopardised.

Having reached this conclusion, the Government has decided to make provision in the Australian Tariff for preferential duties on selected imports from less-developed countries.

This means that, for a range of products of particular export interest to less-developed countries, imports into Australia from those countries will pay substantially lower rates of import duty than are payable on the same products when imported from developed countries.

This will demonstrate by positive action Australia's willingness to help overcome the trade problems of the less-developed countries. It will also give a lead to other countries which may wish to use preferences to assist the less-developed countries.

The Government sees these new preferences as a means of helping to offset the competitive disadvantages faced by the new industries of the less-developed countries, and of putting them in a better position to compete with major industrial countries for a greater share of Australia's import trade.

Preferential duties established on this basis would not conflict with long standing Australian policy of protection for economic and efficient industry. With few exceptions, protective duties in the Australian Tariff have been fixed on the basis of the competition offered by producers in the industrialised countries. They are therefore frequently higher than are needed to afford reasonable protection against the generally less competitive industries of the less-developed countries. So long as duties are not reduced on the products in which less-developed countries are already competitive in international markets, there would be no damage to efficient Australian industries.

The real barrier to the Government taking action along these lines has been the G.A.T.T. provisions on new preferences. The Government had hoped that these would be modified as a result of recent negotiations in the G.A.T.T. and at the United Nations Conference on Trade and Development. However, the position of a few of the major industrial countries has so far prevented any change. Although the question is still being debated in G.A.T.T. and U.N.C.T.A.D., there is, as yet, no assurance that it will be possible to reach early international agreement on arrangements for giving preferences to selected exports of less-developed countries.

The Government has therefore decided to seek a waiver—or dispensation— from the provisions of the G.A.T.T. relating to preferences. The waiver would cover both an initial list of products on which we would introduce preferences as soon as the waiver was granted and additional products which might be added from time to time.

The initial list has been selected after consultation with representatives of Australian industry and after careful examination of the list of products which less-developed countries have indicated as being of special interest to them. From this list, the Government has selected certain products, on which duties on imports from less-developed countries can be reduced without serious detriment to Australian industry. In some cases individual less-developed countries which export some items which are already competitive would have those items excluded from the benefits of the preferences; that is, such items imported from those countries would continue to be dutiable at existing most-favoured-nation rates. In addition, imports from less-developed countries under the preferential rates would be subject to tariff quotas.

These tariff quotas are designed to serve two purposes. They will provide an additional safeguard for Australian industry and will ensure that the preferences do not disrupt or cause serious damage to the trade of third countries.

The Government has been very conscious of both these points in formulating its proposals. It has therefore decided that the preferential rates should be subject to modification as producers in less-developed countries become competitive. Accordingly, Australian industry will be free to seek to have the preferential rates reviewed under the procedures for enquiry and report laid down in the Tariff Board Act.

So far as third countries are concerned, our approach to the G.A.T.T. will envisage the waiver containing provision for prior consultation with other interested supplier countries before introducing a preferential rate of duty. We will also propose to make regular reports to G.A.T.T. on developments under the waiver. These reports will provide an opportunity for countries whose trade may be significantly affected to secure reconsideration of particular preferences. If the circumstances justify it, such international reconsideration might lead to the conclusion that changes in the competitive situation of particular industries in particular less-developed countries were such that the preferences enjoyed by these industries were no longer necessary, or perhaps were higher than needed, to offset the disabilities which affected their competitive position in world markets.

Throughout this statement, I have made frequent reference to the less-developed countries. However, despite the great amount of debate that has taken place in international meetings on what should be done to assist the less-developed countries, there has been little discussion, and no agreement, on which countries fall within this group.

Since a system of preferential tariffs cannot be operated without designating

H

the countries to receive preferences, the absence of international agreement as to which countries are less-developed has posed a problem. The Government would, of course, prefer to adopt a generally agreed list. But in the circumstances that I have explained it has not been able to do this. It has therefore taken the countries which made up the caucus of less-developed countries at the United Nations Conference on Trade and Development and has added Papua and New Guinea, and the British territories or former territories which already receive some preferences under the Australian Tariff.

This seems to us to be reasonable at this point of time. This question will come under discussion when the G.A.T.T. considers our application for a waiver. This may well lead to the emergence of an agreed list of countries which can be regarded as being less-developed for international trade purposes. In this event, the Government would certainly take into account the outcome of the G.A.T.T. deliberations.

The decisions of the Government which I have announced are important. They will enable Australia to play its part in giving practical help to the trade of the less-developed countries thus aiding their growth and development. Our initiative in moving ahead on the important question of new preferences for these countries might well serve as a pattern for others in this field, thus compounding the trade benefits for the less-developed countries.

At the same time, Australian industry, and Australia's growth and development, will be safeguarded in a way which would not be possible were we to accept without reservation the new G.A.T.T. articles.

I now present the following papers for the information of the House:

The Protocol to insert new articles in the General Agreement on Tariffs and Trade

Australia's acceptance of, and reservation to, the protocol

The list of preferential tariff rates which the Government proposes to introduce during the Budget Session[1]

The list of countries which Australia will be indicating to the G.A.T.T. will enjoy the preferential tariff rates under its proposals.

Source: *C.P.D.* (*H. of R.*), vol. 46, pp. 1631-6.

6:5 AUSTRALIA'S CONDITIONAL ACCEPTANCE OF THE PROTOCOL AMENDING GATT

Sir,

I have the honour to inform you that the Government of the Commonwealth of Australia has authorised me by this letter to accept on its behalf the Protocol amending the General Agreement on Tariffs and Trade to introduce a Part IV on Trade and Development, with the understanding that—

(a) because of its own development needs and policies it would be inappropriate for Australia, one of the contracting parties referred to in Article XVIII: 4(b) of the General Agreement, the economy of which is in the course of industrial development and which is seeking to avoid an

---

[1] These tariff rates were to apply to 118 selected imports from developing countries.

198

excessive dependence on a limited range of primary products for its export earnings but which is not a less-developed country, to undertake to give effect to the provisions of paragraphs 1, 2 and 3 of Article XXXVII to the same extent or in the same manner as the other contracting parties to which those paragraphs apply; and

(b) the provisions of those paragraphs of Article XXXVII will be applied to the fullest extent consistent with Australia's development needs and policies and responsibilities.

The reasons for Australia's inability to accept the new Protocol other than on this understanding were explained in the statement of the Australian representative to the Special Session of the Contracting Parties on 8th February, 1965.

> I have the honour to be,
> Sir,
> Your obedient servant,
> (Paul Hasluck)
> *Minister for External Affairs*
> *for the Commonwealth of Australia*

The Executive Secretary to the Contracting Parties
to the General Agreement on Tariffs and Trade,
GENEVA.

> *Source*: Department of Trade, roneoed
> document tabled in the House of
> Representatives on 19 May 1965.

6:6 UNCTAD: AUSTRALIA'S GENERAL ATTITUDE

Statement to the Conference held in March-June 1964 by the Minister for Trade (J. McEwen) on 26 March 1964.

.... To me the problems faced by developing countries are clearly discernible. Australia's own recent experiences in pursuing development, in fostering industrial expansion, of persistent balance of payments problems, of financing the heavy demand for imports of capital equipment, of adverse trends in the terms of trade and of overcoming obstacles in export markets combine to give us a most vivid understanding of the problems facing the developing countries. ...

I welcome the emphasis placed by Dr Prebisch on the need for better quantitative access,[1] on prices which are remunerative, and on the orderly management of any surpluses that may occur.

Australia has been vigorously advocating this approach within the framework of International Commodity Agreements. Currently negotiations are being conducted within the GATT Cereals Group in an endeavour to give practical effect to these very principles for this range of commodities.

Effective planning for development is impossible for developing countries without reasonable predictability in the availability of the foreign exchange resources required for such planning.

[1] Dr Raúl Prebisch, Secretary-General, United Nations Conference on Trade and Development.

Depressed prices for primary products and disruptive fluctuations in these prices have been in large part the cause of the balance of payments difficulties which have bedevilled countries trying to press on with development plans.

This is so important for the developing countries that I urge the conference to declare itself on this issue of stable and remunerative prices. . . .

Care must be taken to avoid freezing patterns of trade or the expectations of the developing countries may be frustrated. . . .

This conference begins with a clear recognition that countries with small domestic markets and new in the field of manufacture face special difficulties in entering export trade in competition with long-established suppliers.

The papers before the conference generally advocate preferences as the solution to these difficulties. . . .

In the past preferences have been employed as a means of giving one exporter an advantage over another. In the present context I see the objective quite differently. What is required is action to offset the initial competitive disadvantage of many developing countries which are or may be newcomers in the business of exporting manufactured products.

Australia is prepared to join in a positive examination of this problem and to contribute within our capacity to a multilateral solution. . . .

Dr Prebisch makes the point that any form of help for developing countries in this field should not require reciprocity. This point of principle is already accepted by and applied by Australia in the preferences which we grant Papua-New Guinea. . . .

There are a number of observations in the documents before us about the means for financing an expansion of international trade. I believe there is need for further study of this. . . .

This is not to say that there is no need for continuing aid. Australia has recognised and will continue to recognise this in a practical way. . . .

We can appreciate why the developing countries are expressing dissatisfaction with the existing international trade institutions. We have said clearly on a number of occasions that GATT has been unsatisfactory in its failure to produce a proper balance of opportunity and obligation as between the industrialised countries on the one hand and the developing countries and the exporters of bulk commodities on the other.

There is, however, no point in seeking to establish new institutions until the detailed objectives required of them are defined and we are satisfied that the existing institutions cannot be made to adequately serve the purpose.

The GATT and other existing organisations have not proved adequate to meet the needs of developing countries. However, there is real advantage in carrying forward the work already under way to strengthen the GATT and I commend as a positive contribution the proposal before us for utilising existing organisations within a wider organisational framework. . . .

The Prebisch Report highlights the importance of the removal, or at least a significant reduction in existing barriers to the trade of developing countries. The report commends the GATT 'Programme of Action' and proposes its adoption in this wider forum. Australia has already indicated acceptance in principle of the action programme and I reiterate that we will implement it in accordance with our capacity to do so.

Australia with a small population of 11 millions has a high living standard and has made progress in industrialisation. However, we face many of the problems of developing countries which need to be dealt with at this conference.

It is sufficient to mention our dependence on primary commodities for the bulk of our foreign exchange, our very large payments for invisible items, our imports of capital, our small exports of manufactures and our continuing industrialisation. . . .

This, we feel, places us in something of a midway position between the developed and developing countries.

While we cannot negotiate policies designed to pursue our own development or policies applied in relation to our primary responsibilities for Papua and New Guinea, I can say that we have already satisfied much of the GATT Action Programme. We have no quantitative restrictions on any items of direct interest to developing countries. Many imports of tropical products already enter free of duty. My Government will remove the duties now operating on bulk tea and cocoa beans and will make a corresponding reduction in the duty on packaged tea. This decision will cost two million dollars in revenue.

We import items to a value of 450 million dollars from developing countries. Over 70 per cent of these imports already enter Australia duty free.

Whilst . . . we are unable to accept a rigid standstill or formula approach to the reduction of duties we are prepared to examine on a case by case basis items of interest to the developing countries. . . .

What we are aiming to do at this conference fits within or is an expansion of the objectives of the Kennedy Round. . . . The Kennedy Round and this conference should together be a monumental forward step uplifting the living standards of millions and lessening international tensions which so often have a relationship to trade opportunities. . . .

Source: Press statement 35/64T issued in
Canberra on 26 March 1964.

6:7 UNCTAD: AUSTRALIA CRITICISES DIVISION OF ALL COUNTRIES INTO TWO CATEGORIES

Statement by Head of the Australian Delegation (A. P. Fleming) at 31st Plenary Meeting of UNCTAD on 10 June 1964, in Geneva.

I have asked to speak at this stage because what I have to say is, from my Government's point of view, an important matter affecting our attitude on many of the resolutions we are dealing with.

Some time ago, the spokesman for the thirty-five sponsors of the draft resolution in the Second Committee of the General Assembly (which duly became resolution 1785 (XVII) launching this Conference) said that the Conference was 'aimed at the urgent trade problems of developing countries amongst which we [i.e. the sponsors] include in so far as trade problems are concerned those countries highly dependent upon a narrow range of primary commodities'.

At an earlier stage in the Second Committee of the General Assembly, it was made clear that Australia fitted that definition.

Yet the tenor of most resolutions before us is to divide all countries into only two categories—developed and developing—and not to recognize stages of development between these two extremes.

They thus do not provide for developing countries to progress from their present status through an intermediate stage to developed status. The concept is static, and there is no transition.

Further, this sharp distinction emphasizes a conflict of interest or confrontation rather than co-operation. The Minister from the Cameroons has also referred to this.

The question can be posed—what are the distinguishing characteristics of developed countries? The answer is that they depend, in the main, upon their export of finished manufactured goods deriving from a mature industrial complex. Their exports of these finished industrial products are, and are likely to continue to be, more than competitive in world markets with the exports of less-developed countries. They have tremendous production and cost advantages in world trade arising either from vitally important economies of scale or from the highly-developed sophistication of their specialized industrial products made possible by a long history of industrial development.

By no stretch of the imagination can Australia be regarded in this trade and development context as having those characteristics. Indeed, in GATT both in 1955 and as recently as in the Ministerial Conference of the 'Kennedy round', it has been formally recognized that Australia is so different from the developed countries currently engaged in negotiations to reduce trade barriers between them that, along with two or three other countries, she is regarded as being in a special category.

Actually, Australia's trade problems are very similar to those of the developing countries, but Australia, in contrast to the developing countries, has already achieved a good standard of living, is a significant donor of aid in grant form and reciprocates or pays for trade concessions. So Australia already accepts many important responsibilities in relation to developing countries.

Just as clearly as we are not a 'developed' country, in the context of this Conference on trade and development, we are not a 'developing' country.

As the Conference has proceeded, we have not attempted to argue our intermediate position point by point. To have injected Australia's special situation into the detailed negotiations could, in our opinion, have prejudiced the possibility of reaching solutions based on the highest common factor of agreement between developing and industrialized countries. We can understand the practical reasons underlying the desire of developing and developed countries to concentrate on their major areas of difficulty and their major interests. We have avoided extending the scope of these difficult negotiations into the area of legitimate exceptions to meet a clearly different set of problems and interests.

But in the circumstances, where neither the great industrialized countries nor the developing countries have been able in the time available to take account of our intermediate position in their proposals, we have no option at this stage but to abstain on many of the recommendations and resolutions of the Conference.

Australia's policy already towards imports from the developing countries is very liberal: there are no quantitative restrictions on goods of interest to them; one-fifth of our total imports come from developing countries; seventy-five per cent of these enter duty free; and we are prepared to do more.

The Australian Government wants to see action pressed forward in those fields which the developing countries have identified as being important to an expansion of their trade in improved access for primary products, in removal of tariff and non-tariff barriers, in preferences on manufactures, in commodity arrangements, and so on. Within the limits imposed by our middle zone position and along with action by other countries, the Australian Government is willing to be constructive in these areas and to make its contribution in expanding the trade of developing countries.

Meanwhile, because of the problems arising from the situation which I have described, my delegation has felt and will find it necessary to abstain on many of the recommendations to be considered in these final plenary sessions.

It is the wish of the Australian Government that the foregoing explanation of its position should be recorded in the proceedings of this Conference.

In conclusion, like some others who have spoken, we too think the need for the future is discussion rather than dialogue, co-operation rather than confrontation. The problem before us is well diagnosed. The measures and actions needed give scope for a major creative task.

Source: Department of Trade, roneoed document.

6:8 UNCTAD: FINAL ACT

8. The United Nations Conference on Trade and Development was convened in order to provide, by means of international co-operation, appropriate solutions to the problems of world trade in the interest of all peoples and particularly to the urgent trade and development problems of the developing countries. In a period when their need for imports of development goods and for technical knowledge has been increasing, developing countries have been faced with a situation in which their export earnings and capacity to import goods and services have been inadequate. The growth in import requirements has not been matched by a commensurate expansion in export earnings. The resultant trade gap, which gold and foreign exchange reserves have been inadequate to bridge, has had to be filled very largely by capital imports. This in itself cannot provide a complete or permanent solution, and indeed the servicing of external debts and the outgoings on other 'invisible' items themselves present severe burdens for developing countries. Moreover, the terms of trade have operated to the disadvantage of the developing countries. . . .

SECOND PART—A CONSOLIDATION OF THE
RECOMMENDATIONS OF THE CONFERENCE

Section V

Institutional Arrangements

78. The Conference has recommended to the United Nations General Assembly that it adopt, at its nineteenth session, the following provisions, *inter alia*:

  (a) that the present United Nations Conference on Trade and Development should be established as an organ of the General Assembly to be convened at intervals of not more than three years and with a membership comprising those States which are members of the United Nations, the specialized agencies, or the International Atomic Energy Agency;

  (b) the principal functions of the Conference shall be:

   (i) to promote international trade, especially with a view to accelerating economic development, particularly trade between countries at different stages of development, between developing countries and between countries with different systems of economic and social organization, taking into account the functions performed by existing international organizations;

(ii) to formulate principles and policies on international trade and related problems of economic development;

(iii) to make proposals for putting the said principles and policies into effect and to take such other steps within its competence as may be relevant to this end, having regard to differences in economic systems and stages of development;

(iv) generally, to review and facilitate the co-ordination of activities of other institutions within the United Nations system in the field of international trade and related problems of economic development and in this regard to co-operate with the General Assembly and the Economic and Social Council in respect to the performance of their Charter responsibilities for co-ordination;

(v) to initiate action, where appropriate, in co-operation with the competent organs of the United Nations for the negotiations and adoption of multilateral legal instruments in the field of trade, with due regard to the adequacy of existing organs of negotiation and without duplication of their activities;

(vi) to be available as a centre for harmonizing the trade and related development policies of governments and regional economic groupings in pursuance of Article 1 of the United Nations Charter; and

(vii) to deal with any other matters within the scope of its competence.

(c) A permanent organ of the Conference, to be known as the Trade and Development Board, shall be established as part of the United Nations machinery in the economic field, consisting of 55 members elected by the Conference from among its membership, with full regard for both equitable geographical distribution and the desirability of continuing representation for the principal trading States.

(d) For the effective discharge of its functions, the Board should establish such subsidiary organs as may be necessary, and in particular three committees—on commodities, manufactures, and invisibles and financing related to trade. . . .

(f) Arrangements should be made, in accordance with Article 101 of the Charter, for the immediate establishment of an adequate, permanent and full-time secretariat within the United Nations Secretariat for the proper servicing of the Conference, the Board and its subsidiary bodies.

(g) The Conference should review, in the light of experience, the effectiveness and further evolution of institutional arrangements with a view to recommending such changes and improvements as might be necessary. To this end it should study all relevant subjects including matters relating to the establishment of a comprehensive organization based on the entire membership of the United Nations system of organizations to deal with trade and with trade in relation to development.

Source: 'Final Act and Report',
Proceedings of the United Nations
Conference on Trade and Development,
Geneva, 23 March–16 June 1964, vol. 1.

7

COMMODITY POLICY

This is one of the few sections in which there is no single key decision which gives unity to the documents. There are important decisions recorded, such as joining the International Wheat Agreements, the International Sugar Agreement, and the long-term Meat Agreement with the United Kingdom. But these are the reflection of a general policy about trade in basic or bulk primary products.[1] This policy is not readily apparent in the documents. Moreover, to attempt a clarification of general policy we will have to refer also to the documents in other sections, especially Sections 2, 3, 5, 9, and 10.

In view of the importance attached to it within such general expositions of trade policy by ministers of the Federal government as there have been, it may seem surprising that the precise meaning of commodity policy comes out so poorly in the documents. While there is a marked absence in the documents of exposition of what commodity policy is, two explanations can be offered. The first, noted further below, is that it is extremely difficult to define the term. The second is that general or overall trade policy has been formulated and objectives pursued with Australia's commodity interests to the fore. These have dominated our export earnings; consequently, total policy, at least on the export side, is in a sense commodity policy. The need has presumably never been felt to expound the principles of commodity policy as a distinct but related field. This is fair comment, but it does not emerge from the documents except perhaps implicitly. What is badly needed is an exposition of the principles or objectives of commodity policy accepted and campaigned for by all post-war governments in Australia. This, we believe, would show not only that general policy strongly reflects our concern with commodities but would also reveal special aims and characteristics which distinguish commodity trade, and therefore policy, from trade in the general run of manufactured goods, both heavy and light.[2] With the growth in importance of Australian trade in manufactures it will be less and less adequate to regard general trade policy and commodity policy as being the same thing.

It would have been easy to assemble many more papers on the subject

[1] The term 'basic' is frequently found in McEwen's statements as a convenient description of the major Australian exports of bulk agricultural and mineral products.

[2] See discussion in Rowe (148), a highly useful book which, however, came too late to my notice for direct use in these comments.

than have in fact been included either in this section or in the other related sections. This would have given more information and viewpoints on various particular war-time purchase contracts with the United Kingdom, the post-war intergovernmental agreements on wheat and sugar, the controversial 1951 long-term meat contract with the United Kingdom, and the many other commodity items receiving only slight mention here and elsewhere in the book. Undoubtedly this would have helped to throw more light on the character of commodity trade. It is unfortunate that space limitations precluded this. Nevertheless, the explicit statement on commodity policy would not have appeared and, for the purpose of this chapter, additional documents may have merely provided more trees to obscure the wood.

It is the purpose of the comment in this section to draw attention to the principles which seem to emerge from the documents in this and the other related sections and from details of Australia's international agreements not reflected in the documents. These principles are important in any attempt to discern what commodity policy appears to mean.

We have suggested that the difficulty of the subject is one explanation of the absence of straightforward exposition in government papers. It is certainly true that it is difficult to offer a straightforward *a priori* definition of commodity policy.[3] We have implied that it is policy concerned with basic commodities which for Australia, and for many other major exporters of primary products, provide the bulk of its export earnings (Section 17: Table VIII).

This unfortunately does not take us very far, for it need not mean more than the application of general trade policy to trade in basic commodities. And certainly there is no aspect of general trade policy discussed in this book which is not relevant to such trade. However, there are some specific reasons for singling out commodity policy for special treatment—reasons which are not normally associated with trade in manufactured goods as this term is generally understood in discussions of trade. These reasons fall in two categories which can be clearly separated.

On the one hand trade in basic commodities, especially agricultural products, seems to be hampered by more difficult commercial and fiscal policies than trade in manufactures.[4] In the more advanced countries (in terms of

[3] There have been several articles contributed by professional economists in Australia on some aspects of commodity policy, but there is scope for much more comprehensive, analytical work in this field. Articles on international commodity arrangements include Wood (168); McMillan (119); Lloyd (110); Strong (154); Maiden (120); Clark (39); Lewis (104)-(107); Riley (145). See also references in Section 7. There have also been several articles on Australia's domestic stabilisation schemes including Lloyd (111), (112); Campbell (33), (34); Downing and Karmel (72); Powell and Campbell (139); Parish (133), (134); Duloy and Nevile (74).

[4] The distinction is not watertight. Textiles, for example, seem to be subject to not dissimilar restrictions on trade and, as we have seen, the LDCs have some reason to complain that their trade in other simple manufactures is similarly hampered. Nevertheless,

income and industrialisation) the farm sectors tend to be strong socially and politically and often to be able to insist on highly protectionist measures designed to limit imports to the amount equal only to the shortfall in local production. This is what we have been calling agricultural protectionism.[5] Fiscal policy sometimes acts in the same way. Protective commercial policy applied to agriculture or minerals is designed to limit or prohibit the competition of imports with domestic production. Fiscal policy may have no relation to home industry; but by imposing high revenue duties on coffee, cocoa, and tea some high income countries have limited consumer demand to the disadvantage of many Latin American, African, and Asian (including Papua and New Guinea) producers.

On the other hand there are special problems associated with the characteristics of supply and demand of basic commodities. These problems are clearly aggravated by restrictive commercial and fiscal policies but would still exist if there were no difficulties about such policies. Thus agricultural products generally do not have the stable supply characteristics of manufactured goods. Seasonal conditions affect short-term supply and hence year-by-year price changes; and, in the longer term, production seems to be cyclical, responding only with a lag to rising and falling price trends, so aggravating both upward and downward trends. In short, greater price stability has become an objective of policy. Again, on the demand side (at least in affluent countries with already high consumption standards) these products seem to suffer more than most manufactures from relatively low income elasticity of demand; relative price inelasticity in some cases, such as wheat; and often from the ready availability of substitutes and from the fact that technological changes in industry have resulted in more economical use of raw materials, especially minerals.

Altogether, trade in basic commodities does present many problems of instability associated with or inherent in the products themselves as well as major problems of protective commercial and fiscal policies. For these two good reasons and for a third, namely that LDCs tend to be the principal sufferers from failure to solve these problems, a great and increasing amount of attention has been given to them in United Nations bodies and GATT. It so happens that Australia, although relatively affluent and better able to live with the problems than the LDCs, does have a direct and proper concern in this large area of trade policy. The reason for interest is discussed in Section 17.

---

the great bulk of trade in manufactures, especially among developed countries, is subject to no hampering except that arising from protective tariffs (and the tendency here is to liberalise, i.e. reduce tariffs) or from periodic balance of payments difficulties.

[5] See particularly Haberler Report (81) and Sections 5 and 6, including the discussion on the new Part IV of GATT.

In dealing with the documents in this section we have not tried to follow the twofold division of the subject just discussed but have rather followed a fivefold division related more closely to the policy measures adopted or advocated by Australia in seeking solutions to the problems noted:

- (a) full employment and economic growth;
- (b) bilateral arrangements between Australia and other governments. These include, for example, understandings with the United Kingdom (war-time bulk contracts, post-war arrangements on meat and wheat), Ceylon (flour), Germany (certain quotas), and the United States (meat). Trade treaties of a more general kind, such as the Australian treaties with the United Kingdom and Japan, may also be regarded, in Australia's case, as an expression of commodity policy;
- (c) attempts to reduce import barriers, particularly non-tariff barriers, to trade in primary products. These attempts have been largely concentrated in GATT but include also more direct dealings with the EEC. A particular item which can be included in this sector is the attempt to contain the adverse effects on Australian trade of United States surplus disposal (PL 480) programs;
- (d) the partially successful attempt to negotiate multilateral inter-governmental commodity agreements which specify the terms and conditions for trade in basic commodities;[6]
- (e) a number of domestic policy measures relevant to our commodity trade. These include efforts through export promotion to stimulate demand for our products; research and development designed to improve or lower the unit costs of our products; and efforts so to influence land use or mineral policy that supply is adjusted to changes in the demand for our products. In this group of policy actions the aim from the viewpoint of export expansion is to influence the decisions of consumers and individual producers of our export goods.[7] Beyond one brief reference in the discussion of international commodity agreements, our comments do not cover another group of domestic policy measures which are highly relevant to export decisions. These are the various stabilisation schemes primarily designed to support domestic prices but sometimes (notably in the case

[6] A newer development, to some extent as an alternative to commodity agreements, is the attempt to devise 'compensatory' arrangements. These are arrangements to stabilise external income by offsetting with special 'insurance' payments or transfers from affluent to non-affluent countries the declines in export returns frequently suffered by countries dependent upon primary products for export earnings. A special function of the International Monetary Fund falls within this subject. While not adopted as a policy objective by Australia, some further brief comment is offered later in this section.

[7] See comments in Vernon Report (11) on 'Policies for Expansion', vol. I, ch. 8, paras. 90-103.

of wheat) also supporting export returns. All influence investment decisions and, although encouraging export, may well distort the best use of resources. The relative over support of the dairy industry is a likely case in point. For reasons given in Section 13 on agriculture this subject falls outside the scope of this book. It is well, however, to note its relevance to commodity policy.

Before taking these subdivisions in turn it may be useful to draw attention to the war-time and early post-war approach to the subject matters reflected in the documents in the early sections. A good many of the relevant policies were anticipated by statements during and immediately after the war. The 1945 White Paper on Full Employment (2:2) gives emphasis to full employment as a necessary condition for rural welfare. While making no direct mention of commodity agreements it does mention international collaboration mitigating fluctuations in prices of primary products and stabilisation of farm incomes. More comprehensive is Chifley's 1946 statement of policy included in Section 2 and also discussed in Section 13. It was inspired a great deal by the work of the Rural Reconstruction Commission.[8] The strong interest in international collaboration in promoting commodity agreements and in curbing the misuse of export subsidies is amply revealed in Dedman's speeches in connection with GATT and ITO (3:14) and in the ready acceptance of FAO (3:21).[9]

The hope for international action was evident in all the negotiations following on Article VII. Yet it was not certain in all minds that the instability of price experience from which Australian exports suffered in the pre-war period would necessarily recur, for, in addition to the benefits of hoped-for full employment, to many the war-time contracts with the United Kingdom pointed the way to a new concept of orderly marketing. Something of this was probably in Scully's mind (7:1) and he certainly spoke for a considerable body of producer opinion. Chifley's actions in 1947 (7:2) and his understanding about meat (7:6) were in line. Even the wool industry held

[8] The Tenth Report of the Rural Reconstruction Commission (12) is an essential starting point for any study of this period. It brings together a great deal of factual material and does present a commodity-by-commodity analysis of likely problems ahead. Its general analysis is premised—and correctly so—on the likely reappearance of a number of difficulties likely to confront Australian trade. It lent its support to orderly marketing and international agreements, but wisely warned those who saw the future wholly in terms of bilateral deals with the United Kingdom. Its review of the problems of international commodity agreements (paras. 2326 *et seq.*) is still highly relevant.

[9] 'Nutrition' was an important approach in early FAO activities which built on Australian initiatives before the war associated with the names of Lord Bruce and F. A. McDougal. The principles of good nutrition remain sound and do affect income elasticity of demand for food, promising increased markets for meat, dairy produce, fruit and vegetables as incomes rise. A great many of the poor countries in Asia and Africa, however, must necessarily concentrate limited resources (especially foreign exchange) on basic foodstuffs. See brief discussion in Section 3.

views which found expression in the Joint Organization of 1945 but which were forgotten by some of the same people in the excitement of a different situation in 1951 (7:19) and again in 1965 (7:20). Nevertheless, all sections of opinion were worried by the prospect of burdensome surpluses after the war.

The analysis offered in the Tenth Report of the Rural Reconstruction Commission was certainly reflected within government ministerial and official thinking of the time. This helpful analysis was less useful than it might have been, since in the immediate post-war period shortages rather than surpluses were the rule.

The experience of the Korean war boom and its collapse, however, served to emphasise the importance of international efforts to stabilise conditions of trade along the lines discussed by the Commission. Moreover, the decision of the United Kingdom in the early fifties to revert to private trade in food imports (see below) seemed to put an end to any expectation that bulk contracts would automatically provide some of the stabilisation needed.

By the mid-fifties, however, policies had clarified along lines that still persist and can be usefully expressed in terms of the five divisions listed above. Further comment is addressed to these in order of their listing.

(a) *Full Employment*

There is little further to add to the documents and comment in Section 2. We have already noted the practical achievement of full employment and, even more important, relatively high rates of economic growth in some of Australia's markets, together with the absence of depressions of the 1930 order. These facts have not lessened the importance of sustained high levels of employment but have served to show up its inadequacy as a single panacea for all export trade problems. For this reason Australian delegations have rather relaxed efforts on the international full employment front and have turned to the other elements of policies for which full employment is not a sufficient substitute.[10] The major policy statements in GATT (5:2) and at Commonwealth conferences, such as that in Montreal (7:16, 7:17) reflect this changing emphasis.

(b) *Bilateral Agreements*

It is not proposed to offer any detailed review of the war-time arrangements. There is a wealth of detailed material available to the student on the war-time marketing arrangements,[11] although he will need access to files of

[10] This has not prevented British delegations from sometimes avoiding these other issues by reminding Australian officials of their post-war affirmation of the high importance of full employment.

[11] See A7:1 which is a brief schedule of these prepared with the assistance of the Department of Primary Industry.

various organisations to ascertain the principles uppermost in producer thinking. Very little help is given in readily available public documents. Government thinking seemed to be a mixture of determination to continue controlled marketing at least at the Australian end, of readiness to continue war-time arrangements with the United Kingdom, and of recognition that wider international action would also be desirable and necessary.

Nevertheless, the economic historian covering this period will probably find the bulk contracts of great interest and worth research. He will find that monopolistic theory does not offer a satisfactory explanation of the immediate post-war relations between the Australian and the United Kingdom governments. British anxiety to obtain Australian produce continued for a short time after the war and during the Korean war boom, but reversion from state to private trading, or open marketing, which took place by the mid-fifties was the signal for the British government to behave like a strong buyer facing an abundant supply position. The return to private trading was made relatively easy by the response of British farmers to a generous protectionist policy and by a rapid increase in world supplies in relation to demand in the high income and viable trading countries (Section 13). The British government was thus able to return to its traditional cheap food policy. It had done well enough in this respect during the war and the early post-war bulk purchase period, but in these years circumstances of war and a strong sympathy for the plight of the British people made it difficult for Australia to behave like a monopoly seller confronting a weak buyer. The documents here presented do not bring this story out, although readers of Hansard from 1945 on will find the argument about Australia's 'cheap' wheat sales to Britain of considerable interest (7:5).[12]

If we classify the Commonwealth Sugar Agreement as an international agreement, the long-term meat agreement with the United Kingdom and the wheat clause of the United Kingdom-Australia Trade Agreement[13] represent continuing bilateral assurances for trade in two important export commodities. Both have been controversial, the latter largely because of doubts about the firmness of the United Kingdom commitment to take 750,000 tons annually (Section 9). The meat contract has also been controversial, because some interests appeared to think that alternative markets were more freely and profitably available than the proponents of the agreement considered to be in fact the case. A full study has yet to be made. There is little doubt in view of the deficiency payments received that the agreement did put a floor

[12] We have already noted one of the relevant factors, namely Chifley's strong humanitarian sympathy for Britain and his understandable reluctance to exploit a shortage situation directly arising from low output in Australia in the face of the difficult economic circumstances of Britain in the early post-war period.

[13] Article 6 of the trade agreement between the government of the United Kingdom and the government of the Commonwealth of Australia (Section 9).

to the market in certain years (7:7), that it did serve as an inducement for investment in the beef industry, and that its flexibility was such that when large-scale entry to the United States market became practicable in the late fifties the development of this new market was not seriously hampered.

On occasion, especially during recent periods of difficulties with the United States, availability of recourse to the United Kingdom market has again proved valuable. Nevertheless, those who have handled this agreement from its negotiation to its now closing years know well how difficult it is to be clear, in advance of unforeseen events, on the precise meaning of complex clauses, to establish unambiguous criteria for floor price determination,[14] and to be sure that growers in the industry affected will be loyal to agreements made with their initial support and enthusiasm. One can sympathise with the efforts of the Minister for Commerce and Agriculture, ideologically not predisposed to long-term bilateral contracts involving bulk purchase, to ascertain and to represent both the growers' and national interests (7:3, 7:4). There seems no doubt about the merit of the contract in the light of the circumstances as appraised in 1951. It is more open to doubt whether the events of subsequent years confirm the initial judgment. For reasons given above they appear to, although the case is open to argument. From the growers' point of view the merits of the post-war wheat contracts and the first International Wheat Agreement are also arguable. Importing members of the agreement gained wheat at prices well below those ruling for purchases outside the agreement.[15]

Bilateral agreements under which governments buy from the Australian marketing authority (China and India for wheat, Ceylon for flour) represent no difficulty of policy: the terms are negotiated, subject to any relevant international agreement, and when agreed the sale proceeds. The United Kingdom wheat arrangement is different in that it requires the concurrence of the millers and persuasion, should they prove reluctant, to take on commercial terms offers of wheat up to 750,000 tons in total (A9:1). Theoretically, too, Australia could offer so much meat that the United Kingdom would find it difficult to honour its undertaking to take all surplus offered on the terms set out in the contract.[16] In this respect, the wheat undertaking has proved the more difficult of the two; the willingness of both United Kingdom govern-

[14] See especially a press statement made by McEwen on 31 January 1951. In announcing the visit of two senior officials from the British Ministry of Food he made some useful comments on price criteria for long-term contracts.

[15] Some partially relevant information is given in the Vernon Report (11), vol. I, Table 8.8, p. 164. In this table the export returns are well above local (fixed) prices. In addition, however, the export prices in 1949-50, 1950-1, and 1951-2 were less than 'free-market' (i.e. non-wheat agreement) prices.

[16] The Meat Agreement expires in 1967. As yet (December 1966) there is no official published indication that it will be renegotiated. The case for it is no longer so strong from the Australian point of view as it was in 1951.

ment and millers to import Australian wheat tends to vary inversely with the size of the domestic crop.

The bilateral agreements and the annual sales to China cover a substantial proportion of Australian wheat export sales. In meat the agreement with the United Kingdom, expanding Japanese quotas, and the opportunities assured for sale to United States importers (7:9) have provided a solid base for the entire export surplus.[17] Quotas for butter regulate our principal market in the United Kingdom.

For the most part, however, even where intergovernmental understandings exist, sales of Australian agricultural and mineral products are subject to the forces of markets in which private, or open, market dealing determines the outcome. Thus even sales of wheat to China, in which prices are determined by direct negotiation with the Chinese government, are inevitably influenced by conditions in the world market.[18] However, these market forces of supply and demand are often subject to tariff and non-tariff barriers to trade which may fall outside the terms of bilateral understanding on a particular commodity. It is towards the reduction of these that some of the most energetic efforts of the Australian government have been directed in the last fifteen years. In addition, attempts have been made in some cases to minimise the range of price fluctuations by international (as distinct from bilateral) commodity agreements. These are items (c) and (d) of our subdivision of commodity policy.

(c) *Reducing the Barriers to Trade*

The story of the government's efforts to reduce the impact of artificial barriers, especially non-tariff quotas and embargoes, on the sale of Australian produce is best studied through the documents given in other sections, supplemented by 7:15 and 7:16 in this section. The most important are those in Section 5, which show the continuing effort by Australia to secure effective measures to contain and reduce agricultural protectionism. The 1954-5 Review Session itself, the Haberler Committee, and the subsequent work of Committee II represent unfinished business. How unfinished is illustrated by the long delays in getting the Kennedy Round over the hurdle of EEC unwillingness or inability to negotiate on agricultural products (Section 5) and by the heavy obstructions to trade so far presented by the Common Agricultural Policy of the EEC (see especially A8:3 and comment in Section 8).

---

[17] It needs to be observed that the meat agreement negotiated bilaterally with the United States Administration (7:8) is subject to the overriding force of later Congressional legislation (7:9).

[18] This point is not vitiated although it may be tempered by the fact that Australian produce is subject to varying degrees of monopolistic marketing practices overseas— e.g. wheat, meat, dairy produce, sugar, dried fruits, wine, and eggs. Wool is a notable exception. See Rural Reconstruction Committee's Tenth Report (12) and Vernon Report (11), vol. I, ch. 8 and vol. II, app. G7.

The story is one of persistence in which Australia is not without friends. The best that can be said, however, is that the problem has been contained and even somewhat ameliorated. If it were not for the possibility—even probability—that the United Kingdom may yet enter the EEC, the worsening of agricultural protectionism would be unlikely.[19] There are two factors, however, which made for slow progress in actually reducing the barriers to trade. These are the strongly entrenched position of highly protected farmers in Britain and Europe and the fact that the United States, which seeks to moderate barriers to trade for its own agricultural surpluses, has rather destroyed its case by strongly protectionist policies of its own in dairy produce and wheat, including in some degree its surplus disposals (PL 480) program.[20] As the documents relating to Commonwealth conferences show (7:16, 8:4), Britain has supported Australian and New Zealand efforts in this field and it can and should be said that in Britain a policy of limiting excesses in its own agricultural protectionism had, a few years ago, begun to bite. Unfortunately, this phase seems to have passed. Support prices have again been raised. Moreover, it is moving away from concepts of open trading to quota arrangements which will continue to put British farmers in a secure position of first priority.[21]

The reference to some amelioration of the problem of agricultural protectionism is justified by steady, if uneven, liberalisation of Japanese import quotas for foodstuffs, by the removal of mineral quotas imposed by the United States (11:13), by the resistance shown by the Administration in Washington to demands for severe import restrictions on meat from Australia (Section 11), and by the evidence that even in Europe there may be more expansive opportunities for important products like meat and fruit. A successful Kennedy Round may yield more scope or at least confirm containment of the problem *vis-à-vis* Europe.

Nevertheless, it would be unwise to expect any great liberalisation of agricultural trade. The high hopes sometimes expressed by McEwen are not

[19] It is true that agricultural support policies in the United Kingdom are more protective for some items than those operating in the Common Market. On the other hand wheat and sugar—two major items of concern to Australia—are more heavily protected in the Common Market. The net effect would be an increase in the aggregate level of protection *vis-à-vis* Australian exports, if the United Kingdom accepts the terms of the Common Agricultural Policy as they now stand (Section 8). In another sense, too, United Kingdom entry would increase the adverse effects of agricultural protectionism, for European farmers will, especially under highly protected conditions, be capable of increasing production to fill the United Kingdom market previously supplied by Australia.

[20] Agricultural policy and the structure of agricultural enterprise in the United States are undergoing changes which may lead to some softening of the protectionism which has characterised the last two decades.

[21] We have always been prone to accept this (9:1). Should Britain fully accept the Common Agricultural Policy of the EEC, the scope for direct competition with British farmers will be considerably less than it is now.

really the prelude to a dramatic reversal of European and foreseeable British policies. The outlook, however, is not unrelated to commodity agreements for, as we shall note shortly, agreements in respect of wheat, meat, and dairy produce, if achieved under the aegis of the Kennedy Round (Section 5), are likely to govern both access to markets and the price behaviour applicable to those markets.

Before turning to this last topic, however, it will be useful to refer to the documents relating to PL 480 surplus disposals (7:11, 7:12), for these have been regarded by Canada, Australia, New Zealand, and Denmark as an unfair trade practice on the part of the United States. Australia's principal concern has been with wheat, although not unaffected by disposals of surplus dairy produce. The documents make clear the FAO principles and Australia's attitude. It ought not to be assumed (and never was by ministers or officials) that the FAO principles (7:11) ensured that these disposals would have no adverse effect on Australia's exports.[22] In circumstances of permanent shortage of foreign exchange and recurring food crises, a country like India was bound to call on PL 480 in lieu of, as well as additionally to, commercial imports. Far from diminishing in importance this problem has grown, although Australia has itself come to live more resignedly with it. The life-saving character of United States wheat supplies to India is too obvious to justify serious criticism; the same circumstances account for Australia's own increasing gifts of wheat. The United States supplies have, until recently, come from otherwise unsaleable stocks—the so-called marriage of convenience.[23] However, this situation is changing. The United States is more likely in future to sell to Russia and even China than it was. In addition its stocks are now falling and it could not maintain current PL 480 supplies to India without easing its curbs on production.[24]

The changing situation in the United States has clearly affected the terms of the 1966 legislation governing PL 480-type operations. The new law lays emphasis on the building up of cash markets and a shift towards financing food aid through long-term dollar credits rather than by means of sales for foreign currencies.[25] In short, there has been a strong trend to world shortages of wheat and other grains, especially rice.

Another reason for some quietness, if not uncertainty, in Australian policy is that surplus disposals to non-affluent countries have become an integral part of the negotiations in the Cereals Group operating within GATT as part of the Kennedy Round. The move owes much to the so-called Baumgartner

[22] See Crawford (61), pp. 390, 394.

[23] See Crawford (61), p. 392.

[24] For India's sake it is to be hoped that her own production program will so succeed that PL 480 imports can be diminished, for these are not costless in terms of scarce foreign exchange.

[25] See 'Public Law 89-808, 89th Congress, H.R. 14929, November 11th 1966'.

215

Plan for international commodity agreements. If these ideas are adopted as the outcome of the Kennedy Round and commodity groups meeting within the GATT framework (see below), agreement would be necessary on prices and market sharing in advanced and poor countries alike. In extreme forms disposal of surpluses on non-commercial terms from all exporters would be incorporated in any new wheat agreement (7:22).[26] It is far too early to say that the problem of surplus disposals as an adverse influence on commercial sales of wheat has disappeared: even if a new wheat agreement incorporates arrangements for them, it may not improve the total export returns available to Australia, since higher prices in markets of limited access (as in Europe) may be offset by the non-commercial terms of sale to less affluent areas. The best hope for these lies not in containment of agricultural protectionism in Europe alone but in the sustained development of commercial markets such as Russia and especially China have recently provided.

(d) *International Commodity Agreements*

While Australian experience under this head has been disappointing, it probably has been less frustrating than the more general effort to lessen barriers to trade. The post-war Joint Organization scheme for disposing of wool was an undoubted success, even though growers twice refused to accept a successor scheme (A7:1, 7:19, 7:20).

The Wheat Agreements (7:23 to 7:25) have been strongly supported by growers even if in retrospect it appears they may have made more money without an agreement. This point cannot be easily substantiated, but it also seems clear that a factor independent of the formal International Wheat Agreement has maintained stable and more or less satisfactory prices since 1954. This is the undoubted fact that since the early fifties 'strong holding' by the United States and Canada (with Australia more or less tagging along) has held world prices within the range specified in the International Wheat Agreements. The agreements have been a convenient way of announcing a sellers' price range. Had they weakened, the agreements (after the initial post-war shortage was over) may well have proved too weak to make floor prices effective. It is probably not too much to say that it is difficult, where burdensome surpluses exist, to negotiate satisfactory prices for sellers unless these sellers are in a semi- or full-monopoly position and have the ability to hold stocks or unless production controls limiting future supply are made effective.

As we have noted in Section 5, a new cereals agreement is being negotiated in the Kennedy Round; such an agreement would completely replace the existing agreement which has been extended pending the outcome of the GATT negotiations.

Australia has certainly benefited from two international sugar agreements

[26] For a good critical account of 'The French Plan' see Lewis (105), (106).

—the Commonwealth (A7:3) and the International (A7:4). The former has stabilised both quantitative access to and prices in major Commonwealth markets; the latter has given periods of stability but has not been adequate to the task of holding floor prices or ceilings at reasonable levels. The Japanese market is the principal free market. The sugar story, regrettably, does not emerge clearly from the documents and we found it impracticable to make good the deficiency fully.[27] Suffice to say the parties to the International Sugar Agreement continue to work for restoration of an effective price range. Until this is achieved the main support for sugar returns is the Commonwealth Agreement and the increased quota presently available in the United States market (11:11).

The Tin Agreement (A7:5) and the Coffee Agreement (A7:2, 7:27)—the latter of importance to Papua and New Guinea—are covered reasonably well in the documents. Document 7:28 merely indicates that Australia has been involved in discussions on lead and zinc which seemed, at one stage, the prelude to an international agreement.

The picture is not clear, even if some objectives of policy are plain enough to be seen. The lack of clarity is not due solely to the relatively few documents here included but rather to the lack of a single comprehensive ministerial statement which would show why we work hard to secure some commodity agreements and far less enthusiastically, if at all, for others.

What follows is not a substitute for such a statement, but tries to indicate the appropriate subject matter.[28] It is clear that 'stability' and 'floor' prices have been key objectives of Australian efforts to secure commodity agreements, but it has perhaps not been sufficiently clear for what purpose stability and 'predictability' in prices have been sought. There are two interests involved: the producers' interest in stable returns and the national interest in a balanced external economy. An international agreement which limits the range of prices, both up and down, may or may not give growers higher incomes over a period than they would have enjoyed in the absence of stability. Nevertheless, if they attach value to security and predictability of prices, as they largely do in the wheat, sugar, dairy, and dried fruit industries, growers will welcome agreements which they regard as reasonable. It is true that for some products governments can and do offer some security through domestic stabilisation schemes which also support export returns wholly or partially. In these cases—the wheat stabilisation scheme, for example—both international and bilateral agreements give an underpinning which governments are likely to welcome.

[27] But see A7:4n. It is rather surprising how little is done in professional journals (both government and academic) to keep public information about the Agreements up-to-date.

[28] This can also be obtained from abundant international literature including the Haberler Report (81), and Blau (25). Among Australian writings listed in n. 3 the work of Lewis is particularly relevant.

Australia has a wide array of exports but it also shares with countries dependent upon fewer primary exports a concern about predictability of total foreign exchange earnings. Thus assured minimum returns per unit for the principal exports of Australia would allow firmer judgments to be made about our ability to sustain a given or rising level of imports.[29] Nevertheless, it is easy to exaggerate this objective. First it is highly unlikely, for reasons given below, that the bulk of our exports will be strongly supported by international price agreements.[30] Secondly, and more importantly, there is an alternative course of policy, namely to hold reserves large enough to ride through year-to-year variations in export earnings. If able to do this, total earnings over a period *may* be greater. In this respect membership of the IMF could prove increasingly important (Sections 3, 15, and 18).

Thirdly, any objective expressed in terms of the national interest has never been pushed in times of peace to the extent of overriding producers' ideas of their own interests. The documents—especially McEwen's statements—give strong voice to the view that if producers prefer the risks of open markets, it is for them to say, for they own the product (7:3). This largely explains Australia's notorious ambivalence in the matter of international agreements—a point to be elaborated below. Orderly marketing may be practised, but it is to help growers and not primarily as a means of serving some definition of the national interest. There may be a national interest in stabilising export earnings, but this objective has been pursued primarily to add to the economic security of the producer—an end in itself for both Labor and non-Labor governments alike.

Should international agreements serve also to improve returns over a period—usually a negotiating objective held distinct from minimising fluctuations—then both national and producer interests are served. As already noted, this has not inevitably been the result in the post-war period.

Again, international agreements have come to have another objective in the situation of agricultural protectionism, namely to ensure access to markets which might otherwise be closed altogether. As already noted, this has particular reference to the negotiations now proceeding in three commodity groups in GATT in association with the Kennedy Round (Section 5). Of these the cereals group is particularly important.

Reference has been made to the ambivalence of the Australian attitude which is not always well understood or accepted internationally. Wool prices

[29] Year by year variations in production would still be unpredictable, especially where seasonal factors are themselves widely variable over time.

[30] With the latest defeat of the Wool Reserve Price Scheme, there is little chance of an international agreement. Had one eventuated, fluctuations in producer returns would be relatively stabilised, but it is more open to doubt whether total export returns would be similarly stabilised. A good deal of literature on this subject exists, partly as the result of the controversial referendum campaign in 1965 (see, for example, Powell and Campbell (139), (140); Parish (133), (134); Duloy and Nevile (74); and Lloyd (112)).

are volatile in behaviour and could do with stabilisation in the interests of both the manufacturers and the producers. Yet we are cold to international agreements for the sufficient reason that adequate grower support has not been forthcoming for the appropriate legislative interference with the auction system. Similarly, no recent government has been willing to work vigorously for an agreement to stabilise prices in lead and zinc, in a situation in which the opinions of producers are divided. In this case the producers (a few large firms) can carry the risks, and any national interest in stability either cannot be, or has not been, argued to the point of overriding their wishes. This concern for producer viewpoints is an important element in our commodity-by-commodity approach in international conferences (7:16, para. 44). However, the more important explanation lies in the widely different conditions of production and marketing which characterise the many commodities of interest to us. It is difficult to devise an all-embracing scheme.

Our interest has been wide enough and will continue to be wide enough to justify continuing effort and initiatives in the international field. Nevertheless, it can now be seen that international commodity agreements in which consumer and producer interests join forces are but one ingredient of our total policies designed to improve the terms and conditions on which our products may be sold abroad. In this particular field our efforts have been vigorous where the light from producers appeared to be green; in others we were less the champion of international agreements than other countries may have expected. On one point we have been consistent: as a consumer of tin and coffee we have accepted agreements and have always been ready to join in tea, rubber, cotton, and other commodity discussions to support our good faith in seeking agreements on wheat, sugar, and dairy produce as producers, and recently on coffee and cocoa representing New Guinea production interests.

Many of the preceding remarks have been beyond the specific content of the documents in this chapter: this has been deliberate, in the hope that professional people both within the government (e.g. the Bureau of Agricultural Economics) and in universities or private enterprise would be encouraged to make a more searching examination of the aims and scope of international commodity agreements in relation to Australia's export industries.

Before turning to the final short comment on item (e) in our break-up of commodity policy, mention may be made (again beyond the scope of the documents) of policies now under discussion as at least a supplement and perhaps an alternative to international commodity agreements. It is difficult to devise an all-embracing commodity agreement which provides the framework for market access, price ranges, and production policies for all commodities. However, much thought has been given to devices for 'compensating' less developed countries dependent on one, two, or three basic commodities for their export income when export returns fall short of some stipulated norm. While Australia might well qualify as an occasional recipient in some schemes, they mostly require a transfer of resources from affluent to less affluent nations. Although it probably has been asked to declare a view, especially at the United Nations Conference on Trade and Development, the Australian government has so far given no real encouragement[31] and, as we have noted earlier, it has made no public statement of Australia's interest. Certainly in any such scheme—even when characterised by a form of insurance—Australia will be expected to act as a net donor of assistance. Compensatory finance is not a sellable substitute for its own interests in commodity agreements, whatever may be its final attraction as a form of international aid to underdeveloped nations.[32]

(e) *Export Promotion*

None of the documents in this chapter is particularly relevant to national policies directed towards the stimulation of consumer demand for Australian produce and towards ensuring an adequate and competitively offered supply. These matters receive some attention in Section 16.

The comment offered in this section has gone beyond the confines of the documents in it. This is in part because commodity policy embraces so much that has been better dealt with in other sections. It is also because government statements tend to be less comprehensive and informative than is desirable in such a complex field of policy. We have noted the need for more research on unanswered questions which arise. We suggest that McEwen might well devote one of his periodical statements on trade policy to this admittedly difficult task: the clarification of objectives of commodity policy. The documents in this book help, but too much is left to speculative interpretation and inference.

[31] Although the Australian government will have supported significant steps taken by the IMF to give extra help of 'compensatory' character to developing countries where circumstances (such as falling export returns) seem to warrant it (7:29). At the UNCTAD meeting in 1964 it supported a resolution favouring further liberalisation.

[32] An introduction to the subject is to be found in United Nations Organization (157). See also IBRD (98); Meier (124); various accounts of IMF work published in IMF Staff Papers and in special documents submitted to the United Nations; and several documents published by UNCTAD. The Resolutions contained in the Final Act of the Conference include a unanimous one in which delegates voted for further liberalisation of IMF's own special arrangements and another which gave rise to the IBRD study (98) mentioned above.

A7:1 BULK PURCHASES OF AUSTRALIAN COMMODITIES BY THE UNITED KINGDOM

PREPARED BY NANCY ANDERSON

Commodity	Bulk Purchases Begun	Bulk Purchases Ceased	Contract Details	Comments
Butter and cheese	Sept. 1939	1955	Intergovernmental contracts negotiated with U.K. Ministry of Food. First five years, 1939–44, annual contracts for definite quantities negotiated. Four years to 30 June 1948, contract for sale of total exportable surplus. Seven years to 30 June 1955, contract extended with new provisions— (1) Annual revision of prices if notice given by either party. (2) Australia could export up to maximum quantity, negotiated annually, to markets outside the U.K. and colonies included in Ministry of Food's colonial program.	
Canned fruits	1940		U.K. government took quantity of apricots, peaches and pears at agreed price.	
	1941	1954	U.K. government agreed to purchase exportable surplus of season's canned fruits. Prices on f.o.b. basis, Australian ports.	Defence requirements meant that commercial shipments virtually ceased from 1942 to 1945.
	1946		Commercial shipments to U.K. under an official arrangement virtually on a merchant-to-government basis.	

(Continued on next page)

221

A7:1 BULK PURCHASES OF AUSTRALIAN COMMODITIES BY THE UNITED KINGDOM—*Continued*

Commodity	Bulk Purchases Begun	Ceased	Contract Details	Comments
Copra	March 1949	Dec. 1957	U.K. bought total production of Papua and New Guinea less Australian domestic requirements and any third-party sales mutually agreed between the contracting governments. Price set for first year, and prices for subsequent years not to be more than 10 per cent higher or lower than in preceding year.	
Dried fruits	Sept. 1939	Dec. 1953	U.K. bought, at agreed prices, whole of exportable surplus after requirements of Australian home market and other regular markets, e.g. Canada and New Zealand, had been met. 1940–5: annual contracts at agreed prices. 1946–8: three-year contract with prices firm for three years. 1948–53: five-year contract. Prices for 1949 and 1950 agreed on in 1948, but prices for remaining years agreed each year. Quantity purchased by U.K. not to exceed value of £2,500,000 stg., f.o.b., which would purchase about 46,000 tons and a free quota of 2,000 tons which was never fully used.	U.K. agreed to support price of Australian fruit in U.K. market for 1954. Agreed to pay Australian government any deficiency between market realisations and the support prices up to 31 March 1955.
Eggs	1939		U.K. bought whole of exportable surplus.	
	1945		Large-scale shipments to U.K. resumed.	
		1953 (shell eggs)	Long-term contract with U.K. to 1950, but this was terminated on 30 June 1948. New contract operated from 1948–9 to 1952–3.	
		1954 (egg pulp)	Envisaged yearly progressive increases in production. If Australian exports not sufficient to provide U.K. equivalent of 4,500,000 cases in 1949 and 1950–1, U.K. had the right to call in January 1951 for review of revision of quantities it was committed to take for balance of period.	1941–2 shipments discontinued because of shipping difficulties.

222

Meat	1939	3 July 1954	Annual agreements at negotiated prices made up to 1944. Four-year Meat Agreement. Later extended to 1951 (beef, veal, mutton, lamb, pigmeat and offal). Fifteen-year Meat Agreement from 1 July 1952 to 30 September 1967. Assures market for whole of Australia's exportable surplus of beef, veal, mutton, and lamb. Australia to encourage expansion of production. Provision also made for: (i) reversion to trader-to-trader marketing, whenever U.K. decided on this; (ii) prices to be negotiated on basis of cost of production whilst government-to-government trading continued; (iii) guaranteed annual average minimum prices on reversion to normal trading methods; (iv) Australia to have right to export full requirements of meat to British colonies and dependencies after end of bulk purchase and to continue to negotiate each year a quantity of 'free quota' meat for export to any market at discretion of Australian government.	Government-to-government prices for mutton and lamb operated to 30 June 1954, those for beef and veal to 30 September 1954. Reversion to trader-to-trader marketing occurred in the U.K. from 3 July 1954. Sheep and lambs killed after 1 July 1954 and cattle, calves and pigs killed after 1 October 1954 could be shipped by exporters direct to importers. Animals killed prior to these dates had to be declared and exported under the bulk purchase arrangements. 1 October 1958: Australia able to export mutton and lamb to any country in unrestricted quantities. 1 October 1961: Australia able to export beef and veal to any country in unrestricted quantities.
Sheepskins	1940	30 June 1946	U.K. government acquired exportable surplus of Australian woolled sheepskins for period to extend and terminate with that of wool arrangement. A periodical review of prices was provided for.	

(Continued on next page)

A7:1 BULK PURCHASES OF AUSTRALIAN COMMODITIES BY THE UNITED KINGDOM—*Continued*

Commodity	Bulk Purchases Begun	Ceased	Contract Details	Comments
Sugar	1939	1 July 1957	U.K. government agreed to purchase Australia's exportable surplus at prices negotiated annually.	
	1949		Commonwealth countries Sugar Marketing Agreement formulated. Included undertaking by U.K. to find a market for Australian exportable surplus sugar to end of 1952.	
	1953		British Commonwealth Sugar Agreement. Effective from 1 January 1953 for 8-year term extendable annually. Currently operative until end of 1973. Provides for: (i) Australian export to preferential markets of a maximum of 600,000 tons per annum. (ii) U.K. purchase of 300,000 tons (increased to 335,000 tons as from 1 January 1964) of the 600,000 tons at an annually negotiated price. This price is determined at a level reasonably remunerative to efficient producers and since 1 January 1965 has included a special payment related inversely to the world price in the case of the less-developed exporting members. As from 1 January 1966 the negotiated price is on a *triennial* basis. (iii) Sale of balance at world market prices plus tariff preferences where applicable.	On reversion of sugar dealings to trader-to-trader basis, U.K. set up Sugar Board to purchase the negotiated price sugar under the British Commonwealth Sugar Agreement.
Wheat and flour	1939	1953	Commonwealth government negotiated with U.K. government for sale of old season's wheat and for 50,000 tons of flour under contract. 1940: 1-million-ton contract for shipment in that year but delivery not completed until 1942. Further quantities purchased from time to time by U.K. government, apparently on an *ad hoc* basis. Reversion to private trading took place in 1953.	Under the 1956 U.K.-Australia Trade Agreement the two governments affirmed their 'desire and expectation' of annual sales of Australian wheat in the U.K. market of not less than 28m. bushels. This target was not achieved regularly.

Tallow	1939	1952	U.K. government purchased Australia's exportable surplus under annual contracts which permitted export of certain grades of tallow to other countries.
Wool	1939	1946	U.K. government agreed to buy whole Australian clip surplus to Australian manufacturers' requirements for duration of war and one year after at agreed price. Australian woolgrowers then to share equally with U.K. in any profit resulting from re-sale outside U.K. of wool thus acquired. Arrangement subject to review in May of each year at instance of either government.
	1942		Purchase price was increased.
	1945		U.K.-Dominion Wool Disposals Ltd. (Joint Organisation) formed by U.K., Australia, New Zealand, and South Africa, to carry out an orderly disposal of the surplus stocks bought by the U.K. under the war-time arrangements.
	1946		Wool auctions resumed in 1946–7. Disposal of stocks made simultaneously with the sales of current clips and these stocks were finally liquidated by December 1951. J.O. was wound up in January 1952. Profits were shared between U.K. and supplying country. During disposal period J.O. maintained a reserve prices scheme aimed at protecting prices of current clips.

SOURCE: Commonwealth Year Books and information supplied by the Department of Primary Industry.

225

A7:2 INTERNATIONAL COFFEE AGREEMENT 1962

PREPARED BY NANCY ANDERSON

The objectives of the agreement are to achieve a reasonable balance between supply and demand of coffee on a basis which will assure adequate supplies to consumers and equitable prices to producers, and which will bring about long-term equilibrium between production and consumption; to alleviate the serious hardships caused by burdensome surpluses and excessive fluctuations in the price of coffee; and to encourage the consumption of coffee.

The agreement is administered by the International Coffee Organisation, whose highest authority is the International Coffee Council consisting of representatives of all importing and exporting members of the Organisation.

There is agreement on the need to prevent coffee prices from declining below their general level in 1962; and to assure to consumers prices which will not hamper an increase in consumption.

Basic export quotas are set for exporting members. Annual export quotas are fixed in the light of Council estimates of total world imports and of probable exports from non-member countries. These quotas are always the same percentage of the specified basic quotas. In addition, quarterly quotas are provided for to keep supply in reasonable balance with demand throughout the coffee year. These may be adjusted to meet market requirements, but without altering the annual overall quotas.

The shipment of coffee from a dependent territory to the metropolitan country does not count as part of its export quota. Also, any exporting member whose average annual exports remain below 25,000 bags is exempted from the quota provisions, as is also a Trust Territory whose annual exports to countries other than the Administering Authority do not exceed 100,000 bags.[1]

To prevent non-member exporting countries from increasing their exports at the expense of members, provision is made for a limitation on the amount which each member country can import from non-member countries.

Producing countries undertake to adjust the production of coffee to the amount needed for domestic consumption, exports, and stocks, the Council recommending production goals for each member and for the world as a whole. In the event of failure to adjust production programs, Council may decide that such defaulting members may not enjoy any quota increases which may apply from the application of the agreement.

> *Source*: Based on text of the Agreement as printed in *International Coffee Agreement, 1962*, United Nations Document E/CONF. 42/7 of 2 October 1962.

---

[1] These provisions mean that both Papua and New Guinea are at present exempt from the quota provisions of the Agreement.

A7:3 COMMONWEALTH SUGAR AGREEMENT 1962

PREPARED BY NANCY ANDERSON

This long-term agreement between the United Kingdom and sugar-exporting countries of the British Commonwealth aims at supplying sugar to the United Kingdom, developing the production of sugar in Commonwealth countries, and at the orderly marketing of that sugar. It was originally negotiated in 1951 with a duration of eight years and an annual right of extension for a further year. It has been so extended every year and at present runs until 31 December 1973.

The exporting countries agree to limit their individual exports in any one calendar year to specified basic quotas totalling 2,535,000 tons,[1] Australia's basic quota being 600,000 tons. Under certain circumstances these quotas may be exceeded by agreement.

The United Kingdom undertakes to purchase each calendar year agreed quantities from each exporting territory up to a total of 1,742,500 long tons,[1] at prices negotiated every three years. Australia's 'negotiated price' quota is 335,000 long tons.

The customary local export of sugar from exporting territories to countries within their respective regions is excluded from the agreement.

Negotiated prices under the agreement take into account principles of uniformity and of reasonable remuneration to efficient producers. Under amendments made in 1965 they are to be fixed at triennial reviews on the basis of annual cost data for the years up to and including the year preceding the review and on other appropriate factors and considerations. If the British government or any exporting territory is dissatisfied with prices, it may apply for the price-fixing method to be varied.

In recognition of the dependence of the economies of the less developed exporting territories upon the export of sugar and the effect on them of depressed world prices, the negotiated prices for those territories also include provision for a special payment related inversely to the world price and taking account of the benefits that formerly accrued to exporters under the Colonial Certificated Preference System.

Source: Based on *The Commonwealth*
Sugar Agreement with Explanatory Notes,
London, 1962, and United Kingdom
Ministry of Agriculture, Fisheries and
Food, press releases of December 1964
and November 1965.

A7:4 INTERNATIONAL SUGAR AGREEMENT

PREPARED BY NANCY ANDERSON

The International Sugar Agreement of 1937 was superseded by the Agreements of 1953 and 1958. In the 1937 agreement each exporting country was given a basic annual quota, which could be increased in proportion to any expansion in sugar consumption. By this means and by limitations on stocks and measures to

---

[1] Rhodesian quotas under the agreement were in suspense as at December 1966.

encourage more consumption it was hoped to hold in balance the supplies and requirements of sugar. In the 1953 agreement basic export quotas were also allocated with provision for reductions or increases to maintain prices within a specified range. In October 1958 a new agreement was negotiated which followed the lines of the 1953 agreement.[1]

The objectives of the 1958 agreement between exporters and importers of sugar are to assure supplies to importing countries and markets for exporting countries at equitable and stable prices; to facilitate steady increases in the consumption and supply of sugar; to contribute to the improvement of the living conditions of consumers throughout the world, and to assist in the maintenance of purchasing power in world markets of producing countries or areas by providing adequate returns to producers; and to further international co-operation on world sugar problems.

The agreement is administered by the International Sugar Council, on which each participating government is represented.

As subsidies may operate to impair the maintenance of equitable and stable prices, any participating government granting or maintaining such a subsidy which increases exports or imports of sugar must notify the Council of its nature, extent, and the circumstances making it necessary. Where a participating country considers it faces serious injury because of such a subsidy, the Council may make recommendations concerning it.

To make sugar more freely available to consumers, each participating government agrees to take action to reduce disproportionate burdens on sugar, including those resulting from private and public controls and fiscal and tax policies.

To prevent non-participating countries from gaining advantage at the expense of participating countries, the governments of participating importing countries agree not to permit the import from the former, as a group, in a quota year of a total quantity of sugar larger than was imported from them during any of the three calendar years 1951, 1952, and 1953.

Participating importing countries also agree that in any quota year their total exports, if any, shall not exceed their total imports.

Participating export countries agree to regulate their exports to the free market so that net exports to that market will not exceed the quantities which such countries may export each quota year; to take all practicable action to ensure that the demands of participating import countries are met; and to give priority in the supply of sugar, on equal terms of sale, to those countries.

Participating export countries also agree to adjust their production of sugar by regulating its manufacture or the acreage of plantings so that production will cover the amount needed for domestic consumption, exports permitted under the agreement, and stocks equal to 20 per cent of their annual production.

Basic export quotas are set for exporting countries. These can be reviewed, in total and then individually, by 1 April each year. The British Commonwealth is allocated a total quota, the distribution of which remains a matter for internal arrangement by the countries and territories concerned.

---

[1] The agreement came into force on 1 January 1959. The quota and price provisions of this agreement cover only the first three years to 31 December 1961. A conference in Geneva in 1961 failed to reach agreement on quota provisions for 1962 and 1963. Attempts are still being made (December 1966) to reach a new agreement. The practical effect of the failure of the 1961 conference is that former export limitations on participating exporting countries, including Australia, do not apply until such time as agreement is again reached.

The price objective is to hold the world price of sugar within a declared range. In attempting to do this, the Council has discretion to increase or reduce quotas to meet market conditions within certain limits, according to various defined prices within the range of U.S. 3·25 cents to 4·00 cents per pound. However, the Council may suspend these limits upon its discretion to increase quotas if it is satisfied that a new situation has arisen which endangers the attainment of the general objectives of the agreement.

If an importing country has experienced or is threatened by a serious deterioration in its reserves, the Council may modify the obligations of that country or of any exporting country under the agreement to permit the importing country to secure a more adequate supply of sugar within its available resources.

The Council is to make representations to the governments of participating countries concerning ways and means of securing appropriate expansion in the consumption of sugar and may undertake studies of such matters as the effects of taxation and restrictive measures and of economic, climatic and other conditions on the consumption of sugar; means of promoting consumption; co-operative publicity programs with similar agencies concerned with the expansion of consumption of other foodstuffs; and the progress of research into new uses of sugar and its by-products, etc. It may also make and arrange for studies of various forms of special assistance to the sugar industry and other studies concerned with the attainment of the general objectives of the agreement.

> *Source*: Based on text of agreement
> printed in *Australia: Treaty Series 1959*
> (Department of External Affairs), and
> *Commonwealth Year Book*, nos. 40, 41,
> 46, and 50.

A7:5 INTERNATIONAL TIN AGREEMENT

PREPARED BY NANCY ANDERSON

This agreement between producers and consumers of tin was formed in Geneva in 1953. It came into force in 1956 and was re-negotiated in 1960 for a further five years from 1 July 1961. A third agreement was re-negotiated in 1965. It does not alter the basic mechanisms of the earlier agreements and took effect from 1 July 1966.

The objectives of the agreement are to prevent unemployment or under-employment and other serious difficulties likely to result from maladjustment between the supply of and the demand for tin; to achieve stability of price on a basis which will be fair to consumers and provide a reasonable return to producers; and to provide a framework for the consideration of measures to promote more economic production of tin.

The agreement is administered by the International Tin Council, on which each participating country is represented.

Floor and ceiling prices for tin metal are established under the agreement, and the Council determines the quantity of tin which may be exported, adjusting the supply to the demand so as to maintain the price between the floor and ceiling prices. The Council also maintains a buffer stock of tin metal and cash equivalent to cover any variance in supply and demand. Producing countries contribute to this buffer stock.

I

The buffer stock manager

> must buy metal at or below £stg 1,000
> may do so between £stg 1,000 and 1,050
> may sell between £stg 1,050 and 1,150
> must sell at or above £stg 1,200.

If the Council considers that a serious shortage of tin is likely to develop, it may make recommendations to participating countries with a view to ensuring the maximum development of production in producing countries, and to assuring to consuming countries the equitable distribution of available supplies at a price no higher than the ceiling price.

Australia is a consuming member of the Council.

> *Source*: Based on text of Second
> International Tin Agreement printed in
> *Australia: Treaty Series 1961*, no. 20
> (Department of External Affairs),
> and a statement provided by
> the Department of National Development.

7:1 POST-WAR MARKETING

Statement by the Minister for Commerce and Agriculture (W. J. Scully) in the House of Representatives on 15 October 1943.

I am entirely in accord with the suggestion that the orderly marketing of primary products should be continued at the conclusion of hostilities. The period of transition from war to peace will be fraught with extreme difficulties for producers unless some form of control remains. Any hasty alteration of marketing methods which have been adopted to meet war-time needs would be to invite loss to producers. This is a happening which must be avoided at all costs, and more particularly at a time when our energies must be bent towards disposing of those commodities, the production of which has been greatly expanded to meet war-time commitments.

Plans have been prepared for the time when the world returns to normal. . . .

I shall be happy to convene a conference of producers' organizations so that primary producers can be given the fullest information concerning the likely trend of post-war demands. It should be the aim of primary producers, whenever possible, to produce to meet export demands, rather than to produce and hope that there will be a demand for the goods produced. I agree that a policy of producing for demand presents many difficulties and that it implies careful organization and long-range planning. However, it can scarcely be argued that this alone is sufficient to cause its abandonment, and that because of difficulties we should revert to the haphazard system of producing goods and hoping that someone overseas will buy them. This system has involved producers in many disasters in the past, and, if perpetuated, would be responsible for similar results in the post-war period. I feel the points raised merit the most earnest consideration of the leaders of primary industry.

> *Source*: *Digest of Decisions and Announcements*, no. 66, pp. 26-7.

7:2 EXPORTS OF FOOD TO UNITED KINGDOM: EXTENSION OF LONG-TERM CONTRACTS

Statement by the Prime Minister (J. B. Chifley) on 17 October 1947.

The Australian Government considers it desirable that Britain should send a small expert mission to Australia to continue exploratory discussions commenced at London between representatives of the two Governments, regarding the production of larger quantities of food in Australia, so that greater supplies will be available for export to the British people.

This view is being conveyed to the British Government through the Australian High Commissioner at London (Mr. Beasley). . . .

The Australian Government will co-operate enthusiastically in a project to further increase output of those foods desired by Britain which can be produced on a commercial scale here, and for which markets for a reasonable term ahead are assured. This will necessarily include extensions of existing long-term contracts, and the negotiation of others—exemplified in preliminary discussions on wheat with Lord Addison when he was in Australia.

Australia has already been able to increase direct exports to Britain since the war ended, and to provide food for British Empire countries in the Pacific and elsewhere. The latter has, no doubt, relieved pressure on Britain's other supply sources. Australia's efforts will be continued and, no doubt, can be augmented with direct aid from Britain. Men and machines are among urgent requirements to stimulate production.

Source: Digest of Decisions and Announcements, no. 131, p. 6.

7:3 BULK PURCHASES: EXPORT CONTROL BOARDS AND GROWERS' RIGHTS

Speech in the House of Representatives by J. McEwen on 11 March 1948.

Both in regard to the dairying industry and the meat industry, statutory boards have been established to control exports, and on those boards there is a majority of producers' representatives. That state of affairs was brought about as the result of pressure exerted over a number of years by members of the Australian Country Party, and by Australian Country Party organizations and producers' organizations in the several States. The producers have always been particularly anxious to obtain representation on statutory bodies set up to ensure the orderly marketing of products. Originally, both the Dairy Export Control Board and the Meat Export Control Board were established by the Lyons Government, and on each board there was a majority of producers' representatives, so that the producers virtually controlled the export side of their industry. Since the Labour Government came into office, the composition of boards has been revised. The principle of majority representation by producers has been preserved, but in each statute introduced by the Labour Government providing for the revision of the boards,

231

the Minister for Commerce and Agriculture has been given complete authority over the disposal of the products of the industries concerned . . . The producers were deluded into the belief that they were to be given control of their industries, whereas, in fact, they have, in a very cunning manner, been deprived of all control. Both the dairy produce agreement and the meat agreement were made by the Minister with another government, and provided for the disposal of the export surpluses of those two great Australian industries. In each case the sale has been made at prices much below then existing world parity . . . On behalf of the primary producers, and of the Australian Country Party, I voice a very strong protest against the establishment of the principle that it is proper for a Government arbitrarily to acquire the product or property of the people and, behind their backs negotiate its sale to any one else . . . Only a few weeks ago the whole of Australia's surplus wheat harvest was sold, not entirely behind the back of the Australian Wheat Board, but in defiance of the advice of that body. The sale was negotiated in secret . . . The proper thing to do when sales are being negotiated is for the Government to take the control boards fully into its confidence and be guided by their advice. Where primary industries are not beholden to the Government for financial assistance, as is notably the case of the dried and canned fruits industries, the control boards should be permitted to negotiate the sales of their products without government interference. . . .

Source: *C.P.D.*, vol. 196, pp. 550-1.

7:4 SALE OF PRIMARY PRODUCTS: GOVERNMENT CONTRACTS

Statement by the Minister for Commerce and Agriculture (J. McEwen) on 7 November 1952.

It is quite easy to understand the criticism that has been quite widely voiced against these contracts. With one single exception all contracts existing were entered into by the previous Labour Government and some of them, such as the dairy contract, have proved to be thoroughly unsatisfactory, while others have been onerous at periods.

Because of this experience there now exists a body of opinion that the Government should decline to enter into any contracts. I myself believe the real test is the test that would be applied by any businessman or company—'Is the particular proposal a good one or a bad one?'

There are two parties primarily entitled to exercise a judgment on that point. First of all, there is the party owning the commodity concerned, and secondly the Government, which must take the responsibility for entering into a contract or the equally serious responsibility for declining to take advantage of an opportunity for a contract.

My own practice, which is in accordance with the Government's policy, at all times is to consult the representatives of the producers concerned on any proposal affecting the sale of their product. This goes for a stabilization scheme as well as a bulk contract.

On the Wool Reserve Price proposals the initiative came from wool grower organizations. The Government constantly co-operated with their chosen representatives in the Australian and international negotiations to compose a plan, and finally put the plan to a ballot of wool growers who themselves rejected it. That was a fair example of the Government's attitude.

We are still in the process of applying exactly the same principle to the extension of wheat stabilization.

During my administration all price negotiations with the Ministry of Food under the Labour Government's contracts have been attended by representatives of the industries concerned. This demonstrates that a non-socialistic Government will not deal arbitrarily with the property of other people, but will make the property owners direct participants in the negotiations.

Working in this manner the arguments of the industry representatives, and the authority and influence of Government together have been successful in securing increases in the Ministry of Food prices for eggs greatly in excess of the price limits imposed in the context of the egg contract. Spectacular increases in dried fruits contract prices have been likewise achieved. Similar representations in the case of the dairying industry were not successful. That lesson, a bitter one, was noted by the Government and all industries as a guide in their attitude to any further contract considerations.

The pig producers' central organization asked that pig meat should not be included in the long term contract. This request was immediately accepted. There had been no representations from the other federal organizations of meat producing interests that beef, mutton and lamb should not be included in the long term meat contract which for two years before its completion the whole world knew was under active discussion and negotiation. The pig producers, however, indicated a desire for a short term contract. When the Ministry of Food declined to approve a price for pig meat which could cover cost of production and a reasonable profit, I immediately declined to conclude any contract and since then pig meat has been free to be exported by anyone to anywhere in the world. It might be noted, however, that this has not made pig producers any better off, for no worthwhile markets for pig meat, other than the Ministry of Food, have been found.

A similar position recently developed with tallow. Long before the annual tallow contract system ended the contract price ruled very much higher than export parity to other markets. When the 1951-52 contract ended the Ministry of Food offered an unattractive contract price for only a six-months' period which was not considered to be good business and so the contract was allowed to lapse. The contract price with the Ministry of Food for copra has similarly over periods produced returns to copra growers very much higher indeed than they would have obtained by selling it in the open market. All this simply illustrates the point that there is nothing good or bad in contracts as such—it all depends upon the particular terms of each contract in the circumstances related to it. The sugar growers obviously rate a satisfactory long term contract as an advantage. In fact the delegation which negotiated the present contract included representatives of both growers and millers.

During the last few weeks growers of canning fruits and all the organized canners of Australia, the big co-operative canners of the Eastern States and the proprietary companies, which included such a representative of successful and independent private enterprise as the important Henry Jones Company, combined to ask me to try to arrange a long term contract with the Ministry of Food for the sale of Australian canned fruits over a period of at least five years. The terms indicated as being desired were, in many ways, almost identical with the terms embodied in the long term meat agreement.

233

It would, indeed, be going a long way to refuse a unanimous and combined request of growers and processors that a long term contract should be sought merely because some people with no business interest at stake had some philosophic or prejudiced opposition to bulk contracts in any form. I have agreed to explore with the Ministry of Food the possibility of such a contract, which, in due course, I will refer to the Cabinet, but in which the Government's position would be no more than that of an agent acting in the interests of the producers and processors concerned.

Of course if any industrial group should ask the Government to bring about a business arrangement which the Government thought was in itself bad business, or contrary to the public interest, then the Government would most certainly decline to be a party to such a proposal.

This brings out the point that if one does not accept a total rejection of all such contract proposals, then the final test, apart from the public interest, becomes a question of business judgment. There will, of course, always be opportunities for differences of opinion on such questions of judgment.

That is exactly the situation which exists in respect of the long term meat agreement. The idea of a long term meat agreement was supported by the Australian Meat Board, which represents livestock producers and meat processors. The producers have majority representation on the Board, while, as regards the processors, the overseas companies operating in Australia, the purely Australian private companies, and the State Governmental meat processing authorities are all directly represented.

During two years of active negotiations with the Ministry of Food, which were virtually conducted in public, because of the progress reports from time to time, and during which period the Meat Board was not only aware of, but was consulted upon every point raised, there is no record of either of the great producers' organizations protesting against the contract.

I refer to the Graziers' Federal Council and the Wool and Meat Producers' Federation, which embody between them every specialized organization of meat producing interests in Australia. Indeed, as late as July, 1951, a couple of months before the contract was signed, the Secretary of the Graziers' Federal Council conveyed a resolution of his Council to the Meat Board urging that there should be no further delay in concluding the contract, all the essential details of which were then known to the Graziers' Federal Council's representative on the Meat Board, and to this day I know of no representative of federated beef producing interests who opposes the contract in principle or in detail.

The day before I left for London for the final negotiations which resulted in the signing of the contract, I attended a meeting of the Meat Board and asked its representatives to confirm support for this very far reaching contract, which, with some deliberation, I had delayed for two years in order to enable industry and public opinion to mature on such an important matter.

Board Members, confronted with this direct request for confirmation, expressed a desire to consult their organizations and it was only after I arrived in London that I was told that the Board on reassembling had confirmed its desire for the contract, but with three dissentients, one representing overseas meat producing interests, and two representing Australian lamb producing interests.

The organizations which every other member of the Board represented—beef, lamb, mutton, Australian private meat exporters and Governmental meat authorities, all combined in confirming support for the agreement in the general form in which it then existed.

234

In these circumstances, it is still quite valid for a newspaper or a political party or any organization or individual to denounce the contract, but the argument must be between the opponent and this solid array of meat producing and processing interests who desired it and still support it. To direct the arguments at the Government, is to imply that the Government should have adopted the attitude of having a superior business judgment to that of this solid phalanx of meat producers and exporters. That is an attitude towards private enterprise which may well be taken by a socialist Government, but I would find it very curious indeed that avowed anti-socialists should be demanding that an anti-socialist government should set itself up as a better judge of what was good for private property interests than the property owners themselves.

I can only add, for what my judgment is worth, that I believe the contract has brought much better immediate returns to the producers than they would have received without it, and as a producer myself, I attach great value to the knowledge that no matter how great our surplus of meat may develop over the next 15 years, a major world power has contracted to take all of it at prices sufficiently satisfactory to justify expanded production. The last two price negotiations on beef, one concluded only this week and one a year ago, in accordance with the price formula which provides a minimum entitlement under the terms of the contract, have given beef producers a 60% price increase within twelve months and their rights go on from year to year. I know of no other business in Australia which is so completely and so adequately protected as this.

New Zealand, although now a vastly more important supplier of meat to the United Kingdom than Australia, but without a similar contract has accepted price increases measurably lower than ours. Of course there are those who describe as world parity the meat prices which prevail in North America, where the equivalent of our basic wage ranges from £30 to £40 per week. That is sheer nonsense. In no other major market in the world is there a comparable price for meat. . . .

During periods of export surplus the Ministry of Food's price, or more correctly in the circumstances which I have just described,[1] the Australian Meat Board's buying schedule determines the floor for livestock values. The additions to these buying schedules establish higher floor values than would otherwise operate. This applies not only in respect of that meat which is exported, but also to the stockyards and paddock transactions and so operates as to raise the level of all meat sold whether for local consumption or export. Thus, under the present system the benefits to producers from any North American profits in the respective accumulated funds are multiplied many times.

There are other factors about the North American market not generally and clearly understood. It is not entirely a gold mine. There has been complete freedom to export pig meat to North America since last February, yet no commercial exports have proved possible. Within the last twelve months the Meat Board exported three hundred tons of good grade mutton purchased at a price only a few pence higher than the Ministry of Food price and from its sale in the United States has shown a loss.

Our hind-quarter beef is permitted entry for sale into the United States—under existing United States laws our fore-quarter beef cannot be sold at all.

Last year we exported, on a trader to trader basis, forty-seven thousand tons of canned meat in respect of which there were no restrictions on country of

---

[1] The omitted paragraphs comprise a detailed exposition of methods and problems of trading with North America within the framework of the Meat Agreement.

destination except for straight canned corned beef and mutton. The United States provided a market for 240 tons only. Our experience in lamb this year has been far from entirely happy. Of 1,700 tons exported in April, really a drop in the ocean, a full clearance had not been effected on my last advice from the Meat Board at the end of October.

The New Zealand Meat Board had 3,600 tons of lamb in New York harbour with no inhibitions on its sale except administration requirements of the United States authorities. New Zealand apparently thought it better business to sail the 3,600 tons, theoretically worth 3/6 or 4/- per lb. in New York, on to the United Kingdom to sell it for 18d. per lb.

Canada has been closed against our meat this year due to an outbreak of foot and mouth disease in that country, which has prevented the export of United States meat to that country and has produced a local glut [*sic*].

All of this indicates problems and uncertainties in the North American market and combines to substantiate the overwhelming majority judgment of Australian meat producing organizations and Australian meat exporting houses. According to their spokesmen they regard the long term contract as better business than to attempt to exploit the North American market to the maximum extent and still expect satisfactory returns from the sale of such residue, i.e. mutton and fore-quarter beef etc., as we would still have to sell to the Ministry of Food at the best price we could negotiate with them, after having deprived them of as much of our choice meat as we could sell elsewhere.

I make one final observation for the benefit of any person, organization or newspaper still unconvinced. It is simply this—neither the Government nor I will be found claiming infallible judgment in these things. The critics may be right, but the time for the critics to speak is before the business has been completed and the contract signed.

During two years of almost public negotiation of this long term meat contract I do not remember any newspaper which is now a critic, publishing a leading article against it. In that period no federal producers' organization protested to me as Minister, nor to my knowledge, to anyone else, against the proposal.

It is easy to be critical after the event.

Source: As printed in Copland and
Barback (eds.), *The Conflict of Expansion
and Stability*, (F. W. Cheshire, 1957),
pp. 621-9. Reprinted by permission.

7:5 CHEAP WHEAT PRICES FOR THE UNITED KINGDOM

*Speech by J. McEwen on the International Wheat Agreement Bill
1948 in the House of Representatives on 2 June 1948.*

This is a piece of legislation introduced on the initiative and with the full backing of the Australian Labour Party to reduce the price on the contracts of sale to the United Kingdom and India by between £12,000,000 and £13,000,000 . . . the growers . . . delivered the wheat under the conditions prescribed by the Wheat Regulations made under the Defence (Transitional Provisions) Act. The Government compulsorily acquired their wheat, and without consulting either them or the Australian Wheat Board . . . entered into contracts to sell to the United Kingdom at 17s. a bushel and to India at 18s. 6d. a bushel. The Australian Wheat Board has been freely selling the available residue at 20s. 6d. a bushel and upwards. The Australian Wheat Board felt so strongly that its responsibilities had been abrogated by the Government that, at its meeting following the announcement of the governmental sale to the United Kingdom, Mr. Everett, the Acting Chairman, stated that the board had unanimously expressed grave concern at the action of the Government in whittling down the board's responsibilities. The board, in a resolution, expressed profound regret at the action of the Government, and declared that the Government should pay to it on behalf of the growers, the difference between the prices to which the Government had agreed and the prices at which the board would ordinarily have sold the wheat. Then, again without consulting either the growers . . . or the Australian Wheat Board, the Government made an arbitrary adjustment of the sale. That is being effected in this bill. In respect of wheat not delivered by the 1st August this year, the effect is to cancel previous contracts, so reducing the price further by about one-third. . . .

In the kind of world we live in at the moment, food supplies furnish the diplomats with one of the most powerful instruments of diplomacy. I shall not argue that our Australian surpluses should not be made available through governmental or international agencies along lines which will show that the western democracies are not indifferent to the needs of humanity and I certainly shall not argue that we should exploit our opportunities to wring the last penny out of the United Kingdom Government in its moment of economic crisis; but . . . I do argue that whatever it is proper for the Australian Government to arrange in either of these respects should be carried through by, and at the cost of the Government, and not by seizing the property of private individuals and carrying out governmental policies at the cost of a limited number of private persons who happen to have chosen one industry as the scope for their activities. Even considerations of sentiment cannot override this as a general principle and certainly national generosity should not be practised at the cost of any one section. . . .

Growers . . . would be prepared to have their product sold to the United Kingdom at a measurable discount. A further concession could and should be provided by a subvention on the United Kingdom sales by the Australian Government. Surely . . . we at least are agreed upon the necessity to aid the United Kingdom through its crisis and help in its re-establishment. . . . I feel that it is not inopportune to remind the United Kingdom itself that when it was not so hard-pressed but when this great industry of ours was in desperate straits at the outbreak of war—I mean literally at the outbreak of war—and before it developed to serious proportions—the United Kingdom drove with Australia what I have always thought to be an intolerably hard bargain in contracting to buy our surplus wheat at that time. The United Kingdom's complete control of shipping at the outbreak of war left us with no freedom to seek alternative purchasers, and the measuring stick which was employed to determine the price at which it could buy from us was the competitive price at which neutral Argentina and the neutral and 'cash and carry' United States of America were then prepared to sell. Another shilling or two a bushel would have made a tremendous difference to our wheat industry, and would have had practically no measurable effect upon the price of bread in the United Kingdom. . . .

Examining this agreement as a commercial transaction, one is guided by the preamble embodying the declaration that high prices resulting from the present shortage, and low prices which would result from future surpluses, are harmful to the interests of both buyers and sellers, and that, therefore, the agreement is to be recognized as an arrangement to rationalize the world wheat trade. Complete confidence in the agreement as such an instrument of rationalization is, from the outset, shaken by two factors. First, some of the most important actual or potential exporting countries, including Argentina, Soviet Russia, and the Danubian countries, are not parties to the agreement. Secondly, those countries which are parties to the agreement as buyers are not bound to it. . . .

I point out that whereas our Government proposes to acquire wheat for the purposes of this agreement, the United States Government on the contrary declares that, insofar as any wheat which is exported in the terms of the agreement is sold for less than its domestic value, the difference will be made good to the American wheat grower. Moreover, the United States has only tied up about one-half of its current exportable surplus to the services of the agreement. The Australian Government has gone the whole hog.

Source: *C.P.D.*, vol. 197, pp. 1582-6, 1593.

7:6 15-YEAR MEAT AGREEMENT

Joint press statement by the Prime Minister (J. B. Chifley) and the British Minister for Food (John Strachey) in London on 27 April 1949.

During the course of his present visit to London, Mr. Chifley has been able to discuss with Mr. Strachey plans for the increase of meat supplies to the United Kingdom from Australia.

Extensive preparatory work has been done in Australia. Plans have been worked out and the necessary capital expenditure approved by the Commonwealth Government for increased cattle production in the Wyndham area of the State of Western Australia. Projects for the expansion of production in big areas in Northern Australia—involving road making, stock route improvements, schemes for water conservation and the like—are also being investigated. Schemes for development in other parts of Australia are to be considered. It is recognised that these developments will require substantial supplies of materials, particularly steel products, and road making equipment beyond those available in Australia itself.

In view of the importance to the United Kingdom of increased meat supplies from Australia the Government of the United Kingdom has urged the Commonwealth Government to promote development schemes designed substantially to raise exports to the United Kingdom to an agreed level within an agreed period.

The Government of the United Kingdom has declared its willingness, in return for an undertaking on the part of the Australian Government to promote development schemes which offer a good prospect of increased supplies of the agreed magnitude, to enter into arrangements that will guarantee a market at reasonable prices in the United Kingdom for the whole of the exportable surplus of meat from Australia up to a specified ceiling during a period of 15 years. The Government of the United Kingdom is also prepared to set limits upon the fluctuation of prices during a period of seven years, as in the case of the contracts for butter and cheese with Australia.

Negotiations for a formal agreement in pursuance of the foregoing will be undertaken as soon as possible.

7:7 15-YEAR MEAT AGREEMENT DEFICIENCY PAYMENTS

Answer by the Minister for Primary Industry (C. F. Adermann) to E. J. Ward in the House of Representatives on 4 April 1963.

QUESTION:

1. What was the total amount received from the United Kingdom Government in each year since the commencement of the current United Kingdom-Commonwealth meat agreement in respect of deficiency payments?

2. How are these payments determined?

3. To whom, and in accordance with what formula, are these moneys distributed?

ANSWER:

1. Since the commencement of the Australia-United Kingdom Meat Agreement in 1952, the following deficiency payments have been received from the United Kingdom Government:—

	A.C. £
Beef—	
Year ended 31st October, 1955	152,125
Year ended 31st October, 1956	3,254,375
Year ended 31st October, 1957	5,927,180
	9,333,680
Lamb—	
Year ended 31st October, 1961	264,680

2. The United Kingdom Government has guaranteed to make good annually any deficiency between the average market price and the agreed minimum prices fixed under the agreement.

3. The method for distributing deficiency payments is set out in the Meat Agreement (Deficiency Payments) Act 1955.[1]

Source: C.P.D. (H. of R.), vol. 38, pp. 470-1.

---

[1] This document is a reminder that there were some tangible benefits received under the agreement in years of low prices, but it would not be possible to make a considered judgment on the operations of the agreement from this one document.

Several documents dealing with the agreement have been omitted and the interested reader will not be able to follow the course of the negotiations from year to year from this selection.

7:8 MEAT AGREEMENT WITH UNITED STATES

A meat marketing agreement between Australia and the United States of America was announced by the Minister for Trade and Industry, Mr J. McEwen on February 18 [1964].

In releasing details of the text, Mr McEwen said that Australia's objectives to safeguard its meat trade with the United States and ensure that this trade would grow in a predictable and assured manner and at a rate commensurate with the future growth of the United States market had been fully achieved. Because of that, the agreement represented a new phase in the trading relations between the two countries.

Over the past six years, Australian exports of beef and mutton to the United States had grown from virtually nothing to about £79,000,000 in 1963. Beef exports to the United States represented about 87 per cent of Australia's total beef exports and the beef and mutton together about 70 per cent of all Australian meat exports.

During recent months there had been growing pressure in the United States from cattle producers and in Congress for the U.S. Administration to impose very restrictive quotas on imports. This had made Australia's major export market a precarious one with no security of continued access and a continuous risk of sudden and severe restrictions of such an order as to threaten the whole stability of the Australian industry. . . .

Under the agreement Australia would have the right to export to the United States this year a total of 242,000 tons (in terms of product weight) of beef, veal and mutton, compared with actual shipments of 132,000 tons, 221,000 tons and 257,000 tons in each of the past three years. The agreement also provided for a quota increase in each calendar year after 1964 corresponding to the estimated rate of increase in the U.S. market. It had been agreed that over the next two years the Australian quota would be increased on this account by 18,000 tons.

This provision for growth in the world's largest meat market represented the first major break-through for agricultural exporting countries in their efforts to get an assurance of expanding access to the major world markets.

The precedent thus established in the United States would be of major importance to Australia and other meat exporting countries in their efforts in the G.A.T.T. Meat Group to negotiate improved conditions of access to world markets as part of the Kennedy Round of International trade negotiations. . . .

Source: *Australia in Facts and Figures*,
no. 81, pp. 26-7.

7:9 UNITED STATES PLACES CEILING ON MEAT EXPORTS

Statement by the Minister for Trade and Industry (J. McEwen) in the House of Representatives on 25 August 1964.

Consequent upon signature of the Compromise Bill by President Johnson last Saturday, legislation has now been enacted which will apply to United States imports of meat from all sources for each calendar year as from 1st January, 1965. The types of meat covered are fresh, chilled or frozen beef, veal and mutton. Lamb and canned meats are not subject to the legislation. As I have

240

said before, it is a very complex piece of legislation which leaves considerable discretion and flexibility with the President and the Administration. The manner in which the powers under the legislation will be exercised will only really be shown should a situation calling for restrictions arise. The legislation does not initially establish any individual country import or export quotas as such. What it does do is to set a total global import ceiling for beef and mutton which, if estimated to be exceeded, would automatically set in train a mechanism which would establish import quotas for individual supplying countries.

Prior to each calendar year an import ceiling for that year will be calculated on a base figure equal to average United States imports for the calendar years 1959 to 1963. This base figure of 323,000 tons will be adjusted annually by a factor which reflects increases or decreases in United States production. For 1965, this factor is 16·5 per cent, which, applied to the base period, gives a figure of 376,000 tons. The import ceiling for each calendar year is 10 per cent above this figure, and for 1965 would be some 414,000 tons. This figure is about 55,000 tons below total imports in the record 1963 import year, but is equal to imports in the previous record year of 1962.

The President has the power to increase this ceiling when he deems it to be in the 'overriding national interest'. There was specific recognition by the United States Congress that such a situation could arise on trade or balance-of-payments grounds. In addition, the President could increase the ceiling if United States meat supplies were inadequate to meet domestic demand at reasonable prices.

It is clear that Australian exporters are subject to no specific restriction under the legislation as regards the level of their exports to the United States in the calendar year 1965 or succeeding years, provided that the prescribed ceiling of imports from all sources is not, on the estimates of the U.S. authorities, expected to be exceeded. If the ceiling is expected to be exceeded, however, country quotas, in total somewhat lower than the over-all ceiling, would be established. If, for example, individual country quotas were to be established in 1965, they would be apportioned within a total quota figure of 376,000 tons. The complicated provisions of the legislation would mean that total imports would be restricted to 376,000 tons, only if total imports were expected to exceed a ceiling of 376,000 tons plus 10 per cent—that is 414,000 tons. . . .

United States authorities do not anticipate that such a situation will arise during 1965.

In short, although the United States meat legislation will become operative from 1st January, 1965, no action has as yet been taken, nor is any action indicated at this stage, which would contravene the provisions of our bilateral agreement.

Source: *C.P.D.* (*H. of R.*), vol. 43, pp. 530-1.

7:10 SURPLUS DISPOSALS POLICIES

Speech by the Treasurer (Sir Arthur Fadden) to Governors of the International Monetary Fund on 27 September 1954.

From the viewpoint of Australia and other primary producers of foodstuffs and raw materials there is a much more immediate and dangerous threat. It is, of course, the growing surplus of agricultural products in the western world, many of them stimulated by uneconomic subsidies in the large producing countries. In compiling their annual report the Executive Directors appear to have paid scant attention to this critical factor . . . Subsequently Congress has, however, provided funds and taken other steps which revive in our minds the ugly spectre of subsidized exports to other countries. No words, no lip service to the commercial interest of allied countries, however genuine and well-meant, can obscure that actual threat to the livelihood of thousands of agricultural producers in other parts of the world. As one who is responsible to a great number of these producers, I say earnestly but without rancour, that such policies may do the world a great disservice. We, in common with many others, lack the power and the long purse with which to withstand such overwhelming competition —at least within the framework of the liberal non-discriminatory world trading system which it is our common purpose to attain. We cannot compete on equal terms if United States domestic surpluses are to be sold abroad from the bargain basement.

The effects of the latest developments in this field have scarcely begun to be felt yet, but we have some past experience which leads us to fear the disruptive effect on our traditional markets of overeager efforts to liquidate the fruits of past domestic policies in the United States. I do not wish to anticipate here the discussions and negotiations which will shortly be opened up within the framework of GATT, and mention this problem because of its intimate connection with the work of the Fund. I mention it also lest there should be some tendency to fear that members of the sterling area are 'dragging their feet' along the road to a freer system of trade and payments. On the contrary, there may be some reason to suggest that the boot in fact is on the other foot. . . .

If faced on the one side by uneconomic subsidized competition, and on the other by embargoes and quantitative restrictions against agricultural products, food exporting countries, however reluctantly, may well be forced to reconsider their whole international position. A framework of international commitments which severely circumscribes quantitative restrictions for balance of payments purposes, and yet freely permits them to protect agricultural interests, must bear inequitably on all but the big exporters of manufactured goods. . . .

Source: International Monetary Fund,
Summary Proceedings of the Ninth
Annual Meeting of the Board of
Governors, September 1954, Washington,
pp. 72-3.

7:11 FAO AND AGRICULTURAL SURPLUS DISPOSALS

General Principles

1. The solution to problems of agricultural surplus disposal should be sought, wherever possible, through efforts to increase consumption rather than through measures to restrict supplies.

2. Member Governments which have excess stocks of agricultural products should dispose of such products in an orderly manner so as to avoid any undue pressure resulting in sharp falls of prices on world markets, particularly when prices of agricultural products are generally low.

3. Where surpluses are disposed of under special terms, there should be an undertaking from both importing and exporting countries that such arrangements will be made without harmful interference with normal patterns of production and international trade.

Principles Governing Sales on Concessional Terms

4. In determining whether or not sales on concessional terms or grants to a given region cause any harmful interference with normal patterns of production and international trade and prices, account should be taken of special factors affecting trade in the commodity concerned, with particular regard to the following aspects:

(1) the extent to which commodities supplied on concessional terms are likely to be absorbed by additional consumption (i.e. consumption which would not have taken place in the absence of the transaction on special terms);

(2) to the extent that sales of the commodities supplied on special terms may constitute some danger of displacement of commercial sales of identical or related commodities, that danger will have to be assessed in the light of relevant factors, particularly the following:

- (a) the exporter's share in the region's imports of the commodity concerned during a representative base period, due allowance being made for factors which lessen the significance of such historical comparisons;

- (b) whether the exports on special terms are likely to form so small (or large) a share of the region's imports of the commodity that the effect of special terms on such trade is likely to be of minor (or major) significance;

- (c) the degree of importance of trade in the commodity to the economy of the exporter concerned, to the economies of competing exporters of the commodity concerned and of closely related commodities and to the importing region's economy;

- (d) the character and extent of the concession offered and their probable effect on (i) the region's usual total imports of the commodity concerned and related commodities, (ii) the exporter's share in the region's imports of the commodity concerned, and (iii) the interference with implementation of treaties or agreements which deal with world trade in these commodities;

- (e) the degree to which commercial market prices are, or are likely to be, affected in the importing region and in world trade;

- (f) the degree, if any, to which effects of the kind mentioned under (d) and (e) above are likely to affect the stability, or desirable expansion, of production and trade of the commodity concerned and of closely related commodities in both exporting and importing countries.

5. In weighing the advantages to countries benefiting from special disposal measures against the possible harm done to other countries, account must be taken of the relationship of possible sacrifices to the economic capacity of the countries concerned, and in particular to the effects of such sacrifices on their rates of development.

6. In accordance with Paragraph 4 above, the following more specific considerations should be taken into account in determining whether or not harmful interference with normal patterns of production and trade is caused, or likely to be caused by some of the most important types of transactions on concessional terms, namely the following:

(1) Sales on Concessional Terms, or Grants in Aid of Development.

Account should be taken in particular of the following aspects:

(a) the extent to which commodities supplied on special terms in aid of economic development are likely to be absorbed by additional consumption, which will depend, *inter alia*, on the net increase in purchasing power resulting from total new development expenditure, and on the extent to which such additional purchasing power will be directed to purchases of the commodities supplied on special terms;

(b) to the extent that export of the commodities supplied on special terms in aid of development programs may constitute some danger of displacement of commercial sales of identical or related products, that danger will have to be weighed against the advantages resulting from such programs to the receiving country and to the world at large.

(2) Sales on Concessional Terms, or Grants, for Special Welfare Distribution Programs.

Account should be taken in particular of the following aspects:

(a) the character, extent and urgency of the emergency;

(b) the effect of the emergency on the stricken country's ability to pay;

(c) the volume of relief and the character and extent of the concessions offered, and their probable effect on the total commercial imports of the stricken country and on the trade of competing exporters.

7. *Assurance Against Resales or Trans-shipment*

(1) In bilateral transactions involving special concessional terms, the intended beneficiary country should make every effort to prevent resale or trans-shipment to other countries, or the use for other than additional domestic consumption of the commodities supplied to it on special terms.

(2) Care should also be taken by the intended beneficiary to prevent exports of supplies of the same or related commodities which might be freed for sale abroad as a result of the country's imports on special terms.

(3) Where a triangular transaction occurs, under which a commodity supplied on special terms is shipped for processing in a third country, the third country should use its best endeavours to ensure that the commodities supplied on special terms are trans-shipped to the intended beneficiary. The same principles should apply when more than three countries are involved.

Principles Governing Sales of Government-Held Stocks in Exceptional Volume, or at an Exceptionally Rapid Rate

8. Harmful interference with normal patterns of production and international trade can be caused not only by sales on concessional terms but also by the quantity of the commodity sold, and/or the rate at which it is moved, seen in relation to other market characteristics.

9. Since it is difficult to agree on any precise definition of 'exceptional' volume or rate of sales, or of 'harmful interference caused by such sales', these aspects need to be ascertained on the merits of each case with the aid of a series of commonsense criteria on the lines of those listed in Paragraphs 4 and 5 above. In the case of very large bulk transactions or sudden drastic changes in governmental sales policies such as the sudden abandonment of price-support measures and large-scale releases of stocks on foreign markets (e.g. liquidation of stockpiles),

it will probably not be difficult to ascertain that the volume or rate of offerings are exceptional. Governments undertaking, or purposing to undertake, such large-scale releases, should, whenever practicable, consult with other countries interested in the possible effects of such transactions.

Guiding Lines for Dealing with Agricultural Surpluses

Within the framework of its general agreement with the findings and recommendations of the Report of the CCP Working Party on Surplus Disposal (CCP 54/2), the Committee on Commodity Problems, in paragraphs 15-21 of the Report of its Twenty-third Session, referred specifically to the following aspects:

(a) Measures to dispose of surpluses already in existence will not solve the surplus problem unless parallel measures are taken to avoid the accumulation of new surpluses.

(b) In general, the adjustment of supply and demand should be sought in the expansion of consumption especially through increased incomes rather than in the reduction of production.

(c) Such output reductions as may appear unavoidable, in the light of existing supply levels and market prospects, should be brought about, as far as practicable, through economic disincentives rather than through physical restrictions.

(d) Steps for improving the international co-ordination of national policies must form an integral part of any sound program of surplus prevention.

(e) The adoption of special measures to dispose of surpluses must not be allowed to overshadow the importance of price adjustments, of policies of full employment and of economic development, of less restrictive trade policies and of the discouragement of uneconomic production, as basic means of dealing with the problem of surpluses.

(f) Special consideration must be given to the economies of less developed countries which depend largely on export receipts for a limited number of primary products.

(g) Consideration must also be given to balance-of-payments problems.

Source: Food and Agriculture
Organization of the United Nations,
Disposal of Agricultural Surpluses.
Principles recommended by F.A.O.,
Rome, 1954.

7:12 GATT RESOLUTION ON SURPLUS DISPOSALS

4. DISPOSAL OF SURPLUSES

(Resolution of 4th March, 1955)

RECOGNIZING

1. That surpluses of agricultural products may be expected to arise from time to time in the territories of certain contracting parties,

2. That the disposal for export of such surpluses without adequate regard to the effect on the normal commercial trade of other contracting parties could

cause serious damage to their interests by restricting markets for their regular competitive exports and by disrupting market prices,

3. That the disturbing effects of such disposals can be substantially diminished, and that the risk of injury can be minimized, if interested contracting parties consult with respect to the disposal of such surpluses,

NOTING that the contracting parties hereby express their intention to liquidate any agricultural surpluses they may hold in such a way as to avoid unduly provoking disturbances on the world market that would adversely influence other contracting parties,

THE CONTRACTING PARTIES

CONSIDER that when arranging the disposal of surplus agricultural products in world trade contracting parties should undertake a procedure of consultation with the principal suppliers of those products and other interested contracting parties, which would contribute to the orderly liquidation of such surpluses, including where practicable disposals designed to expand consumption of the products, and to the avoidance of prejudice to the interests of other contracting parties, and that they should give sympathetic consideration to the views expressed by other contracting parties in the course of such consultations.

Source: *C.P.P.*, no. 91 of 1954-5.

7:13 SURPLUS DISPOSALS POLICIES

From this distance Australians have been able to see only the vapour trails of the battle which several of our Cabinet Ministers have fought in the United States on the future of that country's food surpluses. Indeed, it may have seemed as though the Ministers have been shadowsparring. Not only has no American reply been forthcoming to the appeals and warnings, first by Sir Arthur Fadden and then of the Minister and Acting Minister of Commerce, but the United States authorities have never openly signified any departure from the standing promise of the President that the huge food stockpiles would not be disposed in a way seriously to disturb world trade.

However, two pieces of very recent U.S. legislation—the Agricultural Trade Development and Assistance Act and sections of the Mutual Security Act—have authorised that country's Commodity Credit Corporation to dispose of up to 1,350 million dollars' worth of farm products, either by outright grant or for payment in non-convertible foreign currencies. From the utterances of the U.S. Secretary for Agriculture, Mr. Benson, and his latest negotiations to sell grain in exchange for West German marks, it must be accepted that the new Acts denote some hardening of the U.S. attitude. It is true that they contain clauses to prevent the C.C.C. invading the present export markets of U.S. growers, but this only seems to ensure that the disposal will be concentrated in markets where soft-currency grain is now being sold. . . . There seems to be no complete answer, moral or otherwise, to America's increasing willingness to accept foreign currencies, as well as dollars—in effect, to assume partly the role of a soft-currency seller of wheat, where Australia had hitherto held the stage almost alone. If the prices accepted by the U.S. are broadly in line with the prevailing market—and

Australia itself has indulged in some discreet price clipping—the mere acceptance of non-convertible currencies can certainly not be denounced as dumping. Rather may it appear to be the beginning of a moderate descent towards prewar normalcy in the grain markets.

Source: Leading article in the *Sydney Morning Herald*, 23 December 1954.

7:14 WHEAT SURPLUS DISPOSALS

Statement by the Acting Prime Minister and Minister for Trade (J. McEwen) in the House of Representatives on 30 April 1959, after his return from Washington.

The prime purpose of my mission [was] the statement of Australia's attitude towards wheat surplus disposals. I make it clear that I sought to establish in the minds of U.S. Cabinet Ministers and senior officials the fact that it would not be appropriate or satisfactory ever to examine in isolation U.S. policy in respect of one particular Australian export product. . . . The point that I make is this: Our capacity to earn overseas income is probably, at the present stage, the most inhibiting factor in the whole plan, programme and future of Australian development and the tempo that we have worked up, for we cannot proceed with our internal development without a certain minimum amount of overseas exchange. In fact, on an average, upwards of 70% per annum of our overseas exchange is earned by five products, and there is a trading relationship between these five principal products and U.S. policies. . . .

The U.S. is in fact the only important wool-buyer in the world which maintains a very heavy duty against Australian wool. U.S. surplus disposal activities confront us and inhibit us to some extent in our commercial selling opportunities in respect of wheat which is our second biggest export earner, and, on occasions, of flour. In relation to meat, we have constantly encountered over a variety of fields in that country circumstances obstructive to our opportunities to sell meat there. There is, for practical purposes, a U.S. embargo against the import of Australian dairy products—one of our greatest export earners. We can sell no cheese there, and we can sell only nine tons of butter a year in that market. With respect to lead, which is one of our great export earners, and our principal dollar earner, we have in recent months suffered from a restrictive reduction, amounting to 49 per cent, of our freedom to sell lead compared with the quantity which we sold to the U.S. in the last year when no restrictions applied. These products account for more than 70% of Australia's overall export earnings and this is a pretty serious and important category of trade obstruction. I describe it as being an unparalleled obstruction to our opportunities to sell and I state in this House —as I stated with all the vigour at my command in Washington—that we should not be expected to discuss any single item of trade with the U.S. except with a conscious understanding of the total circumstances of our trading opportunities there.

Now, to put the discussions in respect of wheat surpluses in their setting, the fact of the matter is that in relation to this great export item of ours we have in recent years been operating commercially in the same fields in which the U.S. has been making surplus disposals, sometimes by straight gifts, but more often by

247

disposals from accumulated surpluses under what is known as United States Public Law 480. This means, generally, sale for payment in the currency of the receiving country, and very frequently not merely payment in an unconvertible currency, but also re-lending of the proceeds of the sale for long terms.

Of course, we cannot in a commercial transaction compete with that kind of operation. Notwithstanding that, we have been pursuing our commercial activities. By patient understanding . . . we have achieved a certain level of agreement with the United States. Clearly in recent times there has been an increasing public concern in the United States about the aggregation of surplus farm products and their disposal. Concern has been expressed internally at the cost of the price support system and at the progressive addition, in at least important items, to the already accumulated surpluses. . . .

A new factor is emerging. The under-developed countries . . . almost without exception have a real problem of exchange shortage. Where a country has no capacity to pay but has hungry people and another country has surplus food, the situation is clear. But it is not so clear or simple where a country with a real exchange problem but not entirely without purchasing power seeks to be given, without exchange expenditure, such an important item of food as wheat. . . .

The U.S., not uncommonly, now attaches as a condition to its Public Law 480 concessional transactions a condition that the country benefiting shall purchase a certain stated or minimum quantity at commercial terms. We have agreed that this is very appropriate, but . . . only last year our great friend Canada, which does not have the same kind of exchange earning problem as Australia, was able to sell wheat to India on ten years' terms with nothing to pay in the first three years. Quite frankly I cannot concede that that is in the category of a commercial transaction. . . .

India was for a considerable period Australia's biggest buyer of wheat. In the last nine or ten years we have sold India up to 37,000,000 bushels of wheat annually, but with the advent of surplus disposal programmes and terms sales, last year our share of the Indian market diminished from the high level of 37,000,000 bushels to 500,000 bushels. . . .

Source: *C.P.D.* (*H. of R.*), vol. 23,
pp. 1707-11.

7:15 FORWARD TO FREEDOM?

Whether or not the final communiqué from Montreal of the Commonwealth economic conference contains some last-minute surprise, there have already been sufficient announcements of policy there by Britain and Canada to give it quite an air of achievement. . . . But the real question is whether the Commonwealth is to go forward from Montreal as an active pressure group for freer trade in what ought to be an expanding world economy, or as a cautiously neutral force, or even, in some respects, as an openly restrictionist one. The communiqué has to be very closely studied this weekend for what it says about the four issues where protectionism most blatantly reared its ugly head at Montreal—sometimes in misleading respectable-looking bonnets.

In the crucial field of attitudes towards Asia and Africa, the protectionism showed itself from the start in the clear preference of the richer countries for aid rather than trade.

The second place at which an assault is now most obviously needed against protectionism is on the agricultural front. Few pleas have deserved more sympathy at Montreal than the New Zealand complaint that, while the General Agreement on Tariffs and Trade and other international conventions may have worked only moderately well for industrial exporters, for agricultural exporters they have not worked at all. It was a specific foundation rule of GATT that new restrictive quotas could not be placed upon agricultural imports on protectionist grounds, but only on grounds of balance of payments deficiencies. This rule has been breached by such countries as the United States, Canada and Western Germany, sometimes after securing a waiver with the claim that the production of, say, butter is a defence industry, sometimes with less hypocrisy but more open gall. The barriers which New Zealand and other dairy producers are now facing throughout continental Europe and North America represent one of the most open and widespread contraventions of the spirit of pledged international agreements that has been known in economic history.

There are two ways of redress behind which the Commonwealth ought to be ready to throw its support. One, which has naturally been mooted by Britain at this conference, is that some attempt should be made to make the GATT rules against protectionist import quotas steadily more effective. The other, which has equally naturally not been mooted by Britain, had its source in a recent report by GATT experts at Geneva; they suggested that figures should be regularly published showing the difference between the prices paid to farmers in different countries and the prices which those farmers' products would secure on the open market. The idea is that pressure could then be gradually brought to bear against the countries shown by this clear measure to be more obviously protectionist. The courage of the communiqué in agricultural matters has to be judged by the extent to which it supports, or fails to support, these desirable initiatives.

The third field in which propaganda for protection has been rampant at Montreal has been on behalf of raw material producers by way of stabilisation schemes. If these Australian proposals had been concerned only with genuine buffer stock schemes designed to iron out short term fluctuations in prices, they would have deserved the sympathetic reception they got. But this view of them is a cosy political delusion. What the Australian proposals really envisage is that, when a fall in demand impinges on a commodity produced by a few relatively big concerns, then a fall in price should be averted by cartel arrangements to ration out production among efficient and inefficient producers indiscriminately; when a fall in demand impinges on commodities produced by a lot of small producers (and therefore by a lot of voters) the idea is that a fall in price should be averted by buying up supplies which are not wanted and storing them in some swollen surplus stock or 'food bank' which will dangerously overhang the market. The upshot of the deliberations is that the Australian proposals, tempered by suitable expressions of more business-like intent, will probably be thrown on the laps of the American gods. Unfortunately, it was plainly felt in Montreal that the increasingly protectionist American government will be only too willing to consider at least some of them. . . .

Source: *The Economist*, 27 September 1958, vol. 188, pp. 997-9.

7:16 COMMODITY PROBLEMS CONSIDERED AT MONTREAL CONFERENCE

SECTION II

COMMODITY PROBLEMS AND AGRICULTURE

42. The Conference recognizes the serious problems caused for Commonwealth countries by the prevalence of wide fluctuations in many commodity prices and the impact of protectionism in its varied forms. We agree that the need for remedial action is urgent and important so as to bring about more assured conditions for commodity trade and the mitigation of the difficulties at present facing low-cost producers of both agricultural and mineral commodities.

43. We further agree that this situation calls for—

(a) the maintenance of a high and expanding demand in industrial countries which will promote the economic development of countries primarily dependent upon exports of raw materials; Commonwealth countries are resolved to achieve as high levels of demand as possible, consistent with the need to avoid inflation;

(b) concerted action where appropriate to moderate excessive short-term fluctuations in the prices of primary products;

(c) measures to mitigate the adverse effects of protection afforded to basic agricultural commodities and minerals.

Commodity Arrangements

44. We agree to participate in an examination of the situation, on a commodity by commodity basis, with a view to arriving, wherever necessary, at understanding about how best, consistently with a recognition of long-term trends in supply and demand, short-term price fluctuations could be moderated.

45. We recognize that for the most part effective action will require the participation of the important producing and consuming countries throughout the world. It is our hope that countries outside the Commonwealth will accept our objectives and be prepared to join with us in our work.

46. In the case of many commodities, international machinery already exists for the actual operation of a commodity stabilization scheme (for example, wheat, sugar, tin) or for the study of the situation in respect of a given commodity (for example, rubber, cocoa). There will, however, be other cases where no such specific machinery exists but where a Commonwealth Government considers that a situation calls for examination and that it may be desirable and practicable to concert action to bring about greater stability in the trading conditions of a particular commodity. In such cases, the United Kingdom Government will be prepared to arrange for Commonwealth talks about how best to take the matter farther.

47. Changes in the tempo of Government stockpiling have had important effects upon the stability of prices and upon production of some commodities for some years past. It is clearly most important, especially in present circumstances, that Governments holding such stockpiles should, before making disposals from them, arrange for full consultation with the Governments of countries which may be affected.

Protectionism

48. The Conference considered the problems for many Commonwealth countries arising from policies of protectionism in the fields of agricultural and mineral production. This protectionism may take various forms, not only by the tariff, but also by the protective use of non-tariff measures such as quantitative restrictions, State trading practices, export dumping, export subsidies, high support prices and excessive revenue duties.

49. We recognize that we have certain obligations to our producers. Subject to these we agree on the need to limit and to seek progressively to reduce the level of effective protection afforded to basic agricultural commodities and minerals where this tends to discourage domestic consumption or causes difficulties for low-cost production elsewhere. In addition, we agree that it will be desirable to give urgent consideration to the question of how the GATT can be strengthened so as to make it a more effective instrument for dealing with these problems.

50. We recognize the significance of the work of the independent panel set up in GATT, whose report will provide a valuable basis for consideration of measures to strengthen the GATT. It has demonstrated the need to re-examine critically some of the provisions of the GATT with a view to formulating rules for trade in agricultural and other primary products as effective as those provided for trade in manufactured goods.

51. Excessive protection can lead to the building up of surpluses. Care has to be taken when these are disposed of in world markets on non-commercial terms so as not to cause harm to the legitimate interests of traditional suppliers. We recognize that non-commercial disposal can help to improve the living standards of the less-developed countries. We think, however, that such transactions call for adequate consultations between the Governments affected in order that the legitimate interests of all parties may be safeguarded to the greatest possible extent. . . .

> Source: *Report of the Commonwealth*
> *Trade and Economic Conference,*
> *Montreal,* September 1958.
> Commonwealth of Australia, Paper
> no. 7819/58, Government Printer,
> Canberra.

7:17 AUSTRALIA'S ROLE AT MONTREAL CONFERENCE

Press statement by the Deputy Prime Minister and Minister for Trade (J. McEwen) on 7 October 1958.

The Deputy Prime Minister and Minister for Trade (Mr J. McEwen) described the Commonwealth Trade and Economic Conference at Montreal as an immense success. It would be of historical importance to primary producing countries. . . .

Mr McEwen said Australia was predominantly interested in action to get commodity prices stabilised. That was achieved so far as it could be achieved at Montreal.

The Commonwealth countries alone could not bring about stabilisation of commodity prices. But with the United Kingdom as the biggest Commonwealth importer of food and raw materials pledged to join with all other countries interested in entering a wider international sphere to advocate for long term prices, was an important initial achievement [*sic*].

Export Earnings:

The basis of Australia's economic stability was adequate earnings from her exports. This itself identified as so highly important, the issues Australia was foremost in advancing at Montreal.

A satisfactory level of world prices for commodities, and an assurance that trade could be conducted without dislocations from unfair trading practices by other countries, and assured opportunity to enter overseas markets on the strength of Australia's competitive position was the recipe for Australian stability and expansion.

Australia was recognised for her willingness to give fair protection in her market for the normal trade of her trading partners. Reciprocally there was a constantly widening support for the Australian case against unfair international trade practices.

Mr McEwen said:

Now we have, for the first time in our history, agreement within a highly important international group on an objective of stable commodity prices.

New Era:

If ultimate success can be attached to this agreed objective, a new era of predictability in economic planning would be opened for the raw material exporting countries.

In this objective there is no intention to achieve a rigid price stability, nor is there any intention to try to stultify long term trends in a particular commodity. The purpose will be to modify price extremes.

In introducing this concept at Montreal, I was not proposing from Australia, any grand formula as a 'cure-all'. What I was aiming at first was to achieve a state of mind between all the Commonwealth countries that this objective was highly important. On the basis of this being agreed, as it was, there should then be a procedure of examination, commodity by commodity, of what may be done and in what field this study should take place.

Existing arrangements such as the International Wheat Agreement, International Sugar Agreement and International Tin Council show that in some commodities, machinery already exists where expression may be given to the price stability objective now unanimously agreed upon within the Commonwealth.

Mr McEwen said, 'Now the whole weight of Commonwealth influence will be carried into these existing Councils, where I have made it clear, as much consideration must be given to the genuine needs of the importer as to the genuine requirements of the exporter'. . . .

7:18 INTERNATIONAL COMMODITY AGREEMENTS AND COMMERCIAL POLICY

2324. The earlier commodity agreements were mainly attempts on the part of producing nations to secure a payable price for the commodity concerned. Generally, the need for these agreements arose from a reduction in world demand accompanied, in some instances, by over-production. Their declared objectives were the adjustment of supply to demand and the establishment of a fair price.

2325. The chief criticisms of these agreements were that they were attempts by producers to maintain high prices at the expense of consumers and that, at times, their objectives were unduly influenced by the desire of many interests to maintain the status quo, i.e. high cost producers were kept in production to the detriment of more efficient producers.

2326. *Justification for, and Revised Features of, Government Controlled Commodity Arrangements.*—In spite of the unsatisfactory features of some of the previous international commodity arrangements, there is justification for persistent efforts by the Commonwealth Government to secure, in respect of Australia's most important export commodities, arrangements which will be satisfactory to both producers and consumers. The principal Australian farm industries depend upon the export market for the disposal of a large proportion of their production and it is impracticable to stabilize conditions in those industries without international collaboration. Subject to the overriding importance of buoyant international trade, the most promising and suitable form of international collaboration is through commodity agreements.

2327. Investigations made by those who are attempting to work out the principles of international commodity control show that there have been wide fluctuations in prices of farm products between years of exceptional abundance and those of scarcity. Imposed on these fluctuations there have been disturbing short-term fluctuations on a surprising scale. . . .

2329. These large fluctuations are due to a variety of causes, among which are—

(a) The manufacturer using a primary commodity usually has to make forward contracts for a large proportion of his product. In order to be able to do this, he wishes to know within narrow limits, the price at which he can purchase the commodity; or he must be prepared to take the risk of a fall in the price between the time when he makes the contract and the time when he sells the goods. . . .

(b) Seasonal variations in supply, which naturally cause considerable changes in accordance with the general balance of supply and demand. These are specially important where commodities are partly or wholly perishable. In the former case, storage is fairly costly, as extra handling is involved and the products become of less value as the storage period extends; in this case, if supplies are in excess of demand, the buyer who acquires larger volumes than he can use realizes that he will have to bear these costs and naturally offers a lower price for the goods. . . .

(c) Changes in public fashion, which may lead to sudden changes in demand for primary commodities. Naturally the best examples are in respect of clothing.

(d) Some changes in public demand are normal seasonal occurrences, such as the spring demand for Australian apples in Britain during that period when local fruit is six months old and there is a lack of other fruits to supply popular demand.

(e) Manipulation of markets by middlemen who, in some cases, depress prices artificially in order to make large profits. . . .

2330. This brief analysis of factors leading to variations in the market prices of commodities leads to the conclusion that, while some fluctuation is inevitable, there are reasons for supposing that it could be effectively reduced in the case of some commodities. In the case of commodities which are easily stored, a strong international selling organization could even out many fluctuations but it could not maintain a price unless it had control of the volumes of the product coming on the market. The attempt to maintain steady prices for one commodity may easily result in a switch of public demand to an alternative commodity, with the result that the sales of the former will be reduced . . . Attempts at stabilization in one commodity will be useless unless alternative products are also under control.

2331. As private enterprise is unable or unlikely to provide the mechanism to prevent violent fluctuations in prices, the intervention of Governments is necessary and, as the control required extends to the international field, the international co-operation of Governments is called for. While this aspect of Government intervention relates to the correction of short-term and medium-term fluctuations, the mechanism necessary to achieve the objectives of Governments in this respect is capable of application, with modifications, to the problem of long-term stabilization (subject, as stated previously, to the over-riding importance of buoyant international trade).

2332. Experience has shown that it is necessary to modify short-term fluctuations in prices which occur from day to day and week to week and, also, to provide for the maintenance in the long-term (i.e., throughout each season and over a term of years) of a price level which will ensure a reasonable economic and social standard for the farmer. . . .[1]

2348. Disequilibrium between supply and demand in the case of many agricultural commodities has been caused by the stimulation or maintenance of uneconomic production by means of tariff protection, subsidies, &c. Such devices tend to develop a chronic surplus, to reduce international trade and to restrict consumption through the maintenance of high prices in the protected markets. Two outstanding examples are wheat and sugar. In such cases, there can be no sound solution other than the reduction of tariff barriers and the abolition of subsidies and other aids to production, with corresponding diversions of the farming into other channels and arrangements for dealing with displaced labour. Nevertheless, it is not anticipated that the European countries would be prepared to abandon the production of wheat and sugar but they may be prepared to limit it to an agreed quota. It would be unreasonable to expect the European importing nations to limit or reduce their assisted production of these commodities if the exporting nations were themselves not prepared to limit or reduce their own assisted production of the same commodities. It should be noted here that the provisions of the existing sugar agreement and the draft wheat agreement imply production control in the exporting countries, while the United Kingdom agreed to limit beet sugar production. A note to the draft wheat agreement indicated that, when further consideration was possible, it was proposed to provide for production control in other adhering export countries in addition to Argentina, Australia, Canada and the United States (who have already accepted the principle), and in *importing* countries. The obligation to limit production, however, would not be imposed for the reason that the production was assisted, but simply with the object of relating supply to demand.

2349. The introduction of quota regulation of exports, therefore, implies control of production unless other means can be found for disposal of the surplus. The Commission has pointed out in Chapter I that the Commonwealth

---

[1] Paras. 2335-47 deal with representation in respect of commodity agreements, buffer stock and quota regulations on exports, and production techniques.

has the power to control production for the purpose of implementing an international agreement which has been ratified by the Commonwealth Parliament. . . .

2354. *The Dual Objective—Stabilization of Price and Maintenance of a Reasonable Price.*—It will be clear that the international commodity control plans have two objectives—

- (a) the modification of fluctuations in the short term and the medium term, i.e., stabilization.
- (b) the maintenance, in the long term, of a reasonable price.

2355. The primary, and more easily attained, objective is stabilization around the long-term trend. The form of control necessary, viz., buffer stocks in one form or another, would be capable of utilization for the benefit of many commodities in the short term. . . .

2356. . . . it must be acknowledged that long-term trends in production and prices could not be entirely controlled by the operation of buffer stocks alone. While many people who are concentrating on this problem hope for substantial results from the buffer stocks technique working by itself, it seems that, in any plan having long-term objectives, the quota regulation mechanism must be available to be brought into operation. This is particularly so when the maintenance of reasonable price is aimed at.

2357. The reasonable price would be fixed by the parties to the agreement, i.e., by representatives of producers and consumers. While, in cases of doubt, it is to be expected that the benefit of the doubt would be given to the producer, the equal representation of consumer countries should avoid undue exploitation of consumers. . . .

2359. . . . The primary object of an international agreement is . . . to prevent the fluctuations which take place in prices on world markets and to bring about prices fair alike to producers and consumers.

2360. Having examined, as far as it was able, the principles set out above, the Commission considered whether Australia's rural economy would benefit by such arrangements and came to the view that Australia has probably much to gain by participation in them. It is necessary, however, that each commodity should be considered on its merits and that, whilst stability and security in returns are to be sought, proposals involving restriction in development of our industries should be carefully watched. This is not to mean that Australia would necessarily object to the limitation of production in some special case. We might be quite agreeable to such proposals in one product whilst in another we would wish to look forward to expansion, and the conditions of agreements must leave the way open to secure such expansion if it could be justified. The Commission points out in Chapter VIII. of this Report that over-all guarantees for farm products, accompanied by the necessarily rigid production control, should be avoided.

2361. It is not to be assumed that international arrangements will be easy of accomplishment. There will undoubtedly be difficulty in securing reconciliation of views amongst the various countries and political considerations will also probably enter into negotiations. Time and patience and a spirit of give and take will be needed. The Commission believes, however, that the attempt should be made and, if at first the full measure of collaboration necessary should be found difficult to achieve, some steps forward will still have been made and they will be gradually added to. Because of the outstanding part export plays in the disposal of so many of her primary products, Australia must be particularly interested in this concept of international agreement and the Commission is satisfied that, if such arrangements can be made to achieve the objectives, Australia should do all she can to further their consummation.

2362. The Commission emphasizes here two warnings—

(a) international commodity arrangements cannot be regarded as satisfactory substitutes for buoyant world trade;

(b) agreements covering all of Australia's principal export products, if they involved an unduly rigid control of production, would not be in the best interests of Australian agriculture.

Source: Commercial Policy in Relation to Agriculture, Tenth Report of The Rural Reconstruction Commission, 7 August 1946.

7:19 WOOLGROWERS REJECT RESERVE PRICE PLAN FOR WOOL

Press statement by the Acting Minister for Commerce and Agriculture (Senator G. McLeay) on 24 August 1951.

The Acting Minister for Commerce and Agriculture, Senator McLeay, announced today that the referendum among woolgrowers which closed on 23rd August, had resulted in a majority of growers voting against the proposed reserve price plan for wool.

Senator McLeay said that the result of the poll indicated that a majority in the woolgrowing industry did not favour Australian participation in the Plan for the long-term stabilisation of the industry.

The Minister added that the Plan had been proposed originally by the wool-grower organisations and finally evolved in the course of negotiations embracing the woolgrowers' organisations as well as the governments of the United Kingdom, Australia, New Zealand and South Africa.

7:20 WOOLGROWERS AGAIN REJECT RESERVE PRICE PLAN FOR WOOL

Press statement by the Minister for Primary Industry (C. F. Adermann) on 10 December 1965.

The Minister for Primary Industry, Mr. C. F. Adermann, announced today the final voting figures for the referendum of woolgrowers on the proposed reserve prices plan for wool. The poll closed at noon yesterday.

The Minister said that of a total of 131,485 ballot-papers issued, 113,528 were returned to the Commonwealth Electoral Office which represented a poll of 86·34 per cent. Of the ballot-papers admitted to the count, the YES votes numbered 51,388; the NO votes 59,235; and 303 votes were informal. These figures show that 53·4 per cent of the voters did not favour the plan.

7:21 INTERNATIONAL COMMODITY AGREEMENTS

Report by the Prime Minister (R. G. Menzies) in the House of Representatives on 16 October 1962 on the Commonwealth Prime Minister's Meeting in September 1962.

The second feature concerns the making of international commodity agreements. Australia has, for some years, been perhaps the leading advocate of such agreements, driven on by the steady decline in her terms of trade. It has become, particularly in recent years, a characteristic of world trade that countries exporting primary products have seen a steady decline in the world price of these products, while their imports from the highly industrialized countries of Europe and America have risen in price. I will give one example. In the decade 1951-61, Australia's export prices fell by 42 per cent, while import prices rose 6 per cent.

Under these circumstances, it has not surprised us in the past to encounter on the part of some overseas countries, including Britain, considerable reluctance to make commodity agreements designed to produce a stable and payable price level for primary exports.

In our London discussions, we asked for a dynamic approach to the negotiation of international commodity agreements. We argued that principles be followed on price, on production and on trade access, and on a commodity-by-commodity basis, which would encourage maximum consumption, which would discourage uneconomic production, and which would offer security of access and stability of prices at a level remunerative to efficient producing countries. We argued that the internal price policies of the enlarged communities should be such as not to stimulate internal production so as to reduce the access of outside suppliers to their traditional markets or so as to prevent the expansion of commercial imports as consumption levels rose.

We urged that talks between major countries interested in particular commodities should be called at an earlier date, and certainly before the United Kingdom made its decision whether or not to enter the European Economic Community. . . .

In the result, though we did not secure full acceptance of our views, I think it right to say that a material step in the right direction was taken at the conference, with, in clear terms, the full concurrence of Great Britain.

Source: Current Notes on International Affairs, vol. 33, no. 10, pp. 38-9.

7:22 BAUMGARTNER PLAN FOR COMMODITY AGREEMENTS

Commodity Pacts

I have elsewhere given a detailed explanation of the way in which the proposals for a series of international commodity agreements, known variously as the Baumgartner or Pisani Plan, have developed from the specific devices for agricultural protection selected for CAP and from the problems for non-member countries thereby created.[1] Only a brief summary of the origins and nature of

[1] J. N. Lewis, 'The French Plan. Blueprint for World Trade Without Tears?', *Review of Marketing and Agricultural Economics*, vol. XXX no. 3 (September 1962).

the stimulus provided by this avenue of international commodity policy will therefore be presented here.

The principal feature of CAP, from which this momentum derives, is the provision for using variable import levies as the main protective device for agriculture in the Community. This invites collusion by outside exporters to control supply to EEC so as to eliminate or minimize payments of the levies. The proposed use of part of the proceeds of import levies to subsidize exports to markets outside the Community strengthens this possibility. The Baumgartner Plan for a series of international commodity agreements, each providing for an increase in international prices and for concessional sales to under-developed countries, neatly ties up an incentive to outside agricultural exporters to become reconciled to displacement from traditional market outlets in Europe with other superficially appealing objectives such as the desire to use agricultural surpluses to assist economic development of backward countries.

There are a number of practical difficulties which throw some doubt on the feasibility of the Plan and at a number of points the exposition is not clear. In the first place the effects of higher prices in encouraging production by importing countries and in inducing additional use of substitute commodities requires more explicit consideration. Such supply and demand responses are important enough to suggest that certain commodities will obviously not lend themselves to world-wide commodity agreements unless supply control applies to importing and exporting countries alike and perhaps even embraces substitute commodities. Secondly, there are foreseeable acute difficulties in applying consistent criteria to determine the boundaries of high and low priced markets and, more importantly, in keeping them separate. Leakages of concessional-priced supplies back into higher priced markets would be hard to control—especially indirect leakages through released exports of corresponding quantities of the commodity, or of a close substitute, produced domestically by recipient countries. Thirdly, non-participating exporters present some problems. It would be difficult to persuade importers to adhere to high priced supplies when cheaper non-agreement supplies may well be available from countries not sharing in the costs of the two-price programme but willing to appropriate some of the benefits.

More significant for purposes of our analysis of the implications of the Common Agricultural Policy, however, are the ultimate institutional consequences of such commodity agreements. They would supplant as much as remains of competition in international trade for agriculture with a wholly managed system. Production and marketing decisions would largely be taken out of the market place and settled over the international conference table. Let us beware of condemning this on doctrinaire grounds. If an intergovernmentally managed system for world trade in agriculture will overcome major weaknesses of a competitive system without subrogating weaknesses of its own which are equally or more unacceptable we should not waste time in regrets at the passing of the old order. However, nothing in our experience of international commodity agreements to date suggests that such a change would represent an improvement. There is indeed good reason to fear that a cure essayed through commodity agreements might well prove far worse than the disease currently afflicting world trade in agricultural products.

Clearly current commercial practices have failed to prevent and, rather, have led to, the growing unreality of comparative advantage as a principle explaining the basis of agricultural commodity movements internationally. But there is not anywhere in the exposition of the Baumgartner proposals any hint of an admission that comparative advantage has any relevance in agricultural trade or even that efficient allocation of resources is a valid goal. Indeed the proliferation of international commodity agreements proposed might well be viewed as a denial of these propositions. In this lies one of the Plan's greatest dangers. It implies that agriculture is different, that the principles guiding international action affecting trade in manufactured goods are, for some unexplained reason, inapplicable to agriculture. It would thus tend to perpetuate the bifocal view which has emerged in post-war international trade negotiations as between agricultural and industrial products and would give tacit approval to the very trade practices responsible for our international commodity problems.

From the viewpoint of agricultural exporting countries such as Australia and New Zealand, international commodity agreements along these lines might, prima facie, promise a means of ensuring continued access to markets. The price for such assured outlets—ineffectual as such assurances have proved in the past—could well, however, include acceptance of a strait jacket of international controls. A more formal and rigorous set of constraints upon the growth of their overseas earnings and economic development than is imposed under the current anarchy in international trade may be involved.

Nevertheless, the superficial appeal of the proposals, failure of trade negotiators to analyse their full implications and inappropriate politically imposed decision-making criteria may combine with lack of progress along other lines to bring about the acceptance of an extensive system of commodity agreements. The momentum imparted by CAP to the movement in this direction may thus be one of the most far-reaching implications for Australia and other agricultural exporters.

Source: J. N. Lewis, 'Agriculture and
the European Common Market'.
International Journal of Agrarian Affairs,
vol. IV, no. 2, April 1964, pp. 66-9.
Reprinted by permission.

7:23 MEMORANDUM OF AGREEMENT ON WHEAT

Statement by the Prime Minister (John Curtin) on 2 July 1942.

The wheat meeting recently held in Washington has resulted in the approval by the Governments of Argentine, Australia, Canada, the United Kingdom and the United States of a Memorandum of Agreement as a first step towards the conclusion as soon as circumstances permit, of a comprehensive international wheat agreement. . . .

The Memorandum of Agreement now concluded provides for the convening by the United States, when the time is deemed appropriate, of a conference of all nations having a substantial interest in wheat, whether as consumers or producers, and there is attached to it for consideration at that conference a draft convention prepared by the Washington wheat meeting. In the meantime, the Memorandum of Agreement requires adoption and maintenance on the part of four exporting countries of positive measures to control production with the object of minimizing the accumulated excess of stocks during the war.

The Memorandum of Agreement provides also for the immediate establishment of a pool of wheat for intergovernmental relief in war-stricken and other necessitous areas so soon as the international situation permits. It brings into operation arrangements in the draft convention for contributions to a pool, as they may be required, of 100,000,000 bushels and additional quantities to be determined as the extent of the need becomes known.

In order to prevent disorganization and confusion immediately after the war and pending conclusion of a comprehensive international wheat agreement, the present memorandum provides for the bringing into operation for a limited period provisions of the draft convention relating to control by the four exporting countries of production, stocks and exports, for co-operation by all five countries in stabilizing prices.

The approval of the five governments was notified by the United States Government to the other four Governments on 27th June, 1942, and in accordance with the minutes of the final session of the Washington wheat meeting, the provisions of the Memorandum of Agreement came into effect on that date. . . .

Source: Digest of Decisions and
Announcements, no. 33, pp. 17-18.

7:24 INTERNATIONAL WHEAT AGREEMENT BILL 1959

Second Reading speech by the Minister for Trade (J. McEwen) in the House of Representatives on 12 August 1959.

The purpose of the Bill is to seek the approval of Parliament for the acceptance by Australia of the International Wheat Agreement of 1959.

The first post-war International Wheat Agreement came into force in 1949 and covered a four year period to 31st July, 1953. That Agreement was renewed, with certain modifications, by the Agreements of 1953 and 1956, each of which covered a three year period. The 1959 Agreement, to which this Bill relates, provides for a further three-year extension, with some important variations, of the arrangements covered by the earlier agreements. . . .

In principle, the new Agreement is substantially the same as the earlier Agreements. The basic objective is to provide an element of stability in world wheat marketing. The Agreement seeks to do this by providing that a significant proportion of wheat entering international trade will be bought and sold at prices within a prescribed range.

The previous Agreements operated through a system of guaranteed sales and purchases, or quotas, for both exporters and importers. Each exporting country had an export quota, which represented the amount of wheat it was obliged to make available to importing countries at the maximum price and which it was entitled to sell at the minimum price. Conversely, the quota of an importing country represented the amount of wheat that country was entitled to obtain at the maximum price, and which it was obliged to buy at the minimum price if exporters called on it to do so. Whilst prices were within the specified range, importers were not obliged to purchase their requirements from member exporters.

Although the principle embodied in these provisions worked satisfactorily during the time when the demand for wheat was strong, and the price of wheat sold outside the Agreement was higher than the maximum price under the Agreement, this has not been the case over recent years when the wheat market has been depressed.

There has been a tendency for importing countries to reduce the volume of wheat they committed themselves to purchase at the minimum price, and the 1956 Agreement covered only about 300 million bushels.

The recent negotiating conference therefore examined a number of alternative arrangements with the object of devising a system which would encourage importers to put a greater volume of their wheat purchases within the Agreement. As a result, the old quota provisions have been abandoned and have been replaced by an entirely new arrangement of rights and obligations.

Under the new form of Agreement, the member importing countries undertake to buy from member exporters, at prices at or above the prescribed minimum, not less than a stated percentage of their total commercial imports. These percentages . . . vary from country to country and range from thirty per cent to one hundred per cent. The average is about seventy per cent, and based on the recent level of commercial imports of these countries, constitutes commitments covering about 420 million bushels.

Each importing country is entitled to purchase from member exporters, at prices not higher than the maximum, a quantity of wheat up to but not exceeding its average commercial imports from member exporters over a previous five year period. Conversely, exporting countries have an obligation to supply these quantities at the maximum price. Once these entitlements and obligations have been met, exporters are free to sell at prices higher than the maximum, and importers are free to procure supplies from any source.

What this means for Australia is that whilst prices remain within the prescribed range, we will be selling in normal competition with other exporters. At the minimum price, we have the protection afforded by the importers' commitments to purchase stated proportions of their requirements at not less than the minimum price. Should prices rise to the maximum, our commitment is limited to our average exports to member importing countries over the preceding five years. As with the earlier Agreements, there is of course a provision under which we could seek to be relieved of this obligation in the event of a short crop.

The rights and obligations of member countries relate only to commercial transactions in wheat and flour. At the present time a large amount of wheat is moved under non-commercial terms. This arises from the fact that, on the one hand, very great stocks of surplus wheat are held by exporting countries, particularly the United States, and on the other, many importing countries are unable, through balance of payments difficulties or for other reasons, to pay cash for all their requirements.

Whilst the Agreement does not attempt to regulate transactions of a non-commercial type, the participating countries have agreed that such transactions shall be recorded, and their implications for commercial trade are to be examined annually.

Since the basic prices refer to Canadian wheat, the new agreement includes the same formulae for determining the equivalent maximum and minimum prices for wheat shipped from other exporting countries. These formulae take into account differences in transportation costs, the relative qualities of various types of wheat and different currencies. . . .

The membership of the new Agreement is likely to be somewhat different from the old. By far the most significant change is the re-entry of the United Kingdom which is the world's largest importer of wheat and the biggest single market for

K

Australian wheat. The United Kingdom participated in the 1949 Agreement but not in subsequent Agreements. I believe it is true to say that the return of the United Kingdom Government reflects the importance attached by the United Kingdom Government to the conclusions reached at last year's Montreal Conference, when, largely as the result of Australian initiative, the Commonwealth countries accepted the principle of working towards greater stability of international commodity trade. . . .

The only significant customers for Australian wheat and flour which will not be members of the agreement are Ceylon and Malaya. These countries were not members of the 1956 Agreement. . . .

The Government's view is that international co-operation is essential to the orderly export marketing of wheat. The new Agreement is, necessarily, a compromise of the conflicting interests of exporting and importing countries. Having regard to all the circumstances we believe it is the best Agreement that could be obtained. We have no hesitation in preferring it to the alternative of no Agreement at all which might well lead to a break in world prices and a return to the chaotic marketing conditions of the early 1930's, with disastrous consequences for the Australian wheat-growers and the Australian economy. . . .

It would be misleading to suggest that the new Agreement will effectively take care of all the problems confronting us in the marketing of Australian wheat . . . we must continue the strenuous efforts which we are already making, through the General Agreement on Tariffs and Trade and bilateral arrangements, to reduce the impact of excessive protection, heavily subsidized competition and the disposal of surpluses. . . .

Source: C.P.D. (H. of R.), vol. 24, pp. 150-3.

7:25 INTERNATIONAL WHEAT AGREEMENT BILL 1962

Second Reading speech by the Minister for Trade (J. McEwen) in the House of Representatives on 8 May 1962.

The purpose of the Bill is to seek the approval of Parliament to the signature and acceptance by Australia of the International Wheat Agreement of 1962 . . . The 1962 agreement . . . provides for a further three-year extension, with some variations, of earlier agreements.

The new agreement was negotiated at a conference convened by the United Nations, at which 48 countries participated, including for the first time in recent years, the Union of Soviet Socialist Republics. If all these participating countries sign the agreement about 95 per cent of the world's trade in wheat will be covered by its terms. Trade in flour is also covered by the terms of the agreement. . . .

One aspect of the new agreement is that there have been significant increases in the minimum percentage commitments to which the major importers have been willing to subscribe . . . Moreover, the new agreement gives some protection against low-priced sales through the provision that all transactions between members must be within the price range.

. . . the minimum price has been increased as well as the maximum. This clearly represents a real advance for exporting countries. . . .

Under the present agreement members of the European Economic Community can make sales to each other at prices above the present maximum, . . . provided that both the buying and the selling countries agree.

Under the new agreement countries outside the European Economic Community are not precluded from selling to countries within it at prices above the maximum, provided both countries agree. The significance of this for Australia is that we would not be prevented by the International Wheat Agreement from attempting to negotiate a higher price for the wheat we may sell to present or future members of the European Economic Community.

. . . as we see it, a trading arrangement like the International Wheat Agreement, which does not comprehend such fundamental factors as agricultural production policies and the problem of surpluses, falls far short of our needs and aspirations as a primary producing country . . . An agreement which stipulates a minimum price and which does not cover the cost of 85 per cent of the wheat produced in the world cannot by any stretch of imagination be described as a satisfactory solution of the world wheat problem.

The crux of this problem is that countries like Australia exporting to the United Kingdom, the biggest single import market for wheat, have had to sell there under conditions of cut-throat competition at so-called world prices far below the price received by the vast majority of the world's wheat producers . . . We do not encroach on other countries' share of the market through dumping tactics. In a world where practically every country has a home price for wheat, it would be quite wrong to classify us as dumpers if we are forced by cut-throat competition to sell to our traditional customers at less than our home price.

The situation in which the export prices to our producers are determined by the mechanism of so-called world prices needs to be radically altered. I have become increasingly convinced in recent years that this problem can be solved only if we get some overall world-wide commodity conferences. . . .

Since the Montreal Conference, our Government has more than once reiterated the pressing need for such arrangements. The French Government, in the course of the last year or so, has given the lead internationally in putting forward solutions along lines which I myself have long proposed and advocated. The occasion when the French came forward was the first on which a leading industrial country had given the lead in sponsoring world-wide solutions of commodity problems. . . .

The main lines of the French proposal are: in the first instance the prices paid by industrial countries for their imports of primary products should be fair and adequate. In the second instance the vast potential for food production of the Western countries should be employed constructively to help the hungry millions in the less-developed countries.

. . . it is clear that in the foreseeable future surpluses of basic foodstuffs such as wheat would be commercial surpluses, and not surplus to human needs . . . It is clear to me that a satisfactory world arrangement should, for commercial, and I believe, also for humanitarian and the broadest political reasons, embrace the concept of making surpluses available to those who are without the means to pay for their essential food needs . . . Clearly the financial aspects of this would be for all the wealthier countries to assume—not merely the wheat producers.

As a result of the French initiative at the Ministerial meetings of the General Agreement on Tariffs and Trade, a Cereals Group was set up. This is the first of a proposed series of such groups whose job it will be to develop world-wide solutions for the problems of the major commodities. . . .

Source: *C.P.D. (H. of R.)*, vol. 35,
pp. 2011-14.

7:26 WHEAT: INTERNATIONAL AGREEMENT AND TRADE PROBLEMS AND THE CEREAL DISCUSSIONS IN THE KENNEDY ROUND

Second Reading speech on the International Wheat Agreement (Extension) Bill 1966 by the Minister for Trade and Industry (J. McEwen) in the House of Representatives on 28 April 1966.

The purpose of this Bill is to seek approval of Parliament to the signature and acceptance by Australia of the Protocol extending the International Wheat Agreement 1962 for a further year.

In 1962, Parliament approved the acceptance by Australia of the International Wheat Agreement which had been negotiated that year in Geneva. The terms of the Agreement provided that it would expire on 31st July 1965, and prior to that date it would have been customary to re-negotiate a new Agreement to take effect from that date. However, at that time most of the trading countries of the world were already engaged in the Kennedy round of trade negotiations in Geneva and in the circumstances the International Wheat Council agreed that the existing Agreement be extended for one year. It was expected that if comprehensive arrangements to regulate trade in cereals, including wheat, could be negotiated they would make redundant an International Wheat Agreement of the present type. Unfortunately, progress in the Geneva negotiations has been slower than expected and the International Wheat Council in November last year agreed that the most practical procedure could be to again extend the Agreement for a further twelve months; that is, until July, 1967. . . .

The trade negotiations which are proceeding in Geneva are, for the first time in the history of the General Agreement on Tariffs and Trade, tackling the problems of agriculture. However, because of the complex and sensitive problems of agriculture, progress in the negotiations has been slow. Moreover, the internal difficulties experienced by the European Economic Community over the last 12 months or so have further delayed progress. There are now signs that these difficulties have been largely overcome and that the E.E.C. will soon be in a position to resume effective negotiations on cereals. . . .

At the GATT Ministerial Meeting in May 1963, which I attended, it was agreed that a significant liberalisation of world trade was desirable. It was also agreed for the first time—and this is most significant—that the negotiations should cover all classes of products, including agricultural products, and should not only deal with tariffs but also with non-tariff barriers to trade. The GATT Cereals Group was given the responsibility of negotiating comprehensive arrangements for cereals, including wheat, which could cover national support programmes, international prices, access to markets and non-commercial transactions.

. . . the provisions of the International Wheat Agreement are limited. The Agreement does nothing to inhibit the protection afforded high cost wheat production. Highly protectionist wheat policies pursued by many industrialised countries have led to a shrinking or, at the best, a stagnation of their imports of wheat. Unless these countries are prepared to accept some commitments on domestic production, this trend will almost certainly be accelerated with the application of modern technology to farm production, particularly in Europe.

Equally disturbing is the fact that the price level at which wheat is traded internationally is far from satisfactory. The so-called world price for wheat, which exporters of wheat are obliged to accept, bears little relationship to prices being paid for the great bulk of the world's wheat production. It is an intolerable situation when efficient wheat producing countries are from time to time forced to resort to subsidies in order to maintain the incomes of farmers at reasonable levels. Over recent years world prices for wheat sold on world markets have been largely determined by the subsidy and dumping practices associated with the level of protection afforded high-cost wheat production . . . competition is not between producers or exporters, but between national treasuries.

Another critical area of the international wheat situation is the position of many less developed countries. The food needs of these countries are certain to increase. The famine in India this year has emphasised the gravity of this problem. Over the past two years this Government has provided India with nearly $16 million in emergency food aid, mainly wheat. The Government has taken the view that whilst the needs of the developing countries such as India must be recognised, the responsibility should not fall on the food exporting countries alone. The burden of meeting the legitimate food needs of these countries must be shared by all countries which have the ability to contribute.

. . . an international arrangement which adequately deals with all the issues I have mentioned is obviously not a simple matter to negotiate. However, the effort must be made and Australia has submitted a comprehensive and fully articulated proposal to the GATT Cereals Group. . . .

Source: *C.P.D.* (*H. of R.*), vol. 51,
pp. 1288-9.

7:27 INTERNATIONAL COFFEE AGREEMENT: AUSTRALIA AS CONSUMER, NEW GUINEA AS PRODUCER

Statement by the Minister for Trade (J. McEwen) in the House of Representatives on 4 April 1963.

The International Coffee Agreement . . . was negotiated in 1962 under United Nations auspices . . . The Agreement represents the culmination of much hard and patient work by interested countries—both producers and consumers—largely through the medium of the Coffee Study Group. It has been signed by 54 countries, representing 95 per cent of world trade, and when it enters into force will take the place of, and have much wider scope than, the agreement, also styled the International Coffee Agreement, entered into by producing countries in 1959. . . .

The main purpose of the agreement is to increase the export earnings of coffee-exporting countries by stabilising prices at remunerative levels and by increasing consumption. It aims to do this by controlling world trade through a system of export quotas on member countries, by holding imports from non-members at their present level, by reducing obstacles to trade and by increasing consumption.

Australia signed the agreement last November, and the Government has decided to present it to the House for ratification. Australia will join the agreement as an importing country. However, the Territory of Papua and New Guinea is an exporter of coffee, and special provisions have been included in the agreement which should meet the Territory's needs. . . .

Australia supports the negotiation of commodity agreements for three main reasons. First, our own producers stand to benefit directly from higher returns and more stable market conditions which these agreements bring about. Secondly, a growing proportion of our export trade is done with countries, many of them among the lesser developed ones, whose export returns depend crucially on world price levels for a few commodities like tin, rubber and jute. International commodity agreements which improve the export earnings of these customers of ours will in turn bring benefits to ourselves.

Last . . . economic advancement, and the political stability that goes with it, cannot be achieved in many of these countries in the absence of rising exports to provide the wherewithal for buying essential imports.

Source: *C.P.D.* (*H. of R.*), vol. 38,
pp. 431-2.

7:28 LEAD AND ZINC AGREEMENT

*Statement by the Acting Prime Minister and Minister for Trade
(J. McEwen) in the House of Representatives on 14 May 1959.*

Under the auspices of the governments of the lead and zinc exporting countries and the lead and zinc consuming countries—but in the presence of representatives of the lead and zinc producing industries, or mines and smelters—conferences in New York, initiated in the first place, I think I can claim, by Australia at least a year ago, have culminated in an agreement that there shall be an equitable diminution of the offerings of lead and zinc for sale on world markets so that the quantity available for purchase will approximately equate the consumer demand for these products. This is done in order to produce price stability in world markets, and that stability would, in turn, provide very strong grounds for representations to the United States Government that it should remove the quotas that were imposed six or seven months ago. The actual reductions under the agreement will be such that, for Australia, there will be a very modest restriction of exports beyond the restrictions which the mining and smelting companies had themselves already arranged over the last six or nine months. All of this is in pretty close conformity to the general policies that were propounded for Australia at the Montreal conference—that it was desirable to achieve by agreement stability in world prices for the bulk commodities, and that against that policy decision there should be a commodity by commodity study of what could best be done.

Source: *C.P.D.* (*H. of R.*), vol. 23,
p. 2173.

7:29 INTERNATIONAL MONETARY FUND: COMPENSATORY FINANCING OF EXPORT FLUCTUATIONS

Another important development with respect to members' access to Fund resources was the Decision of the Executive Directors in February of this year regarding the Compensatory Financing of Export Fluctuations. By this Decision, the Fund created a new drawing facility which, we hope, will greatly benefit primary producing countries adversely affected by temporary declines in their export earnings.

It has always been one of the recognized functions of the Fund to provide financial assistance in case of balance of payments difficulties arising from export shortfalls, and there have been many instances of countries drawing on the Fund under such circumstances. Yet it was felt that this problem had become sufficiently pressing to deserve special consideration. The Executive Directors and the staff spent many months in studying and discussing it. Indeed, this was the last major task to which Mr. Jacobsson devoted his efforts. The Decision which finally emerged and which is published in the Annual Report is, in my opinion, a useful further development of the basic principles and aims of Fund policy.

In essence, it establishes a new facility to provide assistance to members experiencing balance of payments difficulties arising from export shortfalls. This facility will become available in cases where the shortfall is temporary and largely caused by circumstances beyond the member's control, and where the member is willing to cooperate with the Fund in an effort to find appropriate solutions for its balance of payments difficulties, where such solutions are needed.

Given these conditions, a country is assured that its request for a compensatory drawing will be met in amounts not normally exceeding 25 per cent of the member's quota. Besides facilities available under these liberal terms, members may, of course, draw under the Fund's ordinary drawing policies for the purpose of meeting difficulties arising from export fluctuations.

Furthermore, in order to enable members to have the full benefit of the facility, the Fund will be willing to exercise its authority to waive the limits which are prescribed in the Articles, firstly, on the amount that a member may purchase within any 12 months and secondly, on the Fund's holdings of a member's currency, which should not exceed 200 per cent of its quota. The latter is a new development in the Fund's policy; hitherto, there has been no waiver of the 200 per cent limit.

I have been glad to note that the Fund's new policy on compensatory financing has been well received both by Fund members and by international organizations. In particular, the United Nations Commission on International Commodity Trade has concluded that the new facility can make a substantial contribution toward solving the problems arising from export fluctuations in primary exporting countries.

Source: International Monetary Fund,
Summary Proceedings of the Eighteenth
Annual Meeting of the Board of
Governors, September 30-October 4,
1963, Washington, pp. 17-18.

THE COMMON MARKET AND THE
EUROPEAN FREE TRADE ASSOCIATION

The documents in this section deal with decisions made by other countries but of great importance to Australian trade policy. The first was the establishment of the European Economic Community by the signing of the Treaty of Rome in March 1957 (A8:1): the second was the effort by the United Kingdom to form a European free trade area (8:2) and the application by the United Kingdom in July 1961 to join the Common Market (8:12). The full impact of all these decisions and of likely future developments has yet to be felt by Australia.

Document 8:10—a leader in the *Sydney Morning Herald* of 5 July 1960 —complains about the lack of public information about economic developments in Europe. In a sense the complaint was justified and even more so a year later when the United Kingdom government, reversing all previous declarations of policy, decided to apply for entry into the European Economic Community (8:11 to 8:14).[1] This was a major shock to the Australian public, even if ministers and officials had been less unaware of a possible change in British policy.

While it is true that before the momentous British decision of 31 July 1961 and the closely preceding visit to Canberra by Duncan Sandys (8:11) there was little public debate in Australia of movements for economic integration in Europe, there were understandable reasons. None of the newspapers made an effort to present the issues, perhaps in part because of their technical complexity but more because Australian interests did not seem to be significantly involved—even a number of leading academics in discussions convened in 1957 showed a similar lack of sense of relevance.[2] Even in Britain before July 1961 there was a relative dearth of public information and debate. What problems for Australia there might be—whether political or economic— could be left to ministers and officials. Ministers had not been inactive, at least from September 1956 when Macmillan, then Chancellor of the Exchequer, first indicated United Kingdom proposals for a European free trade

[1] Cited throughout as EEC or Common Market; for the European Free Trade Association established by the Stockholm Convention of November 1959, EFTA will be used.

[2] On the issues and possibilities for Australia's interest in the two major European trade developments (EEC and EFTA) see, however, Corden (43). Such an article today would receive far more notice in the press, especially in provincial papers and columns, than it did in 1958.

area (8:2). Moreover, there was no veil of secrecy drawn by ministers over their activities: references were frequently made by them to the EEC and EFTA (8:1, 8:3, 8:4, 8:7, 8:9).

It is important, in understanding the course of United Kingdom policy, to distinguish four stages:[3]

(i) its decision (8:2) not to take part in the negotiations of the Messina group which culminated in the Rome Treaty.[4]

(ii) the decision (8:2) to negotiate within the framework of the Organization for European Economic Co-operation for a wide European free trade area, including the SIX.[5]

(iii) it having become plain by November 1958 that negotiations for a full-scale free trade area were unlikely to succeed quickly, if at all (8:5), Britain's decision to go ahead with the SEVEN. This resulted in the Stockholm Convention and the establishment of EFTA on 20 November 1959 (8:6).

(iv) in 1961, for reasons given by Macmillan (8:12, 8:14), Britain's decision to see whether acceptable terms could be negotiated for her entry into the Common Market. These efforts ended abruptly in failure; a speech of General de Gaulle being the sufficient signal (8:21).

Our concern is with Australian trade policy, not with the detailed sequence of events.[6] Step four was the one that by far the most severely threatened Australian economic interests. Before referring to it, however, it is worth noting in passing that Australia had, on political grounds, consistently deplored the economic division of Europe, since this seemed to impair the political unity of the West. It was easier to expound this view before 1961 for two reasons: Britain's ideas for a free trade area excluded agriculture and therefore offered little threat to Australia's interests; and the free trade area concept did not include institutions to promote the integration of economic

[3] See treatment by Menzies (8:15).

[4] See Crawford (54), (56).

[5] The OEEC comprised some eighteen countries including those in the Common Market (the SIX) and those later to form at Stockholm the present EFTA (the SEVEN). It is often overlooked that the Council of OEEC had in July 1956 established a Working Party to 'study the possible forms and methods of association, on a multilateral basis, between the proposed Customs Union (of the SIX) and Member countries not taking part therein'. An encouraging report was submitted in January 1957 on the basis of which formal negotiations were commenced.

[6] Unlike the pre-1961 period, the literature is now considerable. The student interested in the sequence of events should study Camps (35), (36); Beloff (21); and Meade (123). The most comprehensive study from the Australian viewpoint is Gelber (88). Other Australian writings include those of Burns (30); Miller (129); Bowen (26); Barclay (20); Crawford (53); and Sawer (151). Another useful reference is the full text of Sir Robert Menzies's speech in the House of Representatives on 16 August 1961, some extracts from which are given in 8:15. It is to be found both in *C.P.D.* (*H. of R.*), vol. 32, pp. 134-41 and in *C.P.P.* no. 71 of 1961.

and commercial policy on a wide front as does the Treaty of Rome.[7] For the same two reasons the situation after July 1961 was different. Economic interests were now drastically involved, since agriculture was very much part of the Rome Treaty, and at least the Prime Minister (then Menzies) could see a threat to the continued existence and political usefulness of the Commonwealth if Britain were to become 'European' in the terms of the Rome Treaty (8:13, 8:15). The earlier view—apparently well disposed toward British association with Europe (8:3)—was, after all, predicated on association through a free trade area, not membership of the Common Market. Despite Menzies's strongly felt and expressed concern for the fate of the Commonwealth in 1961, the general course of Australian policy in Commonwealth meetings and in GATT had been to deplore the economic division of Europe into two trade blocs. This at least carried the implication that Australia would participate in efforts to promote some form of economic fusion of the two groups. We were willing to discuss our preferences if given an appropriate voice as a principal at the negotiating table at which alternative assurances might be considered.

Three or four other short comments are in order before turning to the direct impact of Britain's changing policy on Australia's trade policy. The first is that the Common Agricultural Policy of the Common Market (A8:3) was seen from the beginning to be a threat to American, Canadian, Australian, and New Zealand agricultural interests.[8] Australia's delegates at meetings of GATT and of Commonwealth officials were at all times explicit on this matter. It is of interest to note that the Americans also saw the threat to American exports but not until 1960 did they actively express concern. Up to that point the political importance to them of Franco-German unity in Europe overrode difficulties of this kind and the larger difficulty of bridging the gap between the SIX and the SEVEN. Not until the Kennedy Round (Section 5) did Washington begin to take a really strong line on agricultural protectionism in Europe. Without this support Australia, which had battled on the point in GATT ever since 1956, had lacked any real prospect of success in containing, let alone reducing, the European barriers to her agricultural export trade.

The second observation is that throughout the period 1956 to 1960 the Commonwealth showed little sense of unity—despite some Australian efforts to promote it. The interests of members were differently affected and, in particular, Britain made it clear that she preferred to conduct her European negotiations alone and, moreover, was, in my experience, rather prone to

---

[7] The documents make plain the difference in tariff systems between EEC and EFTA: both are free trade areas, but the former also builds up a *common* external tariff. In *addition*, EEC provides institutions designed to develop common policies in a wide number of economic and social matters (A8:1). EFTA is confined to an industrial free trade area for its members; EEC includes a Common Agricultural Policy.

[8] See especially Cornish and Hempel (51) and Cornish and Carrington (50).

speak for members of the Commonwealth in the light of discussions held in London and Montreal. This lack of any organised unity certainly made it more difficult to protect Commonwealth interests in the crucial negotiations after July 1961 (8:20). More than members perhaps realised there was no real way of assuring all Commonwealth interests—a fact which might have been convenient in assessing whether the interests of the 'Commonwealth as a whole' had been 'reasonably' safeguarded upon British entry into the EEC. There is no doubt that *sauve qui peut* was a fair description of the policy adopted by the senior Commonwealth members. The only way to operate this was by direct talks in Europe (8:18) and by ventilating the issue in GATT: Australia followed both courses of action. Yet, as *The Economist* pertinently observed (8:8), GATT was not likely to do much before hurt was sustained. Article XXIV of GATT is given practically in full (A8:2). From this it could be argued that neither the EEC nor EFTA complies. For the EEC it may be contended that the highly protectionist Common Agricultural Policy which is an integral part of it is in breach in spirit, if not in letter, of the provision that 'the purpose of a customs union or a free-trade area should be to facilitate trade between the constituent territories and not to raise barriers to the trade of other contracting parties with such territories' (Article XXIV, Clause 4 (A8:2)). A statement by an EEC spokesman quoted in Curzon certainly supports this view. In the case of EFTA it is open to doubt whether the exclusion of agriculture (very much in Australia's interests) enables EFTA to qualify under Clause 8(b)—elimination of duties 'on substantially all the trade between the constituent territories on products originating in such territories'. Neither basis for challenging legal validity matters much; the GATT approach would be to minimise initial damage once its threat is present in concrete terms—a point of considerable advantage to the EEC.[9] In fairness it ought to be said that EEC willingness to negotiate at all on agriculture in the Kennedy Round is a recognition that there is now an issue calling for negotiation.

This is not the place to analyse the changes in British thinking, but part of the apparent indifference in Australia before July 1961 must be put down to Macmillan's 1956 assurances about Commonwealth interests and about the United Kingdom's reliance on preferences for her goods in the Commonwealth (8:2). In July 1961, however, the Australian government naturally

[9] For a brief comment along these lines see Vernon Report (11), vol. I, ch. 12, p. 321. For a more detailed and penetrating discussion of the methods of GATT in dealing with the EEC and the EFTA see Curzon (68). The following exchange between Contracting Parties and the Community spokesman as recorded by Curzon, p. 276, is particularly worth noting. 'The Community spokesman cut short these speculations by stating that "the common agricultural policy of the Community was only subject to discussion within the Contracting Parties, when there was the question of concrete action which would be contrary to the obligations under the General Agreement", and furthermore added "if that should later turn out to be the case, the Community would ask for a waiver under the General Agreement".'

noted the apparent reversal of these assurances and A8:3 gives the basis for the very real concern officially expressed by the government, if not by some individual ministers (8:19).

In A8:3 an indication is given of the threat to Australia implicit in Britain's acceptance of the terms of the Rome Treaty.[10] Moreover, the course of negotiations in 1962 gave little real promise of substantial relief, despite the stated willingness on the part of the SIX to consider commodity agreements and to be 'reasonable' in determining price support policy within the Common Market.

The document shows the amount of trade in 1965-6 which enjoyed the listed preferences in the United Kingdom market and which would not only lose this preference but be subjected to the Common External Tariff (CET) shown. It is to be remembered that Australian producers would pay this CET while producers in member countries of the EEC (e.g. France, Denmark, Holland, and Britain) would enjoy free trade within the enlarged boundaries of the EEC.[11] On top of this, the application of the Common Agricultural Policy in important instances would so control imports that these could *never* seriously compete with domestic producers but only fill any gap between total requirements and domestic production.[12] Since this gap is often marginal only to domestic production,[13] it is not surprising that the Common Agricultural Policy further provides for export subsidies to dispose of 'surpluses' produced in the Community, threatening to turn a 'natural' importing area into an exporting area of the 'hot house' (over-protected) variety.[14]

The usual answer to this protest by those within Australia who saw no real difficulty was that the *growth* of demand in the Common Market would ensure opportunity for exporters (8:19)—and, indeed, some such growth could be expected, particularly for meat. It is true, too, that unless European production expanded there would be no reduction in imports merely by reason of the transfer of Britain to the market.[15] But in the opinion of competent

---

[10] A8:3 is made up from a document originally compiled by J. G. Crawford and used in a different form in the Vernon Report (11), vol. II, Attachment K:1, p. 1039. To that version have been added Australia's exports to the United Kingdom for 1965-6. For further details see Cornish (50), (51); Camps (35), (36); and reports of the EEC.

[11] It is safe to assume that if Britain were to join the EEC at least Denmark, of the other EFTA members, would join with her.

[12] The same effect can be achieved by a deficiency payment system of protection as used by Great Britain (Section 9). It so happens that in the case of the major commodities—wheat and sugar—the supports offered have not been as great as those likely to prevail under the Common Agricultural Policy (A8:3; also Section 7).

[13] Meaning that domestic production in Europe (excluding Britain), e.g. bread, grains, meat, dairy produce, sugar, mostly exceeds 95 per cent of total requirements (see Cornish and Hempel (51), p. 65). Nevertheless, 5 per cent of Europe's requirements often represents a large market for oversea suppliers.

[14] For a good, although technical, explanation, see Curzon (68), pp. 202-5.

[15] We ignore the impact on consumption of the higher prices British householders would have to pay under the European system of price support.

observers there is ample room for further technological development in European agriculture—so that in cereals, sugar, and dairy produce imports could be expected to diminish greatly and even disappear (8:18). Nor could Australia object to this if the method of protection were the one most favoured by GATT, namely a fixed tariff which would allow some competition from abroad.[16] The root of Australian objection was and must remain the non-tariff barriers designed to ensure absolute preference for the marketing of all domestic produce as against would-be competition from overseas suppliers and the export subsidies to assist disposal of surpluses which would threaten Australia's position in other world markets. It is little wonder that McEwen's proposals for retaining the equivalent of our British market (8:18) received little response, especially in France, for whom the best thing (economically) about British entry would perhaps be the enlarged agricultural market.

If a great deal of Australian trade was threatened, what could be done about it? Again there was often a ready answer: direct our trade to new markets—a rather tall order for sugar, butter, dried fruits, and canned fruits.[17] Nevertheless, one of the discoveries made by the Australian public was that a considerable switch was already occurring away from Britain to Japan and other markets. What was overlooked by those who thought that anything up to $200m. loss in trade could be replaced by growth of markets elsewhere was that Australia's economic growth calls for a considerable expansion in exports.[18] This would need to be even greater if losses in Europe (and Britain) proved to be considerable.

In fact Britain did not gain entry (8:21, 8:22) and the furore at least temporarily died down.[19] Before concluding this comment with a reminder that the threat may well confront us again, it needs to be noted that even without Britain's entry into the Common Market, the Common Agricultural Policy remains a threat to external trade with the SIX. Two courses are under discussion inside the framework of Kennedy Round negotiations within GATT which may mitigate the problem. Both are unfinished business. One is to reach agreement with the SIX on limits to be set to agricultural protectionism (see Sections 5 and 7). The other—in which Britain is an important party—is to negotiate commodity agreements (cereals, meat, and dairy produce), also under GATT auspices, which would not only establish prices in high in-

[16] It is possible to argue that variable levies are 'legal' but they are certainly not favoured (see Curzon (68), p. 203).

[17] Threatened more by tougher United States competition once our preferences in the United Kingdom market were abolished than by the barriers erected by the EEC, although the entry of Greece would affect dried fruit.

[18] A8:3 shows $171m. trade affected. No one could estimate the losses. Contrary to some reports, my use of $200m. was as a ceiling, not as a detailed estimate.

[19] In Document 8:20 McEwen gives a good indication of how Commonwealth interests have been dealt with in the negotiations as seen in December 1962 just prior to the veto expressed by General de Gaulle (8:21).

come countries but would also set the pattern for surplus disposals (see Section 7). Such agreements may secure some assured access to Europe for Australian products but they cannot be expected to offer better terms than if Europe were to adopt a tariff protection policy for agriculture equivalent to its policy in the industrial field.

As this note is being written (late in 1966), the views of President de Gaulle seem more amenable to British entry; the election campaign in Britain in March 1966 indicated a willingness of both Socialist and Conservative Parties to try again; and the Prime Minister, Harold Wilson, and his Foreign Minister are making clear preparations for another round of negotiations. To the Australian public a formal decision to negotiate, when announced, will now come as no surprise at all. The possibilities of substantial trade losses will remain, somewhat softened by the continued development of agricultural trade with Japan and China and by the hopes that the Kennedy Round may bring results both for effective limits to obstructions to trade now threatened by the Common Agricultural Policy of the EEC and for reasonably assured terms of access, including price, for stated quantities of produce. The Australian case at the negotiating tables in London, Brussels, and Geneva is a strong one; but neither this nor political concern about the future of the Commonwealth is likely to be accepted if stated in extreme terms as a sufficient cause for non-entry by Britain. Macmillan's belief of 1956 (8:2) that the House of Commons would never agree to

> our entering arrangements which, as a matter of principle would prevent our treating the great range of imports from the Commonwealth at least as favourably as those from the European countries

is now certain to fail in the test should the House of Commons be brought to it. For Australia the only possible course is to negotiate the best terms she can either within GATT or directly with Europe and Britain while further diversifying the geographical range of her export markets.

A8:1 TREATY OF ROME

PART ONE

Principles

ARTICLE 1

By the present Treaty, the High Contracting Parties[1] establish among themselves a EUROPEAN ECONOMIC COMMUNITY.

ARTICLE 2

It shall be the aim of the Community, by establishing a Common Market and progressively approximating the economic policies of Member States, to promote

[1] Belgium, Germany, France, Italy, Luxembourg and the Netherlands, who signed the Treaty on 25 March 1957.

throughout the Community a harmonious development of economic activities, a continuous and balanced expansion, an increased stability, an accelerated raising of the standard of living and closer relations between its Member States.

ARTICLE 3

For the purposes set out in the preceding Article, the activities of the Community shall include, under the conditions and with the timing provided for in this Treaty:

(a) the elimination, as between Member States, of customs duties and of quantitative restrictions in regard to the importation and exportation of goods, as well as of all other measures with equivalent effect;

(b) the establishment of a common customs tariff and a common commercial policy towards third countries;

(c) the abolition, as between Member States, of the obstacles to the free movement of persons, services and capital;

(d) the inauguration of a common agricultural policy;

(e) the inauguration of a common transport policy;

(f) the establishment of a system ensuring that competition shall not be distorted in the Common Market;

(g) the application of procedures which shall make it possible to coordinate the economic policies of Member States and to remedy disequilibria in their balances of payments;

(h) the approximation of their respective municipal law to the extent necessary for the functioning of the Common Market;

(i) the creation of a European Social Fund in order to improve the possibilities of employment for workers and to contribute to the raising of their standard of living;

(j) the establishment of a European Investment Bank intended to facilitate the economic expansion of the Community through the creation of new resources; and

(k) the association of overseas countries and territories with the Community with a view to increasing trade and to pursuing jointly their effort towards economic and social development.

ARTICLE 4

1. The achievement of the tasks entrusted to the Community shall be ensured by:

– an ASSEMBLY,

– a COUNCIL,

– a COMMISSION, and

– a COURT OF JUSTICE.

Each of these institutions shall act within the limits of the powers conferred upon it by this Treaty.

2. The Council and the Commission shall be assisted by an Economic and Social Committee acting in a consultative capacity. . . .

ARTICLE 8

1. The Common Market shall be progressively established in the course of a transitional period of twelve years.

The transitional period shall be divided into three stages of four years each; the length of each stage may be modified. . . .

PART FOUR

The Association
of Overseas Countries and Territories

ARTICLE 131

The Member States hereby agree to bring into association with the Community the non-European countries and territories which have special relations with Belgium, France, Italy and the Netherlands. These countries and territories, hereinafter referred to as 'the countries and territories', are listed in Annex IV to this Treaty.

The purpose of this association shall be to promote the economic and social development of the countries and territories and to establish close economic relations between them and the Community as a whole.

In conformity with the principles stated in the Preamble to this Treaty, this association shall in the first place permit the furthering of the interests and prosperity of the inhabitants of these countries and territories in such a manner as to lead them to the economic, social and cultural development which they expect.

ARTICLE 132

Such association shall have the following objects:

1. Member States shall, in their commercial exchanges with the countries and territories, apply the same rules which they apply among themselves pursuant to this Treaty.

2. Each country or territory shall apply to its commercial exchanges with Member States and with the other countries and territories the same rules which it applies in respect of the European State with which it has special relations.

3. Member States shall contribute to the investments required by the progressive development of these countries and territories.

4. As regards investments financed by the Community, participation in tenders and supplies shall be open, on equal terms, to all natural and legal persons being nationals of Member States or of the countries and territories.

5. In relations between Member States and the countries and territories, the right of establishment of nationals and companies shall be regulated in accordance with the provisions, and by application of the procedures, referred to in the Chapter relating to the right of establishment and on a non-discriminatory basis, subject to the special provisions made pursuant to Article 136.

ARTICLE 133

1. Imports originating in the countries or territories shall, on their entry into Member States, benefit by the total abolition of customs duties which shall take place progressively between Member States in conformity with the provisions of this Treaty.

2. Customs duties imposed on imports from Member States and from countries or territories shall, on the entry of such imports into any of the other countries or territories, be progressively abolished in conformity with the provisions of Articles 12, 13, 14, 15 and 17.

3. The countries and territories may, however, levy customs duties which correspond to the needs of their development and to the requirements of their industrialisation or which, being of a fiscal nature, have the object of contributing to their budgets.

The duties referred to in the preceding sub-paragraph shall be progressively reduced to the level of those imposed on imports of products coming from the

Member State with which each country or territory has special relations. The percentages and the timing of the reductions provided for under this Treaty shall apply to the difference between the duty imposed, on entry into the importing country or territory, on a product coming from the Member State which has special relations with the country or territory concerned and the duty imposed on the same product coming from the Community.

4. Paragraph 2 shall not apply to countries and territories which, by reason of the special international obligations by which they are bound, already apply a non-discriminatory customs tariff at the date of the entry into force of this Treaty.

5. The establishment or amendment of customs duties imposed on goods imported into the countries and territories shall not, either *de jure* or *de facto*, give rise to any direct or indirect discrimination between imports coming from the various Member States.

ARTICLE 134

If the level of the duties applicable to goods coming from a third country on entry into a country or territory is likely, having regard to the application of the provisions of Article 133, paragraph 1, to cause diversions of commercial traffic to the detriment of any Member State, the latter may request the Commission to propose to the other Member States the measures necessary to remedy the situation. . . .[2]

PART SIX
General and Final Provisions

ARTICLE 237

. . . Any European State may apply to become a member of the Community. It shall address its application to the Council which, after obtaining the opinion of the Commission, shall act by means of a unanimous vote.

The conditions of admission and the amendments to this Treaty necessitated thereby shall be the subject of an agreement between the Member States and the applicant State. Such agreement shall be submitted to all the contracting States for ratification in accordance with their respective constitutional rules.

ARTICLE 238

The Community may conclude with a third country, a union of States or an international organisation agreements creating an association embodying reciprocal rights and obligations, joint actions and special procedures.

Such agreements shall be concluded by the Council acting by means of a unanimous vote and after consulting the Assembly.

Where such agreements involve amendments to this Treaty, such amendments shall be subject to prior adoption in accordance with the procedure laid down in Article 236.

Source: Treaty Establishing the European Economic Community and Connected Documents (published by the Secretariat of the Interim Committee of the Common Market and Euratom, Brussels, 1957).

[2] Part V has been omitted from these extracts. It provides for an Assembly to exercise the powers of deliberation and control and for a Council to ensure the co-ordination of the general economic policies of Member States. It also provides for complicated voting rights which have subsequently become an issue between France and her partners. The full text needs to be consulted for details.

A8:2 ARTICLE XXIV OF GENERAL AGREEMENT ON TARIFFS AND TRADE

Text of the General Agreement 1958.

TERRITORIAL APPLICATION—FRONTIER TRAFFIC—CUSTOMS UNIONS
AND FREE-TRADE AREAS

4. The contracting parties recognize the desirability of increasing freedom of trade by the development, through voluntary agreements, of closer integration between the economies of the countries parties to such agreements. They also recognize that the purpose of a customs union or of a free-trade area should be to facilitate trade between the constituent territories and not to raise barriers to the trade of other contracting parties with such territories.

5. Accordingly, the provisions of this Agreement shall not prevent, as between the territories of contracting parties, the formation of a customs union or of a free-trade area or the adoption of an interim agreement necessary for the formation of a customs union or of a free-trade area; *Provided* that:

(a) with respect to a customs union, or an interim agreement leading to the formation of a customs union, the duties and other regulations of commerce imposed at the institution of any such union or interim agreement in respect of trade with contracting parties not parties to such union or agreement shall not on the whole be higher or more restrictive than the general incidence of the duties and regulations of commerce applicable in the constituent territories prior to the formation of such union or the adoption of such interim agreement, as the case may be:

(b) with respect to a free-trade area, or an interim agreement leading to the formation of a free-trade area, the duties and other regulations of commerce maintained in each of the constituent territories and applicable at the formation of such free-trade area or the adoption of such interim agreement to the trade of contracting parties not included in such area or not parties to such agreement shall not be higher or more restrictive than the corresponding duties and other regulations of commerce existing in the same constituent territories prior to the formation of the free-trade area, or interim agreement, as the case may be; and

(c) any interim agreement referred to in sub-paragraphs (a) and (b) shall include a plan and schedule for the formation of such a customs union or of such a free-trade area within a reasonable length of time.

6. If, in fulfilling the requirements of sub-paragraph 5 (a), a contracting party proposes to increase any rate of duty inconsistently with the provisions of Article II, the procedure set forth in Article XXVIII shall apply. In providing for compensatory adjustment, due account shall be taken of the compensation already afforded by the reductions brought about in the corresponding duty of the other constituents of the union.

7. (a) Any contracting party deciding to enter into a customs union or free-trade area, or an interim agreement leading to the formation of such a union or area, shall promptly notify the CONTRACTING PARTIES and shall make available to them such information regarding the proposed union or area as will enable them to make such reports and recommendations to contracting parties as they may deem appropriate.

(b) If, after having studied the plan and schedule included in an interim agreement referred to in paragraph 5 in consultation with the parties to that agreement and taking due account of the information made available in accordance with the provisions of sub-paragraph (a), the CONTRACTING PARTIES find that such agreement is not likely to result in the formation of a customs union or of a free-trade area within the period contemplated by the parties to the agreement or that such period is not a reasonable one, the CONTRACTING PARTIES shall make recommendations to the parties to the agreement. The parties shall not maintain or put into force, as the case may be, such agreement if they are not prepared to modify it in accordance with these recommendations.

(c) Any substantial change in the plan or schedule referred to in paragraph 5 (c) shall be communicated to the CONTRACTING PARTIES, which may request the contracting parties concerned to consult with them if the change seems likely to jeopardize or delay unduly the formation of the customs union or of the free-trade area.

8. For the purposes of this Agreement:
(a) A customs union shall be understood to mean the substitution of a single customs territory for two or more customs territories, so that
  (i) duties and other restrictive regulations of commerce (except, where necessary, those permitted under Articles XI, XII, XIII, XIV, XV and XX) are eliminated with respect to substantially all the trade between the constituent territories of the union or at least with respect to substantially all the trade in products originating in such territories, and,
  (ii) subject to the provisions of paragraph 9, substantially the same duties and other regulations of commerce are applied by each of the members of the union to the trade of territories not included in the union;
(b) A free-trade area shall be understood to mean a group of two or more customs territories in which the duties and other restrictive regulations of commerce (except, where necessary, those permitted under Articles XI, XII, XIII, XIV, XV and XX) are eliminated on substantially all the trade between the constituent territories in products originating in such territories.

9. The preferences referred to in paragraph 2 of Article I shall not be affected by the formation of a customs union or of a free-trade area but may be eliminated or adjusted by means of negotiations with contracting parties affected. This procedure of negotiations with affected contracting parties shall, in particular, apply to the elimination of preferences required to conform with the provisions of paragraph 8(a)(i) and paragraph 8(b).

10. The CONTRACTING PARTIES may by a two-thirds majority approve proposals which do not fully comply with the requirements of paragraphs 5 to 9 inclusive, provided that such proposals lead to the formation of a customs union or a free-trade area in the sense of this Article. ...

Source: *General Agreement on Tariffs and Trade: Basic Instruments and Selected Documents*, Geneva, 1958, vol. III, pp. 47-50.

A8:3   SELECTED EXPORTS

SUMMARY OF TARIFF TREATMENT BY THE UNITED KINGDOM AND THE EUROPEAN ECONOMIC COMMUNITY

PRODUCT	U.K. TARIFF		EEC COMMON EXTERNAL TARIFF	EEC COMMON AGRICULTURAL POLICY	PROPORTION OF PRODUCT EXPORTED TO U.K. Value 1965-6 basis[e] %
	Commonwealth Preference	Most Favoured Nation			
Butter	Free	Free	24%	Yes[a]	78
Cheese	Free	10% and 15%	23%	Yes[a]	30
Eggs (not in shell)	Free	10%	6% (22% with sugar)	Yes[a]	52
Honey	Free	50c per cwt.	30%	No	73
Dried skim milk	Free	10%	18–23%	No	17
Canned mutton	Free	10%	22%	No	54
Other canned meat	Free	10–20% (mainly 20%)	26%	No	40
Meat extracts	Free	10–20%	Free to 24%	No	25
Dried vine fruit	Free	20c to 85c per cwt.	8%	No	45
Dried tree fruit	Free	(Apricots 80c per cwt.) Free	10%	No	18
Canned fruit	Free[c]	28c to $1.50 per cwt. 12–25%	17–25% (mainly 23%)	Potential[b]	65
Fruit juices	Free[c]	10–18%[c]	19–28%	No	11
Jams and jellies	Free[c]	10%[c]	30%	Potential[b]	15
Soups	Free	Canned, excl. tomato or dried, 7½% Other 10%	22%	No	9

Preserved vegetables	Free	10% (asparagus, beans, peas, tomatoes) 15% (other)	18–24%	No	14
Dried peas	Free	10–15%	9%	No	11
Flour	Free	10%	30%	Yes[a]	8
Sugar	Free to 17c per cwt.	20c–22c to 60c–$1.07	80%	Yes[b,d]	47
Wine	$1.60 to $3.90 plus 22c for each degree over 42° proof spirit	$1.85 to $4.90 plus 31c for each degree over 42°	9–40 units of account per hectolitre or for some 1.60 units of account per degree per hectolitre	Yes	53
Wheat	Free	Free	20%	Yes[a]	12

[a] Where a CAP operates, variable levies substantially over and above the stated protective level of the CET could apply. (There are no levies on wine, however.)

[b] The potential CAP is one related to standards such as can sizes, labels, permitted preservatives, etc. A variable levy system is not known to be contemplated.

[c] Plus sugar surcharge of 3 per cent.

[d] A draft regulation has been drawn up but it has not yet been approved. CAP therefore is not yet in force. The common price for sugar is due to come into force on 1st July 1968.

[e] Information added to original table.

SOURCE: Department of Trade and Industry. Derived from Vernon Report, vol. II, app. K, attachment K. 5. Figures for updating (Dec. 1966) of table and data for final column supplied by Department of Trade and Industry.

8:1 AUSTRALIAN REACTIONS TO UNITED KINGDOM PARTICIPATION IN PARTIAL FREE TRADE AREA

Press statement by the Minister for Trade (J. McEwen) on 4 October 1956.

The Minister for Trade, Mr. J. McEwen, stated today that the United Kingdom had asked the Australian Government for its reactions to the suggestion that the United Kingdom should participate in a partial free trade area in Western Europe. This proposal and its implications for Australian trade with the United Kingdom and Europe was under active consideration by the Commonwealth Government at the present time. . . .

Mr. McEwen emphasised that not only were we being consulted but our vital interests in these markets were being carefully watched.

Moreover the decision of the United Kingdom not to participate in the Plan in respect of foodstuffs means that our major trade with the United Kingdom will be protected. Greasy wool, our principal export to United Kingdom and the European continent is not subjected to duty in any important European market and would not be affected by the common market scheme.

8:2 THE UNITED KINGDOM EXPLAINS THE FREE TRADE AREA PROPOSALS

Statement by the Chancellor of the Exchequer (Harold Macmillan) in the House of Commons on 26 November 1956.

When we see a significant movement in Europe, tending to strengthen the old world, we must, I think, at least try to find a way whereby, without weakening or running counter to our other interests, we may be associated with it . . . I believe that we all agree that it is quite impracticable for the United Kingdom to join such a Customs union.

The countries which together will form a Customs union will not only abolish tariffs against all goods within the union, but they will also abolish their separate national tariffs against the outside world and will replace them by a single common tariff. In this process some tariffs will be raised and others may be lowered. If the United Kingdom were to join such a Customs union the United Kingdom tariff would be swept aside and would be replaced by this single common tariff. That would mean that goods coming into the United Kingdom from the Commonwealth, including the Colonies, would have to pay duty at the same rate as goods coming from any other third country not a member of the Customs union, while goods from the Customs union would enter free.

Judged only by the most limited United Kingdom interests, such arrangements would be wholly disadvantageous. We could not expect the countries of the Commonwealth to continue to give preferential treatment to our exports to them if we had to charge them full duty on their exports to us. Apart from that, our interests and responsibilities are much wider. I do not believe that this House would ever agree to our entering arrangements which, as a matter of principle would prevent our treating the great range of imports from the Commonwealth at least as favourably as those from the European countries,

So this objection, even if there were no other, would be quite fatal to any proposal that the United Kingdom should seek to take part in a European common market by joining a Customs union . . . So that is out.

If a Customs union, from our point of view, is out, and we cannot join it, can we be associated with it in some other way? . . .

What are we to do? We would dearly have liked to find some way by which the Commonwealth countries, with their resources of food and raw materials and rapidly developing economies, and Europe, a large manufacturing area with a great market for Commonwealth produce, might, if they wished, join together in some still wider common market. That would have been ideal . . . but it was soon evident . . . that the developing countries of the Commonwealth would not be prepared to remove their tariffs and quotas against European goods, and that, at the same time, the countries of Europe, not having our historical link with the Commonwealth would be reluctant to grant free entry to Commonwealth manufacturers.

So we have turned to some other plan by which we could associate with Europe without injury, and indeed with benefit, to Commonwealth relationships. After all, a strong and expanding Europe is the best guarantee of Commonwealth prosperity. After the most careful examination the Government have worked out a main plan and proposals to this end. Its purpose is to harmonise the interests of Britain, the Commonwealth and Europe. . . . the President of the Board of Trade and I took the opportunity of the gathering of the Commonwealth Finance Ministers, in Washington, at the end of September, to put these ideas before them. As I have already reported, the initial reaction was friendly and sympathetic, and after further discussion their more considered judgment confirms this initial reaction. . . .

The main features of the proposed plan . . . are these. In accordance with the broad lines of the scheme already being studied in the o.e.e.c., the United Kingdom would enter a mutual free trade area with the Messina Powers, would reach it stage by stage with the Messina Powers and—this is important—with other o.e.e.c. countries that wished to participate. The area would then consist of the Customs union, that is the six countries as one unit, together with such other countries, including ourselves, as thought fit to join. . . .

Within this free trade area . . . goods of every sort would eventually . . . be admitted duty free. Each country which is not a member of the Messina customs union—this is the real difference—would retain its own separate and different tariffs on imports from outside the area. There would not be a harmonised tariff; each would have its own tariffs. It would retain its freedom of action to vary that tariff subject to any international agreement by which it might be bound at any time. National freedom of action would be retained in its own tariffs. It would also be retained in the field of duties designed to raise revenue rather than to protect home industry. . . .

We must make it clear from the first that any project we could envisage of a free trade area cannot be extended to foodstuffs, whether for man or beast, whether in the raw, a manufactured, or a processed state. Foodstuffs must be extended to include drink and tobacco. We must remain free to continue to grant to this great volume of imports the preferential arrangements we have built up over the last twenty-five years. This is an essential counterpart to the preferences which we enjoy in Commonwealth markets.

It is absolutely essential that this exception should be made so that the preferential system can remain, but that is not all. Apart from the independent members of the Commonwealth, many of our Colonies rely for their social and economic development to an important extent on the preferential treatment which their exports of foodstuffs receive in this country. So, from the point of view of independent Commonwealth countries and of the Colonial Territories this exception is vital.

. . . we have made a determined effort to build up an efficient agricultural industry in this country. We are all resolved to maintain it. I think we all agree that some measure of support or protection is essential if we are to maintain it. Therefore, for all these reasons—the Commonwealth interests, the colonial interests and support of our home agricultural industry, there is only one way out. . . . it is to treat agriculture as an exception in this scheme. . . .

Source: *P.D. (H. of C.)*, vol. 561, pp. 35-50.

8:3 AUSTRALIA AND THE UNITED KINGDOM'S PROPOSAL TO ENTER THE COMMON MARKET

Statement by the Prime Minister (R. G. Menzies) at his Press Conference, Australia House, London, on 9 July 1957.

The matter I thought I would like to mention is this position of the United Kingdom in relation to the European Common Market and its position in relation to the British Commonwealth countries, because I think it is perhaps too readily assumed in some quarters that these two things are bound to be opposed. I do not think that is true.

So far as the European common market is concerned . . . I have no difficulty in seeing what merits, both politically and economically, it may possess. The United Kingdom has to consider whether to get into this Western European economic organisation or stay out, and the answer to that of course, is to consider why the Messina powers have made this treaty. Plainly, with a growing measure of internal free trade they would hope to have greater access to each other's raw materials, greater fluidity of labour which would enable them to improve production, perhaps get down their costs of production and therefore make themselves more competitive in the world's markets. All these things are, I think, intelligible. But, if that happens and the United Kingdom remains completely aloof, she will find herself meeting very heavy competition, particularly perhaps from great industrial countries like Germany whose competition is already being felt by this country. The United Kingdom Government has, in fact, proposed that it ought to have some organised association with the Western European countries but, at the same time, making it quite plain that it does not want to see agricultural products from the British Commonwealth countries brought into the picture; in other words, they should continue to retain the advantages which they now have. That is important to the United Kingdom and it is important to us. It seems to be taken for granted that we should be hostile. I am not hostile in principle at all. We have a very watchful eye on the future of our agricultural exports, but if the economic strength and therefore the purchasing power of Western Europe is improved by this improvement, we as a trading nation may secure some benefit. If the adoption of the proposals of the United Kingdom tends to improve the economic position and power of this great country then we will clearly benefit from that because the United Kingdom is our best market and we are anxious that it should continue to be so . . . We think, in principle, that Great Britain should not remain aloof from this arrangement, but we also, of course, have the liveliest interest in protecting the position of our own exports which are still, to an overwhelming extent, the products of the farms and pastures of Australia—wool and foodstuffs of a great variety of kinds. . . .

8:4 COMMONWEALTH'S ATTITUDE TOWARDS FREE TRADE AREA

Report of the Commonwealth Trade and Economic Conference, Montreal.

40. The Conference considered the influence which the European Economic Community might have on Commonwealth trade interests and reviewed the progress of the negotiations for a European Free Trade Area. It reaffirmed the conviction of the Commonwealth countries that an outward-looking Free Trade Area in which trade would be increased rather than merely rechannelled would contribute to their common objective of an enlarging world economy. It was the belief of the Conference that the European countries could make an important contribution of their own to the freeing of world trade and payments, the removal of discrimination and the expansion of world trade. Many delegations expressed anxiety lest arrangements for closer economic association in Europe should result in a narrowing of the trading opportunities for outside countries, or in the extension of protection, especially in agriculture, where they feared that existing protectionist tendencies might become reinforced and entrenched. The United Kingdom delegation recognized the importance of making the provisions of the Free Trade Area such as would ensure the widest possible trading opportunities and reaffirmed the undertakings about the safeguarding of Commonwealth interests in the United Kingdom market for foodstuffs including drink and tobacco. The Conference reviewed the arrangements made to ensure effective and continuing consultation on these issues among Commonwealth countries, and noted the progress of consultations in the GATT with the members of the European Economic Community.

Source: Commonwealth of Australia: Paper no. 7819/58, Government Printer, Canberra.

8:5 OEEC FREE TRADE AREA TALKS FOUNDER ON OPPOSITION BY FRANCE

Statement by the Paymaster-General (R. Maudling) in the House of Commons on 17 November 1958.

In October 1957 the seventeen nations of the O.E.E.C. recorded their unanimous determination to secure the establishment of a Free Trade Area that would take effect in time parallel with the Treaty of Rome. The Inter-Governmental Committee, of which I am the Chairman, was appointed to conduct the necessary negotiations.

In these negotiations the French Government have always faced difficulties of quite a special order, as has been generally recognized, and they have felt compelled from the start to enter a number of reservations.'....

On Friday, M. Soustelle announced that it did not seem possible to the French Government to establish the Free Trade Area as it had been proposed and that they were looking for a new solution.[1]

Source: *P.D. (H. of C.)*, vol. 595,
pp. 1958-9.

8:6 EUROPEAN FREE TRADE ASSOCIATION ESTABLISHED

Text of Convention approved at Stockholm on 20 November 1959.

On behalf of their Governments, Ministers from Austria, Denmark, Norway, Portugal, Sweden, Switzerland and the United Kingdom have today initialled at Stockholm the text of a Convention establishing the European Free Trade Association, to consist of the seven founding members together with any other countries which may accede to it.

The purposes of the Association are economic expansion, full employment, the rational use of resources, financial stability and a higher standard of living.

The Convention will establish a free market between the members of the Association. This will be achieved by the abolition of tariffs and other obstacles to trade in the industrial products of members over a period of ten years, or earlier if so decided. Each country will be free to decide its own external tariffs.

Freer trade between the participating countries will stimulate competition and economic expansion. There are provisions to ensure that the effects of the removal of the barriers to trade are not nullified by means of subsidies, practices of state undertakings, restrictive business practices and limitations to the establishment of enterprises.

The Convention also covers agricultural goods, for which special provisions are made and agreements concluded so as to promote expansion of trade and ensure a sufficient degree of reciprocity to the countries whose major exports are agricultural. To the same end there are also special rules for trade in non-processed fish and marine products.

The Convention reaffirms the determination of the seven member countries to facilitate the early establishment of a multilateral association for the removal of trade barriers and the promotion of closer economic co-operation between the members of the Organisation for European Economic Co-operation, including the six members of the European Economic Community. To this end a special resolution was adopted.

As world trading nations, the countries of the European Free Trade Association are particularly conscious of Europe's links with the rest of the world. They

[1] No solution was found and the next step was the formation of the more limited European Free Trade Association formed by the SEVEN at Stockholm in November 1959 (see 8:6).

have therefore chosen a form of economic co-operation which, while strengthening Europe, enables them to take full account of the interests of other trading countries throughout the world, including those facing special problems of development. The Association is a further expression of the post-war drive towards lower trade barriers, and reflects the principles which have been established by the General Agreement on Tariffs and Trade (GATT). The individual freedom of action of E.F.T.A. members in their external tariffs will allow each of them to participate actively in GATT negotiations for tariff reductions. . . .

It was agreed to seek ratification of the Convention not later than March 31st, 1960. . . .

Source: H.M.S.O. Cmnd. 906, 1959.

8:7 DIFFERENCE BETWEEN FREE TRADE ASSOCIATION AND EUROPEAN COMMON MARKET

Statement by the Minister for Trade (J. McEwen) in reply to a question by T. F. Timson in the House of Representatives on 25 November 1959.

An announcement has been made that Ministers representing the seven nations named by the honorable member have signed a convention in Stockholm. It is designed to establish what is called the European Free Trade Association. This so-called European Free Trade Association will not come into existence officially unless and until the governments of the nations named ratify the convention. It is designed to eliminate tariffs between member countries, but will apply mainly—I think almost entirely—to industrial goods. Because the free trade convention will apply to industrial goods, it will not impinge significantly upon Australian preferences with the United Kingdom. Indeed, I should say that the United Kingdom has been very firm in declining to enter into any arrangement that would necessitate the abandoning or serious impairing of the system which has been historically known as the system of imperial preference.

The free trade area differs from the so-called European Common Market, which is comprised of the six countries mentioned by the honorable member, in that a common external tariff is not intended to apply in the case of the free trade area, whereas the European Common Market group of six countries intends, over a period of twelve to fifteen years, to establish free trade within the group of six and also to establish gradually a common external tariff equally applied by all of the six. Those are the main distinguishing features of the two groups.[1]

Source: *C.P.D.* (H. of R.), vol. 25, p. 3068.

[1] The statement fails to be explicit on two other major points: the EEC provides for a managed agriculture and for institutions for developing economic integration in several forms. (A8:1).

8:8 GATT AND THE EEC

The General Agreement on Tariffs and Trade is not the forum in which the differences between the Six and Seven are likely to be fought out. But it has the the task of fitting the special trading relationships between European countries into their broader international obligations. Thus the last two sessions of GATT were mainly preoccupied with the European Economic Community; and the European Free Trade Association is already the centre piece of the quiet working session that began last Monday.

The contracting parties to GATT have already studied the EFTA treaty and have submitted some hundred pertinent questions. In particular, they ask how the Seven reconcile their treaty, which does not provide for the elimination of tariffs, quotas and other barriers to trade in agricultural goods and fish, with the GATT provision that duties and other trade barriers are eliminated on 'substantially all the trade' within a customs union or free trade area . . . The question of compatibility or incompatibility with the General Agreement has not been pressed to a conclusion.

This phraseology covers, of course, one of GATT's weak points. Contracting parties refuse as a rule to discuss situations that might arise. They wish to confine themselves to facts which already exist. GATT is therefore in no position to prevent ill effects of a customs union or free trade area, but only to cure once damage has been done. Thus EFTA has not yet passed GATT's scrutiny, but it legally exists and functions whatever the outcome of this session's discussion. . . .

Source: *The Economist*, 21 May 1960,
p. 766.

8:9 EUROPEAN FREE TRADE ASSOCIATION: AUSTRALIA WAIVES CERTAIN PREFERENCES

Press statement by the Deputy Prime Minister and Minister for Trade (J. McEwen) on 3 July 1960.

The Minister for Trade, Mr. McEwen, commented today on some of the implications for Australia of the first tariff cuts made by some members of European Free Trade Association (EFTA). On 1st July, 1960, the EFTA countries made a 20% reduction in their tariffs between each other on industrial products and on some agricultural products thus beginning the process of progressively moving towards the complete elimination of tariffs between the group on these items. . . .

In the EFTA arrangements the United Kingdom has been to a large extent successful in getting a worthwhile arrangement with its continental EFTA partners without infringing on vital Commonwealth interests in the United Kingdom market. This meant that Australia's major preferences in the United Kingdom market on dairy products, fruits—fresh, canned and dried—canned meat, eggs, wine, barley, sugar, flour and honey were preserved intact.

Mr. McEwen said that at the request of the United Kingdom the Australian

Government had agreed to waive preferences guaranteed to Australia under the U.K./Australia Trade Agreement on the following nine products—

Leather;	Asbestos;	Canned Pork Luncheon Meat;
Lead;	Wattle Bark;	Blue-veined cheese;
Zinc;	Eucalyptus Oil;	Coconut oil (one type only not of interest to Papua/New Guinea).

Mr. McEwen emphasised that the Government had agreed to waive these preferences in respect of the EFTA countries only....

8:10 EEC DEVELOPMENTS: AUSTRALIAN PUBLIC KEPT IN IGNORANCE

Announcing that Australia had agreed to waive preferences on nine products under her trade agreement with Britain, Mr. McEwen said at the week-end that the British Government faced a difficult task in trying to reconcile its commitments to the Commonwealth with its desire not to be completely shut out of the moves for freer trade in Europe. The particular 'move for freer trade' which prompted Britain to ask for the waiving of nine preferences was the formation of the European Free Trade Association. The agreement setting up this organisation was initialled last November; only now, seven months later, is the Australian public told of the British request and of our decision to agree to it.

Mr. McEwen's disclosure is a reminder of how little the public in this country—or in any other country of the Commonwealth—is being told by its rulers about the historic developments which are transforming the trade relations of European nations, both between themselves and the outside world. In the absence of clear indications of policy, it has been widely assumed that it was her Commonwealth obligations which prevented Britain from participating in the powerful European Economic Community (Common Market).

When the British Government, having missed the United Europe bus years before, tried to negotiate a partial association with the Common Market she encountered so much opposition from the Continental Six, particularly France, that she was compelled to join the Outer Seven, or EFTA. But the limitations of this association, and the danger of a permanent trade division in non-Communist Europe, were clear from the beginning.

There is little doubt that the six nations in the Common Market are laying the economic foundations on which a political federation may one day be built. The existence of two trade groups in Europe can only be a hindrance to this tremendously important development. If a decision by Britain to throw in her lot with the Six could really secure the integration of European trade, is it not imperative for the Commonwealth countries—and not least Australia—to examine whether such a decision would damage their basic interests? The assumption that it would has been fostered too long by British politicians concerned not so much for the welfare of Commonwealth agriculture, as for that of Britain's own farmers, or strongly opposed to the idea of a supranational authority in trade.

All aspects of this crucial question should have been discussed at the recent Prime Ministers' Conference in London. Apparently they were not, mainly because the conference was preoccupied with the dangerous implications of the apartheid crisis in South Africa. But the failure of the Prime Ministers to discuss fully the issues raised by the rapid growth of the Common Market cannot be allowed to excuse the Australian or any other Commonwealth Government from putting the facts before the public, and attempting to create an informed opinion. Instead of occasional rather offhand references by one or two Australian Ministers, Mr. Menzies and Mr. McEwen should give a considered judgment on the probable consequences for the Commonwealth of any substantial association by Britain—assuming that it were now possible on fair terms—with one of the world's greatest potential markets.

Source: Leading article in the *Sydney Morning Herald*, 5 July 1960.

8:11 UNITED KINGDOM AND THE EEC

Text of Joint Communiqué issued on 11 July 1961 at the conclusion of Duncan Sandys' visit to Canberra.

The Prime Minister of Australia, Mr Menzies, and other Australian Ministers have during the last few days had discussions with the British Secretary of State for Commonwealth Relations, Mr Duncan Sandys.

Mr Sandys explained the various considerations which had led the British Government to re-examine its attitude towards and relationship with the European Economic Community (the 'Common Market'), established by the Treaty of Rome.

In the course of several meetings, the political and economic implications of such a step were fully discussed.

The Australian Government considered that, should Britain join the European Economic Community, it might well be that she will become increasingly involved in not only the economic policies of the Community but also in matters of an international and political kind. Mr Sandys emphasized that the British Government was convinced that the objective of closer unity in Europe was in no way incompatible with the maintenance and further development of Commonwealth ties, which constitute a valuable and unifying influence in a much divided world. Australian Ministers pointed out that they thought the ultimate political implications of the Treaty of Rome are extremely significant and will tend to possess a developing character in the achievement of some kind of European unity. They saw merit in such unity since a continuing division in rival economic groups would be a source of danger and weakness, while a powerful and experienced group of free European nations can do much to preserve the world's peace. However, they emphasized that although avoidance of a divided Western Europe was a desirable objective it should not be accomplished at the cost of division within the Commonwealth or elsewhere in the free world. Australian Ministers expressed their concern at the weakening effect they believed this development would have on the Commonwealth relationship. Mr Sandys stressed the importance the United Kingdom attaches to maintaining this relationship unimpaired. Indeed, the British Government believed that a closer association of Britain with the continent of Europe might well be an added source of strength not only to Britain but to the Commonwealth as a whole.

290

Full exchanges occurred on the economic advantages and disadvantages which would ensue if Britain were to accede to the Treaty of Rome and the possible effects of this on the trade and industry of Britain and Australia. It was recognized that the issue of Britain's accession to the Treaty of Rome was primarily a matter for Britain and was one which the British Government alone could decide. But Australian Ministers explained the serious adverse consequences for Australian producers and for the Australian balance of payments which would confront Australia if the United Kingdom were to enter the Common Market on a basis which failed to safeguard Australian trade interests for the future.

Mr Sandys assured the Australian Government that the British Government fully shared its concern to maintain the long-established flow of trade between their two countries. If negotiations took place, the intention would be to secure special arrangements to protect these important trading interests.

Mr Sandys made it clear that he did not ask the Australian Government to express an opinion on the question whether Britain should join the Common Market. The British Government itself had as yet reached no decision on this issue. The immediate question was whether or not to open negotiations with the European Economic Community.

As the whole question is of major importance for Britain and for decision by her, Australian Ministers did not feel entitled to object to the opening of negotiations by the British Government should it reach the conclusion that this was desirable. But they made it clear that the absence of objection should in the circumstances not be interpreted as implying approval. They further stressed that, as in any such negotiations various Australian export industries would be materially involved, Australia should be in a position to negotiate direct on Australia's behalf when details and arrangements affecting items of Australian trade were being discussed.

Mr Sandys said he well understood the position of the Australian Government; and he appreciated its understanding of Britain's problem.

It was agreed that these talks, which had been conducted in a most helpful and constructive spirit on both sides, had resulted in a more complete understanding of the important and complex issues involved.

Source: *Current Notes on International Affairs*, vol. 32, no. 7, pp. 21-2.

8:12 UNITED KINGDOM TO NEGOTIATE WITH EEC

Statement by the Prime Minister of the United Kingdom (Harold Macmillan) in the House of Commons on 31 July 1961.

This is a political as well as an economic issue. Although the Treaty of Rome is concerned with economic matters it has an important political objective, namely to promote the unity and stability in Europe which is so essential a factor in the struggle for freedom and progress throughout the world. In this modern world the tendency towards larger groups of nations acting together in the common interest leads to greater unity and this adds to our strength in the struggle for freedom. I believe it is both our duty and our interest to contribute towards that strength by securing the closest possible unity with Europe. At the same time, if a closer relationship between the United Kingdom and the countries of the

European Economic Community were to disrupt the long standing and historic ties between the United Kingdom and the other nations of the Commonwealth the loss would be greater than the gain. The Commonwealth is a great source of stability and strength both to Western Europe and to the world as a whole. And I am sure that its value is fully appreciated by the member Governments of the European Economic Community. I do not think that Britain's contribution to the Commonwealth will be reduced if Europe unites. On the contrary I think its value will be enhanced.

On the economic side, a Community comprising as members or in association the countries of Free Europe could have a very rapidly expanding economy supplying, as eventually it would, a single market of approaching 300 million people. This rapidly expanding economy could in turn lead to an increased demand for the products of other parts of the world and so help to expand world trade and improve the prospects of the less developed areas of the world.

No British Government could join the European Economic Community without prior negotiations with a view to meeting the needs of the Commonwealth countries, of our European Free Trade Association partners and of British agriculture, consistently with the broad principles which have inspired the concept of European unity and which are embodied in the Rome Treaty.

As the House knows, Ministers have recently visited Commonwealth countries to discuss the problems which would arise if the British Government decided to negotiate for membership of the E.E.C. We have explained to the Commonwealth Governments the broad political and economic considerations which we have to take into account. They for their part told us their views and in some cases their anxieties about their essential interests. We have assured the Commonwealth Governments that we shall keep in close consultation with them throughout any negotiations which might take place. Secondly, there is the European Free Trade Association. We have a treaty and other obligations to our partners in this association and my Right Hon. friends have just returned from a meeting of the E.F.T.A. Ministerial Conference in Geneva, where all were agreed that they should work closely together throughout any negotiations. Finally we are determined to continue to protect the standard of living of our agricultural community.

During the past nine months we have had useful and frank discussions with the E.E.C. Governments. Now we have reached the stage where we cannot make further progress without entering into formal negotiations. I believe that the great majority in the House and in the country will feel that they cannot fairly judge whether it is possible for the United Kingdom to join the E.E.C. until there is a clearer picture before them of the conditions on which we would join and the extent to which these would meet our special needs. Article 237 of the Treaty of Rome envisages that the conditions of admission of a new member and the changes in the Treaty necessitated thereby should be the subject of an agreement. Negotiations must therefore be held in order to establish the conditions on which we might join. In order to enter into these negotiations it is necessary under the Treaty to make a formal application to join the Community although the ultimate decision whether to join or not must depend on the result of the negotiations. Therefore after long and earnest consideration Her Majesty's Government have come to the conclusion that it would be right for Britain to make a formal application under Article 237 of the Treaty for negotiations with a view to joining the Community if satisfactory arrangements can be made to meet the special needs of the U.K., of the Commonwealth, and of the E.F.T.A. by whatever procedure they may generally agree.

If as I earnestly hope our offer to enter into negotiations with the E.E.C. is accepted we shall spare no efforts to reach a satisfactory agreement. These negotiations must inevitably be of a detailed and technical character covering a very large number of the most delicate and difficult matters. They may therefore be protracted and there can of course be no guarantee of success.

When any negotiations are brought to a conclusion then it will be the duty of the Government to recommend to the House what course we should pursue. No agreement will be entered into until it has been approved by the House after full consultation with other Commonwealth countries.

Source: United Kingdom Information Service, *Background to Britain Series*, no. B. 26 of 2 August 1961.

8:13 UNITED KINGDOM NEGOTIATIONS WITH EEC: THE ISSUES FOR AUSTRALIA

Statement by the Prime Minister (R. G. Menzies) on 31 July 1961.

The British Government has now made a momentous decision to enter into negotiations with the Members of the European Economic Community with a view to joining the Community if satisfactory arrangements can be made to meet the special needs of the United Kingdom, of the Commonwealth and of the European Free Trade Association. A second, more momentous decision will become necessary when the negotiations conclude and further consultation takes place, as it no doubt will, with the other Commonwealth countries.

I had been made aware through messages from the British Prime Minister of the decision of the British Government prior to the announcement in the House of Commons. Mr Macmillan's messages to me covered both the terms of his Government's decision and also the considerations which led his Government to it.

The issues for Australia are pressing and real. We will, I hope, with the assistance of Great Britain, be participants in a series of negotiations which I believe to be the most important, in time of peace, in my lifetime. They will demand of us both wisdom and patience and constant vigilance.

On the commercial side we have taken the view and have expressed it strongly, that in the negotiations which will now take place arrangements to protect our export trade and commercial interests must be secured. To this end further consultations of a detailed character on trade and commodity questions will take place between the United Kingdom and Commonwealth countries, including Australia, before substantive negotiations with the European Economic Community begin. When those substantive negotiations do begin we will persist in the presentation of our view that nobody can argue the case for our export industries half so well as we can ourselves.

One of the things Great Britain had to decide is whether in fact her membership of the Common Market would strengthen her own economy. It is tremendously important to us that her economy should be strengthened, because if it weakens our own British market will suffer.

293

L

With respect to preferences we have special arrangements which are of immense value to us and we regard ourselves as the Australian Government as having a primary duty to protect those interests. Therefore we have devoted much time to discussing them and to pointing out that you cannot turn a preferential system upside down without exposing our export industries such as wheat, butter, dried fruits etc. to very great danger.

We have also felt that if the United Kingdom were to join the Community it would not be without effect on the close and individual political relations which characterize the Commonwealth. The European Economic Community, besides being a commercial arrangement, is also a great political conception, working towards something resembling a common political organism. It could be a tremendous thing for the world to have a cohesive Europe, but if this common European policy develops with United Kingdom participation one could hardly say that the Commonwealth would remain quite the same. I hope that I may be wrong, but so it seems to me.

Source: *Current Notes on International Affairs*, vol. 32, no. 7, p. 30.

8:14 HOUSE OF COMMONS APPROVES DECISION TO NEGOTIATE WITH THE EEC

Speech by the Prime Minister (Harold Macmillan) in the House of Commons on 3 August 1961.

On Thursday August 3, 1961, the United Kingdom House of Commons approved by 313 votes to 5 the following motion:

That this House supports the decision of Her Majesty's Government to make formal application under Article 237 of the Treaty of Rome in order to initiate negotiations to see if satisfactory arrangements can be made to meet the special interests of the United Kingdom, of the Commonwealth and of the European Free Trade Association; and further accepts the undertaking of Her Majesty's Government that no agreement affecting these special interests or involving British sovereignty will be entered into until it has been approved by this House after full consultation with other Commonwealth countries by whatever procedure they may generally agree.

Mr. Macmillan's Speech

Introducing the motion the Prime Minister said:

We must all agree that the problems involved in the future of our relations with Europe are among the most difficult and most important that this nation has ever had to face. The moment of decision, however, has not yet come. What the House is now asked to do is to support the Government's proposal to initiate negotiations on the Common Market within the terms of the motion. When those negotiations are completed one way or the other, the House will have to pass judgement.

The underlying issues, European unity, the future of the Commonwealth, the strength of the Free World, are all of capital importance and it is because we firmly believe that the United Kingdom has a positive part to play in their development—for they are all related—that we ask the House to approve what we are doing. . . .

Meanwhile there has grown up a practical application of the aspiration towards unity in continental Europe by the formation of the European Economic Community. I ask Honourable Members to note the word 'economic'. The Treaty of Rome does not deal with defence. It does not deal with foreign policy. It deals with trade and some of the social aspects of human life which are most connected with trade and production.

Whatever views are held of what should be our relations with the E.E.C. everyone will readily acknowledge the tremendous achievement involved. Its most striking feature, of course, is the reconciliation of France and Germany. That is on the moral side. But on the political side these countries have made remarkable economic progress in recent years. Of course that is not all due to the E.E.C. Nevertheless the Community has imparted an impetus to the economic growth of the Six; the Community has developed a dynamic of its own. Above all it is an idea which has gripped men's minds.

At the time when the E.E.C. was being discussed most people felt that it would be dangerous to split Europe in this way and a great effort was made for two years, during negotiations in which the President of the Board of Trade played a conspicuous part, to form a Free Trade Area upon an industrial basis, excluding agriculture, thus allowing almost all European countries to take part.

These negotiations which at one time seemed to have encouraging prospects of success, finally broke down. After this setback some of the countries outside the Six formed the European Free Trade Association and one of its declared objects was to work for wider trading arrangements in Western Europe. E.F.T.A. has steadfastly pursued that objective ever since its inception.

I am myself convinced that the existence of this division in Europe, although it is superficially of a commercial character, undoubtedly detracts from the political strength and unity of Western Europe. If we are to be involved in Europe at all then we have a duty—and so have all the countries in Europe—to seek some means of resolving causes of potential division. . . .

I have sometimes heard it asked: 'What would happen if one of the countries with which we might be associated in Europe fell into political difficulties, or even went Communist? Would not this have a grave effect on us if we were members?' Of course, but the effects would be equally grave whether we were members of the Community or not. If a member of N.A.T.O. or W.E.U. went Communist or semi-communist what would be the position of the other member states? If all the countries of Western Europe became satellites of Moscow what would be the position of this island? We have only to pose the question to answer it. We shall not escape from the consequences of such a disaster by seeking in isolation a security which our geographical position no longer gives us. Surely from this point of view it will be better for us to play our role to the full and use the influence we have for the free development of life and thought of Europe? . . .

We shall consult Commonwealth countries at every level and at all stages. If it is desired by the Commonwealth we will have a meeting at an appropriate stage either of Ministers or of Prime Ministers as they may wish. This is really for them. . . .

If I thought that our entry into Europe would injure our relations with and influence in the Commonwealth and be against the true interest of the Commonwealth, I would not ask the House to support this step. I think, however, that most of us recognise that in this changing world if we are not to be left behind and to drop out of the main stream of the world's life, we must be prepared to change and adapt our methods. . . .

Source: United Kingdom Information Service, *Background to Britain Series,* no. B. 27 of 9 August 1961.

8:15 AUSTRALIA AND THE EEC

Statement by the Prime Minister (R. G. Menzies) in the House of Representatives on 16 August 1961.

The decision of the Government of Great Britain[1] to negotiate for admission to the European Economic Community is one of enormous political, economic and historic importance for Great Britain herself, for Europe, for the Commonwealth in general and Australia in particular, and for the world.

It is therefore essential that, at this first opportunity after the visit of the Secretary of State for Commonwealth Relations (Mr. Duncan Sandys) and after Mr. Macmillan's announcement in the House of Commons, I should, on behalf of the Australian Government, set out in this Parliament the nature of the action proposed or taken, and of the issues involved.

But before I do that, there are some matters of history to be recorded.

Not long after the War, movements began for strengthening Western Europe, economically and politically, against new threats to freedom and progress. These took a particular practical form when, in 1950, the European Coal and Steel community was promoted by M. Schumann of France. This was a marked success, and paved the way for the later development of the Common Market.

In 1957 the Atomic Energy Community, known as 'EURATOM', was set up.

Concurrently, on March 25th 1957 the Treaty of Rome was signed, establishing the European Economic Community, sometimes known as 'the Common Market' or 'The Six'. The parties to the Treaty were France, Germany, Italy, Belgium, the Netherlands and Luxembourg. While this Treaty was being negotiated, Great Britain made her first decision, which was not to participate. At that time, she felt that, although she approved of the idea of European unity, she could not go in as a party because of her Commonwealth commitments, her own system of protecting British agriculture and (as I have always supposed) because she did not choose to accept any abatement of her own sovereignty.

But she still took active steps. Her second decision was to propose an Industrial Free Trade Area for the whole of Western Europe, including The Six. This proposal would have met the agricultural and (for the greater part) the Commonwealth considerations which had previously deterred her. But 'The Six' did not favour the proposals, and they failed.

A third decision was then taken. Great Britain formed the European Free Trade Association with Sweden, Norway, Denmark, Austria, Portugal and Switzerland. This group became known, and I shall refer to it, as The Seven. Subsequently, attempts were made to bring about an association between The Seven and The Six but without success.

I mention these matters of history because they will remind us that the decision now taken is the fourth, and that as it involves detailed negotiations with The Six on items some of which concern Australia very greatly, we have now reached a period in which we must all clarify our attitudes on identifiable matters of great practical moment.

It is now necessary to turn to the Treaty of Rome itself. . . .

Clearly, this is a formidable and far-reaching organism, of profound economic significance, and with political objectives to which I shall refer later.

I will first endeavour, with as much brevity as possible, to explain the nature

[1] Taken by both Houses of Parliament on 3 August 1961; formal application for membership made on 10 August 1961.

of the *economic interests* involved in negotiation by Great Britain for membership.

Great Britain herself has, of course, enormous interests at stake. Her decision to negotiate could not have been easy, and we may be sure that it has been arrived at in the light of her immense experience and ripe judgment. It would not be for us to substitute some opinion of our own, even if we had formed one. For we are in no position to assess the elements in the British economy, or the economic arguments this way and that concerning the effect upon her of an achieved membership. We have, of course, a lively interest in the accuracy of her final decision, for we want to see a powerful and prosperous Great Britain, for the good of Australia in all aspects of our national and international life and for the good of the whole free world.

She herself, as Mr Sandys was careful to explain to us in the course of our frank and helpful exchanges, is impressed by the competitive advantages for her own exports and necessary trade balances which she believes would derive from free access to a 'Home Market' of over 250,000,000 people. ...

On the other hand, of course, Great Britain's entry into a European free trade area will mean that her own industries will meet the full blast of European competition, including that from countries like Germany which has a longer working week, a less extensive system of social services, and a high proportion of modern plant erected since the war-time destruction. It is said that such competition will lead to greater efficiency, and no doubt, given sufficient time, it will. In any case this aspect of the matter has beyond question been fully weighed and considered. We ourselves see great scope for an increase, by increased efficiency, in the Commonwealth Market. Commonwealth countries to-day take 42% of British exports, while The Six take 14·5%. While Great Britain clearly hopes that, as a member of the Common Market, she will increase her exports to Europe—which would be a great thing for her economy—we simply direct attention to the undoubted fact that her Commonwealth market must continue and grow if her overall strength is to increase. But the Commonwealth market cannot grow if any conditions of European membership inflict material damage upon the export earnings of Commonwealth countries. ...

There is another aspect of this great matter. We have throughout felt that the Common Market, as it now stands, whatever effect it might have on any individual country, would tend to increase the total prosperity and purchasing power of The Six, and that Australia, among others, might hope to find a growing market in Europe. As I will show later, we have for some time been actively seeking to develop that market. Undoubtedly, the European Economic Community has been succeeding. The economic recovery of France in recent years has contributed to this. Trade exchanges between them have increased 50% since the Treaty of Rome. They have accumulated massive international reserves.

Yet the prospect of Australian benefit from this improvement will depend very importantly upon the internal policies adopted by the Common Market Countries in relation to their own agriculture. If, and there have been suggestions of it, agricultural protectionism prevails, the entry of foodstuffs, from e.g. Australia, will become more difficult. The pricing policy adopted by the E.E.C. for its agricultural products will largely determine the size of the European market for imported agricultural products and the extent to which surpluses in given European countries can be exported. Price stabilization at the high levels now current in some Member States will tend to increase production in the Community area. Under the encouragement of high domestic prices, France is already developing an export surplus in wheat. These matters will be dealt with by my colleague, the Minister for Trade.[2] It is sufficient for me to say that the advantages or disadvantages to Australia, economically speaking, from the success of the Common Market will be largely determined by policies worked out in Europe.

It is difficult to assess the prospects. For example, wool is to enjoy free entry under the common external tariff. But it does not automatically follow that European economic growth will correspondingly increase the demand for wool. We hope that it will, but the fact is that although industrial production in The Six has been rising rapidly since 1957, there has so far been no increase in the volume of our exports of wool to these countries.

Our most definable interest arises in relation to our exports to Great Britain, wheat, meat, dairy products, base metals, sugar, dried fruits, fresh fruit and processed fruits. These constitute the great bulk of our current exports to Great Britain of £198m. stg. They enjoy a preferred entry into the British market, while meat and sugar are the subjects of special long-term agreements. In exchange for these preferences, Great Britain enjoys preferential rates in our Customs Tariff and currently exports goods to the value of £259m. stg. to Australia.

Clearly, this mutual preferential structure comes into the arena of Great Britain's negotiations with The Six. Should the other members of the European Free Trade Association decide also to apply for membership of the Common Market (which seems probable) there will be further important problems to be decided. . . .

I think it most desirable that I should point out to all the negotiators that if they want a strong and growing Australia, they must recognise the peculiar Australian significance of the relevant industries.

The development and populating of the North of Australia, from the Kimberleys in Western Australia through the Northern Territory to North Queensland depends primarily on beef cattle, minerals and sugar. The British market has been of commanding importance in all three. Wheat stands next to wool as our export staple; the welfare of at least two states is bound up in its success. The intensive settlement in the irrigated areas of the Murray and Murrumbidgee regions has been built up on the dried vine fruits, processed fruits, and the production of fat lambs. Not one of these industries could exist on its present scale without large exports. In the case of dried fruits and fat lambs, the British market is vital; for processed fruit it is important.

Our great mineral resources, in relation to which great expansion is in sight, tend to be found in areas remote from the industrial cities and the agricultural areas. They come, when developed, to sustain large communities whose very existence depends upon a growing export for the products of the mines, refineries and smelters.

It follows from all this, and I take leave to emphasize this point, that severe blows to our export primary industries would fall with particular severity upon particular areas, industries, and people. The impact would not be more or less evenly distributed over the whole nation, but would be concentrated and therefore more damaging.

We cannot as yet anticipate the results of the negotiations. We can, I think, reasonably assume that Great Britain will not accede to the Treaty of Rome

[2] The Minister for Trade (J. McEwen) dealt with the likely effects of the Common Market's agricultural policies on Australia's trade in the House of Representatives on 17 August 1961 and on 3 May 1962. Mr McEwen's latter speech is reproduced as document 8:18.

unconditionally. Such an accession would bring to an end the Commonwealth Preferential System which has endured for many years. It would be highly damaging to Australia, and could be disastrous to our neighbour and friend, New Zealand. As the preferential system operates both ways, it could mean the end of B.P.T. rates in our Tariff schedules.

On the other hand, it may be too much to hope at this stage that Great Britain will be allowed (by the necessary unanimous agreement of The Six) to maintain the Commonwealth Preferential System completely unimpaired.

Some compromise will no doubt be sought. We shall, of course, battle for the best possible arrangements for the protection of our traditional and legitimate interests.

We cannot doubt that Great Britain will be on our side in that battle. We also have good friends in Europe, and can be assured of their understanding ... we are not unaware of the suggestions, already being made in some quarters, that the emergence in practical form of the Common Market issue has suddenly made the Australian Government aware of the need to develop new and diversified markets.

The suggestions are quite unfounded, as I shall quite easily show. The matter has not arisen with the suddenness which recent publicity may suggest. We have for some time known that attempts would be made to bring The Seven and The Six together. I myself had some general talk about this with both Chancellor Adenauer and President de Gaulle in 1959. But no detailed proposals were ever put to or considered by us because first, it was the specified object of Great Britain to keep agriculture out of any negotiations, thus preserving our own and British interests, and second, it was made clear that before any negotiations were decided upon, we would be effectively consulted.

In London, immediately after the last Prime Ministers' Conference I proposed (and the proposal was accepted) that our officials should go into preliminary conference in London, so that, 'getting down to brass tacks', we could identify the points of difficulty and try to find common methods of approach.

This Conference preceded the visit of Mr. Sandys; a visit which produced, for the first time on the political level, a specific exchange of views. Meanwhile much official study has been made in the relevant departments.

The matter has, therefore, not come suddenly out of a blue sky. From Australia's point of view, neither time nor ground has been lost. Indeed, we have been active for years in strengthening and diversifying our exports to whatever markets we could find.

When, in January 1956, I announced the creation of the Department of Trade, I pointed out that it would direct its major attention to the stimulation of trade. It has, with the backing of the Cabinet, acted vigorously in this field. ...

There were three passages in the communiqué issued at the end of our talks with Mr. Sandys which deserve special mention.

The first showed that the Australian government took a view of the impact of Great Britain's membership of the Common Market upon Commonwealth Relations different from that of Great Britain.

The second showed that we refrained from giving approval to the opening of negotiations.

The third made it clear that we wished to take an active part in the negotiations affecting our special interests.

These statements have been interpreted by some as indicating a spirit of hostility in our discussions, or at least a lack of a co-operative Commonwealth approach. I want to make it clear that our discussions were conducted on a proper Commonwealth level; our common interests never forgotten, but our particular interests zealously expounded and upheld. . . .

We want whatever decisions are finally taken to bring added strength to Great Britain, for her own sake, for our sake, and for the sake of the world. For we are both British and Commonwealth. . . .

Source: *C.P.D.* (*H. of R.*), vol. 32,
pp. 134-41.

8:16 PROBLEMS RAISED FOR AUSTRALIA BY DECISION OF UNITED KINGDOM TO SEEK MEMBERSHIP OF THE EEC

Statement by the Minister for Trade (J. McEwen) in the House of Representatives on 17 August 1961.[1]

In such a situation, I could see nothing but havoc for many industries of Australia, New Zealand and like countries.

I am not declaring that this is what will happen; but I am portraying precisely what the position would be under the existing Treaty of Rome terms, and illustrating thereby the magnitude of the task that we and the United Kingdom have in securing a sufficient modification of the terms to enable our industries to survive as suppliers to the United Kingdom or the Common Market area.

I am sure that the United Kingdom will try to negotiate modifications of the Treaty of Rome terms against such devastating consequences as I have been illustrating.

But do not let us forget that modifications which would substantially maintain our present position would in fact represent a major part of the case which Great Britain unsuccessfully pressed over a period of four years—a case which she has now apparently been brought to believe is hopeless of achievement.

That is why I regard the present position as most serious.

It is not serious in the sense that our trade with the United Kingdom would be wrecked overnight if she joined the Common Market. It is contemplated in the Treaty of Rome that it will take quite a number of years to achieve the full operation of the Common Market.

But we cannot think only of the well-being of Australia to-morrow; we must think in terms of the capacity for expansion of the nation in the years ahead.

The responsibilities in this situation are not to be carried alone by the United Kingdom and her Commonwealth trading partners. Countries like Australia and New Zealand must not be grievously damaged as part of the price to secure greater political and economic cohesion in Europe.

To whom do our friends of the Western world expect us to sell?

United States policies of protection prevent us from making any worth-while sales into that great and rich area.

[1] The first part of this speech which is not reproduced here gives considerable detail in amplification of the Prime Minister's statement (8:15). It spells out the trade implications for Australia of a liberal application of an unmodified Rome Treaty as a condition for Britain's entry. The extracts quoted refer to this situation.

Without sufficient modifications of the Treaty of Rome, I see the stage set to exclude substantially most of our products from Europe and the United Kingdom.

Are we to become predominantly dependent upon sales to Japan, to the Communist countries and for what sales we can achieve, to the great array of under-developed countries, all of which have desperate balance of payments problems? . . .

The concept of some 300,000,000 people in Europe establishing for the first time in modern history free trading between themselves, with a towering tariff barrier surrounding them to keep the rest of the trading world outside, represents through Australian eyes a picture of the most gigantic obstacle to international trading in world history, and certainly a massive new preference area.

We do not want to be obstructive. We do not want to be dog in the manger; but we do want to be allowed to live and to expand.

Australia is not going to be quietly brushed off by trade policies on the part of industrialized countries which cripple her markets for such an important part of her exports, which strangle her development and which frustrate the plans for our economic growth.

So our fight is a fight for stakes which for us are very, very high. . . .

. . . as I see it, Australia, New Zealand and other exporting countries in and out of the Commonwealth must be assured, at the time that the United Kingdom and other European countries join in a larger Common Market, that we will be permitted to sell adequate and continuing quantities of our traditional items of trade in that area.

By 'adequate quantities', I do not contemplate that the quantity would have to be unlimited in relation to the reasonable needs for protection of member country producers. However, in such a situation I can see no argument against Australia being allowed to enjoy, for the reasonable quantities that we sold, the same prices as those that the Common Market countries considered appropriate for their producers, but not artificially depressed prices.

The world prices of wheat and butter, to take two examples, are set by open market prices in the United Kingdom.

These prices are already artificially depressed by exports from countries which heavily subsidize their production.

Nevertheless, the United Kingdom is the major constant world import market for many of those products.

If the United Kingdom joins a great new economic bloc, that major market could be greatly reduced for outside suppliers, and, for some products, it could even disappear.

The displaced supplies of outside countries would then be in bitter competition for the remaining markets of the world.

Beyond that, this competition would be still further intensified if the agricultural policies of the new, enlarged Common Market tended to thrust added export surpluses on to the remaining markets of the outside world.

I am sure that in this setting we cannot get away from the prospect of surpluses of foodstuffs above the quantities that can be sold commercially.

Here again, it is essential that there should be sanity in the treatment of such surpluses. For as far as we can see ahead, there will continue to be hundreds of millions of ill-fed people in the world.

The use of surpluses so generated must be accepted as a problem that is not confined to those who happen to produce the foodstuffs in surplus supply. It is a problem which demands the co-operation of all countries of goodwill throughout the world which have a capacity to contribute to the cost of making them available—free, or at concessional prices—to those who need them but cannot afford to buy them at a fair and economic price. . . .

Source: C.P.D. (H. of R.), vol. 32,
pp. 259-63.

8:17 EFFECT ON COMMONWEALTH IF UNITED KINGDOM ENTERS EEC

Statement made by the Lord Privy Seal at the meeting with Ministers of Member States of the European Economic Community at Paris on 10 October 1961.

7. In particular, we had to think very deeply about the effect on the Commonwealth of so important a development in United Kingdom policy. I hope you will agree with me that the Commonwealth makes an essential contribution to the strength and stability of the world, and that sound economic foundations and prospects of development go hand in hand with this. We believe that it is in the interests of all of us round this table that nothing should be done which would be likely to damage the essential interests of its Member Countries. Some people in the United Kingdom have been inclined to wonder whether membership of the Community could in fact be reconciled with membership of the Commonwealth. The task of reconciliation is complex, but we are confident that solutions can be found to Commonwealth problems fully compatible with the substance and the spirit of the Treaty of Rome. . . .

The Treaty of Rome

11. Her Majesty's Government are ready to subscribe fully to the aims which you have set yourselves. In particular, we accept without qualification the objectives laid down in Articles 2 and 3 of the Treaty of Rome, including the elimination of internal tariffs, a common customs tariff, a common commercial policy, and a common agricultural policy.

12. We are ready to accept, and to play our full part in, the institutions established under Article 4 and other Articles of the Treaty. . . .

Three major problems

24. I will now turn to the three major problems posed by the particular circumstances of the United Kingdom for which we have to seek solutions together. As you all know, these problems are those of Commonwealth trade, of United Kingdom agriculture, and of the arrangements which could be made for our partners in the European Free Trade Association.

25. I wish to make it clear that we are not seeking a privileged position for the United Kingdom. We fully recognise that the solutions to be worked out must be compatible with, and not disruptive of, the Common Market. . . .

The Commonwealth

26. We believe that you share our view of the value of the Commonwealth, not only to the United Kingdom but also to yourselves and to the whole Free

World . . . I should be misleading you if I failed to say how deeply the British people feel about this association. That, I am sure, is a sentiment which the Members of the Community will fully understand.

27. Commonwealth trade is one of the strongest elements in maintaining the Commonwealth association. It would be a tragedy if our entry into the Community forced other members of the Commonwealth to change their whole pattern of trade and consequently perhaps their political orientation. I do not think that such a development would be in your interests any more than in ours. Nor, looking at it now from the point of view of a potential member of the Community, would any of us wish the Community to be met with the hostility which would flow from a large group of countries strung across the world if they were to feel that their interests had suffered at our hands.

28. The economies of most Commonwealth countries have been built up on the basis of supplying the British market, which has traditionally imported their produce duty free and often on preferential terms. In the last few decades the majority of them have sought to enlarge both the variety of their production and the range of their markets. But the British market is still of great importance to the economies of most Commonwealth countries.

29. I am sure that you will understand that Britain could not join the E.E.C. under conditions in which this trade connection was cut with grave loss and even ruin for some of the Commonwealth countries. For our remaining Dependent Territories we have a special and direct responsibility.

30. The problem of Commonwealth trade has analogies in the problems which faced you when you were negotiating the Treaty of Rome. Your problems concerned a considerable number of countries which were in varying constitutional relationships with Members of the Community. The total volume of trade affected was large. Your problems were dealt with, either in the Treaty or in its accompanying Protocols, without damage to the interests of the countries concerned, and in some cases with considerable advantage to them. It is a striking fact, and very relevant to the Commonwealth problem, that in no case was a tariff imposed on trade where one had not been in force before the Treaty was signed. Broadly speaking, it appears to us that two alternative solutions were applied according to the different circumstances. For some countries—Morocco and Tunisia for example—the problem was solved by maintaining, unimpaired by the Treaty, their right of access to the market of the country with which they were associated. For others, who became Associated Overseas Countries or Territories, not only was their right of access to their metropolitan country preserved, but they gained a preferential position for their products in the Common Market as a whole.

31. We recognise that the problem of Commonwealth trade is more extensive in scale and range than these earlier problems. The differences should not be exaggerated. Thirty-six per cent of our imports come from the Commonwealth; but I think I am correct in saying that over 20 per cent of metropolitan France's imports come from territories having a special relationship with her. Be that as it may, the trade is of very great importance to the Commonwealth countries concerned . . . Of the older Commonwealth countries New Zealand is also heavily dependent on the United Kingdom market, sending 56 per cent of her exports to us. The proportions of their exports which Australia, India, and Ceylon send to the United Kingdom are of the order of 30 per cent. . . .

38. *Materials* should not in general give rise to difficulties, as the common

tariff on most of them is zero. There are, however, a few on which it is substantial. Five of them—aluminium, wood pulp, newsprint, lead and zinc—are of great importance to certain Commonwealth countries; on these five materials we would wish to seek a zero tariff.

39. *Manufactures* are, with a very few exceptions, imported duty-free into the United Kingdom both from the developed countries in the Commonwealth —Canada, Australia and New Zealand—and from the less developed Asian countries. Exporting industries in all these countries have been assisted in their development by free entry and the preferential position they have enjoyed in the United Kingdom. They would be seriously affected, not only by loss of preferences in our market, but also if their position were transformed into one in which the whole of their export trade was affected by reverse preferences in favour of the major industrial countries in Europe. Nevertheless we recognise that indefinite and unlimited continuation of free entry over the whole of this field may not be regarded as compatible with the development of the common market and we are willing to discuss ways of reconciling these two conflicting considerations. I believe that the problem is of manageable proportions. The trade in question is important to the Commonwealth countries concerned but it is not large in total in comparison with European trade.

40. The problem arises in a special form for manufactures from the less-developed countries, the so-called low cost manufactures. It occurs most acutely in relation to Asian Commonwealth countries and the Colony of Hong Kong. There is increasing international recognition that developed countries have a duty to facilitate international trade in their field as much as they can. But what the nature of the solution should be in the context of our joining the E.E.C., must depend on how far it can be dealt with under arrangements for a Part IV Association. You will probably agree that it would not be in the general interest that the United Kingdom should erect fresh tariff barriers to cut back such trade.

41. A major concern of the more fully developed members of the Commonwealth is their trade with us in *temperate foodstuffs*. Australia, New Zealand, and Canada, in particular, have vital interests in their field for which special arrangements must be made.

42. I should like to give you some figures to demonstrate how essential to these countries exports of temperate foodstuffs are. New Zealand's total exports in 1959 were valued at £290 million. Of these £170 million worth, or about 60 per cent, were temperate foodstuffs. £130 million worth, out of a total £170 million, came to the United Kingdom. The bulk of these exports to us consisted of mutton, lamb, butter and cheese. Over 90 per cent of total exports of these commodities came to the United Kingdom. If in the future New Zealand cannot, by one means or another, be assured of comparable outlets for them, her whole economy will be shattered. New Zealand's problem is particularly acute because of her dependence on a relatively limited range of exports. But other Commonwealth commodity problems are the same in kind if not in degree. For example Australia, even though she exports a much more varied range of products, relies on temperate foodstuffs for 35 per cent of her exports. The temperate foodstuffs she sends abroad are valued at £250 million; of these £100 million worth come to the United Kingdom. I hope that these figures will help to illustrate the problem. But figures alone cannot tell the whole story. We must bear in mind the effect of what we do both on particular localities and on individual producers in Commonwealth countries.

43. To many Commonwealth countries the United Kingdom has both moral and contractual obligations, on the basis of which they have planned the development of their economies. I will mention only the Commonwealth Sugar Agreement with which you are all familiar since it is recognised in the International Sugar Agreement. It provides an assured basis for sugar production which is particularly important in the case of our Dependent Territories.

44. The problem therefore is to reconcile our obligations to the Commonwealth with the common agricultural policy as it evolves. We believe that solutions can be found which will prove satisfactory. The Commission's proposals emphasise that trade policy in agricultural products should take into account, not only internal agricultural considerations, but also the need to maintain trade with third countries. This is a liberal approach and one with which we fully agree.

45. I therefore hope that we can reach agreement in principle that full regard should be paid to the interests of the Commonwealth producers concerned, and that they should be given in the future the opportunity of outlets for their produce comparable to those they now enjoy. . . .

Source: The United Kingdom and the
European Economic Community.
Statement reproduced by British
Information Services in Australia, 1961.

8:18 THE UNITED KINGDOM AND THE EEC: AUSTRALIA'S SUGGESTION OF PREFERENTIAL QUOTAS FOR A MINIMUM QUANTITY OF TRADE

Statement by the Minister for Trade (J. McEwen) in the House of Representatives on 3 May 1962.

A very important aspect of my mission in Europe was to form a judgment as to what we should ask for, with hope of success, by way of protection; to decide in what manner the request could best be presented; to see to it that the Governments which had to respond to that request gave their reactions with a full comprehension of the nature of the problems being raised for Australia. Important impressions made on my mind as the result of these most valuable discussions in the capitals of the Six may be briefly summed up in this way. There would be the strongest resistance to securing long-term special arrangements for Australian items, to enter Britain only, on terms different from those under which the same items of trade were being sold in the other Common Market countries . . . So if Britain has no chance of securing continuance beyond a transitional period of our preferences in *her* market alone, and if we cannot have our full preferential opportunity extended to the enlarged Common Market, how then can our trade be protected?

There is one obvious means. That would be an arrangement under which we could sell on preferential terms the same items of trade into the enlarged area but in quantity no greater than the quantity which we sell to Britain. For this situation there would, of course, be no limit to the *quantity* we could sell beyond the quota by meeting the Common External Tariff.

So here is a request which we can make. It is one that ought to be regarded as fair, because it would give us no new advantage but merely preserve our present opportunities. This would be represented by a right to sell on our present preferential terms, a quota into the Common Market—the quantity being equivalent to our recent pattern of trade and with some fair provision for growth.

Such a provision for growth exists now, since our present right of duty free entry is unrestricted as to quantity. . . .

Under this kind of approach our trade would be protected. We would gain no new advantage of preferences. The principles of G.A.T.T. would not be violated. It is clear that Article 234 of the Treaty of Rome contemplates the possibility of some such situation.

That Article says, in effect, that prior obligations to third countries resulting from Conventions—like our Trade Agreement—shall not be affected by the provisions of the Treaty in so far as those obligations are not incompatible with the Treaty. Our existing rights of access to the British market are Britain's obligations to us under our long-standing trade arrangements.

Here is an approach—a principle—which would protect our trade—shaped after my full opportunities to ascertain the views strongly held by the countries which will have the determining decision upon this matter. . . .

In the broadest sense we are concerned with two categories of items which the Common Market itself deals with each in a different manner. These are the items of the common agricultural policy, in abbreviation referred to as the C.A.P. items, and the other category, the list of items whose import into the Common Market would be subject to a common external tariff—the C.E.T. items.

Basically the common agricultural policy items with which we are concerned are those major items of foodstuffs which are produced in bulk quantity within the Common Market area—wheat, barley, butter, meat, sugar, apples and pears, wine, etc.

In regard to these items it is the intention of the Common Market that the producers of the Common Market countries shall receive a price to be agreed between the countries. After a transitional period, the level of prices shall be uniform as between the countries. The producers are assured of receiving these prices because the Common Market Commission will see that the market operates to ensure them.

This policy clearly requires that to protect this objective internal price, imports shall not be permitted to under-sell the local product. So the intention broadly is that an import levy or customs duty shall be imposed which will bring the landed cost of imported wheat or sugar, etc., to a level at which the local product cannot be under-sold.

For us this would mean that if Britain were a member, her producers would not have their returns made up by subsidies, but would receive the higher internal price. And Britain would have to accept these items without restriction when offered for sale from within the Common Market countries. Our wheat, taking wheat as the example, would no longer have duty free entry but would have to pay the levy prescribed at the time. To effectively protect the European producer the levy would have to be high enough to accord protection against the cheapest wheat offering.

Therefore the measure of the levy imposed on our wheat would not, in effect, be determined by the British Government for instance, or by the Common Market countries as a whole. The levy on our wheat could be determined by some other country, perhaps a Communist country, offering wheat at a lower price and attracting, as we now see it, a high levy on all wheat imports.

This, of course, produces a most dramatic change in our circumstances.

We believe that there is likelihood that the Common Market price for internal wheat will prove an incentive to increased production. So we fear a diminished market attracting fierce competition from outside Europe. The more a seller cuts his prices to achieve a sale, the higher would be the levy on him and everyone else. Such wheat sold more cheaply would be of no benefit to British or other European consumers. European Treasuries would gain by collecting the levy in the first place, but in the second place the regulations under the Treaty of Rome contemplate that revenues so collected would be used to aid European agricultural production and, if necessary, provide funds to subsidise exports.

So taxes collected on our own wheat would, under this situation, finally be spent to subsidise competition against us in third markets.

Against this situation, and these contingencies, what should we ask the British to request as special protection for our trade?

Our Trade Treaty with the United Kingdom provides us with the right to have a market there for 750,000 tons of wheat a year at commercial prices. The purpose is to give us price security against competition from subsidised wheat.

This establishes the quantity we may state as our legitimate expectation in the United Kingdom market.

On price I see no reason in logic why British consumers should not pay as much to our growers for our wheat, allowing for quality differentials, as they pay, for example, for French wheat.

On the other hand, I see no reason why, in this artificially diminished market for non-European wheat, we should be forced into acceptance of very low prices through fierce competition. This would be very important as there is a history of the price realized for wheat in Britain being taken as the price guide by importers everywhere else in the world. . . .

Very full and frank discussions in London, taking wheat as a pattern common agricultural policy item, confirm that the interests of Australia and Britain are different, in this situation.

They face their consumers having to pay higher prices for home-produced food, and higher prices for European imports, but they do not want the burden of higher prices for food and raw materials bought from outside the Area. On the other hand many of our exports are not sold at profitable prices and there is our serious balance of payments problem. Therefore we need higher prices.

This situation will show quite clearly why Australia wants satisfactory world arrangements for the bulk commodities.

I have to say that we did not succeed in resolving these differences, but the British became increasingly aware of the strength of our arguments and the firmness of our views that our trade in wheat and the other common agricultural policy items should be sufficiently protected. . . .

The items of our trade with Britain which would be subject to the common external tariff are valued at about £A80 million a year. In respect of this group I was able to reach agreement with British Ministers as to the best method of having our problems considered.

In the first place this would be to seek to have these items considered in four separate groups. The first group would comprise agricultural products, not subject to the common agricultural policy, including the processed foodstuffs; the next group raw materials, including the metals; the third group ordinary industrial factory products or hard manufactures; and the fourth group tropical products.

To the extent that our preferences in Britain operate at present against the products of countries of the Common Market, it is quite clear—I have to say this—that there would be no hope of securing approval of the Common Market countries for the perpetuation of the preferences for *our* products against theirs.

We must strive to preserve the measure of preference which we have against suppliers from outside the Common Market area. This will be of major importance in cases such as canned fruits and meats.

In other cases we must strive to preserve the right of duty-free entry, or aim to achieve the lowest possible common external tariff duties—with the retention of the existing preference margins—against non-member countries—on a given quantity of exports. In effect, we are asking for tariff preference quotas, which will provide Australian exporters with comparable outlets to those currently enjoyed in the British market. In the case of metals, including lead, zinc, alumina, aluminium and cadmium, we have supported Britain's request for a nil rate of duty in the common external tariff. . . .

What we have done is to take the common external tariff products in the four categories and in most cases to request that special arrangements be approved for us to continue to export either to Britain or to the whole Common Market area, on our present preference terms into Britain, a *quantity* representing our present pattern of trade, with a growth factor. This obviously is, and should be recognized as reasonable, and in conformity with our contractual rights with Britain, and with the provisions of the Rome Treaty, and G.A.T.T. . . .

Source: *C.P.D.* (*H. of R.*), vol. 35,
pp. 1969-73.

8:19 AUSTRALIA WOULD GAIN FROM BRITISH ENTRY INTO EEC

Speech by L. H. E. Bury, M.P., at luncheon of the American Chamber of Commerce in Sydney on 8 October 1962.

Australia is likely to gain rather than lose by new developments involving British entry to the Common Market. British entry, coupled with the mutual scaling down of barriers between the Common Market and the United States, should benefit Australia, if all went reasonably well. . . .

One can always point directly to certain items of trade which, instead of enjoying a preferred position in a limited market, may suffer a competitive disadvantage in a larger market. . . .

On any reasonable balance of probabilities Australia will gain much more from higher levels of prosperity in Europe and on expansion in international trade than we should lose by Britain modifying current market arrangements for a limited range of our products.

In matters of trade the Common Market has already bargained from a position of great strength. Outside this new complex the political and economic significance of Britain would shrink even further, even *vis-à-vis* Europe, let alone in the world at large.

However valuable the Commonwealth association may be in other respects, it could not possibly provide for its members the foundations either of their security or trade.

We should be extremely foolish not to recognise this fact or to keep talking about the Commonwealth in terms that suggested that economic relations between its members posed any real economic alternative to the Common Market, either for Britain or Australia. . . .

The post-war drive to reduce trade barriers and restrictions and to expand international trade was originally a strong reaction from the disastrous events of the inter-war period which carried us all into World War II. . . .

Recent events promise to carry the broad process much further and we ought to look at the European Common Market from this angle. The six nations comprising it have all joined in the general international process of liberalisation, but have also been working in even closer association among themselves.

Whether the Six turn inward or outward is the prime economic issue now confronting the world. But the very drive and momentum which has already scaled down so many barriers between the countries themselves has been of an enlightened liberal character. . . .

Source: *Australian Financial Review*,
9 October 1962, p. 3.

8:20 EEC NEGOTIATIONS

*Statement by the Minister for Trade (J. McEwen) in the House
of Representatives on 6 December 1962.*

The purpose of my statement today is to inform the House . . . of the present position in Britain's negotiations for possible accession to the European Economic Community. These negotiations, which had been adjourned on 5th August, were resumed in October following the meeting of Commonwealth Prime Ministers. . . .

At that time—to summarize the position—very few items of interest to Australia had been negotiated by Britain with The Six, though they had of course been extensively discussed between Australia and Britain. It had been provisionally agreed between Britain and the European Economic Community that Commonwealth preferences on 'hard' manufactures would be phased out and disappear by 1970. Imports of these products from Australia into Britain would then be dutiable at the rates laid down in the common external tariff.

Certain broad understandings had been reached about international trade in temperate foodstuffs. First, Britain and The Six, at the time of Britain's accession, would declare their intention to call as soon as possible an international conference to endeavour to negotiate world-wide agreements for wheat and other grains, meat and dairy products, and sugar. Secondly, there would be a declaration by the enlarged community expressing its intention to pursue in respect of its own agricultural production 'a reasonable' price policy. This policy, to use the Community's words, 'would offer reasonable opportunities in its markets for exports of temperate agricultural products.' Since the resumption of the negotiations, discussions have continued on the whole range of issues involved. Little progress has been made. It now seems that the negotiations will continue for at least some time in 1963.

There are, of course, other major questions to be settled besides the complex of trade issues affecting various members of the Commonwealth. There is the question of the adaptation of the British system of agricultural protection, based on a policy of cheap food imports and deficiency payments to its producers, to the Continental system. The Continental system, as it has been applied in individual members of the European Economic Community and as it will be applied under the Community's common agricultural policy, would make subsidies to the United Kingdom domestic producers no longer necessary or permissible because duties and levies would be used in place of subsidies to raise internal market prices to levels high enough to be considered profitable to producers in the enlarged Common Market.

This change in Britain from low prices plus subsidies to high prices protected by tariffs and variable levies would be the most fundamental change in British trade policy since her abolition of the Corn Laws more than 100 years ago.

To cushion this change, Britain has proposed to The Six that deficiency payments to farmers in Britain should be phased out during a transition period of several years . . . If this were not so, a sudden increase in the price of many basic commodities would be inevitable. . . .

The Six have made the counter-proposal that Britain should abandon its present support system and adopt theirs immediately upon entry into an enlarged Common Market. The Six are concerned to see that British farmers are not placed in a more favourable position than those in the European Economic Community countries and that the British economy does not get the benefit of having lower food prices than other members of the community. The Six suggested that temporary consumer subsidies be introduced in Britain to off-set the abrupt effect of higher market and hence higher consumer prices. They have not indicated how these subsidies would operate. Britain . . . has informed The Six that the proposal for consumer subsidies is not acceptable.

. . . the negotiations about safeguards for the treatment of Commonwealth trade in temperate foodstuffs have to take into account the stage reached by the community in the development of its own agricultural policy.

The community has within the past several months brought into effect regulations dealing with trade in cereals, eggs, poultry, pigmeats, wine and fruit and vegetables. These regulations have turned out to be no better from our point of view than I had anticipated. They clearly represent a giant stride towards a completely regulated market, insulated from reasonable competition from efficient and economic traditional exporters. The community has, however, still to settle the regulations that will govern trade in such important products as beef and veal, dairy products and sugar. The prospects in regard to these regulations seem no better at this stage than I have indicated in the past.

It seems that the sugar regulations may not be completed before Britain makes her decision whether or not to join the community. This, of course, is a matter of particular concern to us. However . . . Britain has agreed that the Commonwealth Sugar Agreement should be extended for a further year—that is, up to the end of 1970 . . . I would also mention that Britain in its negotiations is adhering to the position that the Commonwealth Sugar Agreement should be continued, if Britain joins the community, or be replaced by an arrangement giving equivalent benefits to sugar producers in the Commonwealth. . . .

. . . the community has offered associate status to British dependencies and to the independent Commonwealth countries in Africa and the Caribbean. Nigeria, Ghana and Tanganyika have notified Britain that they have no wish to accept this offer. Britain is therefore discussing the position of alternative arrangements for these countries. Britain has proposed, and The Six have agreed, that there could be trade agreements between those Commonwealth countries and the community. The possible form and substance of such agreements, and hence the degree of safeguard they would provide for the trade interests of the countries concerned, has not apparently been discussed. The European Economic Community has also agreed to leave open to these countries the opportunity to apply for association should they opt for it later on, and have agreed to a zero tariff on tropical hardwood timber, which is a major export item from Ghana and Nigeria.

In the context of such arrangements being made for other producers in the Commonwealth of tropical products, this Government is continuing to watch the interests of Papua-New Guinea. We are concerned that means should be found that would enable this Territory to market its exports on fair terms as compared with like exports from British dependencies that may gain associated status. Arrangements for India, Pakistan and Ceylon have also been under further discussion.

The Six had previously offered to negotiate comprehensive trade agreements with these three countries by 1966 at the latest. In the meantime, transitional arrangements were envisaged that would involve the phasing out of preferences in the British market on products produced by these Commonwealth countries. This means that they would face a worsening of their terms of entry to Britain ahead of the completion of negotiations for the comprehensive trade agreements. . . .

Britain has asked that the progressive application of the common external tariff to the trade of India, Pakistan and Ceylon should be suspended until the promised trade agreements are concluded. This request has been refused by the European Economic Community. It has, however, been agreed that negotiations for the trade agreements would begin within three months of Britain's accession to the community.

With regard to the problems affecting Canada, Australia and New Zealand, the provisional agreement regarding what are called 'hard' manufactures . . . still remains the only one which has been completed. This is the only sector of our trade where we have had clearly presented to us the situation we shall face after the end of the transitional period. That means in 1970—no preferences.

. . . all we have at present in regard to our major bulk foodstuff items is a possible framework within which solutions may or may not be found after the whole of our preferences have gone. . . .

Before the Prime Ministers' Conference, the European Economic Community had agreed that transitional arrangements would apply to the trade of Commonwealth countries in commodities for which there is a levy system under the common agricultural policy on those cereals on which there is a preference in the British market—on barley there is 10 per cent., on oats there is £3 a ton, but there is no preference on wheat—the Commonwealth countries would benefit until the end of 1969 from a diminishing proportion of the preference that the members of the enlarged community would extend to one another. This diminishing preference . . . during the transition period would not be as valuable or effective as our existing preferences. Our present form of preference would be lost to us as soon as Britain joined the European Economic Community.

As far as wheat is concerned, all that The Six have offered by way of transitional arrangements is the general assurance that they would review, in consultation with countries of the Commonwealth, the application of the intra-community preference if that preference caused a sudden and considerable

311

alteration of trade patterns in the British market. This assurance is expected to apply to all products for which the community would use a system of import levies. The community has not been prepared to give any undertaking as to what, if anything, it might do by way of remedial action in such circumstances.

It has not yet emerged from the negotiations what The Six may be prepared to do even by way of transitional arrangements, other than the general assurance I have just mentioned, for such important commodities as beef, veal, mutton and lamb and dairy products. . . .

If The Six apply variable levies on these products, as has been proposed in the case of beef, veal and butter, our preferences, on the current proposals, would enjoy a temporary preference of a different type for a limited period only.

. . . Apart from wool, New Zealand's export income depends almost entirely upon these products. The Six have recognized that New Zealand has a special problem but have not agreed to any solution.

. . . There is . . . the prospect that The Six may agree to arrangements for New Zealand products that would not apply to products from Australia. We have made it clear to Great Britain that we would expect that there would be no discriminatory treatment as between Australia and New Zealand. . . .

Up to the time of the Prime Ministers' Conference, there had been no discussion at ministerial level . . . about what arrangements might be made in respect of processed foodstuffs of interest to Australia and Canada and New Zealand.

In our case, this category of items embraces such important commodities as canned and dried fruit. Only recently have the Ministers in Brussels got to grips with this sector of the negotiations. The Six have opposed the proposition of tariff preference quotas which was put forward by Britain in line with our own ideas of what would represent a reasonable solution consistent, as we saw it, with both the General Agreement on Tariffs and Trade and the Rome Treaty.

Their opposition would appear to be based not on any legal grounds but merely on doctrinal dislike of preferences. Their proposition is that all our preferences should be phased out during the transitional period. Again, I refer sourly and wryly to preferences against all the rest of the world outside the European Economic Community, whether as it is or enlarged including associate members. They are disposed to abolish or suspend the common external tariff— we are grateful to hear—on kangaroo meat, rabbits and fish liver oils. This has been their response to Britain's request for safeguards for our important interests in the category of foodstuff items subject to the common external tariff. . . .

In arguing for the continuance of preferences we are opposed not only by The Six but also by the United States. It has its doctrinal objection to preferences —well, to our preferences, anyway. It has also its own trade interests in products like canned and dried fruit . . . we have been able to enlist strong American support for action with The Six which would limit the degree of protection afforded in the Common Market to the production of certain items of critical importance to us and of importance also to the United States. These items embrace the major bulk foodstuffs, the major processed foodstuffs and certain raw materials.

The United States is now willing to put its negotiating strength behind getting worthwhile reductions in the common external tariff on a number of commodities of concern to us. . . .

Another important part of the negotiations concerns the treatment of certain raw materials of interest to Commonwealth countries for which duties are at present provided in the common external tariff. Items of interest to Australia . . .

are lead and zinc metal and aluminium. There is on this matter still an impasse in Brussels. The British requested zero tariffs. The Six opposed this. It cannot be said at present how this impasse may be resolved. But here again, American willingness to enter into negotiations for reductions in the common external tariff may prove of inestimable value. . . .

At the time of the Prime Ministers' Conference there was no evidence that adequate assurances would be obtained for our trade interests. That is still the position. Of course, it will be for the British Government to weigh up the outcome of its negotiations. It rests solely with the British Government to decide whether it has carried out the assurances which it gave to us and others before it began its negotiations and which . . . that Government has repeatedly confirmed . . . We, for our part, have looked for arrangements that would clearly and definitely protect our trade—and not just for a transitional period.

I have mentioned broad understandings about trade in temperate foodstuffs. We do not think that Britain should rest her judgment on what constitutes adequate safeguards for our interest on the basis of general assurances only . . . It is the view of the Australian Government that we are entitled to expect of Britain, and of The Six, that they will demonstrate a willingness to begin to translate their statements of good intent into practical terms before Britain joins the Common Market.

They will have ample opportunities to do this. I mention three that are in the offing. There will be—on the initiative of the United States and Canada—a ministerial meeting of the General Agreement on Tariffs and Trade early next year. That meeting, it is proposed, will pave the way for a further round of tariff negotiations following the recent passage of the United States Trade Expansion Act. It will also consider the equally important questions of how to improve international trading arrangements for primary products . . . and how to ensure better access to international markets for the products of less-developed countries.

Then, there is the G.A.T.T. cereals group. Starting from a French initiative about a year ago, this seemed to offer prospects of getting to grips with the whole complex of problems affecting international trade in wheat. These problems have been thrown into much sharper focus and made more urgent by the common agricultural policy of The Six and Britain's prospective membership of the Common Market. Indeed, many of the problems would be the direct outcome of the formation of an enlarged Common Market responsible for the greater part of existing world trade in many items of concern to agricultural and raw material producing countries. But when this cereals group met last February it was the attitude of Britain that was the factor, more than any other, that frustrated progress. . . .

I believe that progress is possible if Britain will join in further discussions in a constructive and realistic manner. The crux of the problem is simple. It calls for a willingness on the part of Britain and The Six to give to external producers what they have promised to their own domestic producers, that is, remunerative and more stable prices. . . .

Source: *C.P.D.* (*H. of R.*), vol. 37,
pp. 3038-44.

8:21 DE GAULLE ANNOUNCES TERMS FOR UNITED KINGDOM'S ENTRY INTO EEC

PARIS, JANUARY 15

President de Gaulle last night brusquely denied Britain's entry into the Common Market—unless Britain is prepared to jettison all major reservations she has had so far about terms of membership.[1]

[At a Press Conference on 14th January] General de Gaulle asked whether Britain was ready to accept these four conditions for entry into the Common Market:

1. Is Britain prepared to place herself inside 'a genuinely Continental tariff system?'
2. Is she prepared to renounce the system of Commonwealth tariffs at present in force?
3. Is she prepared to renounce her present arrangements with the sterling exchange area and the Outer Seven (European free trade area) nations?
4. Is she prepared to renounce her request for special terms on behalf of British agriculture?

'If she is prepared to do all this, then perhaps she can join. But it is up to Britain and only she can answer', General de Gaulle said. . . .

It would be a different Common Market if Britain were to join. Following Britain we might get a Common Market of as many as 18 nations.

A Europe of seven, or 11 or even 18 countries would no longer resemble the Common Market as conceived by France.

General de Gaulle then revealed another doubt dominating his present thinking. It is that, if Britain did get in, it would lead to a position where the United States could move in with an irresistible take-over bid.

An enlarged Common Market would in the end amount to 'a colossal Atlantic community dependent upon and controlled by the United States' which would tend to absorb the European Community, he said. . . .

For us, agriculture was important [General de Gaulle said.] It was evident that France must have outlets for her agricultural production, and it was absolutely essential to us that agriculture should be properly dealt with by the Common Market.

In January last year we at last got agriculture into the Common Market, but this needed very complex and detailed negotiations.

On top of all that Britain came forward with her candidature. . . .

. . . she exerts actively a commercial and industrial influence, but not an agricultural one.

She has other views, other loyalties, she has original and individual traditions.

Britain buys cheaply in the two Americas and the Dominions. But that is incompatible with the system now set up by the Six of Europe, which have rigorously fixed prices and forbidden price-support and subsidies. . . .

All Britain's interests differ profoundly from those of the Continental nations. How then, to incorporate?

[1] The talks collapsed in Brussels at a meeting of delegates to the negotiations on 29 January 1963. Mr Macmillan acknowledged defeat in a statement to the House of Commons on 11 February 1963. (See British Information Services series 'Background to Britain', 14 February 1963.)

Any pledge to uphold Britain's present agricultural system was clearly incompatible with the agricultural problems of Common Market countries.

The whole point of the Common Market, where agriculture was concerned, was to eat some of the agricultural products of other nations as well as your own. . . .

If Britain could agree to join the Common Market on a purely European basis, giving up all her reservations and her requests for special terms, then the door was still open.

Source: The *Sydney Morning Herald*, 16 January 1963.

8:22 AUSTRALIA'S REACTIONS TO BREAKDOWN OF UNITED KINGDOM'S EEC NEGOTIATIONS

Statement by the Prime Minister (R. G. Menzies) on 5 February 1963.

The Prime Minister, Mr. R. G. Menzies, said on February 5 that the Australian Government had that day considered the latest dramatic developments in relation to the United Kingdom's application to join the EEC. It had throughout the long negotiations presented its interests and views in a constructive and co-operative way, based on two major propositions. The first was that the ultimate decision to join or not would be made by the United Kingdom, since Australia was not a direct party either to the application or the negotiations. The second was that Australia wished to see the United Kingdom secure terms which recognised the continuing importance of protecting long-established and vital trading interests. Those interests and Australia's anxiety to protect them remained.

At the same time, his Government had a sincere feeling of sympathy for the United Kingdom Government in the manner in which the negotiations had been terminated, Mr. Menzies said. It had come as a shock that one of the negotiating parties, France, should have terminated them for published reasons which, had they been stated originally, would probably have rendered the whole process of negotiation unnecessary. The United Kingdom Government would need to sort out the present position. It might take some weeks to discover the effect of France's action on the other members of the EEC and on the policies of the United Kingdom. . . .

Source: *Australia in Facts and Figures*, no. 77, p. 29.

C

BILATERAL TRADE POLICIES

OTTAWA REVIEWED

The war-time and post-war intergovernmental contracts between Australia and the United Kingdom are clearly bilateral in character. In this part, however, our primary interest is in trade treaties and more especially those with the United Kingdom (A9:1) and with Japan (A10:1). These two agreements are given separate treatment, as each is of special significance in the development of Australian trade policy. Although not covered in a formal bilateral treaty, trade relations with the United States also warrant separate treatment. For the rest there is a small miscellany of documents indicating a range of other bilateral treaties and agreements entered into by Australia with other countries, none ranking in importance with the three major countries named.

The decision to renegotiate the Ottawa Agreement of 1932 with the United Kingdom was a 'key' decision.[1] The new agreement represents the first major review of the Ottawa Agreement—a 'replacement' agreement in fact, as foreshadowed by the Prime Minister in May 1956 (9:6). It was negotiated within constraints imposed by the GATT no-new-preference rule and necessarily implied retreat from the political concept of an integrated Empire held dear by many in the thirties and earlier. It brought to light many of Australia's trading difficulties in the fifties and a number of Britain's. Revision promised Australia considerable room for 'manoeuvre', a promise as yet far from fully realised.

The motives for seeking a renegotiation and the results emerge clearly enough in the documents here presented. What is not so clear is the course of the negotiations, of which it can be said that they were sticky and even rugged at times! As McEwen admitted, with unusual understatement (9:14), 'the negotiations were not simple'. As he observed in a speech not included here, 'The United Kingdom had not been prepared for such far-reaching revision of Ottawa as we require and propose'.[2] Much of the detail of the argument and counter-argument is still classified material and must await the interested student and agreement on the part of government to allow the full

[1] Some aspects of this topic are treated in Section 7, Commodity Policy.
[2] Press statement made on 26 August 1956.

story to be told.[3] Also not fully clear from the documents is the use Australia made of the new agreement, partly because there have been disappointing frustrations in attempts to negotiate with other countries but partly, also, because some potential opportunity to use our greater freedom to cut tariffs, as in the Kennedy Round, has not yet been fully tested.

The opening document, the Memorandum of Conclusions (9:1), is included merely to remind the reader of two things. First, there had been a pre-war attempt to review the Ottawa Agreement, which cleared the air somewhat but left the terms of the Agreement unchanged. It did succeed in gaining recognition—reluctantly conceded—by the United Kingdom that Australia must industrialise. The second point is that Menzies clearly saw the dilemma of Empire trade: Australia could not afford (nor could Britain) to ignore the fact that many of its products—not least wool—required markets outside the Empire. Paragraph 4 of the Memorandum states this clearly for both countries.

A third point about the document to be noted in passing is the dissatisfaction with the Ottawa Agreement voiced by British manufacturers about the operation of the Australian Tariff Board which then, as now, gives the benefit of an additional margin to Australian manufacturers in assessing costs *vis-à-vis* the United Kingdom. Document 9:2 conveys the notion that the Agreement made no real difference to Board policy. What is of real interest is that Tariff Board thinking and investigations always had been, and continued to be even in 1952, almost exclusively related to British industry. Most-favoured-nation rates were more or less accidental and mostly liberal additions to the British Preferential Tariff rates. When Ottawa came up for thorough review in 1956 it was found that on a great many commodities the margin of preference extended by Australia on British goods considerably exceeded the contractual margin obligatory under the Ottawa Agreement.[4]

In reading the documents which relate to the renegotiations of Ottawa in 1956 it is well to remember that Britain was a declining rather than a growing market for Australian produce and Australia needed to develop markets elsewhere (A9:2). The Prime Ministers' Conference of 1952 (4:8) had

---

[3] The story is an important chapter in Australian economic history and it will be unfortunate indeed if a long period of years elapses before access is given to the scholar. The documentation is good and no one's reputation is dependent upon continued secrecy.

[4] Margin of preference = MFN rate minus BPT rate. See Section 15 for a fuller treatment of the tariff question raised here: also Vernon Report (11), vol. I, chs. 13 and 14, and vol. II, app. L. (It does not follow that 'liberal' additions to BPT rates for the purpose of determining the MFN rates always overstate the amount of protection required against MFN suppliers. In some cases costs in MFN countries would be low relative to British costs and call for a relatively high rate in the Australian tariff. Any attempt to convert the tariff into a single rate tariff would be vexed by the fact that costs do vary widely among all supplying countries—and not merely between Britain and MFN countries, often wrongly lumped together as a homogeneous group.)

made it clear that adding to the mutual preferential structure was not an acceptable course to the Commonwealth as a whole. Moreover, at its Review Session in 1954-5 GATT rejected the Australian attempt to gain even marginal room to manoeuvre in preferences (Section 5). In the difficult economic conditions of 1956 the Australian government naturally needed to pursue every line of export development open to it. To the government there had seemed, even before this year, room for an improved position in the British markets for Australian goods despite the constraints just noted, and this had been informally taken up in London in 1954, as mentioned in 9:10. In addition the government saw the need to open trade negotiations with other countries and to take cost-reducing actions such as elimination of preferential tariff margins on goods required by Australian industry but not made in Australia. On these two counts, from the point of view of Australia's interests, the Ottawa Agreement appeared restrictive and unbalanced.

To help fill out the argument of the documents (especially 9:9 to 9:12) we have prepared a document of statistical data of the kind used by me in the negotiations to demonstrate imbalance in the Agreement (A9:2). The officials concerned were well briefed, for the decision to seek 'a new and comprehensive agreement to replace Ottawa' (9:6) was not lightly taken by the Australian government, although as noted above the firmness of the decision appeared to surprise the British government.

The data in the first part of A9:2 served to illustrate a growing imbalance: British exports to Australia were expanding much faster than Australian exports to the United Kingdom. Imbalance shown in this way is a little misleading since it omits helpful capital outflow from Britain[5] and would seem to overemphasise the bilateral balance of trade in a situation in which only trends in *total* exports and *total* imports finally matter. Nevertheless, the statistical trend reflected the underlying fact of importance to Australia: a restricted and, indeed, in volume terms, declining market in the United Kingdom for Australian goods.[6] For most products affected other than wool there were not at that time obvious or certain alternative outlets. The trade trends showed the expansive influence on British exports of the rapid population increase and industrialisation in Australia since the war. There could be no objection to the growth of British exports. However, Australia could not indefinitely finance growth of this kind without opening up additional markets for exports: if Britain could not supply these Australia had to turn elsewhere, even if this meant cutting into the liberal preferential position enjoyed by Britain.

[5] By the same token, other 'invisibles'—freight, insurance, tourism, operated then as now heavily in Britain's favour.

[6] This has been pointed out clearly enough by many observers not least in the Tenth Report of the Rural Reconstruction Commission (12), p. 70.

The second part of A9:2 shows something of the rather lopsided balance of preferential concessions as they had developed under the Ottawa Agreement. It indicates conclusively enough that Ottawa was no longer a mutually balancing agreement. It was the task of the Australian ministers to hold this position despite arguments that the Meat Contract and the Commonwealth Sugar Agreements and free entry for most Australian products were advantages not shown in this statistical picture. These arguments were countered by referring to the uncontested fact that free entry (and margins of preference) on many products was vitiated by a heavy and growing incidence of agricultural protection by means of the United Kingdom government's use of non-tariff devices. The meat and sugar compacts stood on their own as mutually balancing and independently regulated agreements.

As already noted, the first objective of the negotiations was to improve access to the United Kingdom market for some products, of which wheat was the chief. As 9:8 to 9:10 show, this was a major difficulty in the negotiations. Not only had total imports into Britain fallen from 1938 to 1956, but Australia's share had fallen. The first fact was due to heavy subsidies given the British farmer (as well as improved farming); the second was due to the impact of subsidised United States and, in the mid-fifties, subsidised French wheat. For the rest the other documents tell the story of United Kingdom reluctance to give the desired assurances. First was the unwillingness to offer the direct affront to France and America (and to her own cheap food policy) involved in imposing countervailing duties against subsidised imported wheat. Second, the government was reluctant to step into wheat purchasing by British millers to ensure that they purchase a guaranteed quantity of Australian wheat 'at commercial prices', especially in years of large domestic crops. The Australian case was not against protection to British agriculture (9:1 still stood) but against the non-tariff device used which virtually assured the home producer against competition at all.[7] Regardless of what millers paid British farmers, the taxpayer, at that time, assured them 30s stg per cwt (*ex farm*) or about 20s Australian per bushel. This compared with the 1956 guarantee to Australian farmers of 13s 1d Australian f.o.r. per bushel, equivalent to an *ex farm* price of about 10s 3d Australian. Even this high protection was not open to attack provided it was not operated to debar efforts to compete. The Australian case was twofold: under the system of protection used, competition was impracticable: virtually no imported wheat was allowed in beyond that amount which ensured that all usable domestic wheat was used; and in competing with other suppliers in a restricted import market Australia was at an 'unfair' disadvantage against subsidies by both France and the United States.

---

[7] In even sharper terms this has become the exporters' concern with the methods used in the Common Agricultural Policy of the EEC to protect European producers (see Section 8).

The outcome on wheat was something better than 'best endeavours' but not a cast-iron guarantee of the 750,000 tons (when offered by the Australian Wheat Board) specified in the difficult terms of the Agreement (A9:1, Article 6). It is not the concern of this comment to trace the difficulties or shortcomings in the operation of the Article: it is worth perhaps expressing the view that the net gain to Australia has been substantial assurance of access to the United Kingdom market but less than originally sought and less than the Article appears to concede. A great deal of the sting has been taken out of the failure to achieve regularly the target of 750,000 tons wheat 'equivalent' by the dramatic emergence in the sixties of China as a much larger market. It cannot be said, however, that the British market is unimportant, especially as many Australians would prefer to avoid 'dependence' on China.

The second objective of the negotiations was to prune the unjustified and inflationary impact on the Australian cost structure of over-generous preferences extended by Australia. Substantial but not complete success attended these efforts, although complete advantage of the new treaty has yet to be taken. It is to be remembered that the old treaty allowed preferential margins for British products on the great majority of Australian imports of 12½, 15, and 17½ per cent and, in some cases, higher again.

In fact, as already noted, many preferences exceeded these contractual margins, so that Australia already had some room within the existing treaty for cutting MFN rates if it wished. But it had little room where it mattered most—on producer goods needed by Australian industry and especially those not made in Australia. The obligatory margin of preference on a list of producer goods was reduced to 7½ per cent and advantage was quickly taken of this in respect of some eight hundred items (9:16). The other change was to speed up the process for by-law determinations under which, if goods in the opinion of the Australian government were not available from Britain, the duty on non-British goods could be waived altogether (A9:1, Article 8). This change has proved of considerable benefit.[8]

The third objective was to secure more room to negotiate with other countries. This was achieved by reducing the obligatory preference margins from the 12½, 15, and 17½ per cent noted above to 7½ or 10 per cent (A9:1, Article 7).[9] This has given room but, except where it has been applied in a few subsequent Tariff Board decisions, no use has yet been made of it in international tariff negotiations let alone to effect unilateral reductions in MFN rates. This almost certainly means that Australia continues to levy

[8] On the more technical aspects of this matter see Vernon Report (11), vol. I, ch. 14, and vol. II, app. L, paras. 11-14.

[9] As noted above the 7½ per cent margin applied to a scheduled list of producer goods; 10 per cent applied to all other items enjoying preference and on which MFN rates were expressed in *ad valorem* terms.

MFN rates at over-liberal levels in many cases,[10] awaiting the opportunity to negotiate concessions with other countries. Bilaterally the opportunity has not occurred, but the Kennedy Round could be a major occasion for mutual tariff (and non-tariff) concessions between Australia and members of GATT.[11] Until this occurs, Australia's third objective in negotiating the new treaty remains frustrated. Should the Kennedy Round fail, it would still be open to Australia to offer concessions to the United States, Japan, and other trading partners in specially negotiated bilateral trade treaties. Should the United Kingdom join the EEC the incentive to negotiate these preferences would be even stronger.[12]

It will be noted that the new agreement (A9:1, Article 9) continues the assurance to British suppliers that the Tariff Board will continue the 'principle' of tariff making assured in Articles 9-13 of the original agreement.[13] The emergence since 1956 of Japan and other suppliers with lower costs than traditional suppliers (Britain included) has made it more and more necessary that the Board also pay heed to cost conditions in MFN countries.[14]

It is important to note that the new agreement reaffirmed the principle of mutual preferential aid. It sought to reduce lopsidedness in this respect, but until Australia makes more use of the adjustments it secured, the United Kingdom continues to enjoy a very considerable advantage in the shape of wider margins of preference than Australia is obliged to give. This requires stress for, despite this advantage, the United Kingdom has continued to lose ground in the Australian market—largely to Japan, Germany, and the United States.[15] It enjoys less help in respect of producer goods than it did before 1957 but in other respects its problems in Australia seem to be part of its general problem of being competitive in world markets.

[10] See Section 15; Vernon Report (11), vol. I, chs. 13 and 14 and vol. II, app. L.

[11] The Tariff Board has twice reported to the government its views on the room that actually exists for cutting MFN tariffs (and hence margins of preference (see 9:17, 5:13). These reports have not been made public.

[12] Nor should it be thought that Japan and the United States would be uninterested on the grounds that we would abolish preferences now enjoyed by Britain once we lost our preferences in the United Kingdom market, for the method of abolishing preferences would be of great importance to all trading partners. We could abolish by raising BPT rates to MFN rates, which course would probably be less helpful to the United States and Japan than if we reduced MFN rates to the lower BPT rates. In fact, a single-tier tariff would almost certainly comprise some reductions in MFN rates and some increase in BPT rates.

[13] See Section 15 and Vernon Report (11), vol. I, ch. 14, para. 8 and vol. II, app. K, para. 195 and app. L, para. 182.

[14] The term is regular shorthand for those suppliers to the Australian market whose goods are subjected to the MFN tariff rates. The need to examine their costs more directly in some commodity fields is not inconsistent with the view that in several instances MFN tariffs are higher than needed to protect Australian industry.

[15] See Vernon Report (11), vol. II, app. K.

Australia has recovered somewhat in wheat but has lost further ground in the United Kingdom in respect of total exports. This is partly because of more profitable opportunities elsewhere (e.g. United States for meat) but on the whole continues to reflect the rather static condition of the market in Britain for the type of goods Australia produces for export.

The further review of this treaty, provided for in Article 15, has been postponed pending the outcome of the Kennedy talks (Section 5).[16] The significance of the postponement is not merely that Australia may yet be able to use its greater freedom to cut preferential margins but rather that negotiations on agricultural products as part of the Kennedy Round may call for a review of the present methods of assuring Australia rights of entry to the British market. Negotiation of new types of cereal and meat understandings on an international scale may require adjustment in the present terms of our agreements with the United Kingdom. In 1963 the Kennedy Round was the clear and adequate reason for postponing review of the treaty. In 1966 the outcome of the Round is uncertain. At the same time prospects for British entry into the EEC have so improved that renewed negotiations to this end might well bring the treaty to an end for all practical purposes, leaving Australia somewhat lamenting, no doubt, but free to secure what negotiating advantage it could from its opportunity to abolish the preferential tariff system.

A9:1 TRADE AGREEMENT BETWEEN THE GOVERNMENT OF THE UNITED KINGDOM OF GREAT BRITAIN AND NORTHERN IRELAND AND THE GOVERNMENT OF THE COMMONWEALTH OF AUSTRALIA[1]

The Government of the United Kingdom of Great Britain and Northern Ireland (hereinafter referred to as the United Kingdom Government) and the Government of the Commonwealth of Australia (hereinafter referred to as the Australian Government), having resolved to replace the Agreement between them signed at Ottawa on 20th August, 1932, except so far as is otherwise provided in this Agreement, have agreed as follows:—

In this agreement—

'Australian goods' means goods grown, produced or manufactured in Australia or in the external territories administered by the Australian Government, being goods which are entitled to Imperial Preference on importation into the United Kingdom;

[16] This was first announced in London in May 1963 in a communiqué issued by the Board of Trade following talks between McEwen and United Kingdom ministers.

[1] Schedules A and B, which deal with preferences on various items, are omitted; the chief preferences are included in A8:3.

M

'United Kingdom goods' means goods grown, produced or manufactured in the United Kingdom which are admissible into Australia at preferential rates of duty;

'margin of preference'—

(a) as applied to Australian goods, means the difference between the rates of Customs duty charged on Australian goods imported into the United Kingdom and the rates of Customs duty charged on like goods imported into the United Kingdom from any other country which are not entitled to Imperial Preference; and

(b) as applied to United Kingdom goods, means the difference between the rates of duty under the Australian Customs Tariff charged on United Kingdom goods imported into Australia and the rates of duty charged under the Australian Customs Tariff on like goods imported into Australia from the most favoured country which are not admissible at preferential rates of duty.

ARTICLE 1

The United Kingdom Government and the Australian Government reaffirm the principle of maintaining mutually advantageous tariff preferences and declare their resolve to facilitate and extend commercial relations between their respective countries.

ARTICLE 2

The United Kingdom Government undertake that Australian goods which at the date of this Agreement were free of duties (other than revenue duties) on importation into the United Kingdom shall continue to be free of such duties. This undertaking shall not apply to goods in which there is no active Australian trade interest.

ARTICLE 3

The United Kingdom Government undertake to accord to the Australian goods listed in Schedule A margins of preference not lower than those specified in that Schedule.

ARTICLE 4

The United Kingdom Government undertake to consult the Australian Government before reducing margins of preference which exceed the margins specified in Schedule A or which are accorded to Australian goods not listed in that Schedule. This undertaking shall not apply to goods in which there is no active Australian trade interest.

ARTICLE 5

The provisions of the Agreement between the United Kingdom and Australian Governments signed at Ottawa on 20th August, 1932, are not affected by this Agreement in so far as they relate to the import of meat into the United Kingdom.

ARTICLE 6

1. The United Kingdom Government, noting that the traditional share of Australian wheat in the United Kingdom market has declined in consequence of changes in world wheat marketing and the increase in the level of wheat production in the United Kingdom, will consider sympathetically any measures which may be found practicable from time to time, having due regard to their domestic policies and international obligations, to improve the opportunities for the sale of Australian wheat in the United Kingdom.

2. The United Kingdom Government and the Australian Government welcome arrangements for periodical discussions between the representatives of the United Kingdom flour millers and the Australian Wheat Board regarding sales of Australian wheat. They affirm that it is their desire and expectation that sales on commercial terms of Australian wheat and flour in the United Kingdom will amount to not less than 750,000 tons per annum of wheat, inclusive of the wheat equivalent of Australian flour imported into the United Kingdom each year.

3. The two Governments agree that if in any year the quantity of Australian wheat and flour imported into the United Kingdom should fall short of 750,000 tons (wheat equivalent) or such smaller quantity as may be offered by the Australian Wheat Board on commercial terms, they will consult together at the request of either Government. In the event that such consultation is requested the two Governments will for this purpose establish an inter-Governmental Committee to meet in London to consider the reasons for the shortfall and possible solutions. The two Governments further agree that if such consultations should not lead to an outcome satisfactory to both Governments either Government may call for a renegotiation of the terms of this Agreement.

4. If at any time the United Kingdom Government should impose countervailing duties which are agreed between the two Governments to be effective on imports of subsidized wheat, the Australian Government will not invoke the provisions of paragraph 3 of this Article so long as such duties remain effectively in force.

5. Grades of Australian wheat of high protein content, superior to f.a.q. and sold at a premium, imported into the United Kingdom for milling, and Australian wheat imported into the United Kingdom for purposes other than milling, shall be regarded as being outside the scope of this Article.

6. The quantity of Australian wheat referred to in paragraphs 2 and 3 of this Article means the quantity of wheat supplied for milling on the basis of being about equal to the customary official standard established for wheat of Western Australia, South Australia, Victoria or New South Wales, according to the season and the State of origin, or wheat sold on sample to millers.

ARTICLE 7

1. The Australian Government undertake, except in respect of goods in which there is no active United Kingdom trade interest or on which no margin of preference was accorded at the date of this Agreement, to accord minimum margins of preference of—

    (a) $7\frac{1}{2}$ per cent. ad valorem on United Kingdom goods specified in Schedule B;

    (b) $7\frac{1}{2}$ per cent. ad valorem on United Kingdom goods which are subject to rates of duty under the Australian Customs Tariff of 10 per cent. ad valorem or less; and

    (c) 10 per cent. ad valorem on all other United Kingdom goods;

except that, on United Kingdom goods on which the margin of preference provided for at the date of this Agreement was lower than that otherwise required under this paragraph, the minimum margin shall be such lower margin of preference.

2. The provisions of paragraph 1 of this Article shall apply to rates of duty and margins of preference expressed in other than ad valorem terms as if they were expressed in ad valorem terms.

3. The Australian Government undertake to consult the United Kingdom Government before reducing any margins of preference which exceed the minimum margins required under paragraph 1 of this Article, except in respect of the goods specified in Schedule B or where such action follows a report by the Australian Tariff Board or where there is no active United Kingdom trade interest.

ARTICLE 8

1. Notwithstanding the provisions of Article 7 of this Agreement, the Australian Government may admit goods under by-law items of the Australian Customs Tariff as at the date of this Agreement.

2. Where such action would have the effect of eliminating a margin of preference required under Article 7, the Australian Government will first consult the United Kingdom Government with a view to establishing whether suitably equivalent United Kingdom goods are reasonably available and will take into account any representations which the United Kingdom Government may make on these points. This undertaking shall not limit the right of the Australian Government to determine whether any particular goods shall be admitted under by-law.

ARTICLE 9

1. The Australian Government undertake that—
(a) protection by tariffs shall be afforded only to those industries which are reasonably assured of sound opportunities for success;
(b) the Australian Customs Tariff shall be based on the principle that protective duties shall not exceed such a level as will give United Kingdom producers full opportunity of reasonable competition on the basis of the relative cost of economical and efficient production, provided that in the application of such principle special consideration may be given to industries not fully established or to industries essential for defence purposes;
(c) except as provided in paragraph 2 of this Article, no new protective duty shall be imposed and no existing protective duty shall be increased on United Kingdom goods to an amount in excess of the recommendation of the Australian Tariff Board; and
(d) United Kingdom producers shall be entitled to full rights of audience before the Australian Tariff Board when it has under consideration matters arising under sub-paragraph (b) of this paragraph.

2. Having regard to the obligations of the Australian Government under the General Agreement on Tariffs and Trade the provisions of sub-paragraph (c) of paragraph 1 of this Article shall not operate so as to prevent the imposition of a most-favoured-nation rate of duty which the Australian Tariff Board recommends as being necessary to protect Australian producers from the competition of most-favoured-nation countries. In such cases the duty on United Kingdom goods shall be fixed at the lowest level consistent with the provisions of the General Agreement on Tariffs and Trade.

ARTICLE 10

1. The Australian Government undertake that, on the basis of the reciprocity afforded by the preferential tariff treatment at present accorded to them, they will maintain, in respect of each of the dependent territories for whose international relations the United Kingdom Government are responsible, all existing

preferences and preferential rights arising under the Agreement between the United Kingdom Government and the Australian Government signed at Ottawa on 20th August, 1932, or otherwise, until such time as further discussions regarding new reciprocal tariff arrangements between those territories and Australia have been held and concluded, whether by the making of a new Agreement or otherwise.

2. The United Kingdom Government have invited the Governments of the said dependent territories to maintain the preferential tariff treatment at present accorded by them under the Agreement of 20th August, 1932, or otherwise to imports of Australian goods, pending the conclusion of discussions as mentioned in the previous paragraph.

3. Paragraphs 1 and 2 of this Article do not apply in respect of the Federation of Rhodesia and Nyasaland.

ARTICLE 11

The provisions of this Agreement do not affect the Agreement between the United Kingdom Government and the Australian Government signed at Ottawa on 20th August, 1932, as in force between the Governments of Ceylon and Australia.

ARTICLE 12

The United Kingdom Government and the Australian Government recognize that industries in each country engaged in trade with the other may be materially injured by the competition of dumped or subsidized exports from third countries. They declare their intention to introduce legislation at the earliest possible opportunity which will enable them, consistently with their international obligations, to impose anti-dumping or countervailing duties where such material injury is caused or threatened. They agree, if after consultation it is established that such injury is caused or threatened, to consider taking action consistent with their own legislation and with their international obligations to remedy the injury or prevent the threatened injury.

ARTICLE 13

The United Kingdom Government and the Australian Government agree that opportunity will be afforded for full consultation between them in respect of their agricultural production and marketing policies and in respect of the food and feeding stuffs import policy of the United Kingdom Government. In particular, the two Governments will each year exchange statements of agricultural production trends; and each Government will give full weight to the views of the other in the formulation of their agricultural production marketing and import policies.

ARTICLE 14

The United Kingdom Government and the Australian Government recognize that there are other matters, such as transport and communications, the disposal of surpluses and restrictive business practices, not otherwise dealt with in this Agreement, which may have a material effect on the level of trade and commerce between the United Kingdom and Australia. The two Governments agree to consult together about any such matters at the request of either.

ARTICLE 15

1. This Agreement shall be deemed to have come into force on 9th November, 1956, and, except as provided in Articles 5 and 11 of this Agreement, supersedes

the Agreement between the two Governments signed at Ottawa on 20th August, 1932.

2. The operation of this Agreement shall be reviewed from time to time at the request of either Government. The terms of the Agreement may be renegotiated in accordance with the provisions of paragraph 3 of Article 6 and in any event shall be the subject of negotiation between the two Governments during the fifth year of its operation.

3. Subject to paragraph 2 of this Article, after the expiration of a period of five years from the date on which this Agreement is deemed to have come into force, either Government may terminate this Agreement by giving to the other Government six months' notice.

IN WITNESS whereof the undersigned, duly authorized by their respective Governments, have signed the present Agreement and have affixed thereto their seals.

DONE in duplicate at Canberra this twenty-sixth day of February, One thousand nine hundred and fifty-seven.

For the Government of the United Kingdom of Great Britain and Northern Ireland:	For the Government of the Commonwealth of Australia:
CARRINGTON.	J. MCEWEN.

Source: C.P.P., no. 5 of 1957.

A9:2 PREFERENCES ON TRADE BETWEEN UNITED KINGDOM AND AUSTRALIA

1. AUSTRALIAN-UNITED KINGDOM MERCHANDISE TRADE

(a) *In value terms (f.o.b.)*

	1938–9 £Am.	1955–6 £Am.	Increase %
Imports from U.K.	46·1	355·9	672
Exports to U.K.	68·7	257·4	274

	Av. for 5 years ended 30 June 1939 £Am.	Av. for 5 years ended 30 June 1956 £Am.	Increase %
Imports from U.K.	43·3	349·3	707
Exports to U.K.	66·9	282·2	322

(b) *In volume (constant price) terms*

	1938–9	1955–6	Increase %
Imports from U.K.	45·6	87·4	91·6
Exports to U.K.	83·8	52·0	– 37·9

	Av. for 5 years ended 30 June 1939	Av. for 5 years ended 30 June 1956	Increase %
Imports from U.K.	44·6	89·0	100
Exports to U.K.	71·2	59·8	– 14·5

2. PREFERENTIAL IMBALANCE

Preferences accorded by Australia to U.K.

	1952–3	1953–4	1954–5
Total Australian imports from U.K. (£Am. f.o.b.)	214·7	331·7	378·7
Preferential imports (£Am.)	180·2	294·4	(327·0)
Preferential % of total	83·9	88·8	(86·3)
Estimated value of preferences (£Am.)	25·2	40·9	(45·8)
Average preference on goods receiving preference (%)	14·0	14·0	(14·0)

Note: Figures in brackets are estimated

Preferences received by Australia in U.K.

	1952–3	1953–4	1954–5
Total Australian exports to U.K. (£Am. est. c.i.f.)	395·2	330·8	314·7
Preferential exports (£Am.)	171·8	166·7	150·7
Preferential % of total	43·0	50·0	48·0
Estimated value of preferences (£Am.)	15·0	15·0	13·6
Average preference on goods receiving preference (%)	8·8	9·0	9·0

SOURCE: Figures prepared for the author's use by the Department of Commerce and Industry at time of Review of Ottawa Agreement.

Note: The figures given for preferences accorded by Australia to United Kingdom imports are in line with the following figures for 1948 given by Donald MacDougall and Rosemary Hutt, 'Imperial Preference: A Quantitative Analysis', *Economic Journal*, vol. LXIV, no. 254, June 1954, p. 241:

AUSTRALIA
Percentage of imports from the U.K. receiving preference	88–91
Percentage average margin of preference on U.K. goods enjoying preference	15–16
Percentage average margin of preference on all imports from U.K.	13–14

9:1 TRADE DISCUSSIONS BETWEEN THE UNITED KINGDOM AND AUSTRALIA: MEMORANDUM OF CONCLUSIONS LONDON, 20 JULY 1938

1. United Kingdom and Australian Ministers have been engaged for some time in a review of various matters arising out of the Ottawa Agreement of 1932. Not only have the existing preferential arrangements between the two countries been examined, but Empire problems have, in a spirit of mutual sympathy and goodwill, been considered in their widest aspects with a view to ensuring the maximum co-operation between the United Kingdom and Australia in their solution. Ministers have reviewed the broad principles which should, in their opinion, be regarded as the charter of United Kingdom-Australia trade relations.

2. The United Kingdom and Australia have a vital interest in each other—Australia in the United Kingdom—

   (a) as a great force for the bringing about and maintenance of international political and economic peace;

(b) as an essential element in the defence of Australia's territory and trade;

(c) as the greatest market for Australian exports of primary products.

The United Kingdom in Australia—

(a) as a sister nation closely linked to the United Kingdom in matters of Empire defence;

(b) as a country which, given adequate population and a full development of resources, will become a great power in continued partnership with the United Kingdom;

(c) as one of the greatest customers in the world for United Kingdom goods;

(d) as the domicile of the largest amount of United Kingdom capital invested in any single overseas country and as a field for future United Kingdom investment.

3. Both the United Kingdom and Australia have certain problems and requirements the existence of which each not only admits but is prepared to treat as the basis of the trade relationship between the two countries. Australian Ministers recognize—

(a) the necessity for the United Kingdom to safeguard and develop her own agriculture;

(b) the position of the United Kingdom as a great international trader, investor and shipowner;

(c) the consequential necessity that the United Kingdom should maintain her position as a great overseas trader and in particular as an exporter of manufactured goods to Empire and foreign countries;

(d) that these facts impose an upward limit upon the extent to which increased opportunities can be afforded to Dominion producers in the United Kingdom market;

(e) that any diminution of total export from the United Kingdom will tend to affect the capacity of the United Kingdom to purchase foodstuffs and raw materials from overseas suppliers, including Australia.

United Kingdom Ministers recognize—

(a) that in the interest of both countries and of the British Empire as a whole it is desirable for Australia to endeavour to bring about as soon as possible a substantial increase in her population;

(b) that it is impossible to achieve this objective solely or principally by an expansion of Australian primary industries;

(c) that there is therefore a necessity to combine with such expansion the sound and progressive development of Australian secondary industries.

4. Both United Kingdom and Australian Ministers are strongly attached to the principle of preferential trade within the British Empire. At the same time they realize that several of the important facts above stated render it not only inevitable but desirable that both the United Kingdom and Australia should from time to time enter into trade agreements with foreign countries. In this way the two countries can assure their own full development and at the same time make an effective contribution to the expansion of international trade. To this end United

Kingdom and Australian Ministers have undertaken to co-operate in every practicable way with a view to assisting each other in arriving at trade agreements with foreign countries. . . .[1]

Signed on behalf of His Majesty's Government in the United Kingdom:	Signed on behalf of His Majesty's Government in the Commonwealth of Australia:
STANLEY	EARLE PAGE
OLIVER F. G. STANLEY	ROBERT G. MENZIES
W. S. MORRISON	THOMAS W. WHITE
20th July, 1938	

Source: *C.P.P.*, no. 16 of 1940.

9:2 TARIFF BOARD REPLIES TO CRITICISM OF ARTICLES 9 TO 13 OF UNITED KINGDOM-AUSTRALIA TRADE AGREEMENT

On occasions, criticism is made by interested parties of what are regarded as the restrictive sections of the Ottawa Agreement, viz., Articles 9 to 13. . . .

The attention of the Tariff Board has recently been drawn to the report of a speech by a leading Australian industrialist in which he commented on the effects of the Ottawa Agreement and, in particular, of Articles 9 to 13 of that Agreement.

In dealing with the Agreement generally, the speaker is reported as having said:—

Prior to Ottawa, it was internationally recognized that Australia had one of the best tariff-making systems in the world. The Tariff Board was able to judge a case purely on its merits and, unhampered by any consideration other than the economics of the Commonwealth, and the desirability or otherwise of fostering a given industry, it forwarded its report to the Government, which, in turn, after examining the Tariff Board's advice, granted whatever tariff it believed was justified. Ottawa took all that freedom of action away, and substituted a set of conditions to which the Australian Government was foolish enough to agree, which made it impossible for the Tariff Board to have any real confidence when recommending a measure of tariff protection, that the measure so recommended would adequately protect.

Regarding Article 9 which requires that 'protection by tariffs shall be afforded only to those industries that are reasonably assured of sound opportunities for success' more than one critic has inferred that Australia should not accept dictation from Great Britain on matters connected with its essential growth and development. It has also been claimed that this Article prevents the actual trial being undertaken without which it cannot be demonstrated that a new industry is reasonably assured of sound opportunity for success.

In dealing with Articles 10 and 11 which require that 'protective duties shall not exceed such a level as will give United Kingdom producers full opportunity of reasonable competition on the basis of the relative cost of economic and

[1] A detailed recognition followed of the difficulties of reconciling opposite interests. Ottawa had difficulties for both the United Kingdom and Australia.

efficient production' and that existing duties shall be reviewed in accordance with these principles, the criticism was based on the claim that these meant that—

Australian tariffs shall eventually be no higher than, what amounts to, the imposition of a duty which represents little, if any, more than the difference the Tariff Board can find between British and Australian costs of production.

. . . even were the Ottawa Agreement cancelled immediately, it would not be likely that there would be any alteration in the Board's method of arriving at its findings. For example, the Board would consider that it was failing in its duties if it were to recommend protection to industries 'not reasonably assured of sound opportunities for success'.

The Board's interpretation of Article 10 in allowing a small margin in favour of Australian manufacturers over competitive imports provides adequate protection without over-protecting. The Board's object in this is to stimulate efficiency in Australian industry and protect the interests of consumers whether they be other manufacturers or retail purchasers. The Board has every confidence that, whether the Ottawa Agreement be in operation or not, it can recommend duties which will really protect. In fact, it would not recommend duties otherwise as it would be most unwise to apply a 'protective' duty which does not protect, because it merely adds to the costs of consumers without being of benefit to local manufacturers. . . .

To sum up, the Board would state—

(a) The obligations of the Australian Government under the Ottawa Agreement have not resulted in the Board recommending lower protection to an Australian industry than it would otherwise have done.

(b) The policy of the Board is to protect, but not over-protect, economical and efficient Australian industries from the competition of similar industries overseas and this policy is followed not only in the interests of the Australian industries themselves, but because the Board realizes its responsibility to protect the interests of consumers in the Commonwealth.

(c) Irrespective of the Ottawa Agreement the Board is not prepared to recommend protection to industries not reasonably assured of sound opportunities for success.

Source: Tariff Board. Annual Report for
the Year Ended 30th June, 1942, pp. 27-9.

9:3 GRAZIERS' FEDERAL COUNCIL ASKS FOR REVIEW OF UNITED KINGDOM-AUSTRALIA TRADE AGREEMENT

Extract from article by W. A. Gunn, President, Graziers' Federal Council of Australia.

The Graziers' Federal Council has requested the Federal Government to press for a review of the system of Imperial preference and has suggested that an opportune time would be during the forthcoming Commonwealth Economic Conference. . . .

The Ottawa conference was held at a stage when the world was suffering under severe depression conditions and the decisions of the conference were aimed at reviving and building up trade within the British Empire. In spite of the fact that the whole situation has changed long since, we have clung blindly to Imperial Preference without pausing to analyse the need and the reasons.

Added to Producers' Costs

Over recent years primary producers have had cause to question the operation of Imperial Preference in so far as it has added greatly to the cost of importing farm machinery and other essential pastoral supplies.

Whilst British manufacturers have been unable to meet our requirements, it was expected that where we could obtain these goods from other countries there would be little difficulty in arranging for the waiving of the very substantial British preferential duties.

This was not the case, however, and in many instances whilst protracted discussions took place between British and Australian officials as to whether or not the goods were available in Britain, our primary producers were required to pay preferential duties which amounted to hundreds of pounds on some items of machinery.

One-Sided Advantages

It does appear that the direct advantages of Imperial Preference are very one-sided in that it only applies to wine, sugar and dried fruits in the British market.[1] On the other hand the preponderance of imports from Britain in the Australian market is worth many millions to British exporters. . . .

It is possible that Imperial Preference is providing shelter which is removing Empire trade from the realities of world trade. It may be that the operation of this agreement places Australia at a decided disadvantage, economically. These are the type of questions which can be answered only by a complete review of the Ottawa Agreement and the system which has been subsequently evolved.

Source: The Leader, 19 November 1952.

9:4 UNITED KINGDOM PREFERENCES DUE FOR REVISION

In telling the people of Britain that our capacity to buy from them depends on their willingness to buy from Australia, the Minister for Commerce lays bare a lop-sided system of trading preferences which events have rendered ineffective, from the standpoint of many Australian export producers.

Britain, as Mr. McEwen said, has been taking less Australian wheat, and is terminating its bulk buying of meat, butter, cheese, dried and canned fruits, and base-metals. Trade in these commodities has passed, or is about to pass, into private hands, and sentiment has little place in competitive open markets.

Our dried fruits industry, which does not lend itself to mechanisation, is meeting subsidised competition in the United Kingdom from Mediterranean countries, where wage and working conditions differ from our own. If the U.S.A. were to subsidise exports of Californian dried fruits when the U.K. discontinues Government trading at the end of this year, the position would be aggravated.

Under greatly changed money values, ocean freights and other charges, the

[1] An inaccurate statement since it omits other important preferences such as canned fruit, canned meat, and dairy products.

preferences accorded Australian dried fruits under the 1932 Ottawa agreement have lost effective value. Other export items incur the same forfeiture when preference rates are expressed in so many shillings or pence for a stated weight, or quantity. All such margins are rendered obsolete and unreal by contrasting commodity price levels. . . .

Effective preferences for Australian products in the U.K. market, by improving our export earnings, would strengthen our ability to import goods from the U.K. A recasting of rates and percentages is clearly needed in the light of modern market values and the mutual benefits of reciprocity between kinsmen. . . .

Source: Age (Melbourne), 5 October 1954.

9:5 ASSOCIATED CHAMBERS OF COMMERCE ASK FOR REVIEW OF THE UNITED KINGDOM-AUSTRALIA TRADE AGREEMENT

The annual conference of the Associated Chambers of Commerce in Sydney yesterday decided to ask the Federal Government to review the Ottawa trade agreement of 1932.

The Minister for Trade, Mr. J. McEwen, in addressing the conference later, said the Ottawa Agreement was of demonstrably greater value to Britain than to Australia.

The conference resolution said that the conference believes that the time is opportune for the Australian Government to decide whether Australia can afford to retain the limitation placed on its choice of purchasing markets by the preferential provisions of the agreement.

It said that such a review should take into consideration as vital principles the retention of Articles 9 to 13 of the agreement. . . .

Source: Sydney Morning Herald,
3 May 1956.

9:6 AUSTRALIA SEEKS NEW TRADE AGREEMENT WITH THE UNITED KINGDOM

Press statement by the Prime Minister (R. G. Menzies) on 24 May 1956.

The Australian Government has informed the United Kingdom Government of its wish that trade discussions with the United Kingdom should take place during my forthcoming visit to London. The Minister for Trade, Mr. McEwen, who will be in London with me, will of course, take a special part in the discussions.

We desire that the talks should cover the whole field of our trade relationship and should not be confined to matters relating to the Ottawa Agreement. The object of the talks will be to reach agreement with the United Kingdom on a set of principles. These principles would provide a framework for a new trade agreement but it would be the task of officials in subsequent negotiations to translate them into the details of a new and comprehensive agreement to replace Ottawa. The negotiations between officials may need to extend over several months.

In reaching its decision to seek a new and broader agreement with the United Kingdom, the Government has been influenced by a number of important factors.

World trading conditions have changed greatly since the Ottawa Agreement was negotiated in 1932. New problems have arisen for which Ottawa does not provide a solution. We are confronted, at present, with particular balance of payments problems and consequently with import licensing controls. We must solve these problems. To assist in this task, it is necessary to reach a wider understanding with the United Kingdom which will take account of present-day conditions. We want to ensure that each party has reasonable access to the market of the other party, and fair opportunities to compete in the market on commercial terms. Each country is the chief export market for the other's products and has much to gain from the accord of mutually advantageous preference. I cannot emphasize too strongly that the Government's wish is to preserve the principle of preference as between the United Kingdom and Australia. At the same time we must pay attention to the effect of preferential arrangements on Australia's cost structure and trade development.

These will, we hope, be the most important trade talks which have taken place between the two countries since the negotiation of the Ottawa Agreement itself. The Government hopes that they will place trading relationships between the United Kingdom and Australia on a basis which will be of lasting benefit to both countries, and that they will open the way for a growing volume of trade not only between the United Kingdom and Australia, but between both of our countries and the rest of the trading world.

9:7 AUSTRALIA'S CASE AGAINST SUBSIDISED PRIMARY PRODUCTION

... the great difference between Australia's latest attitude on the Ottawa tariff schedules and the line it was taking two years ago is that nobody expects Britain to restore the balance by giving new tariff preferences to Australian products. It is recognised that the rules of GATT prevent this. In any case, tariff duties would hardly be applicable to some of the primary export markets that Australia is concerned about. Any lingering hope that Britain may open its doors wider to Australian exports rests mainly on the chances of persuading it to see the case against buying the subsidised exports of countries like Argentina. A second prong of the Australian argument is that Britain itself should not subsidise a greatly expanded home production of foodstuffs in a period of world surpluses.

To distinguish a 'subsidised' primary export from the Simon-pure variety is admittedly an intricate matter these days, and Australian realists acknowledge that the Conservative Government in Britain is not likely to reverse its general policy of leaving the free play of market forces to determine the pattern of commodity purchases. Nevertheless, it is suggested, Australia naturally grows some of the cheapest wheat in the world. Admitting the limitations in the range of grains produced, and possible deficiencies in selling techniques which must be corrected, there is something wrong in a system that prevents that wheat from enjoying its natural advantages in overseas markets. It is argued that there would be nothing inconsistent with the spirit of GATT if Britain took some kind of anti-dumping action against foreign grains to ensure that the Australian product came into its own.

However, many hard heads inside and outside the Australian Cabinet accept the probability that Britain will not be able to open the doors wide enough. From that point, their reasoning is fairly terse. Australia's trading position is becoming desperate; the Imperial preferences are now working much more to Britain's advantage than Australia's, and that is not fully offset by separate trading agreements between the two countries in commodities like sugar, meat and copra; were it not for the tariff preferences, Australia could import some items more cheaply from foreign countries; besides the saving in the imports bill, Australia would be able to re-negotiate mutual tariff reductions with those countries (inside or outside the regular GATT conventions) so as to secure itself better export markets; in its present condition it must be free to 'shop around' in this way.

GULLIVER RAISES HIS VOICE

That is the argument and that is the sense in which Mr. Menzies has said he will seek a new trade agreement to replace the Ottawa schedules. The idea is not to abolish imperial preferences—Australia is conscious of its own advantages from them—but to fix a more accurate *quid pro quo*. . . .

Source: *The Economist*, 30 June 1956, vol. 179, pp. 1294-5.

9:8 AUSTRALIAN WHEAT EXPORTS PROBLEM

One piece of unfinished business lingers on from the Commonwealth Premiers' Conference. Talks are still going on, behind confidentially closed doors, between Australia's Minister of Trade, Mr. McEwen, and the Board of Trade . . . The Australians are most interested in getting more wheat into the British market, and would probably like the United Kingdom to impose an anti-dumping duty on French and American wheat, which they say is subsidised. But apart from the technical difficulties of fixing an anti-dumping duty—and an extremely stiff one would be needed to keep out American wheat—Britain would be reluctant to remove one source of discontent at the risk of creating two others. There is slightly more room for agreement about reducing the subsidies on Britain's own wheat production, but this depends on how much further Britain is ready to go in abandoning its policy of growing all possible food at home regardless of cost. A proposal for some kind of guaranteed price for Australian wheat is not likely to figure very high on Mr. McEwen's list, since it might involve political difficulties for the British Government and in any case would probably not expand the volume (as distinct from the value) of Australian exports to Britain. Ultimately, the matter depends on how firmly Britain has nailed the colours of free trade to its masthead. If the Board of Trade refuses to shift its ground, it should not complain if Australia feels bound to lower the preferences it gives to British goods by cutting the tariffs on some non-Commonwealth imports. Free trade can be a two-edged weapon.

Source: *The Economist*, 28 July 1956, vol. 180, p. 306.

9:9 MUTUAL PREFERENCE BETWEEN UNITED KINGDOM AND AUSTRALIA TO BE PRESERVED

Joint press statement issued by Peter Thorneycroft, President of the Board of Trade and J. McEwen, Australian Minister for Trade, on 5 August 1956.

1. On behalf of the Governments of the United Kingdom and the Commonwealth of Australia, we have engaged in discussions about the trading problems of our countries.

2. Our intention is that a comprehensive agreement shall be arrived at, satisfactory to both, and that the whole field of our mutual trade shall be examined to enable this to be achieved.

3. Both the United Kingdom and Australia are determined to preserve the great principle of mutual preference, which has been the basic feature of their trade relations for so many years. We say this not in a spirit of hostility to the interests of world trade, which we are anxious to expand, but because we believe that the strengthening of Anglo-Australian trade and of our national economies will improve world trade generally.

4. In these discussions we have fully recognised not only the great importance of strengthening Commonwealth trade, but the fundamental inter-dependence of the United Kingdom and Australia in trade matters, illustrated by the fact that each is the other's best customer. We have also recognised that there have been marked changes in the pattern of trade in recent years and that both countries are currently facing new and difficult problems. In particular, we have concentrated on measures designed to help the Australian balance of payments and thus to enable Australian quantitative import restrictions to be reduced. We have considered the level of the mutual preferences and methods of improving consultation between the two countries on trade issues. We have also discussed the problems arising from the use of export subsidies by certain other countries.

5. We are giving special attention to the question of how best wider opportunities can be secured for the expansion of traditional Australian exports to the United Kingdom, especially wheat.

6. The objective of these discussions is a comprehensive agreement. It has not been possible to conclude this in the time available during the visit of the two Australian Ministers. The discussions will be resumed in September, when further study has been completed in both countries.

9:10 REPORT ON TRADE NEGOTIATIONS WITH THE UNITED KINGDOM

Speech of the Minister for Trade (J. McEwen) in the House of Representatives on 13 September 1956.

Of course, the policy of the Government in respect of trade matters is to protect the currency and our overseas reserves, as is necessary by import restrictions and to devote its constructive efforts to enabling the country to escape from the necessity for these restrictions by an expansion of our trade . . . Our proposals to the United Kingdom Government originated through our balance of payment circumstances which had led to the unwelcome necessity for import licensing. As a nation, we are faced with the immediate and urgent necessity of increasing our export earnings. To improve them we clearly must produce, at the right cost, more of those goods which are saleable in the world's markets. We must secure the right to sell them in overseas countries, and we must sell them on the most advantageous terms achievable . . . Wool is our dominant exchange earner. Wheat comes next. The United Kingdom is overwhelmingly our biggest purchaser, and Japan comes next. . . .

Our external trade is dominated by two great trade treaties. One is the General Agreement on Tariffs and Trade, to which Australia, in company with 34 other nations, is a signatory. This agreement is designed to promote a freer flow of world trade and generally to inhibit changes in the pattern of international trade brought about by new preferences being given or protective duties being increased above levels bound in trade negotiations under the agreement. On the other hand, what we call the Ottawa agreement is a trade agreement between Australia and our greatest trading partner, the United Kingdom. The essence of this agreement is a system of mutual tariff preferences. In contrast with the General Agreement on Tariffs and Trade, it prevents the reduction of the Australian tariffs on foreign goods below duties arrived at by adding the stipulated margins of preferences to the British rates in our tariff schedule. In so far as additional trade or better trade is to be achieved by negotiations with foreign governments, these two agreements critically determine our opportunity. Taken in combination, these two trade treaties result in a quite extraordinary rigidity, inhibiting the negotiation of new trade opportunities with foreign countries achieved through tariff bargaining. . . .

Superimposed upon this tariff scene we have at the present time, not by choice, but by inescapable necessity, a wide system of import licensing. In theory this could be used as a bargaining factor in negotiating trade arrangements, but for most powerful reasons we are against this as a policy. Nothing could be more provocative or, in the end, more complicating. But, in addition, we are also engaged contractually as a member of the General Agreement on Tariffs and Trade to operate import licensing in a non-discriminating manner as between countries, although not necessarily as between currencies. To add one more factor to the complexities of our external trade situation, most of our exports are raw materials such as wool, wheat and other grains, and base metals which enter most countries under terms of free or near-free entry, whereas the overwhelming percentage of our imports from foreign countries is subject to tariffs.

My remarks are designed to deal with that aspect of trade opportunity which can be negotiated only by the Government with other governments. At this level, we want, first, assured rights of continued access and opportunity in a market where we now have access, and preferential tariff terms as justified by reciprocal preferences given. We want also the assurance, as intended under the General Agreement on Tariffs and Trade, of protection against discriminatory tariff obstructions to our trade. We want protection against distortion of the normal pattern of our trade through the disposal of surpluses on non-commercial terms, and against distortion by export subsidies. We want stability in world trade in important commodities, which can be assured by contracts such as the International Wheat Agreement. We want an assurance of protection against dumping

340

in an established market, for which we are prepared to guarantee reciprocally the trade of an established customer against dumping in our market. We want sufficient flexibility in our tariff commitments to leave some elbow-room for the negotiation of new export trade opportunities. Finally, and hardly less important than any of these requirements that I have mentioned, we need the opportunity to buy from overseas on terms which will avoid inflating our own costs unless there is a clear balancing benefit to compensate. . . .

We have claimed—and I have not the slightest doubt that we can substantiate our claim—that the Ottawa agreement of 1932 has, for a variety of reasons, come to operate with an advantage to United Kingdom trade in Australia very much greater than the advantages to Australian trade in the United Kingdom. Our thinking on this, and what in our opinion was necessary to re-establish a balance of advantage, was pointed out late in 1954 by the present Minister for the Navy (Senator O'Sullivan), who was then Minister for Trade and Customs, and myself to all the Ministers in the United Kingdom Cabinet who were concerned with our trading or general relationships. We felt that some improvement of our trading relationships could be achieved without the alteration of contractual relations, principally in our wheat trade.

This year, with our balance of payments problem becoming if anything more acute, or at least taking on an air of greater permanence, the Government decided to approach the problem of our external trade situation in more formal contractual terms. Consequently, after months of quite intense study here, the Prime Minister and I opened negotiations with the United Kingdom Government in June. The Australian proposal was that the current Ottawa Agreement should be replaced by a more comprehensive agreement, which would embody the principle of preferences under the Ottawa Agreement, protecting existing Australian rights in the United Kingdom, but modifying the United Kingdom rights in Australia to a level nearer to the balance of advantage. In addition, we proposed that Australian exports to the United Kingdom should be accorded some new protection—by that I do not mean tariff protection—for instance, against the competition of goods sold with the advantage of subsidies by foreign governments, protection against non-commercial transactions made possible by foreign governments, and mutual protection against dumping. One result intended to flow from this was an assured re-establishment of the historic position of Australian wheat in the total pattern of British wheat imports.

Having reached a certain point of understanding late in July, the negotiations were interrupted, principally to permit the United Kingdom Government to engage in certain detailed studies. The Australian request, from the outset, had been that all issues to be negotiated in determining the trade relationship between the two countries should not be negotiated in separable compartments but as one total issue embodied in one trade treaty. In late July agreement was reached with the United Kingdom Government that this should be the objective of the two governments—one comprehensive trade agreement to replace the current Ottawa agreement, and also embody whatever other trade agreements were agreed upon. . . .

Broadly, this trade arrangement at which we aim is designed to achieve three results. First, protection of our normal trade with the United Kingdom. Wheat is our second largest export, and honourable members will be aware of the extent to which our share of the United Kingdom's wheat imports has shrunk over the last few years. Secondly, to secure new or improved negotiated trade opportunities, principally with foreign countries. To negotiate concessions with foreign countries we require greater freedom in our tariff than we now have. Thirdly, to ensure that we do not burden ourselves, through contractual commitments, with greater import costs than are justified by compensating contractual benefits. In a country with indications of inflationary problems at home and which must be cost conscious in exports, this cost factor in our objective is rated as highly important. These are our objectives. In return we offer the United Kingdom continuance of contractual reciprocal preferences, so that her great export industries may continue to enjoy a preferred position in this their most important market. We also offer reciprocal protection against trade disloca-tion by dumped goods. . . .

Source: *C.P.D.* (*H. of R.*), vol. 12, pp. 550-4.

9:11 UNITED KINGDOM-AUSTRALIA TRADE AGREEMENT 1956: HEADS OF AGREEMENT

Joint Communiqué of 9 November 1956.

1. The United Kingdom and Australian Governments announced in August their intention to resume discussions for the purpose of concluding a compre-hensive Trade Agreement.

2. We have initialled the attached Heads of Agreement which will form the substance of a new trade agreement to replace the United Kingdom-Australian Trade Agreement of 1932. This will be drawn up early in 1957.[1]

3. Throughout the discussions, we have been determined to do everything possible to promote the stability and growth of trade between the United Kingdom and Australia believing that this will also serve the interests of inter-national trade generally.

4. We have made a comprehensive review of the trade between the two countries and we have taken fully into account changes in their economic circumstances.

5. We have agreed that the time is opportune for changes in the contractual arrangements between the United Kingdom and Australia which will, however, continue to reflect the joint determination of both Governments to preserve the principle of mutual preference.

6. To this end, the United Kingdom will maintain tariff preferences and duty free entry enjoyed by Australian goods and Australia will maintain tariff pre-ferences for United Kingdom goods subject to reductions in the level of guaran-teed margins.

7. We have recorded an understanding about the opportunity for the sale in the United Kingdom market on commercial terms of 750,000 tons of Aus-tralian wheat and flour annually over the next five years.

8. We have reached policy understandings and have made specific arrange-ments for close consultation between the two Governments about a wide range of

[1] The agreement was signed on 26 February 1957 but was deemed to have come into force on 9 November 1956.

trade and related matters including anti-dumping and countervailing duties, agricultural policies, transport and communications, and disposal of surpluses.

9. We are convinced that the new Trade Agreement will preserve and strengthen the close traditional trade and commercial ties between the United Kingdom and Australia to the continuing benefit of both countries.

(Signed)   J. McEwen
Australian Minister for Trade

PETER THORNEYCROFT
President of the Board of Trade

London
9th November, 1956.

Source: Press statement issued for publication
in Australia on 13 November 1956.

9:12 NEW UNITED KINGDOM-AUSTRALIA TRADE AGREEMENT ANNOUNCED

Press statement by the Acting Minister for Trade (W. McMahon) on 13 November 1956.[1]

The Acting Minister for Trade (Mr. William McMahon) announced today that the Australian and United Kingdom Governments had negotiated a new and comprehensive trade agreement which would replace the Ottawa Agreement of 1932. . . . Mr. McMahon said:

The new agreement preserves the principle of mutual preference which has been basic to the trade policies of successive Australian Governments and on which so much of Australia's overseas trade is dependent. Although this principle has been preserved the Australian Government has been successful in obtaining modifications in the contractual arrangements between the two Governments which take account of the changes in the world trading environment since 1932.

From the Australian point of view, the principles on which agreement has been reached preserve, and in some important cases enhance the position of Australian exports entering the United Kingdom market. On the other hand, by providing the opportunity for Australia to reduce preference margins accorded to United Kingdom goods in the Australian market, it will not only reduce duty paid costs of foreign goods to Australian industry but will also lead to greater scope for developing Australian exports to those countries.

The main provisions of the new Agreement which will be effective initially for a period of five years, are:—

 (i) where Australian goods at present enjoy duty free entry to the United Kingdom market this will be continued;

 (ii) the United Kingdom has agreed to increase the range of Australian goods on which it will guarantee the existing margins of tariff preference in her market;

[1] The student may also be interested to read the later statement of Mr McEwen in the House of Representatives on 9 April 1957 which traverses some of the same ground in a less concise way. Only two paragraphs of this statement are reproduced in these documents (9:14).

(iii) in those cases where the margin of preference accorded Australian commodities is not subject to a contractual arrangement, the Australian Government will be consulted about any proposals to reduce such margins;

(iv) an understanding has been recorded on the opportunity for the sale in the United Kingdom market on commercial terms of a minimum of 28 million bushels of Australian wheat and flour annually over the next five years;

(v) Australia is empowered to reduce the margin of preference accorded to United Kingdom goods to 7½% on a wide range of goods which are basic to Australian industry and irrespective of the level of the present preference margin accorded to the United Kingdom. When the rate of duty applicable to British goods is not in excess of 10%, the minimum margin of preference will also be 7½%. On all other goods, the margin of preference can be reduced to 10%;

(vi) the final decision in respect of the admission of goods into Australia under Customs By-laws rests with the Australian Government;

(vii) special arrangements have been made for consultations between the two Governments on their agricultural production and marketing policies, on the disposal of surpluses, and on the United Kingdom's food import policy. It has been further agreed that the United Kingdom Government will introduce legislation to enable it to impose anti-dumping or countervailing duties should the need arise.

. . . the Government felt that a mutual preference arrangement was still in the best interests of the Australian economy provided that, within such an arrangement, there would be significant opportunities for reducing the cost of imported goods, for developing wider trade possibilities with other countries and for obtaining a degree of protection for our export commodities in a world market subject to a wide range of unfair and restrictive practices.

Just how successful we have been in achieving these objectives, [said Mr. Mc-Mahon] is apparent from an examination of each of these objectives in turn. Under the Ottawa Agreement goods from foreign countries had to pay an additional duty of 12½% when the duty on similar British goods was 15% or less. The additional duty increased to as much as 17½% when the rate on British goods exceeded 25%. The new arrangement will not oblige the Australian Government to maintain these additional duties on foreign goods at levels higher than 7½% for a large and very important section of our imports, and 10% on the balance. The practical importance of this may be illustrated simply. Take, for instance, a commodity which is at present subject to a rate of duty of 27½ per cent when imported from the United Kingdom. If imported from a foreign source, it would, under the Ottawa Agreement, be subject to duty of not less than 45 per cent. Under the new Agreement, it would be dutiable at not less than 37½ per cent, i.e. there is a saving of 7½ per cent. If it is an item in the selected list of basic raw materials and machinery, the minimum rate would be 35 per cent, and the saving to the importer—10 per cent.

It will not be possible to take full advantage of this scope for cost reductions. The Government has no intention of departing from its clearly established policy of providing protection through the tariff for efficient and economical domestic industries. In fact, this policy is written into the new Agreement as was the case in the Ottawa Agreement. Thus, before taking advantage of the scope for reducing preference margins, the Government will, where protection to an Australian industry is involved, ensure that domestic industries are not deprived of proper protection. Australian industries will, in addition, benefit from lower duties which will apply in connection with raw materials and plant imported from foreign countries.

The Government's second objective in seeking a review of the Ottawa Agreement was to obtain some room for manoeuvre in our trade negotiations with other countries, and in particular for those countries who were good customers for our exports. Not only should we look at possible savings in costs in Australia in terms of the reductions in duties made possible under the new agreement, but also indirectly at the potential benefits which can be expected to accrue from increased competition by foreign suppliers in the Australian market. Such competition is particularly important in the case of those commodities where the Ottawa preference margins were so wide as to virtually prohibit effective competition amongst overseas suppliers. Australian imports of goods on which Australia would now be in a position to reduce preference margins amounted to about £350 million in 1954/55 and of this total no less than £100 million were imported from non-preferential sources. The competitive position of foreign suppliers will, of course, be enhanced to the extent that the preferential treatment now accorded British goods is reduced. This opportunity for increased access to the Australian market would, it is hoped, lead to improvements in the treatment of Australian goods entering other overseas markets.

. . . it is not envisaged that the United Kingdom's exports to this market will be impaired in the long run. As experience since Ottawa has shown, United Kingdom exporters can look forward to a growing market for their goods in absolute terms even though their percentage share of the market may decline.

In the trade discussions, the Australian Government sought an assurance of proper access to the United Kingdom market for our agricultural exports. Under present trading conditions, the protection in overseas markets of domestic agriculture, the extensive use of subsidies by our competitors and problems associated with the disposal of accumulated surpluses, have assumed an importance which at times over-rides tariff preference considerations. Under the 'no new preference' provisions of the G.A.T.T., we were not, of course, in a position to seek higher margins of preference for our goods in the United Kingdom market . . . as a means of ensuring Australian exports the maximum protection possible within this framework, the Australian Government has succeeded in obtaining a guarantee of existing preference margins on a wider range of goods than was covered in the Ottawa Agreement. In addition, the two Governments have recognised the importance of non-commercial competition from dumped or subsidised exports, and the United Kingdom Government has agreed to introduce legislation which would permit remedial action to be taken. The United Kingdom has also undertaken to afford the Australian Government full opportunity for presenting its views prior to changes in United Kingdom policy on domestic agriculture, imports of food and particularly on imports of surplus commodities.

In this regard, the commodity most susceptible to these influences has been wheat. Recognising this fact, the United Kingdom has indicated that it is her expectation and a positive policy objective that sales of Australian wheat and flour should amount to not less than 28 million bushels in each of the next five years. This minimum figure does not include higher protein wheat, sales of which would be additional. In recent years, our sales of wheat and flour to the United Kingdom have been significantly below 28 million bushels. This year, largely as a result of adverse climatic conditions in Europe, our sales may reach as high as this level. By contrast, however, they fell in 1954 to as low as 13 million bushels. Such is the importance attached to the wheat arrangement by both Governments that there is provision for opening up the whole Agreement should this figure of imports not be realised.

Mr. McMahon stated that the trade negotiations had covered a wide range of other subjects which, although less tangible in nature than those already referred to were nevertheless of the utmost importance to our overall trade policy. For instance, many manufacturers and importers have drawn attention to the problems and uncertainties which they had faced over many years in so far as the administration of Customs By-laws were concerned. The Australian Delegation, in the London negotiations, had been able to reach the clear understanding that, subject only to consultations with the United Kingdom Government, the decision to eliminate the preference margin on goods eligible for admission under Customs By-laws clearly rests with the Australian Government.

Special attention had also been given to the important effects of restrictive business practices and such other matters as transport and communications on trade between the two countries. The new Agreement recognises the problems associated with these questions and provides for consultation on specific issues as they arise.

In conclusion, Mr. McMahon said:—

The negotiation of this new Trade Agreement between the United Kingdom and Australia brings up to date the provisions of the Ottawa Agreement and is without a doubt the most important development in Australia's overseas trade policy since the principle of reciprocal preferential tariff treatment was placed on a formal basis in 1932. When the major Australian industry organisations were consulted prior to the commencement of the negotiations, almost without exception they stressed two issues as cardinal objectives for Australia; the maintenance of the preferences accorded Australian foodstuffs in the United Kingdom, and the vital necessity of relieving the Australian economy of the excessive costs inherent in the preference margins accorded United Kingdom goods under the Ottawa Agreement. Both these objectives have been achieved. . . .

9:13 PRAISE FOR NEW TRADE AGREEMENT

Mr. McEwen and his vigorous department deserve everybody's thanks. They worked persistently and well to show the British that Australia's case for a new trade agreement was based on more than naive self-interest. To judge from the early reports, they have gained at least as many points as we could have expected, considering the difficulties they were up against: GATT undertakings, Britain's new interest in a European common market, and the dense network of import restrictions in Australia which has tarnished our status as a potential market.

To praise Mr. McEwen's achievement is not to pretend that it goes anywhere near solving Australia's trade deficit. It is still impossible to put a money value on the immediate improvement we can expect to the trade balance when the agreement comes into effect, but a figure of £10 million a year may be distinctly generous. Even the 'understanding and expectation' that sales of wheat and flour to Britain will be not less than 28 million bushels a year for five years will lend itself to different interpretations. Wheat was the biggest single issue for Australia at these talks, and the wheat clause may give the most immediate results. But the question of wheat prices in the British market could still be a subject of lively debate.

Mr. McEwen's second major success has been to reduce the preferential tariff margins granted to British imports. The immediate benefits from this may be small. Everything will depend on the follow-through, especially on the way we use this new freedom to negotiate for better export outlets to foreign countries. Imports should become rather cheaper and the climate for exports rather better,

It is, perhaps, in his attention to this broad question of climate that Mr. Mc-Ewen has shown most originality. It was a very good idea to obtain the full right of discretion to waive the preferential tariff by-laws. It was an excellent idea to have put into writing a joint statement of disapproval of subsidised exports, with a British undertaking to bring down anti-dumping legislation. This may some day prove an important round won in the continuing battle against American methods of disposing food surpluses. . . .

Source: Leading article in the *Sydney Morning Herald*, 14 November 1956.

9:14 UNITED KINGDOM-AUSTRALIA TRADE AGREEMENT: BRITISH ATTITUDE

Statement by the Minister for Trade (J. McEwen) in the House of Representatives on 9 April 1957.

It soon became clear that the United Kingdom authorities were not prepared for such a comprehensive review of the Ottawa agreement as we were pressing for. The issues involved were important and they were certainly complex. There was no easy meeting of views between the two governments. . . .

The negotiations were not simple. Before progress could be made, it had to be strongly emphasised to United Kingdom Ministers that we were determined to secure a thoroughly new basis for our trade relations with the United Kingdom and a new coverage in the replacing Agreement that we sought.[1]

Source: *C.P.D. (H. of R.)*, vol. 14, p. 649.

[1] The full statement made by McEwen on 9 April 1957 gives similar information to that given in 9:12, but spells out in more detail the effect of the new Agreement on some specific commodities.

9:15 CRITICISM OF NEW TRADE AGREEMENT

Speech by R. T. Pollard in the House of Representatives on 30 April 1957.

When we analyse the core of the agreement,[1] we find that the end result is of little importance to the people of this country. The agreement will make a most meagre contribution, if any contribution at all, to the solution of the problem of our adverse balance of trade which has confronted us for the last three or four years, and which the Minister set out, partially at least to solve.

One of the reasons advanced for our adverse trade balance was that in our trade with the United Kingdom we were bound hand and foot by the Ottawa Agreement, which was entered into in 1932 by the then Australian Government and the Government of the United Kingdom. As a result of the march of time, the expansion of secondary industry in this country, and the substantial alteration

[1] Trade in wheat between the United Kingdom and Australia was the main point in Pollard's speech, although he covered other matters too.

in money values, that agreement has no longer any relevant or sensible application to the problems affecting trade between the two countries concerned. For that reason, I agree with the Minister that it was due for some revision. . . .

In Article 6, we have the strangest conglomeration of ideas, statements and so on that I have ever read in any agreement drawn up between two governments. This article concerns wheat . . . The article says that the United Kingdom Government notes that Australia's share of the wheat trade has declined. That is a very interesting observation! We know it only too well. Reasons are given for that decline, the first two being changes in world wheat marketing and the increase in United Kingdom home-grown wheat. That is an obvious observation; everybody knows it or ought to know it, but it is incorporated in an article in the agreement. Then we find this strange paragraph—

> The United Kingdom will consider sympathetically any measures which may be found practicable from time to time, having due regard to their domestic policies and international obligations, to improve the opportunities for the sale of Australian wheat in the United Kingdom.

It goes on to say that both governments welcome arrangements for periodical discussions. Who would not? That has been the ruling modus vivendi ever since responsible government was established in Australia. . . .

Referring to both the governments the article says—

> They affirm that it is their desire and expectation that sales on commercial terms of Australian wheat and flour in the United Kingdom will amount to not less than 750,000 tons per annum.

That is approximately 28,000,000 bushels of wheat. They affirm that that quantity should be taken by the people of the United Kingdom. Of course, 'wheat' includes flour sales. It is very nice to express a desire and have an expectation, but there is no legally binding contract. It is a most visionary arrangement when one takes into consideration that the word 'commercial' is incorporated in that particular article . . . there is no binding obligation whatsoever on the United Kingdom Government to buy any wheat. The reason the United Kingdom will not be buying any wheat is that the Australian Wheat Board, because of ever-rising costs in this country, is not able to offer wheat at a commercial price that would pay Australia, or at a price that would be attractive to United Kingdom flour-millers. . . .

As I have said, the two governments agree to confer if 28,000,000 bushels of wheat have not been sold. If there is no satisfactory outcome of these negotiations, consultations or pow-wows, either side can call for a renegotiation of the agreement. . . .

We find a further reference to this wheat problem . . . I am referring now to paragraph 4 of Article 6, which reads

> If at any time the United Kingdom Government should impose countervailing duties which are agreed between the two Governments to be effective on imports of subsidized wheat the Australian Government will not invoke the provisions of paragraph three of this article. . . .

That is in regard to the renegotiation of the agreement—

. . . so long as such duties remain effectively in force. Let us examine that statement. Some countries are subsidizing the production of wheat. It is exported to the United Kingdom market and the growers are paid a satisfactory price, although the grain is being sold at a price lower than the cost of production . . .

Can anybody in his sound senses imagine the United Kingdom Government imposing a duty of so much a bushel on so-called subsidized wheat—a better term would be dumped wheat—and then facing the electors and saying to them, 'By virtue of the fact that the Australian Government has had a little pow-wow with us we have agreed to impose a countervailing duty so that the price of your bread will go up by 1d., 2d., 3d., or 4d. a loaf'? Such a thing would be the dream of a visionary . . . we see that cost increases in Australia probably are more responsible than any other factor for the grave difficulties that we are encountering in meeting competition by other countries when we seek markets for our products . . . Therein lies one of the basic elements of the problem. Another aspect is the failure of this Government to issue a worth-while challenge to the overseas shipping monopoly. The rise in freight rates is one of the main reasons why the Government is having trouble over the balance of trade. . . .

Source: C.P.D. (H. of R.), vol. 15, pp. 883-8.

9:16 REDUCTION OF TARIFFS

Press statement by the Minister for Trade (J. McEwen) on 22 May 1957.

Duties on over 800 items imported from foreign countries will be reduced as from tomorrow morning. . . .

The action to reduce duties over so extensive and important a field of our imports, said Mr McEwen, flowed from our freedom under the new Trade Agreement with the United Kingdom to narrow the preference margin to 7½% on items where the British Preferential duty is free. . . .

The reduced duties should therefore provide a real cost-relief to wide sectors of Australian industry and overall benefits to the Australian economy.

Apart from the cost relief provided for Australian industry the reduced duties will be of real interest to a number of countries, including some good customer countries for Australian exports. The competitive position of these countries in the Australian market will now be enhanced.

Some 30 of the items on which the foreign duties are to be reduced are subject to primage duties. These primage duties will be eliminated as from tomorrow, Mr. McEwen said.

9:17 REFERENCE TO TARIFF BOARD ON MOST-FAVOURED-NATION RATES OF DUTY

Press statement by the Minister for Trade (J. McEwen) on 13 May 1959.

The Acting Prime Minister and Minister for Trade, the Rt. Hon. J. McEwen, announced to-day that he had forwarded to the Tariff Board for inquiry and report a reference covering over 250 individual items of the Customs Tariff.

Mr. McEwen said he thought that because of the unusual nature of the reference, he should explain its origin and purpose.

Mr. McEwen recalled that, when he signed the new Trade Agreement between Australia and the United Kingdom on behalf of the Australian Government in 1957, he had pointed out that the Agreement allowed for lower tariff preferences to the United Kingdom. This enabled Australia to exercise a greater degree of flexibility in tariff making, which could have important results in two ways.

In the first place, the impact on Australian costs of the wide margins of preference that had operated against imports from foreign countries could be eased as a result of the Agreement. The way became open to make a number of such reductions without impairing protection to Australian industry.

Moreover, the way was open to Australia to negotiate improved export opportunities for Australian products with other countries. This could be by bargaining the reduction of tariff preferences (in cases where those preferences resulted in Most-Favoured-Nation duties which were higher than was necessary to protect local industries) for concessions from other countries.

In May 1957 advantage was taken of the new Agreement to reduce Most-Favoured-Nation rates of duty under some 800 Tariff Items. With one exception, a relatively unimportant By-law item, these items imposed no duty on imports entitled to entry under the British Preferential Tariff. The question of protection of Australian industry had provided no impediment to the action then taken, Mr. McEwen said.

The Government has been examining the best way of taking further steps to derive the maximum benefit from the scope provided by the Agreement for additional reductions of Most-Favoured-Nation rates. There are a number of items where the rates of duty under the Most-Favoured-Nation tariff had been fixed without reference to the protective needs of Australian industry. Many of these rates could, no doubt, be reduced with benefit to Australian industry.

However, the Government had no intention of departing from the traditional policy of affording protection to economic and efficient Australian industries. He had therefore decided to seek the advice of the Tariff Board on the scope for reducing Most-Favoured-Nation duties under such items.

The normal reference asks the Tariff Board to examine and advise on whether assistance should be accorded the production in Australia of the goods concerned and, if assistance should be through the Customs Tariff, the rates of duty under each column of the Tariff. Almost invariably the bulk of evidence submitted concerns competition from the United Kingdom.

Mr. McEwen said that, because of the volume of evidence on U.K. competition, the Board's inquiries on matters referred to it under the normal type of reference took a considerable time. It was because normal references on the large number of items involved could have delayed the consideration of requests for increased protection for Australian industries that he had decided to limit the reference he had just signed to the question of Most-Favoured-Nation rates of duty.

Mr. McEwen added that the reference showed, in respect of each item, the minimum level to which the Most-Favoured-Nation rate could be reduced, under the provisions of the Trade Agreement with the United Kingdom, while the British Preferential Tariff rate remained at the existing level.

10

JAPAN

Any review of Australian trade policy must give high ranking to the decision to negotiate a formal trade treaty with Japan. The rather quiet announcement of the decision by the then Acting Minister for Trade, W. McMahon, was deceptively laconic (10:7). The decision followed what would now be called 'agonising appraisal' in anticipation of a hostile public opinion. In the event, the treaty aroused an even more bitter protest from manufacturers than had been expected. Nevertheless, the general public demur was far less than was expected, for the decision has to be studied against the unhappy pre-war trading relationship and the bitterness of war.[1] Consumers remembered many rather shoddy goods from Japan whose only advantage was cheapness—an advantage naturally not appreciated by Australian manufacturers or Australian trade unionists. The war had given all Australians cause to hesitate about the resumption of ordinary relations of an economic, political, or social character. In the outcome the majority saw the wisdom of the action taken and supported it, even if 'welcomed it' was too generous a term to use in the first year or so after the signing of the treaty.

The necessity to make a decision could not be avoided: it was posed squarely enough in Article 12 of the Peace Treaty (10:1), not least by clause (c) of the Article. This touched on a real difficulty for Australia, which did not accord Japan MFN treatment in the tariff and, in addition, discriminated heavily against Japan in import licensing.[2] There were technical currency reasons for import discrimination since for a while trade with Japan involved the need to convert sterling to scarce dollars.[3] But Japan had reason to protest as time wore on, and the moves to minimise the discrimination against her were inevitably taken. These moves are to be seen as a deliberate part of the cautious economic *rapprochement* culminating in the treaty of 1957

[1] For those interested in the details of the pre-war 'trade diversion policy' and the controversy it aroused, an excellent starting point is given in Copland and Janes (42), pp. 259-346. Valuable material on this period is also available in Nicholson (132), pp. 8-10, 83, 110-15, 120-2, and in the 'Tenth Report of the Rural Reconstruction Commission' (12), pp. 51-2.

[2] Japan was invidiously in a small company of nations subjected to the General Tariff, which on many items of importance to her was significantly higher than the MFN tariff level.

[3] For an account of early post-war trading arrangements with Japan see Nicholson (132), pp. 246-55.

351

which finally removed all discrimination against Japan from the import licensing system (Section 15).

Ambivalence is the correct word to use in explaining Australian steps towards a restoration of normal relations with Japan. The Peace Treaty marked final acceptance of the need to collaborate with other Western powers in an effort to rebuild Japan as a member of the international community and one likely to work with rather than against Western interests. This political objective was of considerable importance in the final decision to negotiate a comprehensive trade treaty with Japan. There is little doubt that the Australian public accepted this aspect of the treaty. Even R. W. Anderson, speaking on behalf of the Associated Chambers of Manufactures of Australia, was at pains to emphasise that they 'were not quarrelling with the Government's political decision to seek a trade agreement with Japan' (10:9). This declaration, however, faithfully echoed in Parliament by Evatt (10:16) and in a remarkably ambivalent statement by the Australian Council of Trade Unions (10:17), was not allowed to soften his version of acceptable terms which were, in fact, too one-sided to be negotiable.

It would be quite wrong, however, to argue that the international political argument alone accounted for the decision to negotiate a trade treaty although it gave powerful support. The economic basis for a treaty was strong and, in the long run, sufficient cause for a treaty. Nevertheless, having regard to the domestic political difficulties expected and the economic fears expressed by manufacturing interests, no treaty was possible without the incorporation of strong defensive economic safeguards.

On the one hand the Australian government could well see that a rehabilitated and economically developing Japan could be of great importance to Australia as a market. The value of this prospect was reinforced by the disappointingly negative development in the volume of our export sales to Great Britain—and the connection between the negotiations with Britain and those with Japan should not be overlooked. The support given to the government by primary producers can be readily understood (10:6). On the other hand, pre-war experience had taught Australian governments and manufacturers alike—and a good many others—to be afraid of the Japanese threat to Australian industry. How strongly felt this fear was is seen in the statements of opposition already noted (10:9, 10:16, 10:17, to which should be added 10:15). It is also evident in the unusual lengths the government went to in preserving its right to act against any threat to Australian industry (A10:1, Article V, 10:18).

Nor could the Australian government sit back and continue to reap the benefits of an expanding market while denying Japan access to the Australian market. Japan had, in the pre-war period, shown that she could divert trade to others. The United States could easily sell wheat from production and surplus stocks. In wool the real fear was that this market (which was predominantly domestic rather than export in character) could give a strong preference to synthetics with probably less strain on its balance of payments. There were (and are) alternative sources of coal, ferrous and non-ferrous minerals. Again, Japan was not easily in total trade balance and, without increasing access to world markets, including Australian, her ability to buy Australian was limited.[4] Finally, Australia's defence policies, immigration program, and other economic and social objectives called for rapid economic development. For this an increasing volume of imports was essential. She therefore had an interest in a rapid, rather than merely a long term, expansion of exports. This was not readily in sight with Britain or anywhere else other than Japan.

All these considerations rendered clause (c) of Article XII of the Peace Treaty of considerable significance (10:1). It was natural that Japan should make early approaches in terms of it and that the Australian government should, in self-interest, finally respond to Japan's overtures.

There is no need to elaborate the general situation further—the Australian interests and reasons for hesitation are well revealed in the documents. It is well, however, to add one observation: Japan, too, had a political as well as economic interest in rebuilding relations with Australia. The American position was clear but Australia was apparently seen by Japan as a potentially important economic partner, important enough also to influence the attitude of other countries (e.g. in GATT) towards the expansion of trade with Japan. In this respect, the issue of recognition in GATT assumed particular importance, as did the agreed relationship under which Japan could share growth in the Australian market provided this was not at the cost of disruption of Australian industry.

These issues are the crucial ones and again are reasonably covered in the documents. The reader may be interested in a few supplementary observations. Regardless of other difficulties of which only one mattered, the refusal by Australia to 'recognise' Japan in GATT was probably necessary politically (10:3, 10:4, 10:10, A10:1, 10:11), for the manufacturers had convinced themselves and would probably have convinced others that Australia's unqualified application of GATT rights to Japan would have made it impossible to protect Australian industry against Japanese competition of disruptive character. There was a difficulty here, for GATT under its Article XIX requires emergency action to be applied to all imports in a non-discriminatory manner: it does not provide for action directed specifically against one member except through the cumbersome procedures of Article XXII, which provides for 'consultation'. As a reading of the documents shows, it was deemed essential to provide for quick action. Article V of the Treaty provided for this

---

[4] This point was made clearly by Russell (150). The same point is developed in Arndt (4), a most useful general reference on the subject of this section. See also Drysdale (73).

while giving scope for remedial action by Japan itself. This article was not strictly consistent with GATT. On its own this point was somewhat 'pure' doctrine, for there were GATT members who recognised Japan without qualification but who nevertheless unilaterally imposed 'un-GATT-like' quotas and restrictions on Japanese exports.[5] Australian restrictions in the event were far less restrictive than those imposed by these GATT members.

Given the fears so strongly held by Australian manufacturers, Article V was essential as a sanction to be seen publicly and to be demonstrated as effective. This is exactly what has happened. I held a private list of rather more than a hundred 'sensitive items' for which there was some reason to fear on behalf of Australian manufacturers the inroads of Japanese imports. In fact, under the special arrangements established there were only fourteen inquiries and action proved necessary only in five.[6]

Experience showed that provided the Australian market was growing, problems of absorption were fewer than would be the case under static conditions. Other factors contributing to the successful outcome pictured in the table in A10:3 were restraint by Japan in difficult cases, the maintenance of high quality, and the discovery that in many lines Japan was not the lowest cost supplier. Also of importance has been Japan's gradual realisation that it has more to gain by competing with Britain, Europe, and America in the many imports (some 70 per cent of the total) which are not subject to protective tariffs.[7] This is especially true of capital goods and components.

Progress was rapid and the changes effected in the review of the Treaty announced in 1963 caused very little stir (A10:2, 10:21). This could be thought remarkable, for in the amended Treaty Australia's recognition of Japan as a partner in GATT became complete and the powerfully discriminating Article V of the original Treaty was dropped (A10:2). But by this time Australian manufacturers had moved from their early position of bitter and even hysterical protest to recognising Japan sufficiently to establish with Japanese businessmen a joint Committee for Australian-Japanese Business Co-operation.[8] Some industries still feared Japanese competition but the community as a whole has come to recognise the expanding mutual interests embodied in the Treaty (10:22). Incidental outcomes have been a large expansion of tourism (as yet largely one way—Australians to Japan) and the growth of Japanese interest (including investment) in Australia's unfolding mineral resources.

[5] This point was made in an address by me to a visiting Sugar Mission from Japan in Sydney on 8 August 1962. Although not published, it is available to interested students.

[6] See Vernon Report (11), vol. I, ch. 12, para. 71.

[7] Ibid., ch. 13, para. 24.

[8] The operations of this committee received good publicity in the daily press and in the *Australian Financial Review*. See, for example, 10:22; Kojima (103); and *Sydney Morning Herald*, Supplement on Japan, 12 April 1965.

A10:3 indicates the very real growth in mutual trade. Any detailed analysis of it here, however, would take us too far beyond the scope of the documents.[9] Japan promises to become for Australia in the future what Great Britain was in the nineteenth century and the first thirty years of the twentieth century. Any analysis supports the view that further expansion in trade between the two countries is inevitable. This will occur despite the occasional question: 'does the fact that Japan has become the Great Britain of the Far East point to too much dependence by Australia on Japan?' This dependence is far from being as complete as the earlier dependence on Britain had been. Moreover, Japan is itself developing a measure of dependence on Australian supplies of essential raw materials, reinforced by its own investment along with Australian and American capital interests in the development of mineral resources in Western Australia and Queensland. There will be problems, including those incidental to price negotiations for iron ore and coal in which Japanese conditional reliance on cartelisation enables it to play off divided and competing interests in Australia, one against another, and all these interests as against suppliers in Asia and Latin America. There will be problems for both countries, each of which has highly protected areas, sensitive to competition. The tariff on Australia's automobile industry is matched by the protection Japan gives its own industry and by some highly protected food producing industries. Japan is still far from being the free trading country many people imagine.

Australia is resisting suggestions from Japanese sources that she should be content to develop raw material and food exports to Japan: Australia will look for openings for processed exports too.[10]

Another problem of importance is both countries' growing awareness that both have problems of political-economic importance in their relations with underdeveloped Asian countries. Even if Australian industry should prove the most efficient producer, Japan cannot afford to divert all its demand for raw materials to Australia, for it already has a surplus of exports with Asian and African countries.[11] Nor can Australia politically afford to take only the attitude of an efficient supplier anxious to displace Asian suppliers of iron ore whose export needs are so much more critical than her own. This political-economic problem must figure more and more in Japanese-Australian

[9] None of the documents in the section offer a detailed review of the course of trade, on which see Drysdale (73); Arndt (4); Vernon Report (11), vol. I, ch. 12, paras. 71-5; and Kojima (102). See also Crawford (59), in which the significance for Australian trade of planned growth in Japanese national income by 1970 is discussed; and *Current Affairs Bulletin* (67).

[10] See Arndt (4) and Kojima (103), for useful discussion on this matter of 'vertical' and 'horizontal' trade. It is interesting that Kojima notes and appears to accept the Australian reluctance to allow exports of its raw materials solely in the unprocessed form.

[11] See Kojima (102).

economic relations. Yet another issue may well come from possible British entry into the Common Market. The ending of British preferences in the Australian tariff would offer new scope for bargaining between Australia and Japan (Section 9).

All these issues are important and now receive increasing recognition in academic research and in press articles. Since our documents largely stop short of expounding these current and future issues, we can be content to note that the 'political' decision to negotiate an agreement with Japan gave full scope to the natural factors making for close trade relations between the two countries. The economic basis was there; but without the agreement of 1957 the course of mutual trade expansion would have been both vastly more difficult and a good deal slower—with adverse effects on Australia's rate of economic growth. It is probably fair to add that, in this case at least, the economic *modus operandi* established in 1957 has greatly facilitated the growth of fruitful political relations.

A10:1 AGREEMENT ON COMMERCE BETWEEN AUSTRALIA AND JAPAN

The Government of the Commonwealth of Australia and the Government of Japan,

Being desirous of improving and developing the commercial relations between the two countries,

Have agreed as follows:

ARTICLE I

1. With respect to customs duties and charges of any kind imposed on or in connection with importation or exportation or imposed on the international transfer of payments for imports or exports, and with respect to the method of levying such duties and charges, and with respect to all rules and formalities in connection with importation and exportation, and with respect to the application of internal taxes to exported goods and with respect to all internal taxes or other internal charges of any kind imposed on or in connection with imported goods and with respect to all laws, regulations and requirements affecting internal sale, offering for sale, purchase, distribution or use of imported goods, any advantage, favour, privilege or immunity which has been or may hereafter be granted by the Government of either country to any product originating in or destined for any third country shall be accorded immediately and unconditionally to the like product originating in or destined for the other country.

2. The provisions of paragraph 1 shall not entitle the Government of Japan to claim the benefit of any preference or advantage which may at any time be accorded by the Government of the Commonwealth of Australia to any member country of the Commonwealth of Nations including its dependent territories, or to the Republic of Ireland.

ARTICLE II

1. No prohibitions or restrictions, whether made effective through quotas, import or export licences or other measures, shall be instituted or maintained by the Government of either country on the importation of any product of the other country or on the exportation or sale for export of any product destined for the other country unless such prohibitions or restrictions are applied to all third countries.

2. In all matters relating to the allocation of foreign exchange affecting transactions involving the importation and exportation of goods, the Government of each country shall accord to the other country treatment no less favourable than it accords to any third country.

3. Notwithstanding the provisions of paragraphs 1 and 2 either Government may take such measures as are necessary to safeguard its external financial position and balance of payments.

ARTICLE III

1. With respect to trade between Australia and Japan,

(a) Each Government undertakes that if it establishes or maintains a state trading enterprise, wherever located, or grants to any trading enterprise, formally or in effect, exclusive or special privileges, such trading enterprise shall, in its purchases or sales involving imports or exports, act in a manner consistent with the general principles of non-discriminatory treatment prescribed in this Agreement for governmental measures affecting imports or exports by private traders.

(b) The provisions of sub-paragraph (a) of this paragraph shall be understood to require that such trading enterprises shall, having due regard to the other provisions of this Agreement, make any such purchases or sales solely in accordance with commercial considerations, including price, quality, availability, marketability, transportation and other conditions of purchase or sale, and shall afford trading enterprises of the other country adequate opportunity, in accordance with customary business practice, to compete for participation in such purchases or sales.

(c) Neither Government shall prevent any enterprise (whether or not an enterprise described in sub-paragraph (a) of this paragraph) under its jurisdiction from acting in accordance with the principles of sub-paragraphs (a) and (b) of this paragraph.

2. The provisions of paragraph 1 of this Article shall not apply to imports of products for immediate or ultimate consumption in governmental use and not otherwise for resale or use in the production of goods for sale. With respect to such imports, the Government of each country shall accord to the trade of the other country fair and equitable treatment.

ARTICLE IV

1. The provisions of this Agreement shall not be regarded as conferring any more favourable treatment on the trade of either country than the Government of the other country is entitled or obliged to accord to those countries in respect of which it applies the General Agreement on Tariffs and Trade. The two Governments shall, so far as practicable and as may be agreed between them from time to time, base their commercial relations upon the provisions of the General

N

Agreement on Tariffs and Trade in respect of matters not covered by this Agreement.

2. The provisions of this Agreement or any action taken under the Agreement shall not affect the rights of either Government under Article XXXV of the General Agreement on Tariffs and Trade nor detract from the freedom of either Government in any negotiations for the application of the General Agreement on Tariffs and Trade between the two countries.

ARTICLE V

1. It is the expectation of both Governments that mutual trade will be increased as a result of this Agreement. It is further expected that this expansion of trade will be achieved without serious injury being caused or threatened to domestic producers in Australia or Japan. If, nevertheless, as a result of unforeseen developments, the Government of either country finds that any product is being imported from the other country under such conditions as to cause or threaten serious injury to producers in the country of importation of like or directly competitive products, that Government may, in respect of such product, suspend obligations under this Agreement to the extent and for such time as may be necessary to prevent or remedy such injury.

2. Before either Government takes action pursuant to the provisions of paragraph 1 of this Article, it shall give written notice to the other Government as far in advance as may be practicable and shall afford the other Government an opportunity to consult with it as fully as circumstances permit in respect of the proposed action.

3. In the event that either Government finds it necessary to take action under this Article which affects such a number of products or such a volume of trade that in the view of the other Government the achievement of the objectives of this Agreement is seriously impaired, the Government which considers its interests adversely affected may request consultations with the other Government on the situation which has developed including the action taken; and may after two months from the time of the action being taken, if no mutually satisfactory solution is reached or at an earlier date if it is agreed that no solution is likely to emerge seek a renegotiation of the terms of this Agreement. Such renegotiation shall be commenced as soon as practicable after a written request has been made. In the event that a satisfactory solution is not reached within two months after such renegotiation is requested, the Government which sought renegotiation may terminate the Agreement on two months' notice, notwithstanding the provisions of paragraph 2 of Article VII.

ARTICLE VI

1. Each Government shall accord sympathetic consideration to representations made by the other Government on matters arising out of the operation of this Agreement and shall afford to the other Government adequate opportunity for consultation.

2. Consultation shall in any event be held annually on the operation of this Agreement.

ARTICLE VII

1. This Agreement shall be ratified by each Government and shall enter into force on the date of the exchange of instruments of ratification.

2. This Agreement shall remain in force until the fifth day of July, 1960, and shall continue in force thereafter provided that it shall be terminated on that date or thereafter if either Government has previously given to the other Government at least three months' written notice of its intention to terminate the Agreement.

In witness whereof the representatives of the two Governments, duly authorised for the purpose, have signed this Agreement.

Done in the English and Japanese languages, both equally authentic, this 6th July, 1957, at Tokyo.

Source: Commonwealth of Australia,
paper no. 3629/57,
Government Printer, Canberra.

In an exchange of letters between the Japanese Minister for Foreign Affairs and the Australian Minister for Trade it was agreed that:

(a) the most-favoured-nation provisions of the Agreement shall not apply to advantages accorded by Japan to areas set forth in Article 3 of the Peace Treaty with Japan signed at San Francisco on 8th September, 1951.

(b) the provisions of the Agreement shall not apply to external territories administered by Australia nor to any advantages accorded between these territories and Australia.

(c) the understandings concerning the implementation of the Agreement embodied in the following Minutes be confirmed.

The 'Agreed Minutes' summarised, are as follows:

Part A

Japan indicated the treatment she intended to accord under her import system to the following Australian goods: wool, wheat, barley, sugar, beef tallow, cattle hides, dried skim milk and dried vine fruits. In general Australia was to be given the opportunity to compete for a substantial share of the Japanese market in these goods. If the opportunity for Australian soft wheat to compete freely in the Japanese market should be impaired, due to transactions not conforming with normal fair trade or commercial practice (e.g. surplus disposals), the Japanese Government would ensure that the Australian wheat which would be purchased through commercial channels and on a competitive basis, represented an equitable share of the Japanese market.

Part B

Australia had already bound against increase the rates of duty on a relatively large number of items to other countries of export interest to Japan, and by extending most-favoured-nation treatment to Japanese goods, Australia assured stability of treatment to those goods. Japan was in a position to vary materially the tariff conditions applying to major Australian exports to Japan. To meet these circumstances Australia requested an assurance that Japan would maintain the present duty-free entry for wool. Japan gave such an assurance for a period of three years after the date of signing the Agreement, having in mind that during that period the Australian Government would endeavour to move towards the application of the General Agreement on Tariffs and Trade between the two countries. The Australian Delegation confirmed that the Australian Government had in mind entering into discussion with the Japanese Government during that period with a view to examining the basis of applying the General Agreement between the two countries.

PART C

The Australian Delegation pointed out that the basis of Article V was the mutual expectation of increased opportunity for expansion of Japanese exports to Australia without serious damage to Australian industry or sudden and serious disruption of the pattern of Australia's imports. It would welcome the co-operation of the Japanese authorities in dealing with such situations if they arose.

The Japanese Delegation stated that under Japanese legislation export was free in principle and that the Japanese Government could only take limited measures to deal with these problems. However, the Japanese Government would use its best endeavours within its constitutional authority to see that exports from Japan to Australia were conducted so as to avoid or remedy the damage or prospect of damage to which the Australian Delegation had referred.

It was agreed that the maximum degree of consultation between the two Governments was essential to the satisfactory solution of any particular problem and that:

(a) effective liaison would immediately be established in Canberra between the Japanese Embassy and the Australian Government and in Tokyo between the Australian Embassy and the Japanese Government;

(b) statistical information would be provided on a continuing basis;

(c) if in the opinion of either Government serious injury were threatened because of imports, immediate consultations would be held to try to remedy the situation;

(d) if a situation required the application of Article V, the procedure provided for in that Article would be adopted.

The Australian Delegation said that the following considerations would apply in respect of any action taken by Australia under Article V. Such action

(i) would not be taken except after consultation, which would be as far in advance as practicable;

(ii) would only be taken where the consultation process failed to provide a mutually acceptable alternative solution to the problem. If urgency required action before the consultation process was completed, consultation would be continued to try to find an acceptable solution;

(iii) so far as administratively practicable, would only apply to those specific goods in respect of which action was necessary;

(iv) would only apply for such time as was necessary to correct the particular situation;

(v) would be limited to cases where serious damage was caused or threatened.

In a further exchange of letters Australia and Japan agreed to the provisional application of the agreements and undertakings set out above as from 6 July 1957.

Source: Commonwealth of Australia,
paper no. 3629/57. Government Printer,
Canberra.

A10:2 PROTOCOL AMENDING THE AGREEMENT ON COMMERCE BETWEEN THE COMMONWEALTH OF AUSTRALIA AND JAPAN

The Government of the Commonwealth of Australia and the Government of Japan,

Desiring to amend the Agreement on Commerce between the Commonwealth of Australia and Japan, signed at Hakone on the 6th July, 1957, (hereinafter referred to as 'the Agreement') as a result of the disinvocation by the Government of the Commonwealth of Australia of Article XXXV of the General Agreement on Tariffs and Trade in respect of Japan,

Have agreed as follows:

ARTICLE I

Paragraphs 1 and 2 of Article IV of the Agreement shall be deleted and replaced by the following:

'Nothing in this Agreement shall be construed so as to derogate from the rights and obligations that either country has or may have as a contracting party to the General Agreement on Tariffs and Trade, so long as both countries are contracting parties to the General Agreement on Tariffs and Trade'.

ARTICLE II

Article V of the Agreement shall be deleted.

ARTICLE III

Paragraph 2 of Article VII of the Agreement shall be amended by replacing the words 'the fifth day of July, 1960' by the words 'the day three years after the date of the entry into force of the Protocol of 5th August, 1963 amending the Agreement'.

ARTICLE IV

This Protocol shall be subject to ratification by each Government and shall enter into force on the date of the exchange of the instruments of ratification which shall take place at Canberra as soon as possible.

IN WITNESS WHEREOF the representatives of the two Governments, duly authorised for the purpose, have signed this Protocol.

DONE at Tokyo in duplicate, in the English and Japanese languages, both equally authentic, this fifth day of August 1963.

For the Government of the Commonwealth of Australia:

J. MCEWEN

L. R. MCINTYRE

For the Government of Japan:

HAJIME FUKUDA

AGREED MINUTES

. The representatives of the Government of the Commonwealth of Australia and the representatives of the Government of Japan, confirming that the General Agreement on Tariffs and Trade will be applied between the Commonwealth of Australia and Japan, hereby record the following understandings which have been reached during the course of the negotiations between their respective

361

Delegations leading to the signing today of the Protocol amending the Agreement on Commerce between the Commonwealth of Australia and Japan, of 6th July, 1957.

The 'Agreed Minutes', summarised, are as follows:

PART A

1. *Wool*

The Japanese Government would not discriminate against raw wool, as compared with raw cotton, in respect to non-tariff matters which might affect its importation. The Japanese Government had no intention at this time of imposing a duty on raw wool, but this did not bind it in any way.

2. *Wheat*

Importation into Japan of soft wheat would continue at a stabilized level. The Japanese Government would study with the Australian Government the possibility of bringing the price differential in Japan between Australian F.A.Q. wheat and U.S. Western White wheat down to the differential in world markets. It was prepared to purchase Queensland and northern New South Wales soft wheat when the necessary requirements had been met.

3. *Barley*

Japan is now self-sufficient in barley production but if emergency imports were necessary, Australian barley would be accorded non-discriminatory access on a most-favoured-nation basis.

4. *Products subject to import restrictions*

The Japanese Government would ensure most-favoured-nation treatment for such products from Australia and would make every effort to expand opportunities for the import into Japan of Australian sugar, canned meat, leather, motor vehicles, butter and cheese.

Both Australia and Japan intended to maintain the scope of import liberalisation currently in force. Any further import restrictions imposed for balance of payments reasons would not be applied so as to prevent the importation of the products concerned in minimum commercial quantities, the exclusion of which would impair regular channels of trade.

PART B

5. *Export of Heavy Industry Products to Australia*

The Japanese Government requested that full opportunities of fair competition be accorded to Japanese products in respect of the purchase of goods abroad by the Australian Government and certain of its Statutory Authorities such as the Snowy Mountains Authority and the Commonwealth Railways. The Australian Delegation stated that equal opportunities of fair and equal competition were accorded by the Government and its Statutory Authorities to Japanese products in regard to public tenders called for overseas purchases. Explanations of the reasons for failure of unsuccessful tenderers were given upon request.

PART C

6. *Temporary Tariff Protection under Article V of the Australian Tariff Board Act*

The Australian Delegation confirmed that such protection was only applied when imports were being imported in such quantities or under such conditions as to cause or threaten serious injury to domestic producers and that it was

362

applied only to such extent and for such time as might be necessary to prevent or remedy such injury.

Before making a reference to a Special Advisory Authority the Australian Government would afford the Japanese Government the maximum practical degree of consultation and if the urgency of the matter required a reference before the completion of such consultation, it could be continued after the reference had been made.

The Japanese Government would cooperate with a view to finding whether the need for action under Part V of the Tariff Board Act could be obviated by measures taken in Japan.

Upon receipt of an application for temporary protection, it was the practice of the Australian Government to notify the Japanese Government immediately and to take full account of any representations made by the Japanese Government before reaching a decision.

The understandings contained in these Agreed Minutes will, as from the date of the coming into force of the Protocol amending the Agreement on Commerce between the Commonwealth of Australia and Japan of 6th July, 1957 signed today, supersede the understandings embodied in the Agreed Minutes attached to the Exchange of Notes of 6th July, 1957.

Tokyo, 5th August, 1963.

Source: Australia: Treaty Series 1964
(Department of External Affairs).

A10:3   TRADE BETWEEN AUSTRALIA AND JAPAN, 1955-6 to 1965-6

(Exports f.o.b., imports f.o.b., including bullion and specie)

Year	Total exports to Japan (A)	Total imports from Japan (B)	Ratio of (A) to (B)	Exports of wool to Japan	Wool as percentage of total exports to Japan	Average wool price at auction
	$Am.	$Am.		$Am.	per cent	cents per lb
1955– 6	173·0	45·2	3·8	129·6	74·9	51·2
1956– 7	277·8	25·8	10·8	207·6	74·7	66·4
1957– 8	205·4	47·6	4·3	148·6	72·3	52·0
1958– 9	204·6	59·8	3·4	137·8	67·4	40·5
1959–60	269·4	83·0	3·2	191·2	71·0	48·2
1960– 1	323·0	130·8	2·5	211·8	65·6	43·4
1961– 2	373·8	99·0	3·8	229·2	61·3	45·1
1962– 3	346·2	129·4	2·7	222·2	64·2	49·1
1963– 4	487·8	162·5	3·0	282·2	57·9	58·1
1964– 5	440·7	258·6	1·7	142·6	55·1	47·8
1965– 6	470·4	280·2	1·7	259·8	55·2	50·1

SOURCE: Derived from Vernon Report (11), vol. I, Table 12:10. Figures for 1964-5 and 1965-6 have been added to the original table and the currency has been changed to $A.

10:1 TRADING RELATIONS BETWEEN JAPAN AND THE ALLIED POWERS

Treaty of Peace with Japan, San Francisco, 8 September 1951.

12. (a) Japan declares its readiness promptly to enter into negotiations for the conclusion with each of the Allied Powers of treaties or agreements to place their trading, maritime and other commercial relations on a stable and friendly basis.

(b) Pending the conclusion of the relevant treaty or agreement, Japan will, during a period of four years from the first coming into force of the present Treaty

(1) accord to each of the Allied Powers, its nationals, products and vessels:

(i) most-favoured-nation treatment with respect to customs duties, charges, restrictions and other regulations on or in connection with the importation and exportation of goods;

(ii) national treatment with respect to shipping, navigation and imported goods, and with respect to natural and juridical persons and their interests—such treatment to include all matters pertaining to the levying and collection of taxes, access to the courts, the making and performance of contracts, rights to property (tangible and intangible), participation in juridical entities constituted under Japanese law, and generally the conduct of all kinds of business and professional activities;

(2) ensure that external purchases and sales of Japanese state trading enterprises shall be based solely on commercial considerations.

(c) In respect to any matter, however, Japan shall be obliged to accord to an Allied Power national treatment, or most-favoured-nation treatment, only to the extent that the Allied Power concerned accords Japan national treatment or most-favoured-nation treatment, as the case may be, in respect of the same matter. The reciprocity envisaged in the foregoing sentence shall be determined, in the case of products, vessels and juridical entities of, and persons domiciled in, any non-metropolitan territory of an Allied Power, and in the case of juridical entities of, and persons domiciled in, any state or province of an Allied Power having a federal government, by reference to the treatment accorded to Japan in such territory, state or province.

(d) In the application of this Article, a discriminatory measure shall not be considered to derogate from the grant of national or most-favoured-nation treatment, as the case may be, if such measure is based on an exception customarily provided for in the commercial treaties of the party applying it, or on the need to safeguard that party's external financial position or balance of payments (except in respect to shipping and navigation), or on the need to maintain its essential security interests, and provided such measure is proportionate to the circumstances and not applied in an arbitrary or unreasonable manner.

(e) Japan's obligations under this Article shall not be affected by the exercise of any Allied rights under Article 14 of the present Treaty; nor shall the provisions of this Article be understood as limiting the undertakings assumed by Japan by virtue of Article 15 of the Treaty.

Source: H.M.S.O. Cmnd. 8392, 1951.

10:2 EFFECT OF GATT ON AUSTRALIA'S TRADE RELATIONS WITH JAPAN

Press statement by the Minister for Trade and Customs (Senator Neil O'Sullivan) on 10 October 1951.

The Minister for Trade and Customs (Senator O'Sullivan) referred today to the recently reported statement by Mr. L. Withall, Director of the Associated Chambers of Manufactures of Australia, on the effect of GATT on Australia's trade relations with Japan.

The Minister added that he desired to correct the erroneous impression that the General Agreement forced Australia into according any particular kind of tariff treatment to Japan in the event that Japan should become a Contracting Party.

The General Agreement provides for the accession of any Government (such as Japan) on terms to be agreed upon between the government desiring to accept the Agreement and the Contracting Parties acting jointly.

At the same time, however, the Agreement [Article XXXV] recognises the essentially bilateral nature of the agreement negotiations and trading relations and provides that the Agreement, or alternatively the concessions negotiated under the Agreement,

shall not apply between any Contracting Party and any other Contracting Party if:
   (a) the two Contracting Parties have not entered into tariff negotiations with each other, and
   (b) either of the Contracting Parties, at the time either becomes a Contracting Party, does not consent to such application.

In simple words all this means is that Mr Withall is entirely mistaken. The position is that in the event of Japan being admitted to membership of GATT it will still remain entirely a matter for Australia to decide on its own account whether and to what extent, if any, it will extend concessions to Japan. Such decision will naturally be made in the light of the corresponding advantages offered to Australia.

10:3 JAPAN'S ACCESSION TO GATT

Press statement by the Prime Minister (R. G. Menzies) on 17 November 1954.

The Prime Minister announced today that the Japanese Government had been informed that Australia was willing to examine in discussions with representatives of the Government of Japan the mutual problems arising from the trading relations between the two countries.

The Prime Minister said:

For some time the Government has been giving careful consideration to the question of our trading relations with Japan, and the proposed talks should be of benefit to both countries.

The Japanese Government had asked some time ago for trade discussions with Australia and concurrently Japan's application for membership to the General Agreement on Tariffs and Trade was before the Contracting Parties to that Agreement.

Australia had been invited to enter into tariff negotiations with Japan under the G.A.T.T. as part of the preliminaries for Japan's accession to the Agreement. Whilst the proposed trade talks with Japan would bear the G.A.T.T. position in mind, Australia would have to continue to reserve its position on the application of the G.A.T.T. principles to Australian trade relations with Japan.

There is still much uncertainty as to the outcome of the review of G.A.T.T. now taking place at Geneva, and as I said in the House of Representatives on September 28 last the results of that review will be one of the factors in determining our attitude to Japanese accession to the G.A.T.T.

10:4 AUSTRALIA SUPPORTS JAPAN'S ACCESSION TO GATT

Press statement by the Prime Minister (R. G. Menzies) on 14 August 1955.

The Prime Minister announced today that the Government had supported Japan's accession to the General Agreement on Tariffs and Trade which had recently been announced from Geneva. The Government, however, could not agree that the General Agreement should apply between Australia and Japan and the necessary formal steps will be taken to secure this result. . . .[1]

Bearing in mind the uncertainties which still exist regarding the strength of Japanese trading competition and the possible effects of such competition on Australian industries and employment, the Government considers that Australia cannot, at this stage, apply the GATT to Japan without special safeguards.

10:5 JAPAN GROPES FOR A STABLE FOOTHOLD

Ten years after the end of the Pacific War, Japan has once again become the object of hard and careful thinking in Australia. The anniversary of her surrender has been marked by two developments of very considerable concern to this country—her accession as a full member to the General Agreement on Tariffs and Trade (GATT) and her Prime Minister's curiously timed announcement that his Government will seek revision of the clause in the Constitution renouncing war as an instrument of policy.

Thanks to the lively and all-too-recent recollections of Japanese trade practices on the one hand and Japanese aggression on the other, the first reaction of most Australians to both these moves can hardly fail to be one of suspicion and alarm. Japanese trade is associated in the minds of Australians with cheap labour, price undercutting, shoddy goods and 'dumping', just as Japanese 'defence policy' still tends to be envisaged in terms of brutal militarism.

. . . there has got to be a realisation that, in a radically altered world situation,

[1] See Document 10:2 for clear statement of Australia's right under Article XXXV of GATT to decline to apply the rules of GATT to its relations with Japan.

Australia's national interest demands the creation of a Japan economically stable and militarily strong.

. . . although Canberra's reaction to the Japanese accession to GATT was no doubt inevitable in all the circumstances, it has to be recognised that Australia has a deep political interest in developing trading relations with Japan, quite apart from such practical considerations as the value of Japanese operations in our wool and coal markets. Again, the new Japanese interest in rearmament should be welcomed here. . . .

Source: Leading article in the *Sydney Morning Herald*, 17 August 1955.

10:6 TRADE WITH JAPAN CALLS FOR REALISM

Statement by the Chairman of the Australian Woolgrowers' Council (W. A. Gunn).

'The importance of our trade with Japan is such that we cannot afford to neglect it or drive Japan away to other markets.'

The Chairman of the Australian Woolgrowers' Council (Mr. W. A. Gunn) made this comment on the Prime Minister's statement that whilst Australia had supported Japan's entry into G.A.T.T., his Government 'could not agree' that the provisions of G.A.T.T. should apply between Australia and Japan.

Mr. Gunn pointed out that Japan now ranked third as a purchaser of our wool and had in fact been a major buyer of our primary produce for a long period.

Over recent years [he said] heavy import restrictions have kept the value of our imports from Japan at only a fraction of our exports to Japan. We must accept the fact that this position cannot continue indefinitely.

Australian manufacturers might give some consideration to the British attitude which is reported to be that a successful commercial treaty and Japanese guarantees to observe international fair trading practices, will clear the way for full G.A.T.T. relationships between the two countries.

I believe the Australian Government should, as a matter of urgency, endeavour to find the necessary safeguards for Australian manufacturers which will enable the drawing up of a realistic bilateral trade agreement with Japan. The removal of unnecessary trade barriers will benefit not only the woolgrowing industry but every corner of our economy.

Source: *Queensland Country Life*, 18 August 1955.

10:7 TRADE NEGOTIATIONS WITH JAPAN TO OPEN

Press statement by the Acting Minister for Trade (W. McMahon) on 25 October 1956.

Trade negotiations between Australia and Japan will open in Canberra towards the end of next week, the Acting Minister for Trade, Mr William McMahon, said today (Thursday). They will be directed towards the conclusion of a trade agreement.

'A Japanese trade delegation will be leaving Tokyo for Australia tomorrow,' Mr McMahon said.

This development followed informal discussions which had taken place with the Japanese Embassy in recent months.

Japan was Australia's second most important export market, taking 11 per cent of our exports in 1955-56. Wool, barley and sugar were among the principal exports, Mr McMahon said.

Australia imported from Japan textiles, steel, canned salmon, crockery and toys. The trade in steel will practically disappear this year owing to greater availability of local supplies, he added.

10:8 THE BALANCED VIEW ON JAPANESE TRADE

In her interest and ours, Japan should be given the chance to sell more goods to Australia. That is proposition number one. Secondly, Australian manufacturers and other exporters to this country should not be violently disrupted by a sudden, overwhelming inflow of impossibly cheap Japanese products. Mr. McEwen's job in economic statesmanship will be to reconcile these two axioms in the coming trade treaty.

To take the first one, it is certainly not our Government's function to interfere with the normal course of competitive trading and to say that Japan or any other nation 'should' sell such and such an amount to Australia. But the point is that the present course of trading is not one of normal competition. Japan alone among foreign countries misses out from enjoying 'most favoured nation' status in our tariff schedules; that phrase has now become so wide in its application that it is contradictory. Moreover, some of our import licensing has deliberately blocked Japan from capturing as much of our markets as she would have done even with the tariff handicaps.

This is the sense in which it is 'wrong' that Japan should be buying some £140m worth of goods from us this financial year while we are buying a mere £12m or £14m worth from her. But Japan is also a potential market for even more Australian products, especially wheat; and she has a genuine problem in finding sterling currency. To that extent, it may be to our advantage, also, if she can sell more here.

Indeed, the acid test of Mr. McEwen's negotiating abilities will be his success in clinching this side of the bargain for Australia. He is not the man to underrate the strength of his own position. He can rightly say that Japan is buying so much wool because it is essential to her processing and re-export industry, whereas she makes few items that are essential to Australia's economy. He should emphasise the importance of giving older-established woolbuying nations a fair chance to sell their products here. He can point out that it is unprecedented to give Japan 'most favoured' status—something she did not enjoy even before the period of wartime enmity—and that safeguards must be applied against dumping.

With these reservations, our local manufacturers will be expected to give the new order a fair trial. In the light of events, Tariff Board or other adjustments may or may not be found necessary. A prospering Japan will be a valuable bulwark against the spread of Communist influence to our north. As for the cheapness of her labour, even by postwar standards, it would be wrong to decry that problem, yet two points must be remembered. That same low-cost Japanese labour has done much to carry the banner of natural wool against the forces of synthetics in the U.S. market. And all the Asian countries, with which we must gradually enter into more intimate trading relations, will inevitably have cheap labour while they are being raised from conditions of severe poverty.

Source: Leading article in the *Sydney Morning Herald*, 25 June 1957.

10:9 MANUFACTURERS PROTEST ABOUT JAPANESE TRADE AGREEMENT

Manufacturers have been quick to protest that they are not sufficiently protected by the provisions of the proposed agreement. Through their national organisation, the Associated Chambers of Manufactures, which is located in Canberra, they have maintained a stream of propaganda on the dangers of low-priced goods coming into Australia. Directing the campaign is the forthright assistant director of the Associated Chamber, Mr. R. W. C. Anderson, who in a couple of months will take over as director from Mr. Latham Withall.

Mr. Anderson said this week that manufacturers were not quarrelling with the Government's political decision to seek a trade agreement with Japan. Nor are there complaints as to the dangers of low-priced imports directed solely against Japan. Instead, the chamber is also calling for further protection against the entry of goods from other low-priced countries such as the United Kingdom, India, Belgium and Italy. The manufacturers want the retention and the extension of quantitative import restrictions limiting the amount of goods brought into Australia from these countries as well as the power for the Government to impose prohibitive duties against low-priced goods.

Although manufacturers are making their complaints general, there is no doubt that they are particularly worried about Japan's possible return on a large scale into the Australian market. Apart from the memories of the thirties, when cheap Japanese goods swamped the world's markets, Australian manufacturers have for the last few years been studying check samples of Japanese goods which could be competitive with Australian products. According to manufacturing sources, these show that Japanese goods will be a very serious challenge to some established Australian industries. . . .

Source: *Sydney Morning Herald*, 27 June 1957.

10:10 AGREEMENT ON COMMERCE BETWEEN AUSTRALIA AND JAPAN: JOINT COMMUNIQUÉ, 6 JULY 1957

An agreement on Commerce between Japan and Australia was signed today in Tokyo by the Minister for Foreign Affairs, Mr. Kishi, and the Australian Minister for Trade, Mr. J. McEwen.[1]

The Agreement follows exploratory talks between the two Governments early

[1] See A10:1 for full text.

in 1956 and preparatory negotiations in Canberra from November 1956. In the course of the discussions a comprehensive review was made of the trade relations between the two countries. The economic conditions in each country have been kept constantly in mind.

Both Governments felt that there were significant mutual advantages to be gained from stabilising in an Agreement the basis of trade between the two countries.

The basis of the Agreement is the exchange of most-favoured-nation rights in tariff matters and reciprocal assurances of non-discriminatory treatment in import control and exchange control matters.

Accordingly all Australian commodities for which there are export opportunities in Japan are assured of most-favoured-nation tariff treatment and non-discrimination in import and exchange controls. In view of the way the Japanese import system affects imports of certain commodities, the Japanese Government has indicated the specific treatment to be given certain major imports from Australia. The Japanese Government has also agreed not to vary the present duty free entry for Australian wool for a three-year period.

The Australian Government will henceforth admit Japanese goods at rates of Customs duty no higher than those applying to goods imported into Australia from other foreign countries. Japanese exports to Australia will not be subject to any discrimination in import licensing. The Australian Government has also agreed to enter into discussions with the Japanese Government within three years (and in the light of the experience gained under this Agreement) with a view to exploring the possibility of applying the General Agreement on Tariffs and Trade between the two countries.

The Agreement provides opportunity for increased mutual trade. Specific arrangements have been made for consultation on a variety of matters and it is recognised that it is important that export trade from Japan to Australia be conducted in an orderly manner.

The Agreement provides, however, that where necessary special action may be taken to prevent serious damage to domestic industry.

The Agreement may be terminated on or after 6th July, 1960, subject to three months' prior written notice.

As it may be some time before formal ratification is effected it has been agreed that the Agreement will operate from today on a provisional basis.

Source: *Current Notes on International Affairs*, vol. 28, no. 7, p. 580.

10:11 JAPANESE TRADE AGREEMENT A PROTECTION AGAINST CHANGING POLICIES

Statement by the Minister for Trade (J. McEwen) on 6 July 1957.

The Agreement on Commerce between Australia and Japan signed today is a notable achievement and a great stride forward in the Government's policy of consolidating in intergovernmental trade agreements Australia's existing export markets and in opening up assured new opportunities for export.

Australia and Japan are major trading partners but since the war trade between the two countries has been carried on without any framework of inter-

Governmental Agreement. Consequently some Australian exports have had no protection against the risks of changing import or economic policies on the part of Japan and others have had little or no access to the Japanese market. The Agreement on Commerce signed today guards against these risks and is a major constructive step towards securing and improving Australia's trade in the Japanese market. As a result of this new Agreement Australia makes real and positive progress in the Australian balance of payments problem, and gets closer to achieving conditions in which we can push ahead with the tasks of national growth and development without the same risk of periodically having to curtail development because of shortage of overseas funds.

It is important to recognise that Japan is Australia's second best customer. She is the second largest wool market and Japanese bidding plays a vital role in the establishment of prices on the auction floor. Should the Japanese Government curtail or manipulate the exchange available for purchases of wool from Australia the result could seriously affect our total export earnings. Such a situation would reflect seriously on the whole Australian economy. . . .

. . . in the absence of a trade agreement a curtailment of Japanese wool buying could come at any time as the result of a deliberate change in Japanese trade or economic policies. If Australia were to continue discriminatory and unfair trade policies towards Japanese goods, especially in the light of such a heavy adverse trade balance as Japan is now running with Australia there would be a constant risk of Japan resorting deliberately to restrictive trade practices and economic reprisals.

Japan maintains a system of bilateral trade agreements and exchange allocation arrangements with other countries. In the absence of a Trade Agreement these arrangements have in some cases narrowed and in other cases blocked Australia's access to the Japanese market. Australian trade has constantly been exposed to the possibility of serious detriment resulting from changes in Japanese trading policy.

Australia's trade relations with many foreign countries are regulated through the General Agreement on Tariffs and Trade. Australia in the absence of a satisfactory period of experience of the problems of reconciling trading difficulties has not been prepared to see the G.A.T.T. apply between Australia and Japan. This position is maintained under the new Agreement on Commerce.

However, as a step towards the establishment of fully normal trade relations with Japan, Australia has undertaken that within the next three years discussions will be entered into with Japan with a view to exploring the possibility and examining the basis of applying G.A.T.T. to trade between Australia and Japan. Nevertheless, without a regular trade agreement there can be no firm expectation on either side as to the treatment to be accorded by one country to the other's trade. This is completely unsatisfactory to both parties.

BENEFITS TO AUSTRALIA

So far as Australia is concerned what have been the constant objectives of our negotiations? There have been two principal goals. We need a trade agreement with Japan to preserve the great stake that we already have in that market. We need an agreement also to gain important new benefits in the Japanese market. Both of these objectives have been achieved to a very large degree.

The Agreement now completed ensures that Australian exports to Japan will receive equal tariff treatment along with other foreign suppliers. It also ensures non-discriminatory treatment in import licensing measures and exchange controls.

371

These clauses in the Agreement give every Australian export product for which a real market exists full rights of competitive entry into the Japanese market. Only when necessitated by Japan's overseas funds position will our exports to Japan be subjected to restrictions . . . If, for balance of payments reasons, Australian exports are restricted on entry into Japan, we now have a guarantee that the Australian product will be treated no less favourably than the product of competing suppliers. This has not yet been the case heretofore. I emphasise that these provisions apply to all Australian exports present or potential to Japan.

These clauses in the Agreement cover the whole of our export trade with Japan. However, because of the way the Japanese import system operates the Australian Government has insisted on specific assurances regarding the treatment to be accorded certain major commodities. Such specific assurances were insisted upon before the Australian Government would accept commitments in return and constituted a major consideration so far as we were concerned, in the whole negotiations.

(a) *Wool*

Japan is buying between 700,000 and 800,000 bales of Australian wool a year. Both this year and last year she has been the second largest buyer of Australian wool.

Under the Agreement the amount of foreign exchange allocated by Japan for imports of wool will be subject to restriction only to the extent that the balance of payments position requires. This safeguards us against restriction of wool for general economic considerations or other reasons.

In addition the Agreement provides that 90% of Japan's total foreign exchange allocation for wool will be in the form of a global allocation and thus available for Australian wool. This insures us against bilateral deals that might force Japanese importers to buy from specific countries other than Australia.

Finally, Australia has successfully negotiated an assurance that the Japanese Government will take no action to vary the present duty free entry for wool for the next three years. During the last year it would appear that the Japanese Government on more than one occasion has been very close to imposing a substantial duty on wool—for fiscal reasons. This assurance of duty free entry of wool for three years should be of particular value to wool, both to the extent that cost of wool in Japan is a factor in the competition between wool and synthetics and in determining the demand itself for wool.

(b) *Wheat*

Virtually the only wheat that Australia has sold to Japan in the post-war period has been premium higher protein wheat which Australia produces in limited quantities. No difficulty is encountered in disposing of this wheat in overseas markets. On the other hand, despite the fact that Japan last year imported over 75 million bushels of wheat all told, roughly half of it soft wheat, Australia although a low-cost supplier exported practically no soft wheat to that country. In fact Japan's imports of soft wheat, averaging about 37 million bushels per annum, have been obtained almost exclusively from the United States. These imports have resulted from surplus disposal arrangements and tied sales.

Because of the threat which surplus disposals hold for marketing opportunities in Japan, Australia in the Agreement has secured assurances that in the event of unfair trade practices or Government disposal operations, we will be assured of an equitable or fair share of the Japanese market based on our ability to compete under normal commercial considerations. As a result of the Agreement signed today it is expected that at least in the early stages of the Agreement under normal commercial considerations Japanese imports of Australian soft wheat will be over 7 million bushels with a yearly increasing trend. Even with the limited availability of Australian higher protein wheat in the past, our exports of this type of wheat to Japan have reached about 7½ million bushels in a season. It is difficult to overestimate the importance to Australia of ensuring continuing and fair access to a grain market with the potential of Japan.

(c) *Sugar*

Japan has bilateral agreements with suppliers of sugar apart from Australia under which she obtains a large portion of her requirements. In past years the Japanese import system has operated in an unpredictable fashion that sometimes prevents us supplying to Japan and at other times permits Australia to sell some of its sugar on that market.

Australia has now obtained a firm position that despite the existence of certain bilateral arrangements which Japan may have with other suppliers, Australian sugar may be imported up to 40% of total sugar imports. On the basis of current import levels this would mean that the Australian industry may compete with other dollar or sterling suppliers to supply up to 460,000 tons.

While the preliminary negotiations were still going on Japan purchased in May last something like £6 million worth of Australian sugar. There would seem to be no reason why we cannot henceforth on a normal competitive basis look forward to regular and substantial exports of sugar to Japan.

(d) *Barley*

Already, under normal commercial conditions, Australia has been supplying something like 30% of the Japanese market. Japan is, in fact, our best market for barley. This position is now assured in the Agreement and the Australian trade is now safeguarded from unfair trade practices and non-commercial arrangements which might threaten our competitive position.

(e) *Other*

Apart from the provisions on wool, wheat, sugar and barley, there is a range of other commodities such as hides, skim milk and dried vine fruit where specific assurances have been secured of reasonable access to the Japanese market. . . .

UNDERTAKINGS BY AUSTRALIA

With regard to what Australia obtains from the agreement we can be pretty well satisfied. But what have we had to give in order to get the assurances we sought? In order to secure these advantages for Australia's export trade and for the whole Australian economy, the Australian Government, having carefully examined the advantages and disadvantages of a trade agreement with Japan (and wider considerations than commercial matters were taken into account) has undertaken to accord to Japan the same tariff and import licensing treatment hitherto accorded to all foreign countries except Japan. This is known technically as most-favoured-nation treatment. This means that the duties charged on certain Japanese goods will no longer be higher than the duties charged on the same goods from other foreign countries; it also means that Australian importers within the existing balance of payments situation and according to whatever import licensing or import quota system is operating, will be just as free to import goods from Japan as they are to import from other countries, apart from the dollar area. Japan is no longer singled out for specially restrictive measures directed against Japanese goods alone.

Over the last few years and especially when imports have been restricted severely, there has in fact been pressure from Australian manufacturers and importers for the removal of the present discrimination against Japan in import licensing. Manufacturers requiring raw materials not available in Australia and importers with quota levels seriously cut down and needing to buy shrewdly in terms of price and quality have been amongst those who have argued for the removal of the present discrimination.

On the other hand some Australian manufacturers fear, on the basis of experience pre-war, that they will be subjected to competition which, under existing levels of tariff protection, they would not be able to meet if Japanese goods were freely licensed. During the course of the negotiations Australia made it very plain that the successful development of future trade relations between Australia and Japan must depend upon adequate protection for Australian industry against serious damage from impossibly cheap imports from Japan.

With this in mind, in the new Agreement we have now an acceptance by Japan of the importance of preventing damage to Australian industry. In this regard Japan assumes a responsibility for action at the stage of export from Japan, to prevent a damaging unrestricted flow of Japanese exports. It is clearly provided under the Agreement that the Australian Government retains full freedom to take action to protect Australian industry from serious damage if that is threatened. The position of Australian industry is fully safeguarded both as to long term tariff action as well as the freedom of Australia to use whatever non-tariff measures may be justified by any particular situation. Australia has this power under Australian legislation and retains this freedom under the new Agreement with Japan.

The Agreement provides for consultation with the Japanese authorities before special action is taken under these safeguards. Such action will only be taken where a satisfactory alternative solution cannot be worked out on a co-operative basis with the Japanese authorities. Moreover, since unreasonable resort to special action of this kind would jeopardise the great advantages secured for Australia as a whole under the Agreement, the Government will act under this provision only in cases where it is satisfied that the facts of a situation fully justify any such action in national interest to protect an Australian industry against serious damage.

The Government expects that this Agreement will give a stimulus to foreign competition in Australia, between foreign suppliers. Suppliers of goods from other countries now competing with Japan under the same tariff and import control conditions will not be able to ignore this new competitive element. This will not be without benefit to Australia's cost position. . . .

Australia will enter into talks with Japan within the next three years on the possibility and the basis of the application of G.A.T.T. to trade between Australia and Japan. Experience under the Agreement will provide a basis for judgment. The Agreement looks to an expanded two-way trade between Australia and Japan. It does not expose Australian industry to a flood of Japanese goods, but it achieves for the Australian economy as a whole a substantial and solid contribution to stability in overseas trade. It reduces to a marked extent the risks of checks and blockages to our programmes of development through severe fluctuations in our overseas financial position.

Source: *Current Notes on International Affairs*, vol. 28, no. 7, pp. 580-3.

10:12 JAPANESE TRADE AGREEMENT: SAFEGUARDS COULD WORK

The terms of the new Australian-Japanese trade agreement, which was formally signed on Saturday, are very much as expected. Each country will extend 'most favoured nation' treatment to the other; and, at least in theory, a substantial and beneficial expansion of trade should result. As usual, however, a good deal will depend upon what happens in practice. 'Much remains to be done', as Mr. McEwen rightly emphasised on Saturday, 'to ensure that a sound basis of co-operation is established so that trade proceeds to the best advantage of the traders and the people of Japan and Australia.'

His statement immediately raises for consideration the agreement's three safe-guards for Australian industries against unfair Japanese competition. The first is a 'voluntary restraint' clause which provides that Japan shall not flood the Australian market with great quantities of low-priced goods. Obviously, Aus-tralian manufacturers are profoundly unimpressed by this variety of moral sanction. Yet, in conjunction with the other two safeguards, it may well contribute to the desired effect.

For the Australian Government has power, under the Customs Tariff (Indus-tries Preservation) Act, to impose a special emergency duty on any cheap goods which threaten Australian industry. It also has power to impose a special quota restriction on Japanese goods. These facts are noted in the agreement; and there is not the slightest doubt that if necessary, the powers will be exercised. They are formidable enough, and Japan has everything to gain by avoiding a situation calling for their use. Australian manufacturers are perhaps over-apprehensive in claiming that, in the event of danger, the powers would be neither speedy enough nor adequate.

The agreement, then, should give considerable satisfaction in both Australia and Japan. Our primary industries—notably wool, wheat, sugar and coal—should benefit significantly; and Japanese businessmen expect that their exports to Australia will double in the first year of the agreement. This will certainly mean very keen competition for Australian manufacturers, but in spite of their forebodings there are sound reasons to suppose that they will meet the challenge successfully. There will also be stringent competition for British textile exporters, and Lancashire is understandably anxious. Here, in particular, Japan will be wise to give unmistakable evidence of her 'voluntary restraint'.

Source: Leading article in the *Sydney Morning Herald*, 8 July 1957.

10:13 AUSTRALIAN MANUFACTURING INTERESTS ATTACK JAPANESE TRADE AGREEMENT

Attacks by Australian manufacturing interests on the Australian-Japanese trade agreement continue unabated. In Canberra, Mr. Latham Withall has scented a 'growing feeling' that Parliament will not 'readily' ratify it. (Not if intensive lobbying by the Associated Chambers of Manufactures has any effect.) In Sydney, Mr. Hall, Director of one of the associated chambers, accuses Mr. McEwen of having 'sold Australian industry's birthright for a mess of pottage, made in this case of soft wheat.' He has also decided that there is 'not a single worthwhile safeguard' against Japanese imports in the agreement.

Both these reactions were, of course, highly predictable. It may well be that Parliament will—as it should—produce the ratification rather more 'readily' than Mr. Withall hopes, for the agreement certainly deserves a fair trial. And Mr. Hall has not helped his case—which in some respects deserves an answer from Mr. McEwen—by his contemptuous reference to the prospective sale to Japan of at least seven and a half million bushels of soft wheat. This kind of export prospect envisages a financial return which cannot be sneezed at. Manufacturers do themselves a disservice when they attack, in exaggerated language, a highly desirable export expansion of this kind.

Mr. McEwen has vigorously defended the agreement for its promotion of 'mutual self-interest.' There is no doubt that our primary industries will benefit by ensuring a more stable market for our main exports. We in turn are to provide valuable opportunities for Japanese businessmen to sell more goods. The Australian consumer should benefit by lower prices; and, much more importantly in the long run, by easing Japan's trade position, we shall be insuring against a recurrence of the painfully familiar Japanese aggression, military in character but born of economic desperation.

Australian manufacturers are, of course, apprehensive of the keen competition which will certainly be forthcoming from Japanese goods. They do not accept the Government's assurances that there are ample and formidable safeguards against unfair competition as a result of cheap labour and dumping. Mr. McEwen says that special emergency duties and quota restrictions are available for immediate use; Mr. Hall thinks there would be nothing immediate about the action, and quotes the actual words of the agreement. On the face of it, these words hardly sustain Mr. Hall's fears. They appear to leave the Australian Government quite sufficient leeway to determine the exact speed of its action, if necessary. All the same, Mr. McEwen would be wise to answer this line of argument.

Source: Sydney Morning Herald,
19 July 1957.

10:14 ASSOCIATED CHAMBERS OF COMMERCE WELCOME JAPANESE TRADE AGREEMENT

CANBERRA, Friday.—The new trade pact with Japan should help the Australian economy, the president of the Associated Chambers of Commerce, Mr. Leon Trout, said today.

'If the agreement has the expected results, we can look forward to substantial progress toward our objective of higher export earnings and more efficient domestic industries with all that implies for a strong Australian economy,' he said.

The pact was prudent and cautious, said Mr. Trout. It clearly had effective safeguards in it.

The three-year term of the pact would enable it to be tried out reasonably without either party being committed permanently.

Time would thus tell how the principles of the pact would work out.

Mr. Trout's statement, published in the Chambers' journal, 'Canberra Comments', is the first official comment from the Associated Chambers of Commerce on the new pact.

His attitude is in marked contrast to that of the Associated Chambers of Manufactures, which is criticising the pact as a threat to Australian industry. . . .

Source: *Sydney Morning Herald*,
17 August 1957.

10:15 ASSOCIATED WOOLLEN AND WORSTED MANUFACTURERS OF AUSTRALIA OPPOSE JAPANESE TRADE TREATY

Press statement by the Minister for Trade (J. McEwen) on 21 August 1957.

The Minister for Trade, Mr. McEwen, today received a deputation from the Associated Woollen and Worsted Textile Manufacturers of Australia.

The deputation expressed great fear of damage that could be done to the Australian woollen textile industry by Japanese imports which the deputation expected would result from the recent Trade Treaty.

The deputation said that the Treaty was not safe 'in its present form'. It asked that in the interests of the Australian woollen and textile industry quantitative restrictions should be established to limit the total importation of woollen textiles, and retained until high tariff protection was provided.

The deputation expressed the fear that lower wage and other costs in Japanese industry would enable the Australian industry to be under-sold under the existing tariff level.

Replying Mr. McEwen said that following the last deputation from the industry, woollen textiles had been referred back to the Tariff Board.

Mr. McEwen said the whole treaty arrangements had been negotiated and devised for the purpose of providing a highly important and necessary stabilising factor for the Australian economy but with a clear intention that no serious damage should occur to established Australian industry from Japanese imports.

A combination of arrangements was designed to guard against such damage. The Japanese engaged to observe a restraint against over-exploitation of the Australian market in items which would cause damage to our industry.

It was the policy of the Australian Government to maintain normal protective tariffs, and to maintain the traditional standard of protection of Australian industry. In addition the treaty acknowledged the existence of the power of the Australian Government to impose emergency duties or quantitative restrictions if it became evident that serious damage was occurring or was imminent to Australian industry.

The Australian Government had retained freedom from the restrictions of the G.A.T.T. so far as Japan was concerned so that there should be no obstruction from that quarter to arbitrary action, if such became necessary, in the protection of Australian industry from Japanese competition.

Mr. McEwen told the deputation that these powers would not be used except in a spirit of good faith in observing the spirit of the Agreement with its reciprocal obligations and mutual advantages.

Mr. McEwen said that in the import licensing system there was a valuable opportunity to have prior warning of the trends of Japanese imports to Australia. If such trends appeared to imply danger to Australian industry there would be an occasion and time for consultation with the Japanese Government so that the agreed objective of restraint from the Japanese end may be given effect to.

Mr. McEwen pointed out that if, on the other hand, it ever should transpire that an unexpected influx of imports menaced Australian industry, protective action could and would be taken just as quickly as was necessary.

It was highly important for Australian importers, in their own interests, to watch carefully that they did not generate such a flow of imports of particular items that they would be confronted with emergency duties on arrival which they had not taken into calculation.

Mr. McEwen said there had been most careful analysis of the details and trends of imports of Japanese woollen textiles over recent years and recent months. The trade agreement did not give the Japanese any preferential treatment whatever in either tariff or licensing—it accorded tariff treatment identical with that accorded to practically all other foreign countries. The treaty accorded the Japanese equal licensing treatment with all non-dollar countries but in the case of woollen textiles the Japanese have enjoyed that position since 1954, therefore the treaty introduced no new advantageous factor in licensing of woollen textiles.

Mr. McEwen then pointed out the actual experience of imports of Japanese woollen textiles since 1954.

. . . figures clearly showed that during a period of years when Australia has been overall a big importer of textiles, though not of woollen textiles, and while Japan has been an important exporter of textiles; while there has been no licensing discrimination against Japan; while Japan had been under very little tariff disadvantage compared with other countries, and while Japanese labour had been at least as low cost as it was now; it was no exaggeration to say that, viewed as a total scene, practically no imports of Japanese woollen textiles to Australia had existed.

On these facts, Mr. McEwen said he could see no justification whatever for the panic erection of obstacles to some imports of Japanese woollens to Australia, merely on the ground of some claims that imports of some uncomfortable dimensions might or could occur.

The deputation accepted the Minister's invitation to keep in close contact with the Department of Trade in studying the imports of Japanese woollen textiles. . . .

10:16 ADOPTION OF JAPANESE TRADE AGREEMENT OPPOSED

Speech by the Leader of the Opposition (H. V. Evatt) in the House of Representatives on 29 August 1957.

. . . Never before has the United Kingdom textile industry, which still trades with us, been faced with the possibility or probability of complete elimination from the Australian market. I do not think the people of Australia would approve of that. I doubt whether those persons who were responsible for negotiating this agreement for Australia contemplated the conditions which are now facing interested manufacturers and the great trade unions concerned in the production of Australian goods by Australians for the use of the Australian people. . . .

We are a people of between 9,000,000 and 10,000,000, whilst the Japanese number 90,000,000 and have a great organisation which receives, first of all, assistance from the military organisation known as S.C.A.P., or the Supreme Command for Allied Powers, as well as American assistance on the technological side.

In those conditions, to give Japanese importations most-favoured-nation treatment, as this Government is doing, is deliberately to sacrifice the industry in this country. . . .

I want to make it clear on behalf of the Opposition that we do not reject all ideas of a trade treaty with Japan or any other country. Whether or not we have a trade treaty must depend on circumstances, such as the safeguards to be applied and other provisions of the treaty. A treaty, in itself, is of no value at all. Its value has to be measured by its advantages and disadvantages. The killing thing about this treaty is the effect it will have on Australian industries that have rendered great service. . . .

I have consulted both the manufacturers and the trade unions and I am told that if this agreement goes through without real safeguards being inserted in it, the industry will suffer. When I say 'real safeguards' I do not mean the provisions that have been put into the agreement to enable one party or the other to get out of it or to vary it; I mean some definite protection. If the agreement contained such protection we could measure it, but nothing of the kind has been attempted. . . .

I submit that the treaty should not be adopted. From an Australian point of view it is a thoroughly bad treaty. It is indefinite and ambiguous; . . . It may be necessary to call upon an international tribunal to give an interpretation of what is called the 'safeguard' clause. I do not think it is a proper safeguard for Australia, at all. Before the agreement is signed and executed, a plan should be drawn up to show how much should come in under all categories, as the English Government has insisted upon in its legislation to which I have referred. . . .

Source: *C.P.D.* (*H. of R.*), vol. 16, pp. 151-71.

10:17 AUSTRALIAN COUNCIL OF TRADE UNIONS CONDEMNS JAPANESE TRADE TREATY

The biennial congress of the Australian Council of Trades Unions in Sydney yesterday overwhelmingly condemned the Australian trade treaty with Japan.

It called on the Government to revoke the treaty and substitute a treaty 'more in keeping with the mutual interest of both countries.'

The motion said:

We condemn the apparent lack of discrimination or effective control which would have assured the entry into Australia only of such products as have a high economic value to us.

The congress declared that effective protection should be given to Australian industries by tariffs or, where necessary, by import restrictions subject to control of prices, the protection of Australian working conditions, and the productive efficiency of such industries.

Regard for World Peace

The motion added:

Subject to this policy, in the interest of world peace and the raising of living standards throughout the world, there should be mutual trade between the nations of the world.

To facilitate such trade, Governments should promote trade agreements and establish the necessary trade organisations on the basis of mutual assistance to all nations.

The congress expressed the view that the treaty

on the one hand exhibits a special concern for the interests of Australian primary producers, and on the other threatens the continued existence of established Australian industries with consequent unemployment to Australian workers.

Source: *Sydney Morning Herald*,
27 September 1957.

10:18 PROTECTION OF AUSTRALIAN INDUSTRIES FROM JAPANESE IMPORTS: PROCEDURAL ARRANGEMENTS

Statement by the Minister for Trade (J. McEwen) in the House of Representatives on 28 November 1957.

In view of the comments that have been made both in Parliament and the Press, I feel that the time is opportune to make a statement to correct certain misunderstandings which have arisen in connection with the operation of the recent Trade Agreement with Japan. I refer more particularly to the extent of the fears and apprehension of various sections of manufacturing industry that damage will be caused because of the removal of the discriminatory treatment of Japanese imports.

As I have previously advised the House, this Agreement was concluded only after a protracted series of negotiations with the Japanese Government. Before these negotiations the Australian Government realised that if imports from Japan were given the same treatment as imports from other non dollar countries, resulting increases in the volume of imports from Japan could cause damage to established Australian industries. I can say that at least a year before the Agreement was signed it was recognised by this Government that effective steps would have to be taken as part of the Agreement that was envisaged to protect Australian industry if these problems should arise.

In 1954, Japan was put on a licensing basis which enabled the Government to observe the impact on local manufacturers of imports from Japan. During this period, imports of some items from Japan were restricted by the Government to ensure that damage was not done to local industry. During this period no item was imported to the full permissible quantity and in no case did imports occasion any damage to the corresponding Australian industry. . . .

The objective of a trade treaty with our second biggest customer was to preserve our place in the Japanese market and gain new trading advantages for Australia. The balancing advantage for the Japanese was to put their sales to us in the same position as those of other foreign suppliers. However, there is one highly important reservation—provision still exists to apply special protection for Australian industry if, as a result of putting Japanese imports on a basis of equality with other foreign importers, serious damage should be caused to Australian industry.

These special arrangements to permit protection of Australian industry would never, of course, be interpreted as justifying the erection of any greater barrier against an item of Japanese trade than that of the kind contemplated by the Parliament when the Customs Tariff (Industries Preservation) Act was amended in 1956.

In other words a treaty which clearly has the intent of increasing mutual trade, would never be interpreted as justifying the erection of any barrier to Japanese trade which would not have been justified had a trade treaty not been negotiated.

Having provided this protective clause in the agreement, the Government has now made the appropriate procedural arrangements to ensure that its objectives will be attained. The Government recently appointed Mr. M. E. McCarthy, the Chairman of the Tariff Board, as an Advisory Authority to examine matters referred to him by the Minister for Trade so that he can advise the Minister whether he considers any serious damage is likely to occur to any industry as a result of the operation of this Trade Agreement. . . .

In this connection, I have invited any industry which feels it is being adversely affected by the operation of the Agreement to form an industry panel on a federal basis and in conjunction with the Associated Chambers of Manufactures, discuss its problems with the Department of Trade. The Department is maintaining a very close watch on imports from Japan and indeed on licences taken out for imports from Japan. Although it will not disclose the import orders of individual importers, it will make available to industry panels details of the overall value of licences which have been issued for particular commodities so that they can assess the prospective volume of imports for these commodities in the future.

If, having had these discussions with the Department, an industry panel feels that the industry is likely to suffer serious damage, it should make representations to the Minister for Trade. The Associated Chambers of Manufactures has also undertaken to advise the Minister on these individual approaches. If the circumstances suggest that there is a threat of serious damage, the matter will then be referred by the Minister to Mr. McCarthy for his assessment of the position and his advice as to what action could be taken to overcome any problem which may arise. . . .

Quite a number of industry panels have already discussed their difficulties with the Department of Trade. These discussions indicate the complexity of the problem. The recent relaxation of import licensing has increased the volume of imports of most commodities from all countries. Indeed, the competition that is being felt from imports in some of the cases that have been discussed is from countries other than Japan. The Government has made it clear on many occasions that it will not retain import licensing for the purpose of protecting local industries so that in these cases, industries should make an approach for tariff protection through the normal Tariff Board procedures. . . .

Source: *C.P.D.* (*H. of R.*), vol. 17,
pp. 2651-3.

10:19 TRADE TALKS WITH JAPAN TO CONTINUE
IN NEW YEAR

Press statement by the Minister for Trade (J. McEwen) on 28 October 1960.

'Australian exports will continue to enjoy all the advantages of the Trade Agreement with Japan, and the safeguards for Australian manufacturing industry will continue unchanged'. The Minister for Trade, Mr. McEwen, said this today when commenting on the announcement in the Joint Communiqué that the Trade talks with Japan had been adjourned and would continue in the early part of 1961.[1]

Mr. McEwen pointed out that the Japanese Government was facing a general election in three weeks' time. Furthermore, the Japanese authorities were in the process of overhauling their import licensing administration and developing programmes of further liberalisation of imports. . . .

The Japanese Government's original undertaking to give duty free entry for wool was for three years only, but this undertaking had now been renewed pending the negotiations planned for the early part of 1961. In addition, the Japanese Government had reaffirmed that it would be placing wool on Automatic Approval from the 1st April, 1961. This meant, said Mr. McEwen, that from that date there would be no restrictions on the amount of Australian wool which could be bought by the Japanese industry.

Mr. McEwen recalled that since the negotiation of the Trade Agreement, Japan had become a market for Australian exports second in importance only to the United Kingdom. In 1959-60, Japan had been the largest buyer of Australian wool, as well as for coal, copper concentrates and hides. In 1959-60 Japan was also the second largest single market for Australian wheat, and there were opportunities for trade expansion in other products.

During the present discussions the Japanese Government had announced more liberal import treatment for a number of products of export interest to Australia. The Joint Communiqué listed a range of both primary products and manufactured goods, imports of which would be licensed up to the level of demand.

Moreover, in the course of these talks, for those items subject to restrictions under global quota the Australian representatives had established the entitlement of Australian exporters to compete in the Japanese market on a non-discriminatory basis to the full extent of total permitted imports. These items are listed in the attachment.

In a number of cases, however, the Australian Government was dissatisfied with the small level of imports permitted. Apart from certain primary products, this applied particularly to some manufactured goods where there was potential for the development of trade. . . .

---

[1] The Joint Communiqué of 28 October 1960 is available in the collection of supplementary documents to this book housed in the R. G. Menzies Library, Australian National University.

10:20 AMENDMENT TO AGREEMENT ON COMMERCE BETWEEN AUSTRALIA AND JAPAN

Joint Communiqué on Protocol, signed 5 August 1963.

A Protocol of Amendment to the Agreement on Commerce between Australia and Japan was signed today in Tokyo by Mr. J. McEwen, the Australian Deputy Prime Minister and Minister for Trade and Mr. H. Fukuda, the Japanese Minister for International Trade and Industry.[1]

The signing of the Protocol completes the discussions between the two Governments which began in November, 1962, in Canberra and in the course of which a comprehensive review of the trade relations between the two countries was made.

As a result, the Australian Government will notify the Executive Secretary of the General Agreement on Tariffs and Trade of the withdrawal of its invocation of Article XXXV of the G.A.T.T. in regard to Japan on the date of the exchange of instruments of ratification of the Protocol of Amendment.

The Protocol will amend the 1957 Agreement to make its provisions fully consistent with the G.A.T.T. relationship which will govern trade between the two countries. The undertaking given by both Governments in the 1957 Agreement to accord to each other's products most-favoured-nation and non-discriminatory import treatment is continued in the amended Agreement.

Both Governments confirmed that Australia and Japan have proved to be natural trading partners because of their basically complementary economies and that the trade between the two countries could be further expanded in both directions through continued co-operation between the Governments and business circles of the two countries. The two Governments would co-operate to ensure that this would continue to take place without serious injury being caused to each other's industries.

The Japanese Government has indicated that it would make efforts to expand the opportunities for the import into Japan of Australian products which are subject to import restrictions. The Japanese Government also recognized that Australia is an important producer, or potential producer, of ores and minerals. Similarly the Australian Government has recognized, in response to the interest indicated by the Japanese Government, that Japan is an important producer and potential supplier of heavy industry products.

During the discussions both Governments considered the obstacles and uncertainties in international commodity trade which confront countries exporting primary products, and the effects of these difficulties upon their economic stability and hence upon the expansion of world trade. The two Governments agreed that, in view of the urgent need to find means of producing a greater degree of stability and predictability in international trade in primary products, they would co-operate, paying due regard to each other's position, for the development of international action to improve the conditions of international trade in primary products of direct interest to either country.

The amended Agreement will be firm until three years after the date of its entry into force and will continue thereafter subject to three months' notice of termination by either Government.

[1] Text of amendment shown in A10:2.

As it may be some time before the Protocol comes into force, both Governments have agreed to apply the new arrangements provisionally as from today.

The two Ministers noted the very great contribution the 1957 Agreement has made to the trade relations between the two countries and expressed their firm belief that the amended Agreement would ensure a continued and mutually beneficial expansion of trade between the two countries.

Source: Department of Trade,
roneoed document.

10:21 JAPANESE TRADE AGREEMENT

Statement by the Minister for Trade (J. McEwen) in the House of Representatives on 19 September 1963.

The document which the Japanese Foreign Minister and I signed in Tokyo on 5th August, is a very significant step in the development of our trading relations with Japan. . . .

The 1957 Agreement was our first Trade Agreement with Japan. It sprang from the need at that time to normalise trade relations between Australia and a country which was becoming a very important market for Australian products. . . .

. . . at that stage, there were real uncertainties as to the danger of Japanese competition—uncertainties arising from trading experiences during the 1930s. For this reason, we wrote into the Agreement that in addition to maintaining our full rights to protect Australian industry, we also reserved the right to discriminate, if necessary, against Japanese imports where this might be necessary to protect Australian industry.

It was for this reason that we refused to disinvoke Article XXXV of the G.A.T.T. and hence did not establish full G.A.T.T. relations with Japan. . . .

The arrangements that were made in 1957 proved successful. Australian exports of wool to Japan have increased from 857,000 bales in 1956/57 to 1,307,000 bales in 1962/63.

In 1956/57 we did not sell any f.a.q. wheat to Japan. Our sales last year were 339,000 tons.

Sugar exports to Japan have increased from 52,000 tons to 298,000 tons.

We exported 300,000 tons of coal to Japan in 1956/57, and in 1962/63 we exported 2·4 million tons.

These increases were very much greater proportionately than the increase in our exports to the rest of the world.

Since 1956/57 imports from Japan increased from £13 million to £65 million. This was done without damage to Australian industry.

Against this background of experience the Government late last year entered into negotiations to review the existing arrangements. Now, six years after the signing of the original Agreement, a Protocol of Amendment has been signed.

Under this Protocol it has been agreed that Australia and Japan will now extend to each other the full rights and privileges accorded to members of the G.A.T.T. Neither country may discriminate against imports from the other country.

This arrangement will become effective when the Protocol has been ratified by the two Governments. Pending this action, both countries have agreed to apply the new Agreement provisionally.

There is nothing in the new Agreement which limits the power of the Australian Government to protect Australian industry against imports from any country.

... in 1960 the Government strengthened the protective machinery available to manufacturers and others who may be concerned by legislating to provide for temporary protection.[1] This has worked effectively and will continue to operate.

In the new agreement the system of voluntary restraint of exports, exercised by the Japanese Government, will continue as it has since 1957.

In line with this, the new Agreement provides that where it appears necessary that urgent action should be taken to protect Australian industry against imports of a commodity of which Japan is a significant supplier, the Australian Government will enter into consultations with the Japanese Government to see if the position can be overcome, and the need for a temporary duty reference obviated, by measures taken in Japan.

The question of a formal commitment of this nature to any other country has not arisen because no other country has undertaken to exercise voluntary restraint so far as its exports are concerned. ...

The only difference between the present Agreement, and the Agreement signed in 1957, is that each country has undertaken not to take any discriminatory action against the other. If it is necessary to protect manufacturers against imports from Japan, the same action would apply to similar imports from all countries.

However, this non-discrimination provision operates both ways, and Japan has also relinquished the right to discriminate against imports from Australia. In view of the level of exports to Japan from Australia this is of major importance, since if each country actively pursued policies of discrimination, Australia would have far more at risk than Japan.

The new Agreement does not accord any tariff reductions or tariff bindings between the two countries.

So far as access into Japan for Australian products is concerned, the new Agreement provides fair and equitable access for Australia's important exports, with the exception of beef.

In the case of wool, a concession has been obtained more meaningful than the temporary duty-free binding which was negotiated in 1957. Because of the importance of wool within the Japanese economy, it is unlikely that the Japanese Government would impose a duty on this raw material.

However, the Japanese system of controlling imports, enables that country to use such restrictive devices as prior deposits, import restrictions, foreign exchange restrictions and other administrative controls.

Japan has undertaken that none of these will be applied to imports of raw wool unless the same action is taken, at the same time, against imports of raw cotton.

Cotton is a commodity which is of even greater importance to the Japanese economy. Exports of cotton goods represent a substantial part of Japanese export income. Therefore it is difficult to imagine the erection of any obstruction to the import of raw cotton into Japan.

For this reason, this provision relating wool to cotton is a commitment very meaningful to the Australian wool industry. It ensures that our major export to Japan will not suffer from any non-tariff type of action, unless the same action is taken against cotton.

The Protocol and accompanying papers, indicate the other undertakings given by the Japanese Government in respect of Australian export to Japan. They

[1] See Section 14.

include a commitment that imports of Australian soft wheat, will continue at a stabilised level.

Last year Japan imported over 330,000 tons of f.a.q. wheat from Australia.

At the same time it has been agreed that the two countries will discuss the possibility of getting rid of the price differential in the Japanese internal trading system which could discriminate against imports of Australian soft wheat had we not received this present quantitative commitment.

So far as other commodities of export interest to Australia are concerned—we are now assured of most favoured nation and non-discriminatory access into Japan.

One of the reasons for the delay in completing the recent negotiations was due to the fact that the Japanese intended to liberalise their import policy. Because this has now been done, a number of important export items are not referred to in the Agreement. For these items we have unlimited opportunities to increase our exports depending only on our salesmanship and competitive position. This is the position, for example, in the case of mutton, lamb, dried fruits, most canned fruits, hides and skins.

In respect of those items which are not freely licensed Japan, in particular, has undertaken, in the words of the Treaty, to make every effort to increase access for our sugar, leather, canned meats, butter and cheese.

The same undertaking applies to motor vehicles, for which the Australian manufacturers see prospects in Japan.

Japan has not imported barley during the last few years, but has undertaken to give Australia non-discriminatory treatment when barley is being imported.

Our exports of ores and minerals to Japan have increased substantially and very satisfactorily during the last few years, and under this arrangement, Australia is recognized as a supplier of ores and minerals. There is included a provision against the imposition of any new import restrictions against ores and minerals for other than balance of payments reasons.

The negotiation to obtain satisfactory access for beef into Japan was largely responsible for the delay in finalising these arrangements. The Japanese Government offered certain concessions, including a small fixed quota, but we were not prepared to record acceptance of an import quota for beef which we regarded as inadequate.

My recommendation to the Government was that we should retain our freedom to pursue discussions on this matter with the Japanese direct, and in the wider negotiations with other importing countries, that are currently being conducted in Geneva, under the auspices of the Kennedy Round on Tariff Negotiations.

The failure to reach agreement on this point does not mean Japan will not be importing beef from Australia. To the extent imports are permitted, we have been assured of most favoured nation treatment. The Japanese Government has just announced that because of shortages it proposes to permit the importation of 5,000 tons of beef during the next few months. Furthermore, it will not inhibit the question of imports of beef into Japan being raised any time during the annual consultations provided for in the Agreement.

. . . as part of the negotiations, the Japanese Government requested that full opportunities of fair competition be given to Japanese suppliers when tenders are called on behalf of the Australian Government, and certain of its statutory authorities.

The Agreed Minutes which have been attached to the Protocol of Amendment, indicate that the Japanese Government was advised, that where the Australian Government proposed to purchase its requirements overseas, equal opportunities of fair and equal competition are accorded to Japanese products in regard to such tenders. . . .

One important reason for the success of the 1957 Agreement was that both parties scrupulously observed the spirit of the Agreement. . . .

I am confident that this new Agreement will be to the mutual benefit of our two countries in matters of trade. . . .

Source: *C.P.D.* (*H. of R.*), vol. 39, pp. 1173-6.

10:22 FREER TRADE WITH JAPAN

A team of about 40 Japanese businessmen will begin talks in Canberra today with representatives of Australian firms. It will be the fourth set of such discussions and the frequency with which they have been held and the high calibre and large number of people who take part are a measure of their importance.

Seven years ago Japan was a relatively insignificant factor in our overseas trade; today she is perhaps the most important. Although Britain is still a slightly larger trading partner, Japan is rapidly catching up and will without doubt soon overhaul her. Japan's rate of economic growth is the highest in the world and the rate of increase in her demand for raw materials and food is, consequently, very rapid too. When considered in the abstract it is indeed surprising that Japan is not already our most important trading partner. She is the closest industrial nation to our shores and transport costs are therefore lower than to North America and Europe. Her population is twice as large as Britain's and her cultivable land much smaller so her demand for food imports should be much larger. The volume of her industrial production is now larger than Britain's so she is a larger market for coal, iron ore, copper, bauxite and other minerals.

Trade between our two nations has, in fact, been held back artificially by restraints on both sides. Until the trade agreement of 1957 we kept out Japanese goods by especially high tariff rates. The Japanese in their turn had a rigid and restrictive system of import licensing which curtailed imports of wool and food-stuffs. Our export embargo on minerals precluded the trade which has since become so important. What is remarkable then is not the size of today's trade but the smallness of trade seven years ago.

There is still a long way to go before all the advantages of trade are realised. On the Japanese side a high cost, old-fashioned farming sector is being maintained by a system of import licensing and quotas and large subsidies, a situation which denies a market to efficient Australian primary producers and keeps the cost-of-living for the average Japanese higher than it need be. On our side the restrictions, on present trends, will become harsher rather than easier. A series of cases recently has produced recommendations from the Tariff Board of substantial rises in tariffs, and in several cases the Government has not only accepted these recommendations, it has imposed rates even higher than those suggested.

If international co-operation generally and co-operation with Japan in particular is to prosper then this trend must be halted and reversed. Businessmen and governments in both countries will have to accept the principle of working towards freer, more mutually beneficial trade. In practical terms this must mean the working out of areas of agreed specialisation among businessmen backed by government measures of tariff reduction and adjustment assistance. This last measure is perhaps the key. It involves a policy of Government assistance to producers whose output becomes unsaleable as a result of tariff reductions, the assistance being used to re-establish workers and management in producing things which can pay their way internationally. In the absence of such help it is not to be wondered that manufacturers form themselves into powerful pressure groups against trade expansion and in favour of ever higher tariffs.

Of course co-operation between Australia and Japan should not be merely for mutual benefit. It should focus too on what can be done to further regional co-operation and the development of the poor countries of the region. Japan and Australia might do more to pool their knowledge of improved agricultural techniques and co-ordinate research. And we should let it be known that we are interested in Japanese moves to encourage a greater sense of regional solidarity. In the shadow of our non-participation in last week's important ministerial talks in Tokyo, it is clear that the Australian Government needs to be encouraged to do more.

Source: Leading article in the
Canberra Times, 18 April 1966.

RELATIONS WITH
THE UNITED STATES

The documents on this subject are less than satisfactory, and there is no key decision around which to group them. Nevertheless, the main grounds for Australian difficulties in the post-war period emerge clearly enough. Two statements—the impersonal reply in answer to Malcolm Fraser (11:12) and the minister's frank review in his characteristic personal style (11:9)—throw the most light on these difficulties. These two documents are far from complete, however, and there is a rich field here for research by contemporary economic historians and students of Australia's foreign economic policy.[1]

The theme of a general review could well be bilateral conflict within agreement on general principles. Pre-war trade relations, it is worth recalling, were characterised more by conflict than by agreement (11:1). Indeed the conflict aroused by the Ottawa Agreement and Australia's own attempt to divert trade from the United States has not entirely disappeared.[2] Nevertheless, since the war the broad framework of American world trade policies—with agreement in GATT to contain but not abandon existing preferences—has been acceptable to Australia. This is the framework stemming from Article VII and finding its principal expressions in GATT and the IMF. To Australia, the major general disappointments about the United States' performance in GATT have been the Administration's inability to persuade Congress to ratify either the ITO (Section 3) or even the far more modest organisation proposed at the GATT Review Session (Section 5), and its uneven (and, in Australian eyes, mostly disappointing) performance in the field of commodity policy generally.

The more direct bilateral troubles between the United States and Australia, as viewed from Canberra, spring from Washington's departures from its own world trade (multilateral) precepts. The documents here have been chosen to illustrate our bilateral relations. The early documents (11:2 to 11:4) remind us that there have been attempts both before Pearl Harbour and in the post-war period to negotiate a bilateral trade treaty. The latter, an

[1] For an account of Australia's economic relations with the United States during 1955-60 see Greenwood and Harper (89), pp. 217-21.

[2] On pre-war trade diversion policies see Nicholson (132), ch. VII, sec. 1.

o

initiative of the United States, came to nothing.[3] There is in fact, however, an agreement representing mutual tariff concessions negotiated within GATT in 1947 (11:12).[4] The negotiations almost broke down over wool (3:7 to 3:9). It is this agreement that has suffered impairment of its value to Australia. It has not provided a satisfactory basis for mutual relations—hence the Vernon Committee proposal for another attempt to negotiate a bilateral treaty similar in scope to the two with the United Kingdom and Japan.[5]

The documents tell the story of impairment. The *waiver* in GATT could not be rejected except at the probable cost of GATT's total rejection by Congress (11:7 and Section 5). The wool story is a constant worry to Canberra. It is true that the United States is the only country of significance imposing a high tariff on wool, but it is not the fact of protecting the American sheep industry that worries Australia. It is rather that the American wool-producing industry is not large enough—imports are essential—to warrant a method of protection calculated, since the tariff raises prices, to restrict American users' consumption of raw wool, especially in competition with synthetics. Hence, Australia has pressed for alternative (price reducing) forms of protection and, in addition, has tried repeatedly (11:9) to 'buy' a further reduction in the level of protection (Section 5, Kennedy Round).

For a long time meat imports were discouraged by one means or another but when meat became available in forms suitable for use in hamburgers, Australia's trade quite suddenly expanded (11:12, table). It grew until it hurt, or appeared to account for hurt to, the local industry. While it is open to doubt whether the hurt, if any, was more than marginal, there was no option but to accept an agreement. This agreement (7:8) between the American Administration and Canberra stands, although subject to interpretative overriding by later Congressional action (7:9).[6] Recent exports, it may be noted in passing, have not raised difficulty with the Administration, being well below quotas—a fact which may not augur well for a lasting partnership with the hitherto willing buyers of Australian meat.

In minerals, a heavy setback was given to Australia's rapidly expanding trade by the quotas introduced in 1958 (11:12, table). These quotas were terminated in October 1965, but at the time the incident added more force to the claim that any products for which Australia had clear natural or comparative advantage were likely to meet with United States import restrictions if offered at prices below those desired by home producers.

[3] There seems no particular reason why there should have been so little public discussion of this subject, except in the period 1942-5 when the pressure being exerted by the United States against the Ottawa preferential system was uncertain in its outcome and politically embarrassing to the Australian government (Sections 1 and 3).

[4] For a full account of these negotiations see Nicholson (132), ch. X, sec. 1.

[5] See Vernon Report (11), vol. I, ch. 12, paras. 76-83, and vol. II, app. K, paras. 57-60.

[6] See also ibid., and accompanying tables together with attachment 2 to app. G, pp. 663-4.

Sugar is a special case of trade preference extended over the years by the United States to Cuba.[7] The position has changed with Cuba's fall from grace and Australia has managed to gain a significant quota for her sugar industry (11:11).

Surplus disposals have been a major point of contention (see Section 7). Australian wheat returns have certainly been affected over the last ten years by the existence of very large stocks in the United States (7:14). The convenience (and pocketbook) of the United States government has, at least up till very recently, been suited by an ability to dispose of large quantities on non-commercial terms. Australia's protests have necessarily been muted by three facts. First, it knows that countries with chronic shortages of food and foreign exchange are helped by PL 480, the point being conceded by Australia's own occasional gifts of wheat to countries in need. Secondly, it has had reason to be grateful that the United States has not dumped its wheat on commercial markets at prices below the minima fixed by the International Wheat Agreement (Section 7). Thirdly, so far Australia has sold its export surpluses despite some large carry-overs in the fifties and despite greatly enlarged acreages in recent years. As we have noted elsewhere (Section 5), the time is approaching when this bilateral point of conflict may be absorbed with a new type of world agreement covering both commercial and non-commercial disposals of wheat. Moreover, as we noted in Section 7, the great fall in stocks in the United States has reduced these below burdensome levels, with the result that the new legislation in 1966 has emphasised a shift to sales for dollars, albeit on generous credit terms, if need be.

Recent American action to curb capital outflow has added to our list of complaints: this one may have some short-term substance on balance of payments grounds—but the reader should not overlook our repeatedly expressed worries about being 'taken over' by American enterprise. The two points are not necessarily inconsistent but can easily appear so.[8]

The grounds for irritation and trade impairment have not always been one-sided, even in the post-war period. Right up to February 1960, discrimination against dollar imports into Australia continued (Section 15); import curbs on the score of shortage of United States dollars had operated, too, in

---

[7] Despite McEwen's taunt (11:9), American Congressmen have shown much concern about the difficult inconsistency of their views on preferences. Their preferences to Cuba and the Philippines in total were breaches of principle but were not of great aggregate importance relative to the British Commonwealth preferential systems.

[8] The story of policy on oversea capital in Australia is not documented more than incidentally in this book. There are many references available including the Vernon Report (11), vol. I, ch. 11, ch. 17, pp. 439-40, and vol. II, app. J and app. N, pp. 1101-2; *Economic Record* (Vernon Report issue) (75), pp. 118-24; *The Australian Balance of Payments, February 1966* (5) pp. 28-9; *Treasury Bulletin on Private Overseas Investment in Australia* (15). Australia's initial reaction to American action to curb capital outflow can be studied in the text of a letter sent by the Prime Minister to the President on 12 March 1965 and tabled in the House of Representatives on 1 April 1965.

the pre-1952 period when non-dollar imports from all countries other than Japan were freely allowed. In the GATT tariff negotiations in 1947 we were not noted for offering liberal cuts in MFN tariff rates and have appeared to Americans over-quick to use Article XIX of GATT for giving emergency protection to goods affected by oversea (including American) competition, and all too willing to use Article XXVIII procedures for quickly raising bound tariff rates following Tariff Board recommendations. We proved rather more than unwilling to abandon wool auctions in 1950, in the interests of United States defence (11:5). Our case was sound and shown to be so when the analysis pointed to United States official buying (emergency and without seeking adequate advice) as a principal cause of the high prices of wool in 1950-1. Our final unwillingness—although after thorough examination, made in good faith, of a range of possibilities—to negotiate some wool allocation scheme seemed inconsistent, too, with our anxiety to negotiate agreements in respect of other commodities (Section 7).

In the background to all our economic relations has been the preference issue (11:8, 11:10). It is still a major issue, for discrimination against the dollar, which for a while matched it in importance, has now happily ended. Our experience in the GATT Review Session made it clear that we had been fortunate (if, indeed, we were) to have the preferential system saved, although limited, in the final outcome of negotiations under Article VII. The fact of preference has been anathema to American interests. Australia has appeared to aggravate the worry by retaining preferences for Britain beyond those obligatory under our agreements, which the Americans may well think has meant larger MFN rates than necessary.

It may well be asked why we have not negotiated direct with Washington on these preferences (see suggestion of Vernon Committee).[9] For we have room to negotiate. Some direct talks are implied in Sir Robert Menzies's exchange with President Kennedy (11:10). We did act on a large list of goods following the new agreement with the United Kingdom (9:16). This significant reduction and the less biased (pro-U.K.) administration of the by-law provisions have undoubtedly helped the large expansion of United States exports to Australia since then. There is a feeling within Australia that Washington has shown very little appreciation of these steps, even though taken primarily with Australia's own industrial costs in mind.

The technical answer to our question is that Washington still approaches Australian-American relations largely as a by-product of GATT negotiations and, more especially now, the Kennedy Round. On this, as noted in Section 5, Australia and America have common interests in seeking to negotiate nontariff barriers to trade imposed by the European Common Market. It remains to be seen whether Australia can persuade Washington not merely to nego-

[9] Vernon Report (11), vol. I, ch. 12, paras. 76-7.

tiate on the wool tariff, but on its own non-tariff barriers to Australia's export trade. The Vernon Committee view implies that an initiative by Australia outside the Kennedy Round may be necessary in an effort to ensure a more lasting and satisfactory framework for Australian-American economic relations. Far from being inconsistent with GATT principles, this may be the best way to secure their mutual application to a resolution of difficulties on both sides.

Despite the scope for a trade treaty to incorporate further improvement in mutual United States-Australian economic relations, it should be stressed that the position in the mid-sixties is much better than it was ten years before. The mineral quotas have gone, the meat position is reasonable, and the Kennedy Round still holds some promises for a reduced wool tariff and for co-operation in seeking reductions in Europe's barriers to trade in agricultural products. Collaboration in wheat marketing has been valuable, although here the future is uncertain. Our exports to the United States have risen in value. Although imports from the United States have risen far more sharply (the United States supplied 23·9 per cent of our imports in 1965-6 as against 11·6 per cent, the average for 1950-5), this in large part reflects specific American capital investment and our general appetite for capital imports.

11:1 AUSTRALIAN TRADE DIVERSION AND TRADE RELATIONS WITH THE UNITED STATES

On 22nd May, 1936, the Minister directing negotiations for Trade Treaties announced in the House of Representatives the decision of the Government to divert portion of Australia's import trade, with the object of increasing exports of primary produce, expanding secondary industry, and bringing about an increase of rural and industrial employment.

Briefly summarized, the Minister's statement indicated that certain imports would be restricted with a view to their manufacture in Australia, including motor chassis, which, it was hoped, would be made in Australia on a large scale within a few years. In the case of certain other imports it was intended to change the present sources of supply to other countries which were great customers of Australia and which it was expected would become greater customers if Australia increased her purchases from them. The Government would proceed in two ways, firstly, by the adoption of a special licensing system over a limited range of imports and, secondly, by the imposition of higher duties where this course appeared more desirable. With the exception of motor chassis all goods of British origin would be exempt from the licensing system. In the case of motor chassis imports of United Kingdom origin only would be exempt from restriction. Upon application licences would be freely granted to countries with which Australia had a favourable balance of trade and to all other countries in regard to which, although the balance might be adverse to the Commonwealth, the Government was satisfied with the position.

The special licensing system was introduced on 23rd May, 1936, in the form of an amendment to the Customs (Prohibited Imports) Regulations which prohibited import, except under special licence, of 84 classified groups of goods from foreign countries. On 7th December, 1937, the Minister for Trade and Customs announced important modifications of the licensing system and the intention to substitute adequate duties to protect Australian industries established or extended under the licensing system. These duties were imposed by Customs and Excise Resolutions of 4th May, 1938, and all licensing restrictions on the 84 groups of goods were removed from that date. Other references to this subject and to restrictions imposed on the import of motor chassis will be found in paragraph 2 above. . . .

The trade diversion policy of the Commonwealth Government . . . adversely affected a wide range of goods from the United States of America, which for a number of years had enjoyed an extremely favourable trade balance with Australia. In reply to this action the United States Government withdrew, as from 1st August, 1936, the most-favoured-nation treatment hitherto accorded to Australian goods including certain trade benefits extended to Australia equally with a number of countries with which the United States had concluded trade agreements. A further step bearing on the trade relations between the two countries was the extension by the Commonwealth Government to 'Proclaimed Countries' as from 1st January, 1937, of intermediate customs tariff rates and certain primage duty concessions. The list of 'Proclaimed Countries' includes the United Kingdom, the Dominions and Colonies, and the principal foreign countries. The principal exception was the United States of America which was not included until 18th February, 1943.

The alteration in the system of import licensing restrictions, which had been in operation since 23rd May, 1936, and the substitution of increased rates of duty where such were considered necessary to provide adequate protection for Australian industries, resulted in the restoration, from 1st February, 1938, of the accord to Australian goods of most-favoured-nation treatment by the United States Government.

As a result of the passing of the Lend-Lease Act in the United States of America the Australian Government took action to obtain from the United States of America, under the provisions of this Act, essential goods which were not available in sufficient quantities in this country or from the United Kingdom.

On the outbreak of war with Japan, large quantities of war materials, raw products for the manufacture of munitions and other goods in short supply were made available to Australia under this Act. In recognition of the great material assistance received from the United States of America, the Australian Government, of its own volition, decided to accord to the United States of America the benefits of most-favoured-foreign-nation treatment. To implement this decision proclamations were made on 17th February, 1943, to include the United States of America in the list of 'Proclaimed Countries' and to accord to that country intermediate Customs Tariff rates and primage duty concessions.

Source: Official Year Book of the
Commonwealth of Australia, no. 36,
1944-5, pp. 320-1.

11:2 ANGLO-AMERICAN TRADE AGREEMENT

Statement by the Minister for Commerce (Sir Earle Page) in the House of Representatives on 18 November 1938.

The Commonwealth Government is very gratified at the successful conclusion of the lengthy trade negotiations between the United Kingdom and the United States of America. It hopes that the Agreement which has just been signed will greatly benefit the trade between those two countries, and that Great Britain and the United States of America may now find it possible to exert joint efforts to establish more liberal conditions of trade throughout the world. . . .

Australia, Canada, India, New Zealand, South Africa and other Empire countries have contributed towards the success of the negotiations by reconsidering some of the preferences they have enjoyed in the United Kingdom market since the Ottawa Conference in 1932.

The commodities affected by the agreement which are most significant in respect of the Australian export trade are fresh apples and pears, canned pineapples, and wheat. The changes of preferences agreed to in respect of these items will not adversely affect the industries concerned.[1]

. . . As was indicated when Ministers returned from abroad early this year, the possibility of Australia commencing commercial negotiations with the United States of America has been discussed informally. The study by both Governments of the problems involved, initiated some months back, is still proceeding, and will, of course, now be continued in the light of the contents and the probable effects of the Anglo-American Agreement.[2]

Source: C.P.D., vol. 158, pp. 1713-16.

11:3 TRADE TREATY WITH UNITED STATES MOOTED

The Prime Minister had talked with the President during his oversea tour early in 1941; an invitation for exploratory talks with a view to a trade treaty was issued by the Americans. Sir Earle Page, putting the position to the Economic and Industrial Committee of Cabinet, advanced cogent reasons for going out of the way to meet the Americans:

The issues involved go far beyond those of an ordinary trade negotiation. We must do our best to develop the most cordial trade and economic relations with the United States which is about to help us under the Lend-Lease arrangement, and whose goodwill towards and cooperation with us are vital to our present and future interests.

He quoted an illuminating piece from the American letter:

I should like to emphasise again my concern regarding the basically unsatisfactory state of commercial relations between the United States and Australia and my conviction that the present uniquely favourable conditions for rectifying the situation should not be allowed to pass without the most serious efforts being made to reach an understanding. It would have been most unfortunate

[1] See Nicholson (132), p. 115, for more precise information.

[2] See Documents 11:3 and 11:4.

if the acrimony engendered by the state of virtual 'trade war' between our countries during 1936 and 1937 had not subsided prior to the outbreak of the present war.

The reference was, of course, to the Australian 'trade diversion' policy of those years. As yet there was no indication of the proposals the United States would make, and in any case the Australian Cabinet was alive to the possibilities of having to surrender advantages elsewhere, for example in the United Kingdom, and of the possible repercussions on tariff arrangements with other Empire countries.

> *Source*: S. J. Butlin, *War Economy 1939-42*
> (1955), p. 433. (*Australia in the War of*
> *1939-1945*, ser. 4, vol. III, Australian War
> Memorial). Reprinted by permission.

11:4 AUSTRALIA-UNITED STATES TRADE AGREEMENT DISCUSSED

Exchanges of views took place from time to time between the Commonwealth Government and the United States Government until after the outbreak of war in September, 1939, with the object of arriving at bases for the negotiation of a mutually satisfactory trade agreement. The similarity in the classes of primary products of the United States with those which entered into the Australian export trade, and the opposition of United States woolgrowing interests to any agreement which would result in a lowering of the United States tariff on wool, made it difficult to arrive at a basis on which negotiations could proceed. There were also difficulties associated with proposals for concessions to the United States. However, during this period quarantine embargoes on Australian fruits and meats were lifted. Further informal discussions were initiated in 1941, but as with pre-war discussions, these did not reach the stage at which a notice of intention to negotiate for a trade agreement was published by the United States Government, as was required under the Reciprocal Trade Agreements Act.

On 19th February, 1943, most-favoured-foreign-nation treatment was extended to the United States by the Commonwealth Government, independently of trade discussions and without any formal request from the United States Government. It was indicated that this action was taken as a gesture of acknowledgment of the great material assistance received by Australia during the period of the war most critical for her. United States goods immediately became subject to the intermediate tariff and primage concessions which had been operative with regard to goods from other countries since 1st January, 1937.

In June, 1943, the Reciprocal Trade Agreements Act was renewed by the United States Congress, but for a period of two years only. Strong opposition to this re-enactment was experienced, the question of an agreement with Australia in relation to wool being raised.

Until the provisional entry into force of the General Agreement on Tariffs and Trade of 1947, Australia had never had any formal contractual relations with the United States which affected her trade with that country. The Convention of Commerce of 1815 between the United Kingdom and the United States, which is still in force, and which contains provisions for most-favoured-nation treatment of each party by the other, applies only to the United Kingdom and to her European possessions, and never applied to the Australian colonies.

Early in 1947 the United States Government approached the Commonwealth Government with a view to the conclusion of a Treaty of Friendship, Commerce and Navigation with Australia. The approaches for such a treaty were made in pursuance of a long-standing policy of the United States State Department to further good relations between the United States and other countries, and had no relation to negotiations embarked on under the provisions of the Reciprocal Trade Agreements Act of the United States.

The prime object of the proposed treaty is generally to obtain reciprocal unconditional most-favoured-nation treatment, and in some cases national treatment, of nationals, corporations, goods and vessels of both contracting parties in their respective territories. The draft submitted to the Commonwealth Government follows on broad lines drafts forwarded for consideration to a number of other countries since 1945, four treaties (with China, Italy, Uruguay and Ireland) having already been concluded.

The draft has been the subject of informal exchanges of views at intervals over several years. Difficulties associated with the reconciliation of existing Australian obligations with those proposed to be undertaken under the treaty, and difficulties arising from the limitation in the constitutional powers of the Commonwealth to implement a treaty covering some matters within the purview of the Australian States, have yet to be resolved before a text satisfactory to both parties can be arrived at.

> *Source*: D. F. Nicholson, *Australia's Trade
> Relations* (F. W. Cheshire, 1955),
> pp. 115-17. Reprinted by permission.

11:5 INTERNATIONAL ALLOCATION OF WOOL: UNITED STATES PROPOSAL REFUSED

Speech by the Minister for Commerce and Agriculture (J. McEwen) in the House of Representatives on 28 November 1950.

An announcement was made on the 26th October last that there had been discussions in London between representatives of Australia, New Zealand, the Union of South Africa, the United Kingdom and the United States of America on the impact which United States military requirements would have on the market for wool. It was stated that the problem would be reviewed and that a system of pre-emption of enough wool to meet the emergency needs of the United States of America—but not such quantities as would harm the auction system—would be examined by missions to be sent from the United Kingdom and the United States of America to the southern Commonwealth countries.[1]

---

[1] In August 1950 the United States first proposed a system of international allocation of wool and that steps be taken to avoid serious price abnormalities, having in mind the effect on the world wool apparel position of its large defence requirements of wool. It proposed suspension of international auctions until international agreement on a system of allocation could be achieved. (This suggestion came at a time of high wool prices.)

The Commonwealth Government stated that it could not agree to any suggestion

(Continued on next page)

That examination was made by delegations from the five countries in discussions that took place in Melbourne from the 15th to the 24th November, when the representatives of the United States were able to give more precise information about their emergency needs than was available at the London talks. ...

... It has been concluded that a system for the pre-emption of wool would not in present circumstances constitute a practicable means of securing the United States military reserve requirements. It was considered that the legal and administrative difficulties, in the United States and in the producing countries, of instituting such a system could not be surmounted in time for pre-emption to assist the United States materially in meeting its requirements. ...

... The opportunity provided by these discussions on wool has been taken to have some general talks on the commodity problems which confront the three southern Commonwealth countries. Information was also provided on the operation of United States priority and allocation powers and on the United States export control system.

That is the statement which has been finally agreed upon between the five countries as setting out the conclusions of the wool talks which began in London in September-October and which were concluded in Melbourne last Friday.

The essential point of interest to the Australian wool industry is that the United States Government has recognised that a system of pre-empting Dominion wools to meet its present special military reserve requirements could not be usefully introduced. Ordinary bidding at auction will be relied upon. That bidding will be through ordinary trade channels. It will be remembered that these wool negotiations originated in August with the request by the United States Government that the International Wool Study Group should consider and devise a system of international allocation of wool, and that some steps should be taken to avoid what were referred to as serious price abnormalities. The United States Government suggested that, in the meantime, the Dominion governments should take steps to suspend public auctions of wool.

The United States Government explained that these requests emerged from the circumstances of a general world shortage of wool and the special huge military requirements of the United States of wool for current use and for an emergency military reserve. The Australian Government declined to take any steps to suspend public auctions and took the stand that, except in a war crisis, maintenance of the public auction system was essential to the well-being of the Australian wool industry. It was pointed out that prices control and public auctions were not compatible, and that, apart from its being undesirable, it was not possible to operate any system of international wool allocations while still maintaining effective public auctions. The Australian Government made it clear that it was prepared to examine seriously the military wool requirements of the United States, and the best means by which those requirements could be satisfied.

In its approach to the problem the Australian Government was conscious of the dominant position of Australia as a producer of wool and of the responsibility pertaining to that position. On the other hand, the Australian Government was no

---

which involved the termination of public auctions, except in a war emergency. It then offered to join with the countries mentioned in paragraph one of this document in confidential discussions on U.S. wool requirements for defence purposes. An earlier account of these discussions is to be found in a statement by the Minister for Commerce and Agriculture (J. McEwen) to Woolgrowers' Organisations in Melbourne on 2 November 1950.

less conscious of the necessity to protect the present and future interests of our most important industry. As a part of those interests it recognises the necessity to avoid such serious disruption of the trade of our traditional principal purchasers —particularly the United Kingdom—as might impair their capacity to continue as our principal purchasers. ...

Source: C.P.D., vol. 211, pp. 3175-7.

11:6 WOOL ALLOCATION AND PRICE CEILING PROPOSALS: AUSTRALIA REFUSES TO PARTICIPATE

Press statement by the Prime Minister (R. G. Menzies) on 22 August 1951.

The Prime Minister, Mr. Menzies, announced today that the Government had decided that Australia would not be a party to an allocation scheme for wool or to any proposal that wool exporting countries should impose price ceilings on wool.

Mr. Menzies said that early this year a Wool Committee had been established as one of a number of commodity committees of the International Materials Conference. The Wool Committee had been given the following terms of reference:—

> To consider and recommend or report to Governments concerning specific action which should be taken in the case of wool in order to expand production, increase availability, conserve supplies and assure the most effective distribution and utilization of supplies among consuming countries.

The Wool Committee had first met in Washington on 2nd April. Since that date, with the exception of an adjournment period of some seven weeks during June and part of July, the Committee had engaged in a close and detailed examination of the world wool situation in recent years and had endeavoured to assess the forward supply and demand outlook in order to ascertain whether a need would appear to exist to change existing wool marketing methods and if so to recommend to Governments what special measures might be necessary and desirable to determine and implement an agreed pattern of world distribution of wool or to regulate wool prices.[1]

The Australian Government, said the Prime Minister, had reached the conclusion after full consideration that the review of statistics and other factors affecting or likely to affect the world wool market did not provide grounds for the adoption of any special wool distribution measures or for action to regulate wool prices. In coming to this conclusion the Government had recognised that technical examination had not revealed the practicability of operating any form of allocations without a possible impairment of the auction system of selling wool. It had concluded also that ceiling prices were not compatible with the effective operation of wool auctions.

[1] More countries took part in the discussions in Washington which were also wider in terms of reference than in the case of the earlier talks reported in Document 11:5. The pressure by the United States continued, however, to be in fairly specific terms, that is, seeking ways and means of assuring her needs a preferential position in the supply of wool.

The Australian Government, said Mr. Menzies, had arranged for its decision to be conveyed to the Wool Committee.

Other Governments, continued the Prime Minister, would form their own views as to whether the wool situation was such as to justify the introduction of any special measures. In view of the fact that the auction selling season in Australia would open next Monday the Australian Government considered it essential that it should make *its* attitude clear not only in the Wool Committee but to all concerned in the production and distribution of Australian wool. . . .

This decision, said the Prime Minister, meant that the Government was satisfied that a case had not been made out for departing from the traditional policy of Australian Governments that the auction system should not be interfered with or suspended except in the event of a war emergency. The merits of the auction system for wool marketing had been recognised by both sellers and buyers of wool.

11:7 UNITED STATES GRANTED GATT WAIVER TO PERMIT IMPORT RESTRICTIONS

Text of GATT *Decision at Review Session on 5 March 1955.*

HAVING RECEIVED the request of the United States Government for a waiver of the provisions of Article II and Article XI of the General Agreement with respect to certain actions by the United States Government required by the provisions of Section 22 of the United States Agricultural Adjustment Act (of 1933), as amended (hereinafter referred to as Section 22) which are not authorized by the Agreement,

HAVING ALSO RECEIVED the statement of the United States:

(a) that there exist in the United States governmental agricultural programmes (including programmes or operations which provide price assistance for certain domestic agricultural products and which operate to limit the production or market supply, or to regulate or control the quality or prices of domestic agricultural products) which from time to time result in domestic prices being maintained at a level in excess of the prices at which imports of the like products can be made available for consumption in the United States and that under such conditions imports may be attracted into the United States in abnormally large quantities or in such manner as to have adverse effects on such programmes or operations unless the inflow of such imports is regulated in some manner;

(b) that the Congress of the United States therefore enacted Section 22 which requires that restrictions in the form either of fees or of quantitative limitations must be imposed on imports whenever the President of the United States finds, after investigation, that such products are being or are practically certain to be imported in such quantities and under such conditions as to render ineffective or materially interfere with any programme or operation undertaken by the United States Department of Agriculture or any agency under its direction with respect to any agricultural commodity or product thereof, or to reduce substantially the amount of any product processed in the United States from any agricultural commodity or product thereof, with respect to which such a programme is being undertaken, and has required the President not to accept any international obligation which would be inconsistent with the requirements of the Section;

(c) that import restrictions can be imposed under Section 22 only when the President finds that imports are having or are practically certain to have the effects for which Section 22 action is required, and then, except as provided by law in emergency situations, only after investigation by the United States Tariff Commission, after due notice and opportunity for hearing have been given to interested parties; that while import restrictions may be imposed in emergency situations before an investigation by the Tariff Commission, the continuance of such restrictions is subject to the decision of the President as soon as the Commission has completed an immediate investigation; and that fees imposed under Section 22 cannot exceed 50 per cent. ad valorem and any quantitative limitation of imports under that Section cannot be such as to reduce the quantity of imports of the product below 50 per cent. of the quantity entered during a representative period as determined by the President; and that except in the case of those products where it is impracticable to limit production or marketings or the United States Government is without legislative authority to do so, the products on which Section 22 controls are now in effect are subject to limitations upon domestic marketings which in turn affect production;

NOTING:

(a) that, to help solve the problem of surpluses of products for which Section 22 import quotas now are in effect, the United States Government has taken positive steps aimed at reducing 1955 crop supplies by lowering support price levels or by imposing marketing quotas at minimum levels permitted by legislation; and that it is the intention of the United States Government to continue to seek a solution of the problem of surpluses of agricultural commodities;

(b) the assurance of the United States Government that it will discuss proposals under Section 22 with all countries having a substantial interest prior to taking action, and will give prompt consideration to any representations made to it;

(c) that it is the intention of the United States Government promptly to terminate any restrictions imposed when it finds that circumstances requiring the action no longer exist, and to modify restrictions whenever changed circumstances warrant such modification;

THE CONTRACTING PARTIES

DECIDE, pursuant to paragraph 5 (a) of Article XXV of the General Agreement and in consideration of the assurances recorded above, that subject to the conditions and procedures set out hereunder the obligations of the United States under the provisions of Articles II and XI of the General Agreement are waived to the extent necessary to prevent a conflict with such provisions of the General Agreement in the case of action required to be taken by the Government of the United States under Section 22. The text of Section 22 is annexed to this Decision,

DECLARE that this Decision shall not preclude the right of affected contracting parties to have recourse to the appropriate provisions of Article XXIII, and

DECLARE, further, that in deciding as aforesaid, they regret that circumstances make it necessary for the United States to continue to apply import restrictions which, in certain cases, adversely affect the trade of a number of contracting parties, impair concessions granted by the United States and thus impede the attainment of the objectives of the General Agreement. . . .

Source: Review of the General Agreement
on Tariffs and Trade at Geneva. 8th
November, 1954, to 7th March, 1955,
Appendix B. *C.P.P.*, no. 91 of 1954-5.

11:8 UNITED STATES ATTITUDE TO BRITISH PREFERENCES IF UNITED KINGDOM ENTERED COMMON MARKET

Speech by the Minister for Trade (J. McEwen) on 26 April 1962.

The American attitude: A most disturbing element in a very complex situation was the American attitude towards retention of the British preferential trading system, Mr. McEwen said. Despite his strong representations in Washington, he was unable to say with any real confidence that the pervasive influence of the United States of America in Europe would not operate in its own self-interest towards the dismantlement of the existing Commonwealth system of preferences. Australia would not be tranquillised with transitional arrangements. Those would be no concession. He was concerned with permanent arrangements that would safeguard Australia's vital trade interests and allow the necessary economic development to continue without serious setback. He had put forward forcibly the view that the General Agreement on Tariffs and Trade, which was the main instrument of the United States' post-war trade policies and which stood for no new preferences, recognised and accepted the existing preferential structure. If it had not done so, no British country could have joined the G.A.T.T. He had argued that Australia and countries similarly placed already had a sense of frustration about the disparity of trading opportunities as between the highly industrialised countries and exporters of primary products. That must turn to a sense of real grievance, if the United States were to use Britain's application to join the Common Market to seek to kill Commonwealth preferences and obtain profit in the process by benefiting at the expense of Australia's trade in the United Kingdom and British trade in the Australian market. . . .

Source: Australia in Facts and Figures,
no. 74, pp. 4-5.

11:9 AUSTRALIA'S TRADING RELATIONSHIPS WITH UNITED STATES

Speech by the Acting Prime Minister and Minister for Trade (J. McEwen) to the American Chamber of Commerce in Australia, Sydney, 11 June 1962.

[The United States] produced the idea of international trade arrangements—the G.A.T.T.; the International Monetary Fund and the doctrine of international freer trade . . . But . . . G.A.T.T. was merely to be part of a bigger scheme, an International Trade Organisation which in concept came out of the United States, which was approved by all the countries but which finally was not adopted by the United States. What was lost . . . was that part of the concept which visualised not only bargaining with the object of reducing international tariffs, but international arrangements to give greater stability to world trade in the bulk commodities . . . The American Administration . . . has opposed until the last year or two proposals for international arrangements to give greater stability to the bulk commodities.

And these are the commodities in which this country is vitally interested . . . the General Agreement on Tariffs and Trade has operated . . . almost exclusively to the benefit of those who trade internationally in industrial products. It has been worth very little indeed, if anything, to those who trade internationally in the great bulk commodities. So we have seen the strengthening of the position of those who trade internationally in the factory products and the deterioration of the international trading position of those who trade in the bulk commodities . . . Since 1953 the terms of trade of the United States have improved from a base of 100 to 108; the terms of the United Kingdom have improved from a base of 100 to 112; the terms of trade of Australia have deteriorated from a base of 100 to 66 . . . this is the factual experience and it is illustrated in the tables of the International Monetary Fund. . . .

This country with the population of New York, is today the 12th biggest international trader in the world. This country is very dependent on its export trade. In a recent period our exports represented about 12% of our gross national product, while United States exports represented about 4% of the gross national product. So here is a country enormously dependent on its export trade. . . .

In some 15 years of this brighter world of freer trading . . . our exports to the United States have fallen from $152 m. a year to $139 m. a year. The United States exports to us have increased from $128 m. a year to $484 m. a year. Ours have fallen in absolute terms; the United States have quadrupled in absolute terms. . . Over the last 10 years Australia has bought $1,200 m. worth more from the United States than the United States with nearly 20 times our population has bought from us. . . And in addition to that, we have run up a debt with the United States over that period for invisible services to the order of $1,300 m. . . .[1]

The United States is the only country in the world, throwing the Communists in, that maintains a duty against Australian raw wool. . . The United States, of course, is a giant producer under Government subsidy of wheat, and a great-giver-away of wheat surpluses. Embargoes and quotas have been imposed against our goods, notwithstanding that in . . . G.A.T.T. we negotiated with the United States and bought a lowering of butter and cheese duties, and paid for it by

---

[1] Figures in this paragraph are all quoted in American currency.

lowering some of our duties . . . then we were told: 'we can't allow your butter and cheese to come in because it would hurt our industry, and we have an agricultural Act which overrides anything else that may operate to the contrary.'

We are the biggest exporter in the world of lead and a very big exporter of zinc. When the United States imposed quotas on lead and zinc, then Australia was the hardest hit and got the biggest quota reduction.

Sugar

Before the Castro regime in Cuba, the United States bought most of its imported sugar from Cuba. . . They bought it on preferential terms, giving to Cuba a higher price than the going world price. Since the Castro regime the United States has imported her sugar from almost every sugar producing country that has a surplus. Since the Castro incident, the United States has bought less than 1%— not much more than half of 1% of her sugar requirements—from Australia, notwithstanding that over recent years we have been destroying an average of more than a million tons of cane a year . . . because we didn't have a market.

These are some of the factors that emerge when one studies why our trading relationship with the United States is less than we would desire it to be.

Butter and Cheese

I went to a Geneva conference and helped the leader of the American delegation . . . to get for America what is technically called a waiver to enable her to impose quotas legitimately under G.A.T.T. because I realised that in the United States there was a surplus of butter and cheese.

Wool

America is the only country that imposes wool duties upon us. I've tried to buy America out in duties [but] . . . what transpires very clearly is that in this freer trading world you can't in the American scene, bargain an agricultural product against an industrial product. . . .

Wheat

In wheat India used to be our biggest market, but a time came when we didn't sell India a bushel . . . because America was giving India all that it wanted. . . Our belief was that while America should be encouraged to give all the wheat and other products she wanted to people who are hungry, it should not be at the price of destroying our legitimate commercial opportunities to the extent that people could afford to buy. I . . . finally got an arrangement under which we sell a modest quantity of wheat and America gives away a very big quantity. . . .

I know that the United States favours the European Common Market, and favours the United Kingdom joining it. Menzies and I have said for years that we see great advantage to the Western World in the greater integration, politically and economically, of Europe. We know that the last two wars America and Australia have been sucked into have largely started between Germany and France. Today these two countries are so integrated economically that I believe we can live out our life time without any danger of being sucked into another war between those two countries. . . .

Menzies and I have said that if the United Kingdom were able to join that would strengthen it. But we have added that Britain ought not to join on terms that would seriously disadvantage this country. . . .

The world won't be made safe by just tying non-Communist Europe into one bundle and getting a liaison with the United States on the one hand together with the rest of the world. That won't make the Free World safe, and we don't want terms out of this European operation that will inhibit the opportunities for countries like Australia to grow.

. . . out of a complex of international policies and experiences, we developed as an act of survival the system of British preferential tariffs, and they still exist today. Now if I have a complaint against the United States it is on this one single ground . . . and it is that the United States should intervene—as I believe her influence is apparent today—to kill the system of British preferences upon which we so much depend. We don't want to have preferences if they are not necessary; but we want to be left alone with what we have contrived as our means of trading survival as long as it is necessary.

Above all if preferences are to be argued they ought to be argued where we have a right to speak and that one place is in the General Agreement on Tariffs and Trade. American influence ought not to be exercised in the place where we have no right to speak—that is in Brussels, where the negotiations are going on between the United Kingdom and the countries of the Six.

Finally . . . I take it pretty ill to be lectured about how bad a system of preferences is by a country that is practising preferences itself today in respect of such a great item as sugar and I quote one example alone. . . .

To sum up . . . I am saying that I would like the United States influence to be exercised to bring G.A.T.T. into balance as visualised in 1946 in the old International Trade Organisation, so that it is capable of being operated, not only to aid international trade in industrial products, but is equally capable of being operated to give stability to the great bulk world commodities of trade. I would like world arrangements on the bulk items—the kind of things that this country depends on for most of its overseas income. That would help us and all other growing countries. Of course, I would like the United States to re-examine its individual policies, particularly those which discriminate against Australia . . . its sugar buying and metal quotas, its dairy products quotas. I hope that no obstacles will be raised against meat and in respect of wool I would hope it would be possible to get down American tariffs against our wool. . . .

And above all . . . I hope that we may have the help of the United States in the European Economic Community negotiations to get a basis where if Britain joins, she joins on terms in which we and other countries like us continue with confidence to trade in our traditional products. . . .

Source: Roneoed statement issued by the
Minister for Trade in Sydney on 11 June 1962.

11:10 THE IMPLICATIONS FOR AUSTRALIA AND THE UNITED STATES IF THE UNITED KINGDOM ACCEDED TO THE COMMON MARKET

Extract from Joint Communiqué issued on 20 June 1962 by the Prime Minister (R. G. Menzies) and President Kennedy, after their talks in Washington.

President Kennedy expressed his strong belief in the importance of the Commonwealth as a source of stability and strength for the free world. At the same time both leaders recognized that European unity could contribute substantially to the strength of the free world.

They reviewed, therefore, the implications for the trade of their two nations of the possible accession of the United Kingdom to the European Economic Community.

It was agreed that in this event the United States and Australia would, as great suppliers to Britain and Europe, face problems in endeavouring to maintain and expand access for their goods.

The Prime Minister offered the view that it would be a grave misfortune if, after the negotiations, it turned out that the conditions laid down for Britain's entry were unacceptable to Commonwealth countries on the ground that they damaged Commonwealth trade and expansion.

The President and Prime Minister took note of the fact that, with respect to certain articles and commodities, Australia's historic terms of access are different from those of the United States. They recognized, however, that Australia competed with the United States in the United Kingdom market with respect to only a relatively small number of these items—though the items themselves are by no means of small importance. They agreed that, with respect to these items, technical discussions would be held between the two governments in an effort to reconcile the trading interests of both nations.

With respect to the great bulk of articles and commodities they noted that, as non-members of the European Economic Community, their countries faced essentially the same problems, and they joined in hoping that the community would pursue liberal trading policies. President Kennedy pointed out that, under the trade expansion legislation now pending before the Congress, the United States Government might be able, through reciprocal agreements, to bring about a general reduction of trade barriers for the benefit of all. Moreover, both leaders agreed that, with respect to a number of key primary products, the problems raised by the expansion of the Common Market might best be solved through international arrangements.

During the course of their interviews the President expressed his warm interest in Australia and his understanding of Australian needs in terms of development and growth, recognizing the problems of particular regions as well as industries. Both he and the Prime Minister were agreed that the problems arising out of Britain's proposed entry should be approached, not on any basis of theory or the use of particular words, but upon a practical basis, examining commodities one by one, having in mind the protection of the interests of both countries.

As a result of their discussions the President and the Prime Minister were encouraged to believe that satisfactory solutions will be found to these problems faced by their two countries.

Source: *Current Notes on International
Affairs*, vol. 33, no. 6, pp. 36-7.

11:11 AUSTRALIA'S ALLOTTED SUGAR QUOTA IN THE UNITED STATES

It was announced on July 22 that Australia had been allotted a quota of almost 40,000 short tons of sugar a year under new United States legislation, which allocated amongst a number of countries a portion of the sugar formerly supplied by Cuba. The allocation followed strong representations to the United States of America made both at Government and industry levels.[1]

The quota is small in relation to total United States requirements of 9,700,000 tons, but Australia will also be able to compete with others for a share of the remainder of the former Cuban quota, which is to be held in suspense and allocated periodically amongst other countries. The Australian industry has already succeeded in selling a further 24,000 tons against this so-called global quota.

The United States sugar market has been one of the most preferential in the world. Until the breach with Cuba, that country supplied the bulk of United States sugar imports and was paid the premium United States price. At the same time, the United States enjoyed preferences on some of its exports to Cuba. Although the new legislation will give to other countries access to the American market on a continuing basis, the price arrangements are not regarded as satisfactory. A levy is being charged on sugar imported under the new arrangements, the effect of which is that the premium over world prices that Australia can expect to receive in the United States market will be partly skimmed off on sugar supplied under Australia's quota and completely taken away on any other sugar that it might export to the United States. Thus, while there is satisfaction at the success in being permitted to enter the world's greatest market, the benefits will not be fully realised until world prices are brought to more realistic levels. The so-called world price is a price set in a residual market for a small part of the world trade in sugar. Prices have been particularly low since the United States breach with Cuba and no country can afford to produce at these prices.

Source: Australia in Facts and Figures,
no. 75, 1962.

11:12 AUSTRALIAN TRADE WITH THE UNITED STATES

Answer by the Minister for Trade (J. McEwen) to questions by Malcolm Fraser in the House of Representatives on 29 August 1962.

Mr Malcolm Fraser asked the Minister for Trade upon notice—

1. What restrictions does the United States of America place on the entry of Australian goods into the United States?

2. What is the nature of the restrictions, and what commodities do they affect?

3. Can he say what restrictions are placed by the United States on the exports of other countries to the United States?

4. What are the major commodities so affected?

5. What has the United States done since the war to reduce restrictions?

6. How has this affected trade from Australia to the United States or from other countries to the United States?

[1] Amended foreign quota provisions under new sugar legislation signed by President Johnson on 8 November 1965 became effective on 1 January 1966. Australia's quota for 1966 was listed as 168,752 short tons out of a total foreign allocation of 3,410,000 short tons.

7. What is the nature of the powers which the United States President is now seeking in relation to tariffs and import restrictions generally?

8. What are the announced aims of the President in seeking these powers?

9. What new restrictions has the United States announced (a) in the last five years, (b) in the last ten years, and (c) in the last fifteen years against (i) imports from Australia and (ii) imports from other countries?

10. Has Australian trade to the United States increased in recent years; if so, in what commodities has it increased?

11. What were the exports of Australian wool, meat, wheat, butter, dried fruits and sugar to the United States during each of the last fifteen years?

12. What was the value of Australian exports of all those commodities during each of those years?

13. What was the value of manufactured exports to the United States during each of the same years?

Mr McEwen—The answers to the honorable member's questions are as follows:—

1 to 4. The entry into the United States of the following products from Australia and other countries is subject to quantitative restriction in addition to the relevant customs duties:— butter, cheese and certain other dairy products; wheat and wheat products; sugar; lead and zinc;[1] peanuts; cotton; stainless steel table flatware; and books (in excess of 1,500 copies for which United States copyright has been obtained). Quantitative restrictions apply also to imports of certain cotton textiles from Hong Kong only.

5. Since the War the United States has removed or relaxed quantitative restrictions on some products. The United States has also reduced and bound under the GATT a range of customs duties.

6. Since the War Australia has been permitted to sell to the United States the following products as indicated below:—

Butter—Australia competes with six other countries for an annual quota of 163,000 lb.

Cheddar Cheese—Australia has an annual quota of 16,910 lb.

Sugar—In 1961 Australia received (for that year) an allocation of 90,000 tons of raw sugar. Recently, Australia was allotted a quota of 15,053 tons for the second half of 1962. Australia has been allotted an annual quota of 39,884 tons for 1963 and 1964.[2] In addition, Australia is entitled to compete with other countries for a share of a global quota. For the second half of 1962 the amount which, to date, has been set aside as global quota is 541,734 tons.

In 1947 Australia negotiated through the GATT reductions in United States customs duties on a number of products, chiefly beef, veal, mutton and lamb, butter and wool. Since then, Australia's exports of meat to the United States have increased substantially; exports of butter to the United States remain subject to the quota restriction referred to above; and exports of wool to the United States have fallen significantly. The value of Australia's total exports to the United States has increased from £47,000,000 in 1946-47 to £102,000,000 in 1961-62. In the same period the value of Australia's exports to the United States as a percentage of exports to all sources has fallen from 16 per cent. to 10 per cent.

[1] In October 1965 the United States terminated import quotas on lead and zinc.

[2] For 1966 Australia's quota was listed at 168,752 tons.

7. In the United States Trade Expansion Bill the President is seeking authority—
  (i) to reduce, in negotiations, existing United States tariffs on some goods by up to 50 per cent. over the next five years;
  (ii) in negotiations with the European Economic Community (E.E.C.) to reduce or eliminate, over the next five years, tariffs on certain groups of products, where the United States and the E.E.C. together account for 80 per cent. or more of world trade;
  (iii) to reduce or eliminate duties and other import restrictions on tropical products, provided that the E.E.C. takes similar action and that the products are not produced in the United States in significant quantity;
  (iv) to eliminate tariffs on products which are dutiable at 5 per cent. or less.

8. In introducing this bill the President indicated that the legislation was aimed at—

Providing negotiating authority which would enable United States products to gain wider access to the European Economic Community.

Accelerating the economic growth of the United States and in improving the United States balance of payments position.

Countering the Communist aid and trade offensive. Assisting the less developed countries of the world to strengthen and expand their economies.

9. During the past five, ten and fifteen years, new quantitative restrictions have been applied on imports from Australia and other countries of the following products:—

Period 1947-51—Nil.

Period 1952-56—(i) Filberts (now removed), (ii) peanuts, (iii) flax seed, linseed oil and peanut oil (now removed).

Period 1957-62—(i) Rye flour and meal (now removed), (ii) almonds (now removed), (iii) tung oil and nuts (now removed), (iv) picker lap cotton, (v) lead and zinc, (vi) cotton textiles (from Hong Kong), (vii) stainless steel table flatware.

10. Australia's exports to the United States have increased in recent years. The main commodities which have shown increases are beef, mutton and lamb, sugar, iron and steel pipes and tubes, and fishery products.

11 and 12. The value of Australian exports of the specified commodities, to the United States and the world, is set out in the table on pp. 410-11.

13. ... The value of manufactured goods exported from Australia to the United States ... was as follows:—

	£Amillion		£Amillion
1952-53	2·3	1959-60	8·5
1953-54	2·6	1960-61[a]	5·1
1954-55	1·5	1961-62[a]	20·1
1955-56	2·9	1962-63[a]	11·2
1956-57	3·7	1963-64[a]	15·9
1957-58	4·0	1964-65[a]	17·4
1958-59	5·6		

[a] Figures supplied by Department of Trade and Industry. The 1960-1 figure has been revised from the figure of £A6·3 in Hansard.

Source: C.P.D. (H. of R.), vol. 36, pp. 852-4.

EXPORTS OF SPECIFIED COMMODITIES T

($A milli

COMMODITY	1946–7	1947–8	1948–9	1949–50	1950–1	1951–2	1952–3	1953–4	1954–
Wool—U.S.A.	71·4	50·6	41·4	80·4	265·2	118·0	61·8	60·4	59·
—TOTAL	252·2	297·4	462·8	626·2	1,266·6	646·8	805·8	820·8	706·
Meat—U.S.A.	0·4	0·4	0·6	1·2	2·0	2·4	3·4	2·2	2·
—TOTAL	42·2	45·2	57·2	68·2	60·8	71·0	131·4	115·6	127·
Wheat—U.S.A.	...	...	...	...	...	...	...	...	..
—TOTAL	12·6	105·6	129·4	124·4	148·2	110·6	104·0	61·8	90·
Butter—U.S.A.	...	...	...	...	...	...	...	...	..
—TOTAL	25·2	41·2	47·6	49·4	37·0	9·2	40·2	32·2	49·
Dried Fruits —U.S.A.	...	...	...	...	...	...	...	...	..
—TOTAL	4·8	5·2	6·8	5·8	9·4	11·4	16·0	14·8	16·
Sugar—U.S.A.	...	...	...	...	...	...	...	...	..
—TOTAL	5·6	6·4	26·6	28·4	29·8	14·0	43·6	63·4	62·
Fish[b]—U.S.A.	...	0·2	0·8	0·8	1·8	2·2	3·0	3·0	3·
—TOTAL	0·4	0·6	1·8	1·4	2·2	2·6	3·4	3·4	3·
Lead[c]—U.S.A.	2·2	4·2	8·2	2·6	6·2	16·0	22·4	16·2	17·
—TOTAL	19·2	22·8	35·2	26·2	33·2	28·2	39·6	45·2	42·
Zinc[d]—U.S.A.	...	...	0·1	0·2	0·1	...	...	...	..
—TOTAL	7·8	7·6	12·2	13·0	23·0	36·0	34·2	13·6	12·
Titanium and Zirconium[b] —U.S.A.	0·6	0·8	0·6	0·4	0·8	1·4	2·2	1·2	2·
—TOTAL	0·8	1·0	1·0	0·8	1·8	3·0	4·6	3·2	5·

HE UNITED STATES AND TO ALL COUNTRIES[a]

.b.)

55-6	1956-7	1957-8	1958-9	1959-60	1960-1	1961-2[b]	1962-3[b]	1963-4[b]	1964-5[b]	1965-6[b]
43·2	41·2	25·6	22·6	24·8	21·4	33·8	45·8	41·2	62·2	68·7
75·2	967·4	746·8	604·4	772·4	668·8	755·0	758·6	961·0	805·8	784·8
2·2	2·4	6·6	46·6	68·8	62·6	102·4	152·2	152·2	102·8	135·6
21·0	102·0	110·4	194·4	177·2	144·6	173·8	225·4	243·2	285·8	287·8
...	...	...	...	...	...	...	...	...	...	...
92·8	120·2	57·0	76·8	123·4	204·8	284·8	216·8	362·0	297·2	264·1
...	...	...	...	...	...	...	...	...	...	...
57·8	51·6	31·2	50·0	57·2	39·2	47·0	47·2	54·6	62.2	50·0
...	...	...	0·2	...	...	...	...	...	...	0·1
15·6	13·2	18·2	25·4	18·2	18·2	20·6	19·0	21·0	24·0	28·4
...	...	...	...	...	2·4	6·8	11·2	20·2	18·2	19·6
49·6	57·8	70·0	64·4	53·4	70·4	67·8	91·0	156·4	112·6	93·9
4·0	5·0	5·2	7·0	8·2	8·2	12·2	11·0	10·6	14·2	18·8
4·2	5·4	5·6	7·4	8·4	8·6	12·8	12·6	14·2	17·8	23·8
20·2	33·0	20·6	14·0	12·0	9·6	16·6	11·2	11·4	17·0	20·4
47·6	56·6	43·2	35·0	31·0	30·2	37·4	35·8	46·0	61·2	61·7
0·8	2·2	0·6	1·4	1·0	0·2	0·8	0·12	0·1	0·2	4·0
17·2	18·8	13·0	13·4	14·2	17·6	22·0	25·0	28·8	39·6	43·9
4·6	9·2	7·2	3·4	3·6	4·0	2·6	4·0	6·2	11·2	11·1
10·4	19·4	14·8	10·2	10·4	11·6	10·6	12·2	17·6	25·8	29·1

[a] ... = nil or less than $A100,000.
[b] Added to original table.
[c] Added to original table. Ores and concentrates, pig and other unwrought shapes.
[d] Added to original table. Ores and concentrates, refinery shapes—ingots, blocks, slabs or cakes.
OURCE: Commonwealth Statistician, *Oversea Trade*.

11:13 REMOVAL OF UNITED STATES IMPORT RESTRICTIONS ON LEAD AND ZINC

Press statement by the Acting Minister for Trade and Industry (Paul Hasluck) on 25 October 1965.

The Acting Minister for Trade and Industry, Mr. Paul Hasluck, commented today on the announcement by President Johnson that the United States import quotas on lead and zinc were being terminated.

Under the terms of the announcement, quotas on lead and zinc ores and concentrates will be removed immediately while those on lead and zinc metal will be removed in 30 days time.

Mr. Hasluck said that Australia welcomed the President's action. Abolition of the United States import restrictions on lead and zinc had been strongly urged by Australia and other producing countries repeatedly over a number of years.

Mr. Hasluck said:

The important restrictions, which were imposed in 1958, had largely isolated the United States market for lead and zinc, thereby aggravating marketing and price problems on world markets outside the United States.

The President's decision will improve the conditions of access for Australian lead and zinc producers in the world's largest market and, by broadening the international market, should add to the stability of the market for these metals.

12

OTHER TRADE TREATIES

The documents in this section give brief reference to other trade treaties and arrangements.[1] The first (12:1) gives an idea of early post-war activity, none of the agreements being of major importance. The arrangement with Germany indicates the practical need to negotiate for quota entry into countries resorting to quantitative restrictions instead of tariffs for protecting their agriculture and food processing industries.

The arrangements with Indonesia have continued to be disappointing: it has not yet been possible to negotiate within a framework of a comprehensive and durable treaty—hence the *ad hoc* character of year-to-year arrangements which have become virtually meaningless. However, with the change in the political situation in 1966 the climate for stronger economic relations between the two countries is bound to improve.

The agreement with New Zealand has been of importance but relations are now covered by the New Zealand-Australia Free Trade Agreement (12:4). Against a background of an adverse trade balance with Australia New Zealand has approached the question of a free trade area with Australia somewhat nervously.[2] There is a natural fear that Australian manufactures would overrun New Zealand 'infant industries'. There is not even an entry to Australia for New Zealand butter to compensate. The list of items of trade published for consideration by interested parties is, at first sight, more impressive in terms of numbers of items of trade than in value.

The agreement is far from complete and the nervousness of both countries about 'sensitive' items is fully reflected in its terms (12:4) and in McEwen's comments (12:3). Australia has less reason to be nervous in terms of total impact on her economy, but the dairy and the paper industries may both give rise to political problems if New Zealand products begin to bite into the Aus-

---

[1] On pre-war and early post-war trade treaties and arrangements generally the best source is Nicholson (132), who includes a list of the large number of such agreements negotiated since Federation, many of them formal rather than of substantial use. In ch. XIII (Post-War Bilateral Trade Arrangements) he makes clear the distinction between comprehensive treaties and agreements on the one hand, and short-term arrangements on the other. The latter are usually confined to understandings about quotas and other conditions of entry for particular products.

[2] Papers on closer economic relations with New Zealand have increased in recent years. See, for example, Robinson (147), Elkan (76), and Holmes (97).

tralian market.[3] Both countries are probably wise to feel their way and there is little to be added to Document 12:3.[4]

The Agreement with Malaya has two novel and interesting features. The first is Malaya's acceptance of the Australian obligation to protect rubber produced in Papua-New Guinea. This acceptance is made easier by the fact that Australia neither seeks nor imposes any *quid pro quo* on Papua-New Guinea in respect of Australian exports.

The other feature is a readiness to protect Malaya against 'unfair' competition from third parties (e.g. China) in Australian markets. The gesture was no more than a reciprocation for Malayan willingness to stand by Australia in its protests against German and French dumping of flour in South-East Asian markets (Section 5). It is worth noting that this type of action is provided for in Article VI of GATT, which allows countervailing or anti-dumping duties by country A against country B not only when the industry of A is affected but also when A is not affected but desires to ensure fair competition for the products of country C. For 'A' read Malaya, 'B' read Germany, and 'C' Australia, the product being subsidised exports of flour from Germany.

For the rest it is of some importance to note that none of the agreements reviewed is in conflict with GATT.[5] There is no need to regard the negotiation of bilateral trade agreements as being in conflict with our GATT obligations. Although the agreement with Japan started outside GATT, the successful experience under it made full partnership in GATT possible. Again, the Malayan treaty showed that two trading partners could make the specific mutual assurances permitted by a particular article of GATT. The wheat deal with the United Kingdom may be regarded in a similar light. Yet again, since many GATT members with which Australia trades enforce import restrictions not fully in accord with the GATT disapproval of non-tariff barriers to trade, it is possible to use bilateral arrangements to minimise their adverse effects. To the doctrinaire purist who may object that it is wrong to negotiate on practices which are in breach of GATT, it may be said that the very spirit of GATT is consultation on difficulties (see Article XXII). If difficulties can be

[3] See, for example, the warning signs in the *Australian Financial Review* for 24 August 1966 reporting the reaction of J. G. Wilson, Managing Director of Australian Paper Manufactures Ltd, to the threat of competitive paper exports from New Zealand.

[4] Since the writing of this comment McEwen announced on 20 December 1966 that early in 1967 the two countries would examine the scope for enlarging the list of items to be included in the Agreement. This at least accords with the decision to review regularly the items at present excluded and listed in Schedule A to the Agreement (12:3). It also recognises the GATT criticism that the Agreement is still more narrowly based than is strictly required by Article XXIV of GATT.

[5] The 1957 treaty with Japan was not in conflict even *de jure*, since Australia's non-recognition of Japan within GATT was quite valid in terms of Article XXXV. Moreover, the *de facto* relations were almost a model of good GATT behaviour.

minimised by mutual agreement so much is gained while the more general battle on principles is being fought.

One document in this section (12:5) refers to trade with China,[6] which is not covered by a treaty and on which political controversy is naturally to be expected. So far the dilemma of trading with a country not recognised diplomatically by Australia and whose policies *vis-à-vis* Australian interests are not to be described as friendly has been solidly settled in favour of trade. This government view would appear to be supported by the public generally and not merely by the wheat and wool producers most affected. A similar view is taken of trade with other Communist countries. We have exchanged formal MFN understandings with Soviet Russia, Poland, Bulgaria, and Korea.

There are several other treaties, mostly of minor order. They call for no particular comment.[7]

12:1 AUSTRALIA'S POST-WAR TRADE ARRANGEMENTS

Memorandum by Department of Commerce and Agriculture, 3 December 1953.

Australia has entered into bilateral Trade Arrangements with seven countries in the post-war period. These Arrangements were aimed at—

(1) Securing import licensing facilities to enable Australian goods to enter the partner country.

(2) Facilitating the exchange of scarce commodities between the two countries.

However, trading conditions have altered radically over the last eighteen months. Most commodities previously in short supply are now entering world trade quite freely. In addition, the Australian Government found it necessary in March, 1952, to impose import restrictions for balance of payments reasons, and as they were administered in a non-discriminatory manner certain of the commitments made by Australia to Trade Arrangement Countries could not be maintained.

[6] For some general comment on Australian ambivalence on this question see Albinski (1).

[7] For some details see Vernon Report (11), vol. I, ch. 12, para. 84, and vol. II, app. K, paras. 199-207. Since this report was printed MFN agreements were concluded during 1965 and 1966 with Korea, the U.S.S.R., Poland, and Bulgaria. In fact, these nations were already receiving MFN treatment and the agreements merely formalised the position. This was done to ensure that they qualified to receive the General Tariff rate which replaced the old MFN rate when Australia in July 1965 adopted the Brussels tariff nomenclature which was already used by most other countries. The General rate is in effect the old MFN rate. Provision is made under Clause 20 of the Customs Tariff Act 1966 for surcharges to be made over and above the General rate in cases where the government may wish to place the goods of some nations on a less favourable tariff than the General rate. Australia has as yet made no use of this provision.

In the light of this policy of non-discrimination, Australia's external trading relations had to be reviewed, with the result that the trade arrangements were either allowed to lapse, or were suspended or revised.

A survey of Australia's post-war trade arrangements is set out hereunder:

Argentina: The Arrangement was signed in April, 1950, and as it was concluded primarily to overcome currency difficulties (since each country regarded the other's currency as 'hard') the main objective was to secure a selection of commodities and a balance of imports and exports which would avoid the transfer of convertible currency.

Provision was made for an exchange of goods worth £500,000 sterling each way. Although Argentine exports to Australia reached this figure, the Argentine authorities had difficulty in granting import licences to Australian exporters and the Arrangement was allowed to lapse in June, 1951.

Brazil: Under the Arrangement signed in September, 1950, it was hoped to establish a new market for Australian goods, especially secondary products such as earth-moving equipment and to obtain import licences for Australian exports otherwise excluded by Brazil. Australian exports were scheduled at £1,500,000 sterling—Brazilian exports at £3,500,000 sterling. Although the Australian export figure was not realized, Australian goods valued at £A918,000 were shipped during 1950-51 as against £160,000 in 1949-50. Our main export item in 1950-51 was wool which accounted for 81% of the total exports, and probably would have been imported without the trade Arrangement.

In recent times, Brazil, like Australia, has experienced balance of payments difficulties, and since neither country is in a position to give undertakings in regard to import licensing, the Arrangement is by mutual consent regarded as inoperative at present.

India: The Arrangement was signed in October, 1951, and was designed to aid the exchange of scarce materials between the two countries. India was to supply jute goods, cotton piecegoods, raw cotton, linseed, etc., in exchange for Australian wheat, zinc and lead, etc.

The Arrangement worked satisfactorily for each country. In June, 1952, it was agreed that the Arrangement had served its purpose and should be allowed to lapse as the supply position of most of the commodities involved had much improved.

Indonesia: The first post-war Arrangement between Australia and Indonesia was concluded in 1950. The main object of the Arrangement from the Australian viewpoint was to overcome difficulties imposed on our exports by Indonesia's policy to restrict imports because of a shortage of exchange.

The Arrangement covered the twelve months ending 30th September, 1951, and each country undertook to issue import and export licences, where applicable, for goods listed in the agreed schedules up to the amounts specified therein.

The Arrangement which was renewed with slight alterations in 1951, continued in force until 30th September, 1952. However, when import licensing controls on a non-discriminatory basis were introduced by Australia in March, 1952, on goods from non-dollar countries other than Japan, it was no longer practicable for Australia to carry out fully her obligations under the Arrangement.

As a result of trade discussions held in Canberra in October, 1953, a new Arrangement to promote Indonesia-Australia trade was concluded. Both countries have agreed to facilitate the import and export of the goods listed in the schedules to the Agreed Minute up to the amounts specified therein, within the limits of their import and export policies.

416

Since the conclusion of the first Trade Arrangement, Australia's export trade with Indonesia has greatly improved. While it is impossible to sort out all the influences on the trade, it is generally considered that the Trade Arrangements have had some beneficial effects.

Pakistan: This Arrangement which was concluded in November, 1951, was an attempt to develop trade between the two countries. Australia hoped to obtain some relaxation of the import licensing treatment accorded certain Australian foodstuffs, while Pakistan hoped to import certain commodities such as iron, steel and copper, which were in short supply and essential to her economy.

The Arrangement has not operated since December, 1952. It was not considered very successful due to Australia's inability to supply the goods required by Pakistan and because import licensing facilities were not provided for Australian goods to the extent hoped for.

Sweden: A series of Trade Arrangements have been negotiated annually with Sweden since 1946. Until December, 1952, they were concerned largely with the supply of scarce materials, with the Swedes bargaining their forest products against our copra, grains and ores. The Arrangements did assist Australia in obtaining increased quantities of newsprint, etc., than might otherwise have been available.

Because of the altered supply conditions of the commodities involved, and the system of import licensing introduced by the Australian Government in March, 1952, a modified form of Arrangement was concluded in May, 1953, between the Swedish and Australian Governments.

Western Germany: The German-Australian Trade Arrangement signed in 1951 and renewed in 1952 and 1953 has proved of assistance to our export trade with the Federal Republic. Import licences have been provided for many items of export interest to Australia. The quotas granted under the Arrangement have enabled our exporters to explore the possibilities of the German market and in a number of instances, e.g. eggs, butter, oranges, whale oil and meat extracts, new business has been secured. The Trade Arrangements have also enabled many items of Australian origin to be guaranteed unrestricted entry subject only to Germany's balance of payments position. Exports from Western Germany to Australia have also been facilitated by these Arrangements.

Under the 1953-54 Arrangements, the Australian Government has given an undertaking that, should there be any material change in our non-discriminatory import licensing policy, an opportunity will be given to the German Government to discuss the effects of the change with the object of maintaining satisfactory trading relations.

In return the Federal Republic of Germany has undertaken to issue licences freely for goods listed in Annex A to the Arrangement and to authorize importation for amounts not less than those specified in Annex B.

Source: Copland and Barback (eds.),
The Conflict of Expansion and Stability
(F. W. Cheshire, 1957), pp. 546-9.
Reprinted by permission.

12:2 AUSTRALIA-MALAYA TRADE AGREEMENT

Press statement released in Malaya by the Minister for Trade (J. McEwen) on 26 August 1958.[1]

'The Trade Treaty signed today brings a new and valuable protection to the important mutual trade between Australia and the Federation of Malaya', Mr. McEwen, the Australian Minister for Trade, said today. . . .

The Australian flour and wheat trade with the Federation of Malaya, worth more than £A3 million a year, has recently been cut into by subsidised and dumped competition from European suppliers.

The new agreement gives assurance that 80,000 tons of Australian flour and 14,000 tons of Australian wheat a year will be protected in the Malayan market against such unfair trade practices.

This is a significant step forward in protecting our normal commercial flour and wheat sales in our South East Asian markets in addition to protection against subsidised competition.

Australian flour and wheat are guaranteed duty free entry. On processed milks and butter, the duty preference of about 1½d. per pound over foreign suppliers will be maintained.

Other important concessions gained for Australia included a reduction in the duty on cheese from 10 per cent to 7½ per cent and a guarantee that the duty preference of 15% on canned peaches, pears and apricots will be maintained.

The 10% preference margin on tanned hides and skins and the duty free entry on both edible and inedible tallow were guaranteed.

As to other Australian exports to the Federation Australia is also assured that whatever changes the Federation might make in its tariff arrangements, specially on preferences, Australia would continue to receive as favourable treatment as the goods of any other country.

In the course of the trade discussions arrangements were made to ensure that Australian manufacturers had full opportunity to compete for the supply of machinery, plant and equipment for the economic development requirements of the Federation.

Australia would reduce the existing duties on natural rubber by 2d. per lb. Rubber would now enter Australia duty free, subject to the satisfactory disposal of the Papua-New Guinea crop.

Just as important to the Federation was Australia's assurance that synthetic rubber would not receive more favourable import treatment than natural rubber. In addition Australia would maintain duty free entry for tin and would protect the Federation's position in Australia's market should it be threatened by dumped or subsidised tin from other sources.

Australia would not increase the preferential rate of duty of 12/- per 100 super feet under tariff item 291 (H) (3), i.e. certain smaller sizes of sawn, un-dressed timber.

Moreover, the margin of preference of 1/- per 100 super feet now extended to Malaya under this tariff item would be continued.

[1] By common consent, the agreement continues in force, applying only to that part of Malaysia which formerly comprised the Federation of Malaya. The agreement continues in force indefinitely, subject to six months' notice of termination by either party. A review of the agreement is due every two years. *Year Book of the Commonwealth of Australia, No. 50*, 1964, p. 513.

Australia and the Federation, as major exporters of bulk commodities have a common interest in international price stability.

The two Governments have indicated in the Agreement that they will actively pursue measures designed to reduce international price fluctuations in all appropriate ways as is usual in Agreements of this type.

Provision has been made in the Agreement for the contingency that either Government may find it necessary to withdraw or modify any particular commitment or concession. Procedures are laid down to enable such necessary withdrawals or modification to be effected.

These are in line with the G.A.T.T. provisions relating to the withdrawal of tariff concessions should this be necessary to protect domestic industries.

. . . It is the first Trade Agreement which the newly independent Federation of Malaya has negotiated. It puts into practical effect the principle of mutual protection against unfair trading practices by other countries. It maintains the preferential structure. It provides a basis for the consolidation and improvement of trade between Australia and the Federation of Malaya.

12:3 NEW ZEALAND-AUSTRALIA FREE TRADE AGREEMENT

Statement by the Minister for Trade and Industry (J. McEwen)
in the House of Representatives on 17 August 1965.

The agreement reached on the formation of a free trade area between Australia and New Zealand, following the negotiations between Mr. Marshall, the New Zealand Minister of Overseas Trade, and myself, has now been confirmed by our respective Governments.[1]

A free trade area has a technical connotation. It is an arrangement between two or more countries which provides for the goods included in it to be traded free of duty between them, but allowing each country to maintain separate tariffs on imports from countries outside the arrangement. It is different from a customs union which requires the members to introduce a common external tariff against imports from other countries. Under the present arrangement Australia and New Zealand will each maintain separate tariffs against imports from third countries.

The General Agreement on Tariffs and Trade requires that, when two countries enter into a free trade agreement, substantially all the trade between the two countries should be subject to the free trade provisions. This indicates that some areas of trade can be excepted. There are no precise rules to indicate the dimensions of the trade which must be included, and there is no strict rule governing the period over which substantially all of the trade must be brought into the free trade agreement.

The arrangement reached between our two Governments has taken these considerations into account. Our agreement includes items covering some 60 per cent. of the total trade between our two countries—not 60 per cent. of the trade of each country, but approximately 60 per cent. of total trade between the two countries.

[1] The Agreement came into operation on 1 January 1966. The text is obtainable from the Government Printer, Canberra. Paper no. 10062/65.

The bulk of the items to be included initially in this 60 per cent. of the trade between the two countries are those already traded on a duty free basis. The balance of the items are at present dutiable—that is, the balance of the items which are initially put in the free trade section. It has been agreed that, where duties are very low—and some are 5 per cent.—they will be removed immediately. In other cases they will be reduced to free over eight years. In certain cases it may be agreed to extend the period beyond eight years.

It has been recognised by both Governments that there are some items which may not be included in the duty free list. Where serious harm or serious unemployment would result from competition by the other country the items concerned will never be traded duty free. The items of trade which have not been included at the outset will come under periodic examination by both countries for decision as to whether, or when, they should be moved into the duty free section which, under the agreement will be known as Schedule A. Where items of trade included in Schedule A are not being produced by one of the countries, that country may, at a later date when production commences, temporarily withdraw an item from the schedule and introduce protective duties. Where the establish·· ment of an industry is essential for economic development an item may be withdrawn permanently from Schedule A.

The greatest single generic item of trade between the two countries—forest products, ranging from timber and paper pulp to paper—will be predominantly duty free when the proposed agreement comes into operation at the beginning of next year. Only a limited range of paper products will remain dutiable.

New Zealand is the biggest customer for our manufacturing industries. The agreement will sustain and over the years develop that position, while not depriving New Zealand of the right or opportunity to establish further manufacturing industries. New Zealand is, of course, predominantly an exporter of primary products. Australia will accept certain of her primary products duty free. In some cases a limit has been set on the quantity to be imported duty free from New Zealand, but in no case at a level which would result in measurable harm to the Australian industry concerned. Provision has been made for the phasing out of duties over as long a period as eight years so that no sharp consequences may result. Before the list of products to be included was finalised the circumstances of the industries concerned were investigated and confidential discussions were held with people who could advise the Government on the competitive position of the industries in Australia and in New Zealand.

Items in Schedule A of importance to New Zealand export industries include frozen peas and beans, dried vegetables, cheese, lamb, pig meats, timber and paper products.

The present duties on these items will be phased out over a period of up to eight years—nine years in the case of frozen peas and beans—after the agreement enters into force. In regard to cheese and certain pig meats there is also provision limiting the quantities to be subject to the duty free arrangement. Duty free imports in the first year will include 3,000 tons of pork. Imports of pork amounted to 2,600 tons in a recent year without dislocation. In the case of cheddar cheese, imports, which have amounted to about 200 tons in recent years, will be 400 tons in the first year and will rise in five years to the ultimate ceiling of 1,000 tons. Special arrangements have been made in respect of the items mentioned above to ensure that New Zealand's quantitative import restrictions will not prevent Australian producers from having an equivalent opportunity to compete in the New Zealand market within their range of production.

I will now describe in more precise terms the provisions in the agreement which will govern the whole character of the new trading relationship between our two countries. The existing Trade Agreement between Australia and New Zealand, which has been in operation since 1933, will form part of the free trade agreement except as superseded or modified by it. This means that the contractual rights we both enjoy under the present Agreement have been maintained.

As already indicated provision is made for the regular review of trade in goods not listed in Schedule A with a view to the inclusion of additional items. The objective of these reviews would be the progressive addition of goods to the Schedule except where their inclusion would be seriously detrimental to an industry in either country or contrary to the national interest. The first of these reviews will take place within two years of the entry into force of the agreement. There are a number of provisions designed to ensure that there will be fair and equitable trading conditions between the two countries in the commodities included. Particular situations in which action might have to be taken by one of the parties to prevent unfair trading have been identified and provisions drafted to deal with them. Where goods are being dumped or are in receipt of a subsidy from the exporting country, provisions allow the importing country to take necessary action to safeguard any affected domestic industry.

There will be an article dealing with deflection of trade which might arise if producers of one country had access to raw materials or machinery at significantly lower prices than producers in the other country. This article will permit the second country, following consultations, to take corrective action to protect its affected producers. Either country, following a consultative procedure, may suspend temporarily its obligations in respect of products which are being imported in such increased quantities and under such conditions as to cause or threaten serious injury to its producers. Rules of origin which determine whether goods included in Schedule A will qualify for reduced duties in terms of the agreement are the same initially as those provided under the existing Trade Agreement. It is proposed, however, that the rules should be reviewed within two years.

The agreement will provide that one country shall not maintain quantitative import restrictions on imports from the other unless it is at the same time applying such restrictions to imports of a third country. Australia undertook not to impose quantitative import restrictions, introduced for balance of payments reasons, on imports from New Zealand. Because of its continuing and serious balance of payments position, New Zealand was not able to give a similar undertaking, but has indicated that it will provide for special arrangements in respect of some imports from Australia. Quantitative import restrictions will be removed on certain products from Australia including timber plywood and veneers from the date of entry into force of the agreement.

The care taken in the selection of items, the quantity limitations prescribed in certain cases and the arrangements to phase out existing duties over a number of years, together with the safeguard provisions to prevent any serious dislocation of trade should ensure there will be an avoidance of serious injury to existing industry in the two countries. In selecting commodities which at the outset would be included in the arrangement particular attention was also given to the interests of third countries. There should be no disruption to the trade of our other trading partners. G.A.T.T. provides for free trade arrangements between members and that organisation will be advised of the details of the agreement as soon as practicable.

421

P

It has also been agreed to set up a consultative committee on forestry products comprising representatives of the two countries. This committee would meet, as necessary, and would advise the two Governments on the steps necessary to develop and co-ordinate all phases of the industry in the two countries to achieve the best use of their forest resources.

New Zealand has undertaken, where import duties levied on goods from Australia are higher than the lowest rate applicable to goods imported under the same tariff item from any third country, to eliminate the difference in the rates at the earliest practicable date. Australia has already eliminated any similar differences which had existed in the Australian tariff.

Special reference should be made to the understanding reached in regard to raw sugar. Raw sugar is not listed in Schedule A but is nevertheless included in the scope of the agreement on the basis that the existing import duties shall be phased out in accordance with the provisions of the agreement but that the non-tariff measures at present in force shall continue. New Zealand, of course, is not a producer of sugar; nor is she likely to be in the foreseeable future.

The agreement will continue for ten years. After that it will remain in force but be subject to termination with 180 days' notice. Time has not yet permitted the agreement reached between the two Governments to be translated into a formal document. It is still necessary to finalise the legal drafting of the articles of the agreement and to ensure that the commodities in Schedule A are defined accurately in terms of the tariff classifications of both countries. The agreement will then be printed. When this is done, it will be signed. These processes will be completed with a minimum of delay and I would expect that the Agreement will be printed and ready for signature within a few weeks. The agreement, in its final form, will be not only a legal document but also a highly technical one. It probably will not use the term 'pork', for example, but will refer to 'tariff item so-and-so'. To the uninitiated, this will perhaps be less comprehensible than the lay description. At the earliest opportunity after signature, I shall arrange for the relevant documents to be tabled in this House. The conclusion of this free trade arrangement represents the culmination of intensive activity by both Governments extending over some two years. It constitutes an historic landmark in the development of trade relations between Australia and New Zealand. Although its immediate results in new trade will not be spectacular, the free trade arrangement is expected to have far reaching long term effects on the welfare, development and growth of the two countries.

Source: *C.P.D.* (*H. of R.*), vol. 47, pp. 11-14.

12:4 NEW ZEALAND-AUSTRALIA FREE TRADE AGREEMENT: BRIEF OUTLINE OF CONTENTS

The Agreement consists of Articles, a schedule listing commodities included in the Agreement, and letters exchanged concerning the Agreement. The following notes describe briefly and in general terms the main features of the Agreement including understandings reached in relation to certain Articles.

Preamble

The Preamble recalls the Australian-New Zealand Agreement 1944, refers to the desire of both countries to strengthen economic relations between them, and recognises their obligations under the General Agreement on Tariffs and Trade.

ARTICLE 1—*Free Trade Area*

The Article formally establishes a free trade area between New Zealand and Australia.

ARTICLE 2—*Objectives*

This Article sets out the objectives of the two countries in concluding the Agreement.
They are:

to further the development of the area and the use of its resources by promoting a sustained and mutually beneficial expansion of trade;

to ensure that trade within the area takes place under conditions of fair competition;

to contribute to the expansion of world trade and to the progressive removal of barriers thereto.

ARTICLE 3—*Scope of Agreement*

This Article defines the scope of the Agreement.

The provisions of the 1933 Trade Agreement between Australia and New Zealand are to continue as part of this Agreement except as superseded or modified by it.

The Article provides also for annual reviews of the trade between the two countries to consider the inclusion of additional items in the Agreement.

Items will be added progressively except where their inclusion would be seriously detrimental to an industry in either country, or contrary to the national interest or inconsistent with the objectives of any commodity arrangement to which both countries are parties.

The Article provides also, in respect of goods not scheduled in the Agreement, for the implementation of special measures beneficial to the trade and development of each country, e.g. the remission or reduction of duties on agreed goods.

It has been agreed also that the rules of origin, which determine whether goods scheduled in the Agreement qualify for reduced duties in terms of the Agreement, will be the same initially as those provided under the existing Australia-New Zealand Trade Agreement 1933. It is proposed, however, that these rules should be reviewed within two years.

ARTICLE 4—*Import Duties*

This Article prescribes the bases on which import duties are eliminated on goods included in Schedule A to the Agreement. These are as follows:
Where goods imported into either country from the other are—

(i) duty free, they remain duty free;

(ii) subject to duties not exceeding 5%, they become duty free on the date the Agreement applies to them;

(iii) subject to duties of more than 5% but not exceeding 10%, they become duty free in two stages—a reduction of 50% on the date the Agreement applies to them with duties completely eliminated two years later;

(iv) subject to duties of more than 10%, they become duty free in five stages over a period of eight years—a reduction of 20% on the date the Agreement applies to them and further reductions each of 20%, each subsequent two years.

Where goods are subject to fixed alternate or composite rates of duty the rates are reduced on the same basis as their ad valorem equivalents.

The method of reducing variable duties will be decided by consultation.

Temporary duties are not to be imposed on scheduled goods when imported from the free trade partner.

Duties may be reduced more rapidly than prescribed or, by agreement, over a longer period. Duties on frozen vegetables will be removed over a nine year period.

ARTICLE 5—*Quantitative Import Restrictions*

This Article provides that one country shall not maintain quantitative import restrictions on imports from the other unless it is applying such restrictions to imports of a third country.

Quantitative import restrictions applied to scheduled goods are to be reduced or eliminated at the earliest practicable date, taking into account the balance of payments situation and the desirability of avoiding any undue diversion of trade.

Following consultations, however, quantitative import restrictions may be introduced or reimposed on scheduled goods where this is necessary for balance of payments reasons.

Where import restrictions interfere unduly with conditions of fair competition, consultations will be held for the purpose of remedying the situation.

In relation to this Article Australia has undertaken not to impose quantitative import restrictions, introduced for balance of payments reasons, on imports from New Zealand. Because of its continuing and serious balance of payments position, New Zealand was not able to give a similar undertaking, but has indicated that it will provide for special arrangements in respect of some imports from Australia.

Quantitative import restrictions will be removed by New Zealand on certain products from Australia including timber, plywood and veneers, frozen peas and beans, dried vegetables, lamb, pork and strawberries from the date of entry into force of the Agreement. It has also been agreed that in the administration of import licensing on specified paper products New Zealand will ensure that Australian producers are given equal opportunity to export to New Zealand where faced with competition from imports from that country.

ARTICLE 6—*Revenue Duties or Taxes*

This Article provides that revenue duties or taxes will not be imposed on imported scheduled goods at rates higher than those applicable to domestic production of the same goods.

ARTICLE 7—*Deflection of Trade*

This Article establishes procedures for dealing with a situation where extreme injury is caused or threatened by deflection of trade which has arisen because producers of one country had access to raw materials, intermediate products or machinery at significantly lower prices than the producers in the other country.

The Article permits the second country to seek a remedy through consultations and, if a solution is not found by this means, to take corrective action to protect its affected producers.

ARTICLE 8—*Development of Industry*

Where necessary for establishing a new industry or extending the range of production of an existing industry, an item may be temporarily withdrawn from the schedule and protective duties imposed. These duties are to be removed within twelve years.

In exceptional circumstances where the establishment of an industry is essential for economic development an item may be withdrawn permanently from the schedule.

Tinplate and steel rails have been included in the Schedule on the understanding that they may be withdrawn, if necessary, once New Zealand production commences.

ARTICLE 9—*Temporary Suspension of Obligations*

This Article provides that where products are being imported in such increased quantities as to cause or threaten serious injury to its producers a country may seek a remedy through consultations. If a satisfactory solution is not found by this means the affected country may suspend temporarily its obligations under the Agreement to the extent necessary to protect its producers.

ARTICLE 10—*Dumped and Subsidised Imports*

Where goods are being dumped or subsidised and are causing or threatening material injury to producers in the importing country provisions of this Article allow that country to seek a remedy through consultation. If a satisfactory solution is not found by this means the country may levy dumping or countervailing duties on those goods to safeguard its domestic industry.

The Article also provides that one country, at the request of the other, may consider taking action to prevent future injury against dumped or subsidised imports from a third country.

ARTICLE 11—*Quantitative Export Restrictions*

This Article prevents the imposition of new export prohibitions or restrictions on exports by either country to the other.

ARTICLE 12—*Exceptions*

This Article lists a number of exceptions relating to security, health, protection of flora and fauna etc., which customarily appear in international agreements.

ARTICLE 13—*Extension to Territories*

This Article provides that territories for which either country is responsible may become associated with the Agreement on terms agreed to by the two countries.

ARTICLE 14—*Association with the Agreement*

This Article provides for the addition of new Members to the Agreement.

ARTICLE 15—*Administrative Co-operation*

This Article is designed to reduce formalities in regard to trade between the two countries.

ARTICLE 16—*Consultation and Review*

This Article provides for consultations other than those specifically covered elsewhere in the Agreement, including annual consultations for the purpose of reviewing the operation of the Agreement.

ARTICLE 17—*Entry into Force and Duration*

Formally, the Agreement will enter into force thirty days after instruments of ratification have been exchanged. The Governments have decided that the Agreement will enter into force on 1st January, 1966.

The Agreement will remain in force for at least ten years. After that it will continue in force but be subject to termination after a consultative procedure with 180 days notice.

OTHER MATTERS

Sugar

Raw sugar is not listed in Schedule A but is included in the scope of the Agreement on the basis that existing import duties will be phased out and that the non-tariff measures at present in force will continue. The duty of 1d. lb. levied by New Zealand is a revenue duty and, in accordance with Article 6, will be retained.

Tariff Rates

In relation to items not included in Schedule A, New Zealand has undertaken, where import duties levied on goods from Australia are higher than the lowest rate applicable to goods imported under the same tariff item from any third country, to eliminate the difference in the rates at the earliest practicable date. Australia has already eliminated any similar differences which had existed in the Australian tariff.

Forest Products

It has also been agreed to set up a Joint Consultative Council on Forest Industries comprising representatives of the two countries. This Council would meet, as necessary, and would advise the two Governments on the steps necessary to develop and co-ordinate all phases of the industry in the two countries to achieve the best use of their forest resources.

Commodity Coverage

Trade involved

The Agreement includes items covering some 60% of trade between the two countries. Items included represent £A42·6m. or 51% of New Zealand's imports from Australia in 1963/64 and £A19·1m. or 85% of Australia's imports from New Zealand in the same year.

Schedule A to the Agreement

The goods covered by the Agreement are listed in Schedule A.

In order to achieve commodity definitions common to both countries, items in the Schedule are described in terms of the Brussels Tariff Nomenclature with appropriate references to Australian and New Zealand Tariff items.

Schedule A needs to be read in conjunction with the Customs Tariff which contains details of the duty, if any, currently applicable. The items mentioned below are described in brief terms which should be taken as indicative only.

Among the several hundred items included in the Schedule are:

Forest products including	Cheese[1]
undressed timber	Dried fruits
most dressed timber	Wheat
plywood	Oranges
veneers	Lactose
pulp, newsprint, most papers	Strawberries
books and periodicals	Frozen peas and beans
Lamb meat, pigmeat[1]	Dried vegetables
Fish	Seeds

[1] Pork and Cheddar cheese have been included subject to quantity limitations.

426

Wool and wool tops
Copper bars and rods
Lead and Zinc
Tinplate
Rails
Petroleum products
Wide range of chemical items

Certain photographic plates and films
Some hand tools
A range of agricultural machinery
Some industrial machinery
A range of scientific and medical instruments and appliances

In the case of pork, duty free imports will be limited to 3,000 tons in the first year with provision for a 5% annual increase. This quota and growth factor will be reviewed at regular intervals. Duty free imports will be restricted to processors who give written assurance that their level and pattern of local purchases will be maintained and that imports will be arranged in an orderly manner. Imports outside this quota arrangement will be subject to normal duties.

Cheddar Cheese imports will be limited to 400 tons a year for the first two years, 800 tons a year for the third and fourth years and 1,000 tons a year in the fifth and subsequent years. Cheese, other than Cheddar, has been included in the Agreement without special conditions.

The following items of major trade interest are not included in Schedule A:

Motor vehicles and most automotive parts
Most iron and steel products
Bacteriological and most pharmaceutical products
Most plastics items.

Source: Department of Trade and Industry,
roneoed document, 31 August 1965.

12:5 TRADE WITH MAINLAND CHINA

Statements by the Minister for Trade (J. McEwen) in the House of Representatives on 31 August 1965.

The policy that the Government follows in this respect is one that is commonly followed by what one might describe as the Western powers, with the exception only of the United States which permits no trade whatever with mainland China. The policy is that the Western powers are agreed upon a list of items—the list is not incapable of being altered—which are classified as strategic items, and there is an absolute embargo on the export of those items to Communist countries. In the list there is a differentiation between China and other Communist countries— the European Communist countries. However, the list exists and there is not only a refusal to permit the export to Communist China of items on that list but also a refusal to permit such items to be exported anywhere, except with a satisfactory assurance that they will not be re-exported to Communist China. Included among the items on which there is an embargo are certain classifications of steel. The embargo does not apply to some other classifications of steel, such as tinplate and certain merchant bars. These may be exported . . . Lead may be exported. . . .

I point out that the Australian Government does not send any items of trade to mainland China. Within the policy I have described, commercial transactions take place. A table has been prepared showing Australian exports to mainland China in the years 1960-61 to 1964-65. Some exports of iron and steel plate and sheet have been made in each year. Exports of lead valued at about £2,000 and £5,000 were made in 1961-62 and 1963-64 respectively. There were no recorded exports in other years. Substantial exports of wheat have been made in each year.

These commodities are, of course, not sent to China by the Australian Government. They are sent by private commercial traders and by the Australian Wheat Board . . . Non-strategic items are freely exportable. . . .

Source: *C.P.D.* (*H. of R.*), vol. 47,
pp. 578, 583.

12:5 EXPORTS TO MAINLAND CHINA
1960-1 to 1965-6[a]

($A'000)

	1960–1	*1961–2*	*1962–3*	*1963–4*	*1964–5*	*1965–6*
TOTAL EXPORTS	79,714	131,912	129,288	168,190	135,633	106,541
Gluten and gluten flour	160	114	...	...	...	...
Wheat	50,826	97,528	105,474	128,154	115,667	100,381
Barley	8,576	5,510	...	906	258	...
Oats	2,266	1,988	1,238	4,290	1,787	...
Wheaten flour	2,824	2	neg.	...	...	1
Tallow	558	1,400	740	1,234	1,831	782
Wool	13,408	23,414	20,756	30,962	14,461	3,475
Hides and skins	118	118	344	284	887	501
Rutile concentrate	14	202	...	364	293	...
Zinc unwrought including spelter	66	382	266	54	...	15
Iron and steel plate and sheet	392	680	284	1,722	246	958
Wire, stranded copper	...	172	...	...	...	...
Copper, unwrought, blocks, etc.	...	116	...	...	...	...
Leather, leather manufactures, and leather substitutes	32	8	4	50	5	49
Vessels	...	...	...	100	...	...
Chemicals, etc.	122	72	4	8	3	1
Other items	352	206	178	62	197	377

[a] Final figures have been substituted for preliminary 1964–5 figures and 1965–6 figures added to the table with the assistance of the Commonwealth Bureau of Census and Statistics. The table has been adjusted to read in $A.

SOURCE: Commonwealth Statistician. As reproduced in *C.P.D.* (*H. of R.*), vol. 47, p. 583.

12:6 IMPORTS FROM MAINLAND CHINA[a]

For the years 1960-1 to 1965-6

	1960-1	1961-2	1962-3	1963-4	1964-5	1965-6[b]
	$	$	$	$	$	$
TOTAL IMPORTS	7,948,344	7,621,222	11,255,510	16,355,078	22,862,360	23,453,849
Animal foodstuffs, nuts, spices and tea, etc.	851,656	768,846	687,404	865,542	991,918	1,087,027
Hides and skins	41,892	95,822	123,516	288,626	331,840	247,164
Bristles and substitutes	1,221,094	888,288	1,243,256	1,399,762	1,474,898	1,269,027
Goat hair other than mohair and cashmere	665,832	116,158	121,802	478,644	666,474	394,268
Textiles	3,007,264	3,044,044	4,903,464	7,156,540	9,004,822	10,721,719
Apparel	263,118	245,844	445,884	1,101,356	1,958,696	1,790,568
Tung oil	395,080	546,590	788,074	551,736	479,882	395,341
Metals and metal manufactures	134,760	198,062	267,530	264,326	478,340	681,415
Chemicals	154,412	201,416	218,058	283,206	426,346	1,148,396
All other articles	1,213,236	1,516,152	2,456,522	3,965,340	7,049,144	5,718,914

[a] This table has been added to the figures supplied by the Minister for Trade.

[b] 1965-6 subject to revision. A new statistical classification of imports was introduced in 1965-6 and thus these figures may not be strictly comparable with those given for previous years.

SOURCE: Commonwealth Statistician.

D

DOMESTIC POLICIES
AND TRADE

13

AGRICULTURE IN DECLINE
AND RECOVERY

The story of agricultural development in the post-war years has yet to be told fully. To document the story adequately would be much beyond the scope of a volume limited to trade policies.[1] Our purpose here is a limited one: to indicate that a key decision was taken in 1952 designed to ensure that the agricultural sector as a whole expanded commensurately with the needs of a growing population and, of more immediately serious moment, with the need for larger export earnings in a rapidly industrialising economy.

Document 7:2 is a reminder that uppermost in everyone's minds in 1947 (for the Prime Minister spoke for the country) was the need to ensure increased food supplies for Britain. There was little argument about extending long-term contracts and, indeed, a powerful group of opinion in the farm sector favoured this method of trading for the future.[2] The pressure from Britain for food supplies continued well into the early fifties,[3] but by 1951-2 there were new reasons for urgent action by the Australian government. High prices associated with the post-war years culminating in the Korean boom (A13:2) had disguised a disquieting production position, even to the point of suggesting to some that exchange rates should be appreciated to equality with sterling.[4]

It could not be said that before 1952 there was no policy. Document 2:3 gives extracts from a little-known statement of rural policy authorised by

[1] On the wider problems of agriculture see Copland and Barback (41), especially chs. 7 and 8. Some of the documents bearing closely on trade policy are repeated in this volume.

For general comment and analysis on agricultural policy, particularly in relation to the period under review here, see Wadham et al. (160); also Crawford (52), some extracts from which appear in Copland and Barback (41); Campbell (32); Belshaw (22); Crawford et al. (63); and Vernon Report (11), vol. I, ch. 8, paras. 17-62.

[2] The attitudes of the United Kingdom and Australian governments in early post-war negotiations are briefly discussed in Section 7 and there are some relevant documents in Copland and Barback (41), ch. 6.

[3] As seen in Section 7, this pressure had abated in the mid-fifties.

[4] At least in retrospect such a decision would have seemed premature in 1952 when it became necessary to impose general import restrictions (see Section 15) and as, concurrently, the terms of trade moved strongly against Australia. No doubt it could be argued that exchange appreciation in 1950 or 1951 could have been followed by exchange depreciation in 1952. However, we have become so used to stable exchange rates that it is difficult to believe that a flexible policy possibly requiring frequent changes in the exchange rate would be acceptable to any Australian government, especially one favourable to high rates of capital inflow from overseas.

Chifley in 1946. It reflected many of the views to be found in the Reports of the Rural Reconstruction Commission[5] and occasional utterances by Labor Ministers speaking on post-war aims. It was a comprehensive policy —more so in many respects than the far more significant announcements in the period January to February 1952 (13:2, 13:3).[6] It lacked the concreteness and urgent relevance of the later 'action program'. Moreover, rural policy was not in fact given the importance attached to full employment in industry. Indeed, as we have noted, full employment—especially abroad— was seen as an important solvent of farm problems. International commodity agreements ranked in importance, too; but there was little evidence, before 1950, of recognition of major problems requiring detailed domestic attention. Given full employment at home and abroad, agriculture might well make its own way. Economically many of the problems of shortage of farm inputs needed to raise production arose in some degree because of, rather than despite, the prevalence of full employment. The other cause was the inability of oversea suppliers to meet Australian import demands despite willingness and ability of Australian farmers to pay for them.

It has been suggested that development of secondary industry was given priority over agriculture in the early post-war years. This is true although, in my view, less from deliberate or planned intention than from the relative impetus of the war-time policies in relation to the two sectors. To quote from the Joseph Fisher Lecture:

> In general terms, there has always been a clearer purpose behind the expressed policy of developing secondary industries than in respect of agriculture. Secondary industry, too, had a better base from which to jump. Whereas farm production was significantly at the expense of farm capital in time of war, secondary production received a great impetus from the needs of war. Much of the gains of war development were held in the peace. Considerable attention was indeed given to market security for primary products, but it has always seemed reasonable to Governments to let production expansion in agriculture take care of itself. This attitude was readily enough reinforced by the fear of the recurrence of burdensome surpluses already noted. In short, there was no clearly recognized driving necessity behind the policy of expansion professed by all parties. In this setting, the voice and pressures of the comparatively unorganized farm bloc were weak alongside the better equipped secondary industry groups.[7]

The shortages of power, materials, and equipment were not confined to agriculture: they were general in the post-war years before 1950 and severely

---

[5] These Reports, ten in all, are too little known and are an invaluable reference for students of agricultural development and policy in Australia in the years before 1946, the year of publication of the Tenth Report (12), which is the one most relevant to this section. The Commission was established by the war-time Labor government. Its Chairman was Hon. F. J. S. Wise, and its members were J. F. Murphy, S. M. Wadham, and C. R. Lambert.

[6] See also statement by the Prime Minister (Menzies) (13:4).

[7] Crawford (52), pp. 12-13.

affected both secondary and primary industries and public enterprises such as power and transport. While detailed evidence is lacking there was, nevertheless, an impression that farm requirements were deliberately placed, by government and private enterprise alike, at the end of the queue.[8] Whatever the exact position as to general attitudes, the result was a general shortage of goods required by farmers anxious to rehabilitate farms and expand production. In the words again of the Joseph Fisher Lecture, the expectation of farmers (in 1945)

> was to get on with production, first making up for the dilapidation of farms, becoming obvious after six years of war, and then to march forward with new practices and new equipment known to the country but impracticable to supply under war conditions.[9]

The war ended in drought and most farmers felt that, given a break in the drought and a removal of shortages, all would be well on the production front. Price incentives, despite the terms of some bulk contracts, were not absent and the stagnation in production must be put down largely to shortages of the necessary physical inputs rather than to financial difficulties which, in any case, largely disappeared during the Korean War boom.

Far from overtaking the backlog of demand, local production of wire, galvanised iron sheets and pipes, steel posts, and most agricultural machinery fell below current requirements and, in most cases, below pre-war production levels. Nor, for the reasons given in Section 15, could imports be obtained to fill the gap, a fact which temporarily made the highly favourable price situation ruling for most farmers a somewhat hollow experience. By 1946-7 superphosphate supplies regained pre-war levels and actually expanded by about 30 per cent in the next three years. From 1949 the capacity of the industry to meet further pressures of demand appeared to lag.[10]

In all the circumstances the outcome was not surprising. By 1948-9 rural production was up by 9 per cent over pre-war and hopes were still high. In fact, however, this percentage was exceeded only once in the next four years and fell to its lowest point (3 per cent only above pre-war) in 1951-2 (A13:1). In 1951-2 returns also fell against a background of inflation of costs, and the serious cost/price squeeze of the fifties and early sixties began (A13:2).[11] In 1950 the stagnation in production had become obvious and, indeed, the first World Bank loan in that year (A15:2) was devoted in significant part to providing an enlarged supply of North American farm equipment. Nevertheless, it was the experience of 1951 that gave the impetus to the decision selected as the key one for this chapter. It was even possible to

---

[8] For a strong reflection of this view see Wadham *et al.* (160), pp. 263-7.

[9] Crawford (52), p. 9.

[10] Material in these paragraphs is drawn from Crawford (52) and (55).

[11] See also a discussion of this matter in the Vernon Report (11), vol. I, ch. 8, paras. 34-47.

speculate in serious terms about the future food supply position for the Australian people, especially of livestock products. Butter shortages in New South Wales in 1950 and the obvious lag of meat production behind population growth (the total tonnage in 1950-1 was about the same as for pre-war years but population had increased 21 per cent) were legitimate causes for concern even if, in retrospect, some other food supply fears seem exaggerated. The statistical picture is reasonably shown in the tables included in 13:5.

A continuing ingredient in the growing worry about agriculture was Britain's as yet (1950) unabated pressure for more food supplies. This was part of a wider concern—not confined to the Australian government—that Australia might not be able to perform an adequate role in war should this again be necessary.[12] The need to earn dollars—either directly or by relieving Britain of the necessity to spend dollars on foodstuffs—persisted. Then, on top of these concerns, in 1951-2 came the realisation, as prices and production fell, that, even without the dreaded recurrence of drought, export earnings would probably prove inadequate to the import needs of a growing industrial economy. It indeed became apparent that industrialisation with its hunger for imported materials and equipment was adding more to trade problems than to their solution. In this situation the needs of the farmers came more to the forefront and there emerged, after some hesitation during 1951, the decision of February 1952 explained in 13:3 and 13:2.

The documents largely speak for themselves, but one or two further observations are in order before turning to the later documents, which reflect conditions a few years after February and April 1952. The first is that although very much a *production* policy (market prospects were not then regarded as a limiting factor), the action of the Commonwealth government was a most important recognition that there could be circumstances in which it must play a major role of leadership in agricultural policy.[13] The second point, which is clear in the documents, is that the States were ready to accept the lead, particularly as the Federal government did act strongly in directions open to it: this last was evident in the tax concessions to farmers, liberalisation of dollar imports, encouragement through appropriate bank credit policy, and, not least in the outcome, the marked stimulus given to research and extension. The details of these matters are beyond our scope; but they deserve to be recognised as a coherent set of policies calling for somewhat less grudging recognition than given by one critic.[14]

The work of the Australian Agricultural Council, both at ministerial and

---

[12] This possibility was not taken lightly by the government, which had established the National Security Resources Board to assist it in some economic aspects of defence preparedness. See 13:7 and Mendelsohn (125).

[13] See Campbell (32), p. 119.

[14] See Wadham's view in Wadham *et al.* (160), pp. 266-7.

official level, was good and was not the least encouraging aspect of the whole episode.[15] This is said with a full recognition that the Commonwealth was supporting its views on policy in an acceptable and financially persuasive way. It is also appropriate to add that secondary industry showed more consciousness of the national situation reflected in the decision to rank agriculture with defence. From April 1952 secondary industry responded more readily to departmental requests for greater output of particular items required for farm production. This, in turn, was facilitated by a substantial enlargement of industrial capacity.

The targets adopted by the Australian Agricultural Council are given in Tables A and B in 13:5.[16] It will be observed that they are general aims rather than year-by-year production goals individually carrying some commitment by governments to the growers concerned. The general aim was expressed by McEwen as the addition of £100m. to export earnings by 1957-8,[17] or an increase in volume of some 21 per cent.[18] The increased volume was solidly achieved well before 1957-8, and the addition in value exceeded the £100m., too. Indeed, the improvement was so rapid that the question has been asked: 'were the measures of 1952 really necessary?' But after 1953-4 export prices again declined substantially, so significantly offsetting production gains (A13:2).

In dealing with this question, even in retrospect, there is little need to qualify the judgment made in March 1953 (13:7). A good season in 1952-3 was followed by others. Nevertheless, the various measures taken (some, such as imports of American equipment under the International Bank loan, preceded April 1952) were, in combination, a stimulus to enlarged investment in improved farming which survived the shock of falling prices after 1953-4. Without these measures and especially the tax concessions and the encouragement given to research and extension, there is no reason to think that growth would have continued at the rate shown in A13:1. As with any industry, growth in agriculture is dependent upon technological advance, appropriate incentives, and capital investment. The immediate response in 1952-3 was partly the accident of a good season, but the results which appear

[15] Rather less effective was the organised voice of farmers. Document 13:1, expressing the views of the National Farmers' Union, indicates promise, but farmers have always been more effective as pressure groups when speaking about commodity problems than on wider issues. The National Farmers' Union has yet to be strongly established. Nevertheless, on some issues like the later trade treaty negotiations with Japan (1957) a rather more effective unity was achieved.

[16] Full explanatory notes concerning these targets are to be found in a pamphlet (No. 5115), issued in December 1952 by McEwen on behalf of the Agricultural Council, entitled *Agricultural Production Aims and Policy* (117).

[17] See his speech, not here reproduced, in the House of Representatives on 7 May 1952. *C.P.D.*, vol. 217, p. 103.

[18] It is regretted that the figure of 35 per cent in the Joseph Fisher Lecture (p. 17) was an error. It should read '21 per cent to 24 per cent'.

for later years require a better explanation than this. It is to be found in a study of all the factors at work, including the great benefits of myxomatosis.[19]

Not all the actual course of events was correctly planned or foreshadowed. Land settlement was given more emphasis in the statement of policies (13:5) than subsequent activities justified. In fact most growth came from more intensive farming, although there were some significant new land settlement ventures, both government and private. Large-scale irrigation has not played the part expected. There is little doubt that some new settlement schemes (including irrigation) will contribute to growth and to export earnings in the future. Nevertheless, growth will continue to be associated principally with the more intensive development of existing holdings.[20]

Another hope that was not realised as early as expected was recovery in wheat acreage to pre-war levels, which did not occur until after 1957-8.[21] At this time additional investment in wheat became more profitable than in wool, a fact assisted by the discovery by many graziers that wheat was a profitable way to use periodically the nitrogen accumulating in their pasture fields.[22]

All told the policies of 1952 did contribute to export expansion without which the balance of payments situation would undoubtedly have proved even more serious than it has been on occasions in the last fifteen years. This brings us back for our concluding comments to the permanent need for growth in agricultural exports. In 1952 there was no great hope that secondary products would rapidly, if ever, replace agricultural products as principal export earners. Yet A13:2 does show a significant change. The falling percentage share of total exports attributable to agriculture is partly due to declining prices relative to other exports, reflecting marketing problems of varying difficulty, but it is more significantly due to rising volume of exports of minerals and manufactured goods. This trend may well continue, but it would be unwise to abandon a strongly positive agricultural policy in the expectation that non-agricultural exports will provide all the additional export earnings required. It is for this reason that the expansion of the Japanese market and of the Chinese market for wheat has become so important at a time when agricultural protectionism in Australia's traditional markets has threatened to seriously limit further growth in agricultural exports.[23]

[19] In this respect some of the material in the Vernon Report (11), vol. I, ch. 8 (and more especially the references there given) will be found helpful.

[20] There remains great scope for serious academic study of the factors in agricultural growth in Australia and of the changes in the relative importance of these factors at various stages.

[21] Since then acreage has expanded rapidly, reaching 16,760,000 acres (preliminary figure) in 1965-6 and promising to be even greater in 1966-7.

[22] See Vernon Report (11), vol. I, ch. 8, paras. 63 *et seq.*

[23] On this see the general argument developed in the Vernon Report (11), vol. I, ch. 12, making due allowance for its understatement of the export potential in mineral development. On this latter point see Crawford (62).

A13:1 RURAL INDUSTRIES, TRENDS IN PRODUCTION, FARM INCOME AND WORKFORCE, 1948-9 TO 1963-4

YEAR	RURAL PRODUCTION		FARM INCOME		RURAL WORK FORCE	
	Quantum Index	*Gross value $A million*	*Income[a] $A million*	*Income as % of national income*	*Census year*	*Number '000*
Average 1936–7 to 1938–9	100	480	202[b]	13[b]	n.a.	n.a.
1948– 9	109	1,218	652	17	1947	467
1949–50	115	1,580	912	21		
1950– 1	109	2,366	1,576	26		
1951– 2	103	1,924	944	15		
1952– 3	121	2,332	1,172	17		
1953– 4	122	2,320	1,026	14	1954	472
1954– 5	123	2,208	898	11		
1955– 6	131	2,314	930	11		
1956– 7	131	2,552	1,110	12		
1957– 8	124	2,258	712	8		
1958– 9	149	2,510	972	10		
1959–60	144	2,646	1,016	9		
1960– 1	152	2,746	1,034	9	1961	446
1961– 2	155	2,734	964	8		
1962– 3	166	3,010	1,108	9		
1963– 4[c]	174	3,378	1,448	10		

n.a. Not available.

[a] Includes income of farm companies. The farm estimates are from the *Australian National Accounts* and incorporate allowances for depreciation based on the provisions of the tax law, which provide for higher rates of depreciation than would be included if based on annual consumption of the fixed assets. F. H. Gruen (*Australian Journal of Agricultural Economics*, vol. 7, no. 2, December 1963) has made estimates of depreciation on the basis of original costs depreciated by the 'straight-line' method. These estimates suggest that the farm income data in the table underestimate farm incomes, because 'official' depreciation allowances were higher by $40 million in 1949–50, and in succeeding years $ million 52, 10, 28, 50, 66, 80, 62, 68, 62, 58 and 60 (in 1960–1).

[b] Aggregate figures for this period are not available. Derived from estimates by H. P. Brown in 'Composition of Personal Income', *Economic Record*, vol. XXV, June 1949.

[c] Estimated by the Commonwealth Bureau of Agricultural Economics.

SOURCE: Unless otherwise stated, Commonwealth Statistician. Derived from Vernon Report (11) vol. I, Table 8.5.

A13:2   RURAL INDUSTRIES, TRENDS IN EXPORTS AND PRICES RECEIVED AND PAID BY FARMERS, 1938-9 TO 1963-4

YEAR	EXPORTS		INDEXES OF PRICES[a]		
	Value of rural exports as percentage of merchandise exports	*Export price index (all groups, excl. gold)*	RECEIVED BY FARMERS		PAID BY FARMERS
			Excl. wool	*Incl. wool*	
	%	1959–60 = 100			
1938– 9	84	21	n.a.	n.a.	n.a.
1948– 9	86	88	112	116	106
1949–50	89	102	123	134	117
1950– 1	91	176	146	208	139
1951– 2	82	126	179	182	175
1952– 3	84	128	178	188	188
1953– 4	85	126	181	189	191
1954– 5	85	115	174	176	191
1955– 6	81	105	183	179	199
1956– 7	80	118	184	190	209
1957– 8	78	102	181	177	215
1958– 9	78	89	184	169	214
1959–60	78	100	191	181	219
1960– 1	75	92	199	182	227
1961– 2	77	97	179	170	230
1962– 3	77	104	178	172	231
1963– 4	77	120	187[b]	187[b]	231[b]

n.a. Not available.

[a] Average of five years ended June 1950 = 100.

[b] Preliminary average of first three quarters.

SOURCE: Commonwealth Statistician and Bureau of Agricultural Economics. As reproduced in Vernon Report (11), vol. I, Table 8.6.

13:1   CAUSES OF AND REMEDIES FOR AUSTRALIA'S LAG IN FOOD PRODUCTION

Statement presented by a deputation from the National Farmers' Union of Australia to the Prime Minister (R. G. Menzies) on 25 February 1952.

The National Farmers' Union of Australia is gravely concerned at the serious trend in this country's food production which has been developing over the post-war years. Recent statements by senior members of the Federal Cabinet, including the Minister for Commerce and Agriculture (Hon. J. McEwen) and the Minister for Labour and National Service (Hon. H. E. Holt) indicate that the

Government is not unaware of the position. The N.F.U. feels, however, that with its wide direct representation of the country's major food producers it can assist the Government by providing an intimate and comprehensive picture of what has caused this serious trend and by advancing recommendations as to how the position might best be remedied.

Over the war and post-war years, Primary Producers have, in spite of tremendous difficulties, been able generally to show some increase in production but this increase has been inadequate to meet a growth in population of 1,620,978 over the last 15 years and an increase in the consumption per head which has occurred in many cases. One way of appreciating the position is by comparing the production per head for the five year period to 1938-39 and the production for 1950-51; these figures indicate a decrease for 1950-51 of most foodstuffs including wheat, meat, butter and whole milk.

The immediate effect of this trend is to reduce our exports which must have a damaging effect on the economy in that it restricts our ability to purchase vital imports. Moreover Australia's primary producers feel that this country with its tremendous resources for food production has an obligation to maintain exports in order to help feed the United Kingdom and other countries, particularly in Asia, which are so urgently in need of food. There is little need to labour this aspect which is of such obvious importance if Australia is to meet her moral obligations within the British Empire and the wider orbit of the United Nations. We would also emphasize the strategic value of Australia's food production in the event of another world conflict.

The problem is not one to be tackled with a quiet philosophical frame of mind—it is urgent and immediate. Australia's population is growing rapidly and on the present trends of natural increase and planned immigration, it is estimated that the population will be 10,500,000 in 1960. It has been further estimated that by 1960, if we are to meet local consumption and maintain exports at the level which has existed over the last two or three years, 1950-51 production will have to be increased for example by some $3 \cdot 15\%$ for wheat, $30 \cdot 7\%$ for meat, $29 \cdot 3\%$ for milk and more than 50% for sugar.

If Australia's export income is to be maintained and the target for 1960 achieved, then steps must be taken by Governments and primary producers in co-operation to ensure that the necessary expansion in food production commences immediately.

Reasons for Lag in Production

The major reason for the lag in Australia's food production has been lack of balance between the growth of primary and secondary industries. During the war, secondary industries were encouraged to meet defence needs and to fill the gaps caused by the sudden curtailment of our normal imports. At the end of the war both State and Federal Governments supported not only the retention of these industries but the development of all types of new secondary industries, at the expense of primary industries. The trend is evidenced by the fact that since 1939 our rural labour force has been reduced by 40,000 whilst our factory labour force has increased by over 300,000.

This lack of balance between primary and secondary industries has been exaggerated by prices policies which aimed at keeping essential foodstuffs at the lowest possible prices, while less essential items were allowed to go uncontrolled. Less essential industries were immediately able to outbid primary industries for both labour and materials.

The effect of these two major factors has been to stultify our food producing industries and prevent producers from replacing or making good the tremendous depreciation of capital equipment which took place over the war years. The story is only too well known in rural areas how fences deteriorated, rabbits and other pests moved in and the producing capacity of our countryside has been seriously impaired. . . .

Summary of Remedies[1]

Australia is on the threshold of a period of tremendous development for her primary industries. Our own growing population and a rapidly increasing population in other parts of the world appear to offer us long term expanding markets for our food production. Capital equipment must be found to enable this development and if it is not forthcoming from sterling areas, then the Government is urged to ensure that it is obtained from dollar sources.

An increase of food production will, however, only come about if food production is profitable relative to other uses of capital and labour. The Government is therefore urged to put into action a policy which will restore primary industries to a status where they can compete with secondary industries for labour and supplies of essential materials. Such a policy does not seek to destroy essential secondary industries but merely to provide some reasonable balance to the economy which must be for the good of the Country as a whole.

Primary producers are willing to play their part in raising Australia's food production and now look to the Commonwealth Government for support and co-operation.

> *Source*: As quoted in Copland and Barback
> (eds.) *The Conflict of Expansion and
> Stability* (F. W. Cheshire, 1957), pp. 575-
> 81. Reprinted by permission.

[1] In some four pages, not reproduced in full here, the deputation suggested government aid to increase the supply of materials to producers; orientation courses for immigrants going on to the land; State Housing Commission projects in rural areas; establishment of new units of agricultural production; improvement of transport facilities; provision of permanent water in rural areas; improvement of rural amenities; pasture improvement; taxation concessions; low interest, long-term loans; fairer price-fixing policies for food products; and fodder conservation.

13:2 FOOD AND AGRICULTURAL PRODUCTION AS IMPORTANT AS DEFENCE AND COAL PRODUCTION

Statement by the Minister for Commerce and Agriculture (J. McEwen) at the 35th Meeting of the Australian Agricultural Council, 25 February 1952.[1]

We are all deeply concerned, I know, at current trends within our agricultural and pastoral industries. Over the past ten years they have failed to expand sufficiently to meet our home requirements and at the same time maintain existing

[1] McEwen had led up to his statement on this occasion in a press statement issued on 14 January 1952, in which he stressed the need for the development of a concrete program to solve Australia's food production problem on the basis of a complete understanding between the Commonwealth government, the State authorities, and the leaders of primary industry.

levels of exports. This is particularly the case in our food-producing industries and, in spite of the run of good seasons since 1947, serious downward trends have become manifest in the last year or two.

In spite of a Commonwealth average yield of some 16 bushels per acre, Australia will be unable this year to meet her commitments under the International Wheat Agreement. As you all know, the acreage in Australia dropped to the low level of about 10,250,000 acres in 1951, a decline not fully explained by the undoubted expansion of other cereal crops and recovery in sheep numbers from the drought years. Exports of frozen beef, which had declined by 35,000 tons since 1947-48 to 70,000 tons in 1950-51, will be further reduced this year as the result of drought conditions in Queensland and increased local demand. Exports of lamb in 1950-51 were only 20,000 tons, which is less than one-third of pre-war average shipments. This year our shipments of lamb may be little more than half as much as last year. Similar declines have taken place in mutton and pork exports. I need hardly mention the decline in butter production, which, however, is by no means the least important of our problems.

Our concern over these trends is not merely in terms of the food requirements of our growing population—although that problem is real enough—it is not merely in terms of our failure to maintain food supplies to the United Kingdom—although there is no room for complacency on this score: there are other serious aspects as well as these. This year there has emerged a huge adverse balance in Australia's overseas trade. Our capacity to earn the credits necessary to sustain our imports of capital equipment and goods at an adequate level is seriously threatened, and, as you well know, there has always been a major dependence by Australia upon rural output. None of us can see any early change in this dependence upon rural industries. On top of all this is the extremely serious sterling dollar crisis. The sterling area is acutely short of dollar credits to finance huge imports of wheat, the feed grains, cotton, sugar, tobacco and other primary products. The more our output of any of these declines, the more acute becomes the problem for the sterling area as a whole. Australia could make a major contribution by expanding any or all of these industries.

In reviewing the cause of the present trends in key rural industries, it is impossible to sort out any one single factor as the major one. There is undoubtedly something far more deep-seated behind the trends than can be ascribed to wool price fluctuations or seasonal conditions. It is obvious that no simple single measure can reverse these trends which are already downward. A comprehensive Commonwealth-wide programme embracing measures within many fields of policy is necessary. Neither the Commonwealth nor the States can embark alone on a programme designed to achieve the results. We have each our role to play, and finally we are dependent upon the reaction of the individual primary producer. It is our joint task to assist him to secure the wherewithal in the form of adequate labour, materials and farm machinery to get on with the job.

It is important that the right incentives should be provided and that the Commonwealth and States work together to achieve this end. I consider the recent Commonwealth-State action in the wheat industry has been a step in the right direction.

There appears no doubt about the market outlook for primary products abroad, particularly for wheat and the feed grains and our meats. Nor can we see ahead any likelihood of world surpluses emerging. On the contrary, responsible opinion suggests that the future is more likely to be marked by more frequent and wider outbreaks of famine in important countries of the world. In such eventualities

443

the contributions which Australia is making to the world's food needs would always come under critical scrutiny.

Out of a consideration of all these circumstances the Commonwealth Government has decided that activities directly concerned with the production of essential items of food and agricultural products in this country shall be classified in importance with defence and coal production. Indeed, food production is one of the important elements of Australia's defence planning, not only to take care of our own needs, but to ensure that in an emergency we are in a position to make an appropriate contribution.

There need be no conflict between policies designed to expand food production in the short term and those which are basic to our long-term programme of development in Australia. The further development of our rural industries, including both the food producing and the dollar saving ones, is necessary to sustain or improve our standards of living under the impact of immigration. Likewise, the further development of our key primary industries is the most promising positive step we can take in making our proper contribution to the solution of the dollar problem.

The Commonwealth Government has, therefore, decided to adopt as its policy objective a Commonwealth-wide programme of agricultural expansion, not only to meet direct defence requirements, but also to provide food for the growing population, to maintain our capacity to import, and to make our proper contribution to relieving the dollar problem.

Source: As quoted in Copland and Barback
(eds.), *The Conflict of Expansion and
Stability* (F. W. Cheshire, 1957), pp. 581-3.
Reprinted by permission.

13:3 AUSTRALIAN AGRICULTURAL COUNCIL'S MOTION ON EXPANSION OF AGRICULTURAL PRODUCTION

Press statement, 26 February 1952.

The following motion was agreed to—

1. The Australian Agricultural Council recognises the serious need for expanded agricultural production and notes with approval the Commonwealth's decision to accord high importance to agricultural production, and, to achieve this objective, recommends a co-operative Commonwealth and State effort in close association with the industries concerned.

2. The Council resolves that a national production aim be immediately formulated and that as a matter of urgency a special meeting of the Agricultural Council be called as soon as possible to formulate a production pattern covering the next 5-year period suitable for the needs of Australian home and export requirements.

3. Council requests the Standing Committee to examine the various related policy matters and suggestions discussed by this Council and to prepare suggestions for Commonwealth, State or Commonwealth/State action for consideration by the Council, conferring as necessary with such established bodies as the Commonwealth-State Allocations Committee.

4. The Council recommends continuance of fullest practicable assistance by the State Governments to the Commonwealth superphosphate programme, and endorsed as a necessary objective the two-year target set for the plant conversion programme.

5. The Council recommends to the State Departments of Agriculture and other State Departments the desirability of continuing to give the fullest assistance possible to the Commonwealth Department of Labour and National Service and Immigration in their current programme of recruitment and placement of migrant labour.

6. The Agricultural Council, having been informed by the Minister for Commerce and Agriculture that the Government is examining the incidence of taxation on agricultural production, hopes such examination will be expedited in the interest of food production.

7. This meeting of the Agricultural Council recognises the need for new farms and recommends that the Commonwealth and the States confer at the earliest possible date on ways and means to achieve this objective.

13:4 ECONOMIC POLICY

Press statement by the Prime Minister (R. G. Menzies) on 28 March 1952.

1. The Government reaffirms its complete belief in the basic principle that the halting of inflation and the stabilisation of costs and prices inside Australia are fundamental to national development, national defence, industrial stability, secure employment, and rising standards of living.

2. This truth may be illustrated by a reference to rural production. Increased prices which are not unusually accompanied by correspondingly increased costs will not only add little or nothing to the farmer's real profit, but will actually expose rural industries to bankruptcy if and when prices fall. Prices of primary products can fall much more rapidly than costs. . . .

5. A series of reports before Cabinet has shown that these measures, combined with the effects of lower wool prices and an exceptional inflow of imports during recent months, are operating to slow down the rate of price and cost increases and to produce some improvement in the availability of labour and materials for basic industries. There has for example been some real movement of labour into the iron and steel industry, transport and power undertakings, the aircraft and other heavy industries.

This is important, for increased production is the positive solution to problems the negative solution of which has had necessarily to receive so much attention. . . .

8. In the face of all these facts, Cabinet has re-affirmed its view that current policy should resolutely continue to aim at checking the inflationary factors which are still at work and that so far from relaxing that policy even greater efforts must be made to avoid a rapid rise in the level of internal demand or an increased resort to inflationary finance through the Central Bank. . . .[1]

[1] Paragraphs 3-4 and 6-7, omitted here, deal with the government's general counter-inflationary policy.

13. The Cabinet has also given careful consideration to the speedy encouragement of primary production, which forms so great a part of our exports. It is only by increasing our export income that we can afford to buy more imports and bring into our country goods and materials which we so badly need for development.

14. We have considered how this encouragement can most wisely be given. We have already announced particular decisions such as those with regard to current provisional tax, the encouragement of material supply, and the placement of migrant labour, which need not be repeated. But at our meeting this week we have also considered how, by some modification of the tax system, we can, without adding to inflation, help the primary producer in such matters as the purchase of farm machinery, the provision of living accommodation for employees, the conservation of fodder, and the effective use of water supply. We have also considered the price to be got for the wheat about to be sown.

15. On these matters we announce the following decisions:

(a) In respect of living accommodation for farm employees commenced on or after April 1st next and before June 30th, 1955, there will be a special taxation provision (i.e. a deduction for income tax purposes) for depreciation at the rate of 20% per annum for five years.

There will be a condition that, to secure the benefit of this concession, buildings commenced but not completed as at June 30th, 1955, must be completed during the financial year 1955-6.

There will be a further condition that any accommodation so built for an employee shall have the benefit of the special depreciation up to a cost of £2000.

(b) In respect of farm implements, buildings for fodder conservation, and irrigation materials such as piping, there will be for a similar period a similar special depreciation allowance of 20% per annum.

(c) The wheat export tax, which is now 2/2d. per bushel, will not be imposed in respect of wheat of the next harvest. Wheat exported will therefore attract the full export price without this special tax deduction. It does not indicate any intention or policy decision in respect of wheat stabilisation, in respect of which our policy of consulting the industry will, of course, be carried out. It is designed solely as a particular concession or benefit for the wheatgrower for the next harvest.

(d) A further matter of concern to wheat growers is the first payment on next season's wheat. We are prepared to facilitate a first advance of 12/- per bushel bulk basis f.o.r. ports, or alternatively, if it is preferred, a sum equal to 85% of the estimated return on the same basis.

(e) The government is actively investigating, for introduction in conjunction with the Budget, new methods of assessing provisional tax which will pay regard to fluctuating incomes. One of the methods under consideration is a system of self-assessment for provisional tax, with proper safeguards against serious error. Such a system now operates in Canada.

Each of these proposals should give material encouragement and assistance to primary producers, while maintaining the Government's over-all counter-inflationary policy. . . .

13:5 PRODUCTION AIMS FOR AGRICULTURE ADOPTED BY AUSTRALIAN AGRICULTURAL COUNCIL

Press statement of 22 April 1952.

The Australian Agricultural Council, after a lengthy examination of Australian food production today, adopted the production aims submitted by the Standing Committee on Agriculture . . . The production aims (set out below . . . are minimum targets and it will be the endeavour of every government to improve on them. . . .

MOTIONS CARRIED:

This Council recognises the States' and Commonwealth's share of the responsibility for increasing the present volume of primary production and the necessity for an increase in the flow of exports of primary products, which contribute 85% of Australia's exports, as well as providing the food requirements of a rapidly increasing Australian population. In order to achieve this, the problem must be approached as a National undertaking. It is necessary to contemplate the developments of land settlement projects, including those requiring irrigation facilities, the development of rural electricity projects and the purchase of machinery and equipment for these purposes. These involve capital investment and raise questions of special grants, such as the Dairy Industry Efficiency Grant to facilitate the implementation of the production drive. Furthermore, the construction of railways in undeveloped areas which will never carry a large population but which are important potential food producing districts must also be financed. Under the present circumstances of uniform taxation these programmes are, in total, beyond the resources of the States. There must, therefore, be consultation between the Commonwealth and States on the financial implications of these necessary programmes.

The Australian Agricultural Council urges the respective Governments at the Loan Council to give special consideration to the requirements of the State Agricultural Finance authorities when preparing the Loan programme. . . .

PRODUCTION AIMS FOR AGRICULTURE

In accordance with the Agricultural Council's direction . . . the Standing Committee on Agriculture has considered the question of a suitable production pattern as an objective over the next five to six years. This is summarised for the Commonwealth as a whole in Tables A and B hereunder.

The aims have been set at limits which are considered to be within the physical capacity of the industries concerned within the period indicated, keeping in mind the need to expand agricultural production to feed our growing population, as a major source of export income, as a contribution to defence preparedness, and as part of the general development of Australian resources.

The production aims postulated hereunder are based on the following general assumptions—

(1) That Commonwealth and State Governments will continue their efforts to expand agricultural production;

(2) That supplies of farm machinery, farm materials, fertilizers and labour will be adequate;

(3) That work on land development schemes, including irrigation projects, will be intensified;

(4) That seasonal conditions are reasonably satisfactory over the next five years;

(5) That the relative prices of individual rural commodities will be such that there will be no undue incentive to the production of any one commodity at the expense of another, such as has occurred in the case of wool in recent years;

(6) That the price for each individual commodity is regarded as attractive. . . .

TABLE A

LIVESTOCK PRODUCTION AIMS—1957-8

Commodity	Unit	Production		
		Av. 1947–8 to 1950–1	1950–1	Aims 1957–8
Butter	'000 tons	166	160	170
Cheese	,,	44	45	40
Processed milk	,,	100	104	190
Total milk (all purposes)	m. gall.	1,206	1,200	1,350
Beef and veal	'000 tons	600	652	672
Lamb	,,	134	113	190
Mutton	,,	179	164	213
Pigmeats	,,	90	85	100
Eggs	m. doz.	115	107	129
Wool	m. lb.	1,052	1,092	1,200

TABLE B
CROP ACREAGE AIMS—1957-8

COMMODITY	AVERAGE 1947-8 to 1950-1			1950-1			1957-8 AIM			
	Area	Production	Unit	Area	Production	Unit	Area	Yield per acre	Production	Unit
	'000 acres	Million		'000 acres	Million		'000 acres		Million	
Wheat	12,090	203·0	bush.	10,500	166·0	bush.	13,650	14 bush.	191·0	bush.
Oats	1,800	29·2	bush.	1,800	25·0	bush.	2,790	15 bush.	42·0	bush.
Barley	980	20·3	bush.	1,000	23·0	bush.	1,400	18 bush.	25·0	bush.
Maize	190	5·5	bush.	150	4·6	bush.	240	30 bush.	7·2	bush.
Grain sorghum	100	2·3	bush.	100	2·3	bush.	300	20 bush.	6·0	bush.
Linseed	20	0·24	bush.	30[a]	0·24	bush.	200	10 bush.	20·0	bush.
Rice	35	3·4	bush.	41	4·2	bush.	40	100 bush.	4·0	bush.
Cotton (raw)	6	0·466	lb.	7[a]	0·366	lb.	60	166 lb.	10·0	lb.
Tobacco	5	3·7	lb.	6	4·75	lb.	16·5	900 lb.	14·9	lb.
Sugar	382	0·854	tons	400	0·929	tons	530	3·25 tons	1·228	tons
Potatoes	132	0·450	tons	128	0·37	tons	140	3·5 tons	0·51	tons

[a] Refers to 1951–2 crop years.

13:6 AUSTRALIA SETS THE SIGHTS

The Australian Government is getting as worried about the decline in its agricultural production as its customers have been for some years past. This week Mr McEwen, the Federal Minister of Agriculture, submitted a five-year plan which could add about £A100 million[1]—or nearly a tenth—to Australia's annual income and save some £A7 million of imports, particularly of tobacco, cotton, and linseed. Products of the land still represent over four-fifths of Australia's exports, and these exports are as vital to it as they are to Britain. A policy of industrialisation should not imply a smaller volume of exports; on the contrary, most of the new industries require imported raw materials and all of them require imported capital goods which have to be paid for in part, at any rate, by the proceeds from exports. What Australia is doing now should have been done immediately after the war—build up its agricultural production to ensure an adequate volume of exports, and then industrialise.

The plan envisages increase in almost all sectors of agriculture. . . . This is undoubtedly a wise policy, but its fulfilment depends on what action the Australian Government takes to stem the flow of labour to the towns, to increase the supply of agricultural machinery and equipment, and to encourage a greater use of fertilisers.

Source: *The Economist*, 26 April 1952,
vol. 163, p. 208.

13:7 REPORT TO NATIONAL SECURITY RESOURCES BOARD ON FOOD PRODUCTION PROGRAM

Press statement by the Prime Minister (R. G. Menzies) on 9 March 1953.

The twentieth meeting of the National Security Resources Board was held in Canberra today when members of the Board heard a particularly heartening report by the Secretary of the Department of Commerce and Agriculture, Mr J. G. Crawford, on the Food Production Programme initiated by the Commonwealth Government.

Mr Crawford made three principal general observations:—

1. Firstly, he reported a growing recognition throughout Australia that there was a practical food policy expressed in production terms and there was a growing acceptance of that policy. As evidence of this acceptance, he quoted the response of farm organisations and of State Government Departments, among which there was a rising momentum of keenness and activity.

2. A good season has certainly contributed to a more optimistic outlook; but apart from this, there is a marked upward trend based on solid factors in production which promises well for the task ahead.

3. Although it would be foolish to claim that there are no difficulties ahead, it is the opinion of competent and responsible Commonwealth officers that the National Food Production drive is significantly gathering way. Except perhaps in

[1] The reference here to £100,000,000 is apparently the figure used by McEwen in two or three speeches at this time.

the case of one or two individual crops there is good reason to anticipate success in the general production aims for 1957-8 proposed last year, and adopted by the Australian Agricultural Council.

Mr Crawford gave members of the Board a full review of the situation which not merely stressed the encouraging factors in it, but dealt with the main difficulties still to be overcome.

On the credit side, he made these points:—

(a) The easing of cost inflation was bringing greater stability to farming throughout Australia.

(b) There is a greater stability in export price conditions and for the great bulk of the Australian food exports prices remain profitable. The terms of trade are improving. Export returns have remained high while import costs are showing signs of decline.

(c) Mechanization and the adoption of other improved farming methods have already given a decided fillip to production. This reflects better technical knowledge, improved supplies of machinery, materials and labour and the generally good economic outlook. The special tax concessions granted to farmers in the last Commonwealth Budget are already a stimulating factor, and there is every reason to believe that they will increase their influence on production as the knowledge of them becomes more wide-spread. The increased availability of labour is also helping, and over the last ten months more than 6,000 workers have been added to the permanent labour force as a result of a special drive. This extra labour is in addition to extra seasonal labour available normally.

(d) Higher wheat yields this year are not entirely a seasonal accident. New high-yielding areas are coming into production and better farming practices in older areas are paying dividends.

(e) Fodder conservation is more wide-spread than for many years. This reflects the general availability of new equipment, silos for grain and fodder storage on farms and increasing interest in mixed farm husbandry.

(f) There is a keener interest among State extension services, assisted by recognition of the clear national purpose in their work. The substantial Commonwealth financial contribution to State extension activities is becoming more widely known and acknowledged.

The cautionary note which Mr Crawford felt it proper to strike was in respect of the following factors:—

A. Some material and equipment shortages still remain to be overcome, especially in harvesting machinery, steel posts and galvanised iron supplies.

B. Although wool is, of course, doing very well, the industry cannot afford to ignore the threat of synthetics.

C. Fertilizer costs are rather too high for comfort.

D. While the momentum behind the food production drive is growing, many farm owners are still cautious about it. More educational work is thus necessary to overcome psychological attitudes and inertia. There is, on the other hand, evidence that more and more farmers are investing in the restoration of fences and buildings in the establishment of new pastures.

E. Large scale improvements are still needed in transport and communications in the beef producing areas of Australia. . . .

451

TARIFF POLICIES AND PROCEDURES

This section is another which, like those on Agriculture and Commodities, could easily be expanded—especially by the detailed use of the Annual Reports of the Tariff Board and the more important reports on specific applications for tariff assistance. What has been attempted in the selection of documents is to indicate the main tariff objectives of Australian governments since 1943 and rather less fully, perhaps, the main principles in use by the Tariff Board.[1] The comments now offered do not attempt to speak instead of the documents. They do little more than invite attention to the early post-war expectations about the role of the tariff; the comparative eclipse of the tariff as a question of public controversy in the fifties; its re-emergence when import restrictions ceased in 1960; the rather sudden awareness of complex problems in the tariff field calling for an enlargement of the tariff advisory machinery; and, not least, increased questioning of ill-defined principles of tariff-making concurrently with general reaffirmation of tariffs as an instrument of economic development in Australia. The documents deal with tariff policies, not with the economic theory of tariffs, although the growing interest in tariff-making principles reflects some interest in whether the tariff can always provide the answer to industry's problems in competing with imports. My views on policy are very largely reflected in the Vernon Report, which largely states conclusions reached, in the course of my administrative experience, on a number of the complex aspects of tariff making.[2]

[1] The bibliographical references are intended to make good the deficiencies in this respect. This applies not least to the Annual Reports of the Tariff Board which, for reasons of space, have not been used in the documentation as fully as they might have been.

[2] Regardless of the acceptability or otherwise of the policy conclusions reached by members of the Vernon Committee, the student of the tariff should be helped by the effort it made to classify the facts about the principal problems of the various aspects of a complex subject. Some references to particular writings will be found in the Committee's Report, but attention is particularly invited to Brigden, *et al.* (28); Corden (45) (46) and (49); Hall (90); Reitsma (143); Cameron (31); and Linge (108). The *Economic Record* of March 1966 (75) is concerned entirely with the Vernon Report. It contains several comments on the tariff sections of the Report including an article entitled 'Protection' by Corden (48). Some useful statements were submitted to the Vernon Committee by individuals and where these have not as yet been published by the persons concerned the Committee itself would not wish a ban to be placed on their use.

As noted in Section 9, tariff making in the post-war period was inevitably guided still by the principles set out in the Ottawa Agreement (9:2, 14:7).[3] This has continued throughout the period under review at least in respect of protection where imports from Britain are involved (14:8). Document 2:2 makes it clear that the Labor governments of Curtin and Chifley intended to continue reliance on the Tariff Board. There was a firm declaration of adherence to a policy of moderately but adequately protecting industries reasonably assured of success,[4] assisting diversification, and contributing to employment and the raising of living standards—a policy which received no less support from ministers of the Menzies administration in the late fifties and early sixties (14:3, 14:4). The early statements also included recognition that policy must be consistent with international obligations[5] and that, except for defence, it is not desirable to establish industries which can only exist behind a high tariff wall.[6] The latter principle and the idea (2:2) that protection is a privilege which carries with it responsibility for efficiency received very severe testing in the 'crisis' in tariff making of the early sixties. One other matter stressed by the post-war Labor government was an interest in price review activities by the Tariff Board (14:2)—a function never enthusiastically accepted by it despite this encouragement.

The fact that Tariff Board activities received little discussion (and certainly aroused little controversy) in the post-war period and up to 1960 requires only brief comment by way of explanation. Up till 1952 import restrictions applied in respect of goods from dollar areas, principally North America, and of imports from Japan. The latter, in particular, curbed competition from the most feared source. Even under these restricted conditions the inflation of 1950 and 1951, relatively greater in Australia than elsewhere, ought certainly to have caused trouble for Australian industry through increased competition from abroad. In fact, however, oversea suppliers could not supply until 1952 and then general import restrictions were imposed (Section 15). Except for a short period in 1953 and 1954, Australian industry felt little chill from foreign competition until 1960, when import

---

[3] See also A14:2 to these comments in which an historical note supplied to the Vernon Committee by the Department of Trade is reproduced as background to the documents.

[4] See comment in Section 2 on the moderation of the approach reflected in the White Paper.

[5] Documents 3:4 and 3:11 make it clear that international obligations as evolved in GATT were not such as to prevent Australia from imposing duties for protective purposes or from taking emergency action. Tariff making, however, remains bound by the no-new-preference rule and by procedures to be followed when unbinding (i.e. increasing) 'bound' duties.

[6] This is not explicitly condemned in GATT but the Preamble, to which Australia adheres, talks of 'entering into reciprocal and mutually advantageous arrangements directed to the substantial restriction of tariffs and other barriers to trade. . . .'

restrictions, both dollar and general, came to an end. Such competition intensified during the domestic recession of 1960-2. It is true that the treaty with
Japan in 1957 aroused great fears, since import restrictions were eased and
tariffs against Japan were lowered from General to MFN; but the worst fears
were never realised, not even after the general end of restrictions (Section
10).

During the period of import restrictions there were suggestions made that
these might be replaced gradually but completely by a tariff more or less
uniform in character (Section 15). The use of the tariff as an instrument of
import control for balance of payments reasons is discussed in Section 15 and
is not further explored here.

One particular aspect of import controls and tariffs may be mentioned,
however, for it reveals that even during the period of severe controls the
tariff rates applicable to various goods had their importance. In determining
whether imports of capital and other goods under administrative control
should be admitted, a relevant consideration was local availability. In deciding this point, too, comparative cost was important; if local goods were very
much dearer than imports this fact constituted one reason for allowing imports. In such judgments, however, the imported value always included the
prevailing tariff and associated landing charges. The tariff, therefore, was not
always irrelevant to the administration of import controls, being the more
relevant the less severe the needed cuts in imports.

During the period 1957-60, import curbs were steadily eased and the
likely return to the tariff as the principal and deliberate instrument of protection became more apparent to those not wilfully deaf to government assurances that import licences would be abandoned in due course. The Board
itself assumed greater initiative in reviewing future problems and its Report
for 1958-9, coinciding in appearance with the end of restrictions in 1960,
offered comments on principles applicable to tariff determination (14:8).
Before dealing with these, however, it is well to note that the period 1960-2
was more troublesome than is satisfactorily explained solely by the ending of
import restrictions.

While the end was comparatively sudden, it did climax steady and obvious
moves to a 'free market' situation in which only the tariff stood between
domestic producers and import competition. More importantly, the period
1960-2 was marked by recession after the 1959-60 boom. In these circumstances vigorous selling by large-scale oversea competitors and, doubtless,
in some cases, dumping too, were the more difficult for smaller-scale enterprises in Australia to combat (14:16, 14:17).[7] The evidence is less conclu-
sive, but in the fifties costs possibly rose more in some Australian industries
than in the oversea countries concerned. In all these circumstances, as noted

[7] The general situation is reviewed in the Vernon Report (11), vol. I, chs. 13 and 14
and paras. 14.30-14.34 in particular.

in the Vernon Report,[8] it is perhaps surprising—pleasantly surprising—that the impact of the end of import licensing was attended by as little difficulty as it was. The number of emergency cases was not really high in relation to the customs schedule and quickly reduced as costs were stabilised and rising productivity was sustained concurrently with recovery from the recession.[9] Rather more complaints about dumping occurred, some overlapping with claims for emergency action. Even so, it seems that the industrial structure survived the ordeal of exposure to competition much better than one would suspect from reading the documents reflecting the spate of policy statements and legislative action in this period.

One point needs to be stressed. A good deal of the clamour of complaints by affected parties about tariff-making 'delays' was due to a confusion between short-term difficulties and the more permanent nature of normal Tariff Board inquiries. On the credit side of governmental activity in this period is the considerable progress made by it in differentiating between short-term or emergency action on the one hand and the properly less rapid process of longer-term judgments by the Tariff Board on the other. A further differentiation not yet completely settled is between anti-dumping measures and other 'emergency' action to combat sudden threats from imports which do not always rise from dumping. In reading the documents (14:15, 14:16, 14:17) it is not always easy to keep the various distinctions in mind.[10] Another recession in Australia, especially if it were to follow a period in which Australian costs rose relative to costs in Europe, Japan, and North America, could produce more pressure on the tariff-making machinery. The inflationary factor alone produces difficulties which are aggravated if domestic demand falls—a situation further aggravated if dumping also occurs.

On the whole the Tariff Board has survived some severe tests as an independent advisory body within the machinery of government (14:4). It has been a useful instrument in Australia's international relations, for it has been widely accepted as a major safeguard against irresponsibility in tariff making. The assurance that all cases of emergency or short-term measures would be

[8] Vol. I, ch. 13, para. 22 and ch. 8, para. 213.

[9] This is shown up in the statistics kindly supplied by the Department of Trade and Industry:

Temporary Protection Cases

Referred to Deputy Chairman		Referred to Special Advisory Authority	
1960	3	1962	32 from 17 April
1961	30	1963	14
1962	7 to 16 April	1964	3
		1965	6
		1966	7

[10] These important problems are the subject of considerable attention in the Vernon Report (11), vol. I, ch. 14. Some suggestions are made for further clarifying procedures and the distinctions between short-term, emergency action, anti-dumping measures and longer-term tariff making. See especially ch. 14, paras. 92-119.

referred to the Board for review has helped in the period 1960-3, when perhaps Australia could have been thought to be acting too frequently and too hastily.

The question of Board independence is still raised from time to time, although rather less since the resignation of Sir Leslie Melville from the chairmanship,[11] Menzies's statement (14:4), and the easing in numbers of applications for emergency help.[12] Even so, it is doubtful whether C. R. Kelly, the most informed critic in Parliament on tariff matters, is yet fully satisfied (14:5, 14:6).[13]

There is little evidence in the documents of the old free trade versus protection controversy—although some speeches in Parliament continue to reflect it somewhat.[14] The reason is not merely the political entrenchment of protectionist interests but the general acceptance of the view reflected so much in the McEwen statements that tariffs, industrialisation, full employment, and immigration go together. As Cameron observes 'if there were not a tariff of this height then some comparable device would have to be used to assure full employment and balance of payments equilibrium'.[15] This general acceptance of the tariff as an instrument of economic growth does not make exporters indifferent to its impact, and these days exporters include, fortunately, an increasing number of manufacturing industries. The latter fact has brought home to some people in secondary industry, if not yet to all members of the government, the fact that indiscriminate tariff making can affect costs and through costs the competitive ability of domestic industry (primary and secondary) to export and to withstand import competition. It cannot be said that all controversy has ceased, and ministerial statements remain inadequate in their lack of sustained emphasis on the relation of tariff protection to competitive efficiency.[16] On the whole, tariff policies have served this country

[11] In selecting documents we have deliberately avoided the particular issues ventilated by the difficulties between Sir Leslie Melville and the government, despite their importance.

[12] See n. 9 above.

[13] The general position of the government on the proper relations between Board and government was stated by the Prime Minister in his Storey Lecture (14:4). See also the second Storey Lecture by J. G. Crawford (58), and the concluding comments in ch. 14 of the Vernon Report (11). The strongest continuing and public voice of scepticism is that of C. R. Kelly, M.H.R., revealed in many speeches to Parliament on tariff matters. These are briefly represented in 14:5 and 14:6. His speeches are the most vigorous and thoughtful in the House of Representatives where the general standard of debate has not lent itself to a wide selection of major documents on tariff policy.

[14] See especially speeches by C. R. Kelly which sometimes have a free trade ring, despite his real position which is that of a moderate protectionist.

[15] Cameron (31), pp. 224-6. See also Corden (44)-(46) and (48). This point of view is developed in the Vernon Report (11), vol. I, ch. 13.

[16] The problem is particularly difficult in capital intensive industries for which the Australian market is not fully adequate. In my view an approach through tariffs alone (especially high tariffs) is not a sufficient solution.

well, but not all particular decisions will stand close scrutiny. There are many highly protected infant industries which stay that way.

This lack is partly due to the difficulty of stating simply and with clear application the principles which govern tariff making. Until recently there had been the one major attempt (14:8) by the Board itself to do this. However, in its Report for 1965-6 (14:11), the Board is again approaching the task in serious and constructive fashion.[17] In 14:3 McEwen illustrated these concepts by extreme examples. In the Vernon Report the subject was taken a good deal further in the belief that the ideas of 'efficient' and 'economic' required further clarification, and this member of that Committee is more than grateful that the Board is accepting the challenge offered it. It is beyond the scope of this book to attempt yet further elaboration.

A particular matter not yet so specifically before the Board, but with which the government has begun to grapple, is the granting of preferential treatment to imports from developing countries (see Section 6). This problem and any further changes in the British preferential system may present difficulties to the Board (Section 9) which, however, would presumably have help in the form of guidance from the government's policy statements.

The Board has had one major role to play of importance in Australia's international economic relations: to serve the interests of Australian tariff negotiations in GATT, there have been, as we noted in Section 5, two general inquiries by the Board. These have been designed to test the room for tariff concessions, especially in the MFN rates, as purchase price for valuable tariff or non-tariff concessions by countries with which Australia trades. Naturally the reports are not yet public. However, when negotiations under the Kennedy Round are complete, or more especially should the United Kingdom enter the Common Market, the reports could be valuable in shaping further adjustments in the Australian tariff structure which the government of the day may think necessary or desirable to eliminate or modify preferences now given to United Kingdom exports (Section 9).

The general impression inevitably left by the documents—of uncertainty and imprecision and of political handling of understandable pressures in the sixties—is correct but incomplete. A careful study, perhaps assisted by the wider reading suggested in the footnotes, will fairly rapidly sort out the different functions of tariff making in short-term emergencies, both general (excessive imports) and for particular products or industries (emergency action); in dealing with dumping; and in the use of the tariff as a permanent weapon in the economic development armoury. Not least is the welcome recognition by the Board itself that there are complex issues which require airing.

[17] The Board devotes a whole chapter to a useful consideration of the views of the Vernon Committee. Its omission from the documentation (except for two paragraphs summarising the views of the majority of the Board and in some particulars the views of all members) is due only to lack of space.

The Annual Reports of the Tariff Board and its specific reports, especially those of industry-wide character, have begun to reflect a need for clearer recognition of problems of tariff simplification, over-capitalisation, use of economies of scale for export as well as for the growing home market, and the need to be sure that actual or potential benefits of very high protection do outweigh immediate cost impact on other industries. Nevertheless, it is fair to conclude this comment with a general observation about the relation of tariff making to trade policy in general.

Import policy as a part of trade policy has two principal objectives. The first is to secure necessary goods on the best terms possible. 'Necessary' here means goods we either do not produce in Australia or are willing to accept in competition with or in supplement to our own production. They include consumer goods as well as producer goods which are not subject to protective duties. A large part of our imports (perhaps 80 per cent) are of this kind, and the total of our requirements is expanding year by year.[18] The other 20 per cent are subject to protective duties but manage to compete effectively for a share of the market. This relates to the second objective of import policy, which is to place a tariff barrier to imports. Some 60 to 70 per cent of Australian industry relies on tariff protection.[19] Clearly a restrictive import policy is of concern to exporting countries and the Australian tariff must therefore be of interest to Australia's partners in GATT.

In terms of the 'rules' the Australian record is reasonably defensible. We prefer tariffs to non-tariff devices as a means of protection. We are not unwilling to negotiate about the rates, but for good reasons not largely of our own making have not been put to any great test in this respect (Sections 5 and 9). The action least defensible in terms of international obligations was the introduction in October 1962 of legislation to enable the Tariff Board to recommend quantitative import restrictions for protective purposes in special circumstances (14:9, A15:4). The 'particular circumstances' under which GATT would approve are very special and limited indeed.[20] Any attempt to introduce quantitative restrictions as a permanent protective measure would put finish to our continued complaint against those who use this method for protecting agricultural production (Section 7). We do take full advantage of special facilities offered us in GATT under Article XXVIII and we do not hesitate to use Article XIX to justify emergency short-term protection when 'need' arises (14:13). This readiness to use our rights does not always gain

[18] Vernon Report (11), vol. I, ch. 13, para. 24. This paragraph, through an ambiguity, overstates the position. Some imports which are not subject to protective duties do compete with Australian production. There are no readily available data giving detailed estimates of the amount of domestic production competing on 'free trade' terms. The 30 to 40 per cent of production not dependent upon protection (see n. 19) certainly includes some Australian products for which there are no competing imports.

[19] Vernon Report (11), vol. I, ch. 13, para. 26.

[20] Ibid., ch. 14, paras. 44-51.

friends and could probably be used with more hesitation. Again we have begun to recognise that our tariff structure will be subject to pressures from countries who regard our affluence as good enough reason for being less sensitive to the protective needs of very high cost industries—that is, a good enough reason for liberalising entry of exports from the less developed countries. We know, too, that we cannot negotiate better access to other affluent markets unless we are genuinely prepared so to shape our tariff structure that exporters in these countries have some real access to our markets. In this respect it is fortunate that so large a share of our imports is open to all comers, especially in supplying producer goods needed for our own relatively rapid economic growth. Nevertheless, this will not fully meet the pressures on us and it is unfortunate that many ministerial statements do give the impression that, while we expect other countries to allow us to compete within their markets, we are unwilling to make any tariff cuts likely to cause pressure on our domestic industries at all (see Section 5: Kennedy Round negotiations).

Yet, if Australian tariff policy has been operated a shade too insensitively to the interests of other countries, there is the greater danger that Australia may nevertheless be operating increasingly against its own interests. It is not only that its interests in expanding export earnings and therefore in access to oversea markets require Australia to be sensitive to similar interests on the part of other nations in the Australian market. It is rather that tariff making (including the granting of margins of preference on goods not produced at all in Australia) does carry costs which may bear directly and through wage-making processes on the costs of actual and potential export industries. This is why so much attention was given to this aspect in the Vernon Report[21] and why the problem of expanding competitive export capacity (as well as capacity to compete with imports) must more and more concern the Tariff Board. The tariff is not the sole factor in these questions, but it is an increasingly important one. If the documents on policy reveal a major lack of understanding it would seem to be in this area. The tariff has been too much regarded as more domestic than international in its implications: this is because it is properly regarded as an instrument of economic growth. We are now beginning to realise that what we do matters for our international relations. We need to recognise even more that what we do matters also because of its impact on our capacity to increase export earnings or to compete with imports without permanently adverse effect on our cost structure and therefore on our economic growth.

---

[21] Ibid., chs. 13 and 14 including especially para. 14.123.

A14:1 FUNCTIONS OF THE TARIFF BOARD

Extracts from the Tariff Board Act 1921-62.

Part IV—Inquiries and Reports by the Tariff Board.

15.—(1.) The Minister shall refer to the Board for inquiry and report the following matters:—

. . . .

(*d*) the necessity for new, increased, or reduced duties, and the deferment of existing or proposed deferred duties;

(*e*) the necessity for granting bounties for the encouragement of any primary or secondary industry in Australia;

(*f*) the effect of existing bounties or of bounties subsequently granted;

. . . .

(*h*) any question whether a manufacturer is taking undue advantage of the protection afforded him by the Tariff or by the restriction of the importation of any goods, and in particular in regard to his—

(i) charging unnecessarily high prices for his goods; or

(ii) acting in restraint of trade to the detriment of the public; or

(iii) acting in a manner which results in unnecessarily high prices being charged to the consumer for his goods.

and shall not take any action in respect of any of those matters until he has received the report of the Board.

(1A.) Where the Minister has referred to the Board for inquiry and report the matter of the necessity for new or increased duties on any goods, the Board may, in its report, recommend the restriction of the importation of those goods (either in addition to or in lieu of new or increased duties on those goods) for such period as is specified in the report.

(2.) The Minister may refer to the Board for their inquiry and report the following matters:—

(*a*) the general effect of the working of the Customs Tariff and the Excise Tariff, in relation to the primary and secondary industries of the Commonwealth;

(*b*) the fiscal and industrial effects of the Customs laws of the Commonwealth;

(*c*) the incidence between the rates of duty on raw materials and on finished or partly finished products;

(*d*) any other matter in any way affecting the encouragement of primary or secondary industries in relation to the Tariff;

(*e*) the classification of goods under all Tariff Items which provide for classification under by-laws.

. . . .

(3.) If the Board finds on inquiry, in respect of any question referred to it under paragraph (h) of sub-section (1) of this section, that a manufacturer is taking undue advantage of the protection afforded him by the Tariff or by the restriction of the importation of any goods it may recommend—

(*a*) that the protection afforded to the manufacturer be reduced or abolished; or

(*b*) that such other action as the Board thinks desirable be taken, but shall, before it makes any such recommendation, consider carefully the conditions obtaining in the industry as a whole.

. . . .

16. The Minister of State for Customs and Excise may refer to the Board for inquiry and report the following matters:—

   (*a*) where any action by that Minister under the *Customs Tariff (Dumping and Subsidies) Act 1961* may be taken only if he is satisfied as to certain facts after inquiry and report by the Board—a question as to the existence of any such facts;

   (*b*) any matter in connexion with the interpretation of any Customs Tariff or Excise Tariff, or the classification of goods in any such Tariff, which has been referred to that Minister for review;

   (*c*) whether goods not prescribed in departmental by-laws made in connexion with any Customs Tariff Item or Excise Tariff Item should be so prescribed; and

   (*d*) the question of the value for duty of goods under section one hundred and sixty of the *Customs Act 1901-1957*.

16A.—(1.) Upon the making of a report by the Board under this Act, the appropriate Minister may, if he thinks fit, take action according to law in respect of any of the matters dealt with by the Board in its report.

(2.) Where a report of the Board contains a recommendation referred to in sub-section (3) of section fifteen of this Act, the Minister shall lay a copy of the report before each House of the Parliament within fifteen sitting days of that House from the date of receipt of the report by the Minister.

17. The Board may on its own initiative inquire into and report on any of the matters referred to in sub-section (2) of section fifteen of this Act or in paragraph (*a*) or (*c*) of section sixteen of this Act.

. . . .

18.—(1.) The Board shall, within sixty days after the first day of July in each year, report to the Minister generally as to the operation of the Tariff and the development of industries, and shall in such report set out the recommendations made by the Board during the preceding twelve months, other than any recommendations whose inclusion the Minister and the Board agree is not in the public interest.

(2.) The Minister shall lay a copy of the report before each House of the Parliament within fifteen sitting days of that House from the date of receipt of the report by the Minister.

(3.) The copy of the report shall be accompanied by a statement by the Minister setting out what action (if any) has been taken in respect of each recommendation of the Board.

Part V—Inquiries and Reports by the Special Advisory Authorities.

18A. Where it appears to the Minister that urgent action may be necessary to protect an Australian industry, in relation to the importation of any goods, pending receipt and consideration of a report of the Board in relation to those goods, he may request a special advisory authority specified by him to undertake an inquiry, either in relation to the importation of those goods generally or in relation to the importation of those goods from a particular country or countries, and to report to the Minister—

(*a*) whether it is necessary that urgent action be taken to protect that Australian industry in relation to the importation of those goods; and

(*b*) if such urgent action is necessary—whether, having regard to the public interest, the protection can appropriately be provided by means of a temporary duty or, if it cannot be so provided, whether it can appropriately be provided—

    (i) by means of the temporary restriction of the importation of those goods; or

    (ii) by means of a combination of both a temporary duty and the temporary restriction of the importation of those goods.

18B.—(1.) Upon receipt of a request under the last preceding section, the authority shall forthwith undertake the inquiry.

(2.) An authority undertaking an inquiry under this section in relation to any goods shall conduct the inquiry in such manner as he thinks fit.

Note: Sections deleted from the Act by amendment are shown by a line of dots.

A14:2 TARIFF: HISTORICAL NOTE

PRE-WAR DEVELOPMENTS

L.135   By the time of Federation, the Australian colonies had been fiscally independent long enough to have developed their own tariff policies. The Australian Colonies Government Act had in 1850 conferred on each the right to levy customs duties as they wished so long as the same rates applied to all sources. From 1873, they were permitted to impose lower tariffs among themselves than on other countries, but the United Kingdom did not agree until 1897 to denounce certain treaties with foreign countries and open the way to the adoption of preferential tariffs throughout the British Empire.

L.136   Because of the differing opinions between the Australian Colonies on tariff policy, tariff questions were amongst the most difficult to settle when Federation was being negotiated. The policy had been strongly free trade in New South Wales and strongly protectionist in Victoria, where a protective tariff was adopted as early as 1866.

L.137   After Federation, the Commonwealth Government was strongly influenced by revenue considerations in creating the first Commonwealth Tariff, because the chief source of funds available to the States was the 75 per cent of customs and excise duties, which the Constitution required the Commonwealth to pay to them. The attitude towards protection was one of moderation and, although it was accepted that worthwhile existing industry must be safeguarded, the Commonwealth was not eager to widen the field of protection.

L.138   The first important extension was the Lyne Tariff of 1908, which was strongly protective and, in particular, raised duties on woollen goods, iron and steel and agricultural implements. Preference for United Kingdom goods was introduced at the same time and the practice of support by bounty was initiated. Revenue tariffs, in particular, were increased during the 1914-18 war, but the Tariff structure was not fully revised until 1921, in the form of the Greene Tariff.

L.139   Prior to the introduction of this Tariff, the Interstate Commission had drawn attention to the disadvantages of Australian manufacturing industry in respect of cost of labour and scale of production. Although impressed with the industrial expansion of the period from 1908 to 1913, the Commission had pointed to the need for greater efficiency, stressing that many manufacturing industries paid below-average wages. It had suggested that the greatest tariff assistance be given to industries employing skilled labour. The danger of creating monopolies by the operation of tariffs had been stressed, and the Commission had considered bounties preferable to duties for the protection of raw materials.

L.140   The existing Tariff had become inadequate because of development during the 1914-18 war. The aim of the revised Tariff was 'to protect industries born during the war, to encourage others that are desirable, and to diversify and extend existing industries'. Industries such as chemicals, iron and steel and metal working were regarded as of key importance and were given increased protection.

L.141   Deferred duties were introduced at the same time, a third column in the form of an intermediate rate was added to the tariff structure and preference margins were increased. Concurrently, an Industries Preservation Act was passed to offset the various forms of dumping.[1] Another important development of this period was the establishment of the Tariff Board. As originally constituted, it consisted of three members, of whom at least the Chairman was required to hold 'administrative office' in the Department of Trade and Customs. The Board was to furnish annual reports, which were required to be tabled in Parliament. The Tariff Board Act set out the matters which the Minister was obliged to refer to the Board for enquiry and report, and also provided that the Board might, of its own initiative, enquire and report on matters which the Minister was not obliged to refer to it.

L.142   The first Pratten Tariff, adopted in 1926, increased the protection for the main branches of the textile and engineering industries to enable them to face increased competition from countries where costs had fallen. Duty increases were mainly as recommended by the Tariff Board. The second Pratten Tariff, introduced in 1928, provided further increases in duties.

L.143   The Scullin Government introduced a number of emergency duties between 1929 and 1931, which very substantially increased protection. These special levies were gradually removed or reduced after the depression eased. The need for protection was reduced by the currency revaluation in November, 1931, though this was, for a time, ignored by the Tariff Board as probably temporary. Part of the excessive protection resulting from the depreciation of the currency was offset in 1933 by the Exchange Adjustment Act, which broadly adjusted rates downwards in the British Preferential Tariff, but not in the General Tariff.

L.144   At the Ottawa Conference of 1932, Australia accepted obligations to grant to the United Kingdom preferences in accordance with agreed formulae, and a completely new Tariff was introduced, with increases in the General Tariff on more than 400 items and provision for the agreed preference margins to British goods. Tariff changes between 1933 and 1939 were generally downwards, and by 1939 the level of tariffs was probably not much greater than the 1929 level, but much higher than in 1920.

[1] Numerous references were made after the removal in August 1922 of restrictions on trading with Germany, but as European conditions stabilised, less use was made of this Act. However, the Tariff Board considered that it played an essential role in safeguarding, in particular, the iron and steel industry.

L.145   Additional duties were imposed, mainly for revenue purposes, during the 1939-45 war, but imports were controlled more by import licensing than by tariff measures.

POST-WAR DEVELOPMENTS

L.146   Tariff-making since 1945 falls into three periods:—The period of post-war shortages culminating in the sharp cost increases from 1950 to 1952; a long period of import restrictions when tariffs were raised gradually and when, because of the import restrictions, the upward pressure on tariff levels was much less than it would otherwise have been; and the period since import restrictions were almost completely removed in February, 1960, during which considerable pressure has been put on tariff machinery. This final period saw the first introduction of temporary tariff procedures and the appointment of a Special Advisory Authority.

L.147   The new machinery arose from the need to provide effective protection at short notice. Legislation in 1960 empowered the Minister to make a reference to the Deputy Chairman of the Tariff Board for a recommendation within 30 days whether temporary duties were justified, and if so, at what level, pending consideration of the normal reference by the Tariff Board. The temporary duties automatically lapsed three months after the Minister had received the final report of the Board. It was intended that temporary duties should be applied only where an industry could show that it would suffer serious damage from imports before the Government could receive and act on a normal report from the Board.

L.148   In February, 1962, provision was made for the reference of requests for urgent temporary protection to a one-man Special Advisory Authority. The Special Authority was empowered to recommend quantitative restrictions for a commodity if he thought that the objective of emergency protection could not be attained by means of duties.

L.149   Further information on the procedures for temporary protection and on other developments in Australia's tariff policy and tariff-making machinery in post-war years is given elsewhere in this report. Important among these have been legislation to deal more effectively with dumping and the effect on Australia's tariff policy of international agreements, in particular, the G.A.T.T. and the United Kingdom-Australia Trade Agreement.

Source: Vernon Report (11), vol. II,
pp. 1058-9.

A. GOVERNMENT POLICY

14:1 TARIFF POLICY AND PROCEDURES

Address by the Minister for Post-War Reconstruction (J. J. Dedman) to a conference of representatives of the Government and of secondary industry, 5 February 1945.

The Government contemplates no break in the traditional Australian policy of protecting industries which are reasonably assured of sound opportunities of success, which have due regard to present and future defence requirements, which assist the diversification of our economy, and which contribute to employment and the raising of living standards in the community, and result in the development of resources. . . .

The granting of tariff protection in the past has been based upon the advice of the Tariff Board. That policy will be continued, but in the post-war period the Government proposes to ask the board to make more regular investigations, reporting on the efficiency of industries receiving protection or other assistance from the Government. Elastic use of the tariff is necessary to nurture infant industries. However, with the exception of industries which are necessary for present and future defence needs it is not desirable to endeavour to establish industries which, even under efficient operation, can only exist permanently behind an excessively high tariff wall. This tends to impose an unreasonably high burden of cost on the community generally, and so limits plans directed to raising standards of living. Further, it is not conducive to the greatest possible development of international trade and it is fundamentally important for Australia that the volume of international trade be maintained at the highest possible level. In the application of Australia's traditional principles of tariff protection to the period ahead, when world trade begins to flow again, our policy must be consistent with international obligations. Some of these obligations are specific; others are generally directed to promotion of employment and consumption and the betterment of world economic relations by agreed action in both international and domestic fields, including the field of commercial policy. Some exploratory discussions of possible lines of agreed action have taken place and may be expected to continue. . . .

Source: *Digest of Decisions and Announcements*, no. 95, pp. 22-5.

14:2 TARIFF BOARD RESPONSIBILITIES

Statement by the Prime Minister (J. B. Chifley) on 11 September 1945.

The Government's White Paper on Full Employment in Australia contains a number of references to cost of production. While investigations towards discovering factors responsible for high cost levels are desirable it would serve no useful purpose now to devote time or attention to factors responsible for cost levels in pre-war years. Cabinet decided that—

The Tariff Board be asked to take note of the contents of the White Paper on Full Employment and the passages expressing the Government's interest in increasing the efficiency of industry.

The Tariff Board be informed that the Government desires the Board, in future inquiries, and in protected industries, to investigate costs of production and selling prices, with a view to ascertaining, as far as practicable, what elements in final cost or selling prices are responsible, or mainly responsible, for high costs or prices in Australia as compared with costs or prices in other countries producing the same article under comparable wage rates.

The Tariff Board be asked to report as to the staffing arrangements necessary to place its organization in a position to carry out routine investigations on this basis, and also make regular reports on the efficiency of protected industries in accordance with paragraph 72 of the paper on Full Employment in Australia.

The Tariff Board be requested to consider the practicability of including in its annual reports, special chapters bearing on the efficiency of protected industries, and high cost of production with special reference to the particular cost elements responsible for the high Australian costs.

The Tariff Board, in conducting these inquiries, will be asked to collaborate with the Secondary Industries Commission.

Source: *Digest of Decisions and*
Announcements, no. 107, pp. 42-3.

14:3 PROTECTION FOR EFFICIENT AND ECONOMIC INDUSTRY

Speech by the Minister for Trade (J. McEwen) in Committee of Ways and Means, House of Representatives, 12 August 1958.

The Government's policy is to provide adequate protection for efficient and economic local industry. This has been the policy of successive Australian Governments for over a generation. 'Efficient' and 'economic' are admittedly somewhat elusive terms. They are not absolute. They do not lend themselves to precise measurement. But this does not mean that this is not a useful and workable concept in the context of Tariff protection for Australian industry.

Despite the lack of precision in the concept it is possible to form a judgment on whether particular industries are efficient and economic—although with greater ease and certainty in some cases than in others. To illustrate. There is, in my opinion, no doubt about the efficiency and the economics of steel production in Australia. There would, I suggest, be considerable doubt about the economics of producing large commercial jet airliners in Australia at this stage of our development.

Whether production is 'economic' or not is particularly important where the industry concerned is one in a chain of industries. I will refer to this point again later in this speech.

The application of the concept of efficient and economic production calls for careful analysis and sound judgment. This is one reason why successive Governments have leant heavily on advice from the Tariff Board when formulating decisions on Tariff matters. . . .

There can, of course, be no absolute reliance on tariffs for the protection of Australian industry. It follows from what I said earlier that tariffs will not be used to protect inefficiency. Industry must therefore set its own house in order before seeking tariff assistance. It can do this by taking all means within its power to reduce costs. But tariffs recognize that individual industries have little or no control over certain elements in their costs. They can, for instance, do little about the higher costs which flow from the relatively limited Australian market for many products. Their wage costs are largely imposed on them by awards and the like.

There is also another side to this question of costs. Because the products of one industry are often the raw materials or components of another, anything

466

which affects the cost of one product has its repercussions throughout the economy. This is particularly so with any increase in costs of basic materials. Such increases have a cumulative effect and tend to be built up as they enter into later stages of production. This is just as relevant to tariffs as it is to other factors which affect costs and prices. . . .

To recapitulate. The Government is for an expanding economy firmly based on diversified production and exports. This will provide increased employment opportunities for our growing population.

The Government will give Tariff protection to efficient and economic production. It will, as in the past, be largely guided by the advice of the Tariff Board on these questions.

With co-operation between Government and industry, further progress is not only possible but assured. . . .

Source: *C.P.D.* (*H. of R.*), vol. 20, pp. 237-9.

14:4 AUSTRALIA'S ECONOMIC OBJECTIVES AND THE TARIFF BOARD

Statement by the Prime Minister (R. G. Menzies) on 8 December 1962.

There has been a fairly common tendency to assume that a Commonwealth Government and Parliament is handicapped by being compelled to sail in treacherous and narrow waters between the Scylla of the Arbitration Commission and the Charybdis of the Tariff Board; the assumption being that each commands and controls the channel. That this is true in the case of the Arbitration Commission with, for all practical purposes, an entrenched constitutional position, cannot hopefully or practically be denied! I have already said something about it. But the Tariff Board is in quite a different position. It is a purely statutory body, created by the discretion of Parliament, and, indeed, subject to the control of Parliament. In this sense, it is an instrument of policy, and in no sense its master.

It has, however, been recognised by successive governments that, though what I have said is constitutionally true, it is important that, for international as well as domestic purposes, the Tariff Board should possess a high measure of independence, that the integrity of its advice should be preserved, and that it should not be subject to any form of day-to-day political instruction. I accept and maintain these propositions. Yet the Tariff Board, our principal adviser on import duties, cannot sensibly be expected to operate in a completely detached intellectual vacuum. It must have in its mind some standards or policies by which to test the cases presented to it.

For a long time it has acted on the principle that it should recommend Tariff protection only to 'economic and efficient industries'. But that principle was, and is, itself an expression of government policy. Of late, indications have been given on behalf of my own Government that the principle needs extension, and that the Tariff Board should have in its mind the national economic policy, meaning by that the national economic objectives, as a whole. There have been sharp criticisms of this by representative, thoughtful, and responsible people. As I

467

think that they have misunderstood these proposals, I will endeavour, without, I hope, wearying you, to make the point clear.

Nobody suggests that an independent but advisory body like the Tariff Board should, in its recommendations, seek to follow every government or legislative application of economic policy in its determination of the case before it. This would be quite impracticable and could lead to strange, anomalous and fluctuating results.

But there are certain features of national economic policy, which I do not regard as the subject of party controversy, which cannot be ignored by any statutory body if the nation is to achieve a dynamic progress, growing in resources, population, employment, industry, and international solvency. For a Tariff Board to ignore their existence would be to detach its work from the great stream of Australian development. This, I am sure, it would not wish to do.

Let me explain what I mean by national economic policy. It includes the encouragement of population growth by substantial immigration. It recognises that such encouragement is an important factor in the future planning of industry and commerce. It calls for a strong development of old and new natural resources, so that a growing population will be fully and usefully employed, and the resources themselves put to full use. It perceives that the achievement of these things will require, in a relatively new country like ours, the fullest possible generation and investment of capital at home, and the attraction of productive capital from abroad. And on top of, and conditioning all these things, it requires that there should be a constant and steady eye upon the costs of production, so that our great export primary industries will not be discouraged by ever-rising costs from attempting that still further enlargement of production on which our export future must continue to depend, and so that our secondary industries may increasingly be able to export to the world's markets in competition with other industrial powers.

These are the great national objectives of economic policy. I am sure that they are accepted by most Australians, and that they have a settled place in our national life.

Who can seriously suggest that they should be ignored by the Tariff Board, or by any other group of people serving the national interest? I would be surprised to learn that the members of the Board wished to ignore these matters, or resented the fact that a clear statement of them was made by any Australian Government.

How these accepted objectives are to be achieved is another and more controversial matter. Particular application of policy may, and does, change from time to time. One government may go out on some particular measure, and another government may come in with an entirely different notion. It would, as I have said, be hopeless to require a Tariff Board to behave like a weather-cock under such circumstances. Nobody suggests that it should do so. What is suggested is that it should do its important work independently, not controlled by sectional pressures, with complete integrity of mind, but with the settled economic objectives of the nation constantly in mind.

Source: *Problems of Management in a Federation*, inaugural John Storey Memorial Lecture, 1962. (Australian Institute of Management.) Reprinted by permission.

14:5 CHANGES IN GOVERNMENT TARIFF POLICIES CRITICISED

Speech by C. R. Kelly in the House of Representatives on 11 March 1964.

When I came into politics in 1958, this Government's policy was based on the protection of economic and efficient industries, on the advice of an independent Tariff Board. We have since seen the impact of emergency protection procedures and the two policy statements in 1962, one made by the present Minister for Trade and Industry (Mr McEwen), who was then Minister for Trade, and the other made by the Prime Minister (Sir Robert Menzies). Even those two statements have not cleared my mind, and I doubt whether the Government really understands what its policy is.

Let us look at these two statements of policy in more detail. The present Minister for Trade and Industry, in his second-reading speech on the Tariff Board Bill (No. 2) 1962, made some observations that I have quoted before and shall quote again. He said—

> The Tariff Board, for its part, has a vital and important role in advising the Government in this direction. Obviously the board in effectively carrying out its advisory duties must keep within its sights the objectives of Government policy—the objectives I have outlined in my remarks to-day and as given in Government statements from time to time.

In the debate that followed on that occasion, Sir, I expressed alarm at the fact that the old measuring stick of economy and efficiency was to be discarded, and at the fact that the board was to be expected to keep within its sights statements of policy made from time to time. I said that this must mean that the board was expected, and must be prepared, to depart from its previous policy of protecting only economic and efficient industries. If the Minister's statement did not mean that, I do not know what it did mean. On 1st [8th] December, 1962, the Prime Minister, in his John Storey Memorial Lecture, dealt with the subject again. He discussed what he called national economic policy, the need for continuing migration, the development of old and new resources, the encouragement of capital investment from sources inside and outside Australia and the need for stability of costs so that export industries could compete on the world's markets. Then he went on to say that surely the Tariff Board should properly keep these matters in mind when making its recommendations.

Apart from these two important policy statements, whatever they may mean, there has also been the impact of the emergency protective procedures. I admit that some such procedures were needed. What I find objectionable in the procedures adopted . . . is the way in which they are frequently used to override the recommendations made in Tariff Board reports. . . .

There are many examples of this. I have given the House many of them before. Probably the worst of the lot is the way in which recommendations concerning the man-made fibre piece goods industry have been shuttled backwards and forwards. All this shuttling necessarily weakens the morale and the status of the Tariff Board when it sees that its recommendations, though only recently made, are altered by the Special Advisory Authority, even though the imports position has not changed.

So it is clear that there has been a change in the old policy that protection should be granted only to economic and efficient industries on the advice of a truly independent Tariff Board. The board's independence is now imperilled by the impact of the emergency protection procedures and by the knowledge that it is expected to keep within its sights policy statements made from time to time . . . What is the new policy? That is far from clear. I challenge the Government to give us a clear statement of its policy. . . . What kind of protection are we to have now? Should we have protection for industries that create employment or protection for industries that lead to development? Is the tariff to be used to promote decentralization, to encourage profitable investment or to strengthen industries that offer the hope of future exports? If the old measuring stick of economy and efficiency is to be abandoned, the purpose must be one of these that I have just mentioned. . . .

We are always told that we must generously protect secondary industry because only secondary industry can employ our people. But this is not so. . . .

We recognize that the Government has the right to expect that any agency—the Tariff Board included—should not hinder a national policy such as full employment. But it is essential that the Tariff Board have full freedom in deciding how this objective is to be achieved. It is dangerously easy to point to increased employment in any particular industry, following high and, perhaps, prohibitive protection, but what about employment provided by dependent industry—the industries that use the goods produced by the heavily protected industries, and ultimately by the export industries that have to sell on the world market? If the position of these industries is jeopardized the employment position may very well become worse.

We all want full employment, but what we must guard against is the attempt to secure this by allowing costs to rise in any particular industry to the general detriment of our whole economy. This is where the independence and the competence of the Tariff Board are so essential. . . .

Is the new policy, whatever it is, to be aimed at inducing growth and development? . . .

What a hopeless philosophy it would be to discard the measuring stick of economy and efficiency in order to promote growth. What kind of growth do we want? Do we want uneconomic, inefficient, or hot-house growth? Is this the kind of development that we have in mind? Let us be clear on this: This is not the kind of development that has made this country what it is. This is the kind of growth that will surely inhibit sound development in the future. To load costs onto the back of the efficient sector of the economy—primary or secondary—in order to protect inefficient primary or secondary industry is just plain economic foolishness. . . .

Source: *C.P.D. (H. of R.)*, vol. 41, pp. 454-7.

14:6 VERNON COMMITTEE'S CRITICISM OF GOVERNMENT TARIFF POLICIES SUPPORTED

Speech by C. R. Kelly in the House of Representatives on 27 April 1966.

I have stated in previous debates that I consider that the Vernon Committee's report bears out the general line of criticism that I have adopted on this subject. . . . The first of my direct quotations from the report is as follows—

A strong, although in our view unwarranted, presumption is gaining ground, that an industry, once in existence, should be protected and that, once protected, should continue to receive the protection it needs, even if its cost disabilities rise to high levels.

... I have said this kind of thing frequently in this House and it has not seemed to carry much weight. I believe that, coming from the Vernon Committee, it will carry much more weight. The next passage from the report that I wish to quote is this—

So much is said about the role of manufacturing in sustaining population increase that, as it was put to us, we may become mesmerised by the thought of bigger and better factories as the only source of future employment. Manufacturing is not the only source of employment; indeed, it employs at present only 27½ per cent. of the work force, and it may become less important relative to tertiary industries . . . Moreover, protected industry accounts directly for only about 15 per cent. of the work force and we should not, therefore, exaggerate its significance. . . .

Here is another quotation on the subject of employment—

We would also stress that, if policies of protection are such as to divert skilled labour away from industries with sound opportunities for expansion to less economic uses, they will damage national productivity. The tariff must not be regarded as an instrument for creating employment of this kind.

... the Vernon Committee seems to think the same as I do. The Committee, after discussing the question of general cost disability, stated—

If the concept of a general cost disability experienced by import competing industries, as we have discussed it in Chapters 13 and 14, is accepted, the aim of tariff making should be to encourage those industries which either have a proven disability less than, or not greatly in excess of, this general disability or which have prospects of reducing their disability to this level. Others should not be encouraged. . . .

Source: C.P.D. (H. of R.), vol. 51, pp. 1209-10.

B. PRINCIPLES

14:7 OTTAWA AGREEMENT AND TARIFF MAKING

Post-War Reconstruction

... One of the most important problems of post-war reconstruction of world trade will be that of control of the trade between countries. The Board, therefore, considers that some comments on the working of the United Kingdom and Australia Trade Agreement, generally called the 'Ottawa Agreement', may give suggestions of value in implementing the general principles set out in the Atlantic Charter and in Article VII of the Mutual Aid Agreement between the United States and Great Britain.

The Ottawa Agreement

The Tariff Board has, since 1932, been engaged mainly in connexion with the implementing of the 'Ottawa Agreement' made in that year. This Agreement represented an attempt to arrive at a code of rules and a procedure to regulate trade between the United Kingdom and Australia in the mutual interests of both.

In various Articles of the Agreement, the Governments of the United Kingdom and of Australia respectively accept certain obligations designed to achieve, by Tariff action and the regulation of imports, preferential treatment to goods supplied by each to the other. Articles 9 to 13, however, lay down certain principles and methods of procedure to be observed by the Commonwealth Government in determining the measure of Tariff protection to be afforded to Australian industry. In the 'Memorandum of Conclusions of Trade Discussions between Representatives of His Majesty's Government in the United Kingdom and the Commonwealth of Australia', dated London, 20th July, 1938, it is recorded that provisions of those Articles 'have, in practice, worked fairly satisfactorily, though they have been criticised from quite opposite points of view in the United Kingdom and Australia' (9:1).

In practice, Articles 9 to 13 have operated as follows:—

Article 9.—His Majesty's Government in the Commonwealth of Australia undertake that protection by tariffs shall be afforded only to those industries which are reasonably assured of sound opportunities for success.

The Australian Tariff Board had, before 1932, recommended to the Australian Government adoption of the principles embodied in Article 9. It was held that no benefit to the nation would ensue from attempts to establish in Australia industries in which the obstacles to success were too great. It was contended that, though the establishment of new industries brings undeniable benefits to Australia, a price must be paid if the products are more expensive than those from overseas; a new industry can only result in net benefit if the total benefits are greater than the resulting excess costs.

The operation of this Article presented no serious difficulty.

Article 10.—His Majesty's Government in the Commonwealth of Australia undertake that during the currency of this Agreement the tariff shall be based on the principle that protective duties shall not exceed such a level as will give the United Kingdom producers full opportunity of reasonable competition on the basis of the relative cost of economical and efficient production, provided that in the application of such principle special consideration may be given to the case of industries not fully established.

The principal ground for complaint from United Kingdom interests arose from the interpretation of Article 10 by the Australian Government. In the Annual Report for the year ended 30th June, 1933, the Tariff Board said that it appeared to have been assumed, both in Australia and the United Kingdom, that 'full opportunity of reasonable competition' entailed finely adjusting duties so as to place efficient manufacturers of the United Kingdom and of Australia on exactly the same price level in the Australian market. The Board characterised such a procedure as 'farcical' and set out its definition of a 'reasonable' duty as one high enough to raise the landed cost of an overseas product to the level which will—

(a) compensate the Australian manufacturer for the higher cost (if any) of Australian labour;

(b) offset the higher costs (if any) of raw materials and overhead charges;

(c) provide a marginal advantage in favour of the Australian manufacturer.

The Board expressed strong opposition to the imposition of prohibitive duties, and proposed that the margin (c) should be wide enough to secure to an efficient

Australian manufacturer that part of the market which it can economically supply, but narrow enough to preclude inefficiency, uneconomic extension and undue profit taking.

This interpretation of Article 10 was never accepted by United Kingdom interests though no alternative reading was proposed other than that which the Board considered unworkable. . . .

Article 11.—His Majesty's Government in the Commonwealth of Australia undertake that a review shall be made as soon as practicable by the Australian Tariff Board of existing protective duties in accordance with the principles laid down in Article 10 hereof, and that after the receipt of the report and recommendation of the Tariff Board the Commonwealth Parliament shall be invited to vary, wherever necessary, the Tariff on goods of United Kingdom origin in such manner as to give effect to such principles.

In the years following the Ottawa Agreement, practically all the Tariff Items covering goods that were produced competitively by United Kingdom and Australian manufacturers were reviewed by the Tariff Board. Many of these reviews arose from requests by the British Government. The Tariff Board followed the principles set out above and also that of recommending the removal of protective duties from goods not being economically manufactured in Australia, except some of a luxury character that it was considered should yield revenue to the Government. . . .

Article 12.—His Majesty's Government in the Commonwealth of Australia undertake that no new protective duty shall be imposed and no existing duty shall be increased on United Kingdom goods to an amount in excess of the recommendation of the Tariff Tribunal.

The wording of this Article purports to impose an unqualified obligation on the Australian Parliament to accept the recommendations of an Authority created by itself but was never accepted in that sense by the Commonwealth legislature. In that respect the Article in question differs from those Articles in which the Governments of the United Kingdom and of Australia undertake to 'invite' their respective Parliaments to take certain action. Actually, in only two instances did Parliament take action to vary the rates of duty recommended by the Tariff Board under the British Preferential Tariff. These cases, however, were of some importance. It is noteworthy that no suggestion is recorded in the Memorandum of Conclusions of the 1938 Conference that the Australian Government should follow the literal meaning of Article 12. Australian Ministers undertook only 'to make every effort to ensure that Tariff Board recommendations under Article 11 are made effective.'

Article 13.—His Majesty's Government in the Commonwealth of Australia undertake that United Kingdom producers shall be entitled to full rights of audience before the Tariff Board when it has under consideration matters arising under Articles 11 and 12 hereof.

The right of United Kingdom producers to audience before the Tariff Board proved one of the most useful provisions of the Agreement. British manufacturers availed themselves of this right in every case in which they were interested and their evidence supplied invaluable information to the Tariff Board. . . . The results of Articles 9 to 13, however, have great significance in that connexion;[1] one of the most important phases of the wide problem of international trade relations

---

[1] This refers to the objectives of the Atlantic Charter.

must be that of the industrial development of younger countries. Such development cannot be prevented; some means of control must be sought and the experience of seven years in applying measures of control must be of great value.

That experience suggests that trade agreements which embody measures of regulation of industrial development must—

(a) recognize that sovereign democratic governments must have full autonomy in the control of internal activities, including industrial development;
(b) set out a basis for framing protective measures;
(c) provide, in particular, that any party have the right to request any other party to review existing protective measures and also the right and opportunity to express itself in regard to proposed alterations[2]. . . .

Source: Tariff Board. Annual Report for
the Year Ended 30th June, 1942.

[2] The balance of the document is of considerable interest. It reflects an expectation that in the post-war world tariff making would be under detailed international scrutiny and makes a number of suggestions. Some of these—such as the right of a country to request another to review its protective measures—found their way into early drafts of the Charter for ITO. This particular one (XVII of the Havana Charter) lapsed when the ITO failed to come into being (Section 3).

14:8 PRINCIPLES OF TARIFF MAKING

In its Annual Report for 1933,[1] the Tariff Board set out certain general principles under which it had operated since its establishment and which, so far as they affect trade relationships with the United Kingdom, had found expression in the Ottawa Agreement in 1932 and have been substantially re-affirmed in the United Kingdom-Australia Trade Agreement of 1957.

Briefly, the provisions of the latter Agreement state that—

(1) protection by tariffs shall be afforded only to those industries which are reasonably assured of sound opportunities for success;

(2) the tariff shall be based on the principle that protective duties shall not exceed such a level as will give United Kingdom producers full opportunity of reasonable competition on the basis of the relative costs of economic and efficient production; and

(3) special consideration may be given to industries not fully established or to industries essential for defence purposes.

In accordance with these principles the Tariff Board recommends assistance, when necessary, to industries on the basis of their being economic and efficient and showing sound prospects for success.

It is sometimes suggested that the Board should elaborate on these principles by listing in full the conditions that must be present before an industry will be classed as 'economic and efficient'. It is doubtful, however, whether such an approach would be practicable even if there were clearer indications of government policy in many fields. The actual criteria vary in importance and usefulness in each case. The conditions that are relevant in one instance may be largely inappropriate in another. The Board has found that the only reasonable approach

[1] An even earlier statement of principles of considerable influence in Australian tariff making appears in 'The Australian Tariff: An Economic Enquiry' (28), para. 11.

is to make on each occasion a separate judgment based on all the relevant criteria. However, it is essential that the various interests giving evidence before the Board should attempt to demonstrate, by factual argument, whether or not the industry concerned is 'economic and efficient'.

In examining what constitutes economic operation, the Board considers broad questions such as the effects of protection on prices to consumers either directly, or indirectly through costs to user industries, whether the industry provides an outlet for economical exploitation of local resources, whether establishment of the industry concerned will assist in the development of other industries, the prospects for further growth of the local industry, the possibility of competing in export markets and so on. In addition, the Board considers particular aspects such as the extent of demand for the industry's product, the proportion of the market that Australian manufacturers can supply and the acceptability of the local product to consumers—in quality, range, variety and availability.

No list of factors relating to the question of whether or not an industry should be regarded as economic could be exhaustive, but enough has been said to indicate that the Board expects an industry seeking protection to demonstrate that it is worthwhile and to indicate why it considers that the gains to the Australian economy from protecting the industry will offset the costs. Such arguments should be an important part of the case presented by industries requesting tariff assistance. Frequently, however, only limited evidence of a general character is given on these aspects and industries thereby fail to do justice to their claim that the industry and its production are economic. Similarly, witnesses opposed to protection sometimes do not make their opposition as effective as they could were they to direct their attention to the question of whether or not production is economic. The Board does not, as a result, receive as much assistance as it might in making its judgment on this question.

The evidence required to establish the efficiency of a local industry is of equal importance. Often a good deal of evidence is presented which is intended to show only the technical efficiency of an industry's manufacturing processes. It is not enough, however, merely to seek to establish technical efficiency in manufacture. Efficiency, as the Board interprets the word, involves not only efficiency in the productive processes relating to the use of materials and labour, machinery and plant, but also efficiency in such things as management, selling, etc. It involves not only a study of efficiency in the context of existing conditions but also under the circumstances that would exist in the future were the industry to be accorded protection. The Board considers that any approach to the measurement of efficiency must be realistic. It does not attempt to impose an absolute measure. Rather, where it is appropriate, the Board looks at levels of efficiency as established by each member of the local industry relative to other members, relative to overseas producers and relative to other industries in Australia.

The members of the Board endeavour to acquaint themselves with the problems of industry. They are informed of the many difficulties that arise, they visit a great many factories in the course of the year, and they are always willing to have witnesses demonstrate the problems of the industry and their bearing on requests for tariff or other assistance.

In its comparisons of efficiency, the Board is interested not only in differences as measured by costs of production, but also in other measures such as output per man-hour, and the explanations that enable it to evaluate these measures. From the financial data various management ratios can be computed and compared, e.g. earnings rates and turnover to funds employed. None of these

475

comparisons is infallible but, considered together, they are of assistance to the Board.

Although fully aware of the difficulties involved in deciding whether or not an industry is efficient, nevertheless, as part of its responsibility, the Board is bound to make the necessary judgment. Witnesses could greatly assist by providing as much data as possible that will aid the Board in making its judgment.

The United Kingdom-Australia Trade Agreement of 1957 also makes special mention of infant industries and of industries that may be important for defence. The Board realizes that some industries require higher tariffs or other forms of assistance initially in order to meet competition from larger overseas manufacturers. This principle is firmly established in tariff policy.

Source: *Tariff Board. Annual Report for the Year Ended 30th June, 1959.*

14:9 QUANTITATIVE RESTRICTION OF IMPORTS FOR PROTECTIVE PURPOSES

Second Reading speech by the Minister for Trade (J. McEwen) on the Bill to amend the Tariff Board Act 1921-1962 in the House of Representatives on 17 October 1962.

Special Advisory Authorities are now provided to advise the Minister for Trade on the need for temporary protection of Australian industries—primary and secondary—against serious damage from import competition, pending review by the Tariff Board of normal protective requirements. The Special Advisory Authorities are authorised, among other things, to recommend temporary safeguarding action by means of quantitative restriction of imports, in cases where the Tariff alone would not be appropriate. The power of the Government to apply quantitative restrictions, as was explained at the time, was not something new; it was a power which had been held for many years under the Customs Act.

Using that means of protecting a local industry is not something remarkably new or novel. Some of the most industrialised countries find it necessary to restrict imports in certain circumstances; . . .

This Bill will extend to the Tariff Board the authority to recommend quantitative restrictions. Other provisions in the Bill will assist in reducing delays in the Board's operations, and will introduce greater flexibility in the Board's administration. . . .

Since the Advisory Authorities can recommend quantitative restrictions for temporary protection, the Board might well conclude that the removal of restrictions imposed on the recommendation of a Special Advisory Authority could result in damaging competition from imports, despite the provision of long term tariff protection. It therefore might wish to recommend that the restrictions be continued or that they be gradually removed. The Government proposes to give it the power to recommend accordingly. The Board would have the right to recommend import restrictions in the special circumstances of any particular case before it, where the Board is satisfied that protection by the Tariff alone would not be appropriate.

It is the Government's intention that protection shall be effective. It is this Government's policy that so long as an industry remains economic and efficient it has an assurance that where necessary it will receive protection. This bill is designed to give additional weight to that assurance. It should remove any uncertainty that may have developed as a result of importing practices aimed at evading or undermining tariff protection. It should help to create an atmosphere where the expansion of local industry can be undertaken with greater confidence.

At the very roots of our national objectives is steady population increase. Hand in hand with that must go solid economic growth at a rate sufficient to provide work for the growing population. I have said before, and I repeat, that we must look to manufacturing industry as a principal source of increased employment.

During the last two and a half years the tariff has stood alone as a protective medium, almost for the first time in over twenty years without the bolstering of the incidental effect of import licensing. Generally speaking it has proved to be effective, but there have been occasions when that has not been so. We have had experience of our intention of giving tariff protection being systematically countered, and not always by means which could be regarded as being entirely ethical. There are circumstances in which tariff protection can be undermined to an extent which can make it an inadequate medium for protection.

Similarly, modern industrial developments have created industries which must have an assured volume of output to maintain production efficiency and a reasonable cost level. Endeavours to avoid serious injury to such an industry by use of the tariff may not be effective where overseas competitors with tremendous advantages of scale can adopt pricing policies aimed at undermining protection. It may on occasions be necessary, where imports above a certain level would make an otherwise stable Australian industry unprofitable and even uneconomic, to use quantitative restrictions of imports to give effective protection to such an industry.

It could, of course, be claimed that in any of these circumstances a tariff could be set sufficiently high to be effective. What this would mean in many if not most cases would be a prohibitively high tariff. That would not be in keeping with our principles of tariff making, and moreover would offer difficulties where part of the demand must be met by imports. It is clear that there are occasions when the use of quantitative restrictions will avoid unnecessary cost increases.

However, I would expect that the need to use quantitative restrictions would arise on very few occasions. But it is worth noting that the right to use quantitative restrictions in particular circumstances is a right no country has foregone, even under the provisions of the General Agreement on Tariffs and Trade. Nevertheless our policy remains that the Customs Tariff is the normal and accepted instrument for protection of Australian industry. The Government intends therefore that the Tariff Board will consider protection by means of quantitative restrictions only in those cases in which the tariff alone would not be an appropriate means of protection. In short, the legislation is to authorise the Tariff Board to recommend quantitative restrictions as a last resort.

In cases where the Board recommends the use of quantitative restrictions it will be required to include in its recommendation an indication of the extent to which protection should be accorded by that means.

Of course unless precautionary measures are taken quantitative restrictions can in certain circumstances lead to cost increases and uneconomic expansion of the protected industry. The Government therefore envisages that the Tariff Board should recommend the use of such restrictions only under conditions in which the Board is satisfied that consumers would be adequately safeguarded. Moreover, the proposed amendment giving the Board this power *requires* that the Board should recommend the period for which the quantitative restrictions will operate in each case in which it recommends their use. . . .

With the Tariff Board able to recommend the use of quantitative restrictions, the protective armoury will be adequate. Adding this to the machinery for giving urgent temporary protection, it will mean that appropriate action can be taken and with whatever rapidity the circumstances call for.

The Government has now decided that the remnant of the former import licensing system which has not in recent times been operated in a restrictive way, can now be removed. As from tomorrow, therefore, the only goods remaining subject to import licensing will be those on which quantitative restrictions have been imposed by the Government for protective purposes pending the receipt of a Tariff Board Report on long term needs. These restrictions cover aluminium ingots and alloys, certain ball bearings, certain classes of timber, and penicillin and streptomycin. In addition, certain classes of second hand and disposals machinery for earthmoving or construction purposes will remain subject to import restriction.

Other amendments are designed to assist in reducing delays in the Board's operations, and to introduce greater flexibility in the Board's administration.

Source: *C.P.D. (H. of R.)*, vol. 36,
pp. 1600-2.

14:10 THE TARIFF BOARD'S METHODS: A STATEMENT OF PRINCIPLES

Statement to the Committee of Economic Enquiry by Sir Leslie Melville.

I believe that the methods worked out by the Tariff Board after 40 years of experience give results that are as good as any tests that can be suggested. The Board compares the costs of local manufactures with the prices of corresponding imported goods to determine what rate of duty is needed, and compares costs of local manufactures with overseas costs to help it make a judgment whether the industry is efficient. It then considers the rate of duty needed against the background of the industry. In examining the characteristics of the industry the Board asks:

(1) Is the industry one that shows prospects of vigorous growth and promises to be able to reduce costs with increasing output?

(2) Is it in some sense a key industry and is it an integral part of a network of firms which are industrially important to Australia?

(3) Will the establishment of the industry be an aid in the further industrialization of Australia?

(4) Does the industry use a high proportion of locally produced materials and parts?

(5) Does the industry give promise of being able to export a significant part of its output?

(6) Will the establishment of the industry be an aid to some export industry either by providing it with equipment or materials or by providing a link in the chain of local research?

(7) Will the industry be able to satisfy a large part of the Australian demand?

(8) Is the industry well-managed and efficient in a technical sense and are its marketing arrangements satisfactory?

(9) Will higher prices for the product of the industry bear heavily on the costs of some promising export industry?

If the Board can give an affirmative answer to the first eight of these questions and a negative answer to question nine, it might recommend the duty that has been shown to be necessary even if it is quite high.

The Board would also take into account a number of other circumstances of the industry in deciding whether to protect it and what rate to recommend. It follows from what I have already said that the amount of employment provided by an industry should not be an important factor in any recommendation made by the Board. Indeed industries which are capital intensive are more likely to be suitable for a country such as Australia where wage costs are high than industries which are labour intensive. Nevertheless the Board would consider the prospects of alternative employment for the workers in a factory if it were closed, particularly in the case of firms in country areas. Similarly it would consider the possibility of the plant being used in part at least for some other product.

If the industry were capable of satisfying only a small part of the Australian market but still seemed to the Board to be promising enough to merit encouragement, the Board might recommend a subsidy instead of a duty. In this way the consumer would not be compelled to pay an unnecessarily high price for the bulk of the commodity which has to be imported.

When the industry does not seem to the Board to be well managed, it might recommend a lower rate of duty than the calculated rate, though sufficient to yield good profits under good management. When there is evidence of excess capacity in the industry the Board might expect the industry to bear some of the costs of the excess capacity and might not recommend a rate of duty so high that the industry would be able to pass all the costs on to the consumer.

If the industry does not have some of the characteristics described above, the Board might refuse to recommend more than a moderate rate of duty and when all the characteristics are absent the industry would be protected only if it could survive with a low tariff protection.

I must now give some indication of what I mean by high and low rates of duty. When the manufacturing process is a substantial one using locally produced materials and parts, a duty of 20 per cent could be given readily. As the duty needed increases above 20 per cent, the Board should expect to find increasing evidence of the favourable characteristics I have described above. Duties in excess of 50 per cent should be given only rarely when there are special circumstances.

A declining industry in an out-dated product or using an out-moded process should rarely be given a duty even as high as 20 per cent.

In recommending duties, the Board must bear in mind the accumulation of costs through the different stages of production. This is becoming an increasingly embarrassing problem on which policy has not always been consistent. *The suggested scale should be applied to test the economics of the final product.* Duties should not be recommended in the early stages of production if they would make the cost of the final product undesirably high as measured by this scale.

Source: Vernon Report (11), vol. II,
p. 1072.

14:11 SUGGESTIONS ON THE OPERATIONS OF THE
TARIFF BOARD BY THE VERNON COMMITTEE

37. As the basis for the comments that follow, and despite the inevitable over-simplification which this involves, the main suggestions made by the [Vernon] Committee on the Board's operations or which affect the Board's work are set down below in summary form:

(i) *Reduce complexity of the Tariff.*—The Board should adopt ad valorem rates as standard practice. Where it recommends variable duties, it should set out the reasons for doing so and, if possible, indicate their ad valorem equivalent.

(ii) *Develop concept of 'economic and efficient'.*—The Board should develop the concept of 'bench mark' or general cost disability rate in deciding whether industries coming before it are 'economic and efficient'. Each case should be decided on its merits, but special reasons for recommending rates significantly higher than the going rate should also be included in the Board's reports. The Board should also comment more frequently on effective rates of protection in its reports.

(iii) *Existence of an industry is not grounds for protection.*—Permanent special protection for an industry which has ceased to be economic and efficient should not be regarded as a matter of right. If rationalisation of such an industry is required in the national interest the Board should give Parliament a full statement of reasons. There is scope, in certain cases, for relatively high protection for a limited period to enable large enterprises with unused capacity to become consolidated.

(iv) *Adopt 'industry' approach.*—The Committee believes there is scope for the development of an 'industry' approach to protection. It does not advocate sudden and dramatic steps in difficult industries but, if the adoption of industry-wide rates requires industries to alter production plans, there should be no hesitation in assisting them with aids to adjustment. Industries of great complexity may need three or four rate 'bands' and some special provisions for very difficult items, but the fewer of the latter the better.

(v) *More frequent reviews.*—The Committee urges the Board to inquire into and report from time to time on the general problems which it faces, as well as reviewing its findings on particular cases. All major inquiries should, if practicable, be repeated about every six years, especially those conducted on an industry basis. A review should also be made, about every three years, of those cases in which special measures are recommended.

(vi) *Economic effects of tariff-making.*—The Board should arrive at decisions after consideration of all the likely consequences for the economy as a whole as well as for the industry immediately concerned. A continuing assessment has to be made of the likely contribution of particular industries to economic growth. The more effectively the Board clarifies and applies its own principles, the more economic benefit is likely to result. It should consider whether particular tariffs are likely to hamper the economic operation of other industries to such an extent that disadvantages outweigh any gain resulting from them.

(vii) *Issue of 'labour intensive' versus 'capital intensive' in tariff decisions.*—The Board should not regard the maintenance of full employment as its

480

direct concern but rather as the responsibility of Government economic policy. Only on few occasions, such as special cases of decentralised industries and employment of persons with particular skills, should the Board give high priority to the effect of its decisions on employment. The issue of 'labour intensive' versus 'capital intensive' should not be the basis for determining Tariff Board policy.

(viii) *Bounties.*—The Committee confirms the Board's policy of considering bounties on their merits, particularly when the cost impact on export or potential export industries is important. It further suggests that profit limitations should be removed from bounty administration and replaced, where necessary for budgeting reasons, by a limitation on the total annual amount of bounty payable. If profit limitations are not removed, the Committee urges a substantial increase in the limit.

(ix) *Anticipatory duties.*—The Committee suggested that the Board make increased use of anticipatory duties. A special hearing in advance of production would reduce risks of investment during the period before protective need can be determined in the normal way. The more difficult it is to form judgements, the more difficult it would be for the Board to give more than a temporary finding. There should be a gradual extension of the n.e.i. principle in association with industry-wide inquiries.

38. Many of these suggestions reflect the Board's present practices. Some have been discussed in previous annual (and other) reports. The Board will comment separately on (ii), in particular, and also on (iv) and (ix). Such reservations as the Board has on the other suggestions result in most cases from differences of emphasis rather than differences of substance.

Source: Tariff Board. Annual Report for the Year Ended 30th June, 1966, summarising the Vernon Report.

C. PROCEDURAL MEASURES

14:12 THE LIFTING OF IMPORT CONTROLS AND THE NEED TO SPEED UP TARIFF PROCEDURES

Details of the Government's relaxation of import restrictions announced by the Minister for Trade (Mr. McEwen) should allay any fears that might have been held by manufacturers that the sudden lifting of this form of control would have adverse effects on industry. Mr. McEwen has made it clear that, although import restrictions are virtually at an end, steps are being taken to see that there is no sudden disruption of trade and that we are to move back as easily as possible to control wholly by the tariff system. . . .

The task of wholly safeguarding Australian industry and maintaining the necessary balance to hold the economy in a healthy state will now rest where it should rest, with the Tariff Board. The only concern which manufacturers might have is that the machinery of the tariff system is too slow to be effective in periods of danger. There can be no regrets that the days of import licensing are over.

No one will argue that import licensing has not had its uses. It has helped the country through some difficult times and played an important part in establishing the healthy position which exists today. But in normal times there can be no support for an arbitrary system of control which upsets the even flow of commerce by its 'stop-and-go' nature. Only those who have been sheltering behind its artificial barriers will regret its passing.

. . . The only concern now is whether the machinery of the tariff system is adequate to hold the position won through the dual use of tariffs and import restrictions.

The Tariff Board is a very efficient body, handling an immense amount of work, and since its reconstruction it has been able to hasten its decisions. But there is still a need for greater speed and flexibility in the system as a whole, particularly in relation to the time which elapses between the board's recommendation and Parliament's decision. Now that greater reliance must be placed on the tariff system to protect our stable and expanding economy, efforts should be made by the Government to speed its processes.

Source: Leading article in the *Age*,
23 February 1960.

14:13 LEGISLATION FOR TEMPORARY TARIFF ASSISTANCE

Second Reading speech on the Tariff Board Bill 1960 by the Minister for Trade (J. McEwen) in the House of Representatives on 16 August 1960.

This Bill is one of three which the Government is bringing forward to adapt Australia's tariff-making machinery to meet the problems which changing world trading and economic conditions raise for Australian industry. The Bills are closely related and it would probably suit the convenience of the House if I were to give a general outline of the total proposals and the Government's reasons for recommending them to the Parliament.

The traditional policy of Government in Australia is that the levels of protective Tariffs should not be determined without the issues involved having been examined and reported on by the Tariff Board.

Australia has progressed tremendously under this long-standing and well accepted policy. It is a tribute to the foresight of those who first introduced it that, after so many years and despite very considerable changes in the industrial scene both in Australia and abroad, the Tariff Board system of tariff-making needs only minor modifications to continue to function effectively, in present day conditions.

At the same time so large a section of the community—indeed, the economy as a whole—is so dependent on exports that we cannot be indifferent to any factor which affects our costs. Our policies of industrialization, including our policy on tariff protection, have to be operated with full consciousness of the fact that tariffs themselves can increase costs although it is demonstrable that they do not always do so. . . .

The rules of the GATT . . . provide that, in certain circumstances, a country can rapidly unbind a bound rate of duty with a view to according increased protection to one of its industries.

But freedom under the GATT has little significance unless our internal procedures allow us to take advantage of that freedom in appropriate circumstances. And, for reasons which I will indicate later, our internal procedures are not completely adequate in today's conditions.

More importantly and even more urgently, the whole question of our future trade relations with Japan has to be reviewed in negotiations with the Japanese Government due to commence shortly. It is essential that the Government take *now* whatever action may be necessary to equip itself with the legislative safeguards necessary to enable it to reach an agreement with the Japanese Government which will be satisfactory to all Australian interests—exporting, importing and manufacturing—and advantageous to the country as a whole. . . .

It has become all the more important to remedy any inadequacies in the present tariff-making machinery now that import restrictions have been removed. There is the possibility that some industries may have to meet sudden unforeseeable competition from overseas suppliers no longer held back from the Australian market by import restrictions. . . .

What is proposed

The Government's proposals are contained in three Bills but the basic objective of those Bills can be stated quite briefly. It is that the Government should, in appropriate circumstances, be able to provide interim or temporary and time-limited Tariff assistance pending inquiry and report by the Tariff Board and Government consideration of the Board's recommendations.

At present duties can be imposed or changed only when this House is in session. Adherence to this procedure would mean that the Government could not take action to apply temporary duties except at times when the House was in session. This would be so no matter how serious might be the consequences of any delay in according short-term protection for the threatened or injured local industry, pending the necessarily lengthy normal inquiry and report by the Tariff Board.

It is proposed therefore, that, subject to a number of important safeguards, short-term assistance be accorded industry where shown necessary by a preliminary Tariff Board inquiry and that the Government be enabled to accord such temporary assistance if the House is in recess at the relevant time.

A comparable point arises in connection with taking action on the normal reports of the Tariff Board. Such a report made after full inquiry may say that the Board is quite satisfied that the industry in question is worthy of and needs protection or increased protection against imports. Experience is that, in the very great majority of cases, such a finding would be acceptable to the Government and the Parliament. But, under present circumstances, if such a finding is received and adopted by the Government just after the House has gone into recess, nothing can be done to give the industry the protection it needs until the House reassembles.

This is a delay which the Government considers to be undesirable and which could be unnecessarily damaging to industry and employment and one which should be avoided. It believes that an industry, which has, in a comprehensive inquiry, demonstrated to the satisfaction of the Tariff Board and the Government that it is entitled to Tariff protection under traditional policies and that it needs such protection, should not be deprived of that protection for a further period if it is unlucky enough to have the Board's report come forward when the House is in recess.

The Government therefore proposes a procedure under which, by the publication of a notice in the Commonwealth Gazette, it can give effect to its decisions on recommendations from the Tariff Board when the House is not sitting. At the same time, and to completely preserve the prerogatives of the Parliament in tariff-making, a clause in the Bill will provide that any Tariff changes introduced when the House is not in session must be introduced as Tariff Proposals in the usual way within seven sitting days of the House meeting.

The Parliament will thus have preserved the traditional opportunity to debate any changes in duties introduced when it is not in session. This will be the case irrespective of whether the new duties are temporary duties, intended to operate only until the Tariff Board can make a final report, or are normal duties introduced following inquiry and final report by the Board.

Provision for tariffs to be changed when the House is not in session is in conformity with normal tariff-making practice in other countries. . . .

Source: *C.P.D. (H. of R.)*, vol. 23, pp. 11-14.

14:14 TEMPORARY TARIFF ASSISTANCE LEGISLATION: VIEWS OF ASSOCIATED CHAMBERS OF MANUFACTURES AND OF COMMERCE

'MAJOR BREAK-THROUGH' IN TARIFF THINKING

Manufacturers yesterday said the Federal Government's proposed tariff legislation was a major 'break-through' in tariff thinking.

Commerce spokesmen said the proposals were undesirable.

They were commenting on the Federal Government's new legislation to give temporary tariff protection to local industries threatened by imports.

Mr. R. W. C. Anderson, the director of the Associated Chambers of Manufactures, said in Canberra it was a major 'break-through' in Australian tariff thinking.

The new powers would prove a deterrent to countries which still had ideas that Australia was a dumping ground for their surplus production.

One of the most important defects in Australia's existing tariff machinery was her inability to take holding or short-term emergency action to safeguard industry inquiries and reports by the Tariff Board.

Another defect had been additional delays caused through the Government not being able to adopt a Tariff Board recommendation until Parliament was sitting.

'These delays have imposed a tremendous financial burden on the companies concerned and endangered the jobs of Australian employees', Mr. Anderson said.

'The new legislation will go a long way to ensuring the future of Australia as a major sophisticated trading nation and act as a "magnet" for overseas investment.'

Source: *Sydney Morning Herald*,
17 August 1960.

14:15 LEGISLATION FOR EXPANDED TEMPORARY PROTECTION

Second Reading speech on the Tariff Board Bill 1962 by the Minister for Repatriation (R. W. C. Swartz) in the House of Representatives on 15 March 1962.

[This Bill] is designed to give the necessary legislative authority for the operation of the expanded temporary protection machinery that the Government intends to make available to industry. . . .[1]

The temporary duty arrangements which resulted from previous amendments to the Tariff Board Act . . . have operated well. The modifications on urgent protection proposed in this bill are procedural and do not involve any change of a fundamental nature. They will, however, provide more clearly for the use of quantitative restrictions as a temporary protection measure and lay down certain safeguards on their continuance. . . .

A special advisory authority will be established to advise on requests for urgent protection against imports. . . .

This bill provides for the special advisory authority to operate within the framework of the Tariff Board Act. The authority will, in effect, replace deputy chairmen insofar as cases for urgent protection are concerned. It is proposed, however, that he will receive references direct from and will report direct to the Minister for Trade. . . .

As the number of urgent cases referred to the authority is expected to fluctuate widely and as the Government will wish to obtain advice on such cases quickly, the Government may determine the number of authorities to be appointed at any time. . . .

Where it is established that imports are causing, or threatening to cause, serious damage to a particular industry, the special advisory authority will be able to recommend that any protection shown as necessary will be given by means of a temporary duty or import restriction or both. This would not conflict with the commitments Australia accepts under G.A.T.T. . . .

The Government has recognized the particular difficulties of certain Australian industries where production efficiency and a reasonable cost level require the maintenance of a continuing high volume of output. Where an inflow of imports has reduced the Australian industry's share of the market so as to make an otherwise stable economy unprofitable and even, perhaps, uneconomic, it may be more appropriate to apply a quantitative limitation of imports, rather than a temporary duty.

Another circumstance which may warrant temporary protection through import restrictions may be that substantial reduction of domestic demand resulting from general economic circumstances operating in Australia may reduce an Australian industry to a serious situation unless the volume of imports is temporarily diminished. . . I must make it clear that the special advisory authority, where he finds grounds for a recommendation for temporary protection, will consider the use of temporary quantitative restrictions only *after* . . . he has considered a temporary duty. This will be the firm approach to our temporary protection machinery—the tariff first; quantitative restrictions where the tariff is

---

[1] Assent to this Bill was reported on 1 May 1962.

not appropriate . . . when temporary protection is accorded an industry it is in the nature of emergency first-aid. It is essentially a holding action pending a full inquiry by the Tariff Board. . . .

Source: C.P.D. (H. of R.), vol. 34, pp. 863-5.

14:16 PROTECTION AGAINST UNFAIR TRADING

Second Reading speech on the Customs Tariff (Dumping and Subsidies) Bill 1961 by the Minister for Customs and Excise (Senator N. H. D. Henty) in the Senate on 4 May 1961.

The purpose of this bill is to impose certain special duties of customs to provide protection for Australian industry against various forms of unfair trading. It also covers emergency action which may be taken against imports which cause or threaten serious injury to domestic producers or to producers in certain third countries. It is proposed that the Customs Tariff (Industries Preservation) Act be repealed. The bill incorporates those parts of the Customs Tariff (Industries Preservation) Act which are in current use and in addition makes provision for some additional measures of protection against unfair trading. Its provisions incorporate the means of dealing with dumping and subsidies which have been internationally agreed in the General Agreement on Tariffs and Trade. It also takes account of comments which have been made by the Tariff Board on problems arising from the Customs Tariff (Industries Preservation) Act.

The bill provides for a dumping duty on goods that are exported to Australia at an export price which is less than the normal value of the goods, where this causes or threatens injury to an Australian industry or may hinder the establishment of an Australian industry. The imposition of dumping duties will continue to be subject to inquiry and report by the Tariff Board . . . the bill does not authorize the imposition of dumping duties if the injury or hindrance is of an insubstantial nature.

The intention of the bill is to introduce dumping legislation which is consistent with Article VI of the General Agreement on Tariffs and Trade, which lays down internationally accepted criteria for the imposition of dumping duties. The General Agreement on Tariffs and Trade states that dumping, by which products of one country are introduced into another country at less than the normal value of the products, is to be condemned if it causes or threatens material injury to an established industry or materially retards the establishment of a domestic industry. . . .

This bill is . . . framed in such a way as to provide for the application of the criteria laid down in Article VI . . . but avoids possible difficulties of legal interpretation which might have been met by using the exact wording of that article.

The provision relating to dumping duty covers the types of cases which are now dealt with under sections 4, 5 and 6 of the Customs Tariff (Industries Preservation) Act—that is, goods sold to Australia at less than their fair market value, goods sold to Australia at less than cost of production plus a reasonable mark-up, and goods consigned for sale in Australia which may be sold at less than a reasonable price. It is, however, broader in scope than these three sections of the Customs Tariff (Industries Preservation) Act in that it empowers the imposition of dumping duties not only where injury to an Australian industry is caused or threatened, but also where the establishment of an Australian industry may be hindered. It is also broader in that 'the normal value' of goods exported to Australia is defined more comprehensively than is done in the two definitions in sections 4 and 5 of the existing act which deal with fair market value and cost of production only. In establishing a fair price, the Minister may take account not only of these factors, but of the price of goods sold in the country of export for export to a third country and of the fair market value of like goods produced in a third country where costs of production are similar to those in the country of export.

These are the general tests which are recognized in the General Agreement on Tariffs and Trade as representing proper means of establishing the normal value of goods entering into international trade; in addition, they provide a means of establishing the normal value of goods in cases where the fair market value or cost of production cannot be readily ascertained.

The bill makes provision, as does the present Act, for imposing dumping duties to protect the trade of third countries against unfair trade practices. The provisions of sections 11B and 11C of the Customs Tariff (Industries Preservation) Act relating to the imposition of countervailing duties on imported subsidized goods are reproduced in this bill. The countervailing duty provisions cover not only subsidies on imported goods, but also subsidized freight rates. The sections of the present Act which relate specifically to subsidized freights are therefore being omitted. The bill also reproduces the provisions of section 11A of the Customs Tariff (Industries Preservation) Act which permits the imposition of emergency duties, in accordance with Australia's international obligations, to prevent serious injury to an industry.

The sections of the Customs Tariff (Industries Preservation) Act which relate to depreciation of currencies have not been brought forward in this bill. Protection against exchange depreciation is available through other channels. Most countries have accepted obligations under the International Monetary Fund which prevent the occurrence of situations of the type which sections 8 to 11 of the Customs Tariff (Industries Preservation) Act were designed to counter. Moreover, there is provision in the Customs Act for the Minister for Customs and Excise to fix a fair rate of exchange in respect of imported goods and there is also provision both in the Customs Act and in this bill to deal with manipulation of exchange rates through the use of multiple currency practices. I might mention that sections 8 to 11 of the . . . Act have not been invoked since the 1920's. . . .

Source: *C.P.D. (S.)*, vol. 19, pp. 771-2.

14:17 LEGISLATION TO COUNTER NEW FORMS OF DUMPING

Second Reading speech on the Customs Tariff (Dumping and Subsidies) Bill 1965 by the Minister for Housing (L. H. E. Bury) in the House of Representatives on 16 September 1965.

The purpose of this Bill is to amend the Customs Tariff (Dumping and Subsidies) Act 1961, to enable action to be taken to counter new forms of dumping which have become evident since the main Act was passed. . . .

. . . In general, the Act has proved to be effective against the usual forms of dumping. However, since it came into operation certain new forms of dumping, apparently designed to circumvent the Act, have been identified. These sophisti-cated trading practices have been causing damage to Australian industry par-ticularly to the chemical and other capital intensive industries. A complete review has been made of the Act and its shortcomings in relation to the dumping practices which were impairing the protection to Australian industry. The present Bill incorporates the results of this review.

. . . Clauses 1 and 2 of the Bill are procedural changes relating to title, citation and date of operation of the Act. Clause 3 vests in the Minister for Customs and Excise the power to determine the export price of goods exported to Australia where, in his opinion, there are reasonable grounds for believing that the documentary export price has been fixed with a view to avoiding dumping duty or other special duties payable in accordance with the provisions of the Act. This is an amendment having a wide effect, and one which introduces into the legislation an element of flexibility necessary to counter all the various practices that have arisen.

The opportunity has been taken to improve the wording of the definition of 'export price'. For example, 'delivery charges'—previously referred to as 'free on board charges'—have been precisely defined. The amendments in this clause are designed to enable counter action to be taken against practices known as 'sales dumping' and 'package deals'. Sales dumping is the export to Australia of goods declared at normal value, i.e. at a fair and reasonable price thereby incurring no dumping duty, which are subsequently resold or costed into production in Australia at an amount which is less than normal value plus overseas freight, insurance, exchange, duty and landing charges, plus a normal or reasonable profit. In sales dumping, the element or act of dumping occurs, not between the exporter and importer, but at a point in the chain between the importer and the user in Australia. There have been, for example, instances of goods which have been imported by companies wholly owned by overseas principals (but separate corporate entities) and which have been the subject of sales dumping after importation into Australia. The wider powers would not be exercised, of course, in cases where the goods are imported in good faith and the importer incurs a genuine loss.

Package deals are transactions in which goods not liable to dumping duties are supplied at reduced prices as an inducement for the purchase of other goods at normal or non-dumped prices, thereby avoiding dumping duty that would other-wise be payable on the latter goods. In this instance, the dumping is transferred, so to speak, from goods which are competitive with Australian products to goods which are not competitive but which form part of the one transaction. These powers of flexibility in the determination of export price should allow the practices I have mentioned to be countered. Anti-dumping legislation needs to be flexible enough to allow the determination of a true export price and a true normal value to ensure that people do not evade the anti-dumping law. The proposed amend-ments to the Act will achieve this objective in regard to export price. The present powers to determine normal value are sufficiently flexible to prevent circum-vention of the Act, insofar as this aspect is concerned.

Clause 4 of the Bill incorporates a drafting change consequent upon the amendment to the definition of 'export price' in clause 3. It also vests in the Minister for Customs and Excise further powers to exempt from payment of dumping duties goods imported under certain circumstances. It is intended that these powers be exercised to exempt goods from the collection of dumping duty in cases where such collection would be contrary to the provisions of international agreements to which Australia is a party. Furthermore, the amendment will allow exemptions in cases where goods are admitted under Customs bylaw on the grounds that suitably equivalent goods, the produce or manufacture of Australia, are not reasonably available, i.e., exemption is granted on the premise that, if there is no production in Australia, there can be no injury to an Australian producer. For example, certain types of paper and paper-boards are not made in Australia but all types are covered by the dumping notice thereby rendering them liable to dumping duty. . . .

The Government is also becoming increasingly concerned with a trading practice which involves inadequate deletion allowances. Inadequate deletion allowances occur when goods—for example, motor vehicle components—are sold in a pack for assembly into a complete article. Importers of component packs pay the price for a complete pack less an allowance for any components which the importer wishes withdrawn from the pack and which he intends to purchase in Australia. This allowance is known as a 'deletion allowance'. If an offered deletion allowance is less than the real value of a component there is a positive financial disincentive to purchase such a component in Australia. In this way, offers of inadequate deletion allowances nullify the protection given by the Government to Australian component manufacturers.

In the case of the automobile industry, this practice has militated against efforts made by Australian manufacturers and assemblers to increase the Australian content of locally produced vehicles. If not checked, the practice may prevent attainment of the objectives of the Government's policy of increasing local content of automobiles. The Government is closely examining the practice of inadequate deletion allowances. If it continues the Government will take steps to regard an offered deletion allowance as the export price of the goods with a view to affording protection under the provisions of the Customs Tariff (Dumping and Subsidies) Act. I commend the Bill to honorable members.

Source: *C.P.D.* (*H. of R.*), vol. 47, pp. 976-8.

15

BALANCE OF PAYMENTS: GENERAL IMPORT CONTROLS, MARCH 1952 TO FEBRUARY 1960

Though two sections (15 and 16) are devoted to documents relating to the Australian balance of payments,[1] the documentation is not complete. This is regrettable, for there is no wish to imply that traffic in 'services' (for example, shipping) and inflow of capital are irrelevant to trade policies or to the actual composition of exports and imports of goods. Given pressing considerations of space and the time available to complete this work we have deliberately chosen to omit the few incomplete documents we had collected on these subjects. Some bibliographical references are given on capital inflow, however, and a brief comment is offered on its bearing on import controls in the fifties.

This section is confined to the general import controls of the period 1952-60 and, in the main, to policies rather than the system of administration. Section 16 gives some documentation on efforts to promote exports and on the key role assigned to external viability and to export policy in particular in government statements of economic policy. But here, too, documentation and bibliographical references will be less than was perhaps possible and will certainly not satisfy a serious student. Altogether there is ample room for a further volume of documents designed to give complete coverage to balance of payments policies since the war.

The 1945 White Paper on Full Employment (2:2) was prescient on the probability that full employment could result in increased imports which could prove excessive in relation to reserves of oversea funds. It also foresaw that declining export earnings would also sometimes require control of imports. In paragraph 91 the White Paper stated explicitly that if 'the fall in export income is one which, although prolonged and severe, is not permanent, the more appropriate method may be quantitative restrictions'.[2]

It fell to the lot of the Menzies government to introduce general import restrictions in March 1952, not because of a fall in export earnings but because a flood of imports threatened to exhaust oversea funds. These general controls were not removed until February 1960 (15:15). They were begun

[1] To which may be added some of the tables and notes in the Statistical Appendix, Section 17.

[2] In the same paragraph the White Paper conceded the possible appropriateness of exchange depreciation in some other circumstances.

as emergency and temporary measures, were substantially eased in 1953 and 1954, and tightened again in late 1955 and early 1956. Although more steadily and precisely eased thereafter (15:11, 15:14), they had seemed to assume in 1956 a rather more permanent air than the government either wished or intended.[3]

The documents tell a straightforward story of government policy—the reasons for the key decision of March 1952, the determination to ease restrictions as soon as possible, and the final unexpected but quite consistent act of removal in February 1960. Incidental to the story are the gradual removal of discrimination against Japan's exports and against imports requiring dollar currency; the attempt to improve the confidence of importers in the fairness of bureaucratic administration; and the growing evidence that many manufacturers were happy to have quantitative controls of imports as a system of protection substantially supplementary to although not replacing the tariff.

In this comment, rather than attempt a chronological review of the period, only certain features of the story are emphasised. Most of these are apparent in the documents but others require a would-be student of the period to dig more deeply into official documents—especially the voluminous Customs Regulations setting out the administrative detail and the available statistical analyses of goods imported in the various licensing categories.[4]

The Situation in 1952

There are some special features to be noted about the situation in 1952. The first is that import restrictions, administered through licensing arrangements, already operated in respect of goods from the United States and from other countries in the dollar area. (On post-war shortage of dollars see Section 4 above.) Protective use was made of this circumstance.[5] For reasons largely associated with American occupation and control of the Japanese economy and Japan's dependence on dollar supplies, trade with Japan in sterling was limited, requiring severe restrictions on imports from that country.[6] As we have seen, however (Section 10), the liberalisation in the mid-fifties of controls on imports from Japan was dictated by the need to come to permanent trading terms as Japan recovered her independence in trade

[3] The varying intensities of the restrictions and the reasons for the variations are usefully summarised in A15:1, prepared by Dr S. F. Harris.

[4] One such student, Harris (93), has gone very thoroughly into the economic aspects of import controls. It is to be hoped that his work will be given the light of day: certainly no historian of the period can afford not to read his thesis. One other useful review of the import licensing system is by Moffatt (130). In his more recent Ph.D. thesis on the subject, he gives rather more emphasis to the nature of the administrative organisation and decisions governing licensing in the years 1952-60.

[5] See Maxcy (121), pp. 504-5.

[6] For a useful account of the early post-war trading arrangements with Japan, see Nicholson (132), pp. 245-52.

policy matters. Domestic political concerns dictated the rather hesitant character of liberalisation prior to the signing of the trade treaty in 1957.

The fact that import licensing was already in operation made the introduction of general controls somewhat easier than might have been expected. It did not lessen the drama of the Prime Minister's announcement, which sets out very clearly the reasons for action (15:2, 15:4). As he said: 'There are . . . none who say that our overall balance of payments can be rectified in time without import restrictions at all' (15:4). Yet, in view of the fact that monthly import figures—reflecting the curbs placed on the boom in Australia—began to fall sharply in June 1952 before the import curbs could have been more than partially effective,[7] it remains a nice, albeit academic, point for argument whether the storm could have been weathered without the curbs. The large increase in exports in 1952-3 was not foreseeable (Section 13) and no one would pretend to have thought in early 1952 that drastic action was unnecessary.[8]

A rather ironical feature of the 1952 situation was the shock given to the United Kingdom. The policy of import controls was consistent with decisions of the Commonwealth Finance Ministers in January 1952 (15:4) and anyone who cares to examine in detail the import figures for the fifties will not easily sustain a case that the United Kingdom was unfairly treated. Indeed, in international circles, particularly in the GATT where she was obliged regularly to consult on and justify her restrictions, Australia gained a deserved reputation for the non-discriminatory administration of her controls.[9] Some United Kingdom industries were hard hit (especially textiles and other consumer products), but in total the United Kingdom managed to retain until 1958-9 more than its pre-war share of Australian imports. Its share was bound to fall from the 1951-2 level of 44·2 per cent as Europe recovered its interest and ability in export trade.

Comments on the Period as a Whole

If we look at the documents and the period as a whole several points call for emphasis. The first is the frequency of ministerial warnings that the import curbs were temporary. Yet actual experience appeared to justify scepticism on the part of importers and manufacturers. Had the substantial easing of restrictions in 1953-4 not been defeated by over-ordering due to the fear

[7] This fall in June gave some point to the nature of the flood of imports in 1951-2, namely, the sudden ability of British and European suppliers to fulfil long outstanding orders, many originating in the halcyon days for importers in 1949-50 and 1950-1, not to mention 1951 itself.

[8] See also pp. 496-7 where the influence of capital inflow (including temporary trade credits) is discussed.

[9] The discrimination against dollar goods was recognised as legitimate, although North America naturally directed criticism at this, with increasing justification, as time wore on.

of reimposition and a continued high level of 'full employment' demand, controls may have gone. In this event, however, the new inflation in late 1955 and 1956 may well have led to their reimposition, as it did to their very severe tightening (15:6, 15:7).[10] From this point on it became difficult indeed to convince traders and manufacturers that licensing would go when oversea reserves permitted. The writer well remembers officially warning investors (domestic and oversea alike) that if they were dependent upon continued import restrictions for success they were taking a major risk. Many took the risk in calculated fashion, relying on tariff procedures as a backstop in the, for some, unhappy event of controls being lifted.[11]

Essential Goods Restricted

Not so clearly evident from the documents is the fact that restrictions were not confined to unessential goods. At no time are consumer goods (usually regarded as unessential) a large enough proportion of Australian imports alone to yield the total 'savings' in imports sought through major cuts like those of 1952 and 1956. Part of the confusion arises from the continual stress on assuring to Australian industry its essential supplies of raw materials, components, and equipment. Preference was given to these goods to ensure full employment. Nevertheless cuts were made even in these categories, so accounting for a good deal of incidental protection (often additional to substantial tariff protection) of, and stimulus to, Australian production. Petrol imports were not curbed at all since the Menzies government was understandably not willing to reintroduce rationing; nor was it likely that the price mechanism would have been allowed to operate as the means of cutting consumption. There was some watch on stocks but failure to cut this item (which, indeed, grew steadily in volume and value of imports) certainly increased the squeeze on other imports, essential and unessential alike. Liberal treatment of tobacco and tea had somewhat similar effects.

The truth is that all but a very few categories of goods contributed to the necessary import 'savings'. The severity of restriction varied with the balance of payments situation, frequently measured by the actual and potential state of oversea reserves. The schedule prepared by Harris (A15:1) gives an indication of the circumstances which led to easing or tightening at particular points of time. Incidental protection to home production was an inevitable

---

[10] The biting reference in 15:5 to the possibility that relaxation was 'an experiment that cannot last' leaves no doubt as to the poor opinion of Australian policy held by *The Economist* in 1953. It is worth noting, however, that inflationary pressures leading to a spillover into demand for imports were more perennially the cause for tightening import controls than were poor export prospects taken alone (A15:1).

[11] As is noted in Section 14, most Australian industries in fact absorbed the shock of February 1960 and the later recession very well indeed. The 'official' voices of industry were somewhat strident in protest in February 1960, but in fact the transition from controls to no controls was not as difficult as industry spokesmen expected (15:16, 15:17).

accompaniment to import restrictions, especially while demand under full employment exceeded the permitted supply of imports. This meant that the longer restrictions continued the more manufacturers would assume some sort of 'right' to their benefit. The prevalence of this view, which was widely held despite the government's clearly stated intention to abolish controls, is shown in the reaction to the February 1960 announcement (15:16, 15:17). Even the weakening of effective incidental protection which accompanied the steady easing of controls from April 1957 on did not appear to lessen this attitude.

Definition of 'Minimum' Reserves

It is worth noting that, although the actual and prospective level of over-seas reserves was the key to decisions on import controls, the government refused to state a figure for basic 'minimum' reserves. This was readily under-standable, since £350m. could be quite healthy if export prospects were good and the 'free' demand for imports judged not to be excessive. Yet reserves at £428m. in June 1955 were thought inadequate in the face of unpromising export prospects and a rising pressure of demand for imports. Australian trade policies operate in a dynamic and variable situation.[12] Accordingly all the major decisions shown in A15:1 were made in the light of both the situation at the moment and the prospects as seen for the twelve months or so ahead. With the enlargement of the second line of reserves (the right to call on the IMF) towards the end of the period, it could be said that primary reserves at £500m. would carry us through at least two years of balance of payments trouble. At least this was the judgment which, in February 1960, finally justified removal of general restrictions.

Ending Discrimination against United States and Japan

Discrimination against Japan in import licensing ended with the signing of the trade treaty (10:10), although some nominal controls affecting Japan and other countries remained after general controls were ended in February 1960 (15:15). In February 1960 all discrimination against goods from dollar areas ceased. The discrimination against the dollar had been a hard necessity for the sterling area in general and Australia in particular (Section 4). A close study suggests that the easing of dollar restrictions might have been more substantial than it was in 1958 (as announced at Montreal (4:12)).[13] The final removal of all dollar restrictions in 1960 left the balance of mutual trade policy complaints very much against the United States. The United

[12] For a useful discussion of the unwisdom of trying to name a figure above which reserves are adequate and below which they are inadequate, see *The Australian Balance of Payments, February 1966* (5), pp. 43-4.

[13] The IMF view of October 1959 (15:13) was probably justified in relation to Australia's continued discrimination at that time.

States' agricultural import embargoes and mineral quotas no longer had a counterpart in Australian restrictions, although the high wool duty might be said to be matched by high tariff duties on some American exports to Australia (Section 11). The change in the licensing provisions covering imports from Japan reflected a growing awareness, already noted, of the need, in Australia's interests, to effect a closer and much less discriminatory trading relationship with Japan. This is discussed in Section 10 above.

Consultation with GATT and IMF

Throughout the licensing period Australia was obliged to 'consult' with both GATT and the IMF. It is not possible to report these consultations adequately in public documents, although the IMF resolutions give some index of their constant but mildly expressed anxiety that the restrictions be retained no longer than necessary. Whether anxiety was the equivalent of the *undue* pressure sometimes attributed to the IMF is a question beyond the scope of this book or my personal competence to pass final judgment. I would, however, personally doubt it. Despite the rather obvious leaning of IMF officials to 'sound finance' (i.e. very strong anti-inflationary policies), I was not, in my official duties, subjected by IMF or GATT officials or national delegates in GATT to any pressure which could be called 'undue'. Having in mind that our international obligation in GATT (Article XII) was (and is) to use quantitative import restrictions virtually for balance of payments reasons only (A15:4), no international body could really attempt to impose unacceptable policies while balance of payments difficulties existed and it was also clear that our policies were directed to resolving those difficulties.[14]

It is worth noting that the IBRD has been an important source of funds needed to sustain capital imports. In this respect it is an important part of the capital inflow story, as we have seen it also to be in the story of agricultural recovery. Document A15:2 gives some interesting detail. The IMF story is

[14] Article XIV, Section 4, of the International Monetary Fund Agreement provides that five years after the date on which the Fund began operations, and in each year thereafter, any member still retaining any restrictions on payments and transfers for current international transactions which are inconsistent with Article VIII, Sections 2, 3 or 4 of the Agreement, shall consult with the Fund as to their further retention. The Fund is entitled 'to influence countries to correct maladjustments in their balance of payments and to fulfil their other obligations under the Fund' (3:17).

It was the practice of the Fund to record its views on action taken by members to reduce such restrictions, constantly to stress the need for such relaxation, and to emphasise the need for moving towards non-discrimination against particular currencies. In document 15:13 the IMF calls on members to proceed 'with all feasible speed in eliminating discrimination against member countries'. The Fund's views on Australia's actions during the 1952-60 import licensing period are recorded in the *Annual Reports by the Treasurer under the International Monetary Agreement Acts* published as Commonwealth Parliamentary Papers. For reasons of space, a document incorporating many of these comments has been omitted. It is available on request. The comments are notable for their mildness. During this period Australia did not have recourse to credits from the IMF.

documented in A15:3, but the main use of our 'rights' with the Fund was in April 1961 and later—that is, outside the period of this section.[15] In 1961 Australia purchased foreign currencies to the value of $U.S.175m. for addition to her reserves and arranged a line of credit for $U.S.100m. which was not used (A15:3). These actions and a marked increase in her quota have clearly established the role of the IMF in providing a second line of foreign exchange reserves.

Capital Inflow

It is worth noting from A15:1 or from Section 17, Table VI, the apparent significance of net capital inflow during the period under comment.[16] No doubt the high 1951-2 and 1955-6 figures include significant temporary trade credits,[17] reflected in the subsequent fall in capital inflow in 1952-3 (actually a small net outflow) and 1956-7. Nevertheless, the high level of new capital inflow in 1957 to 1960 made Operation Slideout—a name given to the gradual easing of restrictions—much easier than it could possibly have been otherwise. Whether capital inflow constitutes an undesirable element of future instability in the apparent need for this item to balance our external accounts is beyond the scope of this book.[18] The final paragraph of 15:12

[15] The 1961 arrangement aroused controversy along the lines of old fears that the IMF might be taking control of our economic affairs. Copies of the relevant correspondence are to be found in *C.P.D. (H. of R.),*vol. 37, pp. 1524-7.

[16] The term 'apparent significance' is used by way of caution. Capital inflow comprises profits on oversea investment retained in the country (i.e. undistributed profits) as well as fresh capital inflow (i.e. foreign exchange) from abroad. It is the latter amount which is significant as a support to the imports of goods and services. Analysis in these terms supports the statements made in this paragraph.

[17] As also in 1960-1 which, too, was followed by a fall in net apparent capital inflow in 1961-2. The 1951-2 figures make it particularly dangerous to assume that, after all, we could have weathered the storm without imposing restrictions. Had there been no restrictions temporary capital inflow may not have materialised so promptly and a greater threat to external value of the currency might well have occurred, forcing devaluation or even more drastic import control measures.

[18] See Vernon Report (11), vol. I, ch. 11 and vol. II, app. J; *Treasury Bulletin on Private Overseas Investment in Australia* (15); *The Australian Balance of Payments, February 1966* (5); and the *Economic Record*, March 1966 (Vernon Report Issue) (75).

My own views are clear. The case for a substantial level of capital inflow continues to be a strong one. Nevertheless, it does constitute an element of instability in the balance of payments situation, since the annual level is not readily predictable in quantitative terms. In these circumstances the level of reserves (primary and secondary) needs to be higher than it would otherwise be, to take account of adverse variations in the level of net capital inflow even if imports may also fall concurrently (but not necessarily commensurately) with capital inflow. An inspection of the balance of payments tables in Section 17 indicates not only the variation in capital inflow but also the steadily rising trend in the proportion of total 'credits', since the low point of 1952-3, represented by net apparent capital inflow. A similar comment applies to capital inflow calculated as a percentage of debits (imports of goods and services on current account) to be met in each year.

can be read to refer to exports or to both exports and capital inflow as the needed 'means to pay for imports' (see also (16:15)).

Administrative Appeal System

Finally, in this catalogue of general observations on the period, we must note the development of a system of appeal to Caesar theoretically against Caesar himself (i.e. the minister), in practice against his minions in the departments (15:8 to 15:10).[19] Three issues were involved: the right of Parliament to review the work of the Executive (the minister); the need to obtain general public understanding and acceptance of the equity of policy—given the fact of import restrictions; and the necessity to have some check on the soundness and fairness of particular administrative decisions.

The Prime Minister had, at the end of March 1952, set up a consultative committee of business people, an Australian Council of Trade Unions representative, consumer representatives, and officials. This played a useful general role as consultant on overall policy but could not pretend to review particular decisions, for which specific means of review were required.

While the whole system was, as time went on, progressively modified to reduce the scope for arbitrary decisions (either by minister or officials), it was not possible to eliminate that scope. Regulations were not capable of legal review process, policies could not be defined in statute with sufficient constancy, and the minister's judgment was final in terms of the relevant statutory powers.[20]

The appeal system finally devised could not lessen the power of the minister, but it did result in effective review of departmental decisions in borderline cases. It is worth stressing that the system not only required a clear understanding of policy on the part of each Import Licensing Advisory Review Board (comprising two business men and one official), but often impelled the department to re-define and modify policies in sensible ways. On the general question I stand by the judgment made in an address published in 1960.[21]

---

[19] Crawford (57), pp. 46-7.

[20] The view that the policies governing the thousands of particular decisions made by the licensing authorities could not be precisely defined was basic in deciding in favour of an administrative system of appeal. A judicial process was rendered the more impracticable by the fact that import control policies were subject to frequent change in nature and in terms of oversea funds available for allocation in accordance with variations in the state of oversea reserves.

The legal authority of the minister rested in Regulation No. 14 (2) and (3) of the Customs (Import Licensing) Regulations Statutory Rules 1939, No. 163 made under Clause 52 (g) of the Customs Act 1901-1950. In 1956, with the repeal of the 1939 regulations, the relevant regulations were nos. 17 and 18 of the Customs (Import Licensing) Regulations Statutory Rules 1956, No. 93. The actual clause reads: 'The following are prohibited exports: . . . (g) all goods the importation of which may be prohibited by regulation.'

[21] Crawford (57).

Were Direct Import Controls the Only Way?

From time to time the view was expressed by some economists that there were other ways open to conserve foreign exchange. This, in fact, is doubtful in the practical circumstances of the period, as some of the economists themselves recognised.[22]

In so far as excessive demand for imports was the result of domestic inflation it can be said that the IMF, although concerned, recognised the efforts of the government to deal with this situation. Exchange depreciation was flatly rejected (15:6).

The other popular candidate was a uniform addition to tariff rates for which Dr Corden was a principal spokesman.[23] Under examination this broke down on at least three grounds, of which the third at least was sufficient in the circumstances of 1952. The first was that a uniform tariff would add to costs of raw materials and goods not made in Australia, whereas admission under import licence arrangements *might* not. The second was that once imposed it could well prove more difficult to remove tariff duties than to dismantle licensing. The history of 'temporary' primage duties imposed in the Great Depression supported this view. The third was that a tariff could not ensure restriction within a close margin of a given target for total value of imports and would therefore require larger reserves to support it. In short, the impact of a tariff on the level of imports was and is unpredictable. Import controls became so accurate by 1956 that a given maximum level of imports could be assured within a relatively small margin of error.

All this is not to say that there are not better and less disruptive ways of curbing imports if action is taken early enough.[24] Given the suddenness of the crises of March 1952 and 1955-6, drastic measures were justified and and at the time direct curbs were the most politically acceptable and effective method available. Moreover, since confident prediction of the elements in a balance of payments situation is difficult indeed, it is rather too much to

[22] Corden (46) noted the need, if reliance were to be placed on a general lift in tariff rates, for a higher average level of reserves, the cost of which must be weighed against the various disadvantages of import restrictions. Karmel (100) was doubtful whether depreciation would have a good effect within a reasonable period and advocated only a uniform *ad valorem* tariff, *if practicable* in the light of international commitments. Arndt (3), after looking at an alternative system of variable selling rates for foreign exchange for imports, said that whether it would be preferable would depend on the extent to which prices of restricted imports rise under a system of administrative licensing; he said that an inquiry was necessary to establish this and if as a result the present system emerged as the lesser evil we must just weigh its advantages against its disadvantages. See also Harris (93) and Moffatt (130).

References in this context to uniform addition to tariff schedules in lieu of direct import curbs are not to be confused with the argument for a uniform tariff in lieu of the present structure of selective tariff rates, on which see Section 16.

[23] Corden (46).

[24] Vernon Report (11), vol. I, ch. 17, paras. 63-6; Corden (46); Harris (93); Moffatt (130).

expect that a general addition to tariff rates or a devaluation will be announced much ahead of a crisis. Given a crisis for which a necessary solution is to cut imports severely, direct controls will always be a strong candidate.[25] The understandable tendency to wait for the crisis may well mean, too, that any long-run pressure, represented by a lag of export earnings in relation to import requirements, will best be dealt with by a steady encouragement to exports, all other action being limited to crisis, whether or not this includes any significant element of longer-term pressure.

The final consequence of the system was inherent in its sudden removal. Perversely, business men took the February 1960 announcement, coupled with the November 1960 anti-inflation measures, as a jolt to their confidence in the long-run economic growth of Australia (15:16, 15:17). In short, despite the government's wishes, import curbs had become an important ingredient in the generally favourable investment climate of the fifties.[26] Some part of the impact of the ending of controls and the recession of 1961-2 is noted in the documents included in Section 14 dealing with Tariff Policies and Procedures.

[25] Useful references on the subject matter of this section not already cited include Lungberg and Hill (113); Meade (122); McColl (114); Perkins (135, 136); Russell (150).

[26] In this sense perhaps the Treasury view (15:12) that 'there is nothing good to be said for import restrictions as such' is an overstatement. There may be better ways of sustaining a favourable investment climate; nevertheless, import licensing did help in this respect, so offsetting some of its costs.

A15:1   SCHEDULE OF VARIATIONS IN IMPORT LICENSING LEVELS, 1952-1960

PREPARED BY DR S. F. HARRIS

Year	Changes During Year	Exports	Imports	Net Capital Inflow	Change in Reserves	Reserves at end of Year	Reasons for Change
1951–2	March— Imposition of Controls	664	−1051	119	−431	373	Rapid rundown of reserves —inflationary and speculative import demand —fall in export income Export prospects not favourable.
1952–3	January— Relaxation—slight April— Relaxation —e.g. 'B' from 20% to 30%	846	−510	−14	188	561	Mainly administrative readjustments —possible in light of improved reserve position. Substantial increase in reserves —import level very low —increase in export income —economy entering recovery stage Need to ease tight licensing position.
1953–4	July— Relaxation —e.g. 'B' from 30% to 40% October— Relaxation —e.g. 'B' from 40% to 50% —6-monthly licensing period introduced	812	−682	9	10	571	Continued improvement in reserve position —strong export position being maintained —low level of imports —no strong inflationary pressures. Trade Balance continuing favourable although margin narrowing —export prospects considered good.

Period / Action		Comments
April— Relaxation —e.g. 'B' from 50% to 60% —'A' Category largely to N.Q.R.		Favourable visible balance to end of January —over £120 m. —expecting to move towards removal of controls —internal demand building up strongly.
1954-5 *October—* Tightening —mainly as *holding* action —'B'—no change —N.Q.R. to 'A' 100%	761 -847 93 -143 428	Reserves falling at fairly rapid rate —imports much above estimate —inflationary demand —speculative demand —export prospects not particularly bright.
April— Intensification —e.g. 'B' cut by 1/3rd		Continued fall in reserves —high import demand —pressure from internal inflation —lower export income.
1955-6 *October—* Intensification —reduction of £80m. p.a. sought —'B' cut another 25%	772 -820 138 -73 355	Reserves fell over £140m. in 1954-5 despite capital inflow—level considered low —imports still well above intended levels —earlier cuts not biting —inflationary demand causing pressures —export prospects not particularly favourable.
1956-7 *July—* Intensification —unachieved ceiling of £650m. raised to £700m. —£40-50m. cut in annual licensing rate	978 -717 97 212 567	Reserves still falling—despite relatively high capital inflow —earlier import cuts not 'biting' sufficiently —1956 Little Budget not yet showing full effects in cutting back inflation —export prospects brighter.

(Continued on next page)

501

A15: 1 SCHEDULE OF VARIATIONS IN IMPORT LICENSING LEVELS, 1952-1960—*continued*

Year	Changes During Year	Exports	Imports	Net Capital Inflow	Change in Reserves	Reserves at end of Year	Reasons for Change
1956-7	*January*— Relaxation—slight —within existing ceiling						Import rate brought under control —need for adjustments/severity of previous measures/anomalies —internal demand quiescent —export position good—prospects not unfavourable.
	April — Relaxation —ceiling raised to £775m. (up £75m.)						Reserves high and increasing rapidly —high export income —imports at low levels —internal demand still at relatively low level.
1957-8	*August*— Relaxation —ceiling raised to £800m.	810	−791	110	−42	525	Reserves high —internal demand fairly slack —export prospects still appeared fairly good.
	December— No Change						More or less balanced position achieved— some downward revision of export prospects —prices tending down —unfavourable seasonal conditions —pressure on ceiling not unduly high.
	April— No Change						Exports well down on previous year —capital inflow maintained —reserves falling but at slow rate from high level. No strong pressures on ceiling—slow pick up in internal activity.

1958–9		810	–796	176	–9	516	
	August— **No Change**						Slight fall in reserves in previous year —export prospects only fair. Pressures developing on ceiling as activity internally picks up.
	December— **No Change**						Export prospects not clearly favourable —internal demand building up —ceiling becoming harder to hold. Reserves holding up.
	April— **Relaxation** (Unannounced) to £830m.						Export prospects favourable. Capital inflow high. Growing inflationary demand internally —strong pressures on ceiling.
1959–60		937	–946	218	–4	512	
	August— **Relaxation** —ceiling raised to £850m.						Pressure on ceiling still relatively strong despite relaxations —high and growing internal demand —export prospects good —capital inflow at high levels.
	December— **Relaxation** —ceiling raised to £875m.						Reserves holding up despite increased imports —high rate of capital inflow —high level of export income —'boom' conditions continuing internally.
	February— **Removed**						Anti-inflation measure —exports high and prospects good —reserves holding up —capital inflow being maintained.

A15:2 SUMMARY OF LOANS NEGOTIATED BY AUSTRALIA WITH THE IBRD

PREPARED BY NANCY ANDERSON

		Principal ($ U.S.)	Duration (years)	Interest Rate (%)	Date Drawings Completed	Purpose
1.	22 Aug. 1950	100,000,000	25	$4\frac{1}{4}$	1953-4	Provide Australia with additional dollar exchange to facilitate importation of capital goods and equipment for her development.
2.	8 July 1952	50,000,000	20	$4\frac{3}{4}$	1954-5	Provide Australia with additional dollar exchange or equivalent in other currencies to facilitate importation of capital goods and equipment for her development. (During 1953-4 Bank agreed that loan could cover portion of cost of aircraft and spare parts being purchased by Qantas Empire Airways Ltd.)
3.	2 Mar. 1954	54,000,000	15	$4\frac{3}{4}$	1955-6	As for 2 above.
4.	18 Mar. 1955	54,500,000	15	$4\frac{5}{8}$	1956-7	As for 2 above.
5.	15 Nov. 1956	9,230,000	10	$4\frac{3}{4}$	1958-9	Provide dollars for Qantas to meet progress payments due on 7 Boeing jet aircraft being purchased in the United States and for purchase of related spare parts and equipment.
6.	3 Dec. 1956	50,000,000	15	$4\frac{3}{4}$	1958-9	As for 2 above.
7.	23 Jan. 1962	100,000,000	25	$5\frac{3}{4}$	Not yet completed[a]	Provide equivalent of $100,000,000 in various currencies to reimburse 50 per cent of expenditure by the Snowy Mountains Hydro-Electric Authority after 30 June 1961, on part of the Murray Development portion of the Snowy Mountains Scheme.
	Total amount of loans	417,730,000				
	Cumulative drawings as at 30 June 1966	417,175,007				

[a] $99,445,000 drawn as at 30 June 1966.

SOURCE: Annual Reports by Australian Treasurer under the International Monetary Agreements Acts.

A15:3 AUSTRALIA'S TRANSACTIONS WITH THE IMF

PREPARED BY NANCY ANDERSON

24 Oct. 1949 $U.S.20,000,000 purchased.

20 Aug. 1952 $U.S.30,000,000 purchased.

1953-4   Above transactions increased Fund's holdings of Australian currency to $U.S.107,843,181 at 30 June 1953 or $18,557,467 in excess of Australia's quota of $U.S.200,000,000 (£89,285,714). By 30 June 1964 Australia made three voluntary repurchases of Australian currency equivalent to $U.S.24,000,000. At that date the Fund's holdings of Australian currency amounted to £97,126,895 and its excess holdings were reduced to £7,841,181.

1954-5   Four voluntary repurchases of Australian currency from the Fund made amounting to the equivalent of $U.S.26,000,000, thus completing the repurchase of Australian currency for the $U.S.20,000,000 and $U.S.30,000,000 purchases in 1949 and 1952 respectively.

1959   Australia's Fund quota increased from $U.S.200,000,000 to $U.S.300,000,000.

1960   Australia's Fund quota increased from $U.S.300,000,000 to $U.S.400,000,000.

28 April 1961   The following foreign currencies equivalent to $U.S.175,000,000 purchased.

Deutschmarks	55,000,000
U.S. dollars	40,000,000
Pounds sterling	30,000,000
French francs	15,000,000
Italian lire	15,000,000
Canadian dollars	10,000,000
Netherlands guilders	10,000,000
	175,000,000

1 May 1961   A stand-by credit with the Fund equivalent to $U.S.100,000,000 became effective for one year.

5 Sept. 1961   The stand-by credit was cancelled at Australia's request. No purchases of foreign currency were made during the period of the stand-by.

22 Mar. 1962   An amount of the Fund's holdings of Australian currency equivalent to $U.S.175,000,000 or £78,125,000 repurchased, thus repaying in full the drawing on 28 April 1961.

8 June 1962   46,013,952 troy ounces of fine gold paid to the Fund, at a cost of £721,245, reducing the Fund's holdings of Australian currency to £718,968. This payment of gold was a result of an increase in Australia's holdings of gold and convertible currencies during the year ended 30 April 1962, when Australia incurred an obligation under Section 7(b) of the Fund Agreement to repurchase a part of its subscription which was originally paid in Australian currency equivalent to $U.S.1,610,342.

11 April 1963   Repurchased with convertible currencies £11,524,702 of the Fund's holdings of Australian currency to bring Australia's 'gold' subscription to the Fund up to the full 25 per cent of its total subscription. (A

country's 'gold' subscription to the Fund is that portion of its total subscription which it is required, under the Fund's Articles of Agreement, to pay in gold and convertible currencies.) The repurchase was effected by payments to the Fund of $U.S.12,907,666 and £stg.4,609,881 at a cost to Consolidated Revenue of £11,556,173.

29 Mar. 1965 Australian currency equivalent to $U.S.12,500,000 (£A5,580,000) made available to the IMF for use in a drawing of $U.S.100,000,000 by India to meet balance of payments difficulties.

28 April 1965 A further Australian currency equivalent of $U.S.12,500,000 was made available for use in a further drawing by India of $U.S.25,000,000. On each occasion India arranged to convert the Australian currency into sterling. Transactions reduced Australia's holdings of gold and foreign exchange by £A11,160,000 and increased, by a similar amount Australia's gold tranche drawing rights in the IMF.

31 Mar. 1965 Fund adopted resolution for 25 per cent increase in quotas of all members. Australia's quota to rise from $U.S.400,000,000 to $U.S.500,000,000. When effective this increase will enlarge Australia's drawing rights to $U.S.650,000,000.

Source: Annual Reports by the Australian
Treasurer under the International
Monetary Agreements Act.

A15:4 TEXT OF ARTICLE XII OF GATT: RESTRICTIONS TO SAFEGUARD THE BALANCE OF PAYMENTS

1. Notwithstanding the provisions of paragraph 1 of Article XI[1] any contracting party, in order to safeguard its external financial position and its balance of payments, may restrict the quantity or value of merchandise permitted to be imported, subject to the provisions of the following paragraphs of this Article.

2.(a) Import restrictions instituted, maintained or intensified by a contracting party under this Article shall not exceed those necessary:

    (i) to forestall the imminent threat of, or to stop, a serious decline in its monetary reserves, or

    (ii) in the case of a contracting party with very low monetary reserves, to achieve a reasonable rate of increase in its reserves.

Due regard shall be paid in either case to any special factors which may be affecting the reserves of such contracting party or its need for reserves, including, where special external credits or other resources are available to it, the need to provide for the appropriate use of such credits or resources.

(b) Contracting parties applying restrictions under sub-paragraph (a) of this paragraph shall progressively relax them as such conditions improve, maintaining them only to the extent that the conditions specified in that sub-paragraph still justify their application. They shall eliminate the restrictions when conditions would no longer justify their institution or maintenance under that sub-paragraph....

[1] Article XI deals with the general elimination of quantitative restrictions.

3.(b) Contracting parties applying restrictions under this Article may determine the incidence of the restrictions on imports of different products or classes of products in such a way as to give priority to the importation of those products which are most essential.

(c) Contracting parties applying restrictions under this Article undertake:

(i) to avoid unnecessary damage to the commercial or economic interests of any other contracting party;

(ii) not to apply restrictions so as to prevent unreasonably the importation of any description of goods in minimum commercial quantities the exclusion of which would impair regular channels of trade; and

(iii) not to apply restrictions which would prevent the importation of commercial samples or prevent compliance with patent, trade mark, copyright, or similar procedures.

Source: General Agreement on Tariffs and Trade: *Basic Instruments and Selected Documents, Volume III, Text of the General Agreement*, 1958.

15:1 AUSTRALIAN GOVERNMENT ENCOURAGES LOCAL MANUFACTURE OF MOTOR VEHICLES

Speech by the Minister for Post-War Reconstruction (J. J. Dedman) in the House of Representatives on 22 March 1945 and letter dated 3 February 1945 from the Prime Minister (J. Curtin) to General Motors-Holden's. Tabled in the House of Representatives on 22 March 1945.

It is the policy of the Government to encourage the local manufacture of motor vehicles . . . Even in peace-time the importation of sufficient vehicles is by no means assured. Our export income from the proceeds of which we must pay for imports, is subject to sudden and largely unpredictable fluctuations. We have no guarantee that our stable exports will be sustained permanently at levels to which we have been accustomed in the past.

Source: C.P.D., vol. VI, p. 821.

(e) The Government will give earnest consideration to any specific request for temporary import of special components under Tariff sub-section 404 A. . . .

(f) (iii) Upon the submission of specific cases, the Government will give earnest consideration to the terms upon which it can facilitate the importation of plant and equipment for the purposes of your proposals. In the approved cases it will facilitate the provision of exchange. . . .

(i) The facilities required for travel and transport and for allocation of manpower, together with foreign exchange, will be granted priority to the fullest extent practicable commensurate with the necessities of the war effort.

Source: C.P.D., vol. VI, p. 825.

15:2 IMPORT LICENSING: GENERAL APPLICATION

Press statement by the Prime Minister (R. G. Menzies) on 8 March 1952.

Today a Gazette notice is being published under which import licensing is applied to all goods passing into Australia, with certain minor exceptions indicated in the notice. The result of this is, as from midnight last night, to extend a system of licensing control such as is now exercised over dollar and Japanese imports to other non-sterling and to sterling imports.

This decision was not an easy one for the Government to take, for we dislike controls, and in particular we are most reluctant to impose restrictions on goods from the United Kingdom, whose exports at this time mean so much to her and to her own balance of trade. But a critical position must be met and overcome. The plain fact is that our import expenditure is so far out-running our export income that unless special measures are taken our overseas funds (which are vital to our solvency and to our international trade) will be seriously threatened, particularly in the period July to October, when our export income tends to slacken off.

I should point out how this position has arisen. It is not the result of a low export income in the ordinary sense. In 1951-1952 if current prices continue our exports will probably bring in about £660,000,000. This will be much the greatest export income we have ever had, with the exception of 1950-1951 which was, of course, the year of the great wool boom. The real reason for the present crisis is to be found in the flood of imports that has come into Australia during this financial year. The present estimate of imports already received and of imports due to arrive before June 30th, is that including freight and insurance they will probably amount to the vast sum of £1250m. There are many reasons for this remarkable fact. Imports have, of course, become more expensive because overseas prices have risen. Supplies of goods from the United Kingdom, Western Europe and Japan have become much more readily available. Many orders for large items of equipment placed overseas, in some cases several years ago, are now at last being fulfilled. There was a good deal of abnormal ordering of goods, when during the wool boom it appeared that almost anything could be sold in Australia. An increasing amount of essential material and equipment is being brought into Australia. Freights have risen very sharply. We have, of course, received some benefit from these importations. Many of them have contributed to the damping down of inflationary pressures by increasing supply relatively to demand.

In this financial year wool prices have fallen very sharply and it was therefore expected that by the beginning of 1952 there would be some natural slackening of import demand and that the deterioration in the trade balance would therefore tend to be halted. But contrary to expectations January and February have seen astonishing levels of imports, with the result that we are forced to intervene with import control in order to prevent an aggravation of the situation.

That situation is, in short, that we are at present spending upon imports far more than we are earning from our exports or receiving from proceeds of overseas borrowing or through private investment of overseas capital in Australia. It follows that, a substantial amount of our overseas reserves having been eaten up by this excess of spending over earnings, we must take steps to reduce our imports to the level of our currently available resources. Upon reflection every Australian will realise that any other course would permit a crisis to develop which would adversely affect most of our people.

Fortunately since one result of this great flood of imports has been that stocks of many imported goods have accumulated to a record level in Australia, import control should not produce immediate shortages for Australian consumers.

I would like to repeat and emphasise that in due time, the current rate of imports would undoubtedly have fallen a long way of its own accord. The very fact that we have received such huge quantities of goods in so short a time would by itself do a great deal to ensure this. Furthermore, the measures taken by the Government to beat inflation and reduce excessive demand within Australia would work, and in fact, are already working, in that direction. As a Government, we would greatly prefer to see the necessary reduction of imports brought about in that way but . . . it is now quite plain that a reduction of imports brought about in this way would not happen soon enough, or go far enough to stop the drain upon our overseas reserves in time. That is why we are reluctantly compelled to fall back upon the method of licensing imports in order to bring the rate of inflow as soon as possible down to a manageable level.

What I have said will indicate that we are not proposing to set up a permanent licensing system. Just so soon as our balance of payments position permits we will be able—and indeed anxious—to modify and eventually remove these controls. The Minister for Customs will, in a separate statement, indicate the nature and extent of the controls which come into operation immediately. I want to make it clear however, that any quotas or standards now established are primarily designed to hold the position for a few months and do not necessarily represent the final word. They are to be regarded as a weapon for holding the fort for the time being. During the next two months, consultations have been arranged between the Treasury and Customs and the other Departments which are concerned with the development of exports and the productive and developmental activities which we want to go on. Means will also be at once worked out for consultation with the Australian industries which will be affected. As a result of this, we would anticipate that proper flexibility will be achieved within the limits of the overall international financial result which must be achieved. Even during the interim period, it is also clear that special consideration will have to be given to special cases, such as, for example, the importation of petroleum products.

Some misapprehensions have arisen because of the banking action already taken. I would like it to be understood that in view of recent rumours about import restrictions it was essential that as a purely interim measure new bank credits should be held up until the full policy could be announced.

Closely associated with our own balance of payments problem is the problem of the whole sterling area. Our main reserves are held as sterling balances in London. But, for the non-sterling currencies which we require over and above our earnings, we must draw on the sterling area pool of such currencies, which is held by the United Kingdom. During recent months that pool has been dwindling at a rapid rate and, as the recent London conference established, prompt and decisive action must be taken to stop the fall. At the London conference the principal countries of the sterling area agreed to co-operate in applying such measures as they might think appropriate to meet the current crisis. Australia is one of the major countries of the sterling group, and we are determined to shoulder our proper share of responsibility. It is, therefore, necessary in any event that we should reduce further the rate of our expenditure upon non-sterling imports, including our imports from the dollar area. But such savings as could be effected by reduction of non-sterling imports would not come anywhere near closing the gap between our own receipts and out-goings, and we have therefore been forced to adopt the grievous expedient of reducing imports from the United Kingdom and other sterling area countries, along with those from countries outside the sterling group.

The Government realises that many problems will be created for business and industry by the present action, even though, as I have pointed out, the position is mitigated by the existence of substantial stocks at this end. I can only say that it will be our desire and policy to minimise these problems and to assist by sensible administration in the making of the necessary economic adjustments with the minimum of injury to businesses and individuals. But the stark fact is that we cannot gamble, or chance the future. The economic position of Australia is basically a sound one. Though the action now announced is necessarily of a negative kind, we are devoting much attention to the positive aspects of increasing our export income. We will hope moreover that the encouragement of overseas investments in Australia will itself contribute greatly in the long term to the stability of our international position.

15:3 IMPORT LICENSING: SCOPE AND OPERATION

Press statement issued by the Department of Trade and Customs on 8 March 1952.

Following upon the announcement by the Prime Minister that the Government had found it necessary to impose import restrictions on a wide scale, the Minister for Trade and Customs (Senator Neil O'Sullivan) has released particulars of the scope and operation of the associated import licensing measures. These measures came into operation at midnight on 7th March, and are promulgated in a Notice by the Minister for Trade and Customs in the Commonwealth Gazette on that date. . . .

Import restrictions already apply to goods of dollar area origin and Japanese origin and the present basis of import licensing on those countries will still continue. Except to the extent covered in the Ministerial Notice, goods imported into Australia from all countries are now subject to the provisions of the Customs (Import Licensing) Regulations.

For the purpose of the new restrictions, imports, other than the exceptions referred to in the Ministerial Notice, have been divided into two main categories of goods. The importation of goods in the 'A' Category will be limited to an annual value equivalent to 60% of the value of similar imports in the year 1950/51, which has been taken as the base year for the calculation of quotas under the new licensing measures. Certain goods in this category which, because of their nature, do not lend themselves readily to quota treatment, will be subject to administrative control. The remaining goods will be included in 'B' category and will be restricted to a total annual value not exceeding 20% of the value of all such goods in the base year 1950/51.

Importers would require to establish their individual quotas, for goods subject to quota control, by supplying to the Collectors of Customs, in their respective States, particulars of their importations during the base year 1950/51 and these particulars must be accompanied by a statutory declaration, in a form to be prescribed, certifying to the accuracy of the figures supplied. Quotas are not transferable and only those goods imported in the prospective quota holder's own name and entered by him at the Customs House may be included in his base year return for quota purposes. In cases where an importer in the base year imported goods into more than one State, separate particulars must be supplied for each State's importations. Details of the particulars required will be available from the Collectors of Customs in each State.

Importers would be at liberty to seek the sources of their supplies within the limits of their quotas from any country except countries in the dollar area and Japan. Also, because it has become necessary to place severe restrictions on category 'B' goods, viz. those falling within the category subject to limitation to 20% of base year values, it has been decided to treat the whole group of these goods as one item for the purpose of licensing administration. Importers who established quotas for the importation of goods in the lower category would be able to exercise freedom of choice in regard to the importation of goods falling within this category, provided the total value of their importations of such goods did not exceed the value of their established quotas. Goods which are included in the higher category, i.e. those which are subject to a 60% limit of the value of importations of similar goods in the base year, will be licensed on an item by item basis. Only importers of such goods in the base year will be permitted to obtain licences on the restricted basis for future importations of similar goods.

No outright prohibitions are being imposed under these new measures. . . .[1]

15:4 IMPORT LICENSING AND GREAT BRITAIN

Press statement by the Prime Minister (R. G. Menzies) on 15 March 1952.

I gather that Australia has been under fire in the House of Commons in consequence of her drastic import cuts. There has even been some suggestion of repudiation. Clearly our position and action have been misunderstood. I therefore make a brief statement of the relevant facts.

Australia is a British country, and is at all times willing and anxious to participate in discussions of overall policy and to accept her share of the burden involved in rectifying the overall position.

The Commonwealth Finance Ministers' Conference in January issued a broad statement of conclusions, two passages from which deserve quotation. They are:—

> It is quite clear that the only way to prevent recurrent drains on the central gold reserves is for every country in the area strenuously to endeavour to live within the means which are, or can be, available to it. The sterling area as a whole must succeed in this endeavour.

> It was also agreed that, where any country in the sterling area was likely to be in overall deficit, corrective measures should be taken as soon as possible, in order to relieve the current pressure on the resources of the area.

[1] The balance of the statement includes some details about licensing arrangements. No attempt has been made to document the methods of and changes in administration of import control over the period. Interested readers should see Harris (93) and Moffatt (130).

Now, in the case of Australia, the plain facts are (as I have previously announced) that, in the absence of any import restrictions save those upon dollar and Japanese goods, our overall deficit was, by June 30, 1952, likely to exceed £500 million.

There are some who say that Australia's imports should have been restricted two months ago; there are, so far as I know, none who say that our overall balance of payments can be rectified in time without import restrictions at all.

The immediately critical period for the sterling area, as the Chancellor has pointed out, is the second half of the calendar year 1952. Since there is always a time lag in the effectiveness of import controls, it is in that period that Australia's import restrictions will become most effective.

I now deal with two criticisms which emerge from the House of Commons debate. The first is that imports from the United Kingdom should have been left alone. The second is that, at any rate, there should have been no interference with the filling of existing orders, whether covered by irrevocable letters of credit or not. I will say something about each of these in turn.

We should have been delighted to leave United Kingdom exports to Australia untouched, and, as soon as our balance of payments position permits, we shall certainly review the measures we have been forced to adopt. We know how important her exports are to the United Kingdom, and how important they therefore are to the whole British Commonwealth. But we had, literally, no option. Our Australian export income for next year is estimated at about £600 million. Save to some extent in wheat, if additional plantings can be promptly made, we cannot quickly expand our exports, which are overwhelmingly of farm and pastoral products. To achieve balance in our international accounts, therefore, involves in the short run a cutting of our imports from their current figure of over £1200 million c.i.f. Of our current financial year's imports, as much as £780 million c.i.f. are estimated to come from sterling sources, as compared with £590 million c.i.f. from the same sources in 1950-51 and £440 million c.i.f. in 1949-50. The great bulk of these sterling imports come, of course, from the United Kingdom. It is thus clear that even if we made the most provocative discriminations against all non-sterling sources—and to do so would be to prejudice our export capacity and achievement most grievously—we would still be compelled either to make substantial cuts in our current imports from the United Kingdom or to run the risk of having to call upon the United Kingdom itself to find the sterling with which to pay for the excess.

The second criticism, that all existing orders should have been left untouched, is equally unsustainable. Many orders by Australian importers are placed for long and spread deliveries. Some were, at the time of our announcement, covered by irrevocable letters of credit. These will be honoured. Some were in course of active shipment. These will be received. Arrangements will also be made to give special consideration to the case of export goods being produced to special specifications and so on so that any proved cases of hardship may be fairly dealt with. To go further than this would be to make import restrictions both inadequate and impracticable. It is quite erroneous to describe an interference with business anticipation as a repudiation. To refuse to make such interferences would have involved not only a repudiation of the decision of the London conference that each member of the sterling area should achieve an overall balance in its international accounts, but also an abandonment by the Australian Government of responsibility for ensuring that what Australia buys Australia can and will pay for.

512

Two other points should, I think, be made. First, we are establishing a committee to review the initial basis of the import cuts and to rectify anomalies consistently with the overall financial objective. Second, it should be realised that interference with some business expectations is to be preferred to an international currency deficiency which could lead to repudiation of liabilities to pay for goods at a later stage.

15:5 AUSTRALIA'S IMPORT POLICY

The relaxation of Australian import restrictions that Mr. Menzies announced this week is expected to add about £A50 million to Australia's import bill in the fiscal year beginning on July 1st next; taken in conjunction with the relaxations announced towards the end of 1952, it will probably bring total Australian imports up to about £A650 million in that fiscal year, compared with a present annual rate of just over £A500 million and with recorded imports of £A1,050 million in the fiscal year 1951-52 and £A742 million in the fiscal year 1950-51. Since the new relaxations do not apply to imports from Japan and the dollar area, much of the benefit from them will accrue to exporters in this country, and the details of the new regulations will therefore be closely studied in Lancashire and the Midlands. . . .

All these relaxations will come into effect on April 1st. It will depend on Australia's general economic policy whether they are to be the harbinger of more good news to come, or merely an experiment that cannot last. It cannot be reiterated too frequently that Australia's present plight—and indeed much of the sterling area's plight as well—is due to that dominion's policy of encouraging a mushroom growth of secondary industries that its cost structure makes it unable to afford. So long as the wool boom kept its external accounts in balance, this predilection for diverting resources from productive to unproductive occupations could be regarded as Australia's own affair; since the wool boom was punctured, it is the rest of the sterling area that has had to make large (though hidden) subventions to keep up Australia's standard of life. Thanks to the import restrictions and some revival of the demand for wool, the dominion's external accounts are now in balance again and the subventions have therefore ceased; but Mr. Menzies announced this week that in determining the import relaxations his government has had clearly in mind the impact of high secondary imports on Australia's employment situation. If this means that the sheltering of an uneconomic and high cost pattern of production is now an immutable aim of Australian policy, then the other sterling area countries should make it clear that in the next wool crisis Australia will not be saved by the fruits of a capital outflow from this country between 1946 and 1952 that many people believe should never have been allowed.

Source: The Economist, 21 February 1953,
vol. 166, p. 504.

Domestic Policies and Trade

15:6 FALL IN AUSTRALIA'S INTERNATIONAL RESERVES AND INTENSIFICATION OF IMPORT RESTRICTIONS

Speech by the Prime Minister (R. G. Menzies) in the House of Representatives on 27 September 1955.

There are four major factors in our present situation. The first is that we have at home a high and growing money purchasing power, which gives rise to a level of demand for goods and buildings and equipment and services higher than ever before in our history. The second is that as such demand cannot, having regard to our population, materials and equipment, be entirely satisfied by Australian products, we have had a vast demand for imported goods; and as that demand exceeds our export earnings, our external balance of payments is in heavy deficit. The third is that any expansion of export earnings is made more difficult by substantially increasing levels of wages and costs, partly arising from the competition for scarce labour generated by excessive demand.

The fourth factor relates to important matters external to Australia. Our true prosperity is deeply affected by international trade and therefore by economic conditions in the countries with which we trade. This exposes us a good deal to what I will call the 'wind and weather' of the world's markets. The fact is that during the past two years the fortunes of international trade have not been as high for us. The terms of trade have moved against us; i.e. the prices of some of our major exports have declined, but the prices of other internationally traded commodities, such as rubber and the non-ferrous metals, have been rising as, indeed, have international shipping freights. On top of this, overseas trading practices are frequently not helpful. Particularly in the export of foodstuffs, we begin to encounter the use of subsidies and bilateral trade deals, as my colleague, the Treasurer, pointed out recently to the governors of the International Monetary Fund. . . .

In April, 1954, a large group of items was put on a 'no quota restriction' basis, which meant that licences were given for any amount so long as it could be shown that goods were genuinely on order and available. The results were so dramatic that in last October it became necessary to discontinue the no quota restriction system, which had proved a major factor in import pressure, and put the goods back on a quota basis. Wool prices fell in the 1954-55 season by about 11d. per lb. There were also some difficulties in selling wheat. Export income fell by £49,000,000, but imports continued to increase. International reserves fell. By March of this year it was clear that something would have to be done. As from 1st April, fairly severe additional restrictions were imposed on all classes of non-dollar imports, though, as honorable members will realize, such restrictions do not bring about an actual reduction of imports for several months. . . .

. . . we have decided that our external payments situation must be brought into full balance not later than the 30th June, 1956.

How can this be done? One immediate measure is, of course, the direct measure of intensifying import restrictions. . . Even when import restrictions are applied it is normally a matter of, at any rate, six months before they take effect in lower imports. It follows that the sooner they are applied the better. The Government has, therefore, decided that further restrictions designed to reduce the total of imports by around £80,000,000 f.o.b. will be brought into effect as from the 1st October. We anticipate that these further restrictions, supplementing the measures applied by the orders of last April, will bring imports down to a level which we can reasonably expect by June, 1956, to finance without further running down our external reserves. . . .

The rapid running down of our international reserves would, if we did nothing or too little about it, give rise to speculative pressures against the currency. In other words, people would begin to gamble on the chances that we would be forced to depreciate our currency by changing the exchange rate. . . On behalf of the Government, I state quite categorically that we are determined to have no depreciation of the currency. . . .

. . . we feel that, unless we are to have a permanently unbalanced economy in Australia, with import restrictions as a chronic feature of life, we must do something to stimulate our export income; we must open up new markets and retain and expand old ones. With our internal cost levels, this is not easy; and, indeed, it becomes more and more difficult as our domestic demands for more and more money and less work proceed. In the case of primary products, we are beginning to confront some growing competition from vendor countries willing to give credit terms to buyers and, in some cases, to support those credit terms by government guarantees at home.

In particular, if a sound basis can be found, and I hope and believe that it can, for an export credit scheme—having regard to some of the special difficulties and peculiarities of Australia's export trade which distinguishes it from that of other countries—such a scheme will be introduced. . . .

We are prepared to send strong missions overseas with special tasks to develop new markets. These missions would comprise practical men who know their goods and are experienced in salesmanship. We will be prepared ourselves to subscribe money liberally for this purpose. We have already given an earnest of this in our approach to trade publicity expenditure. . . .

Source: C.P.D. (H. of R.), vol. 7, pp. 964-74.

15:7 ECONOMIC MEASURES TO REDUCE INFLATION AND HELP DEFICIENCY IN BALANCE OF PAYMENTS

Statement by the Prime Minister (R. G. Menzies) in the House of Representatives on 14 March 1956.

It was therefore made clear, in September, that our objective was to restore our balance of payments by the end of June this year; to assist that object by import restrictions; and to make it certain, if necessary, by adopting fiscal or other measures which would restrain local inflation, diminish import demand, preserve our currency on the international markets and enable us to develop our position as a trading nation.

In my September statement, I discussed in some detail the problem of the *balance of payments* and of our *international reserves*, and endeavoured to explain the importance of achieving a balance by the end of June, 1956. . . .

The dominating cause of our external payments deficiency is the striking increase in the annual value of our imports and this in turn represents a demand which is the inevitable product of internal inflation.

. . . in the light of our experience to date and having regard to our additional import restrictions and to the measures which I am tonight announcing, there is every reason to suppose that our objective, of balancing our external accounts by the middle of this year, will be achieved. . . Measures beyond import restrictions are, of course, necessary if we are to have a lasting cure. . . .

. . . the attack on the productivity problem is still a matter for urgent attention. It is the positive, as opposed to the negative, of economic action. A constant appreciation of its importance induces an active and dynamic attitude, and serves to defeat stagnation. We have not yet fully understood that rapidly increasing population, industrial expansion, adequate national defence, high and stable employment, just social services, and rising real standards for the individual—to all of which we are as a nation dedicated—cannot be simultaneously achieved without increasing skill, organisation, and effort. To put it quite clearly, we cannot have increased development and increased individual consumption without increased individual production, saving and investment. . . .

It is inevitable that properly considered taxation measures should be the most powerful immediate instruments . . . any increases in taxation should be designed as far as possible to reduce inflation. In the light of these considerations we have decided upon the following courses of action.

1. In order to cut expenditure which promotes a high level of imports and also greatly increases an unsatisfied internal capital demand, we propose to have additional taxation upon motor vehicles and petrol.

2. In order to secure added revenue from items which are not the most essential and which should, therefore, make the fullest contribution to the elimination of deficit finance, we have decided to impose additional taxes on beer, spirits, tobacco, cigarettes and cigars.

3. In order to impose a check upon investment spending which although valuable is at present in total beyond the capacity of either saving or borrowing to provide, we propose to increase company taxation.

4. We propose to increase certain sales taxes upon less essential goods. . . .

These measures are not depression measures; they are designed to preserve our existing prosperity by checking inflation and therefore making our prosperity more stable and more secure. . . .

Source: *C.P.D.* (*H. of R.*), vol. 9, pp. 787-90.

15:8 IMPORT LICENSING: CRITICISM OF MINISTER'S POWERS AND LACK OF APPEAL FROM HIS DECISIONS

Speech by Senator R. C. Wright in the Senate on 27 March 1957.

At present, one of the most dynamic forces operating within the Commonwealth set-up is a system of import restrictions. It has been made necessary by an imbalance of the economy of Australia in relation to external trade. Probably all of us will admit that the system was made necessary by the need to protect the currency when other defences are unavailable. But that system of import restrictions is operating to stimulate the inflationary processes that are going on in our economy, and those inflationary processes are having a cruel effect upon many sections of our people. Every member of this Parliament who has expressed his views in this assembly has declared that it is a matter of urgent national duty to dampen down and arrest inflation.

That aspect of import restrictions does not concern me chiefly to-day. I am concerned now with the system by which the restrictions operate, because no measure has been through this Parliament to justify them. So far as I can discover, their ambit and operation are the complete prerogative of a Minister although he is, no doubt, in consultation with the Cabinet or a sub-committee of Cabinet. That executive power determines the volume of national trade that is permitted. It has the authority to vary that volume of trade from time to time. Moreover, it seems to be empowered to discriminate between essentials and non-essentials according to the conception of those terms held by the Minister or, in other words, the department he administers.

When we take our minds from the general matter of trade and focus upon the individual's share in the trade, we find that delay confronts those concerned. There is discrimination, and no rule whereby all persons of the one interest are entitled to equal treatment. The Minister's ipse dixit is the last word on the subject. It is not subject to any review for which there is constitutional provision. One does not need to do any more than state these bleak facts to excite the liberal-minded members of the Senate to the challenge, because that system presents a challenge to anybody who is jealous of either individual rights or parliamentary authority....

Source: *C.P.D. (S.)*, vol. 10, pp. 201-2.

15:9 IMPORT LICENSING APPEAL BOARDS

Statement by the Vice-President of the Executive Council (Senator N. O'Sullivan) in the Senate on 22 May 1957.

It seems to me that the substance of the [Senate Regulations and Ordinances] Committee's objections to the present licensing procedure was that there was no review of departmental decisions. The committee suggested to me that perhaps there could be devised some means, other than the establishment of a court, to review such decisions. I put the recommendations of the committee to my colleague, the Minister for Trade (Mr McEwen)....

As a result of that discussion, the Minister agreed to the establishment, in the various capital cities, of licensing review boards....

I propose to read a letter that I have received from the Minister for Trade... It is as follows:

21st May, 1957

My dear Minister,

I confirm my willingness to establish Licensing Advisory Review Boards to sit in each of the States to hear applicants who have been unsuccessful in applications for import licences and to make a report to the Minister for Trade. There has been a very substantial liberalization of licensing since April 1st and the understanding is that cases submitted to the Review Boards would be restricted to applications made subsequent to the April 1st relaxations.

This would not preclude any application which had been rejected prior to 1st April being re-submitted to the Department.

The present Internal Appeals Committee of the Department which re-examines many cases each week, and which is the quickest method of getting a reconsideration, would continue to function, but failure before that Committee would not preclude appeal to the proposed Licensing Advisory Review Board.

S

A function of the Boards would be to ensure equitable treatment of individual cases within the framework of Government policy decisions.

The Licensing Advisory Review Boards would not hear applications which could be approved only by departure from the current policy of the Government. This is so the operation of the Advisory Review Boards could not have the result of increasing the total licensing ceiling decided by the Government.

It would also mean that the Boards would have to make any recommendations having regard to the allocations by the Cabinet to the 'A' and 'B' categories and the Administrative section of the import budget.

The Boards would be informed by the Minister for Trade of these basic financial policy decisions of the Government and of the details of policy under which the Department is operating.

The Boards would not hear frivolous appeals and would not hear appeals which were based upon any objection by the applicant to the policy of the Government.

The procedure envisaged is that the applicant would first submit to the Board the facts of his case, upon which the Board would consider whether his application could be approved within Government policy. If it could not be approved within Government policy, the applicant would be so advised. If it could be approved within Government policy, the hearing would proceed.

A Board would consist of two non-governmental members chosen for their experience in commercial affairs and an officer of the Department of Trade as Chairman.

Yours sincerely,

J. McEwen

Source: *C.P.D.* (*S.*), vol. 10, pp. 956-7.

15:10 IMPORT LICENSING REVIEW BOARDS

Press statement by the Minister for Trade (J. McEwen) on 25 July 1957.

The Minister for Trade, Mr. J. McEwen, announced today that the recently constituted Import Licensing Advisory Review Boards would begin their first sittings next week in Sydney. Boards have also been set up for the other States, and it is expected that they would also commence hearings within the next few weeks.

Mr. McEwen said the Boards had been set up to supplement the existing machinery within the Department of Trade for reviewing appeals against decisions of the Import Licensing Branch. The Advisory Review Boards whose members are well known in commerce and industry, will provide importers with a final method of appeal, and will ensure that the problems of importers will be reviewed by those who had a first-hand acquaintance with the problems. The Boards will fix their own methods of procedure and will not be bound by formal rules in arriving at an equitable decision. For this reason applicants will normally be expected to present their own case, but may have secretarial assistance or engage a Customs agent to present their case if this has been their practice. . . .

If the appeal is against an original decision of the Import Licensing Branch, it will first be heard by the Departmental Import Licensing Appeal Committee. This will save delay in a large number of cases, as an import licence will be issued immediately if the appeal is upheld.

If the appeal is refused by the Import Licensing Appeal Committee, there is an unconditional right of appeal to an Import Licensing Advisory Review Board. This right of appeal extends to all applications made after 1st April, 1957. The Chairman of the Board will advise each importer of the date when the case will be heard and the venue of the hearing. . . .

When importers make their first appeal, they may indicate whether they wish it to be submitted to the Import Licensing Appeal Committee. If they prefer, they may await the decision of the Import Licensing Appeal Committee before deciding to make a final appeal.

15:11 CEILING RAISED FOR IMPORTS: GOVERNMENT REPEATS WISH TO REMOVE IMPORT RESTRICTIONS ALTOGETHER

Press statement by the Prime Minister (R. G. Menzies) on 1 April 1957.

The Government has decided to raise the ceiling for imports for the financial year 1957-8 to £775m. f.o.b. This is calculated to permit additional imports of £75m.

This decision by the Government follows a close study of the balance of payments situation and prospects. . . .

The Government still aims to get rid of import restrictions altogether. This result will, however, depend on the achievement of a number of conditions including a still further increase in the volume of exports, favourable terms of trade, strong overseas reserves and sound internal policies with the restraints on total demand for goods and services which such policies require. These conditions are by no means impossible. In fact we have made good progress towards achieving them. . . .

15:12 GROWTH AND IMPORT RESTRICTIONS

RESOURCES FROM ABROAD

In recent times it has been argued that our import restrictions are a sign that Australia is trying to expand too fast. The continuance of these controls in a severe form is said to indicate that demand for imports chronically exceeds our capacity to pay for them. From this it is concluded that if we try to maintain a rate of growth as high as that of recent years we shall be forced to attempt still more drastic reductions of imports.

The argument relies to a considerable extent upon the experience of post-war years during which there have always been import restrictions in one form or another. But it is well to bear in mind that, even in the past five years when there have been overall restrictions aimed at keeping down the general level of imports, the circumstances necessitating these restrictions have varied from time to time and could not always be attributed wholly to demands arising from our expansion.

In the earlier post-war years, the restrictions then current were designed to conserve particular currencies, then scarce, rather than to limit total imports.
Supplies were, of course, scarce in that period and we would certainly have taken
more imports if we could have got them; but it is not certain that, even with
greater availability abroad, imports would have run to excessive levels. The effect
of the restrictions then in force was rather to increase the cost of such imports
as we did get by channelling demand to more costly sources of supply. Later on,
there was a period, between 1949 and 1952, when our total volume of imports
was at least equal to our needs, even though dollar imports were scarce; and
there was one remarkable year, 1951-52, when we got far more imports than we
could absorb and excessive stocks built up.

Obviously, of course, our attempted rate of expansion could be pushed so high
that we would have no hope of meeting the import demand it created. But it does
not necessarily follow that because we have had balance of payments difficulties
in recent years our rate of growth must have been too high; nor does it follow that
if we continue to expand at the current rate we must continue to have such
difficulties. It may be that the argument associates too closely the increasing
demands for imports which naturally arise from growth and those which arise
from recurrent but temporary waves of spending such as we have experienced at
least twice in post-war years. Given steady rather than spasmodic expansion and
given also appropriate restraint on total expenditure and a proper relationship
between consumption expenditure and saving, there may be no unavoidable
reason why spending booms, with their consequent excessive demands for imports,
should always accompany growth. It may be too that the argument under-rates
the possibilities of larger export earnings in the future and therefore our future
ability to pay for imports. Much depends here on world prices for raw materials,
and especially on prices for wool, which are always unpredictable; but, as will
be argued later, there seems to be no inherent reason why our export earning
could not grow much further.

The argument is valuable in the emphasis it lays on the harmful nature of
import restrictions and the dangers that lie in a continuance of them. There is
nothing good to be said for import restrictions as such. They are damaging in
their impact on local trade and industry, on the trade and industry of other
countries, and on our relationships with those other countries. They cause
dislocation to some local industries and give arbitrary protection to others, the
result on both counts being to force costs up. Administratively they create the
most intractable problems for which in many cases only arbitrary solutions are
possible. They have had to be used as an expedient to cope with balance of
payments adversities; but all Governments have recognized their drawbacks and
dangers and have sought to eliminate them, or where that could not be done, to
mitigate their incidence.

It is a further merit of the argument that it draws attention to the dependence
of growth upon imports and therefore to the need for a progressive increase in
our means to pay for imports.

Source: *1957 and Beyond: An Economic
Survey*, Commonwealth of Australia, paper
no. 2597/57, Government Printer, Canberra.

15:13 INTERNATIONAL MONETARY FUND ANNOUNCES DECISION ON DISCRIMINATORY RESTRICTIONS ON 25 OCTOBER 1959

TEXT OF DECISION

The following decision deals exclusively with discriminatory restrictions imposed for balance of payments reasons.

In some countries, considerable progress has already been made toward the elimination of discriminatory restrictions; in others, much remains to be done. Recent international financial developments have established an environment favorable to the elimination of discrimination for balance of payments reasons. There has been a substantial improvement in the reserve positions of the industrial countries in particular and widespread moves to external convertibility have taken place.

Under these circumstances, the Fund considers that there is no longer any balance of payments justification for discrimination of members whose current receipts are largely in externally convertible currencies. However, the Fund recognises that where such discriminatory restrictions have long been maintained, a reasonable amount of time may be needed fully to eliminate them. But this time should be short and members will be expected to proceed with all feasible speed in eliminating discrimination against member countries, including that arising from bilateralism.

Notwithstanding the extensive moves towards convertibility, a substantial portion of the current receipts of some countries is still subject to limitations on convertibility, particularly in payments relations with state trading countries. In the case of these countries the Fund will be prepared to consider whether balance of payments considerations would justify the maintenance of some degree of discrimination, although not as between countries having externally convertible currencies. In this connection the Fund wishes to reaffirm its basic policy on bilateralism as stated in its decision of June 22, 1955.

Source: U.S.A. *Department of State Bulletin*, vol. XLI, no. 1063, 1959, pp. 681-2.

15:14 IMPORTS TO BE UNRESTRICTED EXCEPT BY CUSTOMS TARIFF

Statement by the Prime Minister (R. G. Menzies) in Canberra on 21 February 1960.

. . . it is vital to build up resistance to the rise of costs and prices . . . the Commonwealth has decided to intervene in the current Basic Wage Case before the Commonwealth Conciliation and Arbitration Commission. . . .

In the current year we have budgeted for a deficit. But in the circumstances I have described, we propose, for the new financial year, to do all in our power to avoid any deficit finance. . . .

The Government is very much in accord with and will support the policy of restraining the growth of excessive liquidity.

... Along with our review of the internal economy we have this week examined our external trade and payments position. It is one of considerable strength. Whilst imports have risen, exports have risen still further. We have had some success in borrowing abroad, and there has evidently been a quite large inflow of private capital. As a result we now hold considerable reserves of gold and foreign exchange and we have, in addition, our quota in the International Monetary Fund which was increased last year to 300 million dollars. This may be regarded as in the nature of a second line reserve.

Over the past couple of years we have relaxed import restrictions by successive steps and this, I am certain, has been all for the good of the economy. We have now decided to move to a position in which, as nearly as possible, imports will be unrestricted except by the Customs Tariff. It will be necessary for a time to retain some licensing arrangements on certain commodities to meet the special problems arising out of existing commitments, but that will be all the restriction that remains. ...

15:15 IMPORT RESTRICTIONS VIRTUALLY ABOLISHED

Statement by the Minister for Trade (J. McEwen) in Canberra on 22 February 1960.

Sweeping changes in import licensing were announced today by the Minister for Trade, the Rt. Hon. John McEwen. The changes go far towards the complete abolition of import restrictions.

Imports currently worth approximately £800 million a year will now be exempt from import licensing. The items comprise some 90% of our present imports.

Mr. McEwen recalled that it had always been the Government's policy to remove import restrictions as soon as the balance of payments position permitted.

Our external trade and payments position is one of considerable strength. Our overseas reserves are high and our export earning prospects good. That we have reached this position at a time when a number of our important export commodities still face marketing difficulties overseas is evidence, Mr. McEwen said, of the soundness of the Government's economic and trade policies in recent years.

These sound policies and achievements have enabled us to move to a position where nine-tenths of our imports are free of import control. Any person may now import any of these goods.

A small sector of our imports will remain subject to licensing control. In commenting on this, Mr. McEwen said that statistics of licences issued have been of considerable usefulness in the administration of the Trade Agreement with Japan, particularly as regards those provisions which relate to its effects on Australian industry.

The Government considers that it cannot deny itself or industry access to this important information until it can, after consultation with industry and commerce, devise suitable alternative arrangements.

It is therefore proposed that, for the time being, some of the commodities of particular importance in trade with Japan will remain subject to licensing control. However, where the goods are subject to quota restriction the quotas will, in general, be increased by 20% over the previous level. Provision will continue to be made for the admission of new importers.

A few other items must remain under control until special problems associated with them are resolved.

The retention of licensing control over a small field of trade did not, Mr. McEwen said, imply any departure from the established policy of successive Governments of using the Customs Tariff, and the Tariff Board machinery, as the normal method of protecting economic and efficient Australian industries from import competition. On the contrary it is the Government's firm intention to remove licensing from these commodities as soon as various commitments can be met in other ways.

Mr. McEwen said that in November last year he had announced the Government's intention to license timber on a replacement basis as from 1st April, 1960, and to abolish licensing discrimination against Dollar Area motor vehicles as from 1st October, 1960. It had been decided to adhere to that time-table but to exempt the goods from licensing as from the above dates. The last element of discrimination against Dollar Area goods will disappear when North American vehicles are exempted from licensing.

15:16 ASSOCIATED CHAMBERS OF MANUFACTURES' REACTION TO DECISION TO ABANDON IMPORT LICENSING

Press statement by the Director of the Associated Chambers of Manufactures (R. W. C. Anderson) on 23 February 1960.

On the 22nd February the Prime Minister, after a survey by Cabinet of the Australian economy, announced that the Government had decided to virtually abandon import licensing. . . .

ACMA has long recognised the Government's intention to get rid of import licensing when our external position permitted this action. Nevertheless our advice to the Government has been that relaxations should be made cautiously and in such a way as to avoid any 'back-pedalling'.

We would expect the Government's advisors to be confident that our current level of reserves will be sufficient to finance the drain on them which must follow from the virtual abandonment of import licensing. It is difficult, however, to arrive at this conclusion from an examination of available statistical material.

The accumulation (slight though it is) of reserves which has been taking place has been made possible not only because imports have been controlled, but also because of our extremely high rate of capital inflow. This is a pretty tenuous element on which to 'gamble' with the development of Australian industry. Admittedly significant contributions have been received from our capital account in the last few years, but this item is capable of violent fluctuation. And it is by no means impossible that the just announced decision which exposes Australian industry, quite abruptly, to competition from imports, will be followed by a falling away of capital inflow.

To put it briefly, it can surely be argued that our balance of payments position is therefore not one of 'considered strength'. We will all be anxiously watching our import rate and movements in our international reserves.

In announcing its import decision the Government has not referred to the views of the Consultative Committee on Import Policy. This important Committee was set up by the Government to advise on such matters as the overall level of imports; usually their views are recorded by the Minister for Trade when announcing import changes.

Perhaps then this particular decision is one taken basically on 'internal' grounds alone. Having diagnosed the complaint as being one which can be remedied only by a rapid increase in the supply of goods, 'external' or balance of payments considerations become of secondary importance.

But what will this dramatic action mean for Australian industry? Let me speculate. The substantial unused capacity which exists right across a wide range of Australian industry (and this makes it difficult to understand how demand is racing away from supply) will almost certainly be added to. Production costs of manufacturers, already being increased by recent wage increases, will be further increased as their volume of production falls following increased imports.

The Government has in making its new importing arrangements recognised one particular problem of Australian industry. Although increasing the licensing rate whenever the goods have been restrictively licensed the Minister for Trade has announced that licensing will be maintained on all those items which concern the ACMA Japanese Industry Panels. There are some hundreds of items in this category and although they form a relatively small proportion of Australia's import bill they represent a hard core of goods especially 'sensitive' insofar as competition from Japan is concerned.

One last thought; the overnight freeing from licensing of goods now being imported at an annual rate of £400 million will inevitably call for a drastic re-adjustment in Australian industry. The decision which has been taken by the Government must have been taken with a full awareness of this—and of the likely consequences in employment. The Government has a policy of full employment. The next twelve months will present a challenge to the Government in this field.

15:17 MANUFACTURERS' REACTIONS TO ENDING OF IMPORT CONTROLS

The vaunted Australian attribute of self-reliance is nowhere to be seen in the manufacturers' reactions to the virtual ending of import controls. The air is filled with groans of dismay from their group organisations. Disaster is on the horizon, catastrophe is round the corner, and chaos has come again. The consumers—whose problems the manufacturers tend to forget—may be excused for ignoring the din of disagreement with the Government's decision. They have too often heard the 'death knell' proclaimed by the spokesmen of this or that industry.

The manufacturers, of course, are entitled to seek whatever protection they can persuade the Tariff Board to give them. But implicit in their outcry against the abandonment of import controls is the belief that these controls were devised specifically for their benefit. This is nonsense, but the fact that it has taken root in wide sectors of Australian industry is yet another proof of the damage which the imposition of trade restrictions does to a healthy business philosophy.

No country can, under modern conditions, do without a Customs tariff. In Australia enormous benefits have been derived from its existence, but at the same time it provides an undesirable shield for inefficient industries. The import controls, introduced eight years ago to deal with the nation's balance-of-payment difficulties, clearly came to be regarded by manufacturers in this country as an essential addition to the tariff wall. Now that this superstructure is to be dismantled they are 'staggered'.

They need not be. If they are efficient they can count on being safeguarded—by tariff machinery and, in the case of Australian-Japanese trade, by treaty provisions as well—where the national interest clearly requires it. They should demand no more than that if they have any regard at all for the welfare of the Australian consumer, who now appears to have some chance of benefiting from a wider choice of goods and more reasonable quality and prices.

Source: Leading article in *Sydney Morning Herald*, 24 February 1960.

16

BALANCE OF PAYMENTS:
EXPORT PROMOTION AND THE CASE FOR A SUSTAINED EXPORT DRIVE

The documents in this section relate primarily to export policy. Those of wider character have been chosen and edited less with an eye to their revelations of general economic policies held by the Menzies government in the early sixties than to their recognition of the first importance of export policies.

The general documents also emphasise a point appropriate to any consideration of the balance of payments: the relationship between national economic objectives and external viability.

Export policies have received considerable attention already in this book for they permeate our multilateral policies (Part B), our bilateral trading arrangements (Part C), our domestic measures for stimulating agricultural production (Section 13), and the various policy statements on the import position (for example 15:6). All these policies properly belong to the usual meaning of an 'export drive'. In this section, however, the documents for the most part refer to programs of a more directly 'promotional' character. Some documents (for example 16:17) cover the wider aspects as well as the promotional measures more fully reviewed in 16:10. Despite some difficulty in classifying the documents a separation is made into (A) those dealing with specific measures for promoting exports, and (B) those emphasising the inter-relationship of export and other economic policies. The classification is one of emphasis only, for the subjects are not mutually exclusive.

It can fairly be said that all governments since the war have been conscious of the need to promote exports. The Chifley Administration strengthened and expanded the trade commissioner service. It also foreshadowed

the establishment through the Commonwealth Bank of export credit guarantee facilities which would reduce the financial risks to export trade, and the establishment of a joint Government and Commercial Export Trading Corporation which would actively promote Australia's export trade in primary and manufactured goods (2:2; see also 16:1, 16:2).

The first idea was finally given effect by the Menzies Administration in May 1956 when the Export Payments Insurance Corporation (EPIC) was established (16:6). The other proposal has not materialised, although several other forms of export incentive have been introduced. Some of the special promotional programs sponsored by the Department of Trade and Industry, in which private industry and the department are linked in the sales promotion of specific products, are of the character contemplated in the original Chifley proposals.[1]

Export promotion is seen as a need, but out of perspective the term has little meaning. Thus, if goods of the right quality and in quantity are not available to sell or if markets are not open for competitive selling, the impact of special export aids—publicity, trade commissioners, export financial incentives, investment guarantees—are of little avail (16:5). Nevertheless, in a setting of efficient production and growing market opportunities especially for processed goods at least in some regions, export promotion has significance. So while the whole range of policies affecting export production and selling make up the 'export drive' (16:3, 16:5 and especially 16:9, 16:10),[2] the documents here are mostly limited to those which offer stimulus to export selling by offsetting the costs of inexperience in export, by publicising our products, and by insuring against important non-commercial risks.

Unfortunately, the documents do not give adequate information on trade publicity, the extent of the trade commissioner service, the actual operation of trade missions, etc., some discussion of which will be found in the Vernon Report.[3] The Committee, however, found it hard to obtain the kind of material which lends itself to critical appraisal. There is a good deal of room for examination of annual budget papers and departmental papers before the actual magnitude of activities can be gauged, let alone any authoritative comment made on them. No attempt is made to do so here.

The Vernon Committee raised one or two new ideas, including special assistance for investment in export capacity and guarantees for Australian investment abroad.[4] The latter has been substantially met (16:12).

Not the least important part of export promotion is the development of public consciousness of the need, especially on the part of manufacturers, to be active in export. The Department of Trade (16:4)[5] and its two advisory affiliates, the Export Development Council (EDC) and the Manufacturing Industries Advisory Council (MIAC) (16:7, 16:8), especially the former,

[1] For example, the Australian Textile Export Corporation Ltd is an organisation to which the Commonwealth government contributes money, as do a number of private firms. The Corporation offers assistance to all manufacturers of all textile products in the establishment of permanent and profitable export markets.

[2] Indeed, since import policies also affect market opportunities, any 'export drive' has to be set in the total perspective of trade policy. The most obvious *raison d'être* for establishing the Department of Trade arises in this way—as can be seen in the need to have a 'whole' approach in dealing with GATT and important trade treaties such as those with the United Kingdom and Japan.

[3] See especially vol. I, ch. 12, paras. 93-103 and vol. II, app. K, paras. 172-93 (pp. 1032-4).

[4] Vol. I, ch. 12, paras. 97-9.

[5] See Deane (70) for an account of the circumstances leading to the formation of the department.

have carried an important task here. All senior ministers, but especially the Prime Minister, the Minister for Trade and Industry, and the Treasurer, have hammered away at the particular theme of secondary exports as well as the more general need for expanding total export sales. The Prime Minister's comment on 'increasing public awareness' (16:9) is fair and reflects not only the general efforts of himself and ministers but also in even larger measure the steady and cumulative efforts of the EDC and MIAC—especially in industrial and commercial circles. It should be added, too, that many manufacturers are discovering, to their pleasant surprise, that Australia can produce manufactured goods competitively for export: an experience capable of a favourable snowballing action.

As noted in Section 15, we have not attempted to document one highly important aspect of export effectiveness, namely shipping freights. These are naturally of great importance to Australia, whose long distance from major markets makes very substantial the difference between c.i.f. and f.o.b. values. There is some substance, too, in the allegation, often made by would-be exporters, that the advantage of nearness to South-East Asian and Pacific Island markets is offset by the failure to secure from oversea shipping companies freight rates which reflect our advantage in distance compared with European and North American competitors. Heavy freights, particularly if discriminatory, undo much of the comparative advantage otherwise enjoyed in production costs of many products. The subject is one bristling with controversy, both economic and political: suggestions for a national oversea shipping service naturally grow stronger with each increase in export freight rates.

Among the more promising developments is the move towards 'containerisation', but documentation on this and other aspects of shipping policies must await some other volume.[6]

For the rest of the topics strictly within 'export promotion' the documents must speak for themselves, assisted by the bibliographical references given. Two exceptions may be made. The powers of the Export Payments Insurance Corporation have been considerably enlarged (16:11, 16:12). As yet, however, there has been little use made of them although the corporation has done well in terms of its original charter.[7] The other exception is to draw

[6] A short statement on freight determination and the industry bodies engaged in negotiations is contained in the Vernon Report (11), vol. II, app. K, paras. 213-33.

[7] EPIC produces good brochures on its policies and informative Annual Reports. An account is also given in the Vernon Report, vol. II, app. K, paras. 180-91. Since the last sentence of paragraph 188 is ambiguous an explanatory comment is offered. The sentence reads: 'However, an important difference between Australia and some industrialised countries is that its exports generally involve little risk for exporters.' Since a great part of Australia's produce is sold through marketing boards to established markets (wheat, apples and pears, butter and cheese, dried fruit) or is purchased at auction on oversea account through agents in Australia (raw wool), the greater part of Australian

attention to 16:13, which is an extract from a valuable Treasury document. This mentions beef roads, port facilities, and modernisation of railways. This list of aids to exports could have been expanded greatly by referring to CSIRO research, fertiliser subsidies, and assistance to farm extension services. Some Colombo Plan projects could perhaps be regarded as indirect aids to export development, except that the results are incidental to other objectives and, in any case, are too spasmodic to be regarded as consistent stimuli to export expansion.

The Case for a Sustained Export Drive

The balance of the documents in this section arise from the anti-inflationary measures of November 1960 and subsequent declarations of policy, concluding with the announcement of the terms of reference of the Committee of Economic Enquiry, the Vernon Committee (16:19), itself an important reflection of the government's growing concern with the course of economic events after November 1960. It is not our concern to try to reflect the widespread and deeply felt controversies which attended the November 1960 measures and the recession of 1961-2; nor to pass judgment on the measures or the general policies promulgated.[8]

In relation to trade policy the documents confirm a number of important and relevant points. The first is that the Australian community reacts sharply to a recession—the emphasis on the importance of full employment in 1945 was not misplaced. The government's concern with this reaction is reflected in the February 1961 consultations with industry. Secondly, the November 1960 experience merely confirmed the probability that full employment and inflationary pressures will continue to go hand in hand and are often likely to call for corrective measures. Thirdly, the outstanding feature of domestic booms is the spillover into import demand. Sometimes this excessive demand for imports will call for direct curbs of the kind reviewed in Section 15. In any case, the inflationary cause of excessive imports normally requires restrictive internal (credit and fiscal) measures. Yet the 1960-2 experience showed how difficult it is to take corrective action without giving rise to

---

sales carry little risk. Export insurance is relevant to the selling of Australian manufactures (including processed wool and foodstuffs sold by Australian principals). For this reason, EPIC's ordinary transactions are likely to remain a small percentage of total exports but vital in developing an export trade in manufactures. Nevertheless it is open to marketing authorities to insure with EPIC either in the regular way or with EPIC's and the government's consent under the 'national interest' section. EPIC has, in fact, been insuring a substantial portion of the sales of dairy produce by the Australian Dairy Produce Board. With a world trend for governments short of foreign exchange to seek credit terms for bulk purchases of primary products (with attendant risks), it is possible that some of Australia's future supplies of wool and minerals may be sold in this fashion and require insurance. Wheat is already sold to China and India on credit terms.

[8] Tariff policy was an important part of the debate which reached its peak in 1961 and 1962. This debate is partially documented in Section 14.

deflation and loss of confidence. It also gave yet another example of the inter-relationship of problems of ensuring growth and full employment within the constraint of external viability: at least in the short term the two can conflict.[9]

Less easily established is the presence of a continuing strain on the balance of payments associated with sustained economic growth under conditions of full employment. The documents here rather reflect the conviction that export growth is a limiting factor in economic growth than establish it beyond doubt. This problem arises if growth leads to a stronger upward trend in imports and other trade debits than in export earnings or equivalent credits. The documents here and in the earlier chapters do indicate a recognition that while high reserves, including substantial access to IMF 'second line reserves', may reduce the number of occasions for direct curbs (or tightening existing curbs) on imports, the *trend* of imports is likely to be such that there must be matching trend growth in exports or other net credits (16:18). It is interesting to notice Holt's explicit reference to attracting oversea investment as an element in ability to meet import needs (16:15). The terms of reference of the Vernon Committee (16:19) called for some light on this general problem: their Report attempts to offer some. The Report certainly confirms the emphasis given by the Prime Minister (16:18) and the Minister for Trade (16:10), to the need for a sustained export drive. This is a reasonable policy, for while some import replacement may occur it will not be sufficient to obviate the need for rising export earnings; nor can a rising and steady trend in net apparent capital inflow be assured as an alternative. For the one thing that seems certain to be associated with a high rate of growth under conditions of full employment is a rising absolute volume (and value) of imports. The rate of growth may well be a little less than the rate of growth in Gross National Product, but it is likely to require a substantial growth in export earnings which are by no means automatically promoted by full employment or even by capital inflow. An adequate rate of growth in export earnings requires a constant attention to the details of an export drive.[10]

[9] For discussion of the general problem see Vernon Report (11), vol. I, chs. 1, 2, and 17 *passim.*

[10] Although somewhat unsympathetic to the general argument in the Vernon Report and especially to its emphasis on the need to sustain a strong export drive in order to contain long-term pressures on the balance of payments, the Treasury authors of *The Australian Balance of Payments, February 1966* (5), from which Document 16:13 is drawn, do themselves concede the importance of maintaining and expanding competitive export industries. They are a little prone to overlook balance of payments debits sometimes associated with export earnings as, for example, in their otherwise fair criticism of the Committee's understatement of prospective earnings from mineral exports. See also Crawford (62), Perkins (137), pp. 108-18. For an earlier examination of the empirical evidence on relative movements in Australian import and export propensities see Lundberg and Hill (113). The Treasury document gives some useful comments on many other aspects of the subjects of this section, including a particularly

Yet frequent references to the need for a sustained export drive may well worry officials (and their ministers) who realise that progress is necessarily slow, for no magic wands can be waved although the development of mineral exports has something of this character. They are entitled to remind us, as many documents in this book do, that export policy is a complex affair with many strands. The basic need for Australian exports is for other countries to follow expansive policies likely to encourage imports—that is policies of full employment and economic growth. Given this, it is one thing for the Australian government to open up market opportunities—a clear purpose of our international and bilateral trade negotiations; it is another to assist in selling goods by 'promotional' aids of one form or another. It is still another, and no less important, to have an adequate quantity of goods to sell of right quality and price.

Given these three senses of the term 'export drive' a great many of the documents in this book are directly concerned with export policy. What the final half-dozen documents do is to confirm the key importance of export policy not only to continuing viability in the balance of payments situation but also as a major support to 'a high rate of economic and population growth with full employment'.

A. EXPORT PROMOTION

16:1 COMMONWEALTH EXPORTS CORPORATION

Reply by the Prime Minister (J. B. Chifley) to a question by
A. W. Fadden in the House of Representatives on 6 June 1945.

Mr. Fadden—Has the Acting Prime Minister read the press report of a meeting of an exports development group in Sydney, representative of primary and secondary industries, at which concern was expressed at the Commonwealth Government's proposal for the formation of a Commonwealth Exports Corporation? Has the honorable gentleman noted that a resolution was carried, protesting emphatically against the proposed formation of a government or semi-government organization to handle the export trade, and insisting that commercial interests be encouraged to exert every effort, and to apply their wider experience, in the direction of the rehabilitation, expansion and development of Australia's export trade on a sound and economic basis, without government interference? Before

---

useful reminder of the importance, for Australian export hopes, of successful policies of economic growth in other countries.

For an introduction to the general relation between trade and economic growth, the non-professional reader would find helpful a small book by Kindleberger (101). He is likely to enjoy fitting Australia into Table 11-1 (p. 178), which gives the trading and growth characteristics of countries in different stages of development.

further action is taken by the Government, will he ensure that representatives of the interests concerned shall be given an opportunity to submit their views to the Government?

Mr. Chifley—I have not seen the press report referred to. I assure the right honorable gentleman that the Government statement in regard to the proposed corporation was designed to help, not to hinder in any way, Australia's export trade, where it can be conducted without Government advice or assistance. On behalf of the Government, I undertake that discussions will be held with all those who are interested in our export trade. The proposals do not constitute an attempt to obtain a Government monopoly in the export trade. Proposals have been submitted by manufacturers and other bodies, which rather welcome the idea that there should be export guarantees of some sort.

Source: *C.P.D.*, vol. 182, p. 2568.

16:2 EXPORT TRADING CORPORATION PROPOSED

The major proposal made by the Commission for the encouragement of export trade on a permanent basis was for the establishment by the Government of an export trading corporation designed generally to supplement, but not to supplant, other channels of export trade and specifically to assist small firms unable to bear the expense of overseas marketing organisations. Prior to the war there had been limited opportunities for manufacturers and for traders to develop an export .echnique appropriate to the overseas sale of Australian manufactured goods. However, with the expansion which took place during the war, manufacturing had reached a stage of development which warranted particular attention being given to the question of production for export. There were many favourable factors, though special difficulties occasioned by shortages also existed. Apart from these, however, it was considered that many firms which would otherwise be precluded from participation in export trade would be enabled to participate by the establishment of an organisation responsible, inter alia, for obtaining orders overseas and placing them with suitable manufacturers; for undertaking shipment and delivery of orders in accordance with buyers' requirements, with particular reference to adherence to specifications, packing, etc. and for providing a service of guaranteeing bills.

Although it was suggested that both the Commonwealth Government and private interests should jointly subscribe to the corporation, it was not intended that it should have any monopoly, or that there should be any compulsion on exporters to use the facilities provided. For various reasons the proposal has not been pursued.

Source: Department of Post-war Reconstruction, *Memorandum of the work of the Secondary Industries Commission 1943-49*, October 1949, p. 56.

16:3 EXPORT DRIVE

Speech by the Prime Minister (R. G. Menzies) in the House of Representatives on 27 September 1955.

Nevertheless, we feel that, unless we are to have a permanently unbalanced economy in Australia, with import restrictions as a chronic feature of life, we must do something to stimulate our export income; we must open up new markets and retain and expand old ones. . . .

The Government has been positive in the export field, but will now step up still further the tempo of its efforts. It has reason to believe that all industry interests concerned will welcome this and extend their fullest collaboration.

I propose, for one thing, to arrange discussions with farmers' representatives, and I hope that all exporters will be willing, as part of an export drive, to re-examine with us traditional trade practices if the prospect of new markets with old or new customers warrants this. Indeed, I do offer the general observation that as the world becomes more competitive, not less, the placid trade methods of earlier years may have to be modified in more ways than one before we are through.

We are prepared to send strong missions overseas with special tasks to develop new markets. These missions would comprise practical men who know their goods and are experienced in salesmanship. We will be prepared ourselves to subscribe money liberally for this purpose. We have already given an earnest of this in our approach to trade publicity expenditure. . . .[1]

Source: C.P.D. (H. of R.), vol. 7, pp. 972-3.

16:4 DEPARTMENT OF TRADE ESTABLISHED

On 11th January, 1956, His Excellency the Governor-General in Council, under authority of section 64 of the Constitution, abolished the Department of Commerce and Agriculture and the Department of Trade and Customs and established the Department of Trade, the Department of Primary Industry and the Department of Customs and Excise. . . .

In announcing this decision the Prime Minister said:

The principal departmental re-organisation is to be found in the creation, for urgent and obvious purposes, of a new Department of Trade which will not only embrace the trade aspects of the present Department of Commerce and Agriculture, including the work of the statutory marketing boards for certain primary industries, but will also be equipped to ensure that both inward and outward trade are dealt with comprehensively. The new department will take over from Trade and Customs the administration of the Tariff Board and the Central Import Licensing Committee. The normal administration of import licensing, subject to the rules laid down in the new department, will remain with Customs.

In order that the Department of Trade may not, under these circumstances, be overloaded and so that it may direct its major attention to the stimulation of

[1] See also other extracts from the same speech in 15:6.

trade, a new Department of Primary Industry is being created. It will, subject to the activities of the Department of Trade in respect of marketing boards, deal with the Commonwealth's activities in relation to primary industries, including sugar, cotton and wine, which have hitherto been in the Department of Trade and Customs. It will also embrace such matters as the tractor bounty and the sulphur bounty, fisheries and whaling. It will have transferred to it from the Department of the Interior, war service land settlement . . . the circumstances of to-day require very wide reconstruction . . . and the fitting of the Government machine to cope more effectively with the great economic and international problems with which we must urgently concern ourselves.

> *Source*: *Commonwealth Gazette*, no. 3,
> 12 January 1956 and press statement by
> the Prime Minister on 10 January 1956.

16:5 PROMOTION OF EXPORTS BY DEPARTMENT OF TRADE

Extracts from press interview held by the Minister for Trade (J. McEwen) on 11 January 1956.

The Trade Department has been established for the purpose of providing a more concentrated point for thinking and acting in regard to the total problems of trade both import and export. While historically they have been treated as completely separate issues the Government believes that they can no longer be treated as quite separate issues and ought to be thought about at the one point and the Cabinet should receive its advice on import and export issues from a single Minister who has done his thinking against a total background.

In short, we will be treating trade, not as a disconnected series of trading incidents, but as one aspect of the nation's economic life and policy.

The need for this has been long recognised. There has been serious thinking and planning about a Department of Trade ever since this Government was appointed and I think earlier than that. But it is obvious that the balance of payments problem has highlighted the urgency of it.

There will be great weight attached to the balance of payments issue in all the policy thinking.

The balance of payments problem has never been with us in a continuing form before but there is practically no great industrial nation which has not been compelled to maintain an acute consciousness of its balance of payments situation—that goes for the U.K., Germany, Japan and the great industrial countries.

And I think it can be said that as we have become a great and balanced industrial country, the course of events has reached us, and this is an issue now that we will have to be continuously conscious of.

The balance of payments problem . . . does not arise from any fundamental weakness of the Australian Commonwealth. It is clearly a by-product of our tremendous surge of prosperity.

There has been generated a confidence of spending—both consumer and investment spending—in the public sector of development, and in the private sector.

That has set the whole nation—Governments and industries and individuals—spending not only this year's earnings, but spending in anticipation of next year's earnings and next decade's developments. And the result has been that our spending desires, while I would not describe them as undue or extravagant, have in fact outstripped our overseas credits. And so we cannot afford that to continue, and our course is clear—to face the problem, think our way through it as a total problem.

In the short term, preserve our credits with import regulations, and aim determinedly at solving the problem by generating greater export earnings, and that is the function of the Department of Trade—not merely to sell to best advantage and regulate imports, but to compose all its operations towards a solution of this as a problem. . . .

We say we are going to have an export drive. An export drive is imagined by most people, at least by many, as merely a matter of better selling—sheer salesmanship—aggressive presentation, packaging and so on. That is all tremendously important and the Government and industries this year have geared themselves to this end.

The Trade Commissioner Service and the publicity campaign will spend well over £¼ million this year as the Government's contribution to the better selling of products that are not the Government's property.

But important as it is, it is really the least important aspect of an export drive.

By far the most important is ensuring your right to sell and the basis on which you are preparing to enter overseas markets. On this I am talking about international rules of trade—trade treaties—G.A.T.T., Ottawa, special bi-lateral trade treaties or arrangements—the question of whether our exports are confronted with the subsidised exports of another country or with the domestic subsidised production of the buyer country; surplus disposal policies of other countries.

Normally this covers the whole range of our opportunity and whether we sell with advantage or under great disability—that is the real core of the problem that we have to grapple with.

That is almost entirely a matter of inter-governmental negotiations.

I want that to be understood. . . .

16:6 EXPORT PAYMENTS INSURANCE CORPORATION BILL

*Second Reading speech by the Minister for Trade (J. McEwen)
in the House of Representatives on 3 May 1956.*

The purpose of this Bill is to promote Australian export trade. Under the Bill an Export Payments Insurance Corporation will be established which will enable exporters to insure against certain risks in export trading which are not normally insured with commercial insurers.[1]

Experience has shown that the risk of non-payment in export transactions deters exporters from increasing their trade, particularly in markets with which they have not previously done business. Again, some exporters, because of the payment risks involved and because of difficulties of financing sales on credit terms, have not been able to meet their competitors' terms of sale in certain markets. To meet these and other difficulties impeding trade the Government has decided to provide export payments insurance facilities. The provisions of this

---

[1] For some details of the work of the Corporation see Vernon Report (11), vol. II, pp. 1033-4.

535

Bill should be considered against the background of our pressing balance of payments problem and the urgent need to stimulate exports, and as part of the Government's positive attack on the problems of increasing export. It is proposed to provide insurance broadly against the risk of non-payment whether arising from causes such as insolvency of the overseas buyer or his failure to pay within a certain period, or from actions of overseas Governments such as blockage of foreign exchange or the sudden imposition of new import controls in markets abroad. . . .

The function of the Export Payments Insurance Corporation established under this Bill is to offer insurance against certain risks in export trade, in return for payment of a premium by the exporter. The Corporation will not be empowered, nor will it have the funds, itself to extend credit to exporters although as I have explained, the insurance cover issued to the exporter by the Corporation will provide added security for him in the problem of financing his export turnover. . . .

Source: *C.P.D.* (*H. of R.*), vol. 10,
pp. 1760-2.

16:7 MANUFACTURING INDUSTRIES ADVISORY COUNCIL ESTABLISHED

Press statement by the Minister for Trade (J. McEwen) on 3 July 1958.

The Federal Government has appointed Mr. James N. Kirby, of Sydney, who is chairman of a big group of manufacturing companies, as chairman of the Manufacturing Industries Advisory Council.

The Minister for Trade, Mr. McEwen, announced this today.

He said he hoped the new council would become recognised as a body which gave the Government serious and considered advice on the development of efficient manufacturing in Australia.

Twenty other prominent executives of industry and commerce, economists and the secretary of the Trade Department, Mr. J. G. Crawford, have been appointed members.

The council will hold its first meeting on July 22nd in Canberra.

Mr. McEwen said the best possible advice from businessmen was needed on conditions in secondary industry.

The continuing expansion of the Australian economy assumed that there would be a steady growth in manufacturing industries which had made great strides since the war and now employed 28 per cent. of the work force.

Australia was fast becoming a heavily industrialised nation but by world standards the domestic market was relatively small.

Manufacturers faced particular problems in developing thoroughly efficient production. Australia was one of the world's great trading nations and manufacturing development needed to fit into the pattern of a trading policy. The Government aimed to make this policy as liberal as world trading conditions permitted.

In these circumstances there should be closest understanding between manufacturing industry and departments which administered Government trade policy.

In this field the Department of Trade had a wide responsibility including the effects on industry of trade negotiations, import licensing, tariff and overseas trade promotion and publicity.

The new council would in no way cut across the work of existing industry associations with which the Department of Trade maintained a close liaison.

He hoped the council would have the fullest support of industry associations and that those groups would be prepared to provide material help to the council as its work developed. . . .

Source: Sydney Morning Herald,
4 July 1958, p. 7.

16:8 EXPORT DEVELOPMENT COUNCIL ESTABLISHED

Press statement by the Minister for Trade (J. McEwen) on 14 July
1958.

The Minister for Trade (Mr. McEwen) announced today formation of an Export Development Council to advise the Government on all aspects of development of Australia's export trade. . . .

The Government looked to the Export Development Council to be its main advisory body in the field of export development.

The Council would comprise representatives from exporting manufacturers, exporters, Marketing Boards, banks, shipowners and appropriate Government Departments. . . .[1]

16:9 INTENSIFIED EXPORT DEVELOPMENT

Statement by the Prime Minister (R. G. Menzies) on 3 January
1961.

In relation to the economic measures announced last November, the Commonwealth Government made it plain that it would continue to give attention to the need to increase export income. . . .

The Government welcomes the increasing public awareness of the need for a continuing and progressive stepping up of the level of Australian export earnings if Australia is to maintain both a satisfactory rate of development and a rising standard of living.

Throughout recent years there has been evidence on many sides of a lively enterprise on the part of many in developing new kinds of exports, in opening up new markets and in raising the level of export trade.

For its part, the Government has, over the years, introduced a wide range of measures which have enhanced the opportunities of Australian producers to gain profitable export outlets. They include the negotiation of trade agreements with most of our major trading partners; the very substantial strengthening of the Trade Commissioner Service; the organisation of special trade missions; considerable Government assistance in financing export publicity and promotion in the United Kingdom and other important markets; the establishment of the

[1] For some further information see Vernon Report (11), vol. II, p. 1032.

Export Payments Insurance Corporation; taxation concessions to encourage primary production and mining; research aimed at increasing productivity in primary industries; and many others. . . .

The Government is convinced that much more can be done to attain the necessary rate of export expansion. . . .

A major factor in export capacity and performance generally is, of course, the state of the internal economy—not only through the effects on comparative cost levels but also through the impact which internal demand makes, directly or indirectly, upon the volume of goods available for export. The measures which the Government has put in train recently demonstrate its determination to help the competitive position of Australian exports. . . .

The Government recognises that there are difficulties in the way of a very rapid expansion of steel production but it will enter into discussions with the industry with a view to examining how Australia might become a major and continuing net exporter of steel.

. . . As announced by the Minister for National Development on 2nd December, the Government has decided to permit the export of *iron ore* under certain conditions which will ensure that the interests of Australian industry are fully safeguarded. This decision is expected to promote intensified exploration for iron ore reserves and to produce important new exports.

The Committee is studying a number of possible ways, not confined to traditional or orthodox measures, of helping Australian exporters overcome their very real disadvantages of distances from markets, low export volumes, lack of export experience and so on. . . .

. . . The Government will carefully examine proposals for amending some aspects of taxation if they can be shown to offer real prospects of putting Australian industries into a better position to earn substantially increased export income or to develop new lines of export, and if they can be accomplished within manageable limits. . . .

Ministers have also noted the extent to which restrictive export franchises limit or preclude Australian exports. In view of our need to earn more foreign exchange, many restrictive export franchises are clearly not in the national interest.

The Government expects that responsible management of overseas concerns will recognise that it is in their own interests, as well as in the interest of the Australian economy as a whole, that Australian enterprises be permitted and assisted to compete freely in export markets. . . .

. . . Ministers are satisfied that tourism could make a greater contribution to Australia's earnings of foreign exchange.

The Government has therefore decided to take a more active role in overseas promotion of tourist travel to Australia. It will work closely with the State Governments which have important interests in this field. . . It has approved an immediate additional grant to A.N.T.A. to enable it to accelerate some of its existing plans. . . .

The Government has decided to introduce legislation in the next sittings of Parliament to amend the Export Payments Insurance Corporation Act to provide means for the Commonwealth Government to underwrite certain types of transaction through the Export Payments Insurance Corporation in cases where the Government is satisfied that this would be in the national interest. . . .

Source: *Australia in Facts and Figures*,
no. 69, p. 9.

16:10 MEASURES TO IMPROVE AUSTRALIA'S EXTERNAL TRADING POSITION

Speech by the Minister for Trade (J. McEwen) in the House of Representatives on 8 March 1961.

I take this early opportunity to make a statement to advise the House of measures which the Government has taken recently, or proposes to take, in its overall programme, aimed at improving our external trading position. . . .

In January, the Prime Minister (Mr. Menzies) announced that the Government had taken important steps to intensify the drive to increase our export earnings. He announced that a special committee of the Cabinet had been established to carry through a comprehensive and continuous examination of positive measures to increase exports. This committee has undertaken its work against the background of our already real export achievements. Australia, despite its small population, ranks in the first dozen countries as an international trader. Despite this record we have an intransigent balance of payments problem, related not so much to what would appear to be inadequate exports as to unsatisfactory prices for many of them and, above all, this country's enormous appetite to import.

To attack the problem further, the Government has decided to intensify its export drive. The measures which it has adopted for this purpose during the last few months have been announced by the Prime Minister. These, together with a most recent decision to provide taxation incentives to encourage exports, which I will describe presently, should be viewed and judged against the broad requirements of our national export needs. These and other measures, to which I will refer briefly, have been designed with the knowledge that any successful export programme must encompass certain essential ingredients.

In brief, there must be certain inducements, based upon confidence of profitable operations, to produce for export; markets must be discovered, and access to them negotiated; then the product must be adapted to the needs of individual markets, presented well and vigorously promoted. The overseas agents must be serviced effectively. The Government's export planning has always assumed that the great primary and mining industries will continue to earn for Australia the bulk of our foreign exchange. These industries must therefore be assisted to hold and expand their markets. In addition, exports of factory products must be expanded.

The Prime Minister has already announced that certain public works which he mentioned, and to which I shall shortly refer, would require consultation with, and the co-operation of, the State governments and, where necessary, the devising of financial arrangements fair to both parties. These projects are important to the expansion of Australia's export trade. The Commonwealth is discussing with the State Governments concerned the construction of roads in Queensland, the Northern Territory and Western Australia, to aid the beef and mining export industries. In addition, we are examining whether some Commonwealth assistance to the States could ensure the early completion of modern berthing and loading facilities at coal-loading ports.

The results of efforts to sustain and expand coal exports are clearly dependent upon these loading and berthing facilities. The modernizing and standardization of key railway links in Western Australia and South Australia, which could assist the development of important export industries, are at present under active discussion with those States. By planning now, the way should be clear for us to proceed in 1962 on such projects to increase our export earnings. Discussions are proceeding with the appropriate States. It will be evident that this goes a long way towards giving a decided export bent to national development programmes.

Additions to our export earnings are also expected to flow from the recent decision to permit limited trade in iron ore. Much attention has been given to steel as a product which can play an important role in becoming a regular and substantial export. Encouraging discussions have already taken place with the Broken Hill Proprietary Company Limited. But to produce goods is one thing and to sell them is quite a separate task, and continuous energy needs to be devoted to the problem of expanding existing markets and winning new ones.

It has already been announced that legislation will be introduced this session to empower the Export Payments Insurance Corporation to give cover to certain transactions which are at present outside its scope, but which the Government may consider should be covered in the national interest. Large-scale trade development efforts have been authorized in South America and the Middle East. Last year the Government sent a survey mission of businessmen to South America. It reported favourably on prospects for increasing Australian trade, particularly in the countries on the north and west coasts of South America. To permit the pioneering work in these markets to begin, the Government is negotiating with shipping companies for the establishment of a regular shipping service and will do this, even if it entails some financial assistance over a limited period to get the service established. It has been decided that trade commissioner posts will be opened in Lima, Peru, and in Caracas in Venezuela. A trade mission will be sent to the area, and an appropriate trade publicity programme will be undertaken. The Middle East and eastern Mediterranean areas also offer good prospects for the expansion of Australia's export trade.

A trade mission will be sent to the eastern Mediterranean countries this year and, in co-operation with industry and commerce, a trade display ship will go to the Persian Gulf areas early in 1962. A supporting publicity campaign will also be undertaken. The agreement of the appropriate governments is being sought for the opening of new trade commissioner posts in Teheran and Beirut. The trade commissioner's office in Cairo, which is already an important one, is to be strengthened. The cost of the Middle East and South American programmes will be in the neighbourhood of an additional £220,000 a year, which will be in addition to the present cost of the current Budget, of £1,750,000 for trade promotion and publicity abroad.

In these days international tourism is rapidly expanding and is becoming a significant source of overseas funds for Australia. The Australian National Travel Association has estimated that some 68,000 tourists spent £12,500,000 here in 1959. In close consultation with the States and the tourist industry, the Commonwealth Government has decided to take an active role in the development of international tourism. It has given an immediate additional grant to the Australian National Travel Association, and has already turned the resources and facilities of the trade commissioners throughout the world, and of the trade publicity programmes overseas, to support tourist promotion abroad. We have just received from the association a programme to intensify tourist promotion, to which the Government will be giving early attention.

I do not want to leave the impression that we have not been vigorous in this field already. The current Budget contains provision of £100,000 to assist the operations of the Australian National Travel Association, and the additional vote to which I have just referred—a prompt and immediate one—represents, if my memory serves me right, which I am sure it does, an additional £20,000.

The Government has given much attention to the need to trigger off an increased interest in export in which manufacturers must play a bigger part than in the past. It has been decided to stimulate the export drive by certain taxation measures. This is an important decision. First we want to assist the promotion of our products in existing and new markets. To this end the Government has decided to introduce a taxation allowance to give positive encouragement to increased effort in export promotion abroad.

Under prevailing tax laws an expenditure in overseas market development which is accepted by the Commissioner of Taxation is an allowable business expense and, as such, the company is remitted tax at the rate of 8s. in the £1. The incentive proposed is that this rate of remission will now be doubled. This means that—for a period of three years, beginning 1st July, 1961, a company which has expenditure on market development can expect an allowance of 16s. in the £1.

In respect of visits overseas for this purpose, the Commissioner of Taxation must be satisfied that its bona fide purpose is for export market development. In such cases, fares only will qualify for the allowance. Personal expenses will not qualify. There is also a number of other points of importance on which the Commissioner of Taxation will need to be satisfied. The Government expects that this will provide a major stimulus to overseas market promotion and development. It will apply to all products in all export markets. It is expected to give positive encouragement to the further development of the vigorous merchant exporters on whose skills and knowledge of the overseas markets so much of the expanded national export programme will depend.

A way was sought which would further stimulate export of processed and manufactured products. This is a major objective of the export drive, to encourage all Australian processors and manufacturers to seek to enter export markets; to give some aid and incentive to those whose export achievements will be determined by their export costing. To this end the Government has decided to grant a rebate of pay-roll tax related to the value of export sales achieved.

There will be a formula which, up to a point, will increase the benefits of pay-roll tax abatement as the taxpayer lifts the level of his export sales. The rebate will be allowed according to the increase in the value of the exports which an organization achieves over the value of the average of its exports in the base years 1958-59 and 1959-60. The rebate will be calculated having regard to the proportion which increased export sales bear to total income from sales. The rebate will apply for three years from 1960-61. In the light of the experience of those three years the policy will be reviewed. . . .

In choosing a realistic basis for a formula that would give good prospects of achieving the objective of encouraging a worthwhile increase in exports, the Government has decided that where export sales were increased over the base period by 8 per cent. of total income from sales, the exporter would gain exemption from pay-roll tax. This incentive exemption would apply on a pro rata basis for increases up to 8 per cent. The legislation will also include provisions whereby benefits can be obtained by firms supplying materials and components to the final manufacturer. No commodity is excluded from this arrangement.

As a result of these two taxation arrangements there will be both an inducement to search for markets overseas as well as an increased inducement and capacity to bid for business overseas. Legislation to cover these proposals will be introduced.

The Government will, of course, continue, and indeed intensify, all its present programmes of export promotion and market negotiations and is confident that private enterprise will respond with increased energy and activity to the financial stimulus now involved in this.

These, then, are recent developments in the policies which are all integral parts of an intensified export drive. In addition, we are examining proposals further to help the sale of our primary and secondary products abroad by assisting in the development of warehousing facilities for Australian products in important markets. We are calling on the assistance of skilled businessmen and advisers to help us in forming a judgment on this matter. Oil and mineral exploration will be further encouraged and, in general, all possible prospects of earning additional exchange funds will be given close and continuing attention. These are all parts of a positive approach. There is no single touchstone by which all our export problems will be solved. Nothing is more important than the costs and efficiency at point of production and the energy and efficiency of the salesmen. . . .

Source: C.P.D. (*H. of R.*), vol. 30, pp. 46-9.

16:11 EXPORT PAYMENTS INSURANCE CORPORATION BILL 1961

Extract from Second Reading speech by the Minister for Trade (J. McEwen) in the House of Representatives on 13 April 1961.

Over recent months the Government has announced a series of policy measures designed to encourage Australian exporters and to strengthen both the immediate and longer-term export-earning capacity of our primary and secondary industries.

The Government's decision to amend the Export Payments Insurance Corporation Act . . . is one of these measures. The extension of the facilities available as a result of the amendment now proposed will give further inducement to Australian exporters to investigate export possibilities and to gain new business.

The purpose of the bill is to enable export payments insurance cover to be extended to transactions which the corporation would not, or could not, ordinarily cover. Under the bill, the Government would be empowered to authorize cover in such cases where it considered that it would be in the national interest to take such action . . . No attempt is made to give a definition of what would constitute 'national interest'. . . .

At present, under the Act, the Corporation is charged to conduct its operations on a no profit-no loss basis . . . to carry out this policy effectively, the commissioner is obliged to observe orthodox insurance principles where these are applicable. One of these is an acceptable spread of risks between markets. Another is that the payment term involved in a transaction must be such that the risk can be assessed with some confidence.

The bill provides that the commissioner would refer to the Minister for Trade proposals which the corporation would not normally cover but which would merit consideration as national interest propositions. Every case so referred will be considered on its merits by Cabinet Ministers. . . It will be for Ministers to approve or reject each and every individual proposal referred to them.

Some important considerations which would influence the Government in deciding whether cover should be granted, on national interest grounds, to a particular transaction may be stated as follows:—

Whether the proposition holds promise of opening up worthwhile new export markets for Australian products;

Whether an industry with high export potential would be stimulated;

Whether the transaction was important for a particular Australian area or industry from the point of view of development; and

Whether the transaction would confer some obvious and significant benefits for our trade relations with the country concerned. . . .

The corporation has been in operation now for less than four years but has already issued policies to a face value of over £75,000,000. At the present time current policies amount in value to over £24,000,000. . . .

Source: *C.P.D. (H. of R.)*, vol. 30, pp. 823-4.

16:12 EXPORT PAYMENTS INSURANCE CORPORATION BILL 1965

Extracts from Second Reading speech by the Minister for Trade (J. McEwen) in the House of Representatives on 2 September 1965.

This Bill proposes a number of amendments to the Export Payments Insurance Corporation Act 1956-1964. The most important of these are the amendments which I foreshadowed during the last session of Parliament in relation to the insurance of certain classes of Australian investment in overseas countries. This amendment will authorise the Export Payments Insurance Corporation to insure certain types of Australian investments in overseas countries against non-commercial risks which might arise in these countries. The other amendments proposed would authorise—

An increase of £1,000,000 in the capital of the Corporation.

An increase of £25,000,000 in the maximum contingent liability which the Corporation can accept under contracts of insurance and guarantee.

A reduction of the minimum value of export transactions in respect of which the Corporation may provide guarantees.

The investment insurance amendments will authorise the Corporation to insure Australian investors against three categories of risk—

Expropriation.

Damage or destruction of property caused by war, riot, insurrection, and similar happenings.

Inability to transfer capital or earnings back to Australia.

These are risks which are deterrents to investment abroad and against which a number of countries, such as the United States of America, Germany, Japan and Denmark, already provide insurance. Others are considering its introduction. We are proposing that the Australian Government should provide this form of insurance, through the Corporation, because there are certain kinds of overseas investments which we believe Australian investors should be encouraged to make. These are investments which, broadly speaking, are aimed at preserving current and potential overseas markets for our exports, particularly the markets in the developing countries of the world.

The case for encouraging this type of investment can be put fairly simply. It is good business for us and at the same time should provide material assistance to developing countries in pursuing their industrialisation plans. The developing countries are already important markets for our exports—they take roughly 15 per cent. of our total exports. We are convinced that, in the years ahead, they will grow in importance. We are also convinced that, in the process, there will be significant changes in the composition of their imports—changes to which we must adapt ourselves if we are to secure the expanding share of this trade we are seeking.

The developing countries are determined to industrialise as quickly as possible, not only to save imports but also because, like ourselves, they see industrial growth as the main source of increased employment opportunities and incomes. . . .

At present, our exports to the developing countries contain a much higher proportion of processed or finished goods than our exports to other countries. In 1963, for example, over 70 per cent. of our exports to developing countries were processed or finished, while only about 40 per cent. of our exports to Western developed countries were in this group. This is to be expected, of course, since many of the developing countries are still in the early stages of industrial development. However, as the pace of industrial growth quickens, and the production of finished goods expands, they will require a greater proportion of their imports in the form of materials or semi-processed products. In this situation, Australian exporters must be willing, as the need arises, to commence assembly or production operations within the market itself, if they wish to hold their overseas customers. In other cases, investment overseas may be the only real means of breaking into new markets for components or semi-finished products.

In short, exporters may be faced with the need to invest in the market or see their share of it decline . . . we need to be able to remove the new and unfamiliar risks, of a non-commercial character, which might deter Australian manufacturers faced with this situation, from investing abroad. This is what we propose to do in this Bill, by offering insurance against these risks.

There are two further aspects to this general question of development and investment, which I want to raise. The first is that the broad pattern which we expect the developing countries to follow, is basically no different from our own pattern of development, in the post-war years. We have had large scale development of import saving industries, in many cases by overseas firms which recognised that to maintain their sales in Australia they needed to come here and produce the goods in this market. Despite this import saving however, our overall growth has sustained an ever increasing demand for imports. There are solid expectations that this will also happen in the developing countries. As industrial growth generates higher incomes, new import demands will rise and our exports to these countries, though of a changing kind, will continue to grow.

The second aspect relates to our position as a capital importing country. On the face of it, it may seem inconsistent that, as a country which needs and will continue to need developmental capital and know-how from abroad, we should now seek to encourage the outflow of some capital and know-how. There is no inconsistency in this at all. In fact, we see it as a natural development of our industrial and trading growth. . . .

I refer now to the main characteristics of the scheme we are proposing. Firstly, I refer to the kind of investments which will qualify for insurance. Each case will be considered separately and on its merits and not against any rigid set of criteria. Indeed, we realise that because of the wide variety of investment arrangements which occur we will need to have a fairly flexible approach to this and a number of other questions. However, several broad principles will apply. The first is that before insuring an investment we will need to satisfy that it will bring to Australia either current or potential export benefits. . . .

The second principle we intend to apply is that there must be direct participation by the Australian investor in the overseas enterprise. . . .

The Government also intends to administer these insurance arrangements in such a way as to encourage Australian investors to associate with investors in the overseas country in joint, rather than wholly Australian owned ventures. Whenever appropriate, for example, there will be a preferential premium rate for investment in joint ventures. . . .

Insurance will be available not only to companies but also to Australian citizens, Commonwealth statutory bodies, Commonwealth and State marketing authorities, semi-Government institutions, private organisations and partnerships. However, the Government will reserve the right to refuse insurance in cases where, because of the structure or operations of the investing company, it would not be in our best interests to provide insurance. If, for example, the investing company were wholly, or very substantially foreign owned, or were subject to extensive franchise restrictions in its export operations, it would need to be demonstrated that there were very real and substantial export benefits in the investment, before it could be accepted for insurance. We are proposing that, as in the case of similar schemes operating in other countries, insurance should only be available for new investments. However, to avoid any difficulties which this might raise for investors who may have found it necessary to conclude investment negotiations in recent months, it is proposed that investments entered into after 1st January 1965 should be eligible for consideration. . . .

There will be no insurance against normal commercial risks such as failure to make a profit, or devaluation in the overseas country. Three broad categories of risk will be covered—expropriation risks, transfer or convertibility risks, and war and insurrection risks. Separate contracts will be available for each type of risk and an investor may confine his cover to any one of the three risks, that is there will be no compulsory 'blanket' cover of all risks.

Source: *C.P.D.* (*H. of R.*), vol. 47,
pp. 719-22.

16:13 GOVERNMENT ACTION TO STIMULATE EXPORTS

In recent years the Government has intensified action to stimulate exports, in a variety of ways, including:

(a) Actions to assist production for export, such as providing funds for the construction of roads in Queensland, Western Australia and the Northern Territory to aid the beef cattle industry, the construction of modern berthing and loading facilities in a number of coal ports and the modernisation of certain key railroad links throughout the country.

(b) The introduction of taxation incentives. Expenditure on overseas market development is now allowed as a double deduction for income tax purposes. A rebate of pay-roll tax is allowable on a formula related to the increase an exporter achieves in his exports in any year compared with a base period (currently the average of 1958-59 and 1959-60).

(c) The establishment in 1956 of the Export Payments Insurance Corporation and a number of subsequent extensions of the facilities it provides.

(d) Expansion of the Trade Commissioner Service.

(e) Increased emphasis on trade missions abroad and on other forms of trade publicity overseas.

(f) Continuing emphasis, in discussions between the Reserve Bank and the trading banks, on the need to ensure provision of adequate finance for export industries, supplemented in 1962 by the inclusion of export financing amongst the purposes for which loans could be arranged from the Term Loan Fund.

(g) The setting up by the eight major trading banks, with the support of the Reserve Bank, of the Australian Banks' Export Re-finance Corporation Ltd., to assist in financing export sales involving extended terms of payment.

These various measures, designed to reduce export costs, increase export production, strengthen the incentive to export and explore new possibilities in overseas markets, have undoubtedly strengthened our capacity to export.

Source: The Australian Balance of Payments, February 1966, p. 25 (*C.P.P.,* no. 288 of 1964-65-66).

16:14 PAY-ROLL TAX REBATES

Press statement by the Treasurer (W. McMahon) on 28 April 1966.

The Commonwealth Treasurer, the Hon. William McMahon, announced today that in the three months ended March last, pay-roll tax rebates totalling $2,382,000 had been allowed to 292 firms which, by increasing their export sales in 1964-65, had qualified for rebates. This brought the number of firms to which rebates had been allowed to date in respect of 1964-65 exports to 655 and the value of rebates to $6,297,000. A further 394 claims in respect of the 1964-65 financial year, totalling $2,772,000, were currently being handled by the Taxation Office.

Mr. McMahon said that, in addition to rebates in respect of 1964-65 exports, the Taxation Office in the March quarter had allowed rebates totalling $1,296,000 in respect of exports of prior years. To the end of March, 961 firms had been allowed rebates totalling $4,953,000 in respect of 1960-61 exports, 1,256 firms had been allowed rebates totalling $7,846,000 in respect of 1961-62 exports, 1,389 firms had been allowed rebates totalling $8,065,000 in respect of 1962-63 exports, and 1,329 firms had been allowed rebates totalling $10,755,000 in respect of 1963-64 exports. In addition, claims in respect of these years totalling $2,053,000 were currently being handled by the Taxation Office.

Pay-roll tax rebates are part of the taxation incentives for export introduced by the Government in 1961. Rebates are available to firms increasing their exports above the level of their average exports in the two years 1958-59 and 1959-60. If the value of a firm's exports increases by one per cent of its gross business income, the firm is entitled to a rebate of 12·5 per cent of its pay-roll tax liability. This ratio applies proportionately so that when the increase in exports is equal to 8 per cent of the gross receipts of the firm's business, the firm is entitled to a full rebate of pay-roll tax.

B. GENERAL ECONOMIC POLICIES

16:15 THE AUSTRALIAN ECONOMY

Speech by the Treasurer (H. Holt) in the House of Representatives on 15 November 1960.

In February of this year, it will be recalled, we announced four measures directed to check the buoyancy already evident at that time. We intervened in the basic wage case to counsel the commission in the public interest against granting a further general wage increase at that juncture. We removed the great majority of restrictions on imports. We decided to work towards a balanced Budget in 1960-61, and we stated our support for the policy of the Reserve Bank in trying to reduce excessive monetary liquidity in our economic system.

Then, when we came to the Budget after the middle of the year, we followed through on the third of these objectives by providing in our Budget for a cash surplus in 1960-61. To make this possible, we kept additional expenditure down well below the level of 1959-60 and we made substantial increases in taxation. . . .

. . . Nevertheless we have to conserve these overseas reserves, which are so vital to the functioning of our economy, because we cannot be sure what external conditions will be in times ahead. Placed as we are, we can never afford to be extravagant with imports. The Government removed import controls because it held that our economy would benefit from being able to obtain supplies abroad from the widest and best sources. It has always been our view that tariff action, carefully framed to foster only sound industries, is far preferable to the arbitrary protection which import licensing gives. Moreover, import restrictions had always been resented by the community and we had undertaken to get rid of them as soon as we possibly could. Having got rid of them, the Government firmly intends, as I said in my Budget speech, to keep out of them; and we believe that, given reasonable success in trading abroad and in attracting overseas investment, we should be able to do so . . . we expected that there would be an early phase of fairly heavy importing, but that soon thereafter the rate of inflow would begin to fall. So far, it has continued at a fairly high level, and there is one principal reason for this. It is that we have in progress a very strong boom in spending—spending on consumer goods, on motor vehicles, for example, where record sales have been taking place, on building in its various forms, and on other branches of investment. . . .

547

Plainly enough, to safeguard our overseas funds position, we must reduce the excessive internal demands which are the main reasons why imports continue to run so high. That is the external aspect of the matter. . . .

We have come to think . . . that the current measures ought to be reinforced in certain ways. . . .[1]

Source: *C.P.D. (H. of R.)*, vol. 29, pp. 2850-88.

16:16 ECONOMIC MEASURES 1960

Speech by the Prime Minister (R. G. Menzies) in the House of Representatives on 16 November 1960.

It is said by some critics that the Government has a policy that proceeds by fits and starts . . . Our economic policy has remained constant from beginning to end. A policy of the kind which is aimed at stability, at preserving the balance of payments, and preserving employment, is a constant policy.

. . . this country has been very fortunate in having a few people here who understand that unless you are flexible in your treatment of economic circumstances as they arise . . . you are not fit to be entrusted with the responsibility of what I will call . . . economic management.

. . . at the time of the Budget there were many uncertainties. For example, the freeing of imports and the abolition . . . of import licensing had not had time to be fully reflected in the actual imports.

. . . there was a belief in some quarters, that when import licensing came off there would be a sudden, steep rise in imports and then the level would go down again . . . But . . . so high is the purchasing power of this country that there was not a hump in the graph, but a rise to a high plateau, and the volume of importations, as a result, has exceeded what anybody could reasonably have anticipated a few months ago . . . The restrictive directives to the trading banks had been given (at the time of the Budget) . . . the increase in bank advances far exceeded anything which could have been anticipated . . . these elements . . . have brought us to the point of producing supplementary ideas on top of the main Budget. . . .

We recognized that we were called upon to deal with problems arising from prosperity and arising from quick development at home . . . those problems were of two kinds. The first is inflation caused by great pressure on our human and material resources, and the steady fall in our external reserves caused by a fall in export income . . . and a remarkably sustained rise . . . in the demand for imports. The second problem, that of our international trade insofar as it arises from increased import demands is, in a real sense, the outcome of inflation at home. Bank advances not having adequately responded either to the directives or to the fall in the overseas reserves, measures additional were necessary and prudent . . . Our approach is not merely negative or restrictive . . . We believe the balance of payments problem would recur from time to time, having regard to

[1] The balance of the statement outlines the various deflationary measures taken—tightening up of bank credit, various interest rate measures designed to reduce liquidity, increase on sales tax on motor cars, and a minimum of 30 per cent ratio of public investment by life companies. See also 16:18.

inevitable fluctuations in our export income from primary products, unless we maintain, as a major element of policy, the opening and developing of overseas markets, not only for wool, wheat and meat, but also for processed and manufactured goods.

The Department of Trade is well aware of this challenge, and during its relatively brief history has achieved a great deal. Our policy has been and will be to continue to intensify the drive for exports. . . .

Source: C.P.D. (H. of R.), vol. 29,
pp. 2926-30.

16:17 THE AUSTRALIAN ECONOMY

Statement by the Minister for Trade (J. McEwen) in the House of Representatives on 16 November 1960.

The economic strength of the country which we are so determined to preserve is to be found partly in the domestic scene and partly in our economic situation internationally. The very level of our prosperity, from time to time, produces a pressure on costs. This is the situation at the present time. Boom conditions generate a demand for imports and so tend to run down our overseas balances. As a result we seek to place a new emphasis on sustaining the climate that attracts capital into the country, whether for the Government or for private business. This, in turn, enhances the ability of our own industries to export competitively with the rest of the world. That is the kind of job that we have to do in order to assist our economy to maintain our overseas balances.

We need a level of costs that will enable us to produce at competitive prices. We have to produce the right item of the right quality and at the right price for trade overseas. There has to be salesmanship behind these items, and we require access to overseas markets finally to achieve our sales. In all this we have been very successful. True, this success has been achieved only at the price of constant effort by industries that produce for export, but Government aid has been given in prising open new markets and in enabling our products to get to overseas markets. . . .

There have been, of course, immense difficulties experienced from time to time in finding opportunities of selling our goods overseas. Traditionally the great markets for Australian products have been in the United Kingdom and in Western European countries, countries in which prosperity has flowed, but in which the markets for our goods have contracted almost unbelievably. Western Europe and the United Kingdom to-day import 1,500,000 tons less meat and 200,000 tons less sugar. In major food items the United Kingdom and western Europe import 4,000,000 tons less than they did before the war. This change in the situation could have wrecked the Australian economy. It has not done so, because we have geared our policies to meet the situation.

The United States used to be an important buyer of our wool, but it has now almost disappeared from the scene. Our economy has not been shattered, because we have adopted trade policies that have penetrated these contracting markets. Our share of the United Kingdom and western European market to-day is greater than our share was in the 1930's, and in the case of a number of items our

T

exports to those markets are, in the absolute sense, greater than they were in the 1930's.

Then we have turned to other markets, for instance Japan. I can stand here and say that I have a very vivid memory of the night on which I introduced the Japanese Trade Agreement into this Parliament. Predictions of calamity came out of the mouth of every Labour speaker—we were going to be ruined, there was going to be widespread unemployment. That trade agreement has proved to be one of the most effective stabilising actions that have been taken in the recent history of this country. . . .

Throughout our term of office there has not been any device that we have not been willing to have a go at in order to protect our balance of payments position. There have been trade treaties and trade negotiations, arguments in the General Agreement on Tariffs and Trade organization, arguments with the Americans about their surplus disposals, arguments with the French and Germans to persuade them to stand out of our flour markets in the east. In every case we have been successful. We have entered into long-term meat agreements. We have arranged sales of meat to the United States of America which have resulted in a boom in beef values. We have sold 100,000 tons of flour to Ceylon. I am just skipping from point to point to illustrate the kind of successes we have achieved in our trading activity, knowing all the time that the high policy objective we have set for Australia, a policy of expansion and stability, could not be achieved unless we sustained our overseas balances at a satisfactory level. This has been done.

Now we have found that our greatest export product, wool, has fallen in value. This does not fill us with dismay and despair or make us retreat into our shells. It merely leads us to conclude, 'Here is a new challenge.' The machinery that we have devised, the Department of Trade, the Trade Commissioner Service, and the help that we have obtained from industry and commerce, from the Export Development Council and the Manufacturing Industries Advisory Council, will have to be availed of even more freely than has been the case hitherto. We have got to come to grips with the problem, as the Prime Minister (Mr. Menzies) has said, in the traditional manner. We will have to defend our markets and enter new ones. If necessary we will be prepared to adopt any means that appear advisable, even if they be unorthodox, to achieve our end. We have done it before and we will do it again. We went to little New Zealand and made that country the biggest market for Australian manufactured goods, selling £60,000,000 worth a year to that country. This achievement was brought about by the sheer drive of the co-operative efforts of Australian commerce and the Australian Government. Now we are studying markets in other parts of the world. One of our missions has just returned from South America, and we will have a go at that region. It is true, however, that there has been a deterioration in the terms of trade between countries like Australia, which depend on export sales of the great bulk of their commodities, and the industrialized countries to which they sell. We have a sharp problem here, but it will not dismay us. We will tackle it and, I believe, we will overcome it. . . .

We will become even keener in our drive for exports, and I have high confidence that the Australian people, knowing what has flowed from the determination of this Government, and its steady, inflexible drive to ensure the expansion and greatness of our country, will stand behind policies of the kind that have proved so successful in the past.

Source: C.P.D. (H. of R.), vol. 29,
pp. 2936-8.

16:18 GOVERNMENT RESTATES ECONOMIC POLICY

Press statement by the Prime Minister (R. G. Menzies) on 21 February 1961.

We have been closely examining, in Cabinet and Committee, the effects, so far, of our economic policy measures. We have also given much attention to the drive for exports, some general aspects of which I announced at the beginning of January.

We see no reason to alter the substance of our policy which we knew would be, in the short run, unpopular with many people but which we believed, and believe, is in the best interests of the nation. Credit was too easy, and an inflationary boom was under way. Credit therefore had to be restricted so that stability might be restored. The effects of the boom include an increased demand for imports, while our export income, so dependent on primary products, remained somewhat depressed. This, I should point out, is not because primary production has fallen; on the contrary, it has increased. But the 'terms of trade' have moved against Australia very significantly since 1953. By that I mean that the prices of imports, as contrasted with the prices of exports, have not fallen, so that the imports we can buy for a given quantity of exports have been reduced. If our terms of trade are taken as an index figure of 100 in 1953 (itself a relatively normal year), the figure today is 65. This, which is beyond our control, since we cannot fix the price paid by the world for our exports, is at the root of our present problem. The terms of trade have moved against us more than against almost any country in the world. In the result, our overseas reserves, vital to our activities as a great international trading nation were (and are) falling at too rapid a rate. We have been living beyond our means internationally, with the result that reserves are being drawn upon to meet current business payments. This is not good business, as every business man knows.

Another element was the increasing resort to high interest borrowing outside the banking system, for hire purchase and other financial transactions. This growth, which has mushroomed in the last year or two, had two undesirable by-products. First, it increased the burden on the taxpayers, because these high interest payments were treated as business expenses; which meant that up to 40 per cent of the interest was being met by the Treasury, that is by other taxpayers. Second, it attracted money away from savings banks and public loans by out-bidding in interest rates. This has meant that we have not been able to get from the loan market all the funds vitally necessary for national development in power, water supply, transport, schools, housing, and the like, with resultant burdens upon taxpayers who are, broadly, the adult population of Australia. In this current financial year, no less than 65 per cent of the cost of capital works, both Federal and State, is being met out of Commonwealth taxation revenue!

We tackled this matter by some variations in bank interest rates, and by measures to prevent these high outside interest payments from being fully deductible for income tax purposes. We know that there has been much criticism of, and some uncertainty about, our particular measures. At an early date we will resolve this uncertainty by substituting for what we announced as a temporary and somewhat arbitrary measure, a new law on deductibility. I have reason to believe that the new proposals, which the Treasurer will announce in due course, will go a long way towards meeting reasonable and constructive criticism, while not conflicting with the Government's policy objectives.

In order to assist the loan raising which governments must have proper foundations on which to build [*sic*], we announced policies in relation to life assurance societies, superannuation funds, and the like, (which enjoy great taxation benefits); requiring them to subscribe to Government and semi-Government loans 30 per cent of their funds. Since our announcement useful discussions have occurred and certain modifications of our proposal have been worked out. These will be announced by the Treasurer. They will, I believe, be widely acceptable.

In all these and allied matters, it is necessary to make it clear that while we have adopted policies of some severity, we are maintaining a close watch upon results, particularly in the field of employment. That there should be some falling off in employment in the motor car industry, a falling off from a very high peak in 1960, is inevitable; for one of our designs was to reduce inflationary pressure on that section. This must involve some changes in employment, but is not designed, over all, to produce unemployment, which it will be our constant care to resist.

To sum up on these matters, we are conscious of the harm that can be done by the existence of uncertainties in the business world in relation to deductibility of interest and the investment policies of life assurance and superannuation schemes. These uncertainties will be resolved by the Treasurer's statements which I have foreshadowed.

There are four other matters of considerable importance to which I will now refer. . . .[1]

2. There is a good deal of speculation about a possible re-introduction of import licensing, and some speculation about a devaluation by changing the exchange rate. It is therefore necessary to state that we have no intention whatever to restore the import licensing which was abandoned, or to alter the exchange rate.

3. We have been working on practical measures to increase our export income. This is especially important in the field of exports of manufactured goods. We have had the advantage of consultation with representative business men on the immensely difficult question of tax incentives. We are to receive from them, in a few days, further material which will assist us to make decisions.

We have also devised specific proposals for increasing our overseas sales by new promotional means, particularly in the Middle East and South America, in which areas we see very worthwhile opportunities. Our proposals relate to Trade Commissioner services, sales campaigns, and adequate shipping arrangements. They will be stated in detail by my colleague, the Minister for Trade. We have expectations of solid success.

The promotion of the tourist trade is also essential, and holds promise of increased earnings from overseas. In January we made increased grants to the Australian National Travel Association, and asked it to submit a programme designed to ensure that tourist earnings are expanded as quickly as possible. The Association estimates that Australia earned £12,500,000 in overseas exchange from this source in 1959, and that substantial increase is possible by 1963. The financial measures to be adopted by us will be decided when the recommendations of the A.N.T.A. are received and considered.

4. Our economic measures were not lightly adopted, and must, in their substance, be maintained until an adequate impact is made upon the twin problems of internal inflation and an excessive drain upon our overseas funds. . . .

---

[1] No. 1 deals with the sales tax on motor vehicles which was restored (22 February 1961) to the level prevailing before 15 November 1960.

16:19 ECONOMIC ENQUIRY: TERMS OF REFERENCE ANNOUNCED

Press statement by the Prime Minister (R. G. Menzies) on 13 February 1963.

I have already announced the Government's decision to institute an Enquiry into a range of matters that bear directly on the objectives of economic policy as the Government sees them. These objectives, which together constitute the mainspring of our economic policies, are explicitly set out in the Terms of Reference of the Committee of Enquiry now to be established. Their paramount importance is not, I think, to be denied, but a problem of increasing difficulty is to command a comprehensive view of all the complex and interlocking factors that must enter into their achievement.

This problem confronts Governments and their advisers at every turn and we have had constantly before our minds the nature of the questions that the proposed Committee of Enquiry might be called upon to answer. We have now decided that the Terms of Reference of the Committee as previously announced should be given in somewhat greater detail and that certain particular matters that seemed of special importance should be specifically included. In addition, we have decided to make it clear that we expect the Committee, as far as may be possible, to draw together the results of its studies in the form of conclusions as to the bearing of those results on the achievement of our overall economic objectives.

The Terms of Reference for the Enquiry that we have now decided upon are therefore the following:—

Having in mind that the objectives of the Government's economic policy are a high rate of economic and population growth with full employment, increasing productivity, rising standards of living, external viability, and stability of costs and prices, to enquire into and report its findings on the following matters—

(a) The trends in population as a whole, in the work force, and in the distribution of the latter amongst various sectors.

(b) The economic availability of known basic physical resources.

(c) The growth of domestic savings and investment.

(d) Overseas investment in Australia (including likely sources and trends and an assessment of its significance to the Australian economy).

(e) The availability of credit.

(f) Trends in costs, prices and wages.

(g) Trends in productivity.

(h) The pattern of growth and geographical distribution of industry, primary, secondary and tertiary (including the governmental sector).

(i) The consequences of this for the occupational pattern of the work force.

(j) Trends in the standard of living.

(k) The situation with respect to the external balance of payments.

(l) Questions involved in the production in Australia of goods that would otherwise be imported.

(m) Production for export and the securing of adequate export outlets.

(n) The effect of customs tariffs and other forms, direct or indirect, of protection on the disposition of resources and on the broad economic objectives stated above.

The Committee will report the conclusions reached by it as to the bearing which all or any of the matters so ascertained have upon the achievement of the economic policy objectives above stated.

The Committee, which will commence its work in the near future, will comprise:—

Dr. James Vernon, C.B.E. (Chairman)
Professor Sir John Crawford, C.B.E. (Vice Chairman)
Professor P. H. Karmel
D. G. Molesworth, Esq., C.B.E.
K. B. Myer, Esq., D.S.C.

17

STATISTICAL APPENDIX

Some Characteristics of Australian Trade:
Growth and Pattern, 1948-9 to 1965-6

The documents and comments presented in the first four parts of this book have been primarily about policy, although in a few sections some illustrative statistical material has been added as annexes to the documents. Before proceeding to Part E, in which trade policy as a whole is reviewed, it will be useful to present a few statistical tables drawn from official sources and designed to do no more than give point to some of the policy issues discussed in the preceding sections and further reviewed in Part E.[1]

In presenting the tables it must be emphasised that they are not a substitute for the excellent official documents available, especially those issued by the Commonwealth Bureau of Census and Statistics, the special bulletins and supplements now being issued by the Treasury with a welcome increase in frequency, and the various publications of other departments such as Trade and Industry and National Development. The notes which now follow will mostly find backing in the few tables here presented, but at times it will be necessary to go to the official sources mentioned for more ample material. Finally, the notes are descriptive, not analytical in character, although there is an occasional comment on future prospects: their purpose is to present what may be regarded as the facts of Australia's trading situation—facts sometimes the result of policy actions but always to be taken into account by policy makers.

The numbered notes follow a simple classification into Exports; Imports; Balance of Payments.

I *Exports*

(1) Both total value and volume have more than doubled in the post-war period 1948-9 to 1965-6. In the early part of the period total value rose far more rapidly than volume,[2] the disparity reaching its peak at the height of the Korean boom, 1950-1 (see Table XI). Thereafter prices slumped but, thanks mainly to marked advances in farm productivity, volume rose at a

[1] Wherever possible the tables have been brought up to 1965-6; in other cases the latest year available in published sources has been used.

[2] The word 'volume' is used to convey the idea of quantity as measured by 'value at constant prices'. The words 'total value' imply the total quantity measured at current prices.

high trend rate after 1951-2. Prices recovered after 1962-3 (although wool prices fell in 1964-5), but the future rate of growth in quantity of rural exports—especially pastoral products—will for some years be affected by the severe drought of 1965 and early 1966. Generally it can be said that the volume of exports, especially of rural products and minerals, has grown over the whole period at about 4 per cent per annum compound. Prospects for mineral expansion in the future are bright; for manufactures less certain but not unhopeful; and rural exports can be expected to continue an upward trend in volume once the serious drought setback is overcome. Whether values will keep pace with expansion in volume is more problematical.[3] If, as seems likely, an increase in the volume of imports will be needed to sustain future economic growth in Australia,[4] it may be assumed that trade policy will continue, as throughout the post-war period, to predicate a need for increased total values of exports.[5]

(2) The principal categories of exports are those of rural origin (some 81 per cent in 1963-4), minerals (some 7 per cent), and manufactures, including petroleum (11 per cent) (see Table VIII). This represents a significant, although not dramatic shift from earlier years in favour of manufactures. It may be assumed that rural exports will lose further and more substantial ground relative to minerals and manufactures; they will, however, continue to provide the bulk of export earnings and there is no reason for thinking that a policy of expansion of rural exports is any less important than in the past. Regardless of the shift in proportions, more absolute earnings are desirable in all categories. Within the rural category wool still dominates, but wheat, meat, and sugar have risen in relative importance in comparison with the position in earlier years. Within manufacturing, iron and steel products and

[3] The precise figure for past growth naturally depends upon the years selected for analysis. The treatment in the Treasury White Paper on *The Australian Balance of Payments, February 1966* (5), p. 23, tends to be more favourable by reason of the periods selected than the data given in the Vernon Report (11), vol. I, p. 310, Table 12:4. On the other hand, a more favourable view is given, for a different period, in ch. 8, para. 56 of the Report, although the lag of value behind volume is still significant. When it comes to projection, past experience is only one factor to be considered: but a case can be argued for thinking that aggregate value and volume may move more closely together over the next few years. Prices for meats and grains and some minerals may remain buoyant, offsetting relative weakness in wool and dairy produce prices and the recent severe depression in sugar returns. How difficult it is to make judgments may be seen in reading the Vernon Report, vol. I, chs. 8, 12, *passim*, vol. II, app. K, attach. K.1; the Treasury paper (5) and commentaries like those of Perkins (137), pp. 109-11.

[4] Import prices are not likely to fall (see note on terms of trade below); hence the total cost of imports will also rise.

[5] See supporting view in Treasury White Paper (5), p. 16. This view that imports must increase is not an argument that needed 'credits' will not readily increase in total value *pari passu* with the total cost of imports and other 'debits' (see brief discussion in Section 16).

motor vehicles stand out, but a very wide array of goods makes up the total. Minerals represent the glamour prospect for the seventies.[6]

(3) The direction of exports has changed markedly in the post-war period and very much in keeping with what might be expected from a study of the documents and especially from the difficulties now experienced in developing trade with Europe and the more expansive prospects in Japan (see Tables V and IX). The most dramatic and contrasting changes are in the shares of total exports taken by the United Kingdom and Japan. Their respective percentage shares in 1937-8 were 54·8 and 3·7. In 1965-6 they were 17·4 and 17·3. We may expect the Japanese market to continue to expand and probably increase its share in the total of Australian exports (see Sections 9 and 10).

There has been a shift since 1948-9 from Europe (including the United Kingdom) to Asia and the Pacific, but this is associated principally with the expansion of exports to Japan, China (wheat), New Zealand, Hong Kong, and the Pacific Islands. It is not a shift to Asian countries generally. There, future growth of imports from Australia is dependent upon successful programs of economic development and upon Australian ability to provide a share of those goods for which their scarce resources of foreign exchange are allotted by those countries. This observation has a distinct bearing on policies of Australian aid and import policy *vis-à-vis* Asia and underdeveloped countries elsewhere.[7]

(4) Fluctuations in export prices may be seen in Tables IV and XII and Figures 1 and 2. Wool, metals, and 'free market' sugar show up as more volatile in price behaviour than other exports. These fluctuations are an important element and are likely to continue to be so in Australia's drive for some commodity agreements, of which cereals and sugar are the most important (Section 7).

(5) These same fluctuations are the principal component in the rather erratic performance of the terms of trade (Table IV). Since import prices are more stable than export prices and tend to rise steadily,[8] if slowly, the

[6] See Treasury White Paper (5), app. B. In relation to the balance of payments it is well to remember in considering estimates of gross returns from exports that payments for shipping and dividends on oversea capital represent significant offsets. The net result, however, is undoubtedly significantly positive and, in addition, contributes to development and industrialisation in ways consistent with the declared national economic objectives (Document 16:19 and Vernon Report (11) generally).

[7] For discussion of factors affecting Australia's export trade prospects see Vernon Report (11), vol. II, ch. 12 and Treasury White Paper (5), especially pp. 34-6, where the emphasis on the importance of full employment in *developed* countries' growth everywhere is seen as important for Australian exports. But in many underdeveloped countries balance of payments difficulties are so perennial that their import policies must be selective. See also Crawford (59).

[8] See Perkins (137), p. 111.

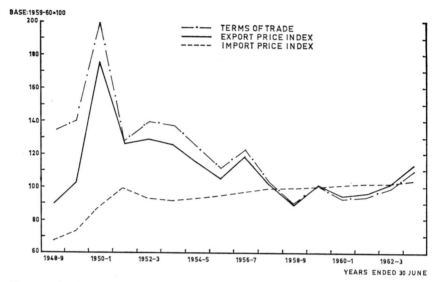

FIGURE 1   IMPORT AND EXPORT PRICE INDEXES AND TERMS OF TRADE,
1948-9 TO 1963-4

Source: Balance of Payments. Derived from the Vernon Report (11), Chart 12.6.

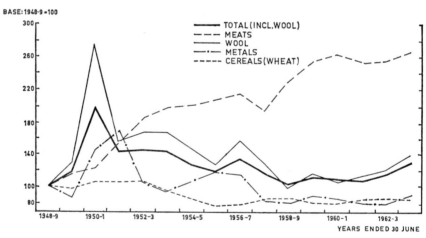

FIGURE 2   EXPORT PRICES OF SELECTED COMMODITIES, 1948-9 TO 1963-4

Source: 1948-9 to 1959-60, based on Commonwealth Statistician's index (base, average
three years ended June 1939 = 100); 1960-1 to 1963-4, based on Commonwealth Statistician's revised index (base, 1959-60 = 100). Derived from the Vernon Report (11),
Chart 12.8.

Note: The indexes have been linked, although they are not fully comparable because of
different weights used and because the revised index covers a greater number of items.

558

terms of trade mostly move against Australia when export prices fall and move in her favour when prices rise. Quite clearly, if there were a discernible (and predictable) persistent long-term trend downwards in export prices, absolutely or relatively to import prices, trade policy decisions would necessarily have regard to this trend as well as to the short-term fluctuations about the trend. Many underdeveloped countries are basing their commodity policies (and their policy demands on the more affluent countries) on the presumption that there is a predictable and adverse trend in the terms of trade for countries dependent upon a few staple primary exports.[9] It is doubtful whether such a confidently predictable trend for any particular grouping of commodities has been established, but the argument will go on. More can be said with confidence, short of certainty, about factors affecting the outlook for particular commodities.[10] The more diversified the exports the more readily can the impact on external economic viability of short-term adverse fluctuations in prices of particular items and any longer-term downward trend be absorbed. It can certainly be said that owing largely to the absence of another depression like that of the thirties and Australia's more diversified array of exports (Tables VIII and X), total earnings by Australian export industries in post-war years have fluctuated less violently than in pre-war years and with less impact on the internal economy.[11] The diversification of export pattern will continue (see paragraph (2) above). It can also be said that the more readily the export sectors are able to respond to permanent shifts in external prices the better.[12] The concurrence of large markets in China for Australian wheat and the relatively greater attractiveness to many individual producers of expanding wheat acreages as against increased investment in wool or other products has been a case in point.[13]

(6) All exports have been subjected to cost price squeeze in varying degree. Rising productivity is necessary at times to offset both falling prices and rising costs. Internal policy in respect of cost price levels is therefore significant for any effective export policy.[14]

[9] Prebisch (159).

[10] See, for example, Balassa (18).

[11] The latter point is, however, due in greater part to better understanding and management of the economy.

[12] See Treasury White Paper (5), pp. 39 *et seq.*

[13] The point made is valid for individual producers but is subject to two observations. In some cases the production of wheat was expanded without impairment of increased wool output. More importantly, the support given to wheat returns by the stabilisation scheme has greatly minimised the risk that oversea prices for wheat would be unprofitable. To the extent that Treasury subsidy has been involved in expanding exports a social cost has been incurred.

[14] This point is not illustrated in the tables here presented. It is extensively discussed in the Vernon Report (11), vol. I, ch. 8, paras. 32-42 and the Treasury White Paper (5), p. 39.

(7) The final observation on exports is to note the relative decline of export earnings in relation to GNP (Table II). This is not merely a matter of decline in traditional export prices relative to prices in the manufacturing and tertiary sectors of the economy; it also reflects the pattern of growth in the economy and the failure of the manufacturing sector to provide exports commensurate with its growth. No great importance need be attached to a decline in the ratio of export earnings to GNP. Total value of imports may also decline as a ratio to GNP; but the absolute increase in these to be associated with further economic growth is, on the whole, more certain than any equivalent increase in export earnings.[15]

II *Imports*

(8) Imports have grown substantially in total value and volume over the period although, in current prices, somewhat more slowly than GNP (Tables II, XV). Some of the contrast between the mid-fifties and the sixties is due to the import restrictions of the fifties. The documents in Section 15 frequently attest to the spillover demand for imports associated with inflationary pressures occurring under conditions of over-full employment. The import restrictions concealed these pressures but were, of course, themselves the reflection of them. Spillover demand has been an important phenomenon in Australia (e.g. 1950-1, 1955-6 and 1960-1). The apparent decline in the ratio of imports to GNP reflects some relative import saving, but it is not possible to make precise predictions about this. As we have observed, it is generally agreed that total value of imports will increase in absolute terms given continued growth in GNP at moderate to high rates.[16]

(9) Table III, taken from the Treasury White Paper on Balance of Payments, indicates Australia's considerable significance as a trading nation. This arises primarily from the high living standards enjoyed by Australians and the relatively high rate of its economic growth. Its high rank as a trader is sometimes puzzling to observers who think of Australia, with some justice, as a rather high protectionist country. Tables XIII, XVI, XVII, and XVIII throw some light on this, as indicated in paragraphs (10) and (11).

(10) Imports are required to supply consumer goods, capital equipment, and producer materials principally for use in manufacturing. Finished consumer goods account for a fairly steady percentage of imports (between 17 and 19 per cent); fuels and lubricants have fallen dramatically from 10 per cent in 1953-4 to under 2 per cent in 1965-6;[17] and producer materials for

---

[15] See discussion in Section 16. For a specific discussion of the relative movements of *export* and *import propensities* in Australia since 1920 see Lundberg and Hill (113).

[16] For discussion of spillover demand see Vernon Report, vol. I, chs. 1 and 2, *passim*; on import replacement and import saving see ibid., ch. 12, paras. 106-8, ch. 13, paras. 68-74, and vol. II, app. K, paras. 124-71. See also Treasury White Paper (5), pp. 19-20.

[17] Because of the rapid development of refineries, imports of high value refined petroleum have greatly fallen in quantity.

manufacturing purposes, together with capital equipment, have risen from 62·2 per cent of imports in 1948-9 to 71·1 per cent in 1965-6 (Table XIII). This is very much a picture of imports geared to the needs of economic expansion in Australia.

(11) As a principal stimulus to industrialisation the Australian tariff is protective in character, for some industries quite highly so (Tables XVI and XVII). As noted in Section 14, it has been estimated that some 60 to 70 per cent of Australian manufacturing industry, whether measured by employment or value of production, is dependent in some degree on the protective tariff.[18] On the other hand, all sectors of the Australian economy rely heavily on imports for capital and producer goods (see Table XIII). The result is that some 70 per cent or more (Table XVII) of imports are not competing with Australian production.[19] Competition for this market is among suppliers to the Australian market and, in this respect, the preferences to Britain and other Commonwealth suppliers, but especially to Britain, are important (Tables XVII and XVIII).

Both these facts are relevant to trade policy. The high degree of dependence of Australian manufacturing industry on the tariff accounts for Australian reluctance to consider across the board cuts in tariff (see references to Kennedy Round in Section 5). On the other hand the high proportion of Australian imports which are assessed at nil BPT and relatively low MFN rates of duties not only provides scope for worthwhile competition among suppliers but gives the existence of preferential margins an added and sharper importance in Australia's international economic relations and negotiations. Moreover, the continued margin of preference of 7½ per cent on producer goods not produced in Australia clearly adds also to Australia's industrial cost structure: this is part of the price of the Trade Agreement with the United Kingdom (Section 9). The tables do not bring out other tariff features relevant to policy and noted in Section 14.

(12) There have been changes in the main sources of supply of Australian imports (see Table XIV). Again, the United Kingdom has declined in relative importance, providing 50·4 per cent of the Australian market in 1948-9 and 25·8 per cent in 1965-6. The share of the United States rose from 10·0 to 23·9 per cent in the same period; while for Japan the rise was from 0·4 to 9·5 per cent. This result is explained by a number of factors: by the final cessation of restrictions on imports from dollar sources in February 1960 (Section 15); by the rise in United States capital investment in Australia; by some loss by the United Kingdom of her preferential margins in the

[18] Vernon Report (11), vol. I, ch. 13, para. 26.

[19] Table XVI suggests 80 per cent or more, but some free-entry imports do compete with unprotected Australian production. See also discussion in Section 14 and Vernon Report (11), vol. I, ch. 13, para. 24.

Australian tariff; the trade treaty with Japan; and the general loss of competitive edge on the part of United Kingdom industry. All these matters are relevant to the future British policy *vis-à-vis* Europe and hence have a bearing on future Australian trade policy, including possible changes in the preferential tariff structure.

III *Trade Balance and Balance of Payments*

(13) A glance at Table VI will show that Australia generally, but not always, has a positive balance of trade, that is a surplus of exports of goods over imports of goods. However, current account items like freight, travel, dividends on foreign investment, and interest on government borrowing— the so-called invisibles (or services)—always represent a large net outgo of funds (Table VI, col. 4). The normal result on current account trade in goods and services is a deficit (col. 5). This deficit is understandably greatest in the years in which the balance of trade is in deficit. For our purposes it is important to note that export earnings from goods and services do not normally meet the cost of imports of goods and services. The table suggests an upward trend of this deficit on current account and this has a bearing on the problem of sustaining a viable external economy under conditions of a high rate of economic growth.

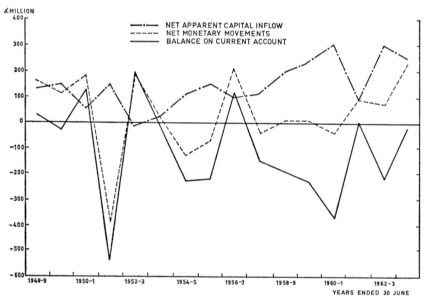

FIGURE 3   THE EXTERNAL BALANCE OF PAYMENTS, IMPORTANT TOTALS, 1948-9 TO 1963-4

Source: Balance of Payments. Derived from the Vernon Report (11), Chart M.1.

(14) If export earnings do not cover the current outgoings, the deficits require settling in some other way. This occurs by public borrowing abroad or running down our reserves or because of an inflow of capital or two or more of these factors together. Since 1950 Federal governments have borrowed significantly, for example, from the International Bank for Reconstruction and Development (Section 15), and oversea firms and individuals (principally British and American) have invested in Australia. This capital inflow (see Figure 3), often accompanied by more advanced technology than otherwise available in Australia, has contributed importantly to economic development and in itself, as already noted, accounts for some of the increase in imports. Important issues, beyond trade policy in the sense of this book, are raised by the rapid growth of capital inflow in the last fifteen years. Our concern is not with these issues but with the simple fact that a large positive net capital inflow has come to be of major importance in overcoming the fact that export earnings from goods and services do not meet annual costs of imports of goods and services. It is clear from Table VI that export and import totals may vary greatly and independently of each other. Net capital inflow is another variable in the sense that the aggregate may vary from year to year, although when it falls there may be some associated and offsetting fall in imports. Since capital inflow creates obligations to pay dividends or interest abroad, these obligations in turn have a further bearing on trade policy. For export earnings must increase or further import replacement occur if such obligations are not to represent a new source of strain on the balance of payments. If, for example, further scope for import replacement were thought to be limited, the case for a strong export drive would be strengthened: it is not always that oversea investment leads directly to export earnings, as is the case with mineral development in northern Australia (Section 16, n. 10).

(15) The function of foreign exchange reserves (Table VI, col. 8) is to tide us through short-term adverse fluctuations in any one or more of the three variables—exports, imports, and net capital inflow. It is, of course, the net position of all three taken together that finally counts. In Section 15 we have discussed what constitutes adequate reserves to cover the kind of variations in exports and imports Australia experiences from time to time. We there noted the importance played by the right to borrow from the IMF and to make stand-by arrangements. While no precise figure can or ought to be stated, it is clear from an examination of Australian experience that large reserves in terms of ability to meet the import bill for several months are desirable.

563

TABLE I

GROSS NATIONAL PRODUCT

Year	Current Prices $A million	Constant Prices (1959–60 base) $A million	Rate of Growth %
1948– 9	4,471	8,608[a]	
1949–50	5,355	9,344[a]	8·6
1950– 1	7,174	9,731[a]	4·1
1951– 2	7,686	10,001[a]	2·8
1952– 3	8,353	9,930[a]	−0·7
1953– 4	9,019	10,532	6·0
1954– 5	9,741	11,152	5·9
1955– 6	10,563	11,672	4·7
1956– 7	11,448	11,908	2·0
1957– 8	11,585	12,129	1·9
1958– 9	12,472	13,008	7·2
1959–60	13,818	13,329	4·0
1960– 1	14,601	14,124	4·4
1961– 2	14,929	14,291	1·2
1962– 3	16,190	15,116	5·8
1963– 4	17,912	16,024	6·0
1964– 5	19,544	16,987	6·0
1965– 6[b]	20,519	n.a.	

n.a. Not available.

[a] 1953–4 prices have been linked to 1959–60 prices.

[b] 1965–6 figure added.

SOURCE: Commonwealth Statistician, *Australian National Accounts, National Income and Expenditure 1948–49 to 1964–65*, Tables 2 and 11; *National Income and Expenditure 1965–66*, Budget Papers, 1966.

TABLE II

EXPORTS, IMPORTS, AND GROSS NATIONAL PRODUCT

Year	GNP[a]	Exports[b]	Ratio exports to GNP	Imports[c]	Ratio imports to GNP
	$A million	$A million	%	$A million	%
1948– 9	4,471	1,082	24·2	821	18·4
1949–50	5,355	1,224	22·9	1,052	19·6
1950– 1	7,174	1,958	27·3	1,448	20·2
1951– 2	7,686	1,330	17·3	2,042	26·6
1952– 3	8,353	1,696	20·3	1,006	12·0
1953– 4	9,019	1,618	17·9	1,328	14·7
1954– 5	9,741	1,512	15·5	1,648	16·9
1955– 6	10,563	1,524	14·4	1,605	15·2
1956– 7	11,448	1,938	16·9	1,389	12·1
1957– 8	11,585	1,601	13·8	1,530	13·2
1958– 9	12,472	1,593	12·8	1,563	12·5
1959–60	13,818	1,830	13·2	1,823	13·2
1960– 1	14,601	1,834	12·6	2,066	14·1
1961– 2	14,929	2,100	14·1	1,710	11·5
1962– 3	16,190	2,102	13·0	2,076	12·8
1963– 4	17,912	2,726	15·2	2,250	12·6
1964– 5	19,544	2,579	13·2	2,755	14·1
1965– 6[d]	20,519	2,648	12·9	2,831	13·8

[a] At current prices.

[b] Merchandise exports.

[c] Imports are shown on an f.o.b. basis, adjusted for balance of payments purposes.

[d] 1965-66 figures added are provisional.

SOURCES: Commonwealth Statistician, *Oversea Trade*; Commonwealth Statistician, *Australian National Accounts 1948-49 to 1964-65*; Commonwealth Treasury, *The Australian Balance of Payments, February 1966*; *National Income and Expenditure 1965-66*, Budget Papers, 1966.

TABLE III

IMPORTS (c.i.f.) BY LEADING IMPORTING COUNTRIES, 1964

Country	Ranking by level of Imports per capita[a]	Total Imports	Imports per capita[b]
		$US million	$US
1. United States	...	20,251	105
2. United Kingdom	...	15,438	285
3. Germany	...	14,618	256
4. France	...	10,070	208
5. Japan	...	7,948	82
6. Canada	(7)	7,556	392
7. Italy	...	7,231	142
8. Netherlands	(3)	7,055	583
9. Belgium-Luxembourg	(1)	5,901	608
10. Sweden	(6)	3,855	501
11. Switzerland	(2)	3,610	602
12. Australia	(11)	3,313	297
13. Denmark	(4)	2,614	554
14. Norway	(5)	1,984	538
15. Finland	(10)	1,505	328
16. New Zealand	(8)	961	370
17. Israel	(9)	826	334

[a] Australia, and countries having a higher *per capita* level of imports than Australia, only.

[b] Based on population at mid-year.

SOURCE: Commonwealth Treasury, *The Australian Balance of Payments, February 1966,* p. 16.

566

TABLE IV

TERMS OF TRADE

(1955-6 = 100)[a]

Year	Export Price Index	Import Price Index	Terms of Trade
Average of 1936–7 to 1938–9	24	25	96
1947– 8	71	67	106
1948– 9	85	70	121
1949–50	97	76	128
1950– 1	168	92	183
1951– 2	120	104	115
1952– 3	122	98	124
1953– 4	120	96	125
1954– 5	110	98	113
1955– 6	100	100	100
1956– 7	112	102	110
1957– 8	97	104	93
1958– 9	85	104	82
1959–60	95	105	90
1960– 1	90	106	85
1961– 2	91	107	85
1962– 3	96	107	90
1963– 4	108	109	100
1964– 5[b]	100	110	91
1965– 6[bc]	102	113	90

[a] Published on bases 1959-60 (Export Price Index) and 1952-3 (Import Price Index). Converted to 1955-6 base.

[b] Figures for 1964–5 and 1965–6 have been added to the original table. Import Price Index published on base 1962–3 has been converted to 1955–6 base. Export Price Index published on base 1959–60 has been converted to 1955–6 base.

[c] Provisional figures.

Derived from Commonwealth Statistician, *Balance of Payments*.

SOURCE: As reproduced in Vernon Report (11), vol. II, Table M.7.

TABLE V   CHANGES IN DIRECTION OF

	1937–8		Average 1950–5		1959–60		1960–1	
	Exps.	*Imps.*	*Exps.*	*Imps.*	*Exps.*	*Imps.*	*Exps.*	*Imps.*
AUSTRALIAN EXPORTS AND IMPORTS								
TOTAL $A million	316	260	1,652	1,528	1,876	1,852	1,940	2,176
PERCENTAGE OF TOTAL TO AND FROM:								
U.K.	54·8	40·6	35·7	45·6	26·4	35·6	23·9	31·4
W. Europe	16·7	9·6	24·4	14·3	20·0	15·8	17·3	16·2
TOTAL	71·5	50·2	60·1	59·9	46·4	51·4	41·2	47·6
Asia and Pacific:								
Canada and U.S.	8·3	22·6	10·9	13·9	9·6	19·4	9·2	24·3
N.Z. and Pacific Islands	6·2	4·6	6·1	2·0	9·2	3·3	9·9	1·8
Japan	3·7	4·7	7·5	2·3	14·4	4·5	16·7	6·0
China (Mainland)	1·2	0·6	1·3	0·5	2·9	1·0	6·3	0·4
India, Pakistan, and S.E. Asia Countries	4·1	11·3	7·4	12·7	7·2	10·6	6·7	10·5
TOTAL	23·5	43·8	33·2	31·4	43·3	38·8	48·8	43·0
All other markets	5·0	6·0	6·7	8·7	10·3	9·8	10·0	9·4

West Europe includes Belgium, Luxembourg, Denmark, France, Federal Republic of Germany, Finland, Gibraltar, Italy, Netherlands, Norway, Portugal, Sweden, Switzerland, Republic of Ireland, Austria, Greece, Spain, Malta, and Yugoslavia. Pre-war figures, which, for example, include East Germany, are not strictly comparable.

Pacific Islands includes the Australian Territories of Papua and New Guinea, Nauru, Norfolk

AUSTRALIAN EXPORTS AND IMPORTS

1961–2		1962–3		1963–4		1964–5		1965–6	
Exps.	*Imps.*	*Exps.*	*Imps.*	*Exps.*	*Imps.*	*Exps.*	*Imps.*	*Exps.*	*Imps.*
2,156	3,770	2,154	2,162	2,786	2,376	2,651	2,905	2,721	2,939
19·0	30·4	18·5	30·4	18·3	27·7	19·5	26·2	17·4	25·8
19·5	16·1	17·3	15·4	17·2	16·1	16·3	16·6	17·6	17·4
38·5	46·5	35·8	45·8	35·5	43·8	35·8	42·8	35·0	43·2
11·5	23·2	14·1	25·5	11·9	26·9	11·5	27·9	14·0	27·6
8·4	2·0	9·3	3·1	9·1	3·4	10·1	3·0	10·3	2·8
17·5	5·5	16·1	6·0	17·5	6·8	16·6	8·9	17·3	9·5
6·2	0·4	6·0	0·5	6·0	0·7	5·1	0·8	3·9	0·8
7·0	11·0	9·7	8·8	8·4	8·0	10·6	7·9	9·8	7·1
50·6	42·1	55·2	43·9	52·9	45·8	53·9	48·5	55·3	47·8
10·9	11·4	9·0	10·3	11·6	10·4	10·3	8·7	9·7	9·0

Island, Cook Island, Western Samoa, Fiji, Gilbert and Ellice Islands, New Hebrides, Solomon Islands, Tonga, New Caledonia, Oceania, Guam, U.S. Samoa and other U.S. islands.

South-East Asia includes Malaya (Malaysia where relevant), Singapore, Brunei, Borneo, Burma, Cambodia, Indonesia, Laos, Philippines, Thailand, Vietnam, Korea, Formosa, Ceylon, Bhutan, Nepal, and Portuguese possessions (Macao and Timor).

SOURCE: Commonwealth Statistician, *Oversea Trade.*

TABLE VI

BALANCE OF PAYMENTS

$A million

Year	Imports f.o.b.[a]	Exports f.o.b.[a]	Balance of invisibles[b]	Balance on current account[b]	Net apparent capital inflow[c]	Net monetary movements[d]	Level of international reserves at 30 June[e]
1948– 9	821	1,043	−160	62	264	326	894
1949–50	1,052	1,186	−205	−71	298	227	1,259
1950– 1	1,448	1,950	−252	250	108	358	1,607
1951– 2	2,042	1,328	−374	−1,088	297	−791	745
1952– 3	1,006	1,692	−297	389	−24	365	1,122
1953– 4	1,328	1,624	−300	−4	45	41	1,141
1954– 5	1,648	1,523	−352	−477	216	−261	857
1955– 6	1,605	1,540	−383	−448	302	−146	710
1956– 7	1,389	1,958	−352	217	205	422	1,133
1957– 8	1,530	1,614	−393	−309	227	−82	1,051
1958– 9	1,563	1,616	−438	−385	401	16	1,033
1959–60	1,823	1,864	−500	−459	474	15	1,024
1960– 1	2,066	1,851	−522	−737	657	−80	1,101
1961– 2	1,701	2,128	−429	−2	178	176	1,097
1962– 3	2,065	2,123	−527	−469	615	146	1,225
1963– 4	2,237	2,732	−548	−53	503	450	1,672
1964– 5	2,739	2,575	−614	−778	481	−297	1,354
1965– 6[f]	2,826	2,636	−640	−830	891	61	1,375

[a] The amounts shown represent the recorded trade figures adjusted for balance of payments purposes. Recorded exports and imports of gold, government exports for armed forces and overseas projects, imports by diplomatic missions, films imported on a rental basis, exports and imports of goods for repair (including value of repairs), and goods intended to be re-imported or re-exported are excluded. Imports and exports of ships and aircraft for use on overseas routes, imports of defence equipment and material, and exports of uranium, for which customs entries are not required, are added.

[b] The minus sign indicates excess of debits over credits.

[c] The minus sign denotes outflow.

[d] The minus sign indicates decrease in international reserves or net IMF position or an increase in foreign holdings of Australian currency. For details see source.

[e] This column has been added. Changes from year to year are not identical with Net Monetary Movements because of the influence of the other two factors mentioned in note (d).

[f] Provisional figures.

SOURCES: Commonwealth Treasury, *The Australian Balance of Payments, February 1966; Treasury Information Bulletin*, no. 43, July 1966; and Commonwealth Statistician, *Balance of Payments 1961–62 to 1965–66*.

TABLE VII

RELATION OF NET APPARENT CAPITAL INFLOW
TO GROSS CREDITS AND GROSS DEBITS

Year	Exports and invisible credits[a]	Imports and invisible debits[b]	Net apparent capital inflow[c]	$\frac{C}{B}$	$\frac{C}{A}$
	A	B	C	D	E
	$A	$A	$A	%	%
	million	million	million		
1948– 9	1,446	1,120	264	23·6	18·3
1949–50	1,655	1,428	298	20·9	18·0
1950– 1	2,253	1,895	108	5·7	4·8
1951– 2	1,839	2,600	297	11·4	16·2
1952– 3	1,885	1,520	−24	−1·6	−1·3
1953– 4	1,898	1,857	45	2·4	2·4
1954– 5	1,985	2,246	216	9·6	10·9
1955– 6	2,109	2,255	302	13·4	14·3
1956– 7	2,475	2,053	205	10·0	8·3
1957– 8	2,177	2,259	227	10·1	10·4
1958– 9	2,355	2,339	401	17·1	17·0
1959–60	2,707	2,692	474	17·6	17·5
1960– 1	2,925	3,005	657	21·9	22·5
1961– 2	2,761	2,583	180	7·0	6·5
1962– 3	3,222	3,074	624	20·3	19·4
1963– 4	3,834	3,375	518	15·4	13·5
1964– 5	3,727	4,015	490	12·2	13·2
1965– 6[d]	4,284	4,223	891	21·1	20·8

[a] Aggregate of figures for exports, invisible credits *and* net apparent capital inflow (treated as a current credit for purpose of this table) given in *The Australian Balance of Payments*.

[b] Aggregate of figures for imports and invisible debits given in *The Australian Balance of Payments*. These debits include earnings from overseas investment payable abroad (i.e. liable to be paid there). Earnings payable include earnings not in fact paid abroad (i.e. are undistributed profits). These reappear on the credit side as portion of the capital inflow.

[c] Source as above. It needs to be noted that here the figure is net, i.e. is gross capital inflow less capital outflow items. See also note b.

[d] Preliminary.

SOURCES: Commonwealth Treasury, *The Australian Balance of Payments, February 1966*, Appendix A; Commonwealth Statistician, *Balance of Payments, 1961–62 to 1965–66*, Table 1.

TABLE VIII

EXPORTS ACCORDING TO INDUSTRIAL ORIGIN AS PERCENTAGE
OF TOTAL EXPORTS[a]

Industrial group	1938–9	1950–1	1955–6	1960–1	1963–4
Agriculture	20	16	20	24	27
Pastoral	44	70	56	49	49
Dairy and farmyard	11	4	7	4	4
Mines and quarries[b]	18	5	8	8	7
Forestry and fisheries	1	1	1	1	1
TOTAL PRIMARY PRODUCE[c]	94	95	92	87	88
Manufactures[d]	6	5	6	10	10
Refined petroleum oils	...	...	1	2	1
Unclassified	...	...	1	1	1
TOTAL AUSTRALIAN PRODUCE[b]	100	100	100	100	100

[a] Columns may not add because of rounding.

[b] Excludes gold exports. The addition to gold and foreign exchange holdings occurs at the time of production, exports merely involving the use or rearrangement of these holdings.

[c] Includes both processed and unprocessed primary produce.

[d] Includes iron and steel, vehicles and parts, rugs and chemicals, and 'other'.

SOURCES: Vernon Report (11), vol. II, Table M.6.; Commonwealth Treasury, *The Australian Balance of Payments, February 1966*, Table 14; *Year Book of the Commonwealth of Australia*, 1953.

TABLE IX   EXPORTS AND PERCENTAGE
COMMODITIES, BY COUNTRY OF

(Exports

Commodity	Year	Total value $A million	United Kingdom %	EEC[a] %	Other West Europe[b] %	Japan %
Wool	1948–9	462·8	34·8	37·4	3·2	2·1
	1963–4	961·0	16·0	28·3	3·3	29·4
Wheat and flour	1948–9	196·8	36·4	2·1	3·6	1·3
	1963–4	404·2	10·7	3·0	2·9	6·8
Beef and veal	1948–9	11·6	74·1	...	5·2	...
	1963–4	176·6	11·8	...	0·3	1·0
All other meats	1948–9	45·8	76·0	...	1·3	...
	1963–4	65·8	37·1	2·4	3·7	10·0
Sugar	1948–9	26·4	78·0	...	...	...
	1963–4	156·6	31·6	...	...	34·2
Butter	1948–9	47·6	87·0	...	0·4	...
	1963–4	54·8	81·3	2·2	...	...
Total dairy products (including butter)	1948–9	68·0	71·5	0·6	0·3	...
	1963–4	88·0	58·6	3·0	0·2	1·6
All fruits	1948–9	21·2	51·9	...	2·8	...
	1963–4	88·4	60·6	11·1	4·5	0·5
Lead and zinc	1948–9	59·2	74·7	6·8	0·3	...
	1963–4	96·2	44·3	13·1	0·2	12·1
Coal	1948–9	0·2	...	...	...	...
	1963–4	32·4	...	...	...	93·8
Petroleum	1948–9	1·0	...	...	...	...
	1963–4	42·4	4·7	1·9	...	6·6
Iron and steel	1948–9	5·4	7·4	...	...	...
	1963–4	66·6	8·7	3·6	1·8	15·6
Other	1948–9	187·0	31·4	14·3	3·3	1·4
	1963–4	604·2	10·7	16·5	2·5	9·8
TOTAL (including bullion and specie)	1948–9	1,085·4	42·3	19·2	2·8	1·4
	1963–4	2,782·4	18·4	14·9	2·4	17·5

[a] Belgium, France, Italy, Luxembourg, Netherlands, West Germany.

[b] Austria, Cyprus, Denmark, Finland, Greece, Gibraltar, Iceland, Malta, Norway, Portugal, Republic of Ireland, Spain, Sweden, Switzerland, Yugoslavia.

[c] 1948–9 figures include Formosa.

[d] Brunei, Burma, Cambodia, Ceylon, Formosa, Hong Kong, India, Indonesia, Korea (North), Laos, Malaya, Nepal, Pakistan, Philippines, Portuguese possessions (Macao, Portuguese India), Republic of Korea, Republic of Vietnam, Sabah, Sarawak, Singapore, Thailand, Vietnam (North), West Irian (1948–9 only).

[e] Christmas Island, Cook Island, Fiji, Gilbert and Ellice Islands, Guam, Nauru, New Caledonia,

OF TOTAL VALUE OF SELECTED
DESTINATION, 1948-9 AND 1963-4
f.o.b.)

China (Mainland)[c] %	Other Asia[d] %	U.S.A. and Canada %	N.Z. and Pacific Islands[e] %	Mid. East and Persian Gulf[f] %	Central and South America[g] %	Other[h] %
0·4	1·0	10·6	0·2	0·9	0·1	9·3
3·2	3·3	4·9	0·2	1·8	1·4	8·2
...	32·1	...	3·4	15·7	0·5	4·9
31·7	11·7	...	0·5	7·0	0·3	25·4
...	...	...	...	8·6	1·7	10·4
...	1·9	80·8	0·5	0·5	0·9	2·3
...	5·7	1·7	2·2	2·6	2·2	8·3
...	5·8	30·7	4·9	2·4	0·9	2·1
...	...	9·1	11·4	...	...	1·5
...	1·0	25·4	7·2	...	...	0·6
...	4·2	1·7	0·4	1·7	2·5	2·1
...	9·1	...	1·5	1·5	2·2	2·2
...	17·3	1·2	0·6	2·1	2·9	3·5
...	24·8	0·7	2·5	3·9	2·0	2·7
...	11·3	18·9	11·3	1·9	...	1·9
...	5·2	10·2	3·4	0·7	0·4	3·4
...	0·3	15·9	2·0	...	...	...
0·2	10·8	15·2	2·1	0·6	1·0	0·4
...	...	...	100·0[i]	...	...	...
...	2·5	...	3·1	...	...	0·6
...	...	...	100·0[i]	...	...	...
...	12·3	...	65·1	1·9	...	7·5
...	14·8	18·5	55·6	...	...	3·7
2·7	11·4	8·1	38·5	...	2·1	7·5
0·4	17·7	7·7	18·2	1·3	1·7	2·6
1·2	17·2	8·6	29·4	1·2	1·1	1·8
0·3	10·9	7·5	5·0	3·8	0·7	6·1
6·1	8·7	11·9	9·3	2·1	1·0	7·7

New Guinea, New Hebrides, Norfolk Island, Papua, Polynesia, Portuguese Timor, Samoa (U.S.), Solomon Islands, Tonga, Western Samoa, other American Pacific Islands.

[f] Afghanistan, Arabia South (Aden), Arabian States, Iran, Iraq, Israel, Jordan, Lebanon, Syria, Turkey, United Arab Republic.

[g] Including Caribbean.

[h] Including European Soviet area. Also including some exports of the commodities shown which, because of aggregation in published statistics, it is not possible to allocate.

[i] Percentages overstated because of rounding.

SOURCE: Oversea Trade.
Derived from Vernon Report (11) vol. I, Table 12.7.

TABLE X

VALUE OF PRINCIPAL EXPORTS AS PERCENTAGES OF ALL EXPORTS, SELECTED YEARS, 1948-9 TO 1963-4[a]

(%)

Year	Wool	Wheat and flour	Beef and veal	All meats other than beef and veal	Sugar	All fruits	Butter	All dairy products	Lead and zinc	Petrol- eum oils	Iron and steel	Coal	Other	All exports
1948–9	42·6	18·1	1·1	4·2	2·4	2·0	4·4	6·3	5·4	0·1	0·5	...	17·3	100·0
1950–1	64·5	10·9	0·7	2·4	1·5	1·6	1·9	3·0	3·5	...	0·1	...	11·8	100·0
1954–5	45·6	8·5	2·8	5·4	4·0	4·2	3·2	5·0	4·5	0·3	0·8	0·1	18·8	100·0
1956–7	48·7	8·2	2·3	2·7	2·9	2·6	2·6	4·1	4·7	1·1	2·7	0·2	19·8	100·0
1958–9	37·2	6·4	6·7	5·2	4·0	4·4	4·1	4·9	3·8	2·0	3·1	0·3	22·0	100·0
1960–1	34·5	12·6	4·1	3·4	3·6	3·0	2·0	3·5	3·1	2·2	2·8	0·8	26·4	100·0
1962–3	35·3	11·5	7·4	3·1	4·2	3·3	2·2	3·7	3·5	2·2	2·4	1·0	22·4	100·0
1963–4	34·5	14·5	6·3	2·4	5·6	3·2	2·0	3·2	3·5	1·5	2·4	1·2	21·7	100·0

[a] Calculated on f.o.b. value of exports. 'All exports' includes bullion and specie.
SOURCE: Oversea Trade.
As reproduced in Vernon Report (11) vol. I, Table 12.5.

TABLE XI

INDEX OF VALUE OF EXPORTS AT CONSTANT AND CURRENT PRICES

(1959-60 = 100)

Year	Constant prices			Total exports	Current prices of total exports[a]
	Foodstuffs	*Minerals, metals and metal manufactures*	*Wool and sheepskins*		
1947– 8	78	38	53	59	44
1948– 9	95	40	60	66	56
1949–50	93	38	70	70	64
1950– 1	82	37	67	66	105
1951– 2	66	40	63	60	71
1952– 3	92	61	75	76	91
1953– 4	83	76	74	75	87
1954– 5	89	62	73	75	82
1955– 6	93	66	81	82	83
1956– 7	94	99	91	93	105
1957– 8	76	94	83	83	87
1958– 9	98	95	91	94	87
1959–60	100	100	100	100	100
1960– 1	109	113	97	105	99
1961– 2	132	142	102	120	114
1962– 3	127	127	99	117	114
1963– 4	160	157	106	137	147
1964– 5	156	161	102	135	139
1965– 6[b]	146	202	102	137	142

[a] Total exports f.o.b. (adjusted for balance of payments purposes) have been made into an index base 1959–60 = 100.

[b] Provisional figures.

SOURCES: Commonwealth Treasury, *The Australian Balance of Payments, February 1966*, Table 16 and Appendix A; Commonwealth Statistician, *Monthly Review of Business Statistics*.

TABLE XII

EXPORT PRICES FOR PRINCIPAL COMMODITIES

(Base of each Index : Year 1959-60 = 100)[a]

Year	Wool	Meats	Cereals (Wheat)	Dairy produce (Butter)	Dried and canned fruits (Dried fruits)	Sugar	Metals and coals (Metals)	All groups
1948– 9	86	40	124	74	46	76	112	88
1949–50	111	45	120	79	50	82	98	101
1950– 1	235	48	130	86	65	91	161	173
1951– 2	133	61	131	92	87	103	189	126
1952– 3	145	73	134	99	85	111	118	128
1953– 4	145	78	123	103	82	106	105	125
1954– 5	127	80	107	99	77	98	119	114
1955– 6	109	82	97	102	82	100	131	105
1956– 7	136	85	98	79	91	111	127	117
1957– 8	111	77	107	69	98	115	93	102
1958– 9	85	91	105	73	110	105	90	90
1959–60	100	100	100	100	100	100	100	100
1960– 1	92	104	99	82	99	101	97	95
1961– 2	97	100	106	81	95	91	91	96
1962– 3	104	101	107	88	90	107	89	101
1963– 4	120	105	107	93	98	175	101	114
1964– 5	102	110	107	94	100[b]	100	123	105[b]
1965– 6	107	120[b]	107	86	102[b]	86[b]	122[b]	107[b]

[a] The indexes 1948–9 to 1958–9 have been linked to the base 1959–60 = 100 although they are not fully comparable with the remaining years because of different weights used and because the revised index covers a greater number of items. Previous category headings are indicated in brackets.

[b] Provisional figures.

SOURCE: Commonwealth Statistician, *Monthly Review of Business Statistics,* 1948–9 to 1958–9 based on Commonwealth Statistician's index (base, average three years ended June 1939 = 100). 1960–1 to 1965–6 based on the revised index (base 1959–60 = 100).

TABLE XIII

IMPORTS OF MERCHANDISE, ECONOMIC CLASSES,
PERCENTAGE OF TOTAL IMPORTS,
1948-9 AND 1953-4 TO 1965-6

(%)

Year	Producers' materials for use in manufacturing[a]	Other producers' materials	Capital equipment	Fuels and lubricants[b]	Finished consumer goods	Other	Total
1948– 9	47·2	4·4	15·0	8·8	17·4	7·2	100
1953– 4	45·0	4·2	21·4	10·0	15·5	3·9	100
1954– 5	47·7	5·1	18·8	6·8	17·2	4·4	100
1955– 6	45·6	4·6	22·0	5·7	17·1	5·0	100
1956– 7	48·3	4·4	21·6	3·9	16·9	4·9	100
1957– 8	48·2	4·0	22·3	3·1	18·0	4·4	100
1958– 9	47·9	3·9	22·4	3·5	17·9	4·4	100
1959–60	47·9	4·4	22·7	2·8	17·7	4·5	100
1960– 1	48·5	4·9	22·0	2·4	17·9	4·3	100
1961– 2	44·6	4·5	23·0	2·9	20·4	4·6	100
1962– 3	46·8	4·3	23·2	2·8	19·0	3·9	100
1963– 4	46–7	4·6	24·2	2·4	17·9	4·2	100
1964– 5	46·3	4·9	26·6	1·9	15·7	4·6	100
1965– 6[c]	42·1	4·6	29·0	1·8	16·3	6·2	100

[a] Includes completely knocked-down vehicles and components and replacement parts for motor vehicles.

[b] Excludes crude and enriched petroleum, which is classified as a producers' material for use in manufacturing.

[c] Figures for 1964–5 and 1965–6 (provisional) have been added.

SOURCES: As reproduced in Vernon Report (11), vol. II, Table M.3; Commonwealth Statistician, *Monthly Review of Business Statistics*, no. 346, September 1966.

TABLE XIV

IMPORTS AND PERCENTAGE OF TOTAL VALUE OF SELECTED COMMODITY CLASSES BY COUNTRY OF ORIGIN, 1948-9 AND 1963-4

(Imports f.o.b.)

Commodity Class	Year	Total Value	United Kingdom	European Economic Community[a]	United States	Canada	Japan	New Zealand	Other countries
		$A million	%	%	%	%	%	%	%
II Foodstuffs of vegetable origin	1948-9	27·8	7·9	...	0·7	...	...	0·7	90·7
	1963-4	61·6	2·9	6·5	5·5	...	0·4	2·9	81·8
III Yarns and manufactured fibres, textiles and apparel	1948-9	218·4	64·8	9·3	2·4	0·8	0·9	...	21·8
	1963-4	234·0	23·3	11·6	9·2	1·5	24·4	...	30·0
IIA Metals and metal manufactures (except electrical appliances and machinery)	1948-9	140·0	72·7	1·7	14·0	6·7	...	...	4·9
	1963-4	437·2	40·8	12·9	27·6	5·7	8·2	0·2	4·6
IIB Dynamo electrical machinery and appliances	1948-9	34·4	87·2	1·2	7·5	2·3	...	0·6	1·2
	1963-4	118·0	39·8	13·2	21·9	3·2	5·9	0·2	15·8
IIC Machines and machinery (except dynamo electrical)	1948-9	81·6	65·2	2·2	25·7	1·7	...	0·3	4·9
	1963-4	392·2	38·8	14·5	38·0	1·8	1·6	0·3	5·0
VI Paper and stationery (incl. pulp, board and paper manufactures)	1948-9	42·2	38·9	1·9	3·3	8·0	...	0·5	47·4
	1963-4	141·6	25·2	4·9	17·4	13·0	2·5	16·8	20·2
IX Chemicals, medicinal and pharmaceutical products, essential oils and fertilizers	1948-9	23·8	49·6	8·4	10·9	1·7	...	...	29·4
	1963-4	163·4	27·9	15·2	30·7	2·9	6·0	0·3	17·0
IX (Part) Petroleum	1948-9	78·2	...	...	14·8	...	...	...	85·2
	1963-4	232·8	0·8	...	...	...	...	...	99·2
All other classes and balance of class IX	1948-9	184·8	33·5	3·6	10·2	3·7	0·8	3·9	44·3
	1963-4	591·8	24·1	11·3	24·9	5·6	7·2	2·8	24·1
Total (including bullion and specie)	1948-9	830·4	50·4	4·1	10·0	2·9	0·4	1·0	31·2
	1963-4	2,372·6	27·8	10·9	22·9	4·0	6·8	1·9	25·7
	1965-6	2,939·5	25·8	11·1	23·9	3·7	9·5	1·6	24·4

[a] Belgium, France, Italy, Luxembourg, Netherlands, Western Germany.

SOURCE: *Oversea Trade.*

Derived from Vernon Report (11) vol. II, Table 12.9. Value changed to dollars and total figures for 1965-6 added.

TABLE XV

IMPORTS: TOTAL VALUE AT CONSTANT PRICES

Year	Imports (f.o.b.)[a] Current prices	Imports (f.o.b.) 1959–60 prices	Index of value at constant prices
	$A million	$A million	
1953– 4	1,328	1,461[b]	79
1954– 5	1,648	1,775[b]	96
1955– 6	1,605	1,683[b]	91
1956– 7	1,389	1,442[b]	78
1957– 8	1,530	1,572[b]	85
1958– 9	1,563	1,572[b]	85
1959–60	1,823	1,849	100
1960– 1	2,066	2,182	118
1961– 2	1,710	1,794	97
1962– 3	2,076	2,219	120
1963– 4	2,250	2,422	131
1964– 5	2,755	2,885	156

[a] Imports are shown on an f.o.b. basis, adjusted for balance of payments purposes.

[b] Based on 1955–6 prices and linked in 1959–60 to a series based on 1959–60 prices.

SOURCES: Commonwealth Treasury, *The Australian Balance of Payments, February 1966*, Tables 11, 12; Commonwealth Statistician, *Monthly Review of Business Statistics.*

581

U

TABLE XVI

DISTRIBUTION OF RATES IN THE TARIFF[a]

Rate of Duty	BPT	MFN
	No. of Sub-items	No. of Sub-items
Free and under $12\frac{1}{2}\%$	1,620	1,184
$12\frac{1}{2}\%$,, ,, $22\frac{1}{2}\%$	418	199
$22\frac{1}{2}\%$,, ,, $32\frac{1}{2}\%$	470	290
$32\frac{1}{2}\%$,, ,, $42\frac{1}{2}\%$	25	359
$42\frac{1}{2}\%$,, ,, $52\frac{1}{2}\%$	16	315
$52\frac{1}{2}\%$,, ,, $62\frac{1}{2}\%$	—	65
$62\frac{1}{2}\%$,, ,, $72\frac{1}{2}\%$	—	7
$72\frac{1}{2}\%$ and over	7 (all 90%)	7 (all 100%)
Total *ad valorem*	2,556	2,426
Other (mainly specific)	595	739
Alternative duties	259	241
Total	3,410[b]	3,406[b]

[a] As at 9 April 1963. Primage and temporary duties excluded.

[b] Apparent discrepancy caused by items applicable to United Kingdom goods only, for example spirits and tobacco.

SOURCE: Derived from table prepared by Department of Trade and Industry. As reproduced in Vernon Report (11) vol. II, Table L.1.

Table XVII

THE TARIFF: CHANGES IN PATTERN OF IMPORTS AND RATES OF DUTY, 1938-9 TO 1962-3

(%)

Item	1938–9	1948–9	1953–4	1959–60	1961–2	1962–3
Dutiable imports as a percentage of all imports	54·4	56·3	53·0	43·1	43·9	43·8
Imports bearing protective rates as a percentage of all imports[a]	39·8	19·0	16·3	15·2	17·3	18·6
Imports from B.P.T. countries as a percentage of all imports	49·0	56·9	52·3	41·0	36·3	37·9
Average duty on all imports	28·1	14·7	13·3	9·3	10·0	10·2
Average duty on imports bearing protective rates	32·1	25·7	27·2	30·5	31·5	31·9

[a] Includes imports bearing (i) *ad valorem* rates above 12½ per cent, and (ii) specific rates, except for revenue items such as tobacco, spirits, petrol, etc., and except, in the years other than 1938–9, for specific rate items with a low *ad valorem* equivalent. Low *ad valorem* equivalent items are those specific-rate duties grouped around the equivalent of 5 per cent *ad valorem*.

SOURCE: Derived from figures supplied by Commonwealth Statistician. As reproduced in Vernon Report (11) vol. I, Table 13.2.

TABLE XVIII

CHANGES IN PREFERENCE IN AUSTRALIAN TARIFF,
1951-2 TO 1961-2

(%)

Item	Year	Average ad valorem incidence		
		BPT rates	*MFN rates*	*Margin*
Goods free from U.K. and dutiable from MFN sources	1951–2	0·09	12·42	12·33
	1961–2	Nil	8·13	8·13
Goods dutiable from U.K. and dutiable from MFN sources at:				
Ad valorem rates	1951–2	18·18	37·07	18·89
	1961–2	20·83	38·62	17·79
Fixed rates	1951–2	10·69	16·52	5·83
	1961–2	10·82	16·64	5·82
Composite rates	1951–2	18·23	36·20	17·97
	1961–2	21·64	37·99	16·35
Ad valorem, fixed, or composite rates	1951–2	16·95	33·57	16·62
	1961–2	19·30	34·91	15·61
Goods free or dutiable from U.K. and dutiable from MFN sources	1951–2	5·71	19·49	13·78
	1961–2	6·38	16·98	10·60

SOURCE: Department of Trade and Industry.
As reproduced in Vernon Report (11) vol. II, Table L.10.

E

TRADE POLICY IN REVIEW

18

TRADE POLICY 1942-66:
RETROSPECT AND PROSPECT

The principal purposes of this final part of the book are to state the trade policy which seems to emerge from the documents; to ask whether that policy has been effective; to draw attention to the evolution of the international framework in which policy matters are principally negotiated and conducted; and to speculate somewhat on possible changes in Australia's future course of action, particularly with reference to the international framework.

Apart from a chart (Figure 4) showing the post-war development of international institutions, there are no documents accompanying this review. What is said is therefore by way of general examination of what may be inferred from the documents in Sections 1 to 17. Certainly a good deal can be readily inferred about policy. It will be shown that the early post-war declarations on policy stand up very well and that, despite important areas of frustration and some change in emphasis on our policies, a good deal has been achieved; that the application of policy, in all its parts, has been reasonably consistent (at least by international standards); and that, of all the international organisations concerned with trade policy, GATT has been the one that really mattered and continues to matter.

What is Trade Policy?

A brief reference to Section 17, the Statistical Appendix, will remind us of some of the important matters which must be encompassed in any trade policy likely to serve Australia's interests. Australia is committed to economic growth: there is no target, but a general expectation would be for a growth rate in GNP of 4 per cent or better. This calls for growth in imports, within the limits of external viability, to serve the needs of expansion in production in all sectors as well as to meet the demands of consumers enjoying rising incomes. Needed imports have to be encouraged, but part of the definition of 'need' lies in determinations by Parliament on the advice of the Tariff Board of tariff protection for some industries. Another part of the definition relates to the necessity to avoid temporary excesses in imports due to spill-over effects of inflationary pressures or, if unable to avoid them altogether, to have adequate reserves to absorb their cost.

Rising import costs together with the costs of services, or invisibles, like freight, tourism, service of oversea borrowing (including dividends to private oversea investors), call for increased export earnings with, in Australia's case, an appropriate recognition of the substantial incidental gain to the balance of payments of continued net capital inflow. However, the last point does not obviate the need for a sustained export drive, and a whole array of policy measures, both international and domestic, assume critical importance in the total complex of measures called 'trade policy'. Many of these measures, including important bilateral trade treaties, seek to open up and develop market opportunities; others seek to expand the supply of exportable goods competitive in price and quality; while yet others seek to minimise the impact of variability in price experience abroad and in seasonal conditions at home. These last again include adequate oversea reserves and also international agreements to stabilise conditions of trade in primary products.

All these subjects have been discussed in the documents as also, although to a lesser extent, has the close interaction between the domestic and external economies (see especially Sections 14 to 17).[1] The last point is worth illustrating. Thus full employment affects the level of imports; it may adversely affect export capacity. Declining export returns impair consumer expenditures and investment within Australia. Forced curtailment of imports because of a threat to external solvency may produce distortions in the allocation of resources. The tariff may wisely assist economic growth but is also capable of distortions and unwanted costs for actual or potential exporters. Capital inflow has major significance for import replacing industries and for investment in other directions, too. Mounting oversea freight costs may hamper export capacity and output. Failure to maintain reasonable internal price stability may put strains on the competitiveness of export industries and of import competing industries. Not least, the character of our natural resources, and new discoveries of such resources, and the quality and numbers of our work-force have a clear bearing on the volume and pattern of our trade.

There is no need to continue this catalogue of illustrations: all post-war governments in Australia have recognised the link beginning with the Chifley government's White Paper of 1945 on Full Employment (2:2); but recognition seemed most complete with the preamble to the terms of reference laid down for the Vernon Committee (16:19). Trade policy and general economic policy are inevitably interlinked.

The meaning of trade policy now becomes clear: it consists of measures designed not merely to promote external viability but also to provide the trade support required by policies of economic growth.[2] The actual trade

---

[1] See Vernon Report (11), vol. I, chs. 2 and 17 *passim*, and *The Australian Balance of Payments, February 1966* (5), pp. 11-12.

[2] As we observed in the Preface, international political aims have not, in Australia's case, been closely associated with trade policy, which by and large has been remark-

results in the period under review have supported a rate of growth in real GNP of a shade better than 4 per cent in the last fifteen years (Section 17). This is not an inconsiderable rate, and trade policies have contributed to the achievement of it and have been affected by it. It is not suggested, however, that trade policies alone or that a mere statement of appropriate policies ensure the desired result. Much depends upon the ability of governments to make their policies effective abroad and even more on collective decisions, within the total scope of policies, of individual producers, firms and government authorities. It is these who invest in export production or import-replacing enterprises and who require, in all sectors of the economy, imports of capital goods and producer goods. In short, policies are not a substitute for actual production and demand decisions which determine both the rate and nature of growth and the magnitude and pattern of trade. But policies on the part of Australian and oversea governments do, by specific measures and agreements, influence the 'climate' in which these decisions are made.

The scope of the documentation in the present book has been a little narrower than this discussion would imply. If we regard trade in its widest sense as traffic in goods and services, then national trade policy could be defined as the objectives and rules laid down or accepted by the national government within which the country's external economic relations are conducted. This is rather too wide to fit with the approach in this book, which has given greatest weight to Australia's export and import trade in goods. Yet we have seen that the full significance of policies apparently related to trade in goods cannot be grasped without some reference to financial and monetary policies and to matters like shipping costs, capital inflow, and other items which go to make up the balance of payments for any given period. Nor have we completely ignored the marked interdependence between the internal and external sectors and therefore the inter-relationship of internal and external policies stressed above. Largely for the sake of limiting the size of this book we have, however, been compelled to limit the range of documentation. We have therefore accepted the wider definition of trade policy here stated but have placed most emphasis in selecting documents and in the commentary on those expressions of policy which most directly impinge on the size and pattern of our export and import trade in goods.

A More Detailed View of Trade Policy

Various documents, including more especially the general policy statements after November 1960 by the Prime Minister and the Minister for

---

ably independent and economic in character. Our policies have been propounded more pragmatically than doctrinally, in some contrast, for example, to the United States, which tends to see competition in international trade in industrial products, at least, as an extension of its views and laws governing competition in industry and commerce within the United States itself.

Trade (Section 16), attempt some spelling out of the trade policies appropriate to the general objectives of 'a high rate of economic and population growth with full employment, increasing productivity, rising standards of living, external viability and stability of costs and prices' (16:19), but none does so more comprehensively and in more detail than three early documents. These are the White Paper of 1945 on Full Employment (2:2), Chifley's 1946 Rural Policy Statement (2:3), and Dedman's speech in 1948 on the International Trade Organization Bill (3:14). To an important extent Dedman's speech sought to correct the overemphasis on full employment, as being in itself an almost sufficient trade policy, which characterised earlier official statements. Nevertheless, with two or three exceptions and some important differences in emphasis, these early statements do cover all aspects of trade policy that might be expected to flow from the general objectives.

From the three documents mentioned, but mainly following Dedman's more systematic review of trade policy, we can list the following policy objectives.

(a) Maintenance of full employment, especially in the major industrial countries, as the means of expanding demand for internationally traded goods.

(b) Australian interests in export trade to be served also by legislating or negotiating for—

    (i) limitations on the unreasonable use of restrictions (especially of a non-tariff kind) on imports of Australian agricultural produce into countries protecting their domestic agriculture;

    (ii) greater stability of external prices for primary products;

    (iii) greater internal stability of prices for export products, 'so as to offset the effect of short-term fluctuations in demand for Australian products';

    (iv) various forms of domestic assistance (credit and market guidance) to exporters;

    (v) international trade treaties;

    (vi) diversification of the range of exports; and

    (vii) an expanded supply of efficiently produced goods for export.

(c) Australian import needs to be ensured by insisting on freedom—

    (i) to protect efficient industry by the tariff as an aid to industrial development;

    (ii) to protect the balance of payments by an appropriate foreign exchange reserve policy and action by resort if necessary (especially to avoid deflationary action likely to produce unemployment) to direct import restrictions; and

(iii) by agreeing, conditionally on international recognition of preferences as an exception to the general most-favoured-nation rule and on adequate reciprocation, to negotiate reductions in tariffs and in preferential margins.

(d) The necessity to promote actively the development of underdeveloped areas and by raising living standards in these territories to increase the demand for imported goods.

It is unlikely that the government of almost two decades later would wish to make major alterations to this statement of trade policies, although it might wish to make some reference to the more obvious omissions. Thus, although the post-war immigration policy began vigorously under Calwell's administration in 1945,[3] the need for expansion in trade to support the program of absorbing migrants under full employment conditions was not mentioned. Again, in declarations on trade policy little was said then about invisibles in the balance of payments such as shipping freights, although this subject especially has proved to be one of continuing importance and difficulty. The Labor government's opposition to borrowing abroad accounts for reticence on this subject although, as we have seen, Chifley appears to have had it in mind to borrow from the World Bank (4:4). Similarly, while private capital inflow was not proscribed there was little deliberate encouragement of it: certainly its subsequent importance to Australia's economic development was not foreseen.[4]

Apart from public and private borrowing abroad and control of the invisibles in the balance of payments, document after document in the period of the Liberal-Country Party ministries confirms the individual objectives listed, even if, for a while, there was perhaps some coyness in using the term 'full employment'.

Perhaps the most important differences between the earlier and later statements are four—and all are matters of relative emphasis only. There is, first, in the later statements a more explicit recognition of the mutual relation between trade and economic growth, a relationship which required growth in trade. Recognition of this truth was not absent from the statements of 1945 to 1948 (see, for example (b) (vii) above); but as we have noted it became more marked as governments in later years saw more clearly the important link between growth and full employment in Australia and capacity to underwrite the needed supply of imports. This evolution of thought accounts for the increasingly stronger emphasis on the export drive. This greater emphasis has in part reflected the increased industrial strength of Australia and the greater possibility for export of manufactured products

---

[3] See *C.P.D. (H. of R.)*, vol. 184, pp. 4913-14.

[4] Encouragement of the motor car industry was, however, one example in which advantage was taken of the necessity to try to replace imports from dollar areas (15:1).

(Section 17: Table VIII). In keeping with this degree of understatement of the significance of export there is not really to be found in the early papers the same persistent recognition of the importance of rising productivity in rural industries and on research and extension as means to this end.[5]

The second difference is again one of developing awareness. There was in the 1945-8 period direct recognition of the problems of underdeveloped countries; but this had more of an abstract quality than the direct awareness, now evident in Australian thinking, of the political and economic implications of mass poverty and inadequate economic growth in large parts of the world. This has begun to affect our trade policies not merely in the sense that aid may mean physical export of goods or that balance of payments problems experienced by the LDCs impair our export prospects, but more importantly in the steps taken to amend our import policies (Sections 5 and 6).

The third difference, one of degree rather than of kind, is difficult to measure but important to state. Australia has always been clear in the expression of its right to protect its industrial development. As we saw in Sections 1 and 3, there is no doubt that more restraint on tariff-making powers was expected than was in fact realised. At the same time it was fairly assumed that agricultural trade would be as free from restraint as trade in industrial products. This assumption has been falsified, leading to the recurring Australian complaint of imbalance in GATT (Section 5). We return to this point again in this review but stop to observe that frustration in the pursuit of Australia's agricultural objectives goes some way to explaining the signs of an unwillingness to approach tariff cutting with the same willingness (McEwen, with some reason, would say 'ability') as other contracting parties in GATT. At least it can be said that if Australia is more protectionist-minded now than the moderate language of the White Paper of 1945 would imply, there has been no great encouragement to be otherwise. And yet there are limits on this apparent growth in protectionism—limits which are becoming more real as Australia's economic growth gathers pace and its economy matures (Section 14). To put it mildly, the very success of Australia's economic policies makes it imperative to negotiate and otherwise encourage market opportunities for its exports of both primary and secondary products (Sections 15 and 16).

The fourth difference is readily enough explained: it is simply that experience has shown a somewhat different evolution of the framework of international organisations, relevant to trade policy, from that negotiated in the early post-war years. The hoped-for International Trade Organization failed to survive the test of Congressional reaction to the first wave of post-war

---

[5] Nevertheless the wool research programs were launched in this period and CSIRO programs were supported. However, greatly enlarged efforts to promote research and extension in farm industries generally came later in response to agricultural decline and continuing balance of payments difficulties (Section 13).

internationalism. With its demise GATT assumed a comprehensive and permanent role not intended for it. Only in 1964 did another world body—UNCTAD—come into being in far different circumstances from those prevailing in the late forties (Section 6). The result is that today we speak of GATT, instead of the expected ITO, and UNCTAD (although with uncertainty about its future). We also speak of the IBRD and the IMF with more confidence than was possible in 1948. But before taking this comment on international framework further it is well to remind ourselves of the substantial and, on the whole, consistent achievement of the policy objectives as outlined above. This, without repeating the detailed comment contained in earlier chapters, will enable us to pin-point the most likely trouble spots for the future. Our purpose is best served by brief reminders of what has happened in respect of each of the policy objectives listed above (see pp. 590-1).

Full Employment

The fullest discussion and recognition of the relation of trade and full employment was in the United Nations Conference on Trade and Employment which resulted in the proposed International Trade Organization. The fact that the Organization did not come into being was not, however, a defeat for Australia's hard work on this subject, for full employment has become an accepted objective and reality in Europe and North America, although it is only recently that the United States has begun seriously to experience some of the economic problems associated with it. The subject is no longer an issue in international trade conferences. This does not belittle its importance for Australian trade prospects: it simply means that there is practical achievement, at least in the developed countries, and no conflict of interest among nations on the question.[6]

Exports

In respect of some of the export objectives there is less ground for satisfaction and a good deal of doubt about future prospects. Agricultural protectionism may be broadly contained, but within that containment it flourishes almost in total disregard of the GATT 'fair trade' rules, especially that limiting the use of non-tariff devices for protecting agriculture. The Kennedy Round involves this issue in a crucial way and as an exercise embracing agriculture may even founder on it, especially if the United States refuses to negotiate its own non-tariff barriers to trade in primary products. Likewise renewed negotiations by Britain for entry into the Common Market again raises the issue sharply for Australia. With Japan some progress has been made in reducing her non-tariff barriers—mainly because Japan needs the

---

[6] We have already had occasion to notice the trouble taken in *The Australian Balance of Payments, February, 1966* (5) to emphasise the importance to Australian trade prospects of economic growth (it does not stress full employment as such) in the industrialised countries of the world. See pp. 34-5 of that publication.

foodstuffs concerned; and even the United States has kept trade open in meat and has recently removed its quotas on minerals.[7] Australia has its own Achilles heel in the shape of a virtual embargo on butter and margarine and an actual embargo on sugar, golden syrup, and treacle.[8]

Partial success has attended efforts to promote stability in export prices. Meat, sugar, wheat, and perhaps butter have had smaller fluctuations than would have occurred without bilateral and international agreements and understandings affecting these commodities.[9] Even more success has attended efforts to improve market opportunities for primary produce by bilateral trade agreements (Sections 9, 10, and 12). Any wide-ranging treaty with the United States, comparable with that represented by the treaties with the United Kingdom and Japan, has yet to come (Section 11), although the Kennedy Round may result in progress here. On a particular item affecting our relations with the United States, surplus disposals, there is now less tension and, indeed, circumstances have so changed that the problem is no longer the same as it was in the fifties and early sixties: less tension because on the one hand we can no longer press countries like India to take large quantities of wheat on commercial terms and because other markets have come to light, notably China.[10] A new cereals agreement is under negotiation in GATT and this may cover both commercial and non-commercial markets— a prospect probably assisted by the fact that under present farm policies the United States does not have stocks large enough alone to continue indefinitely very large scale PL 480 programs in support of the needs of countries like India. Indeed, the outlook for countries in need of food supplies but unable to finance them is now much bleaker unless an international agreement is devised to fill the gap hitherto met almost wholly by the United States.[11]

[7] There has been a move recently (1966) in the United States to relax import restric-strictions on cheddar cheese.

[8] Again, although defensible in GATT, the method of protecting raw tobacco has attracted some criticism. Differential rates of duty are applied to imports, and the concessional lower rate is only allowed when a required proportion of Australian leaf is used in Australian manufacture.

[9] It is particularly important to note that it is not the International Sugar Agreement which really counts (it is in any case in a state of suspension), but rather the more limited but highly effective Commonwealth Sugar Agreement. Unfortunately, it supports a negotiated price for only 335,000 tons out of between 1,400,000 and 1,500,000 tons available for export from Australia. In addition 265,000 tons may be sold at the ordinary market price plus a small preferential margin.

[10] However, in December 1966 the Wheat Board (judging from press reports only) appears to be putting mild pressure on India to take a large quantity of wheat (which it more than badly needs) on credit terms no more favourable than those now regularly applying to China.

[11] It is true that the increasing inability and unwillingness of the United States to meet unaided such problems as India's under the old PL 480 terms (bulk sales for rupees with only a small offset in dollar terms) may have two desirable results. First, it will encour-

594

We need not comment on the various domestic measures that have contributed significantly to improving our export position through promoting greater internal stability of prices for export products, domestic assistance to exporters, diversification of the range of exports, and an expanded supply of efficiently produced goods (objectives (b) (iii), (iv), (vi) and (vii), above). Sections 13 and 16 particularly deal with (b) (iv): measures such as the Exports Payments Insurance Corporation, Trade Commissioner service, beef roads, coal loading facilities, rail unification and modernisation, tax incentives, farm depreciation allowances, fertiliser subsidies, trade publicity, and special reserve and trading bank export finance arrangements. These all have solid worth, even if it is impracticable to assign specific shares of actual export expansion to each of the measures. All these matters and the more general policy of minimising the impact of the cost/price squeeze on export production are important determinants in our ability to compete in available world markets within whatever system of trade rules happens to govern our market operations.

In sum, the major disappointment is in the field of international commodity policy, defining that term broadly as in Section 7. The major frustrations are our failure to make much impact on agricultural protectionism and to secure more adequate market access through commodity agreements. In Section 7 we have discussed whether our aims are sufficiently clear (at least as set out in public documents) and it is possibly true perhaps that we have striven inconsistently. However, the battle is still joined: the future of practical understandings on the marketing of wheat is heavily involved in EEC policy and the Kennedy Round negotiations within GATT.

Import Policy

In respect of all three objectives listed under this heading, Australian governments have, as yet, no grounds for complaint. Australia has freely used its tariff and if its recourse to action under Articles XIX (emergency) and XXVIII (unbinding of bound tariff rates) has been somewhat frequent for its complete comfort within GATT, it has acted within its rights under the GATT contract. It can fairly claim, too, that it has kept its side of the general GATT compact (non-discriminatory MFN tariffs[12] and avoidance of non-tariff restrictions for protective purposes) rather better than the industrial

---

age India in its efforts to become self-sufficient in food. Second, while the need lasts other countries will be under pressure to act collectively with the United States in meeting the need under jointly agreed programs.

In the meanwhile, as we noted in Section 7, Congress has considerably hardened the terms on which United States food 'aid' is to be provided.

[12] With British preferential margins held under firm constraint and actually subjected to considerable reduction following the 1956 United Kingdom-Australia Trade Agreement (Section 9).

countries of Europe and the United States who treat trade in agricultural products (and textiles) so differently from trade in industrial products. Nevertheless our seeming coyness in making, as yet, substantial cuts in our MFN tariff rates rather weakens the willingness of other contracting parties to accept the fairness of our claims.[13] It is not always easy to convince other countries that our ability to cut tariffs is limited by the lack of substantial offers to improve access to their markets for our major exports.

Australia resorted to import restrictions for balance of payments reasons, gave them up when satisfied the need no longer existed, but remains free to use them again in times of severe balance of payments difficulty. While able to avoid them its position as critic of protection of agriculture by non-tariff devices is stronger than it was in the fifties, for the incidental result of import restrictions was undoubtedly a measure of protection which for a period rendered the Tariff Board somewhat inoperative because unnecessary.

On negotiated reductions in tariffs and preferential margins ((c) (iii)), Australia is, at least formally, a willing negotiator. By no stretch of the imagination can Australia be called a free trader, but it has accepted the general GATT objective of *freer* trade (as stated in the Preamble to the GATT articles) and has declared a willingness to make tariff concessions. Moreover, as elsewhere noted, it does offer a large market in goods either not produced at all or in insufficient quantities in Australia. But, as already seen, it has as yet found no takers for its offer to cut preferential margins and MFN rates in return for assured access to markets for its primary produce. Again we must refer to the Kennedy Round—the major current test of this position—as unfinished business at the time of writing. Part of the test for Australia is whether it will really offer significant cuts, valuable to the trade of others, in its tariff rates and preferential margins (see discussion in Section 5). We have noted a tendency to be unduly sensitive to the claims of high cost, highly protected industries in Australia.

To the extent that preferences remain at all on imports of goods not produced in Australia and to the extent that some MFN 'protective' rates are excessive, Australia is still short of a general objective sometimes subscribed to by governments of allowing the Australian consumer and producer, subject only to a reasonable tariff policy, to have full access to the most efficient source of supply, whether local or oversea.[14] The two most important steps

[13] It is difficult to document this observation from published statements: it is based on personal experience as an Australian delegate to GATT and on many conversations with officials in member countries since 1960.

[14] This point is clear enough in respect of producer goods under by-law which attract 7 per cent duty if imported from Europe, Japan, or United States, instead of from Britain, provided only that Britain can supply the goods in question. To talk of 'excessive' MFN rates is to imply that some imports are desirable (i.e. the tariff rates should not exclude them altogether) and that the cost is unduly inflated by the high duties imposed. The competitive pressure on local industry would be greater if rates were

to this end have been the unilateral reduction in preferences on producer goods, together with a less pro-United Kingdom interpretation of by-law arrangements (Section 9) and the virtual abolition of all import restrictions in February 1960. We have, however, taken advantage of the preferential systems allowed under Article XXIV of GATT to establish a free trade area with New Zealand. This, if pursued to a logical conclusion (i.e. a complete free trade area), is likely to be mutually beneficial but may, contrary to the intention of the GATT article, marginally damage the interests of third parties, especially Great Britain.

Underdeveloped Countries

If the Australian tariff system is under specific challenge—a challenge likely to grow with time—it is in respect of the pressures being exerted by the less developed countries.[15] These issues were noted in Section 6 and are important in speculations about the future. In terms of the original objective, as propounded by Dedman, we have played a gratefully acknowledged, although to many too small, part in our aid programs. However, aid has not been an important part of trade policy as it has been in recent years for several advanced countries, including Germany, Japan, France, and the United States. There is scope for this linking of aid and trade in the further development of investment and mutual trade relations with South-East Asia. More rapid growth of the poorer countries of the world remains a vital policy area if significant trade gains are to be made in our economic relations with them. So far the bulk of our export trade is with the richer countries of the world (including Japan) or with China, which has special interests in and ability to buy particular commodities like wheat and wool.

The United Nations Conference on Trade and Development in 1964 may have offered prospect to the Australian government of enlisting support for its drive for intergovernmental commodity agreements.[16] Fervour for agreements was indeed found, but with a natural and very strong bias of interest in

---

reduced, and the outcome would depend on its ability to reduce costs. The term 'excessive' is therefore inexact in this context and is a matter for judgment. See Sections 5 and 14 for references to 'MFN Tariff' reports by the Tariff Board and the bibliographical references given in that section.

[15] This is not intended to underrate the pressure from Japan, which finds objectionable many of our tariffs on consumer goods. Yet there is, in my view, room with Japan especially for negotiation on many MFN rates in the ordinary process of GATT (Kennedy Round) negotiations.

[16] As Curzon (68), p. 33, has pointed out, the title is indicative of the change from the forties to the sixties. When Dedman stated the need to promote the development of underdeveloped areas, he was speaking to the Bill to ratify the International Trade Organization which resulted from the United Nations Conference on Trade and Employment of 1948. With the subsequent emergence of some seventy-five to eighty less affluent but independent nations in United Nations affairs, *employment* gave way to *development* as the issue of the day. Trade continued to hold its major place.

those products—mostly tropical—affecting the less affluent economies. Indeed, Australia's case for consideration of its problems as mid-way between those of the affluent and fully developed economies and those of the non-affluent fell largely on deaf ears. Australia understands and shares the commodity problems of the less affluent nations but must bow, within the Trade and Development Board, to the priority given by these nations to particular commodities of greatest concern to them. Wheat, meat, and dairy produce are not among these, although sugar and minerals are. In respect of minerals our enthusiasm for intergovernmental agreements is rather lacking—in striking and not unnoticed contrast to our interest in wheat and sugar (Section 7). On the other hand, it is difficult for the underdeveloped countries to treat Australia's tariff protection policies as less open to criticism than those of European countries, and most of them are unwilling to do so. Our recent waiver in GATT under which we have offered unrequited preferences to the LDCs is a significant but far from complete concession by Australia to this point of view (Section 6).

General

It can be said, on looking back, that the framework of Australian policy does comprise a mutually consistent set of objectives—unless, of course, the reader is disposed, for example, to argue that Australia would better assist its economic policy objectives by not practising tariff protection at all and that it should not attempt to stabilise export prices on the possible grounds (which, however, cannot easily be tested) that returns in unstabilised conditions would be greater in the aggregate over a period. These arguments do not find much favour in the statements of policy given in this book, although the 1945 statement on tariff policy was certainly more restrained than those of recent years. In any case, tariff protection is not condemned under GATT, and criticism of members can only be directed at excesses in its operation, at undue readiness to unbind undertakings to limit certain duties, or at alleged reluctance on Australia's part to make substantial reductions in tariff rates.[17] Likewise the stabilisation of commodity prices is a widely supported objective even if progress may seem frustratingly slow.

Inconsistencies in our policies can be found, as can shifts in emphasis. We have noted above a few non-tariff barriers and debatable tariff devices of our own erected against the exports of others; Australia may be too prone to meet the admitted export needs of less developed areas at the expense of other suppliers to its market rather than of Australian industries (Section 6); certainly Australia is prone to apparent inconsistency in supporting com-

---

[17] The general argument of the Vernon Report defends the use of the tariff as an instrument of economic growth in Australia, but does observe the ample scope for a more restrained and critical use of very high rates (especially *effective* rates) often supported by the Tariff Board. See vol. I, chs. 13 and 14 and vol. II, app. L.

modity agreements when it suits its interests and rejecting them (as in wool
or minerals) when for reasons which seem good to the government agreements appear impracticable;[18] protection was afforded incidentally under
import licensing and, at least after 1952, unintentionally, as the repeal of
restrictions in 1960 showed; Australia was slower than necessary (or wise
in its own interests) in removing the restrictions imposed on goods from dollar areas; and some (but not in Britain or Europe) might criticise Australian
fertiliser subsidies and our wheat and dairy stabilisation schemes (despite
their clearance in terms of GATT Article XVI) as being unfair aids to our
export trade. Out of frustration of its agricultural export objectives and also
for other more domestic and political reasons, there have been some moves
towards high protectionism in Australia. This will produce economic problems at home and some political ones abroad.

The total record is nevertheless good, especially by comparison with other
members of GATT, and Australia's adherence to the multilateral system is
bona fide. Judging from actual trade results described earlier in this section,
that system has not hampered our growth. The policy objectives as outlined
and discussed in the last few pages are not likely to be seriously altered by
governments within the next few years. If they are, the challenge may come
from stresses within the international system, for there are stresses ahead and
important unsolved problems—not merely in great areas of interest to us,
such as agricultural protectionism, but even by way of threat to GATT, which
has become the bulwark of the multilateral system. Whether the downfall of
GATT would hurt Australia's interests or, what is not quite the same thing,
Australia should abandon GATT, are questions calling for some comment.
Before discussing them, however, some discussion on the evolution of the
framework of international organisations relevant to Australian policy is
appropriate. It is of some importance to our final observations first to remind
ourselves of how far Australia has retreated from the Ottawa system in
accepting the international system which followed upon the initial key decision—the acceptance of Article VII of the Mutual Aid Agreement.

The International Framework for Trade Policy

Figure 4 gives a graphic view of the evolution of the international framework. Perhaps revolution is a better word for the change, for Australia and
for the world, from the economic nationalism of pre-war days to the surprisingly solid multilateral system of today. Indeed Curzon (68, p. 313) under-
states the change in describing it as 'the transition from bilateral commercial
diplomacy to multilateral commercial diplomacy'.

The Ottawa Agreements of 1932 were born of depression and of a series

---

[18] On the other hand, when our interests are those of consumers we have supported
efforts to establish agreements (Section 7) and we may yet be forced to work vigorously
for international agreement on the prices of iron ore!

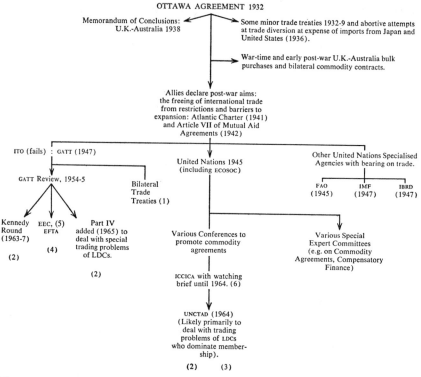

FIGURE 4   EVOLUTION OF INTERNATIONAL FRAMEWORK FOR AUSTRALIAN
TRADE POLICY

Notes:

(1) All Australia's post-war bilateral treaties and arrangements have been negotiated consistently with GATT obligations—e.g. treaties with U.K. (1956), Japan (1957), Malaysia (1958), Indonesia and Federal Republic of Germany (1959), Canada (1960), New Zealand, Korea, and USSR (1965), Poland and Bulgaria (1966).

(2) All three developments—with subscript (2)—bring to fore Australia's claims to be in 'mid-way' position, neither completely an 'advanced country' (economically) nor underdeveloped in the usual sense of LDCs.

(3) UN Trade and Development Board is the continuing arm of the Conference (= UNCTAD).

(4) These and similar regional 'preferential' groupings (e.g. Free Trade Area for Latin America and Australia-New Zealand Free Trade Area) derive international validity from Article XXIV. The British Commonwealth (Ottawa) Agreements are not consistent with this Article.

(5) The EEC's Common Agricultural Policy aggravates agricultural protectionism but EEC may also be a principal in international commodity agreements of importance to Australia.

(6) ICCICA = International Co-ordinating Committee for International Commodity Arrangements = a United Nations body with Chairman provided by GATT. It could and sometimes did advise United Nations action to promote agreements. It also stimulated useful GATT action in wider field of barriers to agricultural trade. It ceased to exist with the establishment of UNCTAD.

600

of nationalistic commercial moves of which the Hawley-Smoot Tariff (United States) of 1930 was not least.[19] The agreements no doubt aggravated the general move towards economic nationalism which was more often characterised by unilateral actions than by 'bilateral diplomacy'. Nevertheless, the Ottawa Agreement, signed by Australia, became basic to Australian trade policy. The trade diversion episodes with Japan and United States (Sections 10 and 11) were in sympathy with Ottawa although, fortunately, unsuccessful.

As we have seen, the war-time and early post-war bulk contracts with the United Kingdom had relatively small permanent significance. The real story of the post-war period stems from acceptance of Article VII, for this committed the country to the course of international collaboration. At one stage, as we saw in Section 1, the article seemed to threaten a complete and abrupt reversal of the pre-war framework of policy, dominated as it was by the preferential system embodied in the Ottawa Agreement of 1932. There had, before the war, been some signs of restlessness with that system.[20] Nevertheless the Australian public would have been shocked had American hopes and, indeed, expectations won the day (Sections 1 and 3).[21] It may have been salutary and, having regard to the cost of the preferences we gave to the United Kingdom, by no means a certain economic loss, after adjusting to the first costly dislocations, to have been forced to abandon our preferences in the United Kingdom completely; but we were not put to the test. Nevertheless, Dedman must, to some extent have had his tongue in his cheek in formulating the objective of negotiating reductions in tariffs and preferential margins outlined in (c) (iii) above.

By 1948 the position was contained in GATT. Australia had begun to operate a somewhat dual system—a largely static system of preferences and a multilateral system which emphasised the virtues and opportunities of an open trading system in contrast to the closed system of Ottawa. Such movement as there has been since—minor tariff concessions in GATT negotiations, minor reductions in preferences following Tariff Board inquiries, and the major revision of the United Kingdom Treaty followed by significant unilateral reduction in preferences on producer goods (Section 9)—has been further away from the Ottawa system. Within Commonwealth Councils agreed decisions and firm rejection by GATT of attempts to gain some flexi-

---

[19] See Nicholson (132), p. 108.

[20] See references to 'Memorandum of Conclusions: U.K.-Australia 1938' in Figure 4 and in 9:1.

[21] The shock would have been not only in terms of damage to our market in the United Kingdom (as it was in 1961) but equally in terms of the affront to the British position in the Australian market—a prospect that must particularly have worried Chifley, whose warm sympathy with Britain's post-war economic plight we have noted from time to time in earlier sections.

bility have emphasised the retreat from Ottawa (Sections 4 and 5). It remains to be seen whether two items of unfinished business,—the Kennedy Round and Britain's relationship with the Common Market—will turn retreat into rout. McEwen (5:12) revealed his anxiety in 1963 about the outcome in his statement, little commented on at the time, that 'the "known" benefits of the United Kingdom-Australian Trade Agreement were for us better than the "unknown" outcome of the Kennedy Round.' He noted rather ruefully the British government's determination to take the Kennedy Round seriously. Recent actions indicate the present United Kingdom government's intention to join the Common Market. Even if little happens under the Kennedy Round and if British entry into the Common Market proves to be a slow business, there is certainly not likely to be a return to the Ottawa system in the sense of enlarging the scope of the preferential arrangement between Australia and Britain. The general position of regional groupings, of pressures by the less developed countries for special preferences, and perhaps the future of GATT itself being so open make it rash to suggest that Australia may not become involved in new forms of preferential arrangements. It has made a cautious beginning in its special preferences for the developing countries (and for Papua and New Guinea) and in its Free Trade Area Agreement with New Zealand.

The most striking thing about the post-war period, reflected in Figure 4, is the dominating position assumed by GATT in matters of importance to Australia. GATT is clearly the principal expression of the international agreements on trade in the minds of those officials who strove to give practical effect to Article VII of the Mutual Aid Agreements of 1942. Yet that position is not without challenge from strong forces discussed in Sections 5 and 6. Part of the challenge has come from Australia itself. It seems appropriate to conclude this review with some further examination of Australia's relations with GATT which, for all its shortcomings, has been the mainstay of a system of 'fair trade rules' which Australia would like to see operate effectively rather than fail entirely. It has to be remembered, too, that the GATT rules permeate our bilateral trading relations. The expansion of market opportunities under our bilateral trade treaties, including those opened up in Japan, have depended significantly on ability to cite the rules of GATT in support of claims or requests addressed to our trading partners.

The Future of GATT

We have chosen therefore to offer comment on the future of GATT and Australia's relation to it not because there is any great case for immediate and significant changes in Australia's trade policy objectives but because there may be doubt about the permanence of GATT or about the wisdom of Australia's continued adherence in any real sense to the articles which form the GATT compact.[22] This doubt is not an attack on the rules so much as persistence of our view that unless all the articles are implemented a stable balance of concessions mutually negotiated under the agreement cannot be achieved. Australia is entitled to point out, as it did in 1954, that the articles were designed to enforce and protect the major agreement negotiated in 1947. The General Agreement makes no distinction between trade in agricultural and industrial products.[23] This is the Australian answer to those countries, such as Germany and France, who have at times appeared to argue that the rules about agriculture should be renegotiated or omitted.

We have used the word 'bulwark' to describe GATT—a word not applicable to its beginnings for, as one observer has put it:

> The GATT was a slender reed on which to base progress toward a multilateral régime. It lacked . . . adequate administrative machinery to deal with problems arising between the periodic meetings of the Contracting Parties. Without provision for a permanent secretariat, it was handicapped in the size and scope of its operations. Its signatories were bound to give effect to most of its trade rules only to the extent not inconsistent with their existing legislation. . . . In short, GATT was permeated by an atmosphere of impermanence.[24]

We can agree with Curzon, who remarked that the 'slender reed grew into a strong plant', for GATT has demonstrated an amazing capacity to deal pragmatically and usefully with a great many problems—but not all problems and not to the satisfaction of all members or potential members. It is under challenge of sufficient seriousness to justify some discussion of the possibility that it might collapse. The mere fact that this might imply a return to the jungle rules of economic nationalism of pre-war decades is not sufficient reason to rule out the possibility, although it is a valuable deterrent.

There are three grounds for questioning the future viability of GATT. One is the development of regional blocs, especially the EEC. The second is the emergence of a new body, UNCTAD; and the third is the fact that some countries like Australia may now see little prospect that GATT will solve the problem of agricultural protectionism.[25]

As to the first it may be argued that in agreeing to Article XXIV (Cus-

[22] The discussion is in terms of membership or non-membership. Membership implies an active effort to live up to the rules. Non-membership clearly implies withdrawal from GATT, but some of the same effect could come from non-membership in the sense of failure to live up to the rules and less effort to have others do so. None of the comments here should be taken as offering any support for this course.

[23] See Curzon (68), p. 166.

[24] Gardner (78), pp. 379-80.

[25] The continued absence of Russia, China, and some other Communist countries is a serious gap but so far has been more significant in the formation of UNCTAD than in breaking down GATT's effectiveness. In my opinion GATT could establish acceptable rules for trade between socialist countries and other types of economies. It is encouraging that Czechoslovakia and Yugoslavia are members and that Poland now enjoys a special relationship and may become a member.

toms Unions and Free Trade areas) the GATT signatories sowed the seeds of the destruction of GATT. It is true that blocs are appearing and that three are strong. Two are regional: the EEC and EFTA can organise bloc votes in GATT and between them give an exceptionally strong voice to Europe as a whole. The third is the informal but strong political grouping of less developed contracting parties. The last group does have an alternative outlet in UNCTAD and in its executive arm, the Trade and Development Board, but for good reasons shows no signs yet of mass desertion from GATT membership. On the contrary, membership has increased.

The good reasons are two. In the recent incorporation of Part IV (Articles XXXVI-XXXVIII) GATT has given a clear indication of specific ways in which the trade of the LDCs can be assisted by more affluent contracting parties, severally and collectively, without reciprocal payment. The recognition that for the LDCs GATT cannot be a mutual contract of balanced concessions is a major departure from its basic premise and significantly changes the character of GATT, at least in this area of world trade policy. There is enough commitment in the articles on the part of signatories to give some hope that the GATT methods of consultation and confrontation will produce results.[26] And this is the second ground for, even on the most intractable subjects such as agricultural protectionism, these methods have yielded some results, even if less than adequate as yet from Australia's point of view. By contrast, although much too early to write it off as a failure, there is not as yet the same *ad hoc* and pragmatic approach to specific problems in the Trade and Development Board. Our comment in Section 6 stands: until the Board grapples with problems in concrete terms it will not begin to satisfy the very real needs of the LDCs. In short, GATT does not provide an easy political forum, but most of the less developed contracting parties continue to recognise its practical possibilities for them, although progress is likely to be slow. As yet any immediate threat to GATT does not come from this quarter, although its claim to be a comprehensive forum and agency for action on all world problems does require early progress under Part IV.[27]

This brings us back to the question whether regional blocs threaten the disintegration of GATT. Already the European Organization for Economic Co-operation and Development (OECD) would seem to offer a threat to the place of GATT. Trade policies and measures *vis-à-vis* the developing countries are discussed in its council and committees. The United States, Canada,

[26] It is sometimes argued that Part IV lacks teeth (see Subhan (155)). There is truth in this, but nevertheless it has been GATT's method of patient consultation and negotiation that has been the basis of the comparative success of other parts of the compact, rather than particular sanctions theoretically applicable.

[27] Should the LDCs leave GATT, the very strong rump of advanced or developed members might well carry on, even if only as a kind of club for advanced countries for supervising *industrial* trade rules which now form its most effective core. In such an unlikely event Australian membership might well be continued.

and Japan are members and it will not be surprising if Australia develops links now begun with its acceptance, in February 1966, of an invitation to join the Development Aid Committee, a special organ of OECD.[28] It certainly is readily possible, therefore, to conceive a situation in which the EEC and EFTA (or an enlarged EEC with Britain and other EFTA members included) decide to abandon GATT in the belief that there exists a suitable alternative organisation for general discussion and formulation of trade policies and for negotiations. Such a strong group might even argue that it had more to gain from freeing trade among its members (the Customs Union) than from trade negotiations with North America and with Japan.

On present indications this is not a likely result. All the members of these blocs value the GATT rules and results achieved to date and, *except in respect of agriculture*, there is a general acceptance of the preamble to the GATT articles which looks to continued lowering of barriers to trade. Far from wishing to withdraw there has been every sign—for example in the acceptance of the new Part IV[29] and in the efforts to make progress with the Kennedy Round—of continued adherence. This indicates a belief in economic gains from external negotiations as well as those inherent in the customs union or free trade area idea. Even if the Kennedy Round fails to achieve much or anything at all—and it is a vital test—it would not follow that GATT would cease operations. Its vitality would be much reduced but it could and probably would continue as a forum for problems arising under Part IV, for problems in agricultural trade not covered in Part IV, and for general application and enforcement of the articles of Parts I-III and tariff agreements negotiated under them. In short, the big powers in trade terms have very little to gain by scuttling GATT and much to gain from making it work in the future as in the past. Moreover, GATT does legitimise, through Article XXIV, their right to form a customs union and/or a free trade area. Withdrawal would not lessen the pressures on them from developing countries to give effect to the principles in Part IV, and the GATT aegis is likely to appeal to them as the appropriate machinery for making progress in contrast to the so far rather more emotionally charged political atmosphere of periodical full-scale United Nations conferences and the regular meetings of the Trade and Development Board.

Australia's Relations with GATT

While it cannot be said that the continuance of GATT is assured, the evidence points that way rather than to disintegration. Even if GATT were to break up, it would be wrong to anticipate a revival of the Ottawa system. Indeed, this event would hasten rather than deter Britain's entry into the

[28] See Arndt (2).

[29] Although France has stood out thus far, so weakening already the effectiveness of the acceptance by the other five members of EEC of Part IV (Section 6).

Common Market. It is conceivable that in these circumstances preferential arrangements could be entered into with Japan in our mutual interests.[30] But the United States would have to be a party to such an arrangement, for both Australia and Japan, but especially Japan, would have much to lose by offending the United States. The position would be so open that further comment here can only be so speculative as to be of no practical value.

It may be different, however, with the question: 'Should Australia continue as a member of GATT?' For, as we have seen (Section 5), this question was seriously discussed and the apparent lack of progress in some matters since the Review Session in 1955 naturally prompts the question again. For reasons given in the documents and comment in Section 5 and in the paragraphs above, the answer in my view is still the same.

The grounds for Australian dissatisfaction, shared, perhaps less vocally, by other countries with a strong interest in exports of agricultural products, remain most strongly centred in the commodity field. There were other difficulties in 1953 when a review was sought but many of these were resolved or have been the subject of change. As shown in Section 5, the agreement remains, for Australia, more balanced than it was in 1953. There are powerful reasons, to be noted later, for remaining in the agreement whatever happens to our agricultural hopes in the Kennedy Round. On the great issue of agricultural protectionism, and especially the unresolved future of the Common Agricultural Policy of the EEC, all is not yet lost, although some prospects are bleak. It is abundantly plain that the EEC members and other contracting parties (including the United Kingdom, if she finally joins the EEC on Rome Treaty terms)[31] will not treat trade in agricultural products in the same manner as industrial products, despite their agreement to do so when entering the original GATT compact.[32] As we have already noted, quantitative restrictions and other non-tariff devices for protection were to be no more applicable (with exceptions not relevant to this comment) to agricultural and mineral products than to manufactured goods. Under the cloak, for a time, of balance of payments difficulties, such restrictions persisted and were multiplied; and with the passing of these difficulties will, for social and political reasons, not quickly be abandoned. Agricultural exporters have sought to press the rules as the fairest way to ensure complete reciprocation

[30] This would, of course, be easier to negotiate in respect of trade items which are not the subject of protection of home industries.

[31] In a press interview reported in the *Australian* on 16 June 1966, McEwen is reported as saying that it will be years before Britain enters the EEC and, more significantly, he does not imagine that Britain could secure terms that will safeguard the Commonwealth, adding: 'If Britain feels it is imperative for her to go in on terms that are less than perfect, then I accept that situation'. The same statement shows a clear recognition of the Kennedy Round as a possible solvent of Australia's problems if Britain were to join the Common Market.

[32] For a good discussion see Curzon (68), ch. VII.

of MFN rights and obligations among the contracting parties. Some victims of their pressure (e.g. Germany) suggested deletion of agriculture from the GATT provisions. Nevertheless, as Curzon remarks, rather more hopefully and comprehensively than is yet justified:

> The discussion on whether to exclude agriculture from GATT or whether to arrive at a negotiated compromise within the organisation has been decided in favour of the latter solution. In meticulous committee work the pattern of a world-wide solution is being woven.[33]

It is worth noting in passing that there is one possible outcome of failure to resolve the problem which arises from the use by advanced countries of quantitative restrictions for protecting agriculture. This is for Australia to make more general use of the same device in protecting key secondary industries. We have noted that Parliament has made legislative provision (14:9) under which the Tariff Board could recommend quantitative restrictions.[34] The possibility is envisaged in Article XVIII of GATT, but a deliberate general use of this method of protection would presumably be justified as a departure from the strict rules of the same character as the departure represented by the use of quantitative restrictions by some contracting parties for protection of agriculture (and sometimes, too, the textile industry). It is a tempting retort to the use by others of protective devices not approved by GATT. If others can use *both* tariffs and quantitative restrictions to protect agriculture there is some logic in the use by Australia of both forms of protection of industrial products. Logic of this superficial kind is no substitute for examining whether economic interests are thereby damaged rather than enhanced, especially if resort to direct protective restrictions also brings to an end Australia's effectiveness in arguing its case against their use by others for agricultural protection (Section 14).

The committees established in GATT are many (Section 5), but of most immediate purpose to Australia are those conducting the negotiations under the Kennedy Round, including the commodity groups on cereals, meat, and dairy produce.[35] At least while negotiations continue, Australia cannot lightly withdraw, for the Kennedy Round in effect postulates that access to markets and the terms of that access are negotiable. Successful negotiations could blunt the economic damage which is threatened if the United Kingdom joins the Common Market, for the United Kingdom would be an important party to commodity agreements. Non-tariff barriers will not be abandoned, but they may be defined and contained or stabilised. Whether containment that will satisfy France and, say, Germany will leave worthwhile room for Australian wheat in Europe is another question and one on which no optimistic

[33] Curzon (68), p. 317.
[34] See Vernon Report (11), vol. I, ch. 14, paras. 44-51.
[35] For a useful listing of GATT committees see GATT (79).

judgment can be offered. Whether a world-wide agreement on wheat which covers both high income and 'needy' countries will be achieved is likewise yet to be answered, but typical GATT methods of negotiated compromise on specific issues give some ground for expecting progress. Withdrawal from GATT at this stage would be a useless gesture, advancing this cause not at all. For reasons already noted, the Trade and Development Board of UNCTAD will give priority to tropical zone products (Section 6) and does not offer the ready-made or experienced forum for negotiations on wheat, meat, and dairy produce.

Altogether the group of advanced countries most adversely affected by agricultural protectionism—Australia, Canada, New Zealand, South Africa, and perhaps, surprisingly, the United States—can hardly hope to do better individually or even collectively outside the GATT framework, and it is quite unlikely that any move by them to withdraw would bring GATT to an end. The possible exception to this view is action by the United States which, however, despite its failure to back a proper GATT organisation, is not likely to desert it because of frustration over agricultural protectionism. It has too much to gain from the backing GATT gives to its ideas (both domestic and international) of competition in industrial production and trade. Certain it is that unilateral withdrawal by Australia would not advance its interests; nor would such action by it alone bring GATT to an end. Membership of GATT is not a burden to carry and continues to offer positive returns which cannot be increased by withdrawal.

Nor has membership seriously hampered Australia's right to protect its industry. If there is room for solid criticism here it is more in terms of Australia's being too ready to offer relatively high protection to all who appear to need it, without sufficient examination of the domestic implications and international reaction. Again, being in GATT ensures a platform and the use of its rules for educating other countries in Australia's problems and for attacking the policies of others where these conflict with the rules and our interests. Being open to the same educational process and even attack is a reasonable price to pay for these privileges.

Not the least advantage of remaining in GATT is that it does not hinder bilateral efforts to improve access to particular markets otherwise subject to highly protective barriers to trade. The treaties with the United Kingdom and Japan have given useful results in respect of wheat, meat, and other products. With the United States, too, direct negotiations have yielded results. Common membership of GATT certainly assists understanding of our problems in a way that helps rather than hinders bilateral negotiations which, we have seen, are quite consistent with GATT obligations and privileges. It would be difficult to gain better terms under bilateral treaties by being out of GATT. Any tariff concessions given us by remaining GATT members would have to be extended to their fellow members. Any reduction in non-tariff barriers can be negotiated at least as well and probably better within GATT. The position outlined by the Prime Minister (then R. G. Menzies) in August 1953 remains valid (5:1).

If there is some discontent and even peevishness in our complaints about the frustratingly slow progress in critical issues, it is understandable. Yet constant iteration of Australia's alleged midway status is probably unnecessary in GATT, which recognised that position in the Review Session in the extra freedom given us in the use of Article XXVIII. Australia was given this concession to modify tariff concessions made in the past as one of a group of countries 'depending in large measure on a relatively small number of primary commodities and relying on the tariff as an important aid for further diversification of their economies' and in special interpretations of Articles XVI and XVIII (Section 5). Australia is right to contest the tendency to divide nations into two groups—affluent and non-affluent—as being too simple and misleading for dealing pragmatically with trade problems. Nevertheless, words like 'midway' or 'middle zone' do not properly describe the Australian position. There are grounds for the special point of view for Australia in GATT. Although affluent, it does have rather more difficult export problems than most affluent countries (but not necessarily Canada, New Zealand, and South Africa). On the other hand, although its export problems (especially for agricultural products) give some common ground with the non-affluent countries, the middle zone position (or neither advanced nor underdeveloped) does not gain acceptance in the Trade and Development Board. Many of the developing countries may value Australian experience and help in commodity matters, but Australia is so far advanced industrially that it must be regarded by them, both in that Board and in GATT, as a principal from whom positive action to liberalise its barriers to trade may be expected under the new Part IV of GATT. That Australia has begun to move under this part is a step forward, but more will be expected.[36]

The point of all this discussion of GATT and Australia's relations with it, including the last paragraph, is simply to indicate that while it continues GATT is the principal international forum for airing, discussing, and hopefully negotiating Australia's problems. Nothing is to be gained by withdrawal, and gains are yet to be made by remaining the active member it is. It is to be remembered that Australia is recognised as a valuable market, ranking eleventh or twelfth in the membership list (see Section 17: Table III). This alone assures a hearing of Australia's special point of view.

These remarks are not to be construed as opposition to membership of UNCTAD which, as it settles down to commodity questions, will be important to Australia's own and New Guinea's interests in tropical products, minerals,

---

[36] For further discussion see bibliographical references in Section 6, and especially the Vernon Report (11), vol. I, ch. 12, paras. 22-3, and Arndt (2).

and, no doubt, in preferential tariff and quota matters. Australia's major interests will continue to be centred in GATT, including the operation of the new Part IV; but the prosecution of our trade policy objectives will also require active membership of United Nations economic agencies, including the Trade and Development Board of UNCTAD, the IMF, and the FAO.

Conclusion

There remains little to add to the two main views expressed in this final section, but a summary restatement may be useful in conclusion. The first view is that the objectives of trade policy as formulated in the post-war period have served our interests and are likely to continue to serve the wider economic aims of Australian governments and to have the support of the Australian people in the next decade. The second is that the international machinery has undergone important modifications and new developments as the balance of forces and urgency of interests among the now much greater number of independent nations have changed. Despite these changes, however, the international centre of trade policy interest and activity for Australia remains the General Agreement on Tariffs and Trade. Its trade policies can and will be pursued in the United Nations itself, but more especially in such agencies as the Trade and Development Board, the IMF, and the FAO. The documents have dealt little with regional organisations of direct interest to Australia, but it is likely that there would be some support for an increasingly active link with the OECD in Europe. Already ECAFE is a venue for ventilating regional interests and problems nearer home and we may expect the informal private committee relations now existing with Japan to continue. There may even develop a type of OECD for Asia,[37] but we need not expect a Common Market to be a serious issue in this part of the world for a considerable time to come, unless it excludes Japan, Australia, and New Zealand.

The objectives of policy and the nature of the international framework are, of course, not unrelated. Changes in the latter may compel modifications to specific objectives. Thus if the Kennedy Round succeeds there will necessarily be a further retreat by Australia from the Ottawa system. This retreat will be considerably greater and will be decisive if the United Kingdom finally embraces the Common Market in Europe. Even if the Kennedy Round fails to solve or greatly soften the agricultural problem and even if Britain also remains aloof from the EEC, our own interests will dictate some further reduction in the importance of the preferential system for our exports to and imports from Britain. This would partly arise from bilateral treaty negotiations and commodity agreements designed to improve access to markets other than Britain and partly from the obligations towards developing countries we have assumed under Part IV of GATT.

[37] This would be undesirable if ECAFE shows itself capable of serving regional needs for trade policy discussions.

With deliberate repetition we conclude with the reminder McEwen offered in January 1955 in the context of the Review Session of GATT:

> To keep the issues which have been argued in proper perspective, it is essential
> . . . [to] remember that world trade is, day by day, becoming both in total and
> for individual industries much less affected by what trade rules exist than by
> ability to compete in cost and quality in international markets (5:3).

One may argue that the point is somewhat overstated; for 'fair trade' rules properly and evenly enforced could do much to improve market opportunities for developing countries with interests in the export of primary products and simple manufactures and for advanced countries with important trade interests in primary products. There is no case for Australia relaxing its efforts to effect advances in its 'market opportunities' (McEwen's own phrase) by means of multilateral and bilateral negotiations. Nor is there room to be indifferent to what others think of Australian policies.

It remains true, however, that to a highly important degree the ability to sell exports in expanding quantities, within the international 'rules' as they exist at any time, rests on the maintenance of full employment and on the rates of economic growth achieved in other countries. This is true even if some trading partners are in breach of some of the rules. At home it rests on Australia's ability to raise productive and marketing efficiency, keep costs down, and provide the will and incentive to expand and develop those old and new export industries its resources and available market opportunities would seem to favour. The documents in this book certainly give full recognition to the importance of all these matters. Close attention to them will enable Australia to weather better whatever frustrations may confront it in pursuing particular ends in GATT, in coping with problems posed by the possible British entry into the Common Market, and in facing the far more complex problems presented to all affluent countries by the trading difficulties of the less developed countries. In resolving these problems, Australia's interests will be best served by continuing to follow the policies of international collaboration which have grown out of its war-time commitments under Article VII of the Mutual Aid Agreement with the United States. This course will also enable it both to take advantage of and to meet the needs of its growing economic strength. There is no case left for a retreat in the direction of Ottawa or to any other extreme form of economic nationalism.

POSTSCRIPT

The documents presented in this volume bring the story of Australian trade policy up to late 1966. The final drafts of the comments and Sections 17 and 18 were completed during 1966. Throughout these pages appear many comments (some speculative) dependent for their relevance upon the outcome of the Kennedy Round negotiations then approaching their climax and upon an expected announcement that the United Kingdom would again seek to join the European Common Market. This announcement has occurred and the Kennedy Round negotiations have ended. During the year that has passed in the preparation of the book for publication, the trends already apparent in the pattern of Australia's trade have also been strongly confirmed by the trading results for 1966-7. During the year, too, public debate on tariff policy, greatly stimulated by the Tariff Board's Annual Reports for 1965-6 and 1966-7, has developed along lines noted in Section 14 and is now likely to be sharpened by the implications for Australia of the Kennedy Round and even more by the determined effort Britain is making to become European. Not least of recent relevant events has been the decision of the United Kingdom government to devalue the pound sterling.[1] It seems useful to offer, in postscript form, some further comment, especially on the Kennedy Round. These events very largely confirm views and predictions offered in the sectional comment concerned.

As suggested on page 602 the formal application to join the EEC, the European Coal and Steel Community and the European Atomic Energy Community (EURATOM), made by Great Britain on 11 May 1967, caused no surprise. Nor did the French reaction which, while short of imposing a veto, remains obstructionist. However, the devaluation of sterling has probably strengthened the British bid, despite the uncompromising, if not virulent, stand of President de Gaulle and his statement on 27 November 1967. Moreover, the British government on this occasion seems far less willing to give up, and although it may have to bide its time, the prospects for entry, despite President de Gaulle, are reasonable. In support of this view is the acceptance by the government, with far fewer pre-conditions than in 1961, of the terms of the Rome Treaty as they now stand, including the

---

[1] As from 19 November 1967 the official rate has been £stg = $US2.40, a depreciation of 14·3 per cent over the old rate of £stg = $US2.80. The Australian government, not without courage in view of the hurt to some primary exports, quickly decided not to devalue. As a result £stg = $A2.143 instead of £stg = $A2.5. The rate on $US remains unchanged at $A1 = $US1.13.

Common Agricultural Policy. Australia's interests on this occasion are receiving, and will receive, scant attention. The only Commonwealth interests Britain will seek to defend with vigour are those of New Zealand, whose special problems still command sympathy, and the sugar interests of the developing countries now safeguarded in the Commonwealth Sugar Agreement. If Australia benefits in this latter respect it will only be incidental to her membership of the Agreement: neither Britain nor the Common Market countries will pay Australia's case much heed on its own merits.[2]

While British entry is, in my view, likely, the negotiations with the Common Market may well prove protracted and the terms of entry must therefore remain somewhat uncertain. On the other hand, the outcome of the Kennedy Round is now sufficiently clear to justify comment. In general terms the negotiations were successful for the advanced industrial countries, but far less so for the developing countries and for countries (developed and less developed) with significant interests in agricultural trade. For Australia the results were disappointing but not useless.[3]

Countries accounting for about 75 per cent of total world trade granted tariff concessions affecting trade valued at just over $40 billion.[4] In Wyndham White's words:

> The industrialized countries participating . . . made duty reductions on 70 per cent of their dutiable imports, excluding cereals, meat and dairy products. Moreover, two thirds of these cuts were of 50 per cent or more. Around one fifth were between 25 and 50 per cent. Of the total dutiable imports on which no tariff cuts have been negotiated (31 per cent of the total), one third are subject to duties of 5 per cent ad valorem or less. The results . . . for the developing countries are less impressive . . . If . . . one bases an appraisal on the goods for which the developing countries presently have significant exports, the results show that of their manufactured exports subjected to duties, some 51 per cent will benefit from tariff cuts by the industrialized countries of 50 per cent or more, and some 25 per cent by tariff cuts of less than 50 per cent. We have not been able to complete our calculation of the results for the de-

[2] The literature attending the British decision to try again is already considerable and no attempt can be made here to review it. The nature of that decision is best given in the White Paper, Cmnd 3345, entitled *The United Kingdom and the European Communities*. This is the text of the statement made by the Secretary of State for Foreign Affairs, George Brown, at a meeting of the Council of Western European Union at The Hague on 4 July 1967. McEwen has discussed the matter on several occasions, two of the most useful statements being addresses respectively to the National Press Club (Canberra, June 1967) and to the United Farmers and Woolgrowers' Association of N.S.W. (17 July 1967).

[3] The most useful references available (November 1967) are GATT Press Releases 992, 993 (a statement by Wyndham White, Director-General of GATT) and 994, all of 30 June 1967, and 995 of 3 August 1967; issues of *The Economist* of 20 May 1967 and of 22 July 1967; press statements by McEwen (Canberra 17 May and 11 July 1967); and a departmental statement in the July 1967 issue of *Current Notes*, published by the Department of External Affairs.

[4] GATT Press Release 992 of 30 June 1967.

v

veloping countries with respect to their agricultural exports but it is known that, as for farm products generally, the results were not impressive. . . .

From the data we have at hand it is clear that the less-developed countries will derive substantial advantages from the Kennedy Round, and equally clear that all their legitimate desires and aspirations are not fully achieved. Those . . . which are heavily dependent upon exports of agricultural products suffer from the general modicity of the results in the agricultural field. We failed to achieve free trade for tropical products, though here the major, if not the only, problem is the difficult one of reconciling the desire of some for larger markets in all developed countries with the reluctance of beneficiaries of existing preferences to surrender these in exchange for free and open competition on open markets. It is also significant . . . that in a major area of manufactures where some less-developed countries have a clear competitive advantage—and despite their concurrence in the extension of the Cotton Textiles Arrangement—tariff reductions fell far short of the 50 per cent target and in some important cases are only granted conditionally.[5]

The results so described by Wyndham White give some force to the heading, 'The Kennedy Round is a Rich Man's Deal', used by *The Economist* in its report of 20 May 1967. Undoubtedly both in GATT and in UNCTAD the poorer countries will renew their pressure for a more effective application of Part IV of the GATT articles. Australia will not escape this pressure despite its initiative in offering one way preferences in its tariff to developing countries on a number of items of importance to them (Section 6). Moreover, this pressure is likely to increase now that it seems probable that the United States administration, in a major change of policy, has become more amenable to some general system of preferences for the less developed countries.[6] In respect of agriculture it can fairly be said that 'the aim was bold, the achievement predictably modest'.[7] Nevertheless, while results were limited,

this difficult sector of economic activity is clearly now within the field of international negotiations and it can no longer be doubted that these negotiations must go beyond tariffs and other commercial devices and embrace all aspects of national policies, production, prices and supports.[8]

For Australia the gains made were limited (but significant in one major respect) and the price paid minimal except for items on which it had little say. In the last category the most important was the substantial cut in preferences hitherto enjoyed in respect of imports of dried fruit into the United

[5] Wyndham White, GATT Press Release 993, 30 June 1967. See also GATT Press Release 995 of 3 August 1967 for preliminary details of concessions for developing countries.

[6] This observation is based on a statement in these terms made by J. N. Schittker, United States Department of Agriculture, at a conference of International Agricultural Economists held in Sydney in August 1967.

[7] 'Whither GATT', address by Wyndham White, Director-General of GATT, to Canadian Club, Toronto, on 23 October 1967 (typed document).

[8] Wyndham White, GATT Press Release 993, 30 June 1967, n.3.

614

Kingdom, Canada, and New Zealand, estimated to cost Australian producers some $A855,000 when fully implemented and set against expected gains through reduction of EEC duties on these products.[9]

Tariff concessions given by Australia covered imports worth $A186 million per annum. They included reductions in the general rates of duty on items covering $A109 million in imports in 1965-6, elimination of primage duties (equivalent to a reduction in the general rate of duty) on items covering imports of $A28 million, and guaranteed duty-free admission of $A4 million of imports. On the remaining items, covering imports of $A45 million, Australia has agreed that its general rates of duty applying to foreign countries will also apply to goods from Britain.[10]

A preliminary examination of the concessions made by Australia indicates two things very strongly. The first is that Japan is the principal beneficiary (as might be expected since most of our gains were concessions made by Japan) while Britain is the principal loser. In forty-seven of fifty-five items in which the margin of preference between General rates (i.e. MFN rates) and British Preferential Tariff rates was abolished, Japan was an important supplier, Britain being important in forty-three cases. The second is that the dilemma whether to raise the BPT rate to the General (MFN) rate or reduce the General rate to the BPT rate was resolved in thirty-two of the fifty-five cases by raising the BPT rate to the General rate. If this is an index to future action on a general scale (as would be stimulated by British entry into the Common Market), the prospect of general reductions in unnecessarily high MFN rates does not seem good. Japan and the United States may be expected to press this point, for while the elimination of preferences is in their interest, it is additionally in their interest to achieve this by reducing the MFN rates to the BPT level.

The principal gain for Australia was a new International Wheat Agreement. Under this it was agreed that the minimum price to be paid by member countries importing from member exporters should be increased by 19 cents to $US1.73 a bushel. McEwen said that estimates in Geneva of the likely increase in average price ranged from $7\frac{1}{2}$ cents (US) a bushel to about 15 cents a bushel, which could mean increases in Australia's foreign exchange earnings of between $US22·5 million and $US45 million.[11] However, recent price behaviour under the pressure of U.S. sales could have an adverse effect on overall prices, and the final benefits are as yet hard to judge.

It was also agreed that participating countries would finance an aid program for developing countries of $4\frac{1}{2}$ metric tons of wheat a year, Aus-

[9] *Forty-third Annual Report of the Australian Dried Fruits Control Board for the Year 1966-67*, p. 14.

[10] Press statement by the Minister for Trade and Industry (J. McEwen) on 11 July 1967.

[11] Ibid., 17 May 1967.

tralia's share being 225,000 tons. This is in line with Australia's representations concerning the need for importers as well as exporters to finance food aid programs and represents a gain in principle and in substance.

Undertakings by Japan covering Australian trade worth more than $A350 million a year represent the other significant gain. Japan guaranteed not to impose duties on a number of products, including wool, hides and skins, coking coal, iron ore and various other ores and concentrates; to improve access for meats and a number of other commodities; and to reduce duties on mutton and lamb, beef, tallow, unwrought copper and zinc, pearls and certain precious and semi-precious stones.

Results with the EEC were limited indeed. There is prospect of reductions in import duties on raisins, sultanas, dried tree fruits, honey, offals, tallow, coal, and other products. An agreement concerning the entry of beef was not reached, but 'consideration is still being given to improving the conditions governing imports of beef'.[12]

The outstanding failure was the refusal of the United States to reduce her tariff on wool, despite our offer of some concessions on tobacco imports from the United States as a *quid pro quo*. There is little doubt that the final offer and demands by the United States were 'tongue in cheek' in character and yet they succeeded in making the Australian public wonder whether the Australian tobacco industry should stand so heavily in need of high protection as to outweigh the needs of the vastly more significant and depressed wool industry.[13] Subsequently, a strong campaign was mounted in the United States for high tariffs and quotas against primary products coming from Australia and other primary exporters. The threat by President Johnson to veto Congressional action on these lines was welcome and at least temporarily effective. All the circumstances point more strongly than ever to the need for a bilateral trade treaty between Australia and the United States to provide a more stable framework for their growing trade and economic relations (Section 11).

The combined effect of the British decision to repeat its bid for entry into the EEC and the limited but significant Kennedy Round result is to confirm the 'retreat from Ottawa' which has been one of the themes emerging from the documents in this book. It is fortunate, in these circumstances, that the strong growth of Australia's trade in the Pacific and especially with Japan has continued and that there is every prospect that it will continue further. The results for 1966-7 are significant. In that year Japan replaced the United Kingdom as Australia's best customer, accounting for 19·4 per cent of Australia's exports as compared with 13·3 per cent in the case of the United Kingdom.

---

[12] Ibid., 11 July 1967.

[13] For a spirited account and defence of his government's stand in these negotiations see address by McEwen to the United Farmers and Woolgrowers' Association of N.S.W. in Sydney on 17 July 1967.

Stimulated in part by the British decision, the Kennedy Round, and the uncertainties still surrounding the future, if any, for the United Kingdom-Australian Trade Treaty, tariff policy has assumed major importance in political and academic debate. There is now far more interest in the detailed conduct, determination, and application of tariff policy than at any other time in the post-war period.

In brief, the historical case for tariff protection or some equivalent has been that expansion of the rural industries and secondary industries able to develop under free trade conditions would not have been enough to provide the industrial base for full employment at present-day living conditions for a population of today's magnitude.[14] A higher standard of living might have been possible under free trade but the population would have been smaller. But tariff protection has had costs, borne by all industries and of critical importance to the export industries and import competing industries which are not able to pass these costs on. Under free trade these industries might not have required protection. Added to these problems, we have today two or three new developments which call for more care in the application of tariff policy. We now have major capital-intensive secondary industries which need a large market for economies of scale. These need to be highly rational in their production structure and high tariffs alone will neither ensure this nor encourage them to enter export.[15] Again, other secondary industries are already competitive in exports (steel is an example), but if such industries are to remain competitive they, like wool, cannot afford unnecessary costs resulting from the protection of less efficient industries. Finally, the upsurge in mineral development adds to the number and strength of export industries with an interest in resisting cost increases resulting from high tariffs. Moreover, these same mineral resources will be the basis of further expansion of processing industries which should have a comparative advantage in export markets.

Altogether, although the time is yet far off for abandoning tariff protection as an instrument of economic development, the Board is fully justified in making a tougher examination of applications for levels of protection which are high relative to the general cost disability level.[16] The detailed proposals of the Board revealed in its Annual Report for 1966-7 may not be the last word,[17] but it was pleasing to read the evidence of intellectual questioning, of greater unity in the Board, and of its apparent determination to keep the cost of tariffs in mind when deciding whether or not protection was justified in particular cases.

[14] See Vernon Report (11), vol. I, ch. 13, paras. 40-43 and the earlier 'Brigden Report' (28).

[15] Vernon Report (11), vol. I, ch. 14, paras. 35-43.

[16] See ibid., ch. 13, paras. 77-78. Also relevant is the Joseph Fisher Lecture of W. M. Corden given in Adelaide on 27 July 1967 (roneoed document).

[17] See *Tariff Board Annual Report for the Year 1966-67*, paras. 55-82.

Postscript

Devaluation by the British government was not followed by the Australian government for generally sound reasons. The immediate effect is some impairment of the returns in Australian currency to those industries whose products sell in Britain for prices fixed in sterling (especially butter and sugar).[18] Nevertheless, the changed pattern of our trade since 1949 adequately explains the Australian reluctance to follow this devaluation: our trading relations are far more heavily oriented to Japan and the United States than to Britain. Another effect will be to make British exports to Australia more competitive with Australian domestic industry. The British Preferential Tariff, hitherto generally adequate, may now offer less complete protection, and some appeals to the Tariff Board on this score may be expected.[19] The devaluation of the New Zealand dollar to parity with the Australian dollar was overdue but may impose some strains on Australian manufacturing industries which have built up an export market there.

A good deal has happened in 1967; but the conclusion reached in Section 18 stands. The retreat from Ottawa has continued; some slight gains in the fight against agricultural protectionism have been registered; and the British devaluation has produced no crisis requiring similar devaluation on Australia's part. But problems remain and threaten. British entry into the Common Market will have adverse effects on Australian exports; the revival of high protectionism in the United States is dangerous; and much remains to be done to promote healthy trade relations between the affluent and non-affluent world. For all these reasons the right course of policy is for Australia to stay with GATT and UNCTAD and, consistently with our obligations in these bodies, negotiate bilateral trade treaties of the type we have with Japan. Not least in this general objective should be a treaty with the United States.

---

[18] Fortunately, it appears that sugar sales had been protected for some months ahead by forward exchange provisions.

[19] Indeed there was an immediate move by the Associated Chambers of Manufactures of Australia to secure compensating exchange adjustments on imports from Britain pending detailed tariff inquiries.

BIBLIOGRAPHY

BIBLIOGRAPHY

(1) Albinski, Henry S. 'Australia and the Chinese Strategic Embargo.' *Australian Outlook*, vol. 19 (1965), pp. 117-28.

(2) Arndt, H. W. 'Australia, Developed, Developing or Mid-way.' (Presidential address to Section G of ANZAAS, Hobart, August 1965.) *Economic Record*, vol. 41 (1965), pp. 318-40.

(3) ———— 'Import Licensing—Are Objections Valid?' *Voice*, June 1955.

(4) ———— 'Observations on the Prospects for Japanese-Australian Trade.' *Hitosubashi Journal of Economics*, vol. 6, no. 2 (1966), pp. 77-90.

(5) Australia. *The Australian Balance of Payments, February 1966.* Issued by Commonwealth Treasury, Canberra, as a Supplement to the Treasury Information Bulletin. C.P.P., no. 288 of 1964-65-66.

(6) ———— Commonwealth Bank. *Annual Report for Year Ended 30th June, 1946.*

(7) ———— *Commonwealth Bank of Australia in the Second World War* [by C. L. Mobbs]. Sydney, 1947.

(8) ———— 'Full Employment in Australia.' C.P.P., no. 11 of 1945.

(9) ———— 'International Monetary Agreements Acts: Annual Reports by the Treasurer.' C.P.P., 1953-66.

(10) ———— *Proposals for Expansion of World Trade and Employment for Consideration by an International Conference on Trade and Employment.* Documents Relating to Anglo-American Finance and Economic Discussions, September-December 1945, Document no. 5, Canberra.

(11) ———— *Report of the Committee of Economic Enquiry* (Vernon Report). 2 vols. Canberra, 1965.

(12) ———— Reports of the Rural Reconstruction Commission [Canberra]:
A General Rural Survey (First Report, 1944).
Settlement and Employment of Returned Men on the Land (Second Report, 1944).
Land Utilization and Farm Settlement (Third Report, 1944).
Financial and Economic Reconstruction of Farms (Fourth Report, 1944).
Rural Credit (Fifth Report, 1945).
Farm Efficiency and Costs (Sixth Report, 1945).
Rural Amenities (Seventh Report, 1945).
Irrigation, Water Conservation and Land Drainage (Eighth Report, 1945).
Rural Land Tenure and Valuation (Ninth Report, 1946).
Commercial Policy in Relation to Agriculture (Tenth Report, 1946).

(13) ———— 'Review of the General Agreement on Tariffs and Trade held at Geneva, 8th November, 1954 to 7th March, 1955.' C.P.P., no. 91 of 1955.

621

(14) ———— Tariff Board. Annual Reports. *C.P.P.*, 1935-36 to 1965-66.

(15) ———— *Treasury Bulletin on Private Overseas Investment in Australia* (White Paper no. F.5714/65).

(16) Australian Institute of International Affairs and Institute of Pacific Relations. 'Australia's Commercial Policy in Relation to Article VII of the Mutual Aid Agreement between the United States and the United Kingdom' by members of the Canberra Branch of the Australian Institute of International Affairs, in *Australia and the Pacific*. Princeton, 1944.

(17) Bailey, K. H. 'Australia's Membership in the British Commonwealth of Nations as Affecting Her Postwar Role Among the United Nations in the Far East', in Australian Institute of International Affairs and Institute of Pacific Relations, *Australia and the Pacific*. Princeton, 1944.

(18) Balassa, Bela. *Trade Prospects for Developing Countries*. Homewood, Ill., 1964.

Balensi, A., *see* GATT (87).

(19) Balogh, T. *Unequal Partners*. Oxford, 1963.

(20) Barclay, F. G. St J. 'The United Kingdom and the Six.' *Australian Outlook*, vol. 15 (1961), pp. 53-72.

(21) Beloff, Nora. *The General Says No*. Penguin Special, 1963.

(22) Belshaw, James P. 'Crisis in Farm Production in Australia.' *Journal of Farm Economics*, vol. XXXIV (1952), pp. 497-508.

(23) Bentick, B. *Prospects of an Australia-New Zealand Economic Union*. (Study No. 4, Committee for Economic Development of Australia.) Melbourne, 1962.

(24) Bernasek, M. 'Dr Corden's Uniform Tariff Proposal: A Comment.' *Economic Record*, vol. XXXVI (1959), pp. 250-7.

(25) Blau, Gerda. 'International Commodity Arrangements and Policies. I.' *F.A.O. Monthly Bulletin of Agricultural Economics and Statistics*, vol. 12 (1963), pp. 1-9; 'International Commodity Arrangements and Policies. II.' Ibid. (December), pp. 1-19.

(26) Bowen, I. 'The European Economic Community.' *Australian Outlook*, vol. 15 (1961), pp. 29-52.

(27) Brigden, J. B. 'Australia's Economic Future.' (Review of Australian Institute of Economic Affairs and Institute of Pacific Relations, *Australia and the Pacific*. Princeton, 1944.) *Pacific Affairs*, vol. XVII (1944), pp. 325-9.

(28) Brigden, J. B. *et al*. *The Australian Tariff: An Economic Enquiry*. Melbourne, 1929.

(29) British Information Services. *The General Agreement on Tariffs and Trade*. R.5470/64, London, 1964.

(30) Burns, Arthur L. *Politics and Administration in the European Economic Community*. (Robert Garran Memorial Lecture, Royal Institute of Public Administration, 1962.) Canberra, 1963.

(31) Cameron, Burgess. 'The Uniform Tariff Proposal.' *Economic Record*, vol. 37 (1961), pp. 224-6.

Bibliography

(32) Campbell, K. O. 'Current Agricultural Development and its Implications as Regards the Utilisation of Resources.' *Economic Record*, vol. XXXII (1956), pp. 119-34.

(33) —— 'Economic Aspects of Agricultural Stabilisation Schemes.' *Journal of Australian Institute of Agricultural Science*, vol. 16 (1950), pp. 144-53.

(34) —— 'National Commodity Stabilisation Schemes: Some Reflections Based on Australian Experience', in Roger N. Dixey (ed.), *International Explorations of Agricultural Economics*. Iowa, 1964, pp. 55-63.

(35) Camps, Miriam. *Britain and the European Community 1955-1963*. Oxford, 1964.

(36) —— *What Kind of Europe: The Community since de Gaulle's Veto* (Chatham House Essays). Oxford, 1965.

(37) Carney, W. R. 'The Ottawa Agreement Now.' *Economic Record*, vol. XXXII (1956), pp. 99-105.

(38) Chambers, F. P., Harris, C. P. and Bayley, C. C. *This Age of Conflict*. London, 1950, pp. 834-6, 921-3.

(39) Clark, John M. 'Development in the Queensland Sugar Industry.' *Quarterly Review of Agricultural Economics*, vol. 12 (1959), pp. 24-31.

(40) Copland, D. B. 'Report on Economic Conditions in the United Kingdom, United States of America and Canada.' *C.P.P.*, F.4086 of 1945.

(41) Copland, D. B. and Barback, R. H. *The Conflict of Expansion and Stability*. Melbourne, 1957.

(42) Copland, D. B. and Janes, C. V. (eds.). *Australian Trade Policy: A Book of Documents, 1932-1937*. Sydney, 1937.

(43) Corden, W. M. 'Australian and European Free Trade.' *Economic Record*, vol. 34 (1958), pp. 160-71.

(44) —— 'The Balance of Payments Problem, Import Replacement and Tariff Policy', in *The Australian Economy and Overseas Trade* (Seventh Summer School of Business Administration, University of Adelaide). Adelaide, 1962.

(45) —— 'The Calculation of the Cost of Protection.' *Economic Record*, vol. XXXIII (1957), pp. 29-51.

(46) —— 'Import Restrictions and Tariffs: A New Look at Australian Policy.' *Economic Record*, vol. 34 (1958), pp. 331-6.

(47) —— 'The Logic of Australian Tariff Policy', in *Planned and Unplanned Development* (Economic Papers no. 15, Economic Society of Australia and New Zealand (N.S.W. Branch)). Sydney, 1962.

(48) —— 'Protection.' *Economic Record*, vol. 42 (1966), pp. 129-48.

(49) —— 'The Tariff', in Alex Hunter (ed.) *The Economics of Australian Industry*. Melbourne, 1963.

(50) Cornish, R. J. and Harrington, D. L. 'Common Agricultural Policy of the EEC.' *Quarterly Review of Agricultural Economics*, vol. XV (1962), pp. 72-86.

(51) Cornish, R. J. and Hempel, J. A. 'The Agricultural Policy of the EEC.' *Quarterly Review of Agricultural Economics*, vol. XIV (1961), pp. 64-79.

(52) Crawford, J. G. *Australian Agricultural Policy* (Joseph Fisher Lecture in Commerce, 1952). Adelaide, 1952.

(53) ——— 'Britain, Australia and the Common Market.' *Australian Outlook*, vol. 15 (1961), pp. 221-39.

(54) ——— 'The Common Market', *World Review*, vol. I (1962), pp. 4-16.

(55) ——— *The Economics of Conservation* (Bureau of Agricultural Economics, Department of Commerce and Agriculture, January 1952). Canberra, 1952.

(56) ——— 'The Impact of the Common Market in Australia.' (Address to Convocation, University of Sydney, 31 August 1962.) Roneoed document.

(57) ——— 'Relations between Civil Servants and Ministers in Policy Making.' *Economic Record*, vol. XXXVI (1960), pp. 46-7.

(58) ——— *Responsibilities of Management in a Growing Economy*. (The Second John Storey Memorial Lecture, 1963.) Sydney, 1963.

(59) ——— 'The Significance of Recent Developments in Asia for the Economic Future of Australia.' (Presidential address to ANZAAS, May, 1961.) *Economic Record*, vol. 37 (1961), pp. 273-93.

(60) ——— 'Trade Policy—Some Emerging Issues', in *The Australian Economy and Overseas Trade*. (Seventh Summer School of Business Administration, University of Adelaide). Adelaide, 1962.

(61) ——— 'Using Surpluses for Economic Development.' *Proceedings of the Eleventh International Conference of Agricultural Economists* (Mexico, 19 August—30 August 1961). London 1963, pp. 377-95.

(62) ——— 'The Vernon Report: Some Wrong Impressions Corrected.' (Address to the National Press Club, Canberra, December, 1965.) Roneoed document.

(63) Crawford, J. G. *et al. War-Time Agriculture in Australia and New Zealand, 1939-1950*. Food Research Institute of Stanford University, 1954.

(64) Crisp, L. F. 'The Australian Full Employment Pledge at San Francisco.' *Australian Outlook*, vol. 19 (1965), pp. 5-19.

(65) ——— *Ben Chifley*. Melbourne, 1960.

(66) Crowley, N. L. and Haddon-Cave, C. P. 'The Regulation and Expansion of World Trade and Employment.' *Economic Record*, vol. XXIII (1947), pp. 32-48.

(67) *Current Affairs Bulletin*. 'Japan and Our Future?' Vol. 30 (4 June, 1962).

(68) Curzon, G. *Multilateral Commercial Diplomacy*. London, 1965.

(69) Dawson, C. 'Outline of U.S. Government Measures for Disposal of Agricultural Surpluses.' *Quarterly Review of Agricultural Economics*, vol. VIII (1955), pp. 56-7.

(70) Deane, R. P. *The Establishment of the Department of Trade*. Canberra, 1963.

(71) Dedman, J. J. 'The Case for Bretton Woods.' *Labour Call*, January 1947.

(72) Downing, R. I. and Karmel, P. H. 'Protection of the Australian Dairying Industry.' *Economic Record*, vol. XXXVI (1960), pp. 351-65.

(73) Drysdale, P. 'Review of Japanese-Australian Trade', in *Papers on Modern Japan, 1965*. Canberra, 1965, pp. 83-98.

(74) Duloy, J. H. and Nevile, J. W. 'The Effects of a Reserve Price Scheme for Wool on the Balance of Payments and Gross National Product.' *Economic Record*, vol. 41 (1965), pp. 254-61.

(75) *Economic Record*. 'The Vernon Report: Reviews of the Report of the Committee of Economic Enquiry.' vol. 42 (1966), pp. 1-180.

(76) Elkan, P. G. *Freer Trade with Australia: Why and How*. (Discussion Paper no. 8 of the New Zealand Institute of Economic Research (Inc.).) Wellington, 1965.

(77) Firth, G. G. 'Article Seven—A Programme for Prosperity?' *Economic Record*, vol. XVIII (1942), pp. 1-15.

(78) Gardner, Richard N. *Sterling-Dollar Diplomacy*. Oxford, 1956.

(79) GATT. *The Activities of GATT 1964-65*. Geneva, 1965.

(80) ——— *Basic Instruments and Selected Documents. Vol. III. Text of the General Agreement 1958*. Geneva, 1958.

(81) ——— *Trends in International Trade: A Report by a Panel of Experts* (Haberler Report). Geneva, 1958.

(82) ——— *GATT Programme for Expansion of International Trade: Trade in Agricultural Products: Second and Third Reports of Committee II*. Geneva, 1962.

(83) ——— *GATT Programme for Expansion of International Trade: Trade of Less-Developed Countries: Special Report of Committee III*. Geneva, 1962.

(84) ——— *GATT Programme for Expansion of International Trade: Trade in Tropical Products*. Geneva, 1963.

(85) ——— Address by Eric Wyndham White, Director-General of GATT, to UNCTAD. GATT Press Release 839, 9 April 1964.

(86) ——— *The Developing Countries and the GATT*. Geneva, February 1965.

(87) ——— Statement by Mr. A. Balensi, Assistant Director-General for External Relations of the GATT. Delivered at the First Session of the Trade and Development Board, UNCTAD, New York, April 1965. INT (65) 139, 10 May 1965.

(88) Gelber, H. G. *Australia, Britain & the E.E.C.* Melbourne, 1966.

(89) Greenwood, Gordon and Harper, Norman (eds.). *Australia in World Affairs, 1956-1960*. Sydney, 1961.

Haberler Report, *see* GATT (81), *Trends in International Trade*.

(90) Hall, G. J. Australian Tariff Board 1922-1956. M. Com. thesis, University of Melbourne, 1958.

(91) Hancock, K. J. 'Australian Balance of Payments Problem', in *The Australian Economy, 1961—Trends and Prospects*. (Sixth Summer School of Business Administration, University of Adelaide, 1961.) Adelaide, 1961.

(92) Hancock, W. K. and Gowing, M. M. *British War Economy*. History of the Second World War, United Kingdom Civil Series. London, 1949.

(93) Harris, S. F. The Control of Imports: Australia 1952-1960. Ph.D. thesis, A.N.U., 1963.

(94) Hasson, J. A. 'Agricultural Home Prices and Income Stabilization.' *Journal of Farm Economics*, vol. XXXIX (1957), pp. 951-7.

(95) —— 'Economic Stabilization in a Primary Producing Country.' *Journal of Political Economy*, vol. LXIV (1956), pp. 226-41.

(96) H.M.S.O. *Provisional Consolidated Text of the General Agreement on Tariffs and Trade and Texts of Related Documents.* London, Cmd.8048, September 1950.

(97) Holmes, F. W. *Freer Trade with Australia?* (Discussion Paper no. 10 of the New Zealand Institute of Economic Research (Inc.).) Wellington, 1966.

(98) IBRD *Supplementary Financial Measures—A Study by the International Bank for Reconstruction and Development, requested by the United Nations Conference on Trade and Development.* Washington, 1965.

(99) Institute of Public Affairs—Victoria. *The Balance of Payments and Development.* Melbourne, 1959.

(100) Karmel, P. H. *Economic Policy in Australia. Ends and Means.* (G. L. Wood Memorial Lecture.) Melbourne, 1954.

(101) Kindleberger, Chas. P. *Foreign Trade and the National Economy.* New Haven, 1962.

(102) Kojima, Kiyoshi. 'Japan's Trade Policy.' *Economic Record*, vol. 41 (1965), pp. 1-22.

(103) —— 'A Japanese View of Australia's Economic Future.' *Australian Financial Review*, 3 June 1966, pp. 2-3.

(104) Lewis, J. N. *Agricultural Price Supports—A Classification of Measures Operating in Australia.* (Economic Monograph no. 207, Economic Society of Australia and New Zealand (N.S.W. Branch).) Sydney, 1958.

(105) —— 'The French Plan.' *Review of Marketing and Agricultural Economics*, vol. 30 (1962), pp. 143-54.

(106) —— The Impact of EEC's Agricultural Policy upon International Commodity Policy. Unpublished paper, 1963.

(107) Lewis, J. N. and Muir, D. A. 'A Note on the FAO Guiding Principles for Price Support Measures.' *Review of Agricultural Marketing and Agricultural Economics*, vol. 30 (1962), pp. 77-87.

(108) Linge, G. J. R. *Index of Australian Tariff Reports 1901-1961.* (Aids to Research Series A/1 (1964), Research School of Pacific Studies, A.N.U.) Canberra, 1964.

(109) Little, A. J. 'Some Aspects of Government Policy Affecting the Rural Sector of the Australian Economy with Special Reference to the Period 1939/45-1953.' *Economic Record*, vol. 38 (1962), pp. 318-40.

(110) Lloyd, Alan G. 'Inter-Governmental Commodity Agreements.' *Review of Marketing and Agricultural Economics*, vol. 20 (1952), pp. 120-40.

(111) —— 'The Marketing of Dairy Produce in Australia.' *Review of Marketing and Agricultural Economics*, vol. 18 (1950), pp. 6-92.

(112) —— 'Reserve Price Scheme for Wool—A Defence.' *Economic Record*, vol. 41 (1965), pp. 505-22.

Bibliography

(113) Lundberg, E. and Hill, M. 'Balance of Payments Problems.' *Economic Record*, vol. XXXII (1956), pp. 28-49.

(114) McColl, G. D. *The Australian Balance of Payments*. Melbourne, 1965.

(115) MacDougall, Donald. *The World Dollar Problem: A Study in International Economics*. London, 1957.

(116) MacDougall, Donald and Hutt, Rosemary. 'Imperial Preference: A Quantitative Analysis.' *Economic Record*, vol. LXIV (1954), pp. 233-57.

(117) McEwen, J. *Agricultural Production Aims and Policy*. Pamphlet no. 5155, issued on behalf of the Australian Agricultural Council, December 1952.

(118) ———— *The Recent Review of GATT*. (Speech to Victorian Chamber of Manufactures on 28 March 1955.) Melbourne, 1955.

(119) McMillan, R. B. 'Organised Marketing of Wool.' *Economic Record*, vol. XXV (1949), pp. 59-72.

(120) Maiden, A. C. B. Some Aspects of Commodity Policy. (Paper presented to the Annual Conference of the Agricultural Economics Society of Australia, Sydney, 1960.) Roneoed document.

(121) Maxcy, G. 'The Motor Industry', in Alex Hunter (ed.), *The Economics of Australian Industry*. Melbourne, 1963, pp. 504-5.

(122) Meade, James. 'The Price Mechanism and the Australian Balance of Payments.' *Economic Record*, vol. XXXII (1956), pp. 239-56.

(123) ———— 'U.K., Commonwealth and Common Market: A Reappraisal', in *Freedom or Free-for-all*, vol. 3 of Hobart Papers (Institute of Economic Affairs). 2nd ed. (revised), 1965.

(124) Meier, G. M. *Leading Issues in Development Economics*. New York, 1964.

(125) Mendelsohn, R. 'The Allocation of Resources as an Administrative Problem.' *Public Administration* (Australia), vol. XVII (1958), pp. 177-93.

(126) Menzies, R. G. *Problems of Management in a Federation*. (Inaugural John Storey Memorial Lecture, 1962.) Sydney, 1962.

(127) Merry, D. H. 'Australia as a Factor in the Sterling Area.' *Lloyds Bank Review*, no. 37 (1955), pp. 34-6.

(128) Merry, D. H. and Bruns, G. R. 'Full Employment: The British, Canadian and Australian White Papers.' *Economic Record*, vol. XXI (1945), pp. 223-35.

(129) Miller, J. D. B. 'Political Implications of the European Economic Community.' *Australian Outlook*, vol. 16 (1962), pp. 229-45.

(130) Moffatt, Graeme. 'The Australian Import Licensing System: 1952-1960.' *Australian Economic Papers*, vol. I (1962), pp. 119-38.

(131) Nakayama, Y. 'Australia in Second and Third Positions.' *Sydney Morning Herald* (Supplement on Japan 1965), 12 April, 1965.

(132) Nicholson, D. F. *Australia's Trade Relations*. Melbourne, 1955.

(133) Parish, R. M. 'Hidden Losses and Gains Once Again.' *Economic Record*, vol. 41 (1965), pp. 457-9.

(134) ———— 'Revenue Implications of a Buffer-stock Scheme: Comment.' *Economic Record*, vol. 38 (1964), pp. 465-6.

(135) Perkins, J. O. N. *Britain and Australia: Economic Relationships in the 1950's.* Melbourne, 1962.

(136) ———— 'How Permanent are Australia's Cuts?' *Banker,* vol. 106 (1956), pp. 566-71.

(137) ———— 'Overseas Investment, Trade Policy and the Balance of Payments.' *Economic Record,* vol. 42 (1966), pp. 105-28.

(138) Plimsoll, James. 'Australia and Ottawa.' *Australian Quarterly,* vol. XIII (1941), pp. 14-21.

(139) Powell, A. A. and Campbell, K. O. 'Revenue Implications of a Buffer-Stock Scheme with an Uncertain Demand Schedule.' *Economic Record,* vol. 38 (1962), pp. 373-82.

(140) ———— 'Revenue Implications of a Buffer Stock Scheme: A Further Comment.' *Economic Record,* vol. 40 (1964), pp. 596-7.

Prebisch, Raúl, *see* United Nations Organization (159).

(141) Prest, Wilfred. 'Australia and the Dollar Crisis.' *Australian Quarterly,* vol. XIX (1947), pp. 57-67.

(142) Reitsma, A. J. 'The Australian Policy of Tariff Protection and Primary Industry.' *Australian Journal of Agricultural Economics,* vol. 6 (1962), pp. 68-79.

(143) ———— *Trade Protection in Australia.* Brisbane, 1960.

(144) ———— 'Trade and Redistribution of Income. Is there still an Australian Case?' *Economic Record,* vol. 34 (1958), pp. 172-88.

(145) Riley, D. L. 'Some Recent Developments in United States Surplus Disposals.' *Quarterly Review of Agricultural Economics,* vol. 16 (1963), pp. 68-75.

(146) Roach, J. R. 'Australian Food Production.' *Far Eastern Survey,* vol. 21 (1952), pp. 85-90.

(147) Robinson, A. D. 'An Australia-New Zealand Community?' *Australian Outlook,* vol. 18 (1964), pp. 5-16.

(148) Rowe, J. W. F. *Primary Commodities in International Trade.* Cambridge, 1965.

(149) Russell, E. A. 'Australia and the European Common Market', in *The Australian Economy and Overseas Trade.* (Seventh Summer School of Business Administration, University of Adelaide, 1962.) Adelaide, 1962.

(150) ———— 'Trade Policy and Australia's Balance of Payments', in *Business and Economic Policy.* (Third Summer School of Business Administration, University of Adelaide, 1958.) Adelaide, 1958.

(151) Sawer, G. 'The Constitutional System of the European Common Market.' (Text of a talk given to the A.C.T. Group of the Royal Institute of Public Administration, Canberra, 1963.)

(152) Shannon, I. *Australian Trade with Asia.* (Study No. 3, Committee for Economic Development of Australia.) Melbourne, 1962.

(153) ———— *Rural Industries in the Australian Economy.* Melbourne, 1955.

(154) Strong, T. H. 'Disposal of Surplus Commodities: Relation to Economic Development of Under-Developed and Agriculturally Dependent Countries.' *Quarterly Review of Agricultural Economics,* vol. VIII (1955), pp. 51-6.

(155) Subhan, Malcolm. 'Third World In.' *Far Eastern Economic Review*, 21 July, 1966.

(156) United Nations Organization. *United Nations Conference on Trade and Employment, Havana, 1947-1948. Final Act and Related Documents.* Havana, 1948.

(157) —— *International Compensation for Fluctuations in Commodity Trade.* Report of a U.N. Committee of Experts under Chairmanship of Sir John Crawford, E/CN 13/40. New York, 1961.

(158) —— *Proceedings of the United Nations Conference on Trade and Development. Geneva, 23 March–16 June 1964. Volume I. Final Act and Report.* New York, 1964.

(159) —— *Towards a New Trade Policy for Development.* Report by the Secretary General of the United Nations Conference on Trade and Development (Raúl Prebisch). New York, 1964.

Vernon Report, *see* Australia (11).

(160) Wadham, S. *et al. Land Utilization in Australia.* 4th ed. Melbourne, 1964.

(161) Ward, E. J. The Case Against the Ratification of the Bretton Woods Financial Agreement, 10 January 1947. Typed document.

(162) Ward, John M. 'Some Implications of the Cessation of Lend-Lease.' *Australian Quarterly*, vol. XVIII (1946), pp. 19-23.

(163) Wilcox, C. *A Charter for World Trade.* New York, 1949.

(164) Wilcyzynski, J. 'Dilemmas in Australia's Trade with the Communist Bloc.' *Australian Quarterly*, vol. XXXVI (1964), pp. 9-19.

(165) —— 'The Economics and Politics of Wheat Exports to China.' *Australian Quarterly*, vol. XXXVII (1965), pp. 44-55.

(166) —— 'Sino-Australian Trade and Defence.' *Australian Outlook*, vol. 20 (1966), pp. 154-67.

(167) Wilson, J. S. G. 'Prospects of Full Employment in Australia.' *Economic Record*, vol. XXII (1946), pp. 99-116.

(168) Wood, G. L. 'International Economic Collaboration and the Australian Economy.' *Economic Record*, vol. XXIII (1947), pp. 159-76.

INDEX

INDEX

Index